lonely planet

Iceland

Paul Harding, Joe Bindloss

Contents

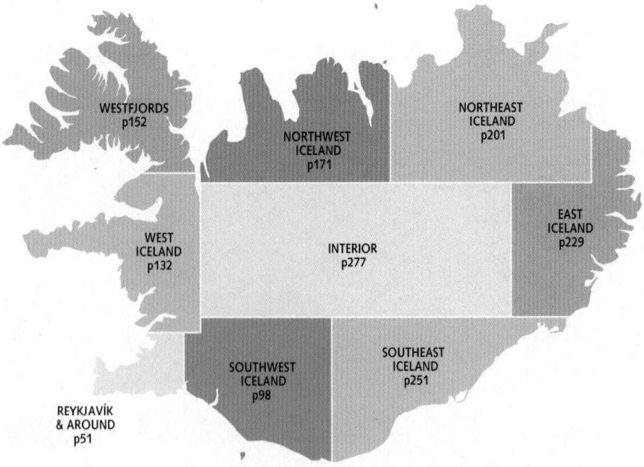

Lonely Planet books provide independent advice. Lonely Planet does not accept advertising in guidebooks, nor do we accept payment in exchange for listing or endorsing any place or business. Lonely Planet writers do not accept discounts or payments in exchange for positive coverage of any sort.

Bækur sem gefnar eru út af útgáfufyrirtækinu Lonely Planet veita óháðar upplýsingar. Lonely Planet auglýsir ekki í ferðahandbókum né þiggur greiðslur fyrir að nefna eða benda á ákveðna staði eða fyrirtæki. Þeir sem skrifa fyrir Lonely Planet þiggja hvorki greiðslur né afslátt af neinu tagi fyrir jákvæða umfjöllun.

Destination: Iceland

Few visitors leave Iceland without a sense of wonder – it's that sort of country. You may be drawn to the awesome diversity of natural phenomena: active volcanoes, valley glaciers, Europe's biggest waterfalls, lava fields, geysers, thermal pools, the aurora borealis on polar nights and the clarity of Arctic light in summer. Or you may be sucked into the unique cultural scene of the compact capital Reykjavík. Either way, there's nowhere in the world quite like it.

Twenty years ago a trickle of tourists came to Iceland for nature and isolation, challenging hiking, adventurous travel and eerily remote wilderness. That's still the case, but now Iceland is one of Europe's hottest travel destinations. It's relatively easy to get around (in summer at least), there's a growing range of quality accommodation (including rustic farmhouses, hostels, cosy guesthouses, modern hotels) and you can organise activities ranging from horse riding, fishing and golf to white-water rafting on glacial rivers and sea kayaking in calm fjords. Ecotourism is developing in Iceland and one of the big attractions is whale watching – in summer this is probably the best place in Europe to see many whale species as well as dolphins and seals. The sea cliffs around the country are a paradise for bird-watchers, but even the most jaded traveller would be mesmerised by the sight of 20,000 puffins nesting on a cliff top.

Iceland is not as cold as it sounds. From June to August it can be quite mild and pleasant and you'll find snow only on the highlands or icecaps. It's true that it does tend to rain a lot and the country's natural beauty is apparent only when the mist clears. It's also one of Europe's more expensive countries in which to travel.

But don't let those things put you off. Iceland is easy to reach (Iceland Express has budget flights from London and Copenhagen daily), and with a little planning it's possible to keep the costs down. Icelanders are a tough, independent bunch, but they're also very warm and welcoming and keen to sha re their little island with tourists. Geologically, Iceland is one of the world's 'hot spots'. As a travel destination it could hardly get any hotter.

GRAHAM BELL

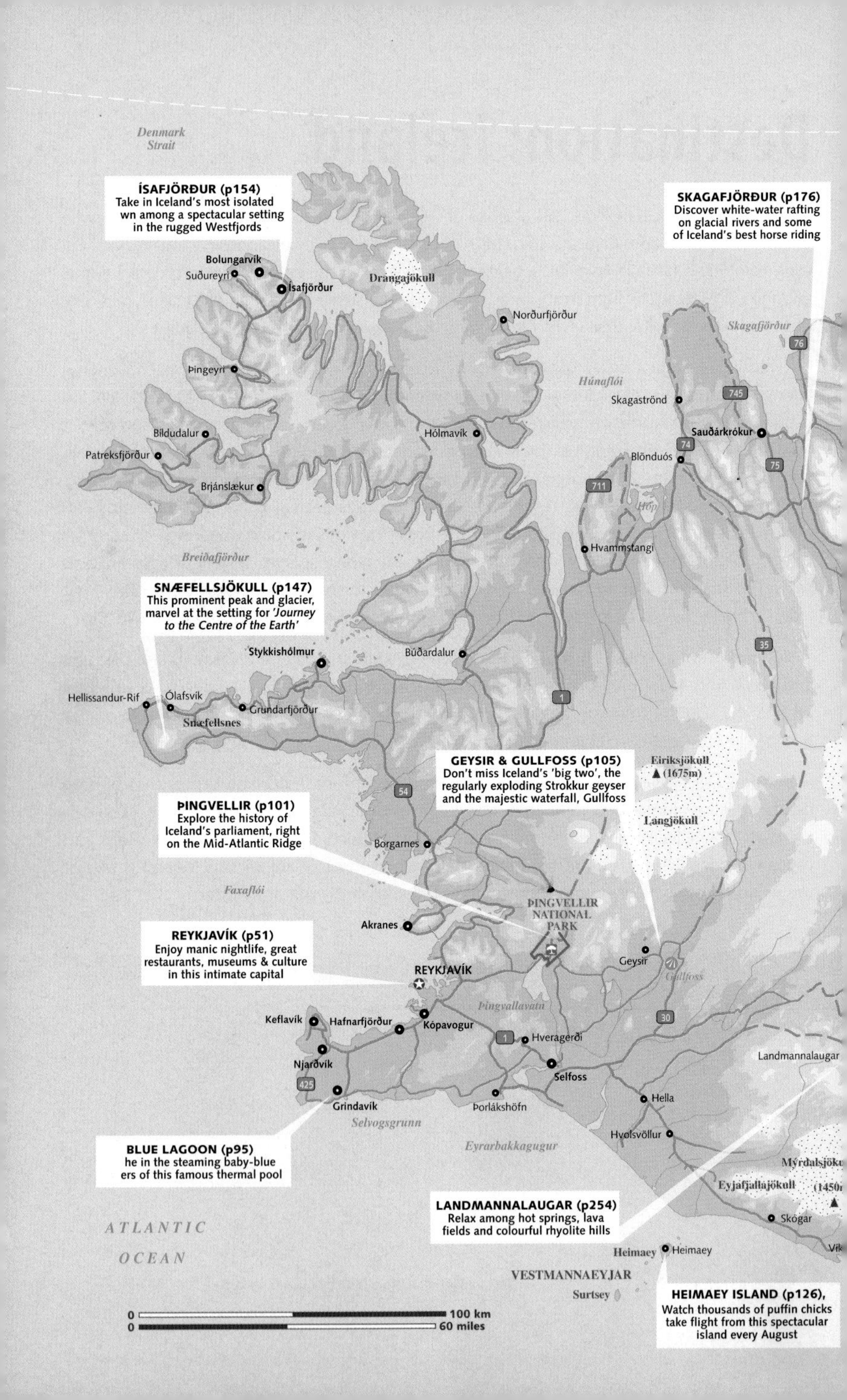

Denmark Strait
ÍSAFJÖRÐUR (p154)
Take in Iceland's most isolated
wn among a spectacular setting
in the rugged Westfjords
SKAGAFJÖRÐUR (p176)
Discover white-water rafting
on glacial rivers and some
of Iceland's best horse riding
Bolungarvík
Suðureyri
Ísafjörður
Drangajökull
Norðurfjörður
Skagafjörður
76
Þingeyri
Húnaflói
Skagaströnd
745
Sauðárkrókur
Bíldudalur
Hólmavík
74
Patreksfjörður
Blönduós
75
Brjánslækur
711
Hóp
Hvammstangi
Breiðafjörður
SNÆFELLSJÖKULL (p147)
This prominent peak and glacier,
marvel at the setting for 'Journey
to the Centre of the Earth'
35
Stykkishólmur
Búðardalur
Hellissandur-Rif
Ólafsvík
Grundarfjörður
1
Snæfellsnes
GEYSIR & GULLFOSS (p105)
Don't miss Iceland's 'big two', the
regularly exploding Strokkur geyser
and the majestic waterfall, Gullfoss
Eiríksjökull
(1675m)
54
ÞINGVELLIR (p101)
Explore the history of
Iceland's parliament, right
on the Mid-Atlantic Ridge
Langjökull
Borgarnes
Faxaflói
ÞINGVELLIR NATIONAL PARK
Akranes
REYKJAVÍK (p51)
Enjoy manic nightlife, great
restaurants, museums & culture
in this intimate capital
Geysir
Gullfoss
REYKJAVÍK
Þingvallavatn
Keflavík
Hafnarfjörður
Kópavogur
30
1
Hveragerði
Njarðvík
Selfoss
Landmannalaugar
425
Grindavík
Hella
Þorlákshöfn
Selvogsgrunn
Hvolsvöllur
Eyrarbakkagugur
BLUE LAGOON (p95)
he in the steaming baby-blue
ers of this famous thermal pool
Mýrdalsjökull
Eyjafjallajökull
(1450m)
LANDMANNALAUGAR (p254)
Relax among hot springs, lava
fields and colourful rhyolite hills
Skógar
ATLANTIC OCEAN
Heimaey
Heimaey
Vík
VESTMANNAEYJAR
Surtsey
HEIMAEY ISLAND (p126),
Watch thousands of puffin chicks
take flight from this spectacular
island every August
0 100 km
0 60 miles

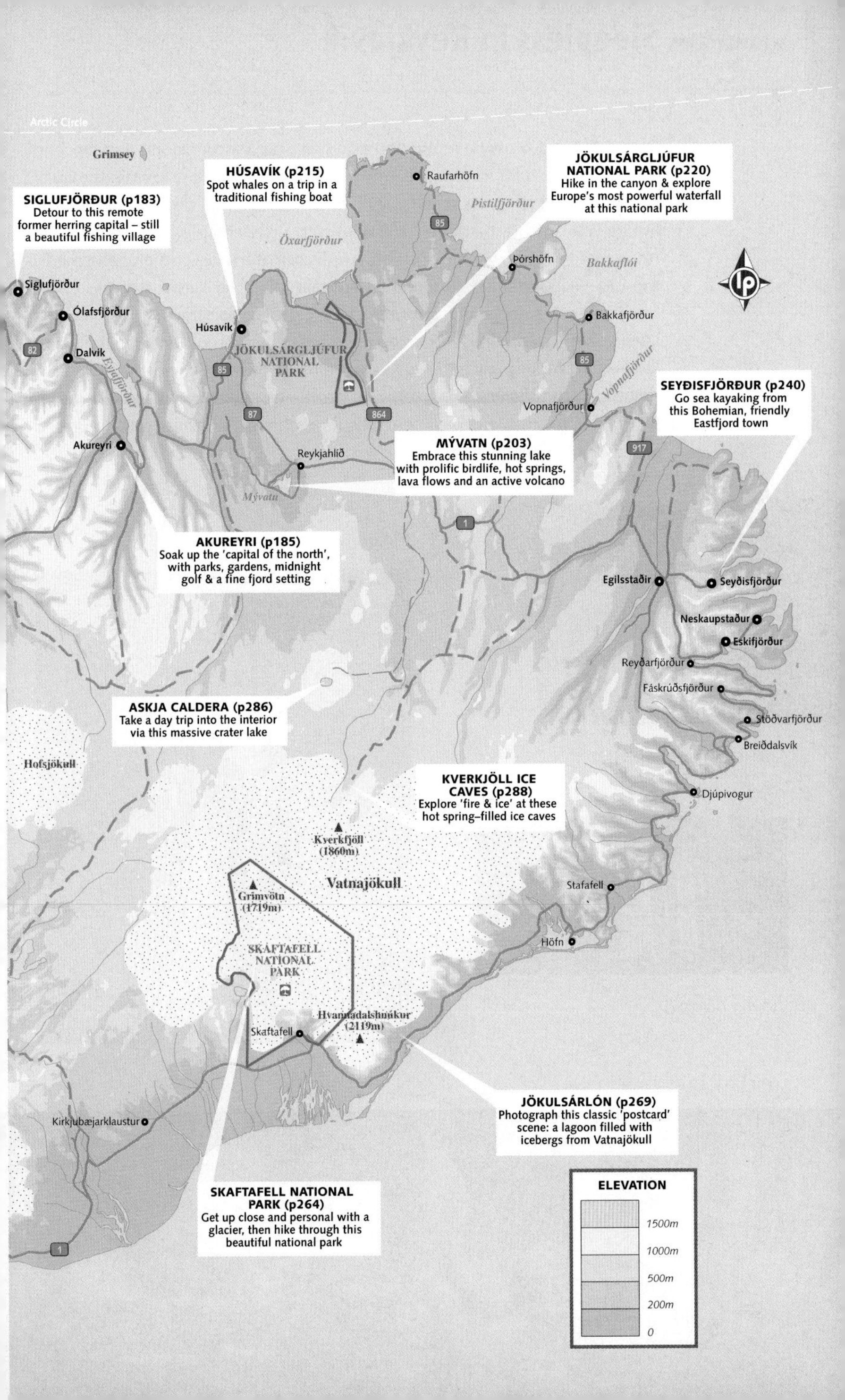

Arctic Circle
Grímsey
SIGLUFJÖRÐUR (p183)
Detour to this remote former herring capital – still a beautiful fishing village
HÚSAVÍK (p215)
Spot whales on a trip in a traditional fishing boat
JÖKULSÁRGLJÚFUR NATIONAL PARK (p220)
Hike in the canyon & explore Europe's most powerful waterfall at this national park
Raufarhöfn
Þistilfjörður
Öxarfjörður
Þórshöfn
Bakkaflói
Siglufjörður
Ólafsfjörður
Dalvík
Eyjafjörður
Húsavík
JÖKULSÁRGLJÚFUR NATIONAL PARK
Bakkafjörður
Vopnafjörður
Vopnafjörður
SEYÐISFJÖRÐUR (p240)
Go sea kayaking from this Bohemian, friendly Eastfjord town
82
85
87
864
917
1
Akureyri
Reykjahlíð
MÝVATN (p203)
Embrace this stunning lake with prolific birdlife, hot springs, lava flows and an active volcano
Mývatn
AKUREYRI (p185)
Soak up the 'capital of the north', with parks, gardens, midnight golf & a fine fjord setting
Egilsstaðir
Seyðisfjörður
Neskaupstaður
Eskifjörður
Reyðarfjörður
Fáskrúðsfjörður
Stöðvarfjörður
Breiðdalsvík
ASKJA CALDERA (p286)
Take a day trip into the interior via this massive crater lake
Hofsjökull
KVERKJÖLL ICE CAVES (p288)
Explore 'fire & ice' at these hot spring–filled ice caves
Djúpivogur
Kverkfjöll (1860m)
Vatnajökull
Grímsvötn (1719m)
Stafafell
SKAFTAFELL NATIONAL PARK
Höfn
Skaftafell
Hvannadalshnúkur (2119m)
JÖKULSÁRLÓN (p269)
Photograph this classic 'postcard' scene: a lagoon filled with icebergs from Vatnajökull
Kirkjubæjarklaustur
SKAFTAFELL NATIONAL PARK (p264)
Get up close and personal with a glacier, then hike through this beautiful national park
ELEVATION
1500m
1000m
500m
200m
0

Sleepless in Reykjavík

Reykjavík has a growing reputation as a hang-out for the young and hip, and it's justly famous for its nightlife. At weekends the whole city joins in the great Icelandic pub-crawl, the **runtur** (p79), which goes on till dawn. When you've finished partying, recharge your batteries with an Icelandic feast at the revolving restaurant **Perlan** (p76), the lobster house **Humarhúsið** (p76) or the unashamedly touristy Viking-themed restaurant **Fjörukráin** (p87). Reykjavík also has some great museums, including the futuristic art gallery **Hafnarhúsið** (p63) and the Viking **Saga Museum** (p62). The capital is full of interesting architecture – our **Architectural Walking Tour** (p65) covers some of the finest buildings, including the grand church **Hallgrímskirkja** (p59). The geothermal field at Nesjavellir provides piping-hot water for Reykjavík's excellent geothermal **swimming pools** (p64) and **Nauthólsvík Geothermal Beach** (p62).

PAUL HARDING

Grand Rokk pub (p80)

PAUL HARDING

Vidalin bar (p79)

Hallgrímskirkja (p59)

GRANT DIXON

Café Paris (p192)

PAUL HARDIN

borealis (Northern Lights) is an attraction from late September to M and activities such as skiing can be organised.

As for climate, Iceland is not always as cold as it sounds. The war waters of the Gulf Stream and the prevailing southwesterly winds fron the Atlantic combine to give the southern and western coasts of Icelanc surprisingly mild temperatures even in winter – often warmer than those of New York or Zürich. The downside of this incoming warmth is that it combines with relatively cold polar seas and mountainous coastlines to form condensation – and plenty of rain. Periods of fierce, wind-driven rain (or wet snow in winter) alternate with partial clearing, drizzle, gales and fog to create an often miserable climate. There's an old saying: 'if you don't like the weather now, wait five minutes – it will probably get worse'.

r more information see mate Charts p295

But don't be put off. In recent years Iceland has benefited from global climate changes and summers have been relatively pleasant – the summer of 2003 was the warmest on record and the previous winter was so mild that the ski season was a disaster. While Reykjavík and the west coast bear the brunt of the North Atlantic wind and rain, as you move north and east, the chances of fine weather increase. It's sunniest around Akureyri and Mývatn in the central north and warmest around Egilsstaðir in the east.

While they're more prone to clear weather than the coastal areas, the interior deserts experience other problems. Blizzards may occur at any time of year, and icy, shrieking winds whip up dust and sand into swirling, gritty and opaque maelstroms. Similar conditions can occur on the *sandur* – grey sand plains formed by glacial rivers carrying silt down from melting icecaps – of the northern and southern coasts.

Even in summer, the mercury rarely rises above 18°C and is usually closer to 12° to 15°C, with overnight temperatures dropping to 5°C. But on clear, windless days this can be T-shirt weather. If only there were more clear, windless days!

OW MUCH ?

amp site
ee–Ikr500

up of coffee
kr200

celand knitted jumper
kr8000–10,000

Museum admission
kr300–500

ne-day car hire
kr6000–8000

oaf of bread
kr200

Reykjavík–Akureyri bus
kr5700

Litre of petrol
kr102

Litre of bottled water
kr200

Pint of beer
kr500–600

Souvenir T-shirt
kr1500

Hot dog
kr190

COSTS

There's no getting around the fact that Iceland is expensive.

Mid-range or 'budget unlimited' travellers staying in guesthouses or hotels, eating in sit-down restaurants and getting around by car will find that Ikr15,000 ($US200) per person per day won't go all that far. Budget-conscious travellers with tents and sleeping bags, who self-cater or eat at cheaper cafés and fast-food places, and who take the bus or share a vehicle, can do it for a fraction of that – perhaps as little as Ikr2500 (US$35). A sensible middle ground – mixing some budget travel with comforts, occasional good food and tours – would be around Ikr7000–8000 (US$100) per day.

Rooms at cheaper guesthouses, farms and summer hotels cost from Ikr1500–2000 for sleeping-bag accommodation and Ikr4000/6000 fo singles/doubles with made-up beds. The best business hotels charge Ikr12,000/15,000 for singles/doubles in summer, with discounts in the of season. Families or groups can get cheaper deals by finding triple, quac or family rooms. Self-contained cottages or cabins in rural Iceland can be great value for groups. You can stay in wonderful timber cabins (sleepin up to six) with kitchen, lounge, bathroom, barbecue deck and a couple o bedrooms for under Ikr10,000 – far better than any hotel room.

To eat well in Iceland – that is, to have a sit-down meal in a decen restaurant – comes at a hefty price. A fish dish averages around Ikr1200–2500; lamb dishes are always over Ikr2000 and as high as Ikr3500. Add a bottle of wine or a dessert and the bill is criminal. Many travellers rel

Iceland has an amazing diversity of natural features, with glacial waterfalls thundering through canyons, powerful geysers, thermal pools, vast lava fields and bubbling geothermal sites. Snowcapped rhyolite and basalt mountain ranges rise from the landscape, active volcanos rumble ominously and glaciers rule. Don't miss the **Jökulsárgljúfur National Park** and the awesome waterfall **Dettifoss** (p223); **Mývatn** and **Krafla** (p203); **Þórsmörk** (p119); **Skaftafell National Park** (p264); and **Landmannalaugar** (p254). Iceland's Southeast is dominated by Europe's biggest icecap, **Vatnajökull**, and its glaciers. The iceberg-filled lagoon **Jökulsárlón** (p269) is a must-see photo stop along the Ring Road. Other 'fire and ice' highlights include the **Askja caldera** (p286) and the ice caves at **Kverkfjöll** (p287), in the northeastern Interior.

In contrast to the desertlike Interior, Iceland's rugged coastline is rich in birdlife. At **Heimaey island** (p126) you can watch thousands of puffin chicks take flight every August. Another highlight is the Arctic light. Few could fail to be mesmerised by the **aurora borealis** (northern lights), visible on clear polar nights. The **midnight sun** means almost continuous daylight in June and July.

GRANT DIXON

Skaftafellsjökull glacier, Skaftafell National Park (p264), Southeast Iceland

Askja caldera (p286), Interior

GRANT DIXON

Heimaey Island (p126), Southwest Iceland

GRANT DIXON

A Whale of a time

The best way to experience Iceland's natural beauty and sublime wilderness is to get off the bus or out of the car and hike, cycle, ride, swim or raft.

In summer, when the midnight sun is shining, it is possible to hike, cycle, play golf or laze in thermal pools throughout the night. **Horse-riding tours** (p30) lasting from one hour to seven days or more (including the famous autumn sheep roundup) can be organised right around the country. **Whale watching** (p33) is Iceland's most popular ecosport and the best spots include Harfnarfjörður, Ólafsvík and Húsavík. **Golf** (p31) can be played on many courses, including as the 18-hole courses at Akureyri and Heimæy island.

Snowmobiling or **dogsledding** (p33) on the icecaps is a great experience. Try it on Vatnajökull, Mýralsjökull or Langjökull. There are some epic opportunities for **white-water rafting** (p32), especially on raging rivers such as the Þjorsá or the Jökulsá Austari. For something more sedate, island-studded Hvammsfjörður is a great spot for **sea kayaking** (p32), as is virtually anywhere in the Eastfjords and Westfjords.

Húsavík (p215), Northeast Iceland

GRANT DIXON

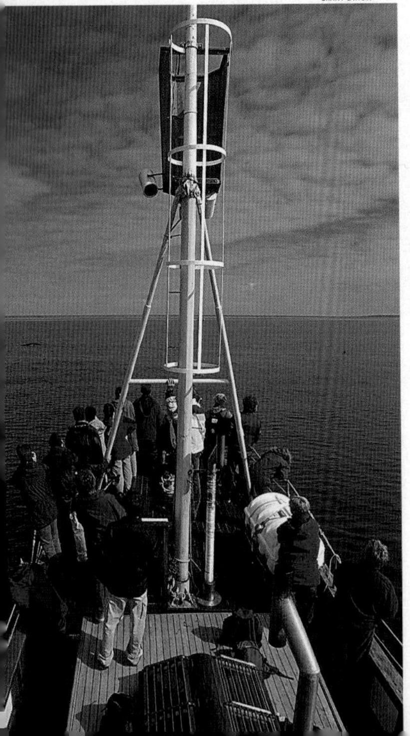

Vatnajökull icekap (p259), Southeast Iceland

PAUL HARDING

STEVE HUTTON

Sprengisandur Route (p282), Interior

Getting Started

If you're expecting more from your trip to Iceland than a weekend in Reykjavík and a quick tour around the Golden Circle, then a bit of forward planning will ensure you're not stuck clutching a soggy timetable for a bus that will never come or driving miles to see a puffin colony that migrated out to sea a month ago.

The summer is relatively short (but the days are long), offering a specific window for popular activities such as hiking, horse riding, whale watching, glacier tours, fishing and river rafting. Reykjavík is at its best in summer but is worth visiting at any time of year. No matter what your budget, watch the costs – Iceland has a habit of draining wallets faster than the flow rate of Dettifoss waterfall.

WHEN TO GO

Iceland's peak tourist season runs from early June to the end of August (summer). As the last of the snows melt and the nights become days, everything gets into full swing – accommodation and camp sites are open, bus services are running and outdoor activities can easily be organised.

May and September (shoulder season) can also be good times to visit, with often crisp, clear days and far fewer tourists. Early- or late-season travellers will find buses running to a reduced winter timetable (some highland bus tours don't operate after late August); summer hotels, tourist offices and museums in smaller towns will shut down. By 30 September, most of the country – apart from Reykjavík and Akureyri – has gone into hibernation. Things are changing though, and the tourist season is beginning to extend well into September, but you'll need to tailor your trip.

'Off-season' winter (October to April) visits to Iceland are gaining popularity, especially during the Christmas season when Reykjavík, in particular, puts on its festive best. The opportunity to see the aurora

DON'T LEAVE HOME WITHOUT...

- Sleeping bag – even if you're not camping, you can sleep for half the price at most hostels, guesthouses and even some hotels if you have your own sleeping bag. A blow-up pillow is also handy.
- Camera and plenty of film – on a fine day Iceland demands to be photographed, but film doesn't come cheap, so bring plenty of your own.
- Swimsuit and towel – essential gear for bathing in natural hot springs or joining in the local passion for geothermally heated swimming pools and hot pots (hot tubs outdoors).
- Eye mask, earplugs and torch (flashlight) – for, respectively, getting some sleep on long, light summer nights; getting some sleep if staying in central Reykjavík or Akureyri on long summer weekend nights; finding things (including your way) on long, dark winter nights.
- Credit card – Icelanders wouldn't know what to do without the plastic.
- Waterproof clothing and thermals – if you're planning on hiking, cycling or hitching, the importance of waterproof gear can't be stressed enough.
- Sense of humour (and adventure) – for when those majestic glaciers are completely lost in the fog, when you're hiking through a blizzard, or when you realise just how much money you spent in Reykjavík bars.

on cheaper, filling alternatives (hot dogs, hamburgers, pizzas) and some restaurants have cheaper lunch-time buffets or tourist menus.

Don't forget to leave room in your budget for things like nightlife (in Reykjavík and Akureyri at least), shopping, museum or sight admission (usually around Ik300–500) and activities such as horse riding (Ikr2000 an hour), whale watching (Ikr3500) or a snowmobile tour (Ikr8900).

TRAVEL LITERATURE

For a country of its size and isolation, there's a wealth of travel literature and photographic coffee-table books about Iceland (or written by Icelanders).

Iceland: Land of the Sagas (1990, Villard), by David Roberts and Jon Krakauer, superbly bridges the gap between coffee-table book and an informative introduction to Iceland's history, landscape and sagas. Krakauer contributes inspirational photographs, while Roberts ties the sagas and historical sites into the modern travel experience.

Letters from High Latitudes (1989, Sheridan House), by Lord Dufferin, is an early travelogue following the voyage of the sailing schooner *Foam* to Iceland, Jan Mayen and Svalbard in 1856. Written in a state of wide-eyed wonder by this adventurous English diplomat and lord, it conjures up images of a simpler, undiscovered Iceland.

Frost on My Moustache (1999, Abacus), by Tim Moore, is a contemporary account following Dufferin's journey. British author Moore writes with pompous but self-deprecating wit about his journey across the North Atlantic via Iceland, the Faroes, Norway and Spitzbergen. Enduring chronic seasickness, hot-dog overdose and a torturous cycling trip through Iceland's Interior, he provides an engaging and insightful look at modern-day Iceland, with reflections of the past.

Letters from Iceland (1937, Faber & Faber), by WH Auden and Louis MacNeice, is an irreverent and facetious collection of poems, letters and narrative about a journey by these two poets as young men. It has now become a travel classic. An update on this tale is provided in *Moon Country – Further Reports from Iceland* (1996, Faber & Faber), by Simon Armitage and Glyn Maxwell. In this unconventional travel book, two modern-day bards follow in the footsteps of Auden and MacNeice, with similarly ludicrous results.

Last Places – A Journey in the North (1990, Houghton Mifflin), by Lawrence Millman, is an entertaining and well-written travelogue recounting a hilarious four-month journey following the Viking route, from Scotland to Newfoundland via the Faroes, Iceland and Greenland. A good read.

The Iceland Traveller – A Hundred Years of Adventure, compiled by Alan Boucher, is another step back in time. This anthology of stories by 15 writers (including Sir Richard Burton) recounts trips and expeditions to Iceland in the 18th and 19th centuries. It contains texts in their original form and is full of romance, history and adventure.

INTERNET RESOURCES

Go Iceland (www.goiceland.org) Iceland's North American Tourist Board site has plenty of travel tips.

Iceland Review (www.icelandreview.is) Excellent site from the magazine of same name. Daily news digest from Iceland, articles and culture.

Icelandic Tourist Board (www.icetourist.is) The official site of the Icelandic Tourist Board, with plenty of travel information in several languages.

Lonely Planet (www.lonelyplanet.com) With a summary of travel in Iceland and the Thorn Tree bulletin board. Plenty of travel-related links.

Nordic Adventure Travel (www.nat.is) Lists some useful practical information and planning tips.

What's on in Iceland (www.whatson.is) Up-to-date information on festivals and special events.

TOP PICKS

MUST-SEE ICELANDIC FILMS

Icelandic feature films have been in regular production only for the last 20 years, but there are plenty of recent offerings (with English subtitles) to whet your appetite. See if you can find these in your specialist video store.

- *101 Reykjavík* (2000)
  Baltasar Kormákur
- *Children of Nature* (1991)
  Friðrik Thór Friðriksson
- *Angels of the Universe* (*Englar alheimsins*; 2000)
  Friðrik Thór Friðriksson
- *Seagull's Laughter* (*Mávahlátur*; 2001)
  Agust Gudmundsson
- *The Icelandic Dream* (*Íslenski draumurinn*; 2000)
  Róbert I Douglas
- *Reykjavík Guesthouse – Rent a Bike* (2002)
  Björn Thors and Unnur Ösp Stefánsdóttir
- *Cold Fever* (1994)
  Friðrik Thór Friðriksson

TOP NOVELS

One of the best ways to learn about contemporary issues and culture and grasp a sense of people and place is to immerse yourself in a good book, and Iceland has an amazing volume of literature, some of it translated into English. Try delving into the following page-turners. See p36 for reviews.

- *Independent People* (1999)
  Halldór Laxness
- *101 Reykjavík* (1996)
  Hallgrímur Helgason
- *Under the Glacier* (1968)
  Halldór Laxness
- *Angels of the Universe* (1997)
  Einar Már Gudmundsson
- *The Atom Station* (1948)
  Halldór Laxness
- *Njáls Saga*
  Translated by M Magnusson (or Robin Cook)
- *Salka Valka* (1932)
  Halldór Laxness
- *Journey to the Centre of the Earth* (1869)
  Jules Verne

OUR FAVOURITE FESTIVALS & EVENTS

Whether it's a celebration of music, culture, history, the changing of the seasons or just an excuse to feast and drink, you'll find that Icelanders love to party. The following list is our Top 10, but for a comprehensive listing of festivals and events see p298.

- Icelandic Independence Day
  (nationwide) June 17 (p298)
- Þorrablót
  (nationwide) February (p298)
- Þjódhátíð Vestmannaeyjar
  (Heimæy Island, Vestmannaeyjar) First weekend in August (p129)
- Verslunarmannahelgi
  (nationwide) First weekend in August (p298)
- Sjómannadagurinn (Sailor's Day)
  (coastal towns) First week in June (p298)
- Airwaves Music Festival
  (Reykjavík) mid-October (p68)
- Reykjavík Culture Night
  (Reykjavík) Second Saturday in August (p68)
- Herring Festival
  (Siglufjöður) early August (p184)
- Akureyri Arts Festival
  (Akureyri) 10 June–mid-August (p191)
- Midsummer
  (nationwide) Around 24 June (p298)

Itineraries

CLASSIC ROUTES

REYKJAVÍK & THE GOLDEN CIRCLE — 3–7 days

Start off with a few days in Reykjavík. Try to come on a Friday or Saturday for the famous **runtur pub crawl** (p79). Splurge on a gourmet Icelandic meal at one of Reykjavík's fine **restaurants** (p74). The next morning, take a relaxing dip in the fantastic **geothermal swimming pool** (p64) at Laugadalur or at the **geothermal beach** (p62) at Nauthólsvík. Admire the view from **Hallgrímskirkja** (p59) and check out Icelandic architecture at street level on our **walking tour** (p65). Make time for the capital's museums – the **Saga Museum** (p62) has incredibly realistic Viking dioramas, while the **Hafnarhúsið** (p63) houses the giant cartoon paintings of Icelandic artist Erró. The following day, head to the Golden Circle. Start at the gorgeous national park at **Þingvellir** (p101), where the Viking parliament used to meet. If you have time on your hands, take an **Icelandic pony ride** (p104). From here head up to **Geysir** (p105) and watch the Strokkur geyser blow its top. Next, visit thundering **Gullfoss** (p106), Iceland's most famous waterfall. If you find the time, loop back via the fishing villages **Stokkeseyri** (p115) and **Eyrarbakki** (p114). On your way out, stop at the idyllic **Blue Lagoon geothermal spa** (p95) – special buses from Reykjavík to the airport stop here.

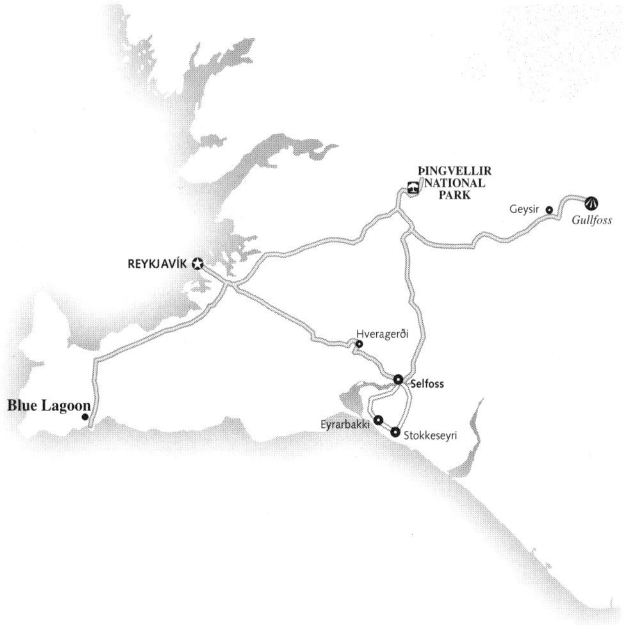

SPECTACULAR NORTHEAST CIRCUIT

3 days–2 weeks

Few parts of Iceland can provide the diversity of landscape and wealth of activities in such a neat little package as this corner of Northeast Iceland. In just a few days you can climb craters, walk across recently created lava fields, cycle around a volcanic lake, spot whales, cross the Arctic Circle and hike through Iceland's most dramatic canyon.

The base for this trip is **Akureyri** (p185), Iceland's second-biggest town. With its lovely position on Eyjafjörður, botanical gardens, fine summer climate and handful of good restaurants and bars, this is an essential stop on a trip around Iceland. From Akureyri it's a scenic 99km drive along the Ring Road to Mývatn, passing the impressive **Goðafoss waterfall** (p200). At **Mývatn** (p203) you could easily spend a couple of days or a week exploring the lake, the nearby geothermal areas and the lunarlike Krafla lava fields and fissures.

Following a clockwise circuit of the so-called 'Diamond Route', the next stop is the lovely fishing village of **Húsavík** (54km; p215), whale-watching capital of Iceland. Follow Route 85 around the Tjörnes Peninsula to Asbýrgi (65km) at the northern end of spectacular **Jökulsárgljúfur National Park** (p220). Do the two-day hike through the canyon or just visit the parts accessible by road: **Asbýrgi canyon** (p222), **Holmatungur** (p223) and **Dettifoss** (p223). It's 26km along unsealed Route 864 from Asbýrgi to Dettifoss, Europe's biggest waterfall. It's another 28km south to the Ring Road, from where you can return to Akureyri via Mývatn or continue east to Egilsstaðir.

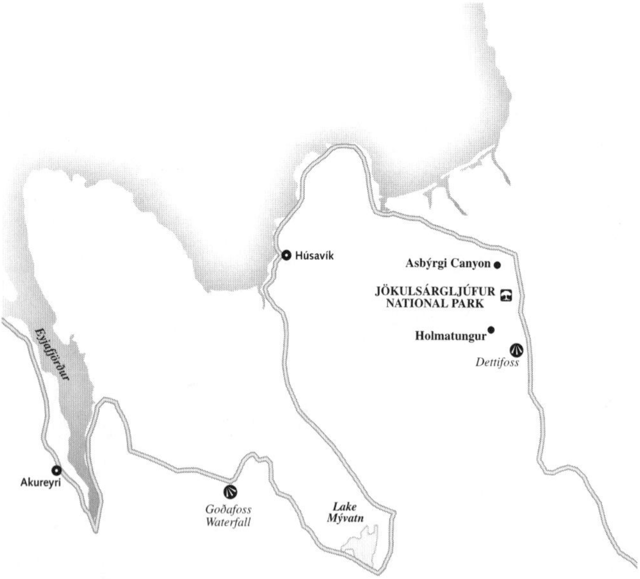

ROADS LESS TRAVELLED

THE EMPTY EAST

3–7+ days

To see the best of the Eastfjords region, you need to leave the Ring Road. From **Egilsstaðir** (p232), the 56km circuit of the long, narrow lake **Lögurinn** (p235) takes you past Iceland's most famous forest, **Hallormsstaður** (p235), the **Skriðuklauster cultural centre** (p235), and the canyon waterfall, **Hengifoss** (p236). Back in Egilsstaðir, it's 69km along Route 94 to the northernmost fjord, **Borgarfjörður** (p238). The road winds over a dramatic mountain pass with fine views down to the *sandur* (sand delta) and river delta on Héraðsflói bay. Backtracking to Egilsstaðir, take Route 93 to **Seyðisfjörður** (27km; p240), the port for the ferry from Europe and the prettiest, friendliest fjord town.

Back in Egilsstaðir, take Route 92 southeast to **Reyðarfjörður** (31km; p244) and **Eskifjörður** (17km; p244), a pair of somnolent fishing villages enveloped by looming, emerald-green basalt mountains. From there the road climbs up and over Iceland's highest mountain pass, before dropping down to the busy fishing port of **Neskaupstaður** (26km; p246).

Returning to Reyðarfjörður, head east along Route 96, which clings to the coast for the rest of the journey south around the fjords. Along the way you'll pass the tiny villages of **Fáskúðfjörður** (50km; p247), **Stoðvarfjöður** (28km; p247) and **Breiðdalsvík** (18km; p248). Don't miss the mineral collection of Petra Sveinsdóttir in Stoðvarfjöður and a meal at Café Margret near Breiðdalsvík. From here you rejoin the Ring Road and follow the coast to the last fjord town, **Djúpivogur** (63km; p249). This is the harbour for boat trips to beautiful **Papey Island** (p250).

INTERIOR BY 4WD

5–10 days

The best way to tackle the rugged central highlands and interior roads is in a 4WD vehicle, but in summer you can also do this loop route from Reykjavík by public bus.

Starting from the capital, head east to **Geysir** (p105) and **Gullfoss** (p106), then continue northeast to the **Kjölur Route** (Route 35; p280). This passes between Langjökull and Hofsjökull glaciers and has some interesting side hikes, before emerging on the Ring Road near Blönduós. From here, head east to **Akureyri** (p185). There are two possibilities for getting onto the **Sprengisandur Route** (p282): either directly south from Akureyri and Eyjafjörður (Route F821), or by turning south at Goðafoss waterfall onto Route F842, then F26 (the latter is easier and is the route taken by BSÍ buses).

Follow the Sprengisandur route through the barren heart of Iceland, with views of Vatnajökull icecap to the southeast. This is a rugged 4WD route with unbridged rivers to ford and virtually no facilities anywhere. There's farm accommodation, food and fuel at Versalir, and from there you can head south to the beautiful rhyolite hills of **Landmannalaugar** (p254) in the **Fjallabak Nature Reserve** (p254). From here you can head southeast to Eldgjá then rejoin the Ring Road near Kirkjubæjarklaustur, or head west to Hella and on to Reykjavík.

TAILORED TRIPS

GLACIERS, GEYSERS & A GOOD SOAK 4+ days

If you're drawn to Iceland by the old 'fire and ice' theme and are keen to get close to glaciers and the underlying geothermal heat, there are plenty of possible options. First stop out of Reykjavík for many visitors is the famous **Blue Lagoon** (p95), a man-made thermal pool. Heading east out of Reykjavík you pass through **Hveragerði** (p110), with the Gufudalar ('Steam Valley') geothermal area, hot springs, mud pots and hothouses. From there head northeast to **Laugarvatn** (p104), a resort with steam baths and naturally heated pools beside a lake, then on to **Geysir** (p105) and the faithfully erupting Strokkur.

Back on the Ring Road, drive east to **Skógar** (p121) for the Eyjafjallajökull and Mýrdalsjökull glaciers. Further east is the awesome **Vatnajökull icecap** (p259). Your first stop should be **Skaftafell National Park** (p264), where you can get close to the glacier tongue. Glacier walks, ice climbing and mountaineering trips can be arranged around **Svínafell** (p268). Further along the Ring Road, **Jökulsárlón** (p269) is the famous iceberg-filled lagoon from pictures and postcards. Further east is the 4WD road to **Jöklasel** (p270), where you can do snowmobile trips on the icecap – they can be organised in the harbour town of **Höfn** (p271).

Other places to consider include the thermal springs around **Landmannalaugar** (p254), the ice caves of **Kverkfjöll** (p288), the Viti crater lake at **Askja** (p286), and the thermal pond, steam bath and geothermal area at **Mývatn** (p203).

IN SEARCH OF SAGAS 1+ weeks

The sagas conjure up a vivid picture of medieval Iceland, and many sites central to those stories can be visited today, although most are nothing more than an abandoned farm, a grave site, a cave, the remains of a hut or church, or nothing at all. However, the most famous sites are very dear to the hearts of Icelanders – start your search with the **Saga Museum** (p62) in Reykjavík.

The richest saga area of Iceland – relating mainly to *Laxdæla Saga* and *Egils Saga* – is the Borgarfjörður and Snæfellsnes peninsula area. Check out **Borgarnes** (p137), Snorri's Pool and the museum at **Reykholt** (p139), and **Laxárdalur** (Salmon River Valley; p141), setting for the *Laxdæla Saga.*

The south, around the valleys of Þórsmörk and Flótsdalur, is the setting for the epic *Njáls Saga* – there are many historic sites around **Hvolsvöllur** (p117) and more sites close to the Ring Road stretching almost to Höfn. In the northwest, Grettir the Strong, of *Grettis Saga*, holed up and was slain on **Drangey Island** (p180) in Skagafjörður. The farms at the centre of *Hrafnkels Saga* can be found in east Iceland, at remote **Hrafnkelstaðir** (p237) and **Aðalból** (p237).

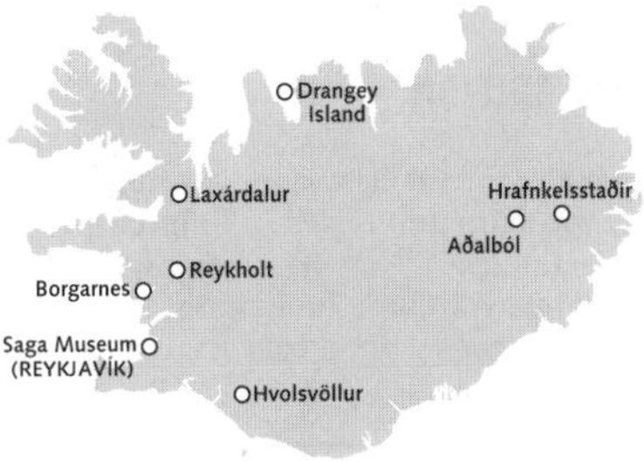

The Authors

PAUL HARDING

Coordinating Author

Paul's interest in glaciers, volcanoes and late-night pub crawls goes back a long way, so exploring Iceland was a natural choice. On this trip, among other things, he joined some Icelandic friends on a memorable *runtur* in Reykjavík, snowmobiled on Vatnajökull, took a dip at the Askja caldera and got attacked by Arctic terns. As a writer and photographer he has travelled extensively in Europe and Asia over the past 10 years and has contributed to numerous books for Lonely Planet, including *Scandinavian Europe* and *Finland*. Paul lives in Melbourne, Australia.

My Favourite Trip

If the weather is cooperating, it's hard to beat Iceland's southeast, with the Vatnajökull icecap always looming over you and the *sandur* stretching out in front. You'll see a little bit of everything travelling from Reykjavík to Höfn via Landmannalaugar and the trip into Fjallabak Nature Reserve and Landmannalaugar is a beauty; soaking in the thermal springs is heaven. The scenery, lava fields and hiking here are among the best in Iceland. From the stark interior you can get back on the Ring Road – I never cease to be amazed at the sight of enormous glaciers snaking down valleys towards the national highway. Stops at Skaftafell National Park and Jökulsárlón, the lagoon full of icebergs, cap off the most interesting road trip in Iceland.

JOE BINDLOSS

Joe first became hooked on Viking culture while growing up in eastern England, where many of the Viking chieftains were buried with their longships. Trips through the Scottish highlands and islands seemed to lead inexorably north towards Iceland, where Joe covered Reykjavík, the Westfjords, West Iceland and Southwest Iceland for this title. Joe has written about volcanic islands all over the world, but he especially rates Iceland for its ice climbing and architecture. He also has a soft spot for whales, seals and puffins.

LAST EDITION

Graeme Cornwallis was the coordinating author of *Iceland, Greenland & the Faroe Islands* 4. He was born and raised in Edinburgh and later wandered around Scotland before coming to rest in Glasgow, where he now teaches mathematics and physics when he's not hiking, climbing, travelling or writing. He has travelled extensively round Scandinavia since the 1980s and has a good background knowledge of Iceland.

Snapshot

The biggest issue to hit Iceland lately is the resumption of whaling 'for scientific purposes'. In 2003 the government decided to end its own 14-year ban on whaling and allow a quota of 38 minke whales to be hunted over a six-week period in August and September, the first of 250 to be killed over several years. Greenpeace sailed in to protest, and foreign governments and animal welfare groups roundly condemned the decision, but the Icelandic government told them all to go and mind their own business.

Despite this international outrage and claims that the growing tourist industry would suffer, many Icelanders on the street agree in principle with the decision. Icelanders, as stoic as ever, say it's their right to hunt whales and they don't give a hoot what the rest of the world thinks. More than a few of them are happy to see whale meat back on supermarket shelves too. That view may be changing though, as Icelanders realise the potential damage to the country's credibility and tourism versus the dubious advantages. The main groups opposing whaling in Iceland are conservationists, students, tourism associations and, of course, operators of whale-watching tours, which are becoming big business in Iceland. See the boxed text on p135 for more information.

Environmental issues are never far from the surface in a country as pristine as Iceland. The controversial Kárahnjúkar hydroelectric project was approved in 2003. By 2005 this project will have dammed and flooded two glacial rivers in the Eastern Highlands, and built a partially underground hydroelectric power plant and (by 2007) an aluminium smelter in the Eastfjords. Environmental groups and some locals protested the development, but others welcomed the boost to the regional economy and employment. Björk's mother, Hildur Hauksdóttir, went on a high profile three-week hunger strike in protest. See the boxed text on p245.

A large part of the workforce on this project will be foreign labour, from Eastern Europe and Italy. This raises another contentious issue: immigration and foreign workers taking local jobs. Although racism is not an obvious problem in Iceland (only 6% of the population is of foreign origin, mostly Polish), some Icelanders express fear and resentment at what they see as increasing immigration. Rules for employing foreign workers require that no qualified Icelander can be found for the job.

The biggest ongoing political issue is whether or not Iceland should join the EU, particularly after Finland and Sweden joined in 1995. It could be argued that Iceland's strong independent streak is enough to keep it out of the EU, but the main issue is one of fishing rights – opponents fear Iceland could lose some of its territorial waters to other member countries at a time when fish stocks are already down. Iceland spent many years during the 'Cod Wars' fighting for its 200-mile exclusion zone, and it doesn't want to lose it now. Still, Icelanders support membership, believing it's vital for future trade and economic stability.

On a lighter note, the talk in Reykjavík's bars is not so much about politics, but who's doing what, which Icelandic films are winning art-house awards, whether Sigur Rós is going to be the next big thing abroad, and when was the last time Damon Albarn was seen hanging out at the bar of Kaffibarinn.

FAST FACTS

Population: 288,201

GDP (million Ikr): 778.96

GDP per capita (US$): 29,619

Inflation: 1.9%

Tourist arrivals (2002): 277,800

Total fish catch (Jan–Jul 2003): 1.6 million tonnes

Unemployment (2002): 2.8%

History

If you skip the geological creation of Iceland, which goes back only about 17 million years, and fast-forward to discovery and settlement by Norse seafarers, you're left with an absorbing millennium of early settlement, sagas and survival, religious conversion, feuding, oppression under foreign rule and finally independence. Throw in centuries of natural disasters and famine, and it's not hard to see where the resilient and fiercely independent Icelandic spirit comes from.

EARLY TRAVELLERS & IRISH MONKS

Between 330 and 325 BC, the Greek navigator Pytheas embarked on a voyage from Massilia (Marseille) through the Pillars of Heracles, and then northward to investigate trade routes to the amber and tin markets of northern Europe. In the process he circumnavigated Britain, is said to have discovered the Orkneys (and possibly the Shetlands), and visited the west coast of Norway.

Northern Sphinx – Iceland & the Icelanders from the Settlement to the Present, by Sigurður A Magnússon, may be a little dated, but it's an easily digestible account of Iceland's people, places, history and issues.

In his report on the journey, Pytheas mentioned the island of Ultima Thule, six days' sailing north of Britain, beyond which the sea 'congealed into a viscous jelly'. This was almost certainly a reference to Iceland. Given the description, it seems unlikely he actually visited the island, but it is significant that the Celts or the Norse knew of its existence at such an early date.

Non-Nordic European perceptions of the North Atlantic region were shrouded in rumour and myth. The great northern ocean, *oceanus innavigabilis*, or the Hyperborean Sea, was a place of maelstrom where the fierce winds of Boreas howled through the Rhipaean Mountains and guarded idyllic lands of plenty like Vinland, the Elysian fields, Avalon, the Hesperides and a host of other enigmatic, but mythical, locales. The borders of paradise were inhabited, they believed, by barbaric dog-headed people (the Cynocephali and the Scythians) who ate raw meat and behaved like bears.

During the 6th century Irish monks set sail for fabled lands to the northwest. They brought back to Ireland tales of the land of Thule, where there was no daylight in winter, but on summer nights, according to the clergyman Dicuil in 825, 'whatever task a man wishes to perform, even picking lice from his shirt, he can manage as well as in clear daylight'. This almost certainly describes Iceland and its midnight sun.

www.mnh.si.edu/vikings/voyage/subset/iceland/history.html – Irish & Viking Discovery of Iceland, a Smithsonian Institute–related site, covers the early settlement of Iceland.

The first monks to settle in Iceland (around the year 700) would have realised that the islands were uninhabited and therefore more suitable as a hermitage than a mission. It's very unlikely that any remained in Iceland when the Norse people began to arrive in the early 9th century; Nordic accounts state that these *papar* ('fathers') fled during the period of Norse settlement.

THE VIKINGS ARE COMING!

After the Irish monks, Iceland's first permanent settlers came from Norway. The Age of Settlement is traditionally defined as the period between

TIMELINE **AD 600–700**

Irish monks voyage to uninhabited Iceland, becoming the first (temporary) settlers.

850–930

Norse settlers from Norway and Sweden arrive, call the island Snaeland ('Snow Land'), and set up scattered farms.

870 and 930, when political strife on the Scandinavian mainland caused many to flee. Although much Icelandic national pride is derived from notions that they're 'children of the Vikings', most North Atlantic Norse settlers were ordinary Scandinavian citizens: farmers, herders, merchants and opportunists. Throughout the Viking Age (800–1066), violent Norse advances were marked by an exodus into the North Atlantic, not only of Scandinavians but also of Britons, Westmen (Irish) and Scots who had intermarried with the fleeing victims of Nordic despotism.

http://viking.no/e – the Viking Network Web is an educational site covering history of the Vikings.

It's likely the Norse accidentally discovered Iceland after being blown off course en route to the Faroes. The first arrival, the Swede Naddoddur, landed on the east coast around 850 and named the place Snæland ('Snow Land') before backtracking to his original destination.

Iceland's second visitor, Garðar Svavarsson, came in search of Naddoddur's reported discovery. He circumnavigated it then settled in for the winter at Húsavík on the north coast. When he left in the spring, some of his crew remained, or were probably left behind, thereby becoming the island's first residents.

Around 860, the Norwegian Flóki Vilgerðarson uprooted his farm and family and headed for Snæland. He navigated with ravens, which, after some trial and error, led him to his destination. This odd practice provided his nickname, Hrafna-Flóki or 'Raven's Flóki'.

Iceland's 1100 Years: The History of a Marginal Society, by Gunnar Karlsson, provides an insightful, contemporary history of Iceland from Settlement to the present. Karlsson also wrote *The History of Iceland*, which covers the same subject in a slightly more academic tone.

Hrafna-Flóki sailed to Vatnsfjörður on the west coast but quickly became disenchanted with the place. Upon seeing icebergs floating in the fjord, he renamed it Ísland ('Ice Land'), which he perhaps considered even less flattering than 'Snæland', and returned to Norway. It was a number of years before he returned to Iceland, settling in the Skagafjörður district on the north coast.

Credit for the first intentional settlement, according to the *Íslendingabók*, goes to a Norwegian called Ingólfur Arnarson, who landed at Ingólfshöfði (Southeast Iceland) in 874, then continued around the coast and set up housekeeping at a place he called Reykjavík (Smoky Bay), named after the steam from thermal springs there. Ingólfur was a true Viking who'd had his day in the British Isles; he and his blood brother Hjörleifur were forced to flee Norway after they encountered some social difficulties there. Hjörleifur settled near the present town of Vík, but was murdered by his slaves shortly thereafter.

Íslendingabók, written by 12th-century scholar, Ari Þorgilsson (Ari the Learned), about 250 years after the fact, provides a historical narrative from the Settlement era. The detailed *Landnámabók*, probably compiled from several sources by Ari the Learned, is a comprehensive account of the Settlement.

As for Ingólfur, the site of his homestead was determined by the custom of the day, which required well-born intending settlers to toss their high-seat pillars, a symbol of authority and part of a Norse chieftain's pagan paraphernalia, into the sea as they approached land. Tradition and prudence dictated that they build their homes at the place where the gods chose to bring the pillars ashore. At times, settlement necessitated years of searching the coastline for stray pillars, and it's likely that Ingólfur was disappointed with the barren, rocky bay he was forced to settle on.

While Ingólfur Arnarson and his descendants came to control the whole of the southwestern part of Iceland, other settlers were arriving from the mainland. By the time Ingólfur's son Þorsteinn reached adulthood, the island was scattered with farms, and people began to feel the need for some sort of government.

874
Norwegian Viking Ingólfur Arnarson sails to the west coast and establishes the first major settlement at Reykjavík.

930
Icelandic parliament, the Alþing (National Assembly), is founded at Þingvellir.

THE VIKINGS

Scandinavia's greatest impact on world history probably occurred during the Viking Age, when the prospect of trade, political stress and an increasingly dense agricultural population inspired many Norwegians to seek out greener pastures abroad. The word 'Viking' is derived from *vik*, which means bay or cove in old Norse and probably referred to their anchorages during raids.

It's suspected that the main catalyst for the Viking movement was overpopulation in western Norway, where polygamy led to an excess of male heirs and too little land to go around. In the 8th century, Nordic shipbuilders developed a relatively fast and manoeuvrable sailing vessel which had a heavy keel, up to 16 pairs of oars and a large square sail, and was sturdy enough for ocean crossings. While Norwegian farmers had peacefully settled in the Orkneys and Shetlands as early as the 780s, it's generally accepted that the Viking Age didn't begin until 793, with the 'Northmen' plundering St Cuthbert's monastery on the island of Lindisfarne off the coast of Northumberland, Britain.

The Vikings apparently had no reservations about sacking religious communities and, indeed, many Vikings believed that the Christian monasteries they encountered were a threat to their pantheist traditions. But the Vikings also realised that monasteries were places of wealth, where a relatively quick and easy victory could result in a handsome booty. Mainly in the more lawless regions of Britain and Ireland, they destroyed Christian communities and slaughtered the monks, who could only wonder what sin they had committed to invite the heathen hordes. Despite this apparent predilection for warfare, their considerable barbarism was probably no greater than the standard of the day – it was the success and extent of the raids that led to their fearsome reputation. The Vikings had no fear of death – only dishonour.

In the following years, the Viking raiders returned with great fleets, terrorising, murdering, enslaving, assimilating or displacing the local population and capturing many coastal and inland regions of Britain, Ireland, France (Normandy was named for these Northmen) and Russia (as far east as the Volga). The Vikings travelled as far as Moorish Spain (Seville was raided in 844) and the Middle East (they even reached Baghdad). Constantinople was attacked six times but never yielded, and ultimately Vikings actually served as mercenaries with the forces of the Holy Roman Empire.

Between the 10th and 14th centuries, the Scandinavian Norsemen also explored and settled land throughout the North Atlantic – including the Faroe Islands, Iceland, Greenland and parts of North America.

A major stepping stone was Iceland, which, unlike Greenland, remained uninhabited. Icelandic tradition officially credits the Norse settlement of Iceland to a single mainland phenomenon. From the middle to late 9th century, the tyrannical Harald Haarfager (Harald Finehair, or Fairhair), the king of Vestfold district of southeastern Norway, was taken with expansionist aspirations. In 890, he won a significant naval victory at Hafrsfjord (Stavanger), and the deposed chieftains and landowners chose to flee rather than submit. Many wound up in Iceland and the Faroes.

While Viking raids continued in Europe, Eiríkur Rauðe (Erik the Red), having been exiled from Iceland, headed west with around 500 others to found the first permanent European colony in Greenland in 987. Eiríkur's son, Leif the Lucky, went on to visit Helluland (the 'land of flat stones', probably Baffin Island), Markland (the 'land of woods', most likely Newfoundland or Labrador) and Vinland (the 'land of wine', probably somewhere between Newfoundland and New Jersey). He had set foot in the New World as early as the year 1000 – Europeans had reached the Americas, but permanent settlement was thwarted by the 'skrælings' (Native Americans), who were anything but welcoming.

The last Viking raids occurred in the 11th century, after King Harald Harðráðl died in battle in England. Almost 300 years of terrorising the seas were coming to an end.

1000

Iceland officially converts to Christianity under pressure from the Norwegian king, though pagan beliefs and rituals remain.

1100–1200

The great literary age of the Sagas.

ASSEMBLING THE ALÞING

After rejecting the political strife at home on the mainland, Icelanders were firmly against monarchy, so they set up a parliamentary system of government. Such a structure had never proved itself before, but they reasoned it could only be better than the fearful and oppressive setup on the mainland.

In the early 10th century, Þorsteinn Ingólfsson founded Iceland's first large-scale district assembly near Reykjavík, placing himself in a strong political position. In the 920s, the self-styled lawyer Úlfljótur was sent to Norway to prepare a code of law for Iceland.

At the same time, Grímur Geitskör was commissioned to find a suitable location for an Alþing, or National Assembly. Bláskógar, near the eastern boundary of Ingólfur's estate, with its beautiful lake and wooded plain, seemed ideal. Along one side of the plain was a long cliff with an elevated base (the Mid-Atlantic Rift) from where speakers and representatives could preside over people gathered below.

In 930 Bláskógar was renamed Þingvellir, the 'assembly plains'. Þorsteinn Ingólfsson received the honorary title *allsherjargoði* (supreme chieftain) and Úlfljótur was designated the first *lögsögumaður* or 'law-speaker', who was required to memorise and annually recite the entire law of the land. It was he, along with the 48 *goðar* (chieftains), who held the actual legislative power.

At the annual convention of 1000 came the decree that made Iceland a Christian nation in a remarkably peaceful conversion. Although conversion came under pressure from Norwegian King Olaf Tryggvason, it provided Iceland with a semblance of national unity at a time when squabbles were arising among the country's leaders and allegiances were being questioned. The first bishoprics were later set up at Skálholt in the southwest and Hólar in the north.

Over the following years, the two-week national assembly at Þingvellir became the social event of the year. Single people came looking for partners, marriages were contracted and solemnised, business deals were finalised, duels and executions were held, and the Appeals Court handed down judgments on matters that couldn't be resolved in lower courts. One such judgment, the pronouncement of exile upon outlaw Eiríkur Rauðe (Eric the Red), led to the Norse colonisation of Greenland.

During its first century, the Alþing was strained by corruption as the *goðar* demanded bribes in exchange for favours. But by this time, Icelandic society and the agrarian economy were well established and the government held. Schools were founded at the two bishoprics and elsewhere, and the resulting educational awareness prepared the way for the great literary era to come.

DID YOU KNOW?

The Alþing, established in 930, is the oldest continuous parliamentary democracy in the world.

www.althingi.is – the official site of the Alþing covers the history and workings of Iceland's parliament.

DID YOU KNOW?

Leif Eiríksson (Leif the Lucky), son of exiled Icelander Erik the Red, is credited as the first European to 'discover' North America (it was already inhabited by Native Americans).

ANARCHY & THE STURLUNG AGE

The late 12th century kicked off the Saga Age, when epic tales of early settlement, family struggles, romance and tragic characters were recorded by historians and writers. But all was not well in Iceland. By the early 13th century, the enlightened period of peace that had lasted 200 years began to wane and the country entered the infamous Sturlung Age, a turbulent era graphically recounted in the tragic three-volume *Sturlunga Saga*. Viking-like private armies ravaged the countryside and competition

1200

Iceland descends into anarchy during the so-called Sturlung Age. The government dissolves and, in 1291, Iceland is absorbed by Norway.

1300, 1341 & 1389

The volcano Hekla violently erupts three times, causing death and widespread destruction.

The Complete Sagas of Icelanders, edited by Viður Hreinsson, is a must for saga fiends. It's a summary translation of 50 saga tales, featuring all the main yarns, along with a few shorter fantasy tales.

Iceland Saga, by Magnús Magnússon, offers an entertaining introduction to Icelandic history and literature, and explains numerous saga events and settings.

between politicians turned into violent feuds and power struggles. Even had it wanted to do so, the failing government was powerless to protect the populace from the ensuing mayhem.

The opportunistic Norwegian King Hákon Hákonarson regarded the strife as his invitation to take control of the situation. The Icelanders, who saw no alternative, dissolved all but a superficial shell of their government and swore their allegiance to the king. An agreement of confederacy was made in 1262. In 1281, a new code of law, the Jónsbók, was introduced by the king and Iceland was absorbed into Norwegian rule.

Norway immediately set about appointing Norwegian bishops to Hólar and Skálholt and imposed excessive taxes. Contention flared as former chieftains quibbled over high offices, particularly that of *járl* (earl), an honour that fell to the ruthless scoundrel Gissur Þorvaldsson who, in 1241, murdered Snorri Sturluson, Iceland's best-known historian and writer. The governorship of Iceland was actually leased for three-year periods to the highest Norwegian bidder, and with that office came the power to extract revenue in any efficient manner.

ENTER THE DANES

In 1397 the Kalmar Union of Norway, Sweden and Denmark brought Iceland, still a province of Norway, under Danish rule. After disputes between church and state, the Danish government seized church property and imposed Lutheranism in the Reformation of 1550. When the stubborn Catholic bishop of Hólar, Jón Arason, resisted and gained a following, he and his two sons were taken to Skálholt and beheaded.

In 1602, the Danish king imposed a crippling trade monopoly whereby Swedish and Danish firms were given exclusive trading rights in Iceland for 12-year periods. This resulted in large-scale extortion, importation of spoiled or inferior goods and yet more suffering that would last another 250 years.

RETURN TO INDEPENDENCE

Five centuries of oppression under foreign rule had taken its toll on the Icelanders. By the early 1800s, a growing sense of Icelandic nationalism was perceived in Copenhagen, but an ongoing liberalisation process in Europe prevented Denmark from tightening its grip. Jón Sigurðsson, an Icelandic scholar, successfully lobbied for restoration of free trade in 1855. By 1874, Iceland had drafted a constitution and was at last permitted to handle its own domestic matters without interference from the mainland.

The Act of Union, which was signed in 1918, effectively released Iceland from Danish rule, making it an independent state within the Kingdom of Denmark, with Copenhagen retaining responsibility for defence and foreign affairs. The Act of Union was to be valid until 1940, when the Alþing could request a review of Iceland's status.

On 9 April 1940, Denmark was occupied by Germany. Since the kingdom was in no position to continue overseeing Iceland's defence and foreign affairs, the Alþing took control of its own foreign relations. A year later, on 17 May 1941, the Icelanders requested complete independence. The formal establishment of the Republic of Iceland finally took place at Þingvellir on 17 June 1944 – now celebrated as Independence Day.

1397
Iceland comes under Danish rule.

1602
Denmark imposes a crippling trade monopoly, giving Danish and Swedish firms exclusive trading rights in Iceland.

WWII & THE US MOVES IN

After the occupation of Denmark and Iceland's declaration of sovereignty in 1940, the island's vulnerability became a matter of concern for the Allied powers. They knew Iceland had no military forces whatsoever and was unprepared to defend its strategic position in case of German aggression. Britain, which would have been most vulnerable to a German-controlled Iceland, sent in forces to occupy the island. Despite declaring its neutrality, Iceland had little choice but to grudgingly accept this help, and was pleased to find that British construction projects and spending bolstered the economy.

Although Iceland didn't fight in WWII, around 300 merchant sailors and fishermen who were assisting the Allied war effort lost their lives as a result of German military action.

When the British troops withdrew in 1941, the government allowed American troops to move in, on the understanding that they would move out at the end of the war. They stayed on, however, and in 1946 asked to be allowed 99-year leases on three bases in Iceland. The far-seeing Alþing rejected the request, but consented to the US use of Keflavík international airport as a refuelling and staging point for cargo aircraft flying between Europe and North America.

Daughter of Fire – a Portrait of Iceland, by Katherin Scherman, is a beautifully written, evocative historical overview of Iceland, covering the land, the people and the sagas.

When NATO was formed in 1949, Iceland was pressured into becoming a founding member by other Scandinavian states, but only on the condition that under no circumstances would foreign military troops be based there during peacetime. The decision prompted riots in Reykjavík among protesters who feared the thin edge of the US military wedge.

By 1951, the US military had completely taken over Keflavík international airport with no obvious intention of budging. They justified their actions by indicating that Iceland required US protection from the Soviet troops that had invaded North Korea, and indeed Iceland served as an important North Atlantic base for monitoring the Soviet Union during the Cold War.

When the Icelanders realised what was happening, they were predictably unhappy, but were powerless to evict the Americans, whose numbers and military technology at Keflavík continued to increase over the next four decades. Small numbers of Icelanders objected and demanded that the 'Yankees go home', but protests have fizzled out.

MODERN ICELAND

Following the Cold War period and the demise of the herring fishing industry, Iceland went through a period of growth, rebuilding and modernisation. The Ring Road was finally completed in 1974 – opening up transport across the remote Southeast – and projects such as the diatomite plant and Krafla power station in the Northeast and the Svartsengi power plant near Reykjavík were developed. Iceland's current situation is one of economic regeneration, and the country is becoming stronger while the fishing industry recovers from the mid-1990s recession. In the recession, problems stemmed primarily from fishing quotas, which in 1992–93 were reduced by 22.5% to allow overfished stocks to regenerate. As a result, in October 1992 unemployment stood at 3% (a previously unheard-of level in Iceland).

1855–74

Iceland moves towards Independence with the restoration of free trade and a draft constitution.

1902

Acclaimed writer and Nobel Prize–winner Halldór Laxness is born in Reykjavík.

COD WARS

For most of its history Iceland has kept to itself, staying out of international disputes. But when it came to fishing – its main source of livelihood and export economy – Iceland was prepared to fight to protect and expand its waters. Iceland's decision to increase its territorial fishing territory, and the resulting skirmishes with British vessels, became known as the 'Cod Wars'.

It all started in 1901 when Britain and Denmark reduced the extent of the country's offshore fishing rights to less than four miles. In 1952, Iceland increased the limit to four miles offshore but expanded it to 12 miles in 1958, sparking the first Cod War. In 1972 they expanded again to 50 miles and finally 200 miles in 1975. The wars were characterised by clashes between Icelandic gunships and British warships and, in 1976, a stopgap agreement was made with Britain. Since then British fishing boats have respected the 200-mile limit, and no new violence has erupted.

Meanwhile, Iceland had to deal with the demise of the lucrative herring industry, which collapsed in the late 1960s as a result of overfishing by both Icelanders and Norwegians.

Interestingly, Iceland claims the tiny islet of Kolbeinsey, 100km north of the mainland in the Arctic Ocean, as part of the country. Although it's little more than a speck (about 40 sq m), and is continually being eroded, it adds 9400 sq km to Iceland's territorial fishing waters – making it the most important piece of offshore rock in the North Atlantic!

The krónur was also devalued by 6% to relieve pressure caused by turmoil in international currency markets. In January 1993, Iceland approved a European Economic Area agreement between the EU and the European Free Trade Association (to which it belongs), but only after the agreement conceded to Iceland's demands for restrictions on fishing in its waters.

In the mid-1990s, the Reykjavík stock market, Verðbrefaþing Íslands, commenced operations. Relatively recently, Icelandic society has started to polarise with the growth of a very wealthy elite.

Politically, Iceland is a democratic republic with a president elected to a four-year term by majority vote. Legislative powers rest with the Alþing (parliament). Current major political parties in Iceland include the conservative Independence Party, or Sjálfstæðisflokkurinn (33.7%), led by Prime Minister David Oddson; the Social Democrat Alliance (31%); and the centrist, agrarian Progressive Party (17.7%).

Vigdís Finnbogadóttir, the first woman elected to the presidency of a democratic country, held office from 1980 until she stood down in 1996 and Ólafur Ragnar Grímsson was elected (he was returned unopposed in 2000).

DID YOU KNOW?

Reykjavík hosted the 1986 summit between Mikhail Gorbachev and Ronald Reagan – a sign of warmer relations between the superpowers and of Iceland's strategic importance to America during the Cold War era.

In the latest parliamentary elections in 2003, there was little change in the distribution of support for the main political parties, and the tradition of coalition government continues with the Independence and Progressive Parties forming the government. The fact that the Left Green Alliance (8.8%) continues to receive support indicates a growing awareness of environmental issues.

Among the big issues affecting Iceland today are the resumption of whaling in 2003, the decision to go ahead with the hydroelectric power plant, dam and Alcoa alumininium smelter in East Iceland, and whether or not to join the EU. See p19 for more information.

1918

The Act of Union makes Iceland an independent state with the Kingdom of Denmark.

1940–41

In WWII, British troops occupy Iceland to defend its strategic position. US troops follow and set up base at Keflavík international airport.

The Culture

THE NATIONAL PSYCHE

Centuries of isolation, hardship and a small, homogenous population have instilled particular character traits in Icelanders. With a population of only 288,000, this is a tightknit nation where everyone seems to know each other, and if not, they're probably distantly related.

Icelanders have a reputation as tough, hardy, seafaring types – witness the recent story of an Icelandic fisherman who wrestled and killed a shark that was threatening his crew – and it's true that rural Icelanders are mainly involved in the fishing industry or farming. But a walk around downtown Reykjavík reveals a very different character among young Icelanders. There's a certain bohemian, creative air among the local urban youth and a feeling that it's possible to achieve anything, without the need to set foot on a fishing trawler or in a fish-processing plant. Meet a group of young Icelanders in a Reykjavík bar and you'll find that most dabble in music (and probably perform in a band), poetry, writing or art. They're proud of their cultural and literary heritage and aim to continue it.

Xenophobe's Guide to the Icelanders, by Richard Sale, is a compact, humorous look at the Icelandic character and foible – everything from customs and driving habits to obsession with material possessions.

Naturally enough for people living on a remote island in a harsh environment, Icelanders are generally self-confident, self-reliant and 'rugged individualists' who baulk at following trends, but still look to the outside world for approval. The international success of people like singer Björk, novelist Halldór Laxness, four-time World's Strongest Man Jon Pall Sigmarsson, and anyone playing football in a European league, elevates them to hero status. At the same time, they don't want anyone telling them what to do – the whaling issue is a prime example.

Icelanders are not as aloof as some of their Scandinavian counterparts in Sweden, Norway and Finland. They're curious about visitors to their country and eager to know what outsiders think of them. 'How do you like Iceland?' is invariably an early question. While most Icelanders speak English very well, they're extremely proud of their language, and to greet them with a little carefully pronounced Icelandic will result in a look of mild surprise (bordering on shock) followed by a broad smile.

While Icelanders are generally quite reserved and stoical, an incredible transformation comes over them when they party. On a Friday or Saturday night inhibitions are let down, conversations flow as fast as the alcohol and downtown Reykjavík has some of the craziest scenes imaginable!

ELVES, SPIRITS & TROLLS

Once you've seen some of the lava fields and eerie natural formations that characterise much of the Icelandic landscape, it will come as no surprise that Icelanders believe their country is populated by hidden races of wee people: *jarðvergar* (gnomes), *álfar* (elves), *ljósálfar* (fairies), *dvergar* (dwarves), *ljúflingar* (lovelings), *tívar* (mountain spirits), *englar* (angels) and *huldufólk* ('hidden people').

Many rock stacks and formations around the country are attributed to trolls who have been caught out at sunrise committing some evil deed and been forever turned to stone. Stories of the hidden people have been handed down through generations, and although some Icelanders today will roll their eyes at the mention of elves, the majority have no doubt about their existence and many claim to have seen them. There are famous stories of workers trying to build a road through a hill occupied by *huldufólk*. The weather turned bad, machinery mysteriously broke down and workers fell ill – until they decided to build around it. Icelanders are content to live in harmony with the hidden people – and that means leaving their homes alone.

WHAT'S IN A NAME?

Icelanders' names are constructed using the patronymic system. That is, a person receives a Christian name from their parents and their surname is constructed from their father's (or occasionally their mother's) Christian name. Girls add the suffix *dóttir* ('daughter') to the patronymic and boys add *son*. Therefore Jón, the son of Einar, would be called Jón Einarsson and his sister, Guðrun, would be called Guðrun Einarsdóttir.

Icelandic telephone directories are alphabetised by Christian name, and as a general rule Icelanders refer to each other – even strangers – by Christian or full names, rather than 'Mr or Mrs Einarsson'. Only about 10% of Icelanders actually have family names, most of them dating back to early Settlement times. These family names are rarely used, however, and the government is trying to do away with them altogether in an attempt to homogenise the system. Currently, nobody is permitted to take on a new family name, nor are they allowed to adopt the family name of their spouse.

It's also forbidden to bestow non-Icelandic or foreign-sounding names upon Icelandic children. Even foreign immigrants must take on Icelandic names before citizenship will be granted. The only exception ever made was for conductor Vladimir Ashkenazy (which led a subsequent immigrant to request the new Icelandic name 'Vladimir Ashkenazy'!).

LIFESTYLE

In the last century, Icelandic lifestyle has shifted from isolated, family communities living on scattered farms and in coastal villages to a more urban-based society with the majority of people living in the southwestern corner around Reykjavík. Despite a more outward-looking nature over the past few decades, family connections are still very strong in Iceland, but young people growing up in rural Iceland are more likely to move to Reykjavík to study and work.

DID YOU KNOW?

Icelanders can use a registry website, *The Book of Icelanders* (www.islendingabok.is), to trace their ancestry and find out who is really related to who.

Icelanders work hard (which may explain why they play so hard on weekends) and enjoy a very high standard of living, but keeping up in the material world comes at a price. It's not unusual for young Icelanders out of school to borrow money to buy a house or 4WD and spend the rest of their days paying off loans and living on credit.

Since there's no stigma attached to unmarried mothers, about a third of children are born out of wedlock. A law was recently passed compelling women to name the father of their child and in late 2003 a special court was set up to deal with custody matters.

POPULATION

Because most Icelanders are descended from Celtic settlers, as well as early Scandinavian, Iceland is the least purely Scandinavian of all the Nordic countries. Immigration is strictly controlled and most foreigners living in the country are either temporary workers or spouses of Icelandic citizens. The population of foreign origin is only about 6%.

The population, just over 288,000, is increasing by only about 0.5% annually. Around 112,500 people, almost half the total population, live in Reykjavík and almost 180,000 live in the Greater Reykjavík area. This is growing at a rate of about 2% annually, mostly due to continuous migration from small towns and the countryside. About 25,000 Icelanders live on farms scattered around the country while the rest live in cities, towns and villages of 200 or more people. The population density of 2.8 per sq km is the lowest in Europe.

www.statice.is – the Statistics Iceland site has facts and figures about Iceland.

Statistically, everyone in Iceland is literate and the average life expectancy – 77.5 years for men and 82.2 for women – is one of the highest in the world.

SPORT

Football (soccer) is the most popular spectator and participation sport in Iceland, with 10 teams in the national premier league – five of them Reykjavík-based. The biggest national venue is the 14,000-seat Laugardalsvöllur stadium in Reykjavík. Iceland doesn't win a lot of international games, but matches are keenly followed and Icelanders will proudly tell you they have several players in top European or English premier league teams. There's also a women's league with eight teams in the premier division.

www.ksi.is – official site of the Football Association of Iceland.

The next most popular team sport is handball, particularly after the world championships were held in Reykjavík in 1995. Iceland has had some success in world championship finals and finished seventh overall in 2003. The game is played by two teams of seven and is similar to basketball, played on the same sort of court but using a smaller ball. Instead of a hoop there's a goal at either end (a bit like soccer or water polo). You can see handball matches at sports halls around the country – Reykjavík, Hafnarfjörður and Akureyri are good places.

The traditional sport is glíma (Icelandic wrestling), a unique national sport with a history dating back to the days of Viking settlement in the 9th century. Icelanders still practise the sport, but it's not common on a competitive level and you're most likely to see it as a demonstration at a traditional festival.

www.ffa.est.is –the Ferðafélag Akureyrar (Touring Club of Akureyri) site also has information on hiking and mountain huts.

OUTDOOR ACTIVITIES

Although Icelanders are great lovers of the outdoors, they tend to spend more time working than playing and they're very independent when it comes to organising activities. City-dwellers living in Reykjavík might escape the city only a few times a year to go camping, hiking or skiing. Most of the organised activities are for foreign tourists, and many of the people you'll pass on hiking trails are also tourists.

Hiking

The best way to see Iceland is on foot, whether on an afternoon hike or a longer wilderness trek, and the opportunities are virtually endless. Even in summer, weather can mean the difference between a miserable, mist-shrouded trudge and some of the most inspiring hiking on the planet, but it's all part of experiencing Iceland on its own terms.

In the highlands, the best months for walking are July and August, since late or early snow is a real possibility; in some places it never melts. May to September are good times throughout the rest of the country, and

TOP HIKES

- Landmannalaugar to Þórsmörk trek (p256)
- Fjallabak Nature Reserve (p254)
- Skaftafell National Park (p265)
- Dettifoss–Asbýrgi Canyon (p223)
- Lónsöræfi (p276)
- Snæfell–Lónsöræfi Trek (p238)
- Hverfell & Dimmuborgir Trail (p209)
- Kjölurvegur trek (p281)
- Hornstrandir peninsula (p169)
- Seyðisfjörður–Vestdalur (p242)

Hiking Trails in Iceland – The Western Fjords (Vikingur Press) was written by Einar Guðjohnsen, a knowledgeable Icelandic hiking buff. Visitors will find it useful for the route maps if nothing else.

a popular trekking route such as Landmannalaugar–Þórsmörk (see p256) may be less crowded late or early in the season. Weather conditions can change in minutes at any time of year, so always be prepared.

Strong boots are essential for walking over lava fields; anything less can be torn to shreds on the rough, jagged rock. When walking with children, especially in fissured areas like Mývatn and Þingvellir, beware of narrow cracks in the ground, which may be hundreds of metres deep.

Apart from national parks, nature reserves and privately owned land, you're free to camp practically anywhere in Iceland. To camp on a private farm, ask the owner's permission before setting up, and wherever you camp, take care to keep toilet activities away from streams and surface water, and use biodegradable soaps for washing up. Due to the shortage of natural fuels and environmental impact, campfires are discouraged and in some places prohibited. Hikers should carry a stove and enough fuel for their entire trip.

Horse Riding

Riding is an integral part of the traditional Icelandic scene – many rural Icelanders own and breed horses and they are still used in the highlands for the traditional sheep roundup. The naturally gentle Icelandic horse (see the boxed text below) is ideally suited for the terrain, even for riders with no experience.

Farmhouse accommodation, tour agencies and individual farmers hire horses and lead riding expeditions through wild and otherwise inaccessible corners of Iceland, including week-long horse packing tours. Short horse rides cost around Ikr2000 per hour. Longer tours, including tent or hut accommodation, guides and meals, cost from Ikr12,000 per day. It's possible to stay in hotels or guesthouses and take day trips from your base. Note that foreign riding clothing or equipment (saddles, bridles etc) must be disinfected upon entry into the country.

The following list includes some of the best operators offering short-term horse hire, as well as longer horse-riding tours:

Arinbjörn Jóhannsson (☎ 451 2938; brekka@nett.is; Brekkulækur, Mið-fjörður, IS-531 Hvammstangi)
Bangahestar (☎ 464 4103; Reykjahlíð, IS-660 Mývatn)
Eldhestar (☎ 483 4884; info@eldhestar.is; Vellir, Ölfus, IS-810 Hveragerði)
Hestaleiga Brattholt (☎ 486 8941; brattholtii@islandia.is; Biskupstungur, IS-801 Selfoss)
Hestasport (☎ 453 8383; www.riding.is; Varmahlíð)
Íshestar (☎ 555 7000; www.ishestar.is; Bæjarhraun 2, IS-220 Hafnarfjörður)
Pólar Hestar (☎ 463 3179; www.polarhestar.is; Stefán Kristjánsson, Grýtubakki II, Grenivík, IS-601 Akureyri)

THE ICELANDIC HORSE

The Icelandic horse *(Equus scandinavicus)*, brought across by early Norse settlers, is a sturdy animal perfectly suited to the rough Icelandic terrain. The horses stand only about 1.3m high, and since no other horses have been imported recently, the breeding stock remains pure.

In early days horse fights were organised as a source of entertainment, and the meat was consumed as a staple and used in pagan rituals. As a result, horse meat was later banned by the Christian church (but is now eaten occasionally).

The horses continue to play a role in the autumn sheep roundup and are widely used recreationally. Like some Mongolian breeds, they have five gaits: *fet* (walk), *brokk* (trot), *stökk* (gallop), *skeið* (pace) and the famous *tölt* (running walk), which is so smooth and steady that the rider scarcely notices any motion.

Swimming

Thanks to Iceland's abundance of geothermal heat, swimming is a national institution. Nearly every city and village has at least one *sundlaug* (public swimming pool), and many cold, rainy and windy afternoons are passed in swirling warm waters with a good book or good company. Hot pots (small heated pools or spa baths) have traditionally been a place where Icelanders gather to meet and chat. Most pools also offer saunas and Jacuzzis of varying temperatures. A session in the pool and/or Jacuzzi costs around Ikr200.

Icelandic swimming pools have a strict hygiene regimen, which involves a thorough shower (with soap and shampoo, usually provided free) in the change rooms *before* you enter the swimming area. Watch what Icelanders do and observe signs and instructions.

Fishing

Fishing is very popular with Icelanders and with visiting anglers who come here expressly for the salmon fly-fishing. What the glossy brochures neglect to tell you about salmon fishing in Iceland is that Icelandic salmon privately caught may well be the most expensive fish on earth.

A licence for one day of salmon fishing on some rivers can cost up to – sit down, fish fans – Ikr200,000. That's per day and doesn't include a guide, transportation or equipment hire – just the licence. If you happen to have that kind of money, you might bump into Eric Clapton or Prince Charles, who reportedly come to fish in Iceland's pristine but pricey streams. The least expensive salmon rivers, under some circumstances, cost as little as Ikr20,000 per day, but you must book well in advance.

The good news is that you can fish for rainbow trout, sea trout and Arctic char on a more reasonably priced voucher system. Some lakes and streams produce more fish and are therefore more expensive than others. Most fishing throughout Iceland is on private farms and fishing time should be booked in advance. Sea fishing and some lake fishing is free.

The salmon-fishing season runs from early June to mid-September. Trout fishing is possible from April to mid-September, and ice fishing is possible in some areas in winter.

For information, pick up the magazine *Veiði Sumar* (Fishing Summer), which is published free annually. It's mostly in Icelandic, but is still useful for the maps of main fishing regions.

Angling and permit details are available from the **Reykjavík Angling Club** (☎ 568 6050; Háaleitisbraut 68) or **Veiðivon** (☎ 568 7090; Mörkin 6), also in Reykjavík. Another source of information is the **Angling Club Lax-á** (☎ 557 6100; www.lax-a.is; Vatnsendabletti 181, 203 Kópavogur).

'You might bump into Eric Clapton or Prince Charles, who reportedly come to fish salmon in Iceland's pristine streams'

Golf

Golf has become increasingly popular in Iceland in recent years, and in the north of Iceland in midsummer, you can try the novel experience of a round under the midnight sun. There are 18-hole courses in Reykjavík, Hafnarfjörður, Garðabær, Akranes, Keflavík, Heimaey (Vestmannaeyjar) and Akureyri, and at least another 20 nine-hole courses spread around the country, as remote as Siglufjörður, Ísafjörður and Eskifjörður. For more information, contact the **Icelandic Golf Club** (Golfsamband Íslands; ☎ 541 4050; www.golf.is; Stofnað 14) in Reykjavík.

Two annual events to look out for are the **Arctic Open** in Akureyri in mid-June, an all-night 36-hole 'midnight sun' tournament that attracts amateurs and professionals from around the world, and the **Volcano Open** at the dramatic Vestmannaeyjar course, played over four days in early July. For entry information, contact the **Akureyri Golf Club** (☎ 462 2974; gagolf@nett.is), the **Vestmannaeyjar Golf Club** (☎ 481 2363; www.eyjar.is/~golf) or the **Iceland Tourist Board** (☎ 535 5500; www.icetourist.is) in Reykjavík.

Skiing

Downhill skiing in Iceland has nothing on mainland Scandinavia, as there's not enough infrastructure or high, accessible slopes, but there are some very enjoyable, little-known slopes offering pleasant, no-frills skiing. In winter, Nordic (cross-country) skiing is possible almost anywhere, and in highland areas it lasts until early July. The main drawback is the limited winter transport.

Reykjavík and Akureyri both have relatively well-organised downhill resorts where you'll spend around Ikr1200 for combination day and evening lift tickets. The slopes at Bláfjöll near Reykjavík are sometimes served by buses from the **BSÍ terminal** (☎ 552 2300), dependent on weather conditions.

Conditions are more reliable at Hlíðarfjall near Akureyri, with runs of up to 2.5km and buses from Akureyri three times daily.

There are also more basic resorts at Ísafjörður (p154; Westfjords), Siglufjörður (p183), Ólafsfjörður (p197) and Dalvík (p196; Northwest), Húsavík (p215; Northeast) and Eskifjörður (p244; Eastfjords).

White-water Rafting & Kayaking

With glacial rivers flowing off Iceland's icecaps and thundering towards the coast, it was only a matter of time before commercial operators discovered the potential for white-water rafting. Some of the best rafting rivers and most established operators are in North Iceland. **Activity Tours** (☎ 453 8383, www.rafting.is) in Varmahlíð offers day trips or multiday safaris of the East and West Glacial Rivers, while **Arctic Rafting** (http://www.travelnet.is/arctic/main.htm) has trips on the Þjórsá river near Árnes.

DID YOU KNOW?

In the summer of 2003, Americans Chris Duff, Shawna Franklin and Leon Sómme completed an unsupported circumnavigation of Iceland in sea kayaks in less than three months. Briton John Burleigh did the same trip solo in 77 days.

Rafting trips include guides, equipment, transport and refreshments, and overnight trips usually include accommodation (tents or huts) and food.

Kayaking is also gaining popularity, particularly in the calm, accessible waters of the Eastfjords and the rugged Westfjords. You can go out on guided kayaking trips in Seyðisfjörður and Neskaupstaður (including midnight-sun paddles in summer), and in the lagoons of Stokkseyri; it's possible to rent kayaks in some places (such as Mývatn). A number of Reykjavík-based adventure-tour operators include kayaking in their programs.

Mountaineering

Unfortunately for rock climbers, Iceland's young and crumbly rock formations don't lend themselves well to technical rock climbing, but experienced mountaineers and ice climbers will find lots of scope for adventure. Anywhere on the ice, however, dangerous crevasses may lurk beneath snow bridges, and even innocent-looking snowfields may overlie rock and ice fissures, so technical expertise and equipment are essential. Crampons, ropes and ice axes are needed for any walk on glacial ice and clothing must be able to withstand extreme conditions, especially on alpine climbs.

Mountaineering in Iceland, by Ari Trausti Guðmundsson, has basic information on ascents of peaks as well as rock- and ice-climbing locations.

Unless you're proficient, experienced and well prepared, the best way to get involved in mountaineering or ice climbing is with a local, organised expedition. Contact the **Iceland Touring Association** (☎ 568 2533; www.fi.is) or the commercial outfit **Mountain Guides** (☎ 587 9999, 899 9982; www.mountainguide.is).

Whale Watching

Iceland is among the premier places in Europe for whale watching, despite the government's decision to resume hunting these creatures, and boat tours to watch whales and dolphins are becoming increasingly popular. The most common are the minke whales, but you can also spot humpback, fin, sei and blue whales. The best places for whale watching are Hafnarfjörður, Keflavík, Stykkishólmur, Ólafsvík, Vestmannaeyjar and Húsavík.

www.icewhale.is – the site of the Húsavík Whale Centre is full of interesting stuff on whales, whale watching and even whaling in Iceland.

Snowmobiling & Dogsledding

Tearing around an icecap on a snowmobile (snow scooter, or 'Skidoo') can be an exhilarating experience, but it's more about having a bit of fun in the snow than actually going on safari. For most travellers, an hour or two on a snowmobile is quite enough and in any case it costs a small fortune. For glacier tours the best places are Mýdalsjökull, Vatnajökull and Langjökull, and the cost is about Ikr7000–9000 for one hour, including transport and gear. It's great fun, especially on a clear day, but follow the guide's instructions and tracks – hapless snowmobilers have disappeared into crevasses in the past.

While high-altitude glacier tours run in summer (April–August), during the winter (January–May) there are possibilities for snowmobiling in other parts of Iceland. Adventure-tour operators in Reykjavík and Akureyri can organise trips. The northern coastal highlands, such as Ólafsfjörður, provide excellent opportunities.

Dogsledding, where you're pulled along behind Greenlandic huskies, is another typically Arctic experience organised for tourists. A one-hour tour costs around Ikr7000. Longer expeditions can be arranged with sufficient numbers. Mush mush!

Operators include:

Arcanum (☎ 487 1500; www.arcanum.is; Árnes, Mýdalsjökull)
Activity Group (☎ 580 9980; www.activity.is; Reykjavík)
Dog Steam Tours (☎ 487 7747; www.dogsledding.is)
Eskimos (☎ 577 4488; www.eskimos.is; Reykjavík)
Glacier Jeeps (☎ 478 1000; www.glacierjeeps.is; Vatnajökull)
Sport Tours (☎ 862 2600; www.sporttours.is; Akureyri)

MEDIA

Iceland's main daily newspapers are published only in Icelandic. The biggest-selling, *Morgunblaðið*, is moderately right wing, but Icelanders generally don't take journalists much more seriously than they do their politicians. Interestingly, a recent international poll studying independence in the media put Iceland at the top of the list.

For snippets of Icelandic news, the *Iceland Review* website (www.iceland review.com) has a free daily news digest (which you can have delivered to your email inbox) and its glossy quarterly magazine has some entertaining, light articles about Icelandic people, culture, history and nature.

An excellent read for Icelandic news, views, reviews and what's hot in Reykjavík is the new *Grapevine* magazine, a fortnightly newsprint magazine distributed free in summer. The editors are not afraid to write at length about big issues in Iceland but it's done with humour and a deft writing style. It's available at the tourist office, hotels and bars in Reykjavík.

TV and radio are more for entertainment than enlightenment, but there are a few news and talkback shows in Iceland. Much of the programming comes from America and the UK.

DID YOU KNOW?

Until 1988, Iceland had only one TV station, state-run, and every Thursday broadcasting was shut down completely.

RELIGION

Norse

Although there were many gods and godlike beings in Norse mythology, the Norse trinity consisted of Þór (Thor), to most Icelanders the king of the gods; Óðinn, the god of war and poetry; and Freyr, the god of fertility and sensuous pleasure.

Óðinn was the patron god of the Viking hordes, and was also the *skáld* (court poet). He was traditionally depicted as a brooding and intimidating presence, the one who doled out both victory in battle and literary talent.

On the Scandinavian mainland, Óðinn was the highest-ranking deity, but in Iceland (which was less concerned with war and raiding) Þór took precedence. This rowdy and rather slow-minded god of the common people controlled thunder, wind, storm and natural disaster, and fended off malevolent outsiders. He was depicted as a burly, red-haired, red-bearded dolt who rumbled through the heavens in a goat-drawn chariot.

Freyr and his twin sister Freyja, the children of the sea god Njörður, served as the god and goddess of fertility and sexuality. Freyr was the one who brought springtime, with its romantic implications, to both the human and animal world and was in charge of the perpetuation of all species.

Since Icelanders peacefully converted to Christianity more than 1000 years ago, pagan religion is now consigned to the history books or to followers of the modern Ásatrú religion – see the boxed text below.

ÁSATRÚ – AN ANCIENT RELIGION REBORN

Ásatrú, which means 'faith in the *Aesir* (the gods of pre-Christian Scandinavia)', has its origins in the ancient religions of most Germanic peoples – Goths, Germans, Dutch, Frisian, Anglo-Saxons – and also appears as far away as India (as described in the *Rig Veda*). The medieval Icelandic text, the *Galdrabók*, reveals that people were calling upon the *Aesir* long after Christianity was adopted by most Germanic peoples. As late as the 1800s, the Lapps (Sami) openly worshipped the god Þór, to whom they'd been introduced by their Scandinavian neighbours in the pre-Christian period.

Modern Ásatrú was organised in the 1970s, almost simultaneously in Iceland, the USA and the UK. The main gods and goddesses of Ásatrú, which are all considered friendly, practicable, dependable and approachable, include Þór, the god of thunder and friend of the common folk; Oðinn (or Allfather), the chief god, poet and wandering wizard; Tyr, the god of war and justice; Ingvi Freyr, the god of peace, fertility and nature (the British images of the 'Green Man' are likely linked to Freyr); Baldur, the bleeding god; Heimdall, the Watchman of Ásgard; Frigga, wife of Oðinn and mother of all the gods and humanity; Freyja, the goddess of fertility, love, magic and war; Idunna, the goddess of renewal; Hela, who rules over the place between death and rebirth or reincarnation; and Nerthus, the Mother Earth goddess, mentioned in Tacitus' *Germania*. Followers also revere *landvættir* (spirits of nature) and various guardian spirits, such as the *álfar* (elves).

The two main rituals of Ásatrú are *blót* (the sacrifice) and *sumbel* (the toast). While scholars debate whether or not the former word is derived from *blóð* (blood), modern Ásatrú followers sacrifice mead (honey-wine), beer or cider. The liquid is consecrated to the god or goddess being honoured, and drinking a portion of it signifies communion with that particular deity. The rest is poured out as a libation. The *sumbel*, a ritualised toasting to the gods, is made in three rounds. The first goes to the god Oðinn, who won the mead of poetry from the Giant Suttung. It's also wise to pour a few drops for Loki, the trickster, to ward off nasty surprises. The second round is to the ancestors and honourable dead, and the third round is open to whoever one wishes to honour.

Magical work is a part of the spiritual life of many practitioners of Ásatrú. Magic involves working with natural but unseen forces, including those embodied in the runes, the early Germanic alphabet, as well as the *galdra* (spellcraft) and *seiðr* (shamanism).

Christianity

Traditionally, the date of the decree that officially converted Iceland to Christianity has been given as 1000, but research has determined that it probably occurred in 999 and was a political decision. In the Icelandic Alþing (parliament), the Christians and pagans had been polarising into two radically opposite factions, threatening to divide the country politically if not geographically. In the session of 1000, Þorgeir the Law-speaker appealed for moderation on both sides in the interest of national unity.

Today, as in mainland Scandinavia, most Icelanders (around 95%) officially belong to the Protestant Lutheran Church.

ARTS

Literature

Iceland boasts one of the purest, most imaginative and most enduring bodies of medieval literature in the world – collectively known as the sagas. Although there was no written literature in Iceland prior to the 12th century, the bulk of medieval Icelandic literature is based upon historical events during the first 250 years of Icelandic history, much of it now translated into English. Medieval poetry, brought from Scandinavia, has also been preserved and handed down through the ages.

But Icelanders are never ones to rest on their literary laurels and the country still produces the most writers and literary translations per capita of any country in the world.

THE SAGAS

Myth & Religion of the North, by EOG Turville-Petre, provides a scholarly outline of the Ásatrú religion.

Without doubt, the most popular early works to come out of Iceland were the sagas. Literally translated into Old English, the word *saga* comes from the Old English translation of *saw* or *secgan*, meaning 'to say', and is from the same root as 'sage'. Most of the sagas were written anonymously, though *Egils Saga* has been attributed to Snorri Sturluson of Borgarfjörður.

During the Saga Age of the late 12th to late 13th centuries, epic tales of early settlement, romance, dispute and development of Iceland were recorded and sprinkled liberally and artistically with dramatic licence. They provided both entertainment and a sense of cultural heritage for Icelandic commoners. Through the difficult years to come, especially on cold winter nights, Icelanders gathered in farmhouses for *kvöldvaka*, or 'evening vigil', a time of socialising and saga reading. While the men spun horsehair ropes and women spun wool or knitted, a family member would read the sagas and recite *rímur* (later reworkings of old material) back into verse.

There were several types of sagas written in medieval Europe, but Iceland was primarily concerned with 'family sagas', tales of early settlers and their struggles, battles, heroics, relations, religion and occupations. While they are derived from nearly equal part fact and fiction, the historical information and the entertainment they have provided over the ages have set them apart as the most developed form of medieval European literature.

One of the best known, *Egils Saga*, is a biography of the Viking *skald* (court poet), Egill Skallagrímsson. Other favourite works include *Grettis Saga*, about a superhuman outlaw, Grettir the Strong; *Laxdœla Saga*, the tragic account of a family in Northwest Iceland (see p141); and *Njáls Saga*, whose endearing characters make it the most popular of all (see p117).

The family sagas were originally told in Old Norse, the common language of Scandinavia. While Norwegian, Danish and Swedish have developed through the centuries and felt the influence of other languages, Icelandic has hardly changed since Viking times, and Icelanders of all ages read the sagas in their original form for both historical and entertainment value.

EDDIC & SKALDIC POETRY

The first literary tradition to emerge from Iceland was poetry. Most early themes probably came from mainland Scandinavia even before the settlement of Iceland, but weren't actually written down until the period of literary awareness in the 12th century.

Icelandic poetry was divided into two categories: Eddic poetry, to modern ears actually more like free-metre prose, and Skaldic poetry, written by court poets employing a unique, well-defined syntax and vocabulary.

The Eddic poems are subdivided into three classes – the Mythical, the Gnomic and the Heroic – and were composed in free variable metres with a structure very similar to that of early Germanic poetry. Mythical poetry was based on the dialogue and antics of the Nordic gods and was probably promoted as an intended affront to growing Christian sentiments in Norway. Gnomic poetry consists of one major work, the *Hávamál*, which both promotes and optimistically extols the virtues of the common life. The Heroic Eddic poems are similar in form, subject matter and even characters to early Germanic works such as the *Nibelungenlied*.

'Skaldic poetry refers to blood as wound dew, an arm as a hawk's perch and

Skaldic poetry was developed and composed by Norwegian court poets, or *skalds*, in veneration of heroic deeds by the Scandinavian kings, but as the genre grew in popularity, other themes were introduced.

The most renowned *skald* was Egill Skallagrímsson, an Icelandic Viking who had run foul of King Harald Haarfager's eldest son, King Eirík Blood-Axe of York. After being captured and sentenced to death at York in 948, Egill managed to compose an ode to the king who had condemned him. The flattered monarch released Egill unharmed and his poem is now known as the *Höfuðlausn*, or 'head ransom'.

The Skaldic poems, far more descriptive than the Eddic, are predominantly dialogue and concerned with the graphic details of battle, an element lacking even in the Heroic Eddas. They also employ *kennings* – vocabulary and descriptions that fitted the metrical requirements and could add colour to the prose. Blood, for instance, is referred to as 'wound dew'. An arm might be described as a 'hawk's perch' and eyes as 'jewels of the head'. The battle itself was often referred to as 'the Valkyries' glorious song'.

DID YOU KNOW?

Iceland publishes the greatest number of books per capita in the world (much of it translated works of foreign authors) in an effort to keep its language alive.

MODERN LITERATURE

Icelandic writers have also made some significant contributions to modern literature. During the early 20th century, the Reverend Jón Sveinsson (nicknamed Nonni), a priest from Akureyri, wrote a vast body of juvenile literature in German that was subsequently translated into 40 languages. Just after him, Jóhann Sigurjónsson wrote *Eyvind of the Hills*, the biography of the 18th-century outlaw Fjalla-Eyvindar; *Eyvind of the Hills* was later made into a film. The best-known modern Icelandic writer is Nobel Prize–winning Halldór Laxness (see the boxed text on p37), whose work deals with daily life in Iceland.

The following modern literature has been translated into English and is worth looking out for. *Devil's Island*, by Einar Kárason, concentrates on Reykjavík life in the early 1950s and '60s. *Independent People*, by Halldór Laxness was voted by Icelanders as the best book of the century. It's one of half a dozen brilliant novels by this Nobel Prize winner.

101 Reykjavík, by Hallgrímur Helgason, is a dark comedy following the torpid life and fertile imagination of out-of-work Hlynur, who lives in downtown Reykjavík with his mother.

Angels of the Universe, by Einar Már Gudmundsson, is a comic drama and winner of the 1995 Nordic literature award.

HALLDÓR LAXNESS – NOBEL LAUREATE

Halldór Laxness is undoubtedly Iceland's most celebrated author of the 20th century, though he was relatively unknown outside Iceland before winning the Nobel Prize for Literature in 1955, and only in recent years have some of his best works been translated into English.

He was born Halldór Guðjónsson in Reykjavík in 1902, but at the age of three moved with his family to the farm Laxness, from which he took his *nom de plume*.

At only 17 he began the travelling that would shape much of his later life. After wandering and writing around Scandinavia, he went to Germany, converted to Catholicism and joined a monastery in Luxembourg. There he wrote his first novel, *Under the Holy Mountain*, but soon became disillusioned with an ascetic's life. After returning to Iceland briefly, he went to Italy, where he wrote of his disaffection with the church and his increasingly leftist leanings in *The Great Weaver from Kashmir*.

When the work reached Iceland it was highly acclaimed, but by this time Laxness had gone to Canada, where he decided to have a go at the fledgling film industry in Hollywood. There he wrote one of his best-known works, *Salka Valka*, as a screenplay. It was during this stay in America during the Great Depression of the 1930s that he became a communist sympathiser. Quickly finding himself facing deportation from the USA, he bought a ticket to Germany.

Laxness became so absorbed with the Communist Party that he attended the 1937 purge trials in Moscow and deliberately misrepresented them in his writings (by his own later admission) lest he in any way defame the system in which he had placed all hope and trust.

Most of Laxness' work during his communist days reflected everyday life in Iceland, often with thinly disguised autobiographical details. *Independent People* describes the harsh conditions under which the average Icelanders lived, especially the common folk on the farms and in fishing villages. Quite a few Icelanders disputed his observations, but their complaints were often motivated by national pride and their reluctance to publicise Iceland's relative backwardness.

His other major novels based on Icelandic life include *The Fish Can Sing* and *The Atom Station*. The former is an exposé of life on the farm and the latter, written almost prophetically in 1948, is about the American military presence in Iceland, conflicting political ideologies and the threat of nuclear proliferation. In 1955 Laxness won the Nobel Prize for Literature.

By 1962 Laxness had settled back in Reykjavík. Apparently mellowed by his experiences with extremism at both ends of the spectrum, he wrote *A Poet's Time*, which recanted everything he'd ever written praising the Communist Party.

He died in 1998.

Music

POP

Everyone under 30 and living in Reykjavík is a musician or songwriter, or so it seems. Iceland's move into the international pop-music scene first came in 1986 with the Sugarcubes. Anyone who'd visited Iceland in the previous five years wouldn't have been surprised by their meteoric rise, since from the early 1980s there were lots of spiky-topped teenagers wandering the streets of Reykjavík. Many seemed to be members of a garage band and frequently put on fairly wild shows in little halls. The Sugarcubes, who formed their own recording label, Bad Taste, had some success abroad, but it was their elfin lead singer Björk who really put Iceland on the international pop charts with her solo album *Debut* in 1993.

Several other Icelandic postpunk pop groups followed, earning their reputations and rites of passage orchestrating Reykjavík's typically obstreperous Friday nights. Such local groups as Reptile, Ham and Bless, all of which appeared on The Sugarcubes' album *World Domination or Death*, performed internationally but have now split up.

The Reykjavík music scene continues to flourish as new bands appear, with big names including Quarashi, Sigur Rós, Singapore Sling, Maus and Emiliana Torrini, who has cowritten songs with Kylie Minogue.

ICELANDIC ROCK: THE COMING OF AGE *By Valur Gunnarsson*

Icelandic rock, so legend has it, grew up in Keflavík on the outskirts of the US Naval base. The town's isolated youth were suddenly able to pick up the new sounds emanating from Armed Forces Radio. When Elvis Presley's 'Heartbreak Hotel' hit Icelandic radio in 1956, the rock 'n' roll craze erupted.

The first rock bands formed in the early 1960s as Beatlemania reached Iceland. Dominating for the entire decade was the band Hljómar from Keflavík, often called the Icelandic Beatles. It was not until 1967 that Hljómar got serious competition from newcomers Flowers – the two eventually merged to form 'supergroup' Trúbrot. Their album, *Lifun*, is often regarded as one of the masterpieces of Icelandic music. As was the trend of the day it was recorded in English, more to disguise the poor quality of the lyrics than in an attempt to make it abroad.

The Icelandic language was soon to make its artistic entrance. In 1972 a man who called himself Megas released his first album full of stories that more often than not mocked Iceland's historical heroes. Some were shocked, but the man's talents were undeniable.

Punk came late to Iceland. At first it seemed to have missed the island completely, but in 1980 it arrived with a vengeance, spearheaded by the bands Utangarðsmenn (The Outsiders) (whose frontman, Bubbi, went on to become the biggest selling solo artist of the past 20 years and whose first album, *Ísbjarnarblús*, remains seminal) and the more hardcore punk band Fræbbblarnir. Suddenly the country was bustling with interesting young garage bands who cared little for the older supergroups. The scene is wonderfully documented in Friðrik Þór's film *Rokk í Reykjavík*, which signalled both the pinnacle and the end of Icelandic punk in 1982.

As the underground went underground once more, and new bands playing mainstream pop and rock emerged to take over the charts, members of some of the foremost New Wave bands, including Þeyr, Purkur Pillnik and Tappi Tíkarrass, formed a supergroup which went on to become the Sugarcubes. When their single, 'Birthday', became *Melody Maker*'s single of the month, they finally got what every Icelandic musician had hoped for but none had yet achieved – international success. Their elfin singer, Björk, went on to even greater success as a solo artist, proving that Icelandic music could reach an audience abroad. No one has as yet managed to repeat her success, but some of the bands currently receiving the greatest attention include avant-garde groups Sigur Rós and Múm, and rap band Quarashi.

Valur Gunnarsson is the editor of Grapevine *magazine*

Iceland also has its own contemporary music legends. Bubbi Morthens, who first came to prominence in 1980 and was in rock bands such as The Outsiders, is still a household name for his anthems championing the common man and life in rural Iceland. Megas, described by fans as a poet and a genius, was a big hit in the '70s and '80s.

You can see bands performing live at venues such as Gaukur á Stöng (p80) and Grand Rokk (p80) in Reykjavík. The best rock-music festival in Iceland is Airwaves, held in Reykjavík in October, which showcases the cream of Iceland's talent along with international acts.

Waking Up in Iceland, by Paul Sullivan, is an insightful journey into Iceland's contemporary and traditional music scenes, analysed through interviews and the author's travel. Focus is on 'cool' Reykjavík and its cultural life.

TRADITIONAL MUSIC

Iceland has hundreds of traditional little ditties which most Icelanders learn before school age and are still singing with relish in their old age. They're dredged up whenever an occasion brings the generations together: family parties, outings, camping. The two favourites (which you'll hear exhaustively) seem to be *Á Sprengisandur*, a cowboy song about sheep herders and outlaws in the desert interior, and a tear-jerking lullaby based on a legend about the wife of outlaw Fjalla-Eyvindar, who threw her starving baby into a waterfall. Several collections of traditional Icelandic music are available from Reykjavík music shops and souvenir shops around the country.

Early traditional instruments included the *fiddla*, a two-stringed instrument played with a bow, but most traditional songs were performed unaccompanied (like *rímur*, a chanted version of poetry or the sagas).

Cinema

Iceland's film industry is young – regular production started only 20 years ago – but it's developing at a cracking pace. Icelandic films have received rave international reviews for their often quirky, dark subject matter and superb cinematography, with Iceland's powerful landscape as a backdrop. In 2003 *Salt*, directed by American Bradley Rust Gray, received plenty of attention, despite being made on a shoestring. It stars four young Icelanders living in a remote fishing village who decide to move to Reykjavík.

www.icelandicfilmcentre.is – catch up on the latest in the Iceland film industry.

In 1992 the film world took notice of Iceland when *Children of Nature* was nominated for an Academy Award for Best Foreign Film. In the film, an elderly couple forced into a retirement home in Reykjavík make a break for the countryside where they belong. The film's director, Friðrik Thór Friðriksson, is something of a legend in Icelandic cinema circles. In 1994 he directed *Cold Fever*, and in 2000 his film version of *Angels of the Universe* received wide critical acclaim.

DID YOU KNOW?

Leatherface in the movie *The Texas Chainsaw Massacre* was played by Icelandic actor Gunnar Hansson.

If one recent film has put Iceland and especially Reykjavík on the cinematic stage, it's *101 Reykjavík*, directed by Baltasar Kormákur and based on the novel by Hallgrímur Helgason. This dark comedy explores sex, drugs and the life of a loafer in downtown Reykjavík.

Seagull's Laughter, directed by Agust Gudmundsson, was, domestically, Iceland's most successful movie of 2001, following the lives of a group of women in a 1950s fishing village.

Icelandic Dream, directed by Robert I Douglas, was another huge film in Iceland's cinemas in 2000. Set against a grey, urban Reykjavík backdrop, this comic drama centres on a man whose life revolves around soccer, juggling current and former girlfriends, and peddling imported cigarettes.

Architecture

People who come to Iceland expecting to see Viking longhouses will probably be disappointed. Icelandic buildings were traditionally built from turf and wood and only the foundations of most Viking-era buildings are visible today. However, the tradition of building turf-roofed farmhouses continued right up to the 19th century and a number of turf-roofed buildings around the country have been preserved as folk museums – there are good examples at Keldur in southwest Iceland and Glambær and Laufaus in north Iceland.

A Guide to Icelandic Architecture (Association of Icelandic Architects, 2000) is the best guide to the history and development of architecture in Iceland. It looks at around 250 buildings and designs.

From the 16th century onwards, Iceland adopted a more familiar Scandinavian style of architecture, constructing houses from wooden planks cut from the timber that washed up along the coast. A remarkable number of these still survive, though most have been clad in sheets of corrugated tin to protect them from the elements. Quite why Icelandic builders ignored the plentiful volcanic rock around them has never really been explained – you can count the number of old stone buildings in Iceland on the fingers of one hand.

Nothing much changed in Icelandic architecture until the 1950s, when Iceland contracted the Scandinavian design obsession and began constructing visionary modern buildings from volcanic stone, glass, concrete and steel. The country is dotted with space-age churches inspired by the surrounding landscape, but the best examples of modern Icelandic architecture are all in Reykjavík – our walking tour (p65) will introduce you to some of the best old and new buildings in the capital.

Painting & Sculpture

Iceland's most successful artists have traditionally studied abroad, in Copenhagen, London, Oslo or elsewhere in Europe. The result is a European influence in style but with Icelandic landscapes and saga-related scenes as key subjects.

'Iceland's most successful artists have traditionally studied abroad, in Copenhagen, London, Oslo or elsewhere in Europe'

The first great Icelandic landscape painter was Ásgrímur Jónsson (1876–1958), who was attracted to impressionism while studying in Italy. He produced a prolific body of oils and watercolours depicting Icelandic landscapes and folk tales. You can see his work at the Ásgrímur Jónsson Museum in Reykjavík.

One of the country's most enduringly popular artists was Johannes Kjarval, who was born in the remote East Iceland village of Borgarfjörður in 1885. His surreal landscapes can be seen at galleries in Reykjavík and Borgarfjörður.

Contemporary artists to look out for in Iceland include pop-art icon Erró (Gudmundur Gudmundsson), who has been honoured with a permanent collection in the Reykjavík Art Museum; mural and glass artist Sjofn Har; and Tryggvi Ólafsson, whose strikingly colourful abstracts depicting Icelandic scenes hang in national galleries in Reykjavik, Sweden and Denmark.

Sculpture is a visible art form travellers can see in parks, gardens and galleries around Iceland. Notable exponents include Einar Jónsson, a mystic sculptor whose work can be seen in a museum and sculpture garden in Reykjavík; Ásmundur Sveinsson, who took inspiration for his concrete abstracts from Icelandic sagas and folk tales; and Sigurjón Ólafsson, who specialised in busts and is also remembered with a sculpture museum in Reykjavík.

Environment

THE LAND

Iceland is not, as its unfortunate name would suggest, covered in ice. Nor is it just a barren lunar landscape of congealed lava flows and windswept tundra. But you will find both those scenarios side by side on this North Atlantic island, along with fertile farmland, rolling hills, glacier-carved valleys and canyons, bubbling, steaming, geothermally active 'hot spots' and the vast, desertlike wasteland of the Interior and Central Highlands.

For geologists, volcanologists and glaciologists, Iceland is surely one of the world's great showpieces. Most of the land is characterised by desert plateaus (52%), lava fields (11%), *sandur* or 'sand deltas' (4%) and ice-caps (12%). More than half the country lies above 400m, which is more significant than it sounds given the northerly latitude. The highest point, Hvannadalshnúkur, rises 2119m from beneath the glacier Öræfajökull.

With an area of 103,000 sq km, Iceland is the second-largest island in Europe, and the northernmost point of its mainland extends to within a few hundred metres of the Arctic Circle; the island of Grímsey off the north coast actually straddles it.

Iceland is a land of coast-dwellers – only 21% of the land (all near the coast) is considered arable and habitable, and most of the population and agriculture is concentrated in the Southwest, between Reykjavík and Vík.

DID YOU KNOW?

Iceland is one of the world's most active hot spots – one-third of all the lava to surface on earth in the last 1000 years is of Icelandic origin.

NATURE'S FURY

Icelanders have had to cope with plenty of hardship in their 1100-year history, not least from some pretty miserable weather and devastating natural disasters.

In 1300, 1341 and 1389, the southern Iceland volcano Hekla erupted violently, causing widespread death and destruction of property. Towards the end of the 16th century, four consecutive severe winters led to widespread crop failure and 9000 Icelanders starved to death while thousands more were uprooted from their homes.

Throughout the 17th and 18th centuries, disaster continued in the form of natural catastrophes. Hekla erupted continuously for seven months in 1636 and again in 1693; Katla erupted violently in 1660 and 1755; and Öræfi, in Vatnajökull, went off in 1727. In 1783, Lakagígar (Laki) erupted continuously for 10 months and devastated much of Southeast Iceland, resulting in a poisonous haze that destroyed pastures and crops. Nearly 75% of Iceland's livestock and 20% of the human population died in the resulting 'haze famine'. The already suffering Icelandic population was then further marginalised by earthquakes and another spell of severe winters.

Natural disasters continue to occur in modern Iceland, but better communications, advance warning systems and a more urban population have reduced their impact considerably. In 1963 the island of Surtsey appeared out of the sea in a submarine eruption just southwest of Vestmannaeyjar. Ten years later, the island of Heimaey, also in Vestmannaeyjar, experienced a terrible eruption that created a new mountain, buried most of the town of 5200 people and threatened to cut off the harbour. In a matter of hours, the island was successfully evacuated and there was only one casualty. The most recent disaster was a series of powerful earthquakes, the first of which hit Southwest Iceland on Independence Day in 2000.

Hekla has erupted (with little damage or destruction) as recently as February 2000; the Krafla fissure north of Mývatn has experienced a lot of volcanic activity; and in late 1996 Grímsvötn went off and released the largest *jökulhlaup* (flooding caused by volcanic eruption beneath an icecap) of the 20th century. Earthquakes and subsurface volcanic rumblings continue in Iceland – stay tuned for the next 'big one'.

Volcanic and geothermal features – geysers, thermal springs, fumaroles, lava flows, mudpots, craters, calderas and igneous plugs – figure prominently in the landscape. Currently dormant or active volcanoes include Eldfell and Surtsey in Vestmannaeyjar, Hekla in the Southwest, Katla beneath the glacier Mýrdalsjökull, Grímsvötn and Öræfi (in Öræfajökull) beneath Vatnajökull and Krafla at lake Mývatn.

In addition to the volcanoes themselves, Iceland has around 250 geothermal areas and a total of around 780 individual hot springs with average water temperatures of about 75°C.

Guide to the Geology of Iceland, by Ari Trausti Guðmundsson and Halldór Kjartansson, is a slim but comprehensive guide to the country's geology, including volcanoes, plate tectonics, geothermal activity, the coast, glaciers, and rocks and minerals.

Geology

Iceland sits squarely on the Mid-Atlantic Ridge, an 18,000km plate boundary running the length of the Atlantic Ocean from north to south. The island itself was created by submarine volcanic eruptions caused by the movement of the plates.

In 1620 Sir Francis Bacon glanced at the most recent map of the Atlantic region and noticed that the eastern coast of South America and the western coast of Africa seemed to fit together like bits of a jigsaw puzzle. This curiosity has now been conclusively ascribed to plate tectonics, which describes the lateral motion of continents on 'plates' of the earth's crust. The theory attributes plate movement to the creation and destruction of crust along plate boundaries. In zones of thin or weak crust (the crust beneath Iceland is only a third the average crust thickness), molten rock (magma) from deep within the earth forces its way upwards, spreading the surface plates apart. To compensate, deep-sea trenches form on opposite plate boundaries where one plate is forced to slide beneath another and

is destroyed by heat. Most of the earth's volcanism and seismic activity occur in hot spots on or very near these plate boundaries.

Iceland is cleanly cut into northwest and southeast halves by the resulting system of fissures and volcanoes between the North American and Eurasian plates.

Glaciers & Icecaps

Much of Iceland's landscape has been carved and shaped by rivers of ice flowing down from permanent icecaps. Icecaps are formed as snow piles up over millennia in an area where it's never allowed to melt. It's slowly compressed, from bottom to top, into ice. When the weight of the ice becomes so great that the underlying land cannot support it, the land beneath the centre compresses and the ice around the edges begins to flow downward in glaciers – rivers of ice – which may reach the sea and form icebergs.

Beginning three million years ago, during the Pleistocene epoch, the northern hemisphere experienced a Great Ice Age. Only parts of Iceland's icecap remain and they weren't formed during the Great Ice Age, but in a cool period beginning 2500 years ago. Today they cover only about 15% of the country. The largest – and the world's third-largest after Antarctica and Greenland – is the 8400 sq km Vatnajökull in the Southeast, which covers almost 13% of the country. Other major icecaps are Mýdalsjökull in the Southwest, and Langjökull and Hofsjökull in the Interior.

Plants & Animals of Iceland, by Benny Génsböl and Jon Feilberg, is an illustrated guide to all of Iceland's flora and fauna, including birds, marine mammals and 220 species of plants.

WILDLIFE

Birds & Animals

Although there are a few land mammals to be seen in Iceland (other than sheep, cows and horses), it's the bird life that really captures the imagination. On coastal cliffs and islands right around the country you can see a mind-boggling array of sea birds, often in massive colonies. Most sea birds visit Iceland to nest and breed in summer.

Most impressive for their sheer numbers are gannets, guillemots, razorbills, kittiwakes, fulmars and puffins – which reach saturation point on high, coastal cliffs. Less numerous birds include wood sandpipers, arctic terns, skuas, Manx shearwaters, golden plovers, storm petrels and Leach's petrels. In addition, there are many species of ducks, ptarmigans, whooping swans, redwings, divers, gyrfalcons – and two species of owl.

DID YOU KNOW?

Colonies of puffins can only be seen around Iceland's coast during nesting season from around May to mid-August. After that they take off en masse to breed out at sea.

Another drawcard is the rich marine life, particularly whales. On whale-watching tours from Hafnarfjörður, Keflavík and Ólafsvík in western Iceland, and Húsavík in northern Iceland (among other places), you'll have an excellent chance of seeing minke, humpback, sperm, fin, sei, pilot and blue whales. Orcas (killer whales), dolphins, porpoises and seals are also spotted. Seals (common and grey) can be seen in waterways around the Eastfjords, on the Vatsnes Peninsula in Northwest Iceland, in the Mýrar region on the southeast coast (including at Jökulsárlón), in Breiðafjörður in the west, and in the Westfjords.

A useful little book for identifying whales is *Whale Watching in Iceland*, by Ásbjörn Björgvinsson and Helut Lugmayr. With colour pictures, it includes background, habitat, a description of whales you might see in Icelandic waters, history of whaling and whale watching.

The only land mammal indigenous to Iceland is the arctic fox, which is smaller than the European fox and may have a bluish-brown or white coat. Polar bears, which occasionally drift across from Greenland on ice floes, might be indigenous if they weren't considered undesirable immigrants. Bears in Iceland have a very short life expectancy, thanks mainly to armed sheep farmers.

Introduced animals include reindeer (wild and often hunted), mink, field mice and several species of rat.

Plants

One of the first things you'll notice about Iceland is the dearth of trees. The hills and meadows are bare – even in fertile coastal areas – except for low shrubs and the ground-hugging dwarf willows, which grow all over Iceland. As the old joke goes, if you're lost in an Icelandic forest, just stand up!

A Guide to the Flowering Plants & Ferns of Iceland, by Hörður Kristinsson, is the best all-round field guide to Icelandic flowers.

The sagas record that newly discovered Iceland was 'wooded from the sea to the mountains', but since the Old Norse word *við*, for 'woods', was the same as the word for 'willow', it's conceivable that the first settlers actually encountered nothing but dwarf willows. If the island really was wooded, the forests were clearly wiped out by early inhabitants, who would have cut them down for fuel and allowed their sheep to nibble down the tender new shoots of young trees. Thanks to more recent reafforestation schemes, however, the country now enjoys several recreational forests and stands of birch, particularly around Akureyri and Egilsstaðir.

New lava flows in southern and eastern Iceland are first colonised by mosses, while those in the east and at higher elevations are first colonised by lichens. The coastal areas are characterised by low grasses, bogs and marshlands. At higher elevations, the ground is covered with both hard and soft or boggy tundra, and arctic cotton blooms during the spring months.

Icelandic Geographic Glossy annual magazine on the most interesting and unique aspects of the Icelandic landscape; can be ordered online at www.icelandgeographic.is

INTRODUCED SPECIES

Some flowering plants, many of them European, have managed to take root in Iceland. The arctic fireweed grows around riverbeds, while in northern Iceland you'll find arctic harebell, upright primrose and mountain heath. The northern green orchid can be found in the grassy lowlands, along with varieties of saxifrage and daisy.

NATIONAL PARKS & NATURE RESERVES

For a country of such pristine wilderness, it's surprising that there are only three fully fledged national parks in Iceland – Þingvellir (South Central Iceland), Skaftafell (Southeast Iceland) and Jökulsárgljúfur (Northeast Iceland). These parks preserve areas of historical and natural importance and can't be settled or developed. Another 80 nature reserves, natural monuments, country parks and wildlife reserves are scattered around the country.

Þingvellir (www.thingvellir.is), which is administered directly by the prime minister's office, is the oldest national park, declared in 1930. The 84-sq-km lake and Almannagjá rift are interesting natural features, but it's the historical significance as the site of the original Alþing (parliament) that attracts many Icelanders (see p23).

Skaftafell, at the foot of Vatnajökull, is a classic wilderness park with superb hiking trails and glacier views. The best time to visit is from May to September (see p264). Jökulsárgljúfur, with a canyon carved out by a glacial river, bizarre rock formations and the awesome Dettifoss waterfall, protects 120 sq km of rugged land (see p222). Both national parks are administered by the **Nature Conservation Agency** (☎ 570 7400; fax 570 7401; www.natturuvernd.is) in Reykjavík.

DID YOU KNOW?

Marimo balls – golf-sized balls of algae – are found naturally in only two places in the world: Lake Akan in Japan and Iceland's Mývatn lake.

A proposal is currently before parliament to have the entire Vatnajökull icecap declared a national park. Nature reserves include hiking areas such as Fjallabak, Lónsöræfi and the Kverkfjöll mountains, islands such as Hrísey, Surtsey and Flatey, and waterfalls such as Gullfoss. Mývatn is classed as a 'special conservation area'.

ENVIRONMENTAL ISSUES

In Iceland it's possible to be environmentally conscious without really trying. With a small population, little heavy industry, large areas of uninhabitable wilderness and a lot of wind to blow away anything that might taint the fresh, clean air, pollution is not a big problem here. And with a wealth of geothermal and hydroelectric power at its disposal, Iceland is aiming to become the first country in the world to completely do away with fossil fuels.

But multinational companies are also looking to Iceland as a place to throw up factories, offering employment and economic benefits to struggling communities as the carrot. The prime example is the Alcoa aluminium smelter in the Eastfjords. The controversial project has been approved and involves first building a dam and hydroelectricity plant, which will flood part of the Eastern Highlands. See p245 for more information.

One of the natural environmental concerns in Iceland at present is the erosion caused by overgrazing of sheep, which chew vegetation down to the roots and expose the underlying soil to the forces of water and the fierce winds. In parts of the country, particularly around Mývatn lake, the results are most dramatic. Iceland was possibly deforested by overgrazing shortly after settlement. Forestry programs are still thin on the ground, but there are more (and taller) trees in Iceland as the years go by.

Despite the low population, there is a small and growing market for recycled products, and some recycling programs have appeared in Reykjavík.

Earth in Action, by Ari Trausti Guðmundsson and Halldór Kjartansson, is an excellent introduction to the complex geological forces at work in Iceland. It explains, in lay terminology, the geological history and composition of Iceland's most prominent natural attractions.

Useful Websites

Iceland Nature Conservation Association (www.inca.is) The site of this independent conservation organisation covers environmental issues affecting Iceland.

Kárahnjúkar Hydroelectric Project (www.karahnjukar.is) Official site of Iceland's largest and most controversial energy project.

Nature Conservation Agency (www.natturuvernd.is) Information on Iceland's national parks and nature reserves.

Food & Drink

Historically, eating in Iceland was more about survival than a celebration of national cuisine. Farmers and fishermen lived isolated lives, and long, harsh winters meant the time for harvesting food and successfully growing crops was limited. Food preparation was simple and practical, and the ingredients came only from what they could glean from the land and sea. In terms of the staples, little has changed over the centuries – fish, seafood, lamb and mutton, bread and simple vegetables such as potatoes form the basis of a typical Icelandic diet.

A Taste of Iceland, by Úlfar Finnbjörnsson, is a full-colour book on Icelandic cuisine and recipes.

Many foods had to be preserved so that they could be eaten throughout the winter. Drying, salting and smoking of fish, pickling in whey and burying shark meat underground were common methods. What wasn't stored was eaten fresh and that's still the hallmark of Icelandic food today – freshness.

A big change in the last decade or so is the innovation in preparation of fish and meat dishes and the increasing number of quality restaurants, especially in Reykjavík but also in some surprisingly out-of-the-way places. Traditional soups and stews are making way for more imaginative culinary exploits. Pasta, salads and rice dishes have also made their way onto Icelandic tables. Although the importation of meat, fish and dairy products is restricted, most other foods such as fruit and vegetables are imported – one reason for the high prices.

New Icelandic Cookbook, by Atli Vagnsson, is an impressive 144-page book with traditional and modern Icelandic recipes and plenty of photographs from around the country. It's available in English, Swedish and German.

There's no denying that dining out in Iceland is expensive, or that the American fast-food influence is very heavy here. To the casual traveller Icelandic cuisine can appear to be an endless menu of hot dogs, hamburgers, pizzas and simple fish dishes, but don't leave without splashing out on a meal here. You won't regret it.

STAPLES & SPECIALITIES

Fish & Seafood

Fish has always been the mainstay of the Icelandic diet. Fish served in restaurants or on sale in markets is always fresh and usually comes boiled, pan-fried, baked or grilled. The most common types of fish on Icelandic menus include *þorskur* (cod), *lúða* (halibut), *bleikja* (Arctic char) and *ýsa* (haddock), but you'll also find *steinbítur* (catfish), *sandhverfa* (turbot), *skarkoli* (plaice), *sild* (herring), *skata* (skate) and *skötuselur* (monkfish). During the summer, you can sometimes get *silungur* (freshwater trout) and *lax* (salmon). Wild salmon is called *villtur* and farmed salmon is *eldislax*.

Icelandic Food & Cookery, by Nanna Rögnvaldardóttir, has a short introduction to the history and types of Icelandic cuisine and is full of interesting recipes.

A common staple is *harðfiskur*, haddock which is cleaned and dried in the open air until it has become dehydrated and brittle. It is torn into strips and eaten with butter as a snack. You can find it in supermarkets and at market stalls.

Lobster, shrimp, oysters and mussels are also caught in Icelandic waters, particularly in the Southeast (Höfn has an annual Lobster Festival – see p273), and can be found in decent seafood restaurants.

Meat

Icelandic lamb is hard to beat. During summer sheep roam free to munch on chemical-free grasses and herbs in the highlands and valleys, before being rounded up in the September *rettir* and corralled for the winter. The result of this relative life of luxury is very tender lamb with

TRAVEL YOUR TASTEBUDS

The most Icelandic of specialities are also some of the most frightening – traditionally no part of an animal was wasted, so sheep's brains, eyes and heads commonly find their way to the dinner table in some homes, although most are reserved for festivals and traditional feast days, and you'll rarely see these popping up on restaurant menus.

You could try:

- **Brennivín** Sledgehammer schnapps made from potatoes and flavoured with caraway.
- **Hervabred** A rich, dark rye bread baked underground using geothermal heat; try it at Mývatn.
- **Lundi (puffin)** It's a cute little sea bird but Icelanders have no qualms about eating it.
- **Svið** Singed sheep's head, complete with eyes but minus the brain, sawn in two, boiled and eaten either fresh or pickled. When the meat is removed from the bone and pressed into gelatinous loaves and pickled in whey, it's known as **sviðasulta** (head cheese).
- **Skyr** Delicious concoction made of pasteurised skimmed milk and a bacteria culture similar to yoghurt, sweetened with sugar and berries.
- **Slátur** (Yes, it means 'slaughter'.) A mishmash of sheep leftovers tied up in a sheep stomach and cooked. One form is known as **blóðmör**, sheep's blood pudding packed in suet and sewn up in the diaphragm or stomach. In another variation, **lifrapylsa**, sheep's liver rather than blood is used.
- **Súrsaðir hrútspungar** Rams' testicles pickled in whey and pressed into a cake.

We dare you to try…

- **Hákarl** Iceland's most famous stomach churner – putrefied shark meat buried underground for up to six months. Icelanders evidently discovered a particular type of shark couldn't be eaten fresh because of an unpleasant acid in the flesh. So they decided to bury it in sand, let it decompose, then eat it. It can be left anywhere because even carrion birds won't touch it. Most foreigners find the stench (a cross between ammonia and week-old roadkill) too much to bear, but it actually tastes better than it smells. It's the aftertaste that really hurts. We sampled it chopped into cubes and served with toothpicks like a cheese platter – comparisons with very strong blue cheese (with a fishy taste) could easily be drawn. A shot of *brennivín* is traditionally administered as an antidote.

a slightly gamey flavour. You'll find lamb fillets or pan-fried lamb on most restaurant menus.

Beef steaks are also excellent but are not as widely available and consequently more expensive. Horse is still eaten in Iceland but it's regarded as something of a 'delicacy' rather than a staple. It tastes a bit like stringy, gamey beef. So if you see 'foal fillets' on the menu, you're not imagining things.

Other unusual meat dishes include *lundi* (puffin), that cute, awkward sea bird that most visitors come to observe on the sea cliffs through a pair of binoculars, rather than smoked or broiled on a plate. *Rjúper* (ptarmigan), a plump but tough bird related to the grouse, is the turkey of Iceland – the popular choice for the traditional Christmas dinner table, served in a milky gravy. It's officially protected but ptarmigan hunting is still a popular pastime.

www.isholf.is/gullis/jo – Jo's Icelandic Recipe is a great independent website full of recipes, customs and a great love of food.

Whale meat isn't as common as it once was, but some Icelanders love it and, since the small-scale resumption of whaling in 2003, it has found its way back onto supermarket shelves. You can try it at a few gourmet restaurants in Reykjavík.

Sweets & Desserts

Traditional Icelandic sweets are simple affairs, but don't miss *skyr*, a delicious concoction made of pasteurised skimmed milk and a bacteria culture similar to that used to make yoghurt. Despite its rich and decadent flavour, it's actually low in fat and is often mixed with sugar, fruit flavours (such as blueberry) and cream to give it a wonderful flavour and texture. *Skyr* in many different forms can be found in any supermarket (it's a great snack for kids) and as a dessert in restaurants.

Pönnukökur (Icelandic pancakes) are traditionally thin, sweet, flavoured with cinnamon and rolled up. *Kleinur* (doughnuts) are another popular sweet – a unique Icelandic variation is *ástar pungur* (love balls), deep-fried spiced balls that you'll find in some bakeries.

DID YOU KNOW?

Icelanders drink more Coca-Cola per capita than any other country (about 115 litres each a year). The fizzy stuff was first bottled here in 1941, around the same time American troops arrived.

DRINKS

Nonalcoholic

Kaffi (coffee) is a national institution in Iceland. Every café and petrol station will usually have an urn full of filter coffee by the counter. A cup costs anywhere from Ikr150 to Ikr250, but you'll normally get at least one free refill. European-style cafés where you can get espresso, latte, cappuccino, mocha and imported coffee are becoming popular in Reykjavík. Tea is available, but clearly doesn't offer the caffeine fix Icelanders need.

Surprisingly for a country with such a brief summer, soft drinks are incredibly popular – what else do you have with that hot dog but a Coke? Bottled water is widely available but tap water is fine and free.

The only traditional nonalcoholic drink (although it may be spiked with alcohol) is *jólaöl* or 'Christmas brew', which is fortunately served only around Christmas. The taste has been generously described as de-alcoholised Guinness seasoned with Marmite.

Alcohol

Icelanders love to drink but they generally don't drink alcohol to savour the taste. Young people tend to drink heavily on weekends and during holidays and festivals – the scene on the streets of Reykjavík at 3am on Friday and Saturday nights must be seen to be believed.

DID YOU KNOW?

Something you might hear around Reykjavík on the weekend is an Icelandic saying for being drunk, *'sauddrukkin'*: 'as drunk as a sheep'!

You must be at least 20 years old to buy beer, wine or spirits, and alcohol is available only from licensed bars, restaurants and the government-run **Vín Búð** liquor stores. Most towns of any size have one, and Reykjavík has five. Opening hours vary, but are usually from 11am to 6pm Monday to Thursday, 11am to 7pm on Friday, and 11am to 2pm on Saturday (closed Sunday). Expect queues around 5pm on a Friday. You can pick up a bottle of imported wine for around Ikr1000 (and up) and beer is about a third of what you'll pay in a bar. Petrol stations and supermarkets sell the weak and watery 2.2% brew known as Pilsner, but most Icelanders would sooner not drink at all.

www.vinbud.is – site of the government liquor stores Vín Búð

There are three brands of Icelandic beer: Egils, Thule and Viking, all fairly standard lager or Pils brews, but you can also get imported beers such as Carlsberg and (in Irish bars) Guinness. A pint of beer in a pub costs around Ikr600; a glass of house wine or a shot of spirits in a restaurant costs from Ikr500 to Ikr800.

The traditional Icelandic alcoholic brew is *brennivín* (meaning 'burnt wine'), a sort of schnapps made from potatoes and flavoured with caraway. Its nickname *svarti dauði*, or 'black death', may offer some clues about its character but it's actually a clear liquid usually taken as a shot. It can be a blessing since it's normally administered therapeutically to those who manage to choke down a bite of *hákarl*, but don't underestimate its potency.

PUBS WITH NO BEER

Never one to follow what the rest of the Europe was doing, Iceland got in first and in 1912 set the international prohibition bandwagon rolling by outlawing alcohol in any form.

In 1933 wine and spirits were legalised, but, as a consolation to the temperance societies, beer with greater than 2.2% alcohol remained illegal. For the next 50 years, beer was either smuggled in or clandestinely brewed at home.

In response, several Reykjavík pubs took to spiking the watery local brew with vodka and began serving it on tap. This stuff flowed freely until September 1985, when a new law banned the mixture. The nation gathered in protest, held mock funerals and sang dirges for the swill that had become a national staple, but the government was not swayed.

Suddenly, in 1988, a vote was taken to legalise real beer in a year's time, and on 1 March 1989 the amber fluid finally flowed again. 'Beer Day' (1 March) is now celebrated in Reykjavík with packed pubs and all-day partying.

WHERE TO EAT & DRINK

Restaurants

Iceland's best restaurants are in the Reykjavík area (p73) and Akureyri (p192), but there a few gems popping up in other places, such as Lónkot in Northwest Iceland (p182) and Café Margret in the Eastfjords (p248). In rural Iceland, however, the only restaurant is often the dining room of the local hotel (if there is one) or the cafeteria of a petrol station. All restaurants will have at least one fish dish on the menu (from Ikr1200 to Ikr2500), and usually several entrée or main course options. There are also meat dishes (usually lamb; from around Ikr2000). Outside Reykjavík and Akureyri, most restaurants will offer pizzas, salad bars, soups and burgers. Hotel restaurants usually have a Scandinavian-style buffet breakfast which is free to guests, but nonguests can join in for around Ikr1000. Some also have lunch or dinner buffets. Although some budget travellers would hesitate to enter a fancy restaurant for fear of expensive menu prices, bear in mind that the price difference between an exceptional restaurant and an average one is often not much, so it's worth checking out recommended places.

For an honest rundown of places to eat, drink and be merry in Reykjavík, pick up a copy of the free fortnightly magazine *Grapevine*.

Some city restaurants and petrol-station cafeterias may serve food all day, otherwise restaurants usually serve breakfast from 8am to 10am, lunch from noon to 2pm and dinner from 6pm to 10pm.

In Reykjavík, and to a lesser extent Akureyri, there's an increasing number of ethnic restaurants, including Thai, Vietnamese, Italian, Mexican, Indian and Chinese.

Cafés & Pubs

European café culture is slowly gaining ground in Iceland, and Reykjavík, Akureyri and a few other towns have small and intimate pub-style cafés where you can drink beer, eat a relatively inexpensive meal or just sit, talk and drink coffee for hours on end without attracting comment. Downtown Reykjavík has a great range of bohemian, smoky cafés such as Svartakaffi (p74), and it's hard to resist spending a rainy day in Akureyri on the leather couches of Karolína Café (p192). Typically creative menus range from simple soups, bagels and gourmet burgers to fish dishes, and offer some of the best-value meals in Iceland.

Pubs or bars that are mainly for drinking can be found in the Reykjavík area and Akureyri – in rural Iceland the local bar is usually in a restaurant or hotel. Pubs and bars, even in Reykjavík, are usually busy only on Friday and Saturday nights and stay open till 3am – after about midnight the queues start to form at popular places.

ICELANDIC PÝLSUR

The *pýlsur* (hot dog) is a fast-food institution in Iceland. Whether you get your hot dog at a mobile kiosk or petrol-station diner, the toppings are always the same (though you'll be asked which ones you want): raw onion, crunchy deep-fried onion (not to be missed), ketchup, mustard and (the secret ingredient) a mysterious tangy rémoulade. These are arranged on a warm bun with your hot dog and there you have Iceland's cheapest snack for around Ikr200.

Locals in Reykjavík reckon the world's greatest hot dogs come from Bæjarins Bestu, a busy but unassuming hot-dog stand (that's all it sells) opposite the Kolaportið flea market (p67).

Quick Eats

Icelanders love fast food and you'll soon discover a cheap way to stave off hunger until dinner is to have a *pýlsur* (hot dog). Most towns have a kiosk serving hot dogs, burgers and chips, or you can head to the nearest petrol-station cafeteria. Pizzas can also be found everywhere – a medium pizza with some decent toppings costs around Ikr1500. Pizza 67 is the most common local chain but practically every restaurant has pizza on the menu.

Bakari (bakeries) are another good place for a meal on the run. Every town has one and as well as fresh bread, buns and cakes, they usually do inexpensive filled rolls and coffee.

Self-Catering

Every town and village has at least one *kaupfélagið* (cooperative supermarket) – your key to inexpensive dining in Iceland. Nýkaup and Hagkaup are large chains, with stores in southwestern Iceland and Akureyri. Bónus and Strax are smaller but often more economical.

Iceland produces few of its own consumer goods, so groceries and grain must be imported from all over the world. Although prices are roughly three times what you'd pay in North America, Australia or Europe, tinned fish is reasonably priced, as are dairy products. Bread, which seems to be mostly air, is extortionate.

Icelandic greenhouse produce is very good, but imported vegetables may be past their peak when they hit the supermarkets. Street stands offer the best value for fresh fruit and vegetables.

VEGETARIANS & VEGANS

Strict vegetarians won't find much joy in Iceland. There are at least three good vegetarian restaurants in Reykjavík and quite a few restaurants in large towns offer a vegetarian meal on the menu, but unless you eat fish, pickings will be slim outside the capital. Vegetarian pizzas are always a fast-food option and supermarkets stock some vegetables, bread, pasta and possibly some soya products.

HABITS & CUSTOMS

Icelandic eating habits are similar to elsewhere in northern Europe and Scandinavia. Breakfast is usually light (often just coffee), as is lunch (soup and bread or a snack). Dinner is the main meal of the day.

You're most likely to see traditional customs at a festival such as Þorrablót, an annual feast day in February featuring traditional foods; Sprengidagur, on Shrove Tuesday, when Icelanders have a traditional meal of salted mutton and pea soup; and Bolludagur, the Monday before Shrove Tuesday, when children pester adults for *bollur* (cream buns). On Christmas Day *hangikjöt* (hung meat) – which is normally smoked lamb – is served, as well as *flatkökur*, unleavened bread charred on a grill or griddle without fat.

Reykjavík

CONTENTS

At first glance, Reykjavík can seem more like a small town than a capital city, but by Icelandic standards, this is a teeming metropolis. More than 62% of Iceland's 288,201 people live here and the city is expanding rapidly – swallowing up towns and villages on all sides. Culturally, Reykjavík is upbeat and youth-oriented, with a vibrant art and music scene, loads of cafés and restaurants, and a famously uninhibited nightlife. During the long summer nights, the streets are packed with young revellers who spill out from the bars and clubs into the midnight sunshine.

Generations of young architects have filled the capital with intriguing modern buildings, which sit neatly juxtaposed against the ancient wooden houses of the old town. Every house is different and the sea of coloured tin roofs that sprawls around the huge Hallgrímskirkja church in the centre of town is undeniably picturesque. The setting is also superb – from the harbourside, you can gaze out over the wave-licked ocean and the snow-topped ridge of Mt Esja (909m).

From a tourist perspective, Reykjavík is a place to eat well, party through the night and soak up the local culture in museums, theatres, cinemas and music venues. You'll certainly appreciate the lively atmosphere and cosmopolitan mood after spending time in the volcanic wilderness outside the capital. To get the best out of the capital talk to the locals – they're an eccentric bunch and you'll soon realise that even Björk, arguably Iceland's most famous export, is fairly down to earth by local standards!

TOP FIVE

- Joining the **runtur** (the great Icelandic pub crawl) through Rekyjavík's bars (p79)
- Gorging on an Icelandic feast at an upmarket Reykjavík **restaurant** (p74)
- Taking a dip at **Nauthólsvík geothermal Beach** (p62) or the Laugadalur **geothermal swimming pool** (p65)
- Admiring the view from the tower of **Hallgrímskirkja** (p59)
- Viewing the Erró painting collection in the funky **Hafnarhúsið** art gallery (p63)

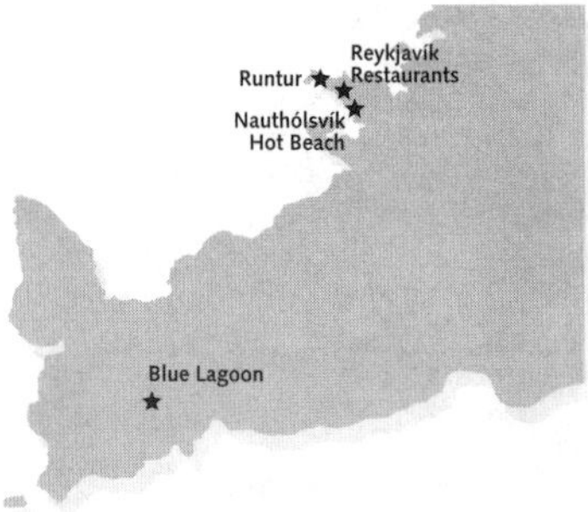

HISTORY

Reykjavík was first settled in AD 874, when Ingólfur Arnarson threw the carved pillars from his Viking high seat over the side of his boat and vowed to settle wherever they washed up on the shore. This happened to be at the site of modern-day Reykjavík, beside lake Tjörn. He called the place Reykjavík, or 'Smoky Bay', after the steam rising from geothermal vents in the surrounding countryside.

Over the years, many more settlers arrived and an Augustinian monastery was established on the nearby island of Viðey in 1226. The manor farm of Bessastaðir, now the official residence of Iceland's head of state, became crown property when Iceland was absorbed by Norway in 1262. The government took over the Viðey monastery in 1613, and in 1752 local sheriff and businessman Skúli Magnússon established weaving, tanning, rope-making and wool-dyeing factories in a bid to overcome the trade barriers imposed by the Danish Trade Monopoly.

On 18 August 1786, the Royal Danish government granted Reykjavík a charter as a market town. After the rural bishoprics were abolished and Iceland converted to Protestantism, Reykjavík became the theological centre of Iceland. The Lutheran cathedral at Dómkirkja was completed in 1796 and, shortly afterwards, the Alþing (Icelandic parliament) was moved from Þingvellir to Reykjavík. Despite this, Reykjavík remained something of a second-tier town right up until the 19th century. There were just 2000 people here at the end of the 19th century, but by 1911 the population had swelled to 12,000 and by the time of Icelandic independence in 1944, it had ballooned to 45,000.

Today, Reykjavík has all the trappings of a modern capital city, including theatres, cinemas, an opera house, designer-clothes shops, upmarket restaurants, hotels, museums and the nation's best nightlife. The old part of town is concentrated around Austurvöllur, and is still full of old tin-clad wooden homes. In a neat bit of historical irony, Reykjavík is now known as the 'smokeless city' due to its complete adoption of geothermal heat and power.

ORIENTATION

Reykjavík is spread out along a small peninsula facing west. The picturesque old town and harbour occupy the north coast, while Reykjavík Domestic Airport takes up the southern half of the peninsula. Over the years, Reykjavík has absorbed a number of outlying towns including Kópavogur, Garðabær and Hafnarfjörður.

The centre of Reykjavík is divided in half by Lækjargata. To the west are the old town squares of Austurvöllur and Ingólfstorg, and the shopping street Austurstræti, crammed with historic buildings and places to eat, drink and shop. At the harbour end of Lækjargata is the Lækjartorg bus terminal for Reykjavík city buses. The domestic airport and the terminal for long-distance buses (BSÍ) are southeast of the centre, while the international airport is 48km away at Keflavík (a special airport bus provides connections to the centre of Reykjavík).

On the west side of Lækjargata, Austurstræti changes name to Bankastræti and then to Laugavegur. This is Reykjavík's main shopping street and is jam-packed with clothes shops, restaurants and bars. Skólavörðustígur runs uphill from Bankastræti to Hallgrímskirkja, the distinctive grey church that looms over the city. If you head east along Laugavegur, you'll reach Snorrabraut, which divides the old town from the new part of Reykjavík, and then the Hlemmur bus terminal, another important stop for city buses.

Maps

Several commercially produced maps of Iceland have insets of Reykjavík, but there are plenty of free tourist maps that do the job just as well. All of Reykjavík's tourist information centres can provide free copies of *Reykjavík, Hafnarfjörður, Kópavogur*, which features all the important tourist sites, and *Enjoy More of Reykjavík,* which also shows the city bus routes. For road maps and trekking maps of Iceland, try the official tourist office or any of the bookshops listed in the Information section below.

INFORMATION

Bookshops

For maps, books on Iceland, and foreign-language novels and periodicals, try these.

Bókabúddin Hlemmi (Map pp54-5; ☎ 511 1170; Laugavegur 118) Good independent bookshop with maps and Icelandic books.

REYKJAVÍK

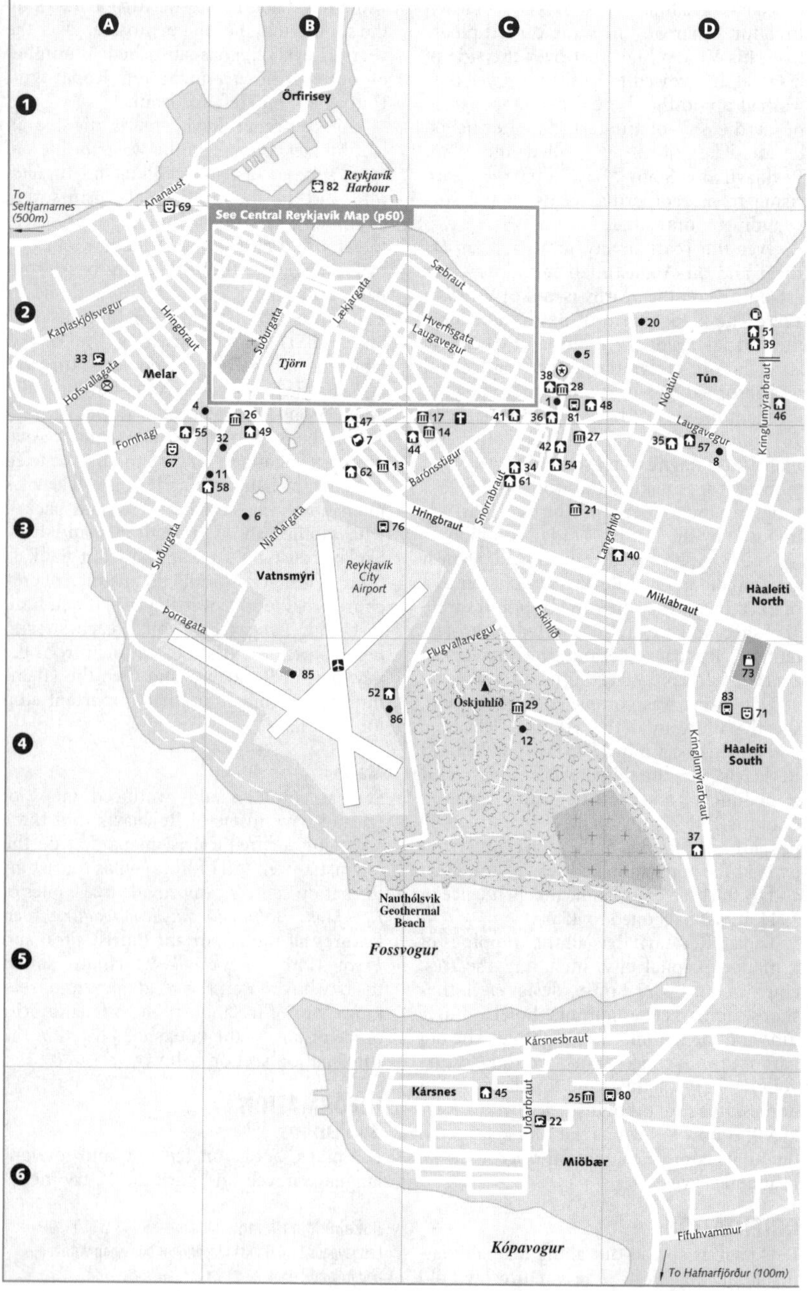
A
B
C
D
1
2
3
4
5
6
Örfirisey
Reykjavík Harbour
82
To Seltjarnarnes (500m)
Ananaust
69
See Central Reykjavík Map (p60)
Sæbraut
Lækjargata
Suðurgata
Tjörn
Hverfisgata
Laugavegur
Kaplaskjólsvegur
Hringbraut
33
Hofsvallagata
Melar
20
5
51
39
38
28
1
48
Nóatún
Tún
Kringlumýrarbraut
46
4
26
47
17
41
36
81
Laugavegur
Fornhagi
55
32
49
7
14
44
27
42
35
57
8
67
11
58
62
13
Barónsstígur
34
61
54
Snorrabraut
6
Njarðargata
76
Hringbraut
21
Langahlíð
40
Suðurgata
Vatnsmýri
Reykjavík City Airport
Miklabraut
Hàaleiti North
Þorragata
Eskihlíð
Flugvallarvegur
73
85
52
86
Öskjuhlíð
29
12
83
71
Hàaleiti South
Kringlumýrarbraut
37
Nauthólsvik Geothermal Beach
Fossvogur
Kársnesbraut
Kársnes
45
25
80
Urðarbraut
22
Miöbær
Fífuhvammur
Kópavogur
To Hafnarfjörður (100m)

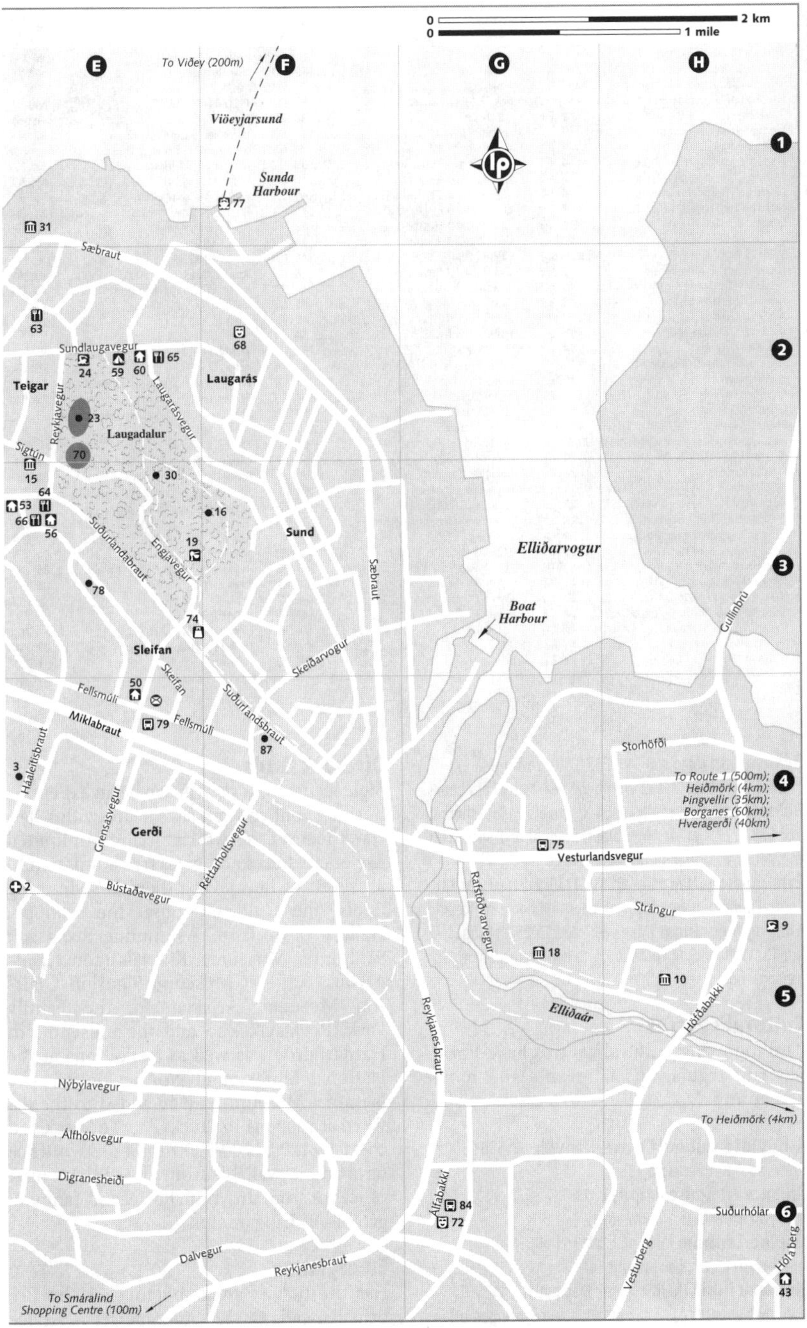
0 2 km
0 1 mile
E
F
G
H
To Viðey (200m)
Viðeyjarsund
Sunda Harbour
77
31
Sæbraut
63
68
Sundlaugavegur
24
59
60
65
Laugarás
Teigar
Reykjavegur
Laugarásvegur
23
Laugadalur
Sigtún
70
15
30
64
53
66
56
16
Suðurlandabraut
Engjavegur
19
Sund
Elliðarvogur
78
Sæbraut
Boat Harbour
74
Gullinbrú
Sleifan
Skeiðarvogur
50
Skeifan
Fellsmúli
Suðurlandsbraut
Miklabraut
79
Fellsmúli
87
Storhöfði
3
Háaleitisbraut
To Route 1 (500m);
Heiðmörk (4km);
Þingvellir (35km);
Borganes (60km);
Hveragerði (40km)
Grensásvegur
Gerði
75
Vesturlandsvegur
Réttarholtsvegur
2
Bústaðavegur
Rafstöðvarvegur
Strángur
9
18
10
Elliðaár
Höfðabakki
Reykjanesbraut
Nýbýlavegur
To Heiðmörk (4km)
Álfhólsvegur
Digranesheiði
Álfabakki
84
72
Suðurhólar
Hólaberg
Dalvegur
Reykjanesbraut
Vesturberg
43
To Smáralind Shopping Centre (100m)
1
2
3
4
5
6

INFORMATION
Bókabúddin Hlemmi 1 C2
Bóksala Stúdenta (University Bookshop) .... (see 49)
Kringlusafn (Reykjavík City Library) .. (see 71)
Landspítali University Hospital (Emergency Ward) 2 E4
Lyf og Heilsa - Austurveri (24-hour Pharmacy) 3 E4
National & University Library of Iceland . 4 A2
Nature Conservation Agency 5 C2
Norræna Húsið (Nordic House) 6 B3
Norway Embassy 7 B3
Útivist 8 D3

SIGHTS & ACTIVITIES (pp59-65)
Árbæjarlaug Swimming Pool 9 H5
Árbæjarsafn Open-Air Museum 10 H5
Árni Magnusson Institute 11 B3
Artificial Geyser 12 C4
Ásgrimur Jónsson Museum 13 B3
ASI Art Museum 14 C3
Asmundursafn (Reykjavík Art Museum) 15 E3
Botanic Gardens 16 F3
Einar Jónsson Museum 17 C2
Electric Museum 18 G5
Fjölskyldugarðurinn og Húsdýragarðurinn (Children's Park & Zoo) 19 E3
Höfði House 20 D2
Kjarvalsstaðir (Reykjavík Art Museum .. 21 C3
Kópavogur Swimming Pool 22 C6
Laugardalur Sports Stadium 23 E2
Laugardalur Swimming Pool 24 E2
Listasafn Kópavogs 25 C6
Menningarmiðstoð Kópavogs .... (see 80)
National Museum 26 B2
Numismatic Museum 27 C3
Náttúrufræ-ðistofnun Íslands 28 C2
Perlan & Saga Museum 29 C4
Reykjavík Skating Hall 30 E3
Sigurjón Ólafsson Museum 31 E1
University of Iceland 32 B3
Vesturbæjarlaug Swimming Pool 33 A2

SLEEPING (pp69-73)
Flöki B&B 34 C3
Fosshótel Höfði 35 D3
Fosshótel Lind 36 C2
Gesthús Dúna 37 D4
Gistiheimilið 101 .... 38 C2
Gistiheimilið Borgartún 39 D2
Gistiheimilið Central 40 D3
Gistiheimilið Centrum 41 C2
Gistiheimilið Egilsborg 42 C3
Gistiheimilið Hólaberg 43 H6
Gistiheimilið Sunna 44 C3
Gisting BB44 .... 45 C6
Grand Hótel Reykjavík 46 D2
Guesthouse Baldursbrá 47 B2
Guesthouse Regina 48 C2
Hotel Garður 49 B3
Hótel Atlantis 50 E4
Hótel Cabin 51 D2
Hótel Loftleiðir 52 B4
Hótel Nordica 53 E3
Hótel Reykjavík 54 C3
Hótel Saga 55 A3
Hótel Ísland 56 E3
Hótel Örkin 57 D3
Park Hótel 58 B3
Rekjavík Camping Ground 59 E2
Reykjavík City Hostel 60 E2
Snorri's Guesthouse 61 C3
Travel-Inn Guesthouse 62 B3

EATING (pp73-8)
10-11 Supermarket 63 E2
Askur Brasserie 64 E3
Carpe Diem .... (see 36)
Fljótt Og Gott .... (see 76)
Kaffisetrið .... (see 38)
Kringlan Food Court .... (see 73)
Lauga-Ás 65 E2
Múlakaffi 66 E3
Ning's .... (see 64)
Perlan Restaurant .... (see 29)
Vox Restaurant .... (see 53)

ENTERTAINMENT (pp80-1)
Broadway .... (see 56)
Háskólabíó Cinema 67 A3
Iceland Symphony Orchestra .... (see 67)
Laugarásbíó Cinema 68 F2
Loftkastalinn 69 A2
Próttur Football Ground 70 E2
Reykjavík City Theatre 71 D4
Sambíóin Cinema 72 G6

SHOPPING (p81)
Antikbúðin .... (see 38)
Kringlan Shopping Centre 73 D4
Útilíf 74 E3
Útilíf .... (see 73)

TRANSPORT (pp81-3)
Ártún Bus Stand 75 G4
BSÍ Long-distance Bus Terminal 76 B3
Ferries to Viðey 77 F1
Ferðaþjónusta Bænda (Icelandic Farm Holidays) 78 E3
Flybus Terminal .... (see 52)
Grensás Bus Stand 79 E4
Hamraborg Bus Stand 80 D6
Hlemmur Bus Terminal 81 C2
Jetty for Whale Watching Tours 82 B1
Kringlan Bus Stop 83 D4
Mjódd Bus Stand 84 G6
Reykjavik City Airport Terminal 85 B4
Reykjavik Excursions 86 B4

OTHER
Destination Iceland .... (see 76)
Ferðafélag Islands 87 F4
Icelandair .... (see 73)

Bókavarðan (Map p60; ☎ 552 9720; Vesturgata 17) Second-hand book dealer with huge selection of old books.
Bóksala Stúdenta (Map pp54-5; University Bookshop; ☎ 570 0777; Garður, Hringbraut) Student bookshop with translations of Icelandic books.
Eymundsson (Map p60; ☎ 511 1130; Austurstræti 18) Central bookshop with loads of maps and books on Iceland.
Máls og Menningar (Map p60; ☎ 515 2500; Laugavegur 18) Well-stocked bookshop with good selection of Icelandic books.

Cultural Centres

The following cultural centres have libraries, run regular special events and movie screenings.

A-Hús Intercultural Centre (Map p60; ☎ 530 9300; www.ahus.is; Hverfisgta 18)
Alliance Française (Map p60; ☎ 552 3870; http://af.ismennt.is; Hringbraut 121)
Goethe-Zentrum (Map p60; ☎ 551 6061; goethe@simnet.is; Laugavegur 18)
Norræna Húsið (Nordic House; Map pp54-5; ☎ 551 7030; www.nordice.is; cnr Sæmundagata & Hringbraut)

Discount Cards

Sightseeing in Reykjavík can be an expensive business, but you can save heaps with a **Reykjavík Tourist Card**, which permits unlimited use of city buses and gives free admission to all seven of Reykjavík's thermal swimming pools, the Culture House, the National Gallery of Iceland, Ásmundur Sveinsson Sculpture Museum, Kjarvalsstaðir, Hafnarhús, ASÍ Art Museum, Sigurjón Ólafsson Museum, Árbæjarsafn, the Family Park, Reykjavík Zoo and the museums in Hafnarfjörður, as well as exhibitions at the National Library and Nordic House. The National Museum may be added to the list when it reopens in 2004. The Tourist Card costs Ikr1200/1700/2200 for one/two/three days and is available from any of the tourist offices or from the youth hostel and camping ground at Laugardalur.

Emergency

For the police, an ambulance or the fire brigade, call ☎ 112. For rape crisis advice call the women's organisation **Stígamót** (☎ 562 6868).

Internet Access

Reykjavík has a handful of commercial Net cafés, but the cheapest places to access the Internet are Reykjavík's many libraries, which charge Ikr200 per hour – see Libraries in this section for more information. Of the private Net cafés, **Reykjavík Travel Service** (Map p60; ☎ 552 2300; Lækjargata 2) is central and charges Ikr250 for 30 minutes. For after-hours Internet access, head to the Net café and LAN-gaming centre **Ground Zero** (Map p60; ☎ 562 7776; Vallarstræti 4), at the south end of Ingólfstorg – it's open until 1am and charges Ikr300 for 30 minutes. There is also Internet access at many hotels and guesthouses, including the youth hostel.

Internet Resources

Good websites for information on Reykjavík include the following:

Complete Reykjavík (www.visitReykjavík.is) Official Reykjavík website
Explore-Reykjavík.com (www.explore-Reykjavík.com) Private site with general information
Randburg.com (www.randburg.com/is/capital) Reliable independent information site

Laundry

Most people rely on their hotel or guesthouse for laundry; the youth hostel has washers and driers for guests. For fast-service laundry, try **EMLA Laundrette** (Map p60; ☎ 552 7499; Barónsstígur 3). A 6/11kg wash will cost Ikr1700/2800 and they can deliver your clothes to where you are staying.

Left Luggage

There is a left-luggage desk at the **BSÍ terminal** (Map pp54-5; ☎ 591 1000; 🕑 7.30am-10pm) for Ikr150/700 per day/week. Guests at the Laugardalur camping ground and the youth hostel can store bags for free in the hostel luggage room.

Libraries

The following offer Internet access for Ikr200 (30 minutes) and have books, novels and periodicals in English, French and other languages.

Aðalsafn (Reykjavík City Library; Map p60; ☎ 563 1717; www.borgarbokasafn.is; Tryggvagata 15; 🕑 10am-8pm Mon-Thu, 11am-7pm Fri, 1-5pm Sat & Sun)
Kringlusafn (Reykjavík City Library; Map pp54-5; ☎ 580 6200; www.borgarbokasafn.is; cnr Borgarleikhús & Listabraut; 🕑 10am-7pm Mon-Wed, 10am-9pm Thu, 11am-7pm Fri, 1-5pm Sat & Sun)

REYKJAVÍK IN…

Two Days

This will give you time to see the best sites. On day one get up early and take a swim at one of Reykjavík's **geothermal swimming pools** (p64) or at **Nauthólsvík Geothermal Beach** (p62). Visit the **Perlan** complex (p62) and **Saga Museum** (p62), and take time for lunch in one of the **cafés** around Austurvöllur (p73). In the afternoon, stroll around the streets looking at the historic and modern **architecture** (p65). In the evening, have a seafood feast at one of the upmarket **restaurants** (p74) around Laugavegur. If you're here at the weekend, join in the **runtur pub crawl** (p79). The next day, check out the **Kolaportið flea market** (at the weekend; p67) or visit lake **Tjörn** (p59) to feed the ducks and geese, and see the giant Iceland map in the **Ráðhús** (City Hall; p59). Then take the lift up the tower of **Hallgrímskirkja** (p59) for the views and visit the excellent **Hafnarhúsið art gallery** (p63). In the evening, try the fusion cuisine at one of Reykjavík's trendy **bars** (p78).

Four Days

With more time on your hands, you can visit the **National Museum** (p62) and browse the bizarre sculptures at the **Ásmundursafn** (p63). Pay a visit to the **Þjóðmenningarhúsið** (p62) to see the ancient manuscripts of Icelandic sagas. In the evening, visit the **Volcano Show** (p61) for an introduction to Iceland's violent geology. The following day, visit the suburb of **Hafnarfjörður** (p84) to see places where elves are rumoured to live and the over-the-top architecture of the **Viking Village** (p87). In the afternoon, take a **horse-riding trip** (p64), or spoil yourself and take a tour to the **Blue Lagoon** (p95) near the international airport.

National & University Library of Iceland (Map pp54-5; ☎ 525 5600; Arngrímsgata 3; www.bok.hi.is; ⏲ 9am-5pm Mon-Fri, 10am-2pm Sat May-Aug; 8.15am-10pm Mon-Thu, 8.15am-7pm Fri, 9am-5pm Sat, 11am-5pm Sun Sep-Apr)

Medical Services

The most useful hospital is **Landspítali University Hospital** (Map pp54-5; ☎ 525 1000; Fossvogur), with a 24-hour casualty department. Non-urgent cases should consult the **Health Centre** (Map p60; ☎ 585 2600; Vesturgata 7); a visit to the doctor will cost around Ikr700.

A reliable central pharmacy is **Lyf og Heilsa** (Map p60; ☎ 562 9020; Austurstræti 12). Outside business hours, visit **Lyf og Heilsa – Austurvegi** (Map pp54-5; ☎ 581 2101; Háaleitisbraut 68; ⏲ 8am-midnight Mon-Fri, 10am-midnight Sat & Sun). Ask at your hotel for a list of dentists.

Money

All the major Icelandic banks offer commission-free currency exchange of cash or travellers cheques in British pounds, US dollars, euros, etc. Most also sell Danish kroner for travel to Greenland or the Faroes. There are central branches of Landsbanki Íslands, Íslandsbanki and Sparisjoðurinn on Laugavegur and Austurstæti. For after-hours foreign exchange, you have the choice of the exchange desks at big hotels, which offer poor rates, or the **Change Group** (Map p60; ☎ 552 3735; Geysishús, Aðalstæti 2; ⏲ 8.30am-6pm daily Jun-Aug, 9am-5pm Mon-Fri & 10am-2pm Sat & Sun Sep-May) at the main tourist office, which will hit you for a staggering 8.75% commission.

With an international credit or debit card, you can withdraw cash from *hraðbanki* (ATMs) at all the major banks and also at numerous hole-in-the-wall ATMs dotted around the town centre (for example, at the corner of Austurstræti and Lækjargata).

Post

The **main post office** (Map p60; Pósthússtræti 5, ⏲ 9am-4.30pm Mon-Fri) handles poste restante – get your correspondents to address letters to the Post Restante, Posthúsið, Reykjavík 101. There's also a fast and efficient parcel service where you can buy boxes, padded envelopes and other packing materials. There are several other post office branches around the capital, including one in the Kringlan Shopping Centre, which also opens on Saturday.

Telephone

You can make expensive phone calls from most hotels and guest houses, but payphones are plentiful in the town centre – try at the Lækjartorg bus terminal.

Tourist Information

Reykjavík has an excellent official tourist office and a number of smaller private tourist information centres that can book tours and accommodation. If you'll be spending any time in the capital, pick up the free booklets *Reykjavík This Month* and *What's On in Reykjavík*, which have all sorts of information on things to see and do in the capital. All of these offices also have brochures covering other parts of Iceland, including the useful booklet *Around Iceland.*

Reykjavík's main tourist office is **Upplýsingamiðstöð** (Reykjavík Complete; Map p60; ☎ 562 3045; www.visitReykjavík.is; Geysishús, Aðalstræti 2; ⏲ 8.30am-7pm Jun-15 Sept, 9am-6pm Mon-Fri & 10am-2pm Sat & Sun 16 Sep-31 May), housed in an attractive old building on Ingólfstorg. Staff are friendly and informed, and there are mountains of free brochures and leaflets. Several walking-guide maps are available for Ikr200, which lead you around Reykjavík's parks, statues and old buildings. The guide *A Literary Walking Tour* takes tourists around sites that have been mentioned in Icelandic literature. There's also a souvenir shop and a foreign exchange desk (see Money, earlier).

From May to September, there's a smaller Reykjavík information desk at the **Rádhús** (City Hall; Map p60; ☎ 563 2005; Vonarstræti; ⏲ 8.20am-4.30pm Mon-Fri, noon-4pm Sat & Sun).

Another good source of information is **Reykjavík Travel Service** (Map p60; ☎ 552 2300; www.icelandvisitor.com; Lækjargata 2; ⏲ 9am-10pm Jun-Aug, 10am-6pm Mon-Sat Sep-May), which has a tour and accommodation booking service, an Internet café and bike rental. It publishes a handy information booklet with a fold-out city map. Another private information office worth checking out is **Kleif Travel Market** (Map p60; ☎ 510 5700; www.kleif.is; Bankastræti 2; ⏲ 8am-8pm in summer, 9am-7pm in winter).

You can also get tourist information from the reception desk at the youth hostel and the booking desk at the BSÍ bus station.

Travel Agencies

There are numerous travel agents and tour companies in Reykjavík that specialise in day tours around Iceland by bus or plane, but you can often save money by hiring a car and undertaking the same trips independently. A few agents can also arrange international travel.

The local agent for Smyril Line, which runs the ferries to the Faroes, Shetland Islands, Norway and Denmark, is **Norræna Terra Nova** (☎ 587 1919; smyril-iceland@isholf.is; Stangarhyl 3a).

Other travel agencies include:

Destination Iceland (Map pp54-5; ☎ 552 2300; www.dice.is; BSÍ Bus Terminal, Vatnsmýrarvegur) BSÍ-owned travel agent offering lots of Iceland tours.
Ferðaþjónusta Bænda (Map pp54-5; Icelandic Farm Holidays; ☎ 570 2700; www.sveit.is; Síðumúla 13) Arranges farm holidays around Iceland.
Stúdenta Ferdir (Map p60; ☎ 562 2362; www.exit.is; Bankastræti 10) Student travel agency specialising in international travel.
Urval Utsyn (☎ 569 9312; www.urvalutsyn.is; Lagmula 4) Mainstream travel agency specialising in international travel.
Útivist (Map pp54-5; ☎ 562 1000; www.utivist.is; Laugavegur 178) Owns huts at Þórsmörk and Landmannalaugar, and runs guided treks.

DANGERS & ANNOYANCES

Icelanders are famously law abiding, but petty theft is a minor risk – just use common sense and don't leave your camera or mobile phone unattended. Alcohol is more of an issue, and while deliberate violence is not really a problem, accidental injury at the hands of drunken revellers is a possibility. Due to rising unemployment, drunks have taken to hanging out at the Hlemmur and Lækjartorg bus stands and harassing tourists for loose change. Another blight on the capital is chewing gum – it's everywhere in town, on pavements, bus seats and park benches. Watch where you sit!

SIGHTS

Hallgrímskirkja

At the top of Skólavörðustígur, **Hallgrímskirkja** (Map p60) looms over Reykjavík like a set from a Norse opera. The 75m-high steeple is flanked by concrete representations of volcanic basalt columns – you can see it from 20km away. The church took an incredible 34 years to be completed, starting in 1940 and finally opening in 1974, and was named in honour of Reverend Hallgrímur Pétursson, who wrote Iceland's most popular hymnal. Although the church is very grand from the outside, the interior is quite stark, but the view from the top of the tower is spectacular. An 'elevator to heaven' with taped choral music runs up to the viewing level for Ikr300. You can visit daily from 9am to 6pm (to 5pm in winter).

In front of the church is an equally eye-catching statue of Leifur Eiríksson, the Viking explorer who first discovered Vinland (modern-day America). Leifur is depicted in a suitably noble pose, standing at the prow of a Viking longboat. The statue was presented to Iceland by the USA in 1930 on the 1000th anniversary of the Alþing.

Dómkirkja

Reykjavík's main cathedral, **Dómkirkja** (Map p60) was built by the Danish king Christian VII in 1796 after the Catholic diocese of Hólar and Skálholt were abolished. Although it played an important role in the conversion of Iceland to Protestantism, the church is fairly modest compared to the looming bulk of Hallgrímskirkja and the current incarnation only dates back to 1847.

Ráðhús & Tjörn

Reykjavík's postmodern **Ráðhús** (City Hall; Map p60; ☎ 563 2005; Vonarstræti; admission free; 🕒 8am-7pm Mon-Fri, noon-6pm Sat & Sun) is in the middle of the old town, on the edge of lake Tjörn ('the pond'). The architecturally interesting building is a blend of concrete blocks, thick green glass and running water. Inside, you can see exhibitions of Icelandic art and a huge 3D map of Iceland that comes apart into sections and slides into a hole in the wall.

Behind the Ráðhús, **Tjörn** (Map p60) is visited by more than 40 species of migratory birds; locals often come to feed the ducks and geese. A short walk through the little park surrounding Tjörn will take you to the BSÍ Bus Terminal and domestic airport.

Alþingi

Although Iceland has a population smaller than some towns in neighbouring nations, it has a fully functional parliament, the **Alþingi** (Map p60; ☎ 563 0500; www.althingi.is; Túngata), which met for the first time at Þingvellir in west Iceland in AD 930. The parliament lost its powers in 1262 when Iceland joined the Kingdom of Norway

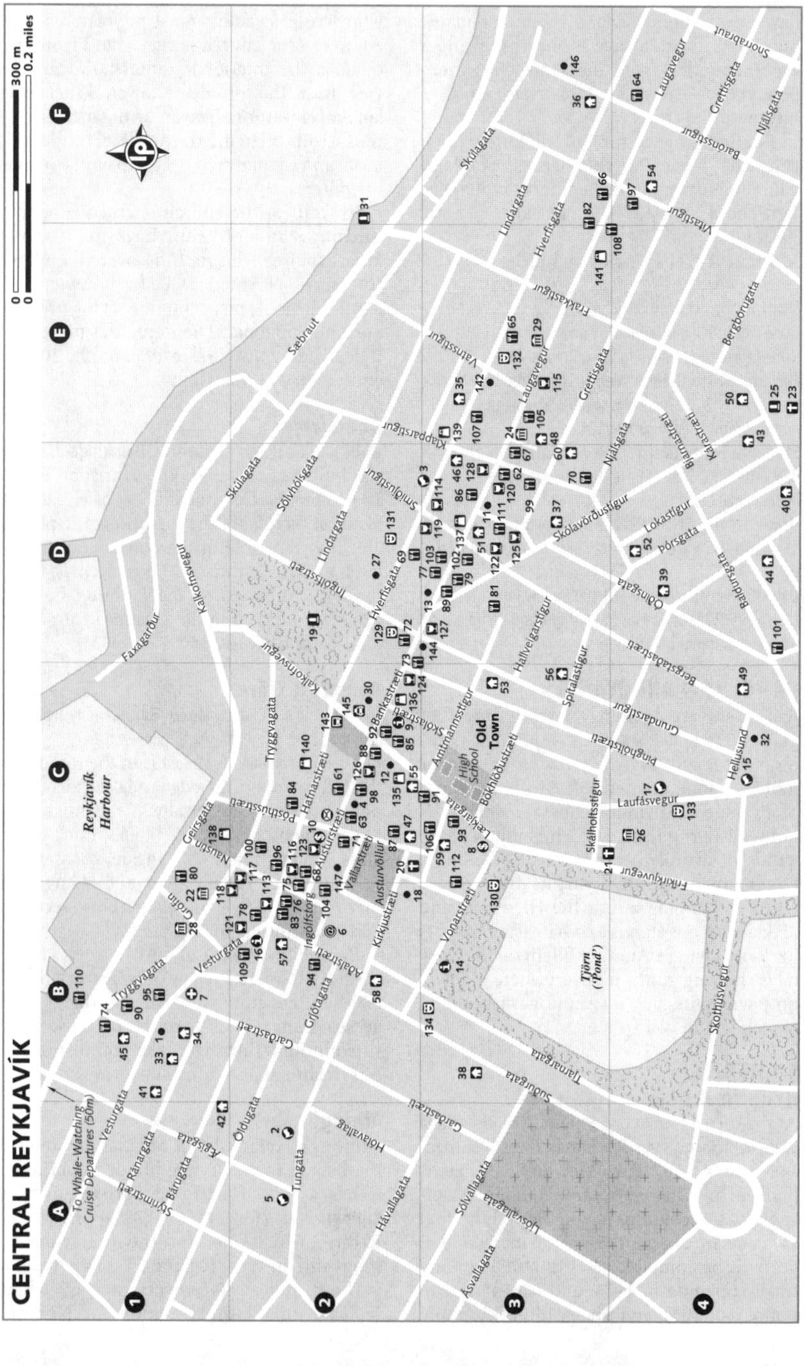
CENTRAL REYKJAVÍK
0 300 m
0 0.2 miles
A
B
C
D
E
F
1
2
3
4
To Whale-Watching Cruise Departures (50m)
Reykjavík Harbour
Old Town
High School
Tjörn ('Pond')
Austurvöllur
Ingólfstorg
Sæbraut
Skúlagata
Faxagarður
Kalkofnsvegur
Tryggvagata
Geirsgata
Naustin
Grófin
Hafnarstræti
Pósthússtræti
Austurstræti
Vallarstræti
Kirkjustræti
Aðalstræti
Grjótagata
Vesturgata
Garðastræti
Öldugata
Ránargata
Bárugata
Ægisgata
Túngata
Hólavallag
Hávallagata
Sólvallagata
Ásvallagata
Ljósvallagata
Suðurgata
Tjarnargata
Vonarstræti
Lækjargata
Bókhlöðustígur
Amtmannsstígur
Skólastræti
Bankastræti
Lindargata
Sölvhólsgata
Ingólfsstræti
Hverfisgata
Smiðjustígur
Klapparstígur
Laugavegur
Vatnsstígur
Frakkastígur
Vitastígur
Barónsstígur
Snorrabraut
Grettisgata
Njálsgata
Bergþórugata
Skólavörðustígur
Lokastígur
Þórsgata
Óðinsgata
Baldursgata
Bergstaðastræti
Hallveigarstígur
Spítalastígur
Grundarstígur
Þingholtsstræti
Laufásvegur
Skálholtsstígur
Hellusund
Fríkirkjuvegur
Skothúsvegur
Kárastígur
Bjarnastígur

(and subsequently Denmark), but was moved to Reykjavík in 1798 and regained its powers in 1845. The Alþingi moved into the current grey basalt building on Austurvöllur in 1881. Parliament meets from 1 October each year and the public is welcome to attend debates at 3pm on Monday, 1.30pm on Tuesday and Wednesday, and 10.30am on Thursday.

Volcano Show

If you are interested in the incredible forces bubbling away just below Iceland's surface, visit Reykjavík's **Volcano Show** (Map p60; ☎ 551 3230; Hellusund 6a; adult/student/child 1hr show Ikr750/650/200, 2hr show Ikr950/800/250). This small cinema features the work of Vilhjálmur and Ósvaldur Knudsen, a pair of eccentric filmmakers who have been rushing to the scene of Iceland's

INFORMATION
A-Hús.....(see 69)
Aðalsafn (Reykjavik City Library).....(see 28)
Bókavarðan Book Shop..... 1 B1
Búnaðarbankinn.....(see 123)
Canadian Embassy..... 2 A2
Danish Embassy..... 3 D3
Eymundsson Bookshop..... 4 C2
French Embassy..... 5 A2
Ground Zero..... 6 B2
Health Centre..... 7 B1
Íslandsbanki..... 8 C3
Kleif Travel Market..... 9 C2
Landsbanki Islands..... 10 C2
Lyf & Heilsa Pharmacy.....(see 147)
Lyf og Heilsa.....(see 28)
Mals og Menningar Bookshop..... 11 D3
Reykjaví Travel Service..... 12 C2
Samtökin '78..... 13 D3
Summer Tourist Information Desk..... 14 B3
UK & German Embassies..... 15 C4
Upplýsingamiðstöd (Tourist Information)..... 16 B2
US Embassy..... 17 C4

SIGHTS & ACTIVITIES (pp59-65)
Alþingi (Parliament)..... 18 B2
Árnarhóll & Ingólfur Arnarson Statue.. 19 D2
Domkirkja..... 20 C2
Fríkirkjan í Reykjavík..... 21 C3
Hafnarhúsið (Reykjavík Art Museum).. 22 B1
Hallgrímskirkja..... 23 E4
Iceland Phallogical Museum (Reðasafn)..... 24 E3
Leifur Eiríkson Statue..... 25 E4
Listasafn (National Gallery of Iceland).. 26 C4
þjóðmenningarhúsið (Culture House).. 27 D2
Reykjavik Museum of Photography..... 28 B1
Ráðhús (City Hall).....(see 14)
SAFN Gallery..... 29 E3
Stjórnarráðið (Government House)..... 30 C2
Sun-Craft (Sculpture)..... 31 F2
Volcano Show..... 32 C4

SLEEPING (pp69-73)
Alfholl Guesthouse..... 33 B1
City Hótel..... 34 B1
Domus Guesthouse..... 35 E3
Fosshótel Barón..... 36 F3
Gistiheimilið Jörd..... 37 D3
Gistiheimilið Krían..... 38 B3
Gistiheimilið Oðinn..... 39 D4
Gistiheimilið Sunna..... 40 D4
Gistiheimilið Vikingur..... 41 B1
Gistiheimilið Ísafold..... 42 A1
Guesthouse Adam..... 43 E4
Guesthouse Aurora..... 44 D4
Guesthouse Butterfly.....(see 33)
Guesthouse by the Sea..... 45 B1
Hótel Klopp..... 46 D3
Hótel Borg..... 47 C2
Hótel Frón..... 48 E3
Hótel Holt..... 49 C4
Hótel Leifur Eiríksson..... 50 E4
Hótel Skjaldbreið..... 51 D3
Hótel Óðinsvé..... 52 D4
i12 Guesthouse..... 53 C3
Lighthouse Apartments..... 54 F4
Litli Ljóti Andarunginn..... 55 C2
Luna Hotel Apartments..... 56 C3
Plaza Hotel..... 57 B2
Room With a View.....(see 11)
Salvation Army Guest House..... 58 B2
Skólabrú Guesthouse..... 59 C3
Tower Guesthouse..... 60 D3

EATING (pp73-8)
10-11 Supermarket..... 61 C2
10-11 Supermarket.....(see 36)
Á Næstu Grösum (One Woman Vegetarian Restaurant)..... 62 D3
Amigos.....(see 55)
Apótek..... 63 C2
Argentina..... 64 F4
Austur India Félagið..... 65 E3
Brasserie Borg.....(see 47)
Bónus Supermarket..... 66 F3
Cafe 22..... 67 D3
Cafe Cosy..... 68 C2
Caffé Kúlture..... 69 D2
Café Garðurinn..... 70 D3
Café Opera.....(see 12)
Café Paris..... 71 C2
Café Sólon..... 72 D2
Caruso..... 73 D2
Casa Grande..... 74 B1
Einar Ben..... 75 B2
Emmessis og Pylsur..... 76 B2
Enrico's..... 77 D3
Galileo..... 78 B2
Gallery Restaurant.....(see 49)
Gott í Gogginn..... 79 D3
Grillhúsið..... 80 C1
Grænn Kostur..... 81 D3
Hereford Steakhouse..... 82 F3
Hlölla Bátar..... 83 B2
Hornið..... 84 C2
Hressingarskálinn.....(see 126)
Humarhúsið..... 85 C2
Indókina..... 86 D3
Kaffi Brennslan..... 87 C2
Kebabhúsið..... 88 C2
Kofi Tómasar Frænda..... 89 D3
Krua Thai..... 90 B1
Kína Húsið..... 91 C3
La Primavera.....(see 123)
Lækjarbrekka..... 92 C2
Mama's Tacos..... 93 C3
Maru..... 94 B2
Naust..... 95 B1
Nonnabiti..... 96 C2
Nuðluhúsið..... 97 F4
Ömmu Kaffi..... 98 C2
Pasta Basta..... 99 D3
Pizza 67..... 100 C2
Þrír Frakkar..... 101 D4
Restaurant Asía..... 102 D3
Restaurant Tjarnbakkinn.....(see 130)
Ristorante Ítalía..... 103 D3
Shalimar..... 104 B2
Si Señor.....(see 93)
Siggihall.....(see 52)
Sjanghæ..... 105 E3
Skólabrú Restaurant..... 106 C3
Sommelier Brasserie..... 107 E3
Svarta Kaffið..... 108 E3
Tapas..... 109 B2
Tveir Fiskar..... 110 B1
Vegamót..... 111 D3
Við Tjörnina..... 112 C3

DRINKING (pp78-9)
Café Victor (Fálkahús)..... 113 B2
Celtic Cross Pub..... 114 D3
Dillon..... 115 E3
Dubliner Pub..... 116 C2
Gaukur á Stöng..... 117 C2
Glaumbar..... 118 B2
Hverfisbarinn..... 119 D3
Kaffi List..... 120 D3
Kaffi Reykjavík..... 121 B2
Kaffibarinn..... 122 D3
Metz..... 123 C2
Nelly's Café..... 124 C2
Ölstofa..... 125 D3
Pravda..... 126 C2
Prikið..... 127 D3
Sirkus..... 128 D3
Thorvaldsen Bar.....(see 104)
Vidalin.....(see 94)

ENTERTAINMENT (pp81-1)
Grand Rokk.....(see 114)
Íslenska Óperan..... 129 D2
Iðnó Theatre..... 130 B3
National Theatre..... 131 D2
Regnboginn Cinema..... 132 E3
Skemmtihúsið..... 133 C4
Tjarnarbíó Leikhús..... 134 B3

SHOPPING (p81)
66° North..... 135 C2
Aurum.....(see 136)
Friða Frænka.....(see 109)
Hans Petersen Photo Shop..... 136 C2
Japis..... 137 D3
Keramik.....(see 141)
Kólaportið Flea Market..... 138 C1
Ömmu Antique..... 139 E3
Rammagerðin..... 140 C2
Rosenthal..... 141 E3
Skífan.....(see 24)

TRANSPORT (pp81-3)
Borgarhjól SF..... 142 E3
Lækjartorg Bus Terminal..... 143 C2
Studenta Ferdir (Student Travel)..... 144 D3
Taxi Rank..... 145 C2

OTHER
Alliance Francaise.....(see 74)
Change Group.....(see 16)
EMLA Laundrette..... 146 F3
Goethe-Zentrum.....(see 11)
Vin Búd (liquor store)..... 147 C2

volcanic eruptions for more than 50 years. Visitors have the choice of a one-hour programme, featuring footage from all the eruptions since 1947, or a two-hour programme that includes a detailed documentary about the creation of the island of Surtsey in 1963 and the Heimaey eruption in 1973.

Shows in English start at 3pm and 8pm daily from May to September (8pm only October to April). From July to August, there's an extra show in English at 11am, a German show at 6pm and a French show at 1pm every Saturday. At other times of the year, all shows are in English but simultaneous translation is available in French and German.

Nauthólsvík Geothermal Beach

Close to Perlan on the south coast of the peninsula, **Nauthólsvík** (Map pp54-5) has a small constructed beach served by an artificial hot spring. It's often called the 'Hot Beach' and the ambient water temperature is around 20°C year-round. Beside the beach is a complex with hot tubs – heated to 30–35°C – where locals come to chat. There's another hot pot out in the bay. The crescent of yellow sand is gorgeous in summer and there's no charge for using the facilities. You can buy snacks and drinks, including alcohol, at the service centre **café** (🕑 10am-8pm 15 May–15 Sep) or at nearby **Kaffi Nauthóll** (☎ 562 9910; Nauthólsvegur).

Museums

Reykjavík is packed with museums that are well worth a browse if you're spending any time in the capital.

NATIONAL MUSEUM

The **National Museum** (Map pp54-5; ☎ 552 8888; Hringbraut) has a huge collection of Norse and Icelandic artefacts. The museum closed for renovations for most of 2003 but is set to reopen in summer 2004. If the museum does reopen as planned, the displays should be better than ever as exhibits have been recalled from regional museums around the country. Among the more interesting items here are the Valþjófs-staður church door, which dates from around 1200 and is carved with Norse battle scenes, and an ancient wooden mask that should look rather familiar to fans of the Jim Carey movie *The Mask*. Contact the tourist office (p58) for the latest information, including opening times and rates. An hour should give you enough time to browse the collection.

ÞJÓÐMENNINGJARHÚSIÐ

Housed in a grand old stone building on Hverfisgata, the **Þjóðmenningjarhúsið** (Culture House; Map p60; ☎ 545 1400; www.thjodmenning.is; Hverfisgata 15; adult/concession/under-16 Ikr300/200/free, free Sun; 🕑 11am-5pm) has rotating exhibits about Vikings and other aspects of Icelandic cultural heritage, including an impressive display of Icelandic manuscripts and sagas from the collection of the Árni Magnússon Institute. Árni Magnússon was sent to Iceland in 1702 by the Danish government to preserve the surviving vellums of the Icelandic sagas, and shipped almost the entire history of Iceland over to Denmark. Tragically, many of the documents were destroyed in the great fire of Copenhagen in 1728, but the remaining texts were finally returned to Iceland in 1971. If you are interested in seeing more Icelandic sagas, contact the **Árni Magnússon Institute** (Map pp54-5; ☎ 525 4010; www.am.hi.is; Suðurgata).

REYKJAVÍK MUSEUM OF PHOTOGRAPHY

Reykjavík's interesting **Museum of Photography** (Ljósmyndasafn; Map p60; ☎ 563 1790; www.ljosmyndasafn reykjavikur.is; Grófarhús, Tryggvagata 15; admission free; 🕑 10am-4pm Mon-Fri) is above the Reykjavík City Library in Grófarhús. The exhibitions change regularly and the displays often include early photographs of Icelandic life.

PERLAN & THE SAGA MUSEUM

The huge water tanks that supply Reykjavík with its hot water have been developed into a tourist complex known as Perlan. The main attraction here is the **Saga Museum** (Map pp54-5; ☎ 511 1517; www.sagamuseum.is; Perlan, Öskjuhlið; adult/concession/child Ikr800/600/400; 🕑 10am-6pm Jun-Aug, 10am-6pm Sat & Sun Sep-May), which features some eerily realistic dioramas depicting key moments in Icelandic history. Don't be surprised if you see some of these characters wandering around town – the silicone rubber figures were based on real-life Reykjavík residents.

In the pearly dome on top of the tanks is the swish restaurant **Perlan** (The Pearl; Map pp54-5). On the same level there's a cheaper canteen and a viewing deck that offers fantastic views over the city. Surrounding the Perlan complex is a natural park with numerous walking trails, including a path down to the hot beach at Nauthólsvík. Next to the water tanks an **artificial geyser** (Map p60) blasts off every few minutes. The complex sits on Öskjuhlið hill overlooking the domestic airport, about 2km from the centre; take bus No 7 from Lækjartorg. Allow a couple of hours to explore.

ÁRBÆJARSAFN

The historic farm at Árbær dates from 1464 and now houses an **open-air museum** (Map pp54-5; ☎ 577 1111; www.arbaejarsafn.is; Kistuhyl; adult/under-18 Ikr500/free; 🕑 10am-5pm Tue-Fri, 10am-6pm Sat & Sun Jun-Aug). The grounds feature various 19th-century houses that have been decked out with period furniture. Staff in traditional costume demonstrate various Icelandic arts and crafts, and there are guided tours at 11am and 2pm. On Monday, most of the museum is closed, but you can still visit the church and farm from 11am to 4pm. You can also visit out of season by appointment.

The museum is about 4km from the centre of Reykjavík – take bus No 10 or 11 from Hlemmur or bus No 110 from Lækjartorg (Monday to Saturday).

OTHER MUSEUMS

The **Náttúrrufræ-ðistofnun Íslands** (Institute of Natural History; Map pp54-5; ☎ 590 0500; www.ni.is; Hlemmur 5; adult Ikr300, concession & under-17 free; 🕑 1-5pm Tue, Thu, Sat & Sun Jun-Aug, 1.30-4pm Sep-May) has a decent selection of displays on Icelandic geology, fauna and flora. There's also the small **Numismatic Museum** (Map pp54-5; ☎ 569 9964; Einholt 4; admission free; 🕑 9am-5pm Mon-Fri), which displays banknotes and coins from around the world.

There are several small museums in the surrounding suburbs – ask at the tourist office for more information. Reykjavík Energy maintains the small **Electric Museum** (Map pp54-5; ☎ 567 9009; www.or.is; Rafstöðvarvegur; admission free; 🕑 1-5pm Tue-Thu Jun-Aug, 3-5pm Sun Sep-May) near Árbæjarsafn by the Elliðaár river. The displays on the development of hydroelectric power in Iceland are interesting, but it's a bit of a trek to get out here.

Galleries

Reykjavík has loads of art galleries featuring work by Icelandic artists.

REYKJAVÍK ART MUSEUM: HAFNARHÚSIÐ

Housed in a very stylish steel and concrete warehouse conversion, **Hafnarhúsið** (Map p60; ☎ 511 5155; www.listasafnReykjavíkur.is; adult/concession/child Ikr500/250/free; 🕑 10am-5pm) is a modern art gallery that's worth a look for the building. Within the industrial interior are changing displays of painting, sculpture and installations, and a permanent exhibition of giant comic-book paintings by the highly political Icelandic painter Erró (Guðmundur Guðmundsson). If you buy a ticket for any of the Reykjavík Art Museum properties, it will get you into the other two for free.

REYKJAVÍK ART MUSEUM: ÁSMUNDURSAFN

Housed in a bizarre igloo-like building, **Ásmundursafn** (Ásmundur Sveinsson Sculpture Museum; Map pp54-5; ☎ 553 2155; Sigtún; adult/concession/under-18 Ikr500/250/free; 🕑 10am-4pm May-Sep, 1-4pm Oct-Apr) is dedicated to the sculptor Ásmundur Sveinsson (1893–1982). Born on a remote farm in west Iceland, Ásmundur moved to Reykjavík to study wood-carving, but ended up studying sculpture in Paris instead. His huge concrete and bronze abstractions are mostly inspired by Icelandic sagas. The artist also designed the rather unique building; xin the spirit of things, the council later added an igloo-shaped bus shelter in front of it. You can get here on bus No 5 from Hlemmur.

REYKJAVÍK ART MUSEUM: KJARVALSSTAÐIR

Although not as impressive as Hafnarhúsið, **Kjarvalsstaðir** (Map pp54-5; ☎ 552 6131; www.listasafnReykjavíkur.is; Flókagata; adult/concession/under-18 Ikr500/250/free; 🕑 10am-5pm Thu-Tue, 10am-7pm Wed) is worth a visit for the collection of paintings, drawings and sketches by Iceland's most popular artist, Jóhannes Kjarval (1885–1972). Kjarval started out as a fisherman, but his fellow crewmen organised a lottery to pay for him to study at the Academy of Fine Arts in Copenhagen.

LISTASAFN

The **Listasafn** (National Gallery of Iceland; Map p60; ☎ 515 9610; www.listasafns.is; Fríkirkjuvegur 7; adult/concession/child Ikr450/250/free; 🕑 11am-5pm Tue-Sun) is in a converted ice house overlooking Tjörn, beside the Fríkirkjan church. The gallery has a huge collection but only a small portion of these are ever put on display. Visiting exhibitions provide a bit of variety from the landscape paintings that dominate the gallery.

SIGURJÓN ÓLAFSSON MUSEUM

Fans of abstract sculpture may be interested in the **Sigurjón Ólafsson Museum** (Map pp54-5; ☎ 553 2906; www.iso.is; Laugarnestangi 70; adult/under 18 Ikr300/free; 2-5pm Tue-Sun Jun-Aug, 2-5pm Sat & Sun Sep-May), which houses works by the sculptor Sigurjón Ólafsson (1908–82). On summer Tuesdays, there are classical concerts at 8.30pm. The gallery is on the shore on the main coast road, near Laugardalur.

EINAR JÓNSSON MUSEUM

Across from Hallgrímskirkja is the **Einar Jónsson Museum** (Map pp54-5; ☎ 551 3797; www.skulptur.is; Eiriksgata; adult/concession/under-16 Ikr400/200/free; Tue-Sun 2-5pm Jun-Sep, 2-5pm Sat & Sun Sep-May), dedicated to Iceland's foremost modern sculptor. The Teutonic works draw heavily from Icelandic folklore and religion. Jónsson was responsible for the Sigurðsson statue in Austurvöllur Square.

NORRÆNA HÚSIÐ

Close to the domestic airport and Reykjavík University, **Norræna Húsið** (Nordic House; Map pp54-5; ☎ 551 7030; www.nordice.is; adult/concession/child Ikr300/150/free; noon-5pm Sun-Thu) is a Scandinavian cultural centre with a gallery, a library of Scandinavian literature, and a pleasant little café. There's a regular programme of concerts, lectures and films, all with a Nordic theme – see their website for details.

OTHER GALLERIES

Hidden away in a residential area is the **Ásgrímur Jónsson Museum** (Map pp54-5; ☎ 515 9600; Bergstaðastræti 74), which has a collection of paintings by the landscape painter Ásgrímur Jónsson (1876–1958) but it's only open by appointment.

Several small galleries display contemporary modern art. **SAFN Gallery** (Map p60; ☎ 561 8777; www.safn.is; Laugavegur 37; admission free; 2-6pm Wed-Sun) is full of conceptual art of the kind that people either love or hate. Opposite Hallgrímskirkja, **ASÍ Art Museum** (Map pp54-5; ☎ 511 5353; Freyjugata 41; admission free; 2-6pm Tue-Sun) is owned by the Icelandic Federation of Labour Unions, and shows installations and other modern works by Icelandic and visiting artists.

Parks & Gardens

The valley of **Laugadalur** (Map pp54-5) is lined with parks and geothermal vents, and runs down to the sea just north of the city centre. Before the harnessing of the Nesjavellir geothermal area, the hot springs here were the main source of Reykjavík's hot water. In the middle of the park are the remains of the old **wash house** where washerwomen used to scrub the capital's laundry in the sulphurous pools, with an interesting display of old photos. The valley is increasingly being taken over by sporting facilities – Laugadalur now has a football stadium, athletics stadium, sports hall, ice-skating rink and a huge geothermal pool – see Activities below.

Also at Laugardalur are Reykjavík's **Botanic Gardens** (Map pp54-5; ☎ 553 8870; admission free; 10am-10pm in summer; 10am-5pm in winter), which contain around 65% of naturally occurring Icelandic plant species. There are walking trails and water features, and a small café in the greenhouse serves coffee and waffles during the summer. Also here is a popular children's park and zoo – see Reykjavík for Children (p67) for details.

Other parks include the small area of grass at **Austurvöllur** (Map p60), sometimes used for open-air exhibitions, and the parks around lake **Tjörn** (Map p60).

ACTIVITIES

Horse Riding

Several horse farms around Reykjavík offer horse-riding tours and will pick up riders from hotels. Over in Hafnarfjörður, **Íshestar** (☎ 555 7000; www.ishestar.is; Sörlaskeið 26) is one of the better operators, and offers half-day tours to Mt Helgafell and the surrounding lava fields for between Ikr4200 and Ikr5300. You can also take longer tours to Reykjanes and Þingvellir. In the same area is **Þyrill** (☎ 588 7887; thyrill@thyrill.is; Víðadal), which offers various tours around Reykjavík, including trips to Raudholar volcano (Ikr3500, 1½ hours) and Elliðavatn lake (Ikr4500, 3½ hours).

Swimming

Reykjavík has a series of excellent geothermal swimming pools that are kept at a toasty 35°C by a series of vents leading from the Nesjavellir geothermal field. Admission to all the Reykjavík pools for adults/children is Ikr220/100. Towels and swimming costumes can be rented for a few hundred krónur. In summer, most pools are open from 6.50am until at least 9.30pm Monday to Friday, and from 8am to 8pm or later at weekends. The largest pool in town is the **Laugadalur swimming pool** (Map pp54-5; ☎ 553 4039; Sundlaugavegur; 🕑 6.50am-9.30pm Mon-Fri, 8am-8pm Sat & Sun), with Jacuzzis, a steam bath, solarium, mud baths and a large waterslide. For more on geothermal pools see www.reykjavík.is/spacity.

Other city pools include:

Árbæjarlaug (Map pp54-5; ☎ 567 3933; Fylkisvegur, Elliðaárdalur) Bus Nos 10 and 110.
Sundhöllin (☎ 551 4059; Barónsstígur) Bus No 140 from Hlemmur.
Vesturbæjarlaug (Map pp54-5; ☎ 551 5004; Hofsvallagata) Bus No 3 or No 6 from Lækjartorg or Hlemmur.

You'll also find geothermal pools in Mosfellsbær, Kópavogur and Hafnarfjörður.

Walking

Quite a few people just enjoy walking around the old town and appreciating the architecture; see the walking tour following. It's also worth taking a stroll along Laugavegur for the posh clothes shops, along Skólavörðustígur for the upmarket arts and crafts shops, and down to the harbour for the view across the fjord to Mt Esja (909m).

There are also several places within easy reach of the town centre where you can soak up a bit of nature. One popular option is the area of parkland around **Perlan** (see p62). You can continue from here to the hot beach at **Nauthólsvík** (see p62).

Further afield, Reykjavík's salmon river, **Elliðaár** (Map pp54-5), empties into the sea just east of the centre in the suburb of Ártúnsholt. The river is surrounded by parks and is pleasant for walking at any time of year. In early August you can watch the leaping salmon making their way upstream to spawn. You can reach Elliðaár on bus No 10 from Hlemmur or bus No 110 from Lækjartorg.

If you follow the river east you'll reach Elliðavatn lake, which is surrounded by the 2800-hectare **Heiðmörk** (Heath Woods). It's full of walking trails, picnic areas and tree plantations, which are something of an obsession in largely treeless Iceland. A hiking and cycling track runs from Seltjarnarnes to Heiðmörk, but there's no public transport into the park. You could walk here from Elliðaár or take bus No 10 or 11 from Hlemmur (Monday to Saturday), which will get you within 2km of the park entrance.

ARCHITECTURAL WALKING TOUR

Icelanders are obsessed with design and architecture. The capital is awash with futuristic buildings made from abstract combinations of concrete, glass, steel and lava, juxtaposed against the historic houses of the old town, which were built from timber washed up on the shores of Iceland from as far away as Siberia and South America. Most of these architectural heirlooms are clad in sheets of corrugated tin to protect them from the elements and many date back to the early 19th century when Reykjavík was a tiny fishing village playing second fiddle to the then metropolis at nearby Eyrarbakki.

You don't have to be an architecture buff to appreciate Reykjavík's landmark buildings – the following walking tour will guide you around some of the capital's most impressive and unusual houses and monuments. It should take around one to two hours to complete.

The logical starting point for any tour of Reykjavík is **Austurvöllur (1)**, where the first settler, Ingólfur Arnarson, had his hayfields. The statue in the centre of the grassy square is of Icelandic nationalist **Jón Sigurðsson (2)**, who led the campaign for Icelandic independence. The old stone building with the stylish glass and stone annex is the **Alþingi** (**3**; p59), home to the Icelandic parliament – the old part dates from 1881 while the new part was completed in 2002. Next door, the wooden **Dómkirkja** (**4**; p59) cathedral dates back to 1847, and across the square is the striking Art Deco **Hótel Björg (5)**, built in 1930.

From here, stroll north onto Austurstræti to the stone square at **Ingólfstorg (6)**, which is surrounded by old wooden houses and has fountains and a steam vent releasing pent up energy from below the ground. Next, head northeast along Naustin and Tryggvagata to the ultramodern **Hafnarhúsið (7)**, a fantastic creation of rusted steel, concrete and glass that now houses part of the Reykjavík Art Museum (p63). Loop around the block along Vesturgata, which is lined with historic wooden houses, including **Fálkahús (8)** at Hafnarstræti 1, where Icelandic falcons were once stored before being shipped to Europe. Next, head south down Aðalstræti to the site of Ingólfur Arnarson's original farm. The bar **Vidalin (9)** at Aðalstræti 10 is housed in the oldest building in Reykjavík.

Cut across on Tjarnargata to Vonarstræti, passing the space-age **Ráðhús (10)** or City Hall (p59), an angular construction of concrete, glass and carved lava. Water trickles down the moss-covered walls and into lake **Tjörn** (**11**; p59). Further along Vonarstræti, you'll pass the imposing wooden **Iðnó Theatre (12)**, built in 1891, where the first motion picture ever shown in Iceland screened, and the schoolhouse **Tjarnaskóli (13)**, built in 1906 as the administrative offices of the Dómkirkja.

Next, skirt around the lake on Fríkirkjuvegur to the **National Gallery (14)** (a former ice house; p63) and the tin-clad **Fríkirkjan í Reykjavík (15)** church (1899) and turn up Skalhóltsstígur. As you turn north along Þingholtstræti, notice the fantastic wooden **tower house (16)** on the corner, with its onion dome, fretwork balconies and carved window frames – it's very *Hansel & Gretel* and now houses a community of actors.

From here, stroll up through the attractive residential streets of Spítalastígur and Þórsgata – home to several grand townhouses – until you reach **Hallgrímskirkja** (**17**; p59), the vast modernist church that lords over Reykjavík. Take the lift up the tower for the best view in town. In front is a **statue of Leifur Eiríksson (18)**, the Viking chief who almost certainly discovered America 500 years before Columbus. If you look down Frakkastígur from here, you'll see Jón Gunnar Árnason's sculpture **Sun-Craft (19)**, which falls somewhere between a Viking ship and a giant silver centipede.

Stroll past the posh galleries and ceramic shops on Skólavörðustígur and down Smíðjustígur to Hverfisgata, where you'll find the wonderful **A-Hús (20)** from 1906, perhaps the finest example of Icelandic wood and tin architecture . The tall turrets are topped by swirling Arabesques and the wooden struts supporting the balconies are carved with whale depictions. Across the road is the Teutonic **National Theatre (21)**, from 1950.

If you stroll west, you'll pass the stone **Culture House (22)** from 1906, and the hill Arnarhóll (Eagle Hill), with its **statue of Ingólfur Arnarson (23)**. Across the road is **Stjórnarráðið (24)**, built as a jail in the 1700s and home to the offices of the president

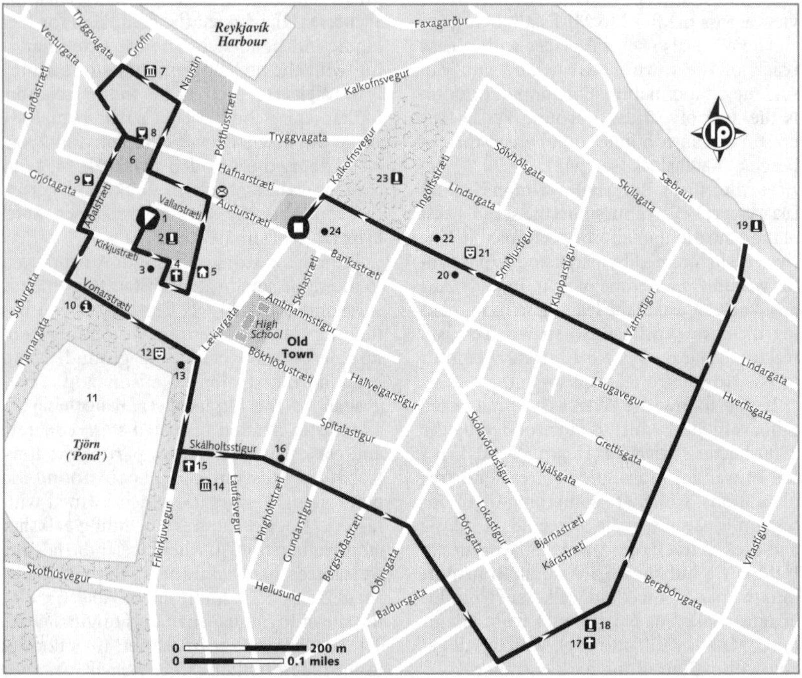

and prime minister. It's lit up a slightly incongruous purple colour at night. Finally, turn onto Lækjargata and head west along Austurstræti, which will take you back to where you started.

For some other walking tour ideas, the tourist office publishes a series of guide maps, including a *Literary Walking Tour* and guides to the *City Parks* and *City Statues* (Ikr200 each).

REYKJAVÍK FOR CHILDREN

Although Reykjavík is probably the most child-oriented place in Iceland, there are only a handful of attractions specifically aimed at children. Children get discount rates at the theatre and cinema, and can travel free or at discount rates on many tours and excursions. One thing all kids will enjoy are Reykjavík's geothermal **swimming pools**. Best is the pool at Laugurdalur (see p65 for details), which has lots of waterslides and hot pots where you can unwind while the little ones frolic. The **Volcano Show** (p61) and the **Saga Museum** (p62) should also capture young imaginations.

Reykjavík's main attraction for kids is **Fjölskyldugarðurinn og Húsdýragarðurinn** (Map pp54-5; ☎ 575 7800; www.mu.is; Laugardalur; adult/child/under-5 Ikr450/350/free; ⏲ 10am-6pm, 10am-5pm 24 Aug–15 May), a children's park and zoo in the middle of Laugardalur. The zoo features animals such as seals, reindeer, foxes, cows and goats – it's more like a city farm. The animals are fed at set times throughout the day. The attached fun-park has an old-fashioned carousel, a miniature train, an adventure playground and a 'science museum' with activities for kids. The **Árbæjarsafn** museum (p63) is also good for youngsters.

If you have an afternoon to kill, why not go ice-skating at **Reykjavík Skating Hall** (Map pp54-5; ☎ 588 9705; www.skautaholl.is; Laugardalur; adult/child Ikr500/400; ⏲ noon-3pm Mon-Thu, 5-7.30pm Wed & Thu, 1-10pm Fri, 1-6pm Sat & Sun). Skate hire costs an extra Ikr300. In a similar vein, you can go lane-bowling at **Keiluhöllin** (☎ 511 5300; www.keiluhollin.is; Öskjuhlið; ⏲ noon-midnight Sun-Thu, noon-2am Fri & Sat) beside the Hótel Loftleiðir.

Little riders will enjoy the Icelandic-pony rides offered by horse farms around Reykjavík – see p64 for details. Over in Hafnarfjörður, younger children will enjoy searching for elves and other little folk on a Hidden Worlds tour (p86).

QUIRKY REYKJAVÍK

Easily Reykjavík's strangest museum is the **Icelandic Phallological Museum** (Reðasafn; Map p60; ☎ 561 6663; Laugavegur 24; adult/child Ikr400/free; ⏲ 2-5pm Tue-Sat May-Aug, 2-5pm Thu-Sat Sep-Apr), tucked away on an alley off Laugavegur. This is rumoured to be the only museum in the world with a collection of penises from all the mammals in a single country – and homo sapiens is soon expected to join the collection. The stated aim of the museum is to make people take the science of phallology seriously; we leave it up to you to decide if the collection of stuffed and mounted Johnsons does the trick.

Held in a vast industrial building by the harbour, the **Kolaportið Flea Market** (Geirsgata; Map p60; ⏲ 11am-5pm Sat & Sun) is a Reykjavík institution. Every weekend, hundreds of locals flock to this vast indoor garage sale to browse through piles of second-hand clothes, old CDs, lampshades, children's toys, plastic Christmas trees – you name it. Several food stalls sell Icelandic delicacies, including *hákarl* (cured shark meat) and *harðfiskur* (dried fish). Part of the cult Icelandic movie *101 Reykjavík* was filmed here and it's definitely worth a visit.

Another unusual Reykjavík experience is the lift ride to the top of the **Hallgrímskirkja church** (p59). The brilliant white elevator resounds with choral music and when it stops you expect to walk out onto a landscape of clouds and angels! Reykjavík has a deserved reputation for architectural innovation, but next to the Kringlan Shopping Centre, you'll see one of the city's more obvious gaffes. The office building **Hús Verslunaninnar** was conceived as a skyscraper with four towers of different heights – unfortunately, locals think the finished construction looks like a giant hand giving Reykjavík the finger!

TOURS

Dozens of companies offer tours around the city and further afield.

A popular option is a whale-watching trip from the main harbour at Reykjavík, just west of the centre on Suðurbugt. Trips run from April to October and do a three-hour tour of the bay searching for whales, porpoises and dolphins, often with a visit to the puffin colonies on Lundey. Most tours leave at 9am and 1pm (also at 5pm from June to August) and cost Ikr3500/1500 for adults/under-12s. If you don't see any whales, you'll usually get another tour free. Hotel pick up is an extra Ikr500. The main operators are **Elding** (☎ 555 3565; www.elding.is) and **Whale Watching Centre** (☎ 533 2660; www.whalewatching.is).

Various companies offer city tours lasting three hours or so for around Ikr2400, but Reykjavík is a small place and it's easy to see most things under your own steam. A more interesting option is to take a cultural tour with **Menningarlylgd Birnu** (☎ 862 8031; www.birna.is; per person Ikr3000, min 2 people), which aims to show visitors the real Reykjavík by visiting artists and local characters, as well as mainstream sights.

Loads of companies offer day trips to the volcanic hinterland around the capital, visiting geothermal areas, waterfalls and other natural wonders. Tours must be booked in advance and may be cancelled if there are insufficient numbers. Children under 12 generally travel free and some companies offer discounts to children from 12 to 15 years old.

The most popular operator is **Reykjavík Excursions** (☎ 562 1011; www.re.is; Hótel Loftleiðir), which runs tours to the Golden Circle, Reykjanes and the Blue Lagoon, Nesjavellir, Kaldidalur, Þjórsárdalur and loads of other possibilities. Similar tours are offered by **Destination Iceland** (☎ 591 1020; www.dice.is; Vatnsmýrarvegur 10), based at the long-distance bus terminal, which also runs longer trips to Þórsmörk and Landmannalaugar. Many of these run in conjunction with adventure-tour operators, so you can often tag on snowmobile tours of glaciers, horse riding, kayaking, rafting and other activities. The other big operator is **Iceland Excursions** (Allrahanda; ☎ 540 1313; www.icelandexcursions.is; Funahöfði 17), which specialises in guided coach tours, including Reykjanes, the Golden Circle, the interior and Snæfellsnes.

The following are some suggested day tours from the capital.

Destination	Price
Golden Circle	
Þingvellir, Skálholt, Geysir, Gulfoss waterfall	Ikr6100
Reykjanes & Blue Lagoon	
Lava landscapes, geothermal springs, Blue Lagoon	Ikr5000
Nesjavellir	
Geothermal field & power plant	Ikr5000
Kaldidalur	
Þingvellir, Borgarfjörður, Snorrastofa museum	Ikr7000
Landmannalaugar	
Þjórsárdalur valley, Landmannalaugar geothermal area	Ikr8900
Þjórsárdalur	
Stöng ruins, Haifoss falls, Hekla volcano	Ikr7800
Snæfellsjökull	
Glacier, Snæfellsnes coast	Ikr7400
South Coast & Þórsmörk	
Selfoss, Hella, Hvolsvöllur, Seljalandsfoss waterfall, Þórsmörk	Ikr7800

For other tour operators, see p303.

FESTIVALS & EVENTS

February

Winter Lights In late February, Reykjavík celebrates the end of the dark days of winter.

Festival of Lights Held in late February/early March, Laugardalur is the setting for this festival, where locals display their enthusiasm for the cheap electricity and hot water they get as a perk for living on top of a geothermal field.

Food and Fun (www.icelandnaturally.com) The accompanying festival to Festival of Lights, when most restaurants in town offer discount meals.

May

Listahátíð í Reykjavík (Reykjavík Arts Festival; www.artfest.is) Held from late May to early June in even-numbered years, Reykjavík features films, dance, theatre, concerts and art exhibitions from around the world.

August

Reykjavík Marathon (http://web2.toto.is/rmar) In mid-August, the capital hosts this event along with a number of shorter runs.

Menningarnott (www.menningarnott.is) This evening of cultural events follows the marathon and includes cultural and artistic performances and a massive fireworks display.

September

Reykjavík Short Film Festival (www.this.is/shortcut) Screening entries from around the world.

October

Iceland Airwaves Music Festival (www.icelandairwaves.is) Iceland's biggest pop festival attracts bands and DJs from around the world.

November

Jazz Festival (www.go.to/Reykjavíkjazz) Attracts a range of international talent.

Young Arts Festival A showcase of the best arts, music, theatre and fashions from Reykjavík's youth.

SLEEPING

Reykjavík has loads of hotels and guesthouses covering all budgets, but mid-range places predominate. Almost all offer seasonal rates, with significant discounts from September to May, and most close from 21 to 28 December.

Budget

Thanks to Reykjavík's increasing popularity, budget travellers now have plenty of accommodation options. However, from July to August, demand sometimes outstrips supply and finding a bed at the HI hostel or a budget guesthouse may be difficult. To avoid risking literally being left out in the cold, bring a tent or make advance bookings.

YOUTH HOSTEL

Reykjavík City Hostel (Map pp54-5; ☎ 553 8110; www.hostel.is; Sundlaugavegur 34; bed in 6-bed dorm with shared bathroom for members/nonmembers Ikr1550/1900, bed in 3- to 6-bed dorm with bathroom Ikr2150/2500, bed in double with bathroom Ikr3500/3000) The only youth hostel in Reykjavík has space for 170 people and the facilities are excellent. The hostel sits on the edge of Laugardalur, a 30-minute walk from the Hlemmur bus stand, and also serves as the reception for the Reykjavík camp site. There are three well-equipped guest kitchens, two TV lounges (videos of Icelandic movies are available at reception), an Internet café, and a guest laundry with self-service washers and dryers. Reykjavík's biggest geothermal pool is right next door.

As this is the best budget option in town, it's often full from June to September, so book in advance. You'll need to show your Hostelling International (HI) card to get the members reduction. From October to May, rates for members/non-members drop to Ikr1550/1900 for dorm beds, or you can pay an extra Ikr1000 for a room to yourself. The hostel is closed from 20 December to 5 January.

The hostel reception is a great source of information on things to do around Iceland

SLEEPING-BAG ACCOMMODATION

As well as the youth hostel, several guesthouses around town offer sleeping bag spaces in rooms or dorms for Ikr1900 to Ikr2700 and most provide a kitchen and lounge for guests. It's best to bring a sleeping bag from home, though a few places can provide a blanket for a fee.

One option is the **Salvation Army Guest House** (Map p60; ☎ 561 3203; www.guesthouse.is; Kirkjustræti 2; sb Ikr1900, s/d/tr in summer Ikr4200/5900/7400, in winter Ikr3900/5500/7000). This pleasant Christian guesthouse is the most central budget place in town and the Flybus stops right outside. The private rooms are a little cramped, but the dorms are spacious, and Reykjavík's best bars and restaurants are right on the doorstop. Book ahead in summer. Breakfast is Ikr800.

The guesthouses following offer sleeping-bag accommodation and guesthouse rooms (see the Mid-Range section for full details), so you should specify that you want a sleeping-bag space when you book.

Domus Guesthouse (Map p60; ☎ 561 1200; www.domusguesthouse.is; Hverfisgata 45; sb in summer/winter Ikr2800/2100) 30 spaces and a kitchen for guests.
Hótel Garður (Map pp54-5; ☎ 551 5656; www.icelandichotels.is; Hringbraut; sb Ikr2300) Summer hotel from May to Sep in student halls of residence; rates include breakfast.
Guesthouse Aurora (Map p60; ☎ 552 5515; aurorahotel@isl.is; Freyjugata 24; sb Ikr1800)
Flóki B&B (Map pp54-5; ☎ 552 1155; www.eyjar.is/guesthouse; Flókagata 1 & 5; sb summer/winter Ikr2700/2200) Guest kitchen and lounge.
Gistiheimilið Egilsborg (Map pp54-5; ☎ 561 2600; egilsborg@vortex.is; Þverholt 20; sb Ikr2400) Offers sleeping-bag space if the rooms aren't taken by B&B guests.
Guesthouse Regina (Map pp54-5; ☎ 551 2050; www.guesthouseregina.is; Mjölnisholti 14; sb Ikr2200)
Snorri's Guesthouse (Map pp54-5; ☎ 552 0598; www.guesthouseReykjavík.com; Snorrabraut 61; sb Ikr2500) Guest kitchen and TV lounge rooms.
Gistiheimilið Central (Map pp54-5; ☎ 552 2822; Bólstaðarhlíð 8; sb Ikr1900)
Hótel Örkin (Map pp54-5; ☎ 568 0777; www.hotel-orkin.com; Brautarholt 29; sb summer/winter Ikr2000/1700)
Gesthús Dúna (Map pp54-5; ☎ 588 2100; www.islandia.is/duna; Suðurhlíð 35d; sb Ikr2100) Guest kitchen.

and hire cars are available at discount rates. Bikes are rented out during the summer. There is a small family restaurant, **Lauga-Ás** (☎ 553 1620), and a snack bar in the arcade behind the hostel.

You can get here directly from the international airport on the Flybus, or take bus No 5 from the domestic airport, Lækjartorg or Hlemmur. If you're coming from the BSÍ terminal, a taxi will cost around Ikr1000.

CAMPING

There's only one camping option in Reykjavík, **Reykjavík Camping Ground** (Map pp54-5; ☎ 568 6944; www.citycamping.is; Sundlaugavegur 34; camping per person Ikr750), but it shares the excellent facilities at the youth hostel, including the guest kitchens and laundry – see p69 for more information. The site is open from 15 May to 15 September but it gets very busy in summer. There's a free shuttle bus to the BSÍ Bus Terminal at 7.15am every morning from 1 June to 31 August. Reception is at the youth hostel.

Mid-Range

Most options in Reykjavík fall into this bracket.

GUESTHOUSES

Reykjavík is packed with *gistiheimili* (guesthouses) and there are new places opening every year. Most are in converted houses, so rooms often have shared bathrooms, kitchens and TV lounges. Some of these guesthouses also offer sleeping-bag accommodation – see p69 for details.

Gistiheimilið 101 (Map pp54-5; ☎ 562 6101; www.iceland101.com; Laugavegur 101; s/d with shared bathroom Ikr3900/4900) The cheapest guesthouse in town is this converted office building. Spacious white rooms are spotless and the Hlemmur bus stand is around the corner.

Skólabrú Guesthouse (Map p60; ☎ 551 5511; www.skolabru.is; Skólabrú 2; s/d with shared bathroom Ikr6900/8900) Just behind Dómkirkja, this very central guesthouse is good value and the rooms are full of old wooden furniture.

Litli Ljóti Andarunginn (Map p60; ☎ 552 2410; Lækjargata 6b; s/d Ikr4900/5900) Just around the corner, this little family-run guesthouse has a good restaurant and economic rooms with shared bathrooms.

Domus Guesthouse (Map p60; ☎ 561 1200; Hverfistgata 45; s/d with TV & breakfast in summer Ikr7300/9800, in winter Ikr5700/7300) The owners of this excellent, central guesthouse try harder than most and have decked out the rooms with leather armchairs and stylish wooden furniture. It's housed in the former Norwegian Embassy.

Gistiheimilið Jörd (Map p60; ☎ 562 1739; Skólavörðustígur 13a; s/d in summer Ikr4000/6000, in winter Ikr3000/4000) This place is tucked away among the posh galleries and shops on Skólavörðustígur and offers simple, good-value rooms. Breakfast is an extra Ikr600.

Guesthouse Adam (Map p60; ☎ 896 0242; www.adamhotel.com; Skólavörðustígur; s/d in summer Ikr8000/10,000, in winter Ikr6000/8000) Just downhill from Hallgrímskirkja, this guesthouse has small singles and larger doubles, all with bathroom and TV.

Gistiheimilið Sunna (Map p60; ☎ 551 5570; www.sunna.is; Þórsgata 26; s/d Ikr7200/9200; with bathroom Ikr8800/11,500) This tidy, modern guesthouse occupies several floors of an apartment building close to Hallgrímskirkja. The spotless wood-floored rooms have TVs and the best of the old town is just a short walk down Skólavörðustígur. Rates drop by 25% in winter.

Guesthouse Aurora (Map p60; ☎ 552 5515; aurorahotel@isl.is; Freyjugata 24; s/d Ikr6500/8500) This recommended guesthouse is in a large purple townhouse just south of the centre.

Guesthouse Óðinn (Map p60; ☎ 552 2313; Óðinnsgata 9; s/d/tr Ikr6100/8100/9900) This long-established guesthouse has simple, comfortable rooms and a kitchen for guests. The owners knock up a good buffet breakfast.

Several guesthouses are clustered together just west of the centre.

Guesthouse by the Sea (Map p60; ☎ 691 7794; Nýlendugata 4; s/d with shared bathroom Ikr5200/6750) Set in a quiet mews close to the harbour, this little tin house offers simple rooms, and a kitchen and hot pot for guests.

Gistiheimilið Vikingur (Map p60; ☎ 562 1290; www.simnet.is/ghviking; Ránargata 12; s/d/tr Ikr5300/7900/9900) This tall red house is in a peaceful residential area west of the centre. Rooms have sinks, fridges and phones, and rates include breakfast.

Guesthouse Butterfly (Map p60; ☎ 894 1864; butterfly@simnet.is; Ránargata 8a; s/d with shared bathroom Ikr5300/7300, 2-bed apt Ikr11,000) In a green townhouse nearby, Guesthouse Butterfly has neat wood-floored rooms and a two-bedroom apartment with a bathroom

GAY REYKJAVÍK

Reykjavík is the only place in Iceland that has an active gay scene – the main source of information is **Samtökin '78** (Map p60; ☎ 552 7878; www.samtokin78.is; Laugavegur 3; 🕑 8-11pm Mon & Thu, 8pm-midnight Sat), which doubles as an informal gay community centre. Another useful information source is the website of the gay student organisation **FSS** (http://gay.mis.is). The lesbian organisation **Konurmedkonum** (www.geocities.com/konurmedkonum) arranges regular activities, such as bowling and volleyball evenings. Since the closure of the only gay nightclub, the main gay hangout in town is **Café Cosy** (Map p60; ☎ 511 1033; Austurstráeti 3; snacks from Ikr300), a quiet little coffee shop and bar near Ingólfstorg. Reykjavík has a lively Gay Pride march every year in early August.

There are several good gay-friendly guesthouses close to the centre.

i12 Guesthouse (Map p60; ☎ 692 9930; www.guesthouses.is/i12; Ingólfstræti 12; s/d with shared bathroom Ikr4000/6000, 4-/6-bed apt Ikr19,900/25,000) This little gay guesthouse is central, and has a guest kitchen and lounge.

Room with a View (Map p60; ☎ 552 7262; www.roomwithaview.is; Laugarvegur 18; studio apt Ikr6000; 1-/2-bed apt Ikr9120/12,920) This apartment hotel is on the main shopping street and offers apartments with private bathrooms and kitchenettes. There's a Jacuzzi with a city view on the balcony.

Tower Guesthouse (Map p60; ☎ 896 6694; www.tower.is; Grettisgata 6; d/ste/apt Ikr7300/11,020/20,140) A slightly more upmarket option is this smart guesthouse on a quiet residential street just uphill from Laugavegur. There's a rooftop Jacuzzi.

Luna Hotel Apartments (Map p60; ☎ 511 2800; www.luna.is; Spítalastígur 1; apt in summer Ikr11,900-17,900, in winter Ikr7900-14,900) This apartment hotel is open all year and offers six modern apartments with kitchenette, TV, fridge, phone and small bathrooms. The penthouse on the top floor has a balcony with city views.

and kitchen. It's open from 1 June to 31 August.

Alfholl Guesthouse (Map p60; ☎ 898 1838; www.islandia.is/alf; Ránargata 8; s/d Ikr6230/8460, studio apt Ikr12,030) This welcoming guesthouse is run by a family of elf enthusiasts – the name means 'hill of the elves'. It's used as a student house from September to May.

Gistiheimilið Ísafold (Map p60; ☎ 561 2294; isafold@itn.is; Bárugata 11; s/d/tr Ikr6900/8900/11,900, 2-bed apt Ikr16,000) This stately white house has good rooms with shared bathroom. Two-bedroom apartments with kitchenettes and bathrooms are available in an old wood and tin house on Nýlendugata 19b. It's a short walk from Austurvöllur.

Gistiheimilið Krían (Map p60; ☎ 511 5600; www.krian.is; Suðurgata 22; s/d with phone & TV Ikr7900/9900, ste with bathroom Ikr13,900) Overlooking Tjörn, this grand house has large rooms with big windows, some of which have good lake views (ask for a room at the front of the house). There are singles and doubles with shared bathrooms, and suites with bathrooms. Rates drop 40% in winter.

Lighthouse Apartments (Map p60; ☎ 551 6580; www.lighthouse.is; Vitastígur 11; apt from Ikr8300-16,400) Just off Laugavegur, this big red house contains six self-catering apartments with TVs, kitchenettes and bathrooms. Prices are a little high, but the location is good. Rates drop by 40% in winter.

Gistiheimilið Centrum (Map pp54-5; ☎ 511 5602; www.guesthouse-centrum.com; Njálsgata 74; s/d with shared bathroom in summer Ikr5900/7900, in winter Ikr3900/4900) Uphill from the Hlemmur bus stand, Gistiheimilið Centrum is quite a convenient option and the rooms are tidy and good value. Rates include breakfast.

Gistiheimilið Egilsborg (Map pp54-5; ☎ 5612600; egilsborg@vortex.is; Þverholt 20; s/d Ikr4900/7650) Set in an old house surrounded by modern apartment buildings, Egilsborg is central and won't break the bank. From September to May, it is used by visiting students.

Guesthouse Regina (Map pp54-5; ☎ 551 2050; www.guesthouseregina.is; Mjölnisholti 14; s/d/tr Ikr6500/8500/11,000, studio apt Ikr10,000) This huge guesthouse is close to Hlemmur in the same area as Egilsborg and is good for the money.

There are more guesthouses on Snorrabraut in a slightly drab area of grey pebble-dashed houses.

Flóki B&B (Gistihúsið Flókagata; Map pp54-5; ☎ 552 1155; www.eyjar.is/guesthouse; Flókagata 1 & 5; s/d summer Ikr7200/10,300, winter Ikr5000/6300) Spread over two buildings, this friendly guesthouse has good rooms with a fridge, kettle, TV, phone and

* Hotel Reykjavik Centrum → in hist. bldgs; price = ?
Hotel Holt - $319 (holt.is)
* Hotel Plaza → $192 (plaza.is)

sink. There are also sleeping bag spaces – see p69.

Snorri's Guesthouse (Map pp54-5; ☎ 552 0598; www.guesthouseReykjavík.com; Snorrabraut 61; s/d Ikr6500/8000, with bathroom Ikr8000/9800) Nearby, Snorri's is housed in another large pebbledashed house. Rooms are bright and have a TV, sink, fridge and coffee-making facilities.

Guesthouse Baldursbrá (Map pp54-5; ☎ 552 6646; baldursbra@centrum.is; Laufásvegur 41; s/d with shared bathroom Ikr6250/8750) Close to Tjörn and the BSÍ Bus Terminal, this quiet guesthouse has a TV lounge and a hot pot for guests, and rates include breakfast.

Travel-Inn Guesthouse (Map pp54-5; ☎ 561 3553; www.dalfoss.is; Sóleyjargata 31; s/d Ikr7500/9500, with bathroom Ikr8900/10,900; ⊠) A short walk from the BSÍ Bus Terminal, this guesthouse is run by a friendly family and has large bright rooms. Rooms can be arranged at a nearby private house if the main building is full. Bike hire costs Ikr500 per day.

Gistiheimilið Central (Map pp54-5; ☎ 552 2822; Bólstaðarhlíð 8; s/d/tr Ikr3600/4800/6000; 🖳) Although it isn't really close to the centre, this place is handy for Perlan and the BSÍ Bus Terminal. There's also a kitchen for guests.

Gistiheimili Borgartún (Map pp54-5; ☎ 511 1515; www.gjtravel.is; Borgartún 34; s/d/tr with bathroom & breakfast Ikr8300/11,000/14,300, in winter Ikr5000/6700/9500) Owned by a local tour operator, the Borgartún is large and institutional, but the rooms are pleasant enough.

There are several options miles from the centre that may be worth considering if you have a hire car.

Gesthús Dúna (Map pp54-5; ☎ 588 2100; www.islandia.is/duna; Suðurhlíð 35d; s/d from Ikr5300/6900, with sink from Ikr6950/9600) Close to Perlan on the way to Kópavogur, this large B&B has spacious rooms with shared bathrooms. Several buses stop nearby on Kringlumýrarbraut. Dúna also offers sleeping bag accommodation – see p69 for details. Book online.

HOTELS

Reykjavík has a handful of mid-range hotels, ranging from guesthouses that have gone upmarket to custom-built places catering to business travellers. Unless stated, the following offer rooms with private bathrooms.

Plaza Hotel (Map p60; ☎ 590 1400; www.icelandichotels.is; Aðalstræti 4; s/d Ikr14,800/18,500) The most central hotel in Reykjavík, the Plaza overlooks Ingólfstorg and has neat rooms with tasteful modern furniture.

City Hótel (Map p60; ☎ 511 1155; www.icelandichotels.is; Ránargata 4a; s/d Ikr9100/13,100) Just west of the centre, City Hótel has decent rooms with minibar, phone and satellite TV, but several guesthouses on the same street offer similar rooms for less.

Hótel Frón (Map p60; ☎ 511 4666; www.hotelfron.is; Klapparstígur 35a; s/studio/2-bed apt Ikr8500/11,900/14,000) Tucked away on an alley just off Laugavegur, this bright blue hotel has well-equipped modern-looking apartments with kitchenette, minibar, phone and TV. Breakfast costs Ikr800. Rates drop by 40% in winter.

Fosshótel Barón (Map p60; ☎ 562 3204; www.fosshotel.is; Barónsstígur 2-4; s/d/apt from Ikr9800/13,100/16,900) This business-like hotel is convenient to the restaurants and shops on Laugavegur. It's worth paying extra for the rooms in the new building at the front. Rates drop by 30% in winter.

Hótel Leifur Eiríksson (Map p60; ☎ 562 0800; www.hotelleifur.is; Skólavörðustígur 45; s/d summer Ikr12,700/15,600, winter Ikr8300/10,400) Opposite Hallgrímskirkja, but with slightly grumpy staff. Rooms have phone and TV, and rates include breakfast.

Hótel Óðinsvé (Map p60; ☎ 511 6200; www.hotelodinsve.is; Þórsgata 1; s/d in summer Ikr15,900/21,000, in winter Ikr10,900/13,900) This boutique place makes a nice change from the chain hotels and has a great restaurant. Rooms have minibars, TV, phones and Internet connections for guests with laptops. Rates include a big buffet breakfast.

Hótel Garður (Map pp54-5; ☎ 551 5656; www.icelandichotels.is; Hringbraut; s/d Ikr6900/8100) From May to September, the student accommodation hall at Reykjavík University transforms into a summer hotel. Rooms have sinks inside, but bathrooms are shared. Rates include breakfast and children under-12 can stay free in the same room as their parents.

Park Hótel (Map pp54-5; ☎ 511 1154; www.icelandichotels.is; Suðurgata 121; s/d Ikr8100/11,500) This summer hotel (open May to September) has rooms with bathrooms, balconies, phones and small kitchenettes.

Fosshótel Lind (Map pp54-5; ☎ 562 3350; www.fosshotel.is; Rauðarárstígur 18; s/d Ikr8800/11,900) Close to the Hlemmur bus stand and Laugavegur, this is a standard business-class place and offers comfortable rooms with TVs, phones and minibars. The restaurant here is also pretty good.

Hótel Reykjavík (Map pp54-5; ☎ 562 6250; www.hotelreykjavik.is; Rauðarárstígur 37; s/d with TV, phone & coffee-making facilities from Ikr9700/12,300) In a commercial area close to the Hlemmur bus stand, the Reykjavík is a no-nonsense business hotel and rates aren't bad for the facilities.

Hótel Cabin (Map pp54-5; ☎ 511 6030; www.hotelcabin.is; Borgartún 32; s/d Ikr6100/7100) Out of the centre near Laugardalur, this place has small but quite nice rooms with TV and phone. Rates include breakfast.

Other options include the summer hotel **Fosshótel Höfði** (Map pp54-5; ☎ 552 6477; www.fosshotel.is; Skipholt 27; Ikr 7600/9800, with bathroom Ikr9800/13,100; open Jun-Aug); the **Hótel Örkin** (Map pp54-5; ☎ 568 0777; www.hotel-orkin.com; Brautarholt 29; s/d in summer Ikr9300/12,800, in winter Ikr6900/9900), close to Laugardalur and the restaurants on Suðurlandsbraut; and the **Hótel Atlantis** (Map pp54-5; ☎ 588 0000; www.atlantis.is; Grensásvegur 14; s/d Ikr6600/8900, with bathroom Ikr10,000/12,500, apt Ikr14,700), close to the Grensás bus stand.

Top End

Reykjavík has a good selection of top-end hotels, and rates are comparable with overseas. All rooms in this category have bathrooms, TV, phone and minibar, and rates include breakfast.

Hótel Borg (Map p60; ☎ 551 1440; www.hotelborg.is; Pósthússtræti 9-11; s/d in summer Ikr15,900/22,900, in winter Ikr11,200/16,000) Overlooking Austurvöllur, this neoclassical place has been restored to its original 1930s grandeur and has far more character than most hotels in the capital. The location, rooms and restaurant are all excellent.

Hótel Skjaldbreið (Map p60; ☎ 511 6060; www.centerhotels.is; Laugavegur 16; s/d in summer Ikr13,500/17,200, in winter Ikr9000/11,300) Right in the thick of things, this place has large floral-decorated rooms in an old townhouse overlooking Laugavegur and is owned by the same people as Hótel Klöpp. Rates include breakfast in the rooftop breakfast room.

Hótel Klöpp (Map p60; ☎ 511 6062; www.centerhotels.is; Klapparstígur 26; s/d in summer Ikr13,500/17,200, in winter Ikr9000/11,300) The partner hotel of Hótel Skjaldbreið, this modern place has spacious wood-floored rooms and the décor is refreshingly restrained. Rates include breakfast.

Hótel Loftleiðir (Map pp54-5; ☎ 505 0900; www.icehotel.is; Hlíðarfót; s/d/tr in summer Ikr14,900/19,500/22,500, in winter Ikr11,700/14,500/17,500) This huge Icelandair hotel is right beside the domestic airport and is also the main departure point for the Flybus to Keflavík international airport. There's a pool and fitness centre, a business centre, a bank, a good restaurant and bike hire in summer.

Hótel Nordica (Map pp54-5; ☎ 505 0950; www.icehotel.is; Suðurlandsbraut 2; r in summer from Ikr17,000, in winter from Ikr12,900) Formerly the Hótel Esja, the Nordica is the flagship hotel of Icelandair, which owns hotels all around Iceland. It's a stylish place and the service is the best in town. Rooms have all the expected amenities and there are grand views from the upper floors.

Hótel Ísland (Map pp54-5; ☎ 595 7000; www.hotel-island.is; Ármúli 9; s/d in summer Ikr15,600/20,350, in winter Ikr8500/10,500) One of two hotels owned by the SAS Radisson group, Hótel Ísland offers the usual international facilities. Lots of businesspeople stay here, but it's a bit of a hike from the centre.

Grand Hótel Reykjavík (Map pp54-5; ☎ 568 9000; www.grand.is; Sigtún 38; s/d from Ikr11,500/14,000) Out of the centre, near the junction of Kringlumýrarbraut and Laugavegur, this huge business hotel has good facilities and rooms have all the expected mod cons, but it's fairly bland as these places go.

Hótel Saga (Map pp54-5; ☎ 525 9900; www.hotelsaga.is; Hagatorg 1; s/d in summer Ikr18,000/22,900, in winter Ikr12,400/14,800) Owned by the SAS Radisson group, this luxury place has top facilities and a good restaurant. It's one stop before the domestic airport on the No 5 bus route.

Hótel Holt (Map p60; ☎ 552 5700; www.holt.is; Bergstaðastræti 37; s/d in summer Ikr20,000/23,200, in winter Ikr17,400/20,300) It doesn't look very grand from the outside, but the interior has loads of character, with Afghan rugs spread around the lobby and leather armchairs in the rooms. The largest private art collection in the country is displayed throughout the hotel.

EATING

Reykjavík is full of places to eat, but remember to budget at least Ikr1000 per person for a meal (without alcoholic drinks). Keep an eye out for cheap special offers at lunchtimes.

Cafés

There are dozens of small cafés in Reykjavík serving grilled sandwiches, soups, salads and other light meals in upbeat surroundings.

Most cafés serve alcohol and many transform into bars during the evening.

Café Paris (Map p60; ☎ 551 1020; Austurstræti 14; snacks Ikr450-700) This relaxed coffee shop overlooking Austurvöllur is usually the busiest place in town. There's a good menu of snack dishes, including *kleina* (Icelandic fried dough), soup and grilled sandwiches. You can get a huge pot of tea or a cafetiere of real coffee for Ikr250. Tourists and locals pack the place out all day and many stay on into the evening.

Kaffi Brennslan (Map p60; ☎ 561 3600; Pósthússtræti 9; meals Ikr390-1790) This popular, unpretentious café serves excellent coffee and a good selection of sandwiches, pasta and other light meals. It becomes a popular bar at night.

Ommu Kaffi (Map p60; ☎ 552 9680; 20 Austurstræti; snacks from Ikr250-500; closed Sun) This cosy coffee shop sells waffles, cakes, hot soup and real espresso coffee; soya milk is available.

Hressingarskálinn (Map p60; ☎ 561 2240; Austurstræti 20; mains Ikr980-1180) This spacious modern bar and café serves up imaginative and good-value meals, including various kinds of *moules marinières* (mussels). It's more bar than restaurant at weekends.

Litli Ljóti Andarunginn (Map p60; ☎ 552 9815; www.andarunginn.is; Lækjargata 6b; mains Ikr600-1990) For good homestyle cooking, this cosy little café serves up hearty Icelandic food at reasonable prices. There's a nightly fish buffet with salad and soup for Ikr1990.

Caffé Kúlture (Map p60; ☎ 530 9314; A-Hús Intercultural Centre, Hverfisgata 18; light meals Ikr350-990) Housed in an atmospheric old building on Hverfisgata, this funky café is full of knick-knacks from the Middle East and serves tasty Mediterranean and Arabic cuisine.

Café Sólon (Map p60; ☎ 562 3535; www.solon.is; Bankastræti 7e; sandwiches Ikr450-980, mains Ikr890-1690) Part restaurant, part nightspot, this trendy place offers tasty international dishes at reasonable prices. The egg noodles with teriyaki chicken are strongly recommended.

Kofi Tómasar Frænda (Koffin; Map p60; ☎ 551 1855; Laugavegur 2; light meals Ikr390-890) This Bohemian place is a favourite hang-out for students and is a great place to retreat to for a coffee, snack or beer. The menu includes nachos, lasagne and loads of sandwiches, and there's usually some interesting art on the walls.

Vegamót (Map p60; ☎ 511 3040; www.vegamot.is; Vegamó-tastígur 4; mains Ikr890-1890) Another chic nightspot, Vegamót serves good-value global cuisine during the day – the menu runs to blackened chicken, sesame chicken, and pasta with lobster and blue cheese.

Café 22 (Map p60; ☎ 511 5522; cnr Laugavegur & Klapparstígur; mains Ikr550-1980) In a large red house on the main shopping street, this café serves good coffee and light meals, including the cheapest steak in town (Ikr1980).

Svarta Kaffið (Map p60; ☎ 551 2999; Laugavegur 54) For Reykjavík's best soup, head to this cosy café in an old house. Soup of the day served piping hot in a bread bowl costs Ikr850, or Ikr1150 with a 500ml beer.

Restaurants

ITALIAN

Italian food is very popular in Iceland, but it varies widely in quality. The following is our pick of the best pasta and pizzas in capital. The following places also offer pricier main courses such as lamb fillet and steaks.

Pizza 67 (Map p60; ☎ 561 9900; Tryggvagata 26; pizzas from Ikr900-2000) Close to the harbour, this hippy-themed pizza restaurant and pub has branches all around the country and prices are pretty reasonable.

Galileo (Map p60; ☎ 552 9500; www.galileo.is; Hafnarstræti 1-3; mains Ikr1200-3650) This stylish place has a night-sky mural on the ceiling and plenty of tasty seafood dishes on the menu.

La Primavera (Map p60; ☎ 561 8555; Austurstræti 9; mains Ikr1600-3650) Above the Metz bar is this sophisticated place with elegant décor, and upmarket pasta and seafood dishes.

Hornið (Map p60; ☎ 551 3340; Hafnarstræti 15; mains Ikr870-3340) This bright art café is full of houseplants and serves pizza and pasta, as well as home-cooked Icelandic food.

Ristorante Ítalía (Map p60; ☎ 562 4630; www.Italia.is; Laugavegur 11; Ikr1500-3000) One of the better Italian options, this family-run place has good pizza, pasta and *secondi piatti* (mains). It's a romantic option for a candlelit dinner.

Caruso (Map p60; ☎ 562 7335; Þingholtstræti 1; mains Ikr1300-3590) Near the corner with Bankastræti, this is a popular place for Italian and Icelandic dishes. It's cosy inside and the food is quite good value, though the pasta is better than the pizza.

Pasta Basta (Map p60; ☎ 561 3131; Klapparstígur 38; meals Ikr1300-2250; from 5pm) This home-spun pasta place has a broad selection including a good range of Italian salads.

ASIAN

Reykjavík has a handful of Thai and Chinese takeaway restaurants that offer good prices, and usually have a few tables and chairs so you can eat in.

Ning's (Map pp54-5; ☎ 588 9899; Suðurlandsbraut 6; mains Ikr550-1450) Handy for the City Hostel, this fast-food Chinese place has a good, cheap menu of noodles and stir fries, and you can eat in or takeaway.

Nuðluhúsið (Map p60; ☎ 552 2400; Vitastígur 10; mains from Ikr780-970) City workers flock to this Thai takeaway every weekday for cheap Thai lunches. **Krua Thai** (Map p60; ☎ 561 0039; Tryggvagata 14) and **Kaffisetrið** (Map pp54-5; ☎ 552 5444; Laugavegur 103) are similar.

There are several restaurants on Laugavegur and Lækjargata serving pretty good Chinese, Japanese and Thai food.

Restaurant Asía (Map p60; ☎ 562 6210; Laugavegur 10; dishes Ikr990-3100) Restaurant Asía prepares reasonably authentic Chinese and Japanese food, and offers a lunch buffet for Ikr1190 and bargain noodle soups for Ikr690 (Ikr990 in the evening). **Sjanghæ** (Map p60; ☎ 551 6513; www.sjanghai.is; Laugavegur 28b; mains Ikr980-2500) and **Indókína** (Map p60; ☎ 552 2399; Laugavegur 19; mains Ikr1350-2295) are very similar.

Kína Húsið (Map p60; ☎ 551 1014; Lækjargata 8; mains Ikr1100-2500, discount lunch menu from Ikr750) Housed in a little red house on Lækjargata, this simple Chinese place serves no-nonsense budget lunches and quite authentic Chinese food.

Maru (Map p60; ☎ 511 4440; Aðalstræti 12; Ikr1090-2990) For upmarket Japanese and Thai cuisine, head to this very stylish restaurant in a fine old building just off Ingólfstorg. The menu features finely prepared sushi and sashimi, and all manner of noodle dishes, curries and *yakitori* (Japanese kebabs).

Shalimar (Map p60; ☎ 551 0292; Austurstræti 4; Ikr750-1550) Shalimar cooks up tasty Indian-cuisine at reasonable prices, like tandoori chicken with rice and salad for Ikr1290. Stuffed naan bread costs just Ikr590 and a lunchtime curry with rice is Ikr850.

Austur India Félagið (Map p60; ☎ 552 1630; Hverfisgata 56; mains Ikr1500-2500; 🕑 from 6pm daily) This upmarket Indian place was voted the best Indian restaurant in Europe by the EU ambassador to Iceland, so they must be doing something right. The chef whips up tasty north-Indian treats and the food is very authentic.

MEXICAN & SPANISH

Every other restaurant in Reykjavík seems to serve Mexican food these days, but most places offer a fairly tried-and-tested menu of nachos, tacos and burritos.

For cheap Mexican fast food, try **Mama's Tacos** (Map p60; ☎ 551 5513; Lækjargata 8) – meals cost from Ikr250-600.

Casa Grande (Map p60; ☎ 511 1333; Tryggvagata 8; mains Ikr1500-2600; 🕑 from 6pm) Down by the harbour, this place has sombreros on the walls, plastic cactuses in the windows and the usual tortillas on the menu.

Si Señor (Map p60; ☎ 552 6030; Lækjargata 10; Ikr1200-2000) Housed in an old house near Tjörn, Si Señor cooks up standard Tex-Mex options with a degree of flair.

Amigos (Map p60; ☎ 511 1333; Lækjargata 6a; mains Ikr1590-2690) Probably the nicest of the Mexican places, Amigos has good enchiladas, fajitas and fine frozen margaritas (Ikr750).

Tapas (Map p60; ☎ 551 2344; www.tapas.is; Vesturgata 3b; tapas plates from Ikr300) For good Spanish tapas, head to this little restaurant around the back of Ingólfstorg. Expect to spend around Ikr2900 per person for a full meal.

STEIKHÚSIÐ (STEAKHOUSES)

Most restaurants in town can cook up a succulent steak, but beef is unfailingly the most expensive thing on the menu. Die-hard carnivores should head for the following places that specialise in steak dinners.

Hereford Steakhouse (Map p60; ☎ 511 3350; Laugavegur 53b; mains Ikr2150-4950) This modern steakhouse grills up top-class steaks, priced by weight and cut. You can pick from fillets, T-bones, rib-eyes and entrecotes. There's a good red wine list to compliment all the red meat.

Argentina (Map p60; ☎ 551 9555; www.argentina.is; Barónsstígur 11a; mains Ikr2600-4280) Housed in an atmospheric basement close to Laugavegur, Argentina serves tasty chargrilled hunks of beef, lamb, pork and chicken. The food is delicious and tasty.

Grillhúsið (Map p60; ☎ 562 3456; www.grillhusid.is; Tryggvagata 20; burgers from Ikr845, other mains from Ikr1295-2195) For Reykjavík's best burgers, freshly made from lean minced beef, head to this popular restaurant down near the harbour. The house burger is topped with cheese, bacon and guacamole, and the menu includes steaks and fish and chips.

VEGETARIAN

Reykjavík has a handful of decent vegetarian restaurants, most serving daily set meals with salad and bread.

Á Næstu Grösum (One Woman Restaurant; Map p60; ☎ 552 8410; Laugavegur 20b; lunchtime meals Ikr550-1190, evening dish of day Ikr1190; closed lunch Sun) Reykjavík's best vegetarian restaurant serves up daily vegetarian specials with exotic and unusual salads. Evening meals are just Ikr900 if you come before 6pm.

Grænn Kostur (Map p60; ☎ 552 2028; Skólavörðustígur 8; meals Ikr900) Tucked away in a small shopping arcade off Skólavörðustígur, this friendly little café serves good pure-veg food and the menu changes daily. The dish of the day comes with salad and bread.

Café Garðurinn (Map p60; ☎ 561 2345; Klapparstígur 37; dish of day with/without bread & soup Ikr1200/850; 11am-6pm Mon-Fri, noon-6pm Sat) This bright little café near Laugavegur offers a different fresh veg menu daily.

FINE DINING

Reykjavík has no shortage of upmarket venues, many housed in old wood and tin buildings in the old town. Most offer broadly similar menus of *bacalao* (salt cod), smoked lamb, seafood and steak, though a few places branch out with more unusual Icelandic dishes such as guillemot, puffin, reindeer or *hákarl* (putrid shark meat).

Naust (Map p60; ☎ 552 3030; www.naustid.is; Vesturgata 6-8; mains Ikr1500-4500; from 6pm) Housed in an old wooden house clad in metal plates, this seafood place has a heavily nautical theme and offers a pretty good selection of seafood and traditional Icelandic oddities.

Við Tjörnina (Map p60; ☎ 551 8666; Templarasund 3; mains Ikr1800-3600) Tucked away on an alley near Tjörn, this recommended seafood place serves up familiar dishes such as baked salt cod, and less familiar dishes such as plaice with banana. The two-course set lunch/dinner costs Ikr1700/2900.

Skólabrú (Map p60; ☎ 562 4455; Skólabrú 1; mains Ikr1940-2250; from 6pm) The cosy Skólabrú is in an old house just off Austurvöllur and makes home-style Icelandic food such as *lambakjötsúpa* (traditional lamb stew).

Restaurant Tjarnarbakkinn (Map p60; ☎ 562 9700; www.idno.is; Vonarstræti; mains Ikr2120-4340) Set in a

SIX OF THE BEST

As you would expect from a capital city, Reykjavík has some of the finest restaurants in the country. The following is our top six of the capital's gourmet eateries.

Perlan (Map pp54-5; ☎ 562 0200; Öskjuhlíð; mains Ikr1390-4190) Housed in the dome on top of the Perlan complex, this posh revolving restaurant has great views and serves European dishes with a French and Italian flavour, and delicacies such as reindeer and guillemot. If you have the money and the appetite, the seafood feast is a whopping Ikr5490.

Humarhúsið (Map p60; Lobster House; ☎ 561 3303; www.humarhusid.is; Amtmannsstígur 1; Ikr1190-3440) Housed in an old grey wooden tower house just off Lækjargata, the Lobster House more than lives up to its name. The crawling crustaceans feature in most dishes on the menu, including the recommended Icelandic lobster tail soup (Ikr1190).

Siggihall (Map p60; ☎ 511 6677; Hótel ÓðinsveÞórsgata 1; mains Ikr2700-4900) This upmarket seafood restaurant is run by Iceland's leading TV chef and is regarded by many as the finest restaurant in Reykjavík. The menu features plenty of Icelandic favourites such as panfried cod served with a French twist.

Lækjarbrekka (Map p60; ☎ 551 4430; www.laekjarbrekka.is; Bankastræti 2; mains Ikr2880-4370) This very posh place is housed in a building dating from 1834 and serves the holy trinity of Icelandic cuisine – pepper steak, lamb fillet and salt cod. The food is excellent, but the restaurant firmly targets well-heeled tourists, so you pay for the privilege.

Einar Ben (Map p60; ☎ 511 5090; www.einarben.is; Ingólfstorg; mains Ikr1490-2590, 4-course dinner Ikr5950) Upstairs in an old red house on the east side of Ingólfstorg, Einar Ben is often used for diplomatic dinners, and the food and service are top-class. The food is Icelandic with a continental twist – think puffin terrine and ravioli stuffed with smoked cod.

Tveir Fiskar (Map p60; ☎ 511 3474; www.restaurant.is; Geirsgata 9; mains Ikr2450-3950) Right on the harbour, this posh seafood place serves anything and everything from the sea, from caviar and crab to *bacalao* (salt cod). The seafood is as fresh as it comes and is highly recommended, though whale meat is a questionable addition to the menu.

stately old building overlooking the Tjörn lake, this place offers fine Icelandic cuisine and lake views. In the summer, there are theatre dinners that include performances in the theatre downstairs.

A number of posh seafood places can be found just west of the centre, close to the harbour.

Apótek (Map p60; ☎ 575 7900; www.veitingar.is; Austurstræti 16; Ikr2250-4590) This sophisticated restaurant and café is housed in an old pharmacy from 1916 and serves up interesting Asian-Icelandic fusion dishes such as catfish with wasabi. Braver souls can sample Icelandic pony!

Café Ópera (Map p60; ☎ 552 9499; www.cafeopera.is; Lækjargata 2; mains Ikr1390-4300) Upstairs near the Reykjavík Travel Service, this long-established place has an extensive menu of Icelandic seafood, and you can also sample fish and meat cooked the traditional Scandinavian way – on a hot slab of rock.

Þrír Frakkar (Map p60; ☎ 552 3939; www.3frakkar.is; Baldursgata 14; lunch Ikr1350-1560, dinner Ikr2310-4200) Lots of Japanese tourists come to this cosy little seafood restaurant just west of the centre. As well as seafood, you can sample seal and puffin, though quite how 'scientifically harvested' whales ended up on the menu isn't fully explained.

Enrico's (Map p60; ☎ 552 0077; Laugavegur 3; lunch specials Ikr850-1300, evening mains Ikr1500-2700) Enrico's has a classy dining room with flowing curtains but prices are lower than you might expect. The menu has food from all over the world – the lunchtime soups, noodles and sandwiches are good value.

Sommelier Brasserie (Map p60; ☎ 511 4455; www.sommelier.is; Hverfisgata 46; 3-course meals around Ikr3900; 🕑 closed Sun) For modern Icelandic cuisine, try this super-sophisticated wood and concrete place. The food is quite inspired and the wine list is top-notch.

● **Askur Brasserie** (Map pp54-5; ☎ 553 8550; www.askur.is; Suðurlandsbraut 4; mains Ikr1490-3500) Close to the big hotels on Suðurlandsbraut, this popular Icelandic restaurant serves steak, lamb fillets, fish and other local favourites. The weekday lunch buffet is good value at Ikr1390 and comes with soup and salad.

All the big hotels have upmarket restaurants offering almost identical menus of seafood, lamb and beef from around Ikr2500 upwards. Try **Vox** (Map pp54-5; ☎ 444 5000; Suðurlandsbraut 2) at the Hótel Nordica, **Carpe Diem** (Map pp54-5; ☎ 552 4555, Rauðarárstígur 18) in Fosshótel Lind, or the **Gallery Restaurant** (☎ 552 5700; Bergstaðastræti 37) at Hótel Holt.

Brasserie Borg (Map p60; ☎ 551 1247; Hótel Borg, Pósthússtræti 11) This place serves a good-value gourmet lunch for Ikr1690, including soup, lemon sole and chocolate mousse.

Quick Eats

Fast food in Iceland generally means *franskar* (chips), *pýlsur* (hot dogs), *hamborgarar* (hamburgers), *samloka* (sandwiches) and pizzas, and there are numerous snack bars or *skalinn* dotted around the town centre. You'll pay around Ikr200 for a small order of chips or a hot dog with all the trimmings (mustard, ketchup, and fresh and fried onions) and Ikr350–500 for a burger or a sandwich.

There are several options along Austurstræti and Lækjartorg. In Ingólfstorg, the kiosk **Hlölla Bátar** (Map p60) sells long 'boat' sandwiches for Ikr690 and stays open until 2am to cater for hungry drinkers. In the same square, the **Emmessis og Pylsur kiosk** (Map p60) serves good hot dogs from Ikr190.

Nonnabiti (Map p60; ☎ 551 2312; Hafnarstræti 18; snacks Ikr190-690; 🕑 9am-2am, 10am-2am Sat & Sun) This cheap, cheery snack bar is a good option for burgers, sandwiches and hot dogs.

Gott í Gogginn (Map p60; ☎ 552 4444; Laugavegur 2; snacks Ikr460-690) For slightly healthier fare, visit this little takeaway place on the main shopping street, which serves various light meals including lasagne, small pizzas and pasta salads.

Kebabhúsið (Map p60; ☎ 561 3070; Lækjargata 2; snacks Ikr400-700) Across the square from Lækjartorg, this snack bar offers the added variety of falafel and kebabs to the usual chips, pizzas, hot dogs and sandwiches.

Another good option for fast food is the **Kringlan Food Court** (Miklabraut; Map pp54-5; 🕑 10am-6.30pm Mon-Wed, 10am-9pm Thu, 10am-7pm Fri, 10am-6pm Sat, 1-5pm Sun) on the 2nd floor of the Kringlan Shopping Centre – there are several fast-food kiosks, including Chinese and Mexican places.

Other possibilities for fast food are workers' cafeterias – there are several near the centre.

Fljótt Og Gott (Map pp54-5; ☎ 555 1288; Vatnsmýrarvegur 10; mains Ikr1090-1490; 🕑 7am-11.30pm) Inside the BSÍ Bus Terminal, this cafeteria has big roast dinners and Icelandic delicacies such as *svi* (singed sheep's head) at bargain prices (for Iceland).

Múlakaffi (Map pp54-5; ☎ 533 7737; Hallarmúli; canteen meals Ikr890-1090; 8am-8pm Mon-Fri) An old-fashioned no-frills, workers' restaurant, this place serves up hearty local meals such as salt cod and roast pork.

Self-Catering

If you are on a budget, think about self-catering. The cheapest supermarket is **Bónus** (Map p60), with stores on Laugavegur, near Vitastígur, and inside the Kringlan Shopping Centre. **10-11** has branches on Austurstræti (Map p60), Hverfisgata (Map p60) and Laugalækur (Map pp54-5; near the youth hostel and camp site). Most residential areas have convenience stores.

Alcohol is prohibitively pricey in all bars and restaurants, but you can save heaps by buying from the government-owned liquor store chain **Vín Búd**. This is the only place licensed to sell alcohol for consumption off-premises and there are six branches in Reykjavík – the most central is on Austurstræti (Map p60; 11am-6pm Mon-Thu, 11am-7pm Fri, 11am-4pm Sat). There are also branches in the Kringlan and Smáralind Shopping Centres.

DRINKING

Reykjavík has a famously energetic and uninhibited nightlife, which takes place at dozens of bars and pubs in the town centre. The line between bars and clubs is blurred in Iceland and many nightspots are coffee shops during the day, restaurants in the early evening, and then bars or clubs at night. On Friday and Saturday, practically the entire population of Reykjavík goes out on the town and joins in the great Icelandic pub crawl or *runtur* – see p79. Things don't get going until 11pm, but once it begins, the party rages till dawn and many snack bars stay open all night to cater for hungry revellers. In comparison, weekday nights can feel ominously quiet – the liveliest places to drink from Sunday to Thursday are usually Reykjavík's small cafés and coffee shops, which open until 1am.

Most of the action is concentrated on Laugavegur and Austurstræti. Budget for Icelandic prices – you'll pay upwards of Ikr600 for each beer and around Ikr1000 for that Icelandic staple, vodka-spiked lager. Some of the larger bars also charge Ikr500-1000 admission after midnight. To save money, do as the locals do and pop into the government alcohol shop on Austurstræti (see previous Self-Catering section) and start the evening in your hotel room. Places change names every few years, so don't be surprised if new bars have opened up in the same location as some of the following nightspots.

Bars

As well as the serious clubs, there are plenty of small, trendy bars that attract a sophisticated crowd and offer more elbow room.

Sirkus (Map p60; ☎ 511 8022; Klapparstígur 31) This Bohemian bar looks a bit dingy from outside but it has a loyal local following and scores highly for atmosphere. DJs play here at weekends and wine is available by the glass.

Kaffibarinn (Map p60; ☎ 551 1588; Bergstaðastræti 1) Björk and other celebrities have been known to frequent this trendy bar in an old house just off Laugavegur. Rumour has it that Damon Albarn from the pop band Blur is one of the owners, which may explain the London Underground symbol above the door.

Vegamót (Map p60; ☎ 511 3040; Vegamótastígur 4) Vegamót is another café by day, bar by night sort of place. It's very popular and trendy and gets busy early at weekends.

Thorvaldsen Bar (Map p60; ☎ 511 1413; Austurstræti 8) An older set hang out at this understated modernist bar – there are DJs from Thursday to Saturday.

Other bars popular with older drinkers include **Kaffi Reykjavík** (Map p60; ☎ 551 8900; Vesturgata 2), which sometimes has a miniature version of the Stockholm ice bar inside, **Apótek** (Map p60; ☎ 575 7900, Austurstræti 16) and **Metz** (Map p60; ☎ 561 3000; Austurstræti 9).

Pubs

You don't have to dress in your best to go out in Reykjavík – the following is our pick for a more relaxed night on the town.

Kaffi Brennslan (Map p60; ☎ 561 3600; Pósthússtræti 9) One of the most relaxed places for a drink is this unpretentious Deco café and pub on Austurvöllur. It's a coffee shop by day and a bar by night and pulls in a crowd throughout the week. You can usually get a 500ml bottle of the beer of the day for Ikr390.

Café Victor (Map p60; ☎ 561 9556; Ingólfstorg) More bar than café, Victor has a Mexican/American menu during the day but lets its hair down and becomes a bar at night.

Ölstofa (Map p60; ☎ 552 4687; Vegamótastígur 4) Next door to Vegamót, this bar is deservedly popular with locals and has a refreshingly relaxed atmosphere. This is one of the few places in the capital where you can hear yourself speak.

Prikið (Map p60; ☎ 551 3366; Bankastræti 12) Many people end up at this cosy little pub on the main street at the tail end of the night, but it can be noisy and crowded.

Nelly's Café (Map p60; ☎ 562 1250; Þingholtstræti 2) This student pub on the corner of Þingholtstræti and Laugavegur serves the cheapest beer in town and offers student discounts. The crowd is young and alternative, bands perform regularly, as do DJs. You can get a half-litre draught beer for as little as Ikr300.

Dillon (Map p60; ☎ 511 2400; Laugavegur 30) This atmospheric bar is housed in an old wooden house on Laugavegur. It looks a lot like an English pub and is recommended on weekday evenings when the larger, trendier places can be spookily empty.

Reykjavík has several Irish-themed pubs that offer the usual folksy décor, Celtic bric-a-brac and Guinness on tap. The **Dubliner** (Map p60; ☎ 511 3233; Hafnarstræti 4) and **Celtic Cross** (Map p60; ☎ 511 3240; Hverfisgata 26) are both cosy places to sink beer.

Clubs

The following clubs and bars should be the first port of call for 24-hour party people.

Vidalin (Map p60; ☎ 551 0962; Aðalstræti 10) This well-established bar is a popular place to shake your tail feather and the dancefloor is packed out all weekend. It may change name soon, but the new owners have promised to retain the party mood.

Pravda (Map p60; ☎ 552 9222; Austurstræti 22; ⏲ 8pm-1am Thu, 8pm-5.30am Fri & Sat) The latest on the club scene, Pravda is full of brushed steel and has a massive dancefloor upstairs. Clubbers queue round the block at weekends and the bar is crammed to the rafters until the early hours. Entry costs Ikr500 after midnight.

Café Sólon (Map p60; ☎ 562 3535; www.solon.is; Bankastræti 7e) This ultratrendy café and nightspot has moody subdued lighting and a dancefloor upstairs that is packed with beautiful people at weekends.

Gaukur á Stöng (Map p60; ☎ 551 1556; Tryggvagata 22; ⏲ 8pm-1am Sun-Thu, 8pm-5.30am Fri & Sat) This historic pub near the harbour is one of the most popular places in town; bands play regularly during the week and there are club nights at the weekend. Most people have a great time here, but it's a notorious pick-up joint and it positively heaves at weekends.

Glaumbar (Map p60; ☎ 552 6868; Tryggvagata 20) This American-style sports bar is boisterous and lively, with a huge video screen and deafening pop music.

Hverfisbarinn (Map p60; ☎ 511 6700; Hverfisgata 20) A strong contender for the title of Reykjavík's most popular bar, this trendy bar and club attracts a young and showy crowd, and there are long, long queues to get in at weekends.

Kaffi List (Map p60; ☎ 562 5059; Laugavegur 20a) Dedicated followers of fashion flock here to see and be seen. There's a dance floor, but dress to the hilt if you want to fit in.

THE RUNTUR

Every Friday and Saturday night, Reykjavík becomes the setting for the famous *runtur* – the great Icelandic pub crawl. This Bacchanalian orgy begins at around 11pm and continues right on through the night, lubricated by copious quantities of vodka-spiked beer. People from more staid cultures may find the Icelanders' lack of inhibition a bit intimidating, but it's mostly good-natured fun and things rarely get aggressive. Most of the action takes place on or around Laugavegur in the town centre and bars generally stay open until at least 3am – some push right on through until 5.30am or later.

Rather than settling into one venue for the evening, Icelanders like to cruise from bar to bar, getting progressively louder and less inhibited as the evening goes on. Because of this, a night on the town can be quite an expensive proposition – budget around Ikr5000 for drinks and Ikr500-1500 for the entry fees to the trendier bars after midnight. You should also set aside another Ikr1500-2000 for a quick hot dog and a taxi home. Friday is generally busier than Saturday, and most locals like to dress up when they go out – ties and suits aren't unheard of in the posher bars. This said, foreigners can usually get away with a more relaxed dress code, particularly if you stick to the quieter pub-type venues.

ENTERTAINMENT

In addition to the buzzing pub and bar scene, Reykjavík has several multiplex cinemas and a good selection of cultural activities, including theatres, concert halls and an opera house.

Cinemas

The cinema is one of the best entertainment options on weekday nights and there are seven multiplexes in Reykjavík. All Icelandic cinemas charge Ikr800 and films are usually shown at 6pm, 8pm and 10pm. The free newspaper *Morgunblaðið* lists shows and times. Most movies are screened in their original language with Icelandic subtitles.

Háskólabíó (Map pp54-5; ☎ 530 1900; opposite Hótel Saga, Hagatorg)
Laugarásbíó (Map pp54-5; ☎ 553 2075; Laugarás)
Regnboginn (Map p60; ☎ 551 9000; Hverfisgata 54)
Sambíóin (Map pp54-5; Kringlan Shopping Centre ☎ 588 0800; Mjódd ☎ 587 8900; Alfábakka 8)
Smárabíó (☎ 564 0000; Smáralind Shopping Centre, Kópavogur)

Cultural Activities

Reykjavík has several theatre groups, an opera house and a symphony orchestra. Information on current events can be found in *What's On in Reykjavík*, or in the daily papers.

OPERA & CLASSICAL MUSIC

The **Íslenska Óperan** (Icelandic Opera; Map p60; ☎ 511 6400; www.opera.is; Ingólfstræti) has a busy programme of international operas. Matinees cost Ikr1000 and evening shows Ikr2000-2500.

The **Iceland Symphony Orchestra** (Map pp54-5; ☎ 545 2500; www.sinfonia.is; Háskólabíó, Hagatorg) is based at the Reykjavík University cinema and has a regular programme of classical performances. Shows are normally on Thursday at 7.30pm and tickets cost from Ikr1900.

THEATRE

Reykjavík has several theatre venues – the most important is the **National Theatre** (Map p60; ☎ 585 1200; www.leikhusid.is; Lindargata 7), which puts on more than 300 performances a year, from modern Icelandic plays to Tennessee Williams and Shakespeare. Most shows are at weekends and tickets cost Ikr2500 (Ikr1900 for seniors and under-16s).

The other important theatre is **Reykjavík City Theatre** (Map pp54-5; ☎ 568 8000; www.borgarleikhus.is; Kringlan, Listabraut 3), behind the Kringlan Shopping Centre. This theatre puts on plays and musicals from around the world at around 8pm from Thursday to Sunday. Tickets cost Ikr2500 for adults, Ikr1900 for the disabled and seniors, and are free for under-12s.

Other theatres include:

Iðnó Theatre (Map p60; ☎ 551 9181; Baldursgata 37) Tourist-oriented performances from Icelandic sagas and folk dances in summer.
Loftkastalinn Theatre (Map pp54-5; ☎ 522 3000; Seljavegur 2) Youth-oriented amateur performances.
Tjarnarbíó Leikhús (Map p60; ☎ 561 0280; Tjarnargata) Small theatre company with contemporary plays.

SAGA OF GUÐRIÐUR

This interesting one-woman show was designed for tourists and has been running since 1998. The story recounts the discovery of Vinland (North America) by the Vikings in the year 1000 and gets good reviews from most people who see it. Performances are held in **Skemmtihúsið** (Map p60; ☎ 864 5963; www.skemmtihusidtheatre.is; Laufásvegur 22) throughout the summer. English-language shows are at 8.30pm on Tuesday, Thursday and Sunday, and 6pm on Friday; shows in German start at 6pm on Tuesday and Sunday. There are shows in French on set dates in August.

DINNER SHOWS

The main venue for dinner shows is **Broadway** (Map pp54-5; ☎ 533 1100; www.broadway.is; Hótel Ísland; Ármúli 9), which offers Broadway-style extravaganzas and musicals. Dinner and show costs around Ikr5400 per person and shows are usually only on Friday and Saturday. The venue is also used for some large concerts.

Live Music

Many of the bars and pubs have band performances – particularly **Gaukur á Stöng** (Map p60; ☎ 551 1556; Tryggvagata 22) and **Nelly's Café** (Map p60; ☎ 562 1250; Þingholtstræti 2). Another stalwart of the live-music scene is **Grand Rokk** (Map p60; ☎ 551 5522; Smiðjustígur 6), a down-to-earth bar just off Laugavegur. Several bands play every weekend and the hugely popular **Hrokurinn Chess Club** (www.icechess.is) meets here during the week. It's a relaxed place and there's no need to dress up.

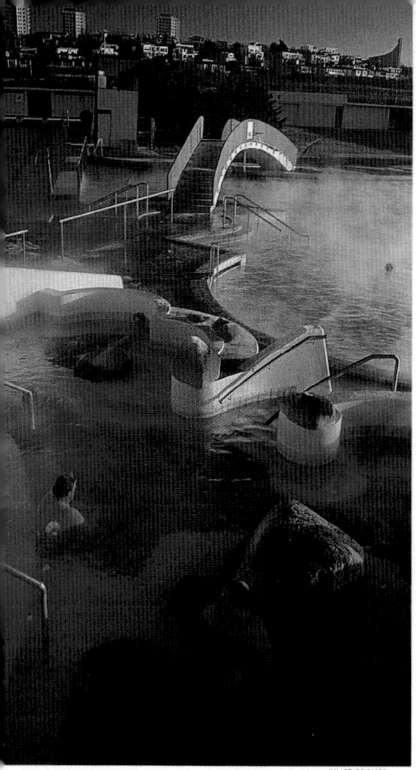

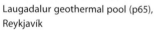

JULIET COOMBE

Laugadalur geothermal pool (p65), Reykjavík

PAUL HARDING

Reykjavík wall graffiti

Reykjavík's old town and harbour (p53)

PAUL HARDING

WADE

Blue Lagoon (p95), near Reykjavík

GRAEME CORNWALLIS

Krísuvík (p97), near Reykjavík

Hafnarfjörður (p84), near Reykjavík

STEVE H

Many rock bands are now including Reykjavík on their international tours – check the local press to see if anyone big is in town. For listings of live music in Reykjavík, see the free listings paper *Reykjavík Grapevine*, available from most cafés and the tourist office.

Sport

Football is Iceland's most popular spectator sport, and local and international games are played at the **Þrottur Football Stadium** (Map pp54-5; ☎ 580 5900; Engjavegi 7), home to the soccer team Þrottur Reykjavík. For information, see the sports sections of Reykjavík newspapers.

SHOPPING

Although Reykjavík is packed with designer clothes stores, these are mostly international chains and you can often get the same thing for less back home. For genuinely Icelandic souvenirs, good buys include Icelandic knitwear, jewellery and ceramics. However, be aware that few Icelanders would be seen dead in an Icelandic sweater! Icelandic delicacies such as dried fish and Brennivín (Icelandic schnapps) make interesting souvenirs and are available from most supermarkets.

Ceramics & Antiques

Several places sell high-quality ceramics and glassware. **Rosenthal** (Map p60; ☎ 562 4244; Laugavegur 52) has a good selection of imported brand-name stuff. **Keramik** (Map p60; ☎ 552 2882; Laugavegur 48b) makes its own ceramics on site. Skólavörðustígur is lined with shops selling pricey arts, crafts and ceramics – some are quite tasteful but there's plenty of overpriced chintz too.

Loads of shops in town sell antiques, but a lot of these are basically junk shops and all are overpriced. Some of the more interesting places to browse include **Antikbúðin** (Map pp54-5; ☎ 552 8222; 101 Laugavegur), **Ömmu Antique** (Map p60; ☎ 552 0190; Hverfisgata 37) and **Friða Frænka** (Map p60; ☎ 551 4730; Vesturgata 3). It is also worth a visit to the weekend **Kolaportið Flea Market** on Geirsgata – see p67.

Clothes & Jewellery

For brand-name clothing by Prada, Hugo Boss and other top names, trawl along Laugavegur or head to the **Kringlan Shopping Centre** (Map pp54-5; ☎ 568 9200; www.kringlan.is; Miklabraut). While you're here, check out the huge mural by the artist Erró. There are similar stores in the **Smáralind Shopping Centre** (☎ 528 8000; www.smaralind.is; Hagasmári) in Kópavogur.

Various shops along Laugavegur specialise in Icelandic jewellery. One of the more interesting designers is **Aurum** (Map p60; ☎ 551 2770; Bankastræti 4) – the whisper-thin gold and silver jewellery is very sophisticated.

Film & Photography

Reykjavík has plenty of photo shops, but prices for film are astronomical. **Hans Petersen** (Map p60; ☎ 570 7560; Bankastræti 4) is the best place to go for slide or print film. Processing and printing of a 24 exposure print film costs Ikr1820 for one-hour service or Ikr1470 for the two-day service. Hans Petersen also has branches near the Nordica Hotel on Suðurlandsgata and in the Kringlan and Smáralind Shopping Centres.

Icelandic Souvenirs

Many places sell tourist tat, like souvenir mugs, Brennivín shot glasses, lava paperweights and plastic Viking helmets. Probably the most tasteful souvenir is Icelandic knitwear; try the well-stocked **Rammagerðin** (Map p60; ☎ 551 1122; Hafnarstræti 19) or the shop at the Reykjavík tourist office. For Icelandic music (including Björk's entire output) try **Japis** (Map p60; ☎ 511 1185; Laugavegur 13) or **Skifan** (Map p60; ☎ 525 5040; Laugavegur 26). Skifan also has branches at Kringlan and Smáralind Shopping Centres. Often, CDs on promotion sell for under Ikr1000.

Outdoor Equipment

Climbing, camping, cycling and fishing equipment and repairs are available from **Útilíf** (Map pp54-5; ☎ 511 2030; www.utilif.is; Miklabraut), formerly Nanoq, in the Kringlan Shopping Centre. It also sells white gas, butane cartridges and other stove fuels. There are branches at the Smáralind Shopping Centre and the small Glæsibær arcade. Iceland's own outdoor equipment company, **66° North** (Map p60; ☎ 561 6800; Lækjargata 4) produces trendy outdoor gear.

GETTING THERE & AWAY

Air

Reykjavík's domestic airport, **Innanlandsflug**, is busy from dawn to dusk with flights to destinations across Iceland, as well as to Greenland and the Faroe Islands. The main airlines providing internal flights are **Flugfélag** (Air Iceland; ☎ 570 3030; www.flugfelag.is) and **Íslandsflug** (Icebird Airlines; ☎ 570 8090; www.islandsflug.is). Seats on both airlines can be booked at the Flugfélag desk at the domestic terminal. You can usually save money if you book over the Internet – a computer terminal is provided for booking near the check-in desks.

For international flights to destinations other than Greenland or the Faroes, you'll need to go to Keflavík International Airport, 48km west of the city. The easiest way to get here is on the Reykjavík Excursions Flybus – see under Bus in the following section. For contact details of other airlines, see the Transport chapter.

Bus

Almost all long-distance buses use the **BSÍ Bus Terminal** (☎ 591 1000; www.bsi.is) on Vatnsmýrarvegur, near the domestic airport – the locals pronounce it *Bee Ess Ee*. The booking desk here can book you onto all the different bus companies that have services around Iceland. Also here is the popular tour agent, Destination Iceland (see p59). There's a good cafeteria and a Net café charging 250kr for 30 minutes.

Bus services around Iceland include:

Destination	Duration	Price
Akranes	50 mins	Ikr850
Akureyri	6hrs	Ikr5700
Blue Lagoon	40 mins	Ikr850
Borgarnes	1¼hrs	Ikr1600
Geysir	2½hrs	Ikr1870 (daytour Ikr3470)
Höfn	8hrs	Ikr7310
Hveragerði	40 mins	Ikr650
Keflavík (town)	40 mins	Ikr800
Kirkjubælarklaustur	5hrs	Ikr3830
Landmannalaugar	4hrs	Ikr3950 (daytour Ikr7900)
Ólafsvík	2¾hrs	Ikr2650
Þorlákshöfn (for the Vestmannaeyjar ferry)	1hr	Ikr1020
Þórsmörk	3¼hrs	Ikr3200
Selfoss	1hr	Ikr850
Skaftafell	6hrs	Ikr4690
Staðaskáli (for Westfjords buses)	3¼hrs	Ikr2800
Stykkishólmur (for the Westfjords ferry)	2½hrs	Ikr2450
Vík í Mýrdal	3hrs	Ikr2750

For other destinations on the north and east side of the island, you'll need to change buses in Höfn or Akureyri, which may involve an overnight stop. Buses to Reykjanes, Snæfellsnes and the main towns on Hwy 1 run year-round, with the exception of the section from Akureyri to Höfn. Services are less frequent on all routes from September to May. Buses to the Westfjords only run from 1 June to 31 August, and most routes across the interior also close down for winter.

Ferry

For information on the Viðey ferry, refer to p89.

GETTING AROUND

To/From the Airport

The only long-distance bus that doesn't use the BSÍ terminal is the **Flybus** (☎ 562 1011; www.re.is) to Keflavík International Airport, which departs from the Hótel Lofteiðir about two hours before each international flight. All the hotels and guesthouses in Reykjavík can provide up-to-date schedules and make bookings. Transfers to the Hótel Loftleiðir are free if you are staying at any of the major hotels, the youth hostel or the Salvation Army Guesthouse.

In the reverse direction, buses are waiting at the main concourse to meet passengers from all arriving flights. The journey to Reykjavík lasts about an hour and costs Ikr1000, which you can pay on the bus in cash or by credit card. The Flybus will also drop off and pick up in Garðabær and Hafnarfjörður if you book in advance.

Expect to pay at least Ikr8000 for a taxi from the city centre to Keflavík International Airport.

Bicycle

Bicycles are a great way to get to the attractions outside the centre, but be prepared for some steep hills, particularly if you intend to head up to Perlan. Reykjavík has a network of cycle lanes, but these are not well integrated, so you'll often end up on busy roads. Be very cautious of the traffic as drivers show little consideration for cyclists.

Several companies rent out mountain bikes to visitors, including **Reykjavík Travel Service** (☎ 511 2442; Lækjargata 2), which charges Ikr700 for three hours, Ikr1100 for six hours, and Ikr1600 for 24 hours. You can also rent bikes from **Borgarhjól SF** (☎ 551 5653; Hverfisgata 50) for Ikr1200/1700 per half/full day. In summer, this company also rents out bikes at the youth hostel and camp site on Sundlaugavegur.

Bus

Reykjavík's excellent **Stræto city bus network** (☎ 551 2700; www.bus.is) offers regular and easy transport around downtown Reykjavík and out to the suburbs of Seltjarnarnes, Kópavogur, Garðabær, Hafnarfjörður and Mosfellsbær. Buses run from 7am until midnight daily (from 10am on Sunday) and services leave at 20-minute intervals from 7am to 7pm on weekdays, and at 30-minute intervals every evening and at weekends. Buses will pick up and drop passengers only at designated stops, these are marked by a yellow sign with the letter 'S'.

There is a flat fare of Ikr220 for all rides on city and suburban buses regardless of the length of the journey, and you'll need exact change. If you need to change buses, ask the driver for a *skiptimiði* (transfer) valid for up to 45 minutes from the time of issue. You can also buy books of nine tickets for Ikr1500 at the main bus stands. The Reykjavík Tourist Card (see p56) offers free travel on all Stræto buses.

The main bus stands for city buses are at **Hlemmur** (Map pp54-5), just outside the town centre on Laugavegur, and **Lækjartorg** (Map p60), right in the centre of town at the corner of Lækjargata and Hafnarstræti. Important suburban bus stands include **Grensás** at the corner of Grensásvegur and Miklabraut, **Hamraborg** at Kópavogur, **Fjórður** at Hafnarfjörður, **Ártún** in the suburb of Höfðar and **Mjódd** in the suburb of Breiðholt. It may be the case that you have to change buses at one of these terminals if you are heading from one suburb of Reykjavík to another. Most free maps of Reykjavík that are available include bus maps.

Useful routes include:

No 5 Domestic Airport, Reykjavík University, Lækjartorg, Hlemmur, Laugardalur (youth hostel/camp site)
No 7 Lækjartorg, Hótel Loftleiðir, Landspítali (hospital)
No 25 Ártún, Mosfellsbær
No 140/150 Lækjartorg, Hlemmur, Kópavogur, Hafnarfjörður

Car & Motorcycle

A hire car is a great way to get around Iceland, but to get out to the countryside, you'll have to fight your way through the Reykjavík traffic. The capital's drivers are notoriously inconsiderate and many people drive around with a mobile phone permanently locked to their heads – beware of people wandering across lanes and cutting corners at junctions.

Getting out of town is fairly easy – just keep your eyes peeled for the signs to Hwy 1, but getting back into Reykjavík can be a little confusing as there are dozens of exits from the highway and road-signs are marked with abbreviations rather than full street names. To help you out, the main road into Reykjavík is Vesturlandsvegur, which turns into Miklabraut and then Hringbraut. Exit by the Kringlan Shopping Centre for the Laugardalur area, at Snorrabraut for the Hallgrímskirkja area, and at Suðurgata for the old town and town centre.

For information on hiring a car in Reykjavík, see p313.

The youth hostel, camp site and all top-end hotels have parking for guests; you can park in the street in front of many suburban guesthouses. Parking in central Reykjavík is regulated by coin-operated parking meters, but you better not rely on the locals to refill your meter when it expires, as happens in the cult movie *101 Reykjavík*.

Taxi

Central Reykjavík is small enough to comfortably walk around and the bus network is excellent, but taxis may be useful if you have a lot of luggage or are staying out until the early hours. Tipping is not required, but prices are high. From the youth hostel to downtown, expect to pay at least Ikr1000. You'll find taxis loitering around in front of the BSÍ Bus Terminal, the domestic airport, Lækjartorg, the youth hostel, and around the pubs and bars on weekend nights. Alternatively, call one of the following taxi companies:

Borgarbílastöðn (☎ 552 2440)
BSH (☎ 555 0888)
BSR (☎ 561 0000)
Hreyfill-Bæjarleiðir (☎ 553 3500, 588 5522)

AROUND REYKJAVÍK

In recent years, Reykjavík has ballooned outwards, absorbing a number of nearby towns, including Seltjarnarnes, Kópavogur, Garðabær, Hafnarfjörður and Mosfellsbær, all of which can be reached on city buses from Reykjavík. Immediately offshore are several interesting and unspoilt islands, providing a taste of Icelandic nature just minutes from downtown Reykjavík. Seltjarnarnes, Kópavogur and Hafnarfjörður all have good swimming pools – see p64 for details.

SELTJARNARNES

pop 4662

The small suburb of Seltjarnarnes occupies the western end of the Reykjavík peninsula, about 1.5km from Lækjartorg. If you don't feel like walking, you can take bus No 3 from Lækjartorg. There are good views across the fjord to Mt Esja (909m) and on clear days you can even see Snæfellsjökull. Lots of people come here specifically to drink in the glass-domed square **Rauða Ljónið** at Eiðistorg, which is alleged to be the largest pub in the world – it's more like a covered market square with beer vendors. Seltjarnarnes is also home to the small **Nesstofa Medical Museum** (☎ 561 1016; Neströð; adult/concession Ikr300/free; 1-5pm Sun, Tue & Thu 15 May–14 Sep) housed in a stone building originally constructed for Iceland's first surgeon-general; the collection of old medical artefacts is worth a look if you're in the area.

KÓPAVOGUR

pop 24,229

The first suburb south of Reykjavík is Kópavogur, which was once a separate township but is now just a dormitory town for Reykjavík. Buses stop near the modernist church at Hamraborg, near the cultural complex **Menningarmiðstoð Kópavogs** (Map pp54-5), which contains a library, gallery, museum and concert hall. On the street opposite you'll find banks, shops, restaurants and other amenities.

Sights

Within the cultural complex is Kópavogur's **Natural History Museum** (☎ 554 0630; admission free; 10am-5pm Mon-Thu, 11am-5pm Fri, 1-5pm Sat & Sun), which has an orca skeleton, and a good collection of stuffed animals and geological specimens. The attached **library** (☎ 570 0450; Hamraborg 6a) has Internet access for Ikr200 per 30 minutes. Also within the cultural complex, **Salurinn** (☎ 570 0401; www.salurinn.is; Hamraborg 6) is a brand new classical music venue with fantastic acoustics, built entirely from Icelandic materials – see the website for details of their concert programme.

Closer to the church is the **Listasafn Kópavogs** (☎ 554 4501; Hamraborg 4; adult/child Ikr300/100; 11am-5pm Tue-Sun) a small gallery with regularly changing exhibitions of modern art.

Kópavogur has a good **thermal swimming pool** (☎ 570 0470; Borgarholsbraut; adult/child Ikr220/100; 6.30am-10pm Mon-Fri, 8am-6pm Sat & Sun).

Sleeping & Eating

If you want to stay over, B&B accommodation is available at **Gisting BB 44** (☎ 554 4228; www.bb44.is; Borgarholtsbraut 44; sb from Ikr1900, s/d Ikr5400/7900), a large and cosy suburban house with a kitchen and TV lounge for guests.

Getting There & Away

To get there, take city bus No 140 or 150 from Hlemmur or Lækjartorg.

HAFNARFJÖRÐUR

pop 20,223

Although it's basically a suburb of Reykjavík, Hafnarfjörður has managed to retain its identity and is worthy of a visit in its own right. It's a tidy little place and sprawls over the cave-riddled lava flows of the 7000-year-old Búrfell eruption, overlooking a small bay. The town was a trading centre for the British in the early 15th century, and the German Hanseatic League took over in the 16th century until the imposition of the Danish Trade Monopoly in 1602. There are still lots of old tin-clad wooden houses in town and Harfnarfjörður trades heavily on its Viking and maritime past. The numerous lava caves and parks dotted around town are rumoured to be occupied by elves and other little folk.

Information

The friendly **tourist office** (☎ 565 0661; www.lava.is; Vesturgata 8; 9am-6pm Mon-Fri, 9am-2pm Sat & Sun 15 May–15 Sept; 1-4pm Mon-Fri in winter) is in a 19th-century timber building, Riddarinn. Ask for copies of the walking trail

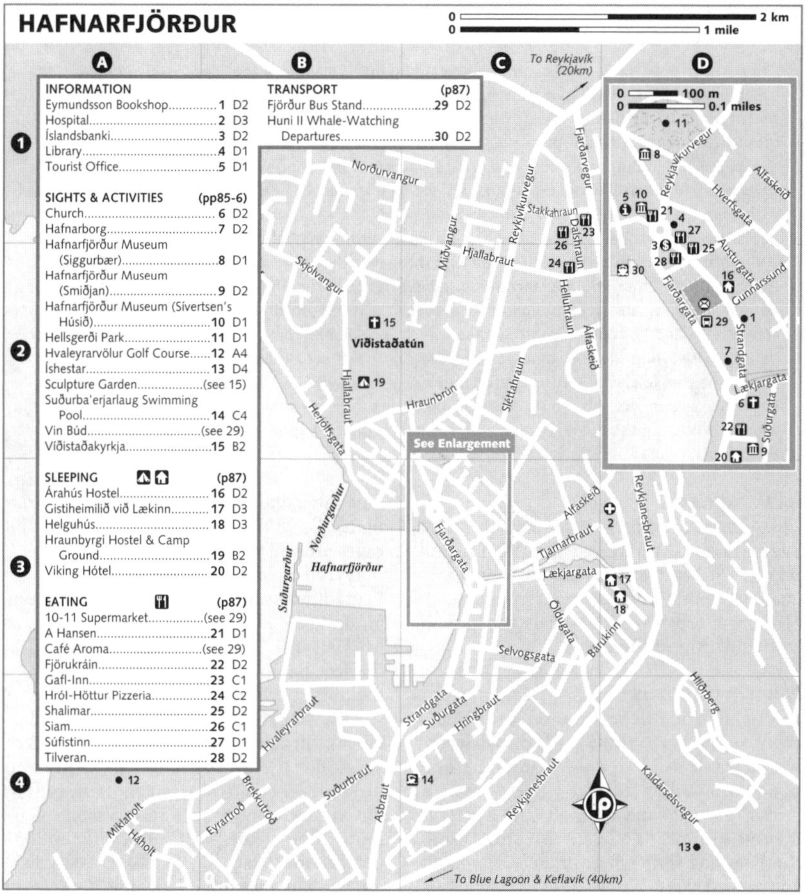

map *Ratleikur* and the photocopied guide for city walks. Internet access is available at the **library** (☎ 585 5690; Strandgata 1; 10am-7pm Mon-Thu, 11am-7pm Fri) for Ikr200 for 30 minutes.

There are banks with foreign exchange desks and ATMs at the Fjórður shopping centre on Fjarðargata. **Eymundsson** (☎ 555 0045; Strandgata 31) is the best bookshop in town.

Sights

HAFNARFJÖRÐUR MUSEUM

There are three museums in town, collectively known as the **Hafnarfjörður Museum** (☎ 555 5420; Vesturgata 6). The same ticket covers you for all three museums and costs Ikr300 (children under 16-years and seniors are free). Hafnarfjörður Museum consists of the following.

Sívertsen's Húsið (Vesturgata 6; 1-5pm Jun-Aug, Sat & Sun only Sep-May) The local folk museum is housed in the town's oldest building, which dates from 1803.

Smiðjan (Strandgata; 1-5pm May-Sep) Next to the Viking Hotel, this museum has exhibits on whaling and the history of Hafnarfjörður. The collection here may move to the location of the old maritime museum – next to the tourist office and Sívertsen's Húsið.

Siggubær (cnr Hellisgata and Kirkjuvegur; 1-5pm Sat & Sun Jun-Aug) Next to the park at Hellisgerði is this little restored fishing hut, but it's only open in summer at weekends.

HIDDEN WORLDS

Once you've seen the eerie lava formations and geothermal fields that characterise much of the Icelandic landscape, it will probably come as no surprise that many Icelanders believe their country is populated by hidden races of little folk – *jarðvergar* (gnomes), *álfar* (elves), *ljósálfar* (fairies), *dvergar* (dwarves), *ljúflingar* (lovelings), *tívar* (mountain spirits), *englar* (angels) and *huldufólk* ('hidden people'). Although only 10% of Icelanders admit to believing whole-heartedly, most Icelandic gardens feature small wooden cut-outs of *alfhol* (elf-houses) to house the little people in case the myths are true.

Hafnarfjörður is believed to lie at the confluence of several strong ley lines (mystical lines of energy) and seems to be particularly rife with these twilight creatures. In fact, construction of roads and homes in Hafnarfjörður is only permitted if it has been determined that the site in question is not already populated by little folk. A local seer, Erla Stefánsdóttir, is particularly attuned to their wavelength and has come up with a map, which is available from the Hafnarfjörður tourist office for Ikr980, showing the best spots to catch a glimpse of these Hidden Worlds. She also leads tours to find the wee folk, which are great fun for kids – see Activities & Tours below. The Hellisgerði lava park and garden, near the town centre, is perhaps the best known and most densely populated Hidden Worlds outpost, and serves as a popular meditation spot with local humans.

HAFNARBORG

This upbeat **art gallery** (☎ 555 0080; www.harnarborg.is; Strandgata 34; adult/concession/under-12 Ikr300/200/free; 🕑 11am-5pm Wed-Mon) has regularly changing exhibitions of modern art, much of it produced by resident artists from Iceland and around the world.

PARKS & GARDENS

Just uphill from the seafront on Reykjvíkurvegur is the pretty little park of **Hellisgerði**, which is full of lava caves, shady trees and ponds. As well as full-sized trees, there's a bonsai garden, and a small café operates here in summer. You can also stroll up to the **Hamarinn Cliffs** where there's a lookout and view disk.

Not far from the camp site is the green valley of **Víðistaðar**, home to the semicircular Víðistaðakyrkja church and an interesting **sculpture garden**, full of interesting artworks commissioned for the Hafnarfjörður art festivals of 1991 and 1993.

Activities & Tours

Some of the most popular tours revolve around the hidden worlds occupied by Hafnarfjörður little people. **Hidden Worlds** (☎ 565 0661) offers guided walks to various spots where elves and other spirits are said to gather, led by local clairvoyant Erla Stefánsdóttir. (See also the 'Hidden Worlds' boxed text above.) Various locals in costume put in an appearance and the tours are great fun for kids. You can also buy the rather overpriced *Hidden Worlds* map (Ikr980), which marks various elf caves around town.

Inland from Hafnarfjörður, there are loads of walking trails in the tree plantations around lake Elliðavatn and on the slopes of Mt Helgafell (338m) – these are detailed in the free pamphlet *Ratleikur*, available from the tourist office.

The range of tours available from Hafnarfjörður has decreased rapidly in recent years, but the tourist office is still keen to promote new activities, so check in to find out if any new tours are available. Currently, one of the most interesting options is **whale-watching** (☎ 555 2758; huni@islandia.is) on the old oak-hulled fishing boat *Húni II*. Trips leave at 10am daily from May to October and cost Ikr3000/1500 adults/under-12.

There are two good swimming pools in town – the better pool is east of the centre at **Suðurba'erjarlaug** (☎ 565 3080; Hringbraut 77; adult/child Ikr220/100; 🕑 6.30am-9.30pm Mon-Fri, 8am-6.30pm Sat, 8am-5.30pm Sun). There's also a **golf course** (☎ 565 3360) surrounded by lava at Hvaleyrarvöllur.

Festivals

In early July, Hafnarfjörður remembers its Viking past with a **Viking Festival**, centred on the Viking Hotel and Fjörukráin restaurant, with parades, horse shows, Viking sports competitions and even the occasional pagan marriage.

Sleeping

Camping and hostel-style accommodation is available at the Icelandic Boy Scouts camp at **Hraunbyrgi** (☎ 565 0900; Hjallabraut 51; camping per person Ikr750, sb Ikr2000; 🕑 1 May–31 Aug) by the park Víðistaðar. The building is a rather stylish construction of decking, glass and concrete, and there's a guest kitchen, laundry and Net café.

Árahús (☎ 555 0795; www.hostel.is; Strandgata 21; sb member/non-member Ikr1600/1950) Hafnarfjörður HI hostel is on the pedestrian main street and is open all year. It's upstairs, behind the Koffortið souvenir shop.

Gistiheimilið Við Lækinn (Guesthouse on the Lake; ☎ 565 5132; olgunn@simnet.is; cnr Hringbraut & Lækjarkinn; sb Ikr2000, s/d with shared bathroom Ikr4400/6800) Near the hospital and overlooking the lake, this family home has decent rooms and low prices.

Helguhús (☎ 555 2842; fax 565 4700; Lækjarkinn 8; s/d with shared bathroom Ikr4400/6800) Up the street from Við Lækinn, this is a slightly tidier, cosier option, but prices are higher.

Viking Hotel (☎ 565 1213; www.vikingvillage.is; Strandgata 55; s/d Ikr9900/12,800) Part of the Fjörukráin restaurant and similarly styled, this wooden hotel has surprisingly smart and modern rooms with TVs, phone and bathroom. The complex is often known as the Viking Village. Rates drop by up to 45% between September and May.

Eating

For self-caterers, there's a large **10-11** supermarket and a **Vin Búd** liquor shop in the Fjórður centre, plus several more supermarkets on Reykjvíkurvegur.

For cakes, snacks and coffees, try **Café Aroma** (☎ 555 6996; Fjórður Centre; Fjarðargata) or **Súfistinn** (☎ 565 3740; Strandgata 9).

Fjörukráin (☎ 565 1213; www.fjorukrain.is; Strandgata 55; mains Ikr1850-3700) Housed in a totally over-the-top reconstruction of a Viking long house, complete with carved pillars and dragons on the roof, Fjörukráin offers Icelandic meals served up by Viking warriors and maidens in full costume. You may even get serenaded with Viking folk songs. It's all good fun and the menu has loads of Icelandic specialties. There's a Ikr4900 set menu, which includes *hákarl*, dried fish, braised lamb shank, fish soup and *skyr* (Icelandic yoghurt), served with a big glass of beer and a shot of Brennivín.

A Hansen (☎ 565 1130; www.ahansen.is; Vesturgata 4; mains Ikr1500-4200) Housed in an old house built in 1880, this upmarket restaurant has fine Icelandic food and a nice old-world atmosphere. During happy hour from 8pm to 10pm Sunday to Thursday, you get two beers for the price of one.

Tilveran (☎ 565 5250; Linnetstígur 1; meals Ikr1200-3000) On the main pedestrian street, this gourmet place serves pizza, pasta and Icelandic favourites.

Shalimar (☎ 544 2019; Strandgata 11; mains Ikr750-1550) This good-value Indian restaurant serves tasty Mughlai food, including stuffed naan bread and chicken tikka.

In the endless commercial estates east of the harbour are all sorts of fast-food restaurants, including a branch of **Hrói-Höttur Pizzeria** (☎ 565 2525; Hjallahraun 13).

Siam (☎ 555 4435; Dalshraun 11; mains Ikr900-1900) This cosy little restaurant has a good selection of spicy Thai dishes and an attached shop for Asian ingredients.

Gafl-Inn (☎ 555 4477; Dalshraun 13) This simple Icelandic restaurant serves a familiar menu of grills, fish and lamb.

Getting There & Away

The bus terminal is in front of the Fjórður shopping centre on Fjarðargata, by the harbour. From Reykjavík, take bus No 140 or 150 from Hlemmur or Lækjartorg. There's a special late service in the wee hours of Saturday and Sunday mornings.

If passengers have booked the **Flybus** (☎ 562 1011) to Keflavík airport it stops in Hafnarfjörður, but you'll need to confirm the exact location of the bus stop on booking. Buses to Keflavík also stop here if you book through Reykjavík's **BSÍ Bus Station** (☎ 591 1020; www.bsi.is).

Getting Around

Hafnarfjörður is small and easy to get around on foot. For a taxi, phone **BSH** (☎ 565 0888).

MOSFELLSBÆR

pop 6293

Mosfellsbær is one of Iceland's fastest growing towns and is teetering on the edge of becoming yet another Reykjavík suburb. Stræto buses run here from the Ártún bus stand in Reykjavík, and the town has all the usual amenities, including a geothermal pool, banks and restaurants and a camp site. The town has several crafts workshops and there is good walking in the surrounding hills, including long day treks to Þingvellir and the geothermal field at Nesjavellir – see the pamphlet *Útivist í Mosefellsbæ*, available from the town library.

There are several horse-riding schools in the area including the recommended **Laxness** (☎ 566 6179; www.laxness.is), just off the road to Þingvellir (Route 35). Two-hour trail rides cost Ikr3500 and all sorts of longer day-tours are available.

Sleeping

The town **camp site** (☎ 566 6754; camping per person Ikr400) is next to the river Varma and has toilets, sinks and showers. **Fitjar** (☎ 586 8337; www.fitjar-guesthouse.com; s/d Ikr4500/6500, with bathroom Ikr5500/7500, self-catering apt from Ikr8000) Just north of Mosfellsbær on a dirt road off Route 1, this stylish modern house has views over towards Reykjavík and is surrounded by wonderful countryside. There's a guest kitchen and laundry, and breakfast is Ikr900.

VIÐEY ISLAND

The tiny island of Viðey (Wood Island) lies 1km north of Reykjavík's Sundahöfn Harbour and is actually the tip of a long-extinct volcano. Although it only covers about 1.7 sq km the island has figured prominently in the history of Reykjavík and Iceland. Viðey was originally part of the estate of Iceland's first settler Ingólfur Arnarson and an Augustinian monastery operated here from 1226 to 1539, when it was sacked by Danish Lutherans. Iceland's last Catholic bishop, Jón Arason, seized the island by force in 1550 and built the fort Virkið to protect the island, but he was captured and beheaded during the Reformation and Viðey became crown property.

The sheriff Skúli Magnússon built the stone mansion Viðeyjarstofa here in 1751, following the designs of Nicolai Eigtved (who also designed the Amalienborg royal palace in Copenhagen). The house is the oldest stone building in Iceland and now houses an upmarket gourmet restaurant. The wooden Viðey church was constructed in 1774 and still contains all its original fittings. Over the next few centuries, Viðey was home to Iceland's first printing press and then a small

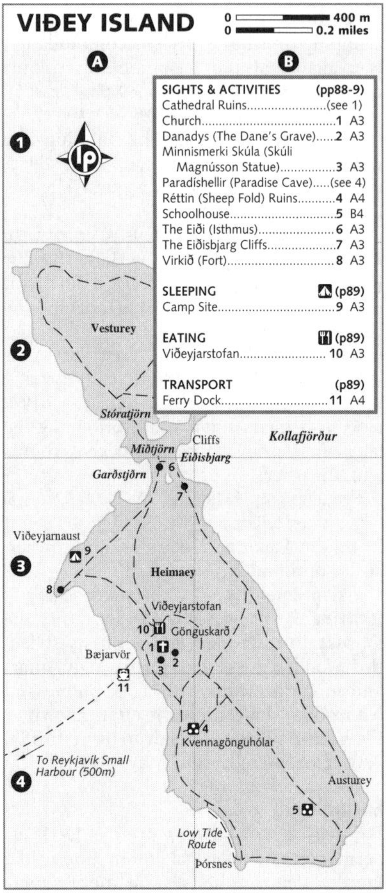

fishing cooperative, before it was donated to the city of Reykjavík in 1986, on the 200th anniversary of its municipal charter.

Sights

You can walk wherever you like on the island, but because of the nesting birds, it's usually best to stick to the marked walking tracks. The ferry docks by Viðeyjarstofa, where you'll find the **church** and **Danadys** (a grave for several Danish citizens who died here in times past). Several ruins have been uncovered and there's a small **monument to Skúli Magnússon**. The **Virkið fort** stood on the coast further north but there's nothing to see today. If you head southeast, you'll find the natural sheep fold **Réttin** and the tiny grotto **Paradíshellir** (Paradise Cave), and then the old **schoolhouse** at Sundbakki. Most of the south coast is a protected area for birds and is closed to visitors from May to June. In the north, you can see several ponds, the low cliffs of Eiðisbjarg and **basalt columns** at Vesturey at the northern tip of the island.

Sleeping & Eating

The quaint and sophisticated restaurant **Viðeyjarstofa** (☎ 568 1045; www.videyjarstofa.is; mains Ikr1690-3000) is housed in the old farmhouse; it serves gourmet Icelandic lunches and evening meals on Friday and Saturday. Advance reservations are required. It may be possible to camp at Viðeyjarnaust – ask permission from the restaurant.

Getting There & Away

The **Viðey ferry** (☎ 892 0099) operates from 1 June to 1 September. On weekdays, it leaves Sundahöfn at 1pm, 2pm and 3pm, returning half an hour later. On Saturday and Sunday, services run hourly from 1pm to 5pm. For restaurant patrons, there are evening sailings to Viðey at 7pm, 7.30pm and 8pm on Friday and Saturday, returning at 10pm and 11pm and midnight. Special sailings can be arranged for groups. The trip from Sundahöfn to Viðey takes about five minutes and the return fare is Ikr500/250 per adult/child.

LUNDEY AND AKUREY

The tiny islands of Lundey and Akurey are the only places near Reykjavík where you can see puffins. The puffin season is May to August – every year, about 10,000 pairs visit Lundey and 15,000 pairs visit Akurey. The **Viðey Ferry** (☎ 581 1010) offers puffin-spotting cruises lasting two to three hours, which leave from Reykjavík's small harbour daily at 10.30am and 4.45pm. Tickets cost Ikr2000/1000 adult/under-12s. Whale-watching tours from Reykjavík also do a circuit around Lundey (see p67 for details).

REYKJAVÍK SKI AREAS

From November to April, the highlands east of Reykjavík are cloaked in snow and many of the best slopes have been developed for skiing. Refreshingly, skiing in Iceland is no more expensive than in many other parts of Europe. There are three main ski areas close to Reykjavík – Bláfjöll, Hengill and Skálafell – and all have ski lifts, ski schools, and heated chalets with cafés. Ski passes are available on the slopes for Ikr1000/500 per adult/child per day, or you can buy a one-month pass for Ikr5000/2500. All the slopes are managed by the organisation **Skídasvædi** (☎ 510 6600; www.skidasvaedi.is; Fríkirkjuvegur 11, IS-101 Reykjavík), which can also provide passes. The ski schools can hire out skis, poles, boots and other gear at reasonable rates.

All these ski areas are popular for walking in the summer, particularly Hengill, which is a possible starting point for walks up to the Hengill volcano and lake Þingvallavatn. From mid-June to mid-August, **Reykjavík Excursions** (☎ 562 1011; www.re.is) runs three-hour evening tours to Bláfjöll (and Heiðmörk) for Ikr2900.

Bláfjöll

Iceland's premier ski area is the 84-sq-km **Bláfjallafólkvangur reserve** (☎ 561 8400), about 25km southeast of Reykjavík on Route 417, just off Route 1. It has nine ski lifts providing access to 11 ski slopes and there are also three cross-country ski trails up to 10km in length. Lifts operate 2pm to 9pm from Monday to Friday and 10am to 6pm at weekends. The service centre has a snack bar, several ski schools and a ski-hire shop.

Hengill & Skálafell

The ski area at **Hengill** (☎ 570 7711) is also about 25km southeast of Reykjavík on Route 378 (just off Route 1) and has five ski lifts, several ski schools, ski-hire and a chalet with a café. The small ski area at **Skálafell** (☎ 566 7095) is about 21km northeast of Reykjavík, near Mosfellsbær, just off Route 36. This is one of the smaller ski areas, with just three ski lifts, but there is good cross-country skiing in the area and Skálafell has several ski schools and a chalet with ski-hire and a café.

Getting There and Away

In the winter, there are special buses to the ski area at **Bláfjöll** (Ikr800) from the Mjódd bus terminal in Reykjavík. Inquire at the **BSÍ Bus Terminal** (☎ 552 2300). Buses between Reykjavík and Hveragerði pass within a few kilometres of the ski area at Hengill, while Reykjavík to Þingvellir buses pass close to Skálafell.

REYKJANES PENINSULA

The Reykjanes Peninsula is often the first, and sometimes only, bit of Iceland that many visitors see. From the bus between Keflavík airport and Reykjavík, it can seem like a barren and lifeless place, but the vast expanse of black lava has a mournful beauty that grows on you. Most of the settlements are squeezed into Miðnes, a small spur on the north coast of the peninsula, with the exception of Grindavík, which sits alone in the lava on the south coast of Reykjanes.

The largest town here is Keflavík, which is also the location for Iceland's main international airport. A road loops around the top of the spur to the fishing villages of Garður and Sandgerði, which are good places to see migrating birds. Southwest of Keflavík, a back road runs along the rugged west coast to Reykjanestá, a wonderful wild spot surrounded by strange lava formations. You can continue from here to Grindavík and then take the tarmac road back up to Keflavík, passing Iceland's most famous tourist attraction, the Blue Lagoon geothermal spa.

The southeast part of Reykjanes is mostly uninhabited, but the Reykjanesfólkvangur wilderness reserve is full of wild lava landscapes and geothermal springs. Public transport to Keflavík, Grindavík and the Blue Lagoon is fast and frequent, but you'll need private transport to reach more remote parts of the peninsula.

Buses within Reykjanes are provided by **SBK** (☎ 420 6000; www.sbk.is).

KEFLAVÍK & NJARÐVÍK

pop 10,944 (combined)

The twin towns of Keflavík and Njarðvík lie about 48km west of Reykjavík on the north coast of Reykjanes, in the small, flat Miðnes peninsula. Keflavík is the largest town on the Reykjanes peninsula, and was once one of Iceland's busiest trading centres. English and German traders established depots here as early as 1513 but the Danes established a trade monopoly in 1602 and Keflavík faded into the background until the monopoly was lifted in 1855. The modern town owes

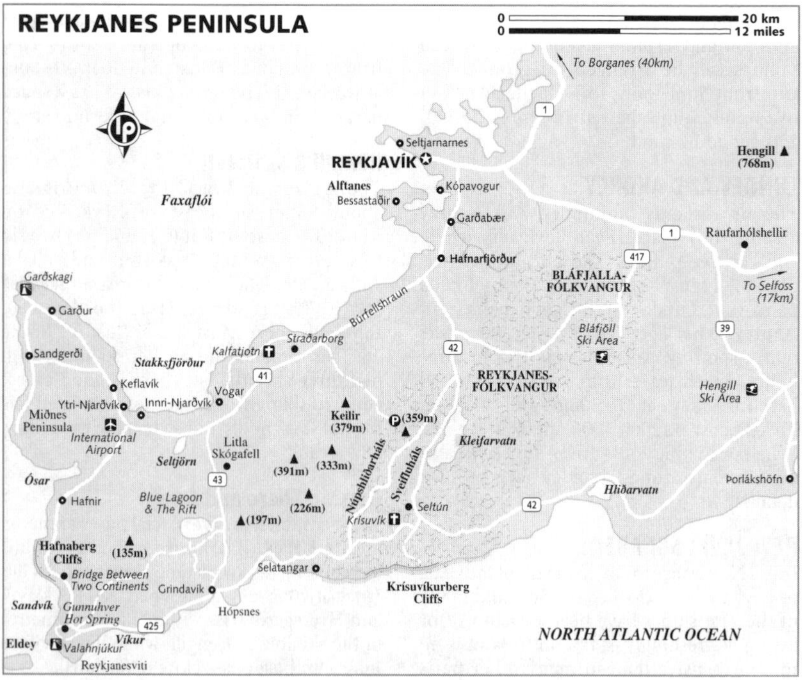

most of its prosperity to fishing, the nearby international airport and NATO military base, which has brought loads of investment into the area. There have been various attempts to oust the US military from the area over the years, but NATO operations were scaled back massively at the end of the Cold War and the issue has largely fallen off the political agenda.

East of Keflavík are the suburbs of Ytri-Njarðvík (Outer Njarðvík), which has a camp site, youth hostel and swimming pool, and forlorn little Innri-Njarðvík (Inner Njarðvík), which also has a youth hostel. The three settlements are often known simply as Reykjanesbær. This is probably the best place to base yourself on the peninsula, and there are good facilities for tourists, including a cinema, hotels, restaurants and bars.

Information

The main **tourist information centre** (☎ 425 0330; www.reykjanesbaer.is; 6am-8pm Mon-Fri, noon-5pm Sat & Sun) is at the Keflavík International Airport, but in summer there's a small tourist office in the **library** (☎ 421 5155; Hafnargata 57; 10am-8pm Mon-Fri, 10am-4pm Sat). Net access is available for Ikr250 per 30 minutes and staff can provide a free map of Keflavík and the map booklet *Enjoy More of Reykjanes*. ATMs and foreign exchange desks are located at the Íslandsbanki and Landsbankinn on Hafnargata.

Sights

An old house by the docks now houses the local folk museum **Byggðasafn Suðurnesi** (☎ 421 3796; Vatnsnesvegur 8; adult/under-18 Ikr 450/free; 12.30-7pm May-Sep). In a nearby warehouse, the **Duushús** (☎ 421 6700; Grófin; adult/under-18 Ikr450/free; 11am-6pm May-Sep) has an exhibition of miniature ship models, collected by a local sea captain. In the harbour itself, keep an eye out for the *Íslendingur*, a reconstruction Viking longship built in 2000 by a direct descendent of Leifur Eiríksson. He successfully sailed it from Iceland to America, proving that it was indeed possible that the Vikings were the first Europeans to reach North America.

Close to the Bonus supermarket at Ytri-Njarðvík is a reconstructed turf farmhouse containing a small **folk museum** (Stekkjarkot; ☎ 421 3796; admission Ikr300; by appointment). The church at Innri-Njarðvík is one of only a few stone churches in Iceland and you can walk from here to the nearby sea cliffs, which have nesting seabirds.

If you have your own transport, it's worth a detour to **Keflavík International Airport** to see the interesting sculptures in front of the terminal. Magnús Tómasson's Þotuhreiður (Jet Nest), resembles a Concorde emerging from an egg, while Rúrí's Regnbogi (Rainbow) is a glittering arch of steel and coloured glass. Many people regard these as the best public sculptures in the country.

Activities

Keflavík has the inevitable **geothermal swimming pool** (Keflavík Swimming Pool; ☎ 421 1500; Sunnubraut; adult/child Ikr200/100; 6.45am-9pm Mon-Fri, 8am-5pm Sat, 9am-4pm Sun), with all the usual facilities.

You can go scuba diving with **Sportkofunarskóli** (☎ 411 7100; www.dive.is; scuba dives min 2 people from Ikr1500). Dry-suit dives are possible in the spooky rift between the North American and European plates at the bottom of lake Þingvellir or off the coast at Keflavík. Snorkelling with dolphins can also be arranged.

Whale-watching trips (☎ 421 7777; www.dolphin.is) are available on the M/S *Moby Dick* for Ikr2700/1400 per adult/child. Trips leave at 10am daily from April to October, and also at 1.30pm in July and August – whales are seen on 97% of trips. Fishing trips can be arranged through **Sjóstangaveiðiferðir** (☎ 897 3332) or **Kaffi Duus** (☎ 699 5625), which also offer whale-watching tours. For a morning of deep-sea fishing, you'll pay around Ikr5000 per person. Both companies are based at the small harbour on Duusgata.

Sleeping

BUDGET

The well-equipped **camping ground** (☎ 421 7800; camping per person Ikr500) is next to the Samkaup supermarket in Ytri-Njarðvík, about 1km south of central Keflavík. However, it may move so inquire first at the tourist office.

There are two hostels in rather inconvenient locations in Njarðvík, but both offer free airport transfers.

Strönd Hostel (☎ 421 6211; strond@centrum.is; cnr Tjarnargata & Njarðvíkurbraut; sb/s/d Ikr190/2100/3800) Down by the shore in Ytri-Njarðvík, this building houses a slightly run-down but cheap youth hostel. There's a guest kitchen and the hostel is open year-round.

KEFLAVÍK & NJARÐVÍK

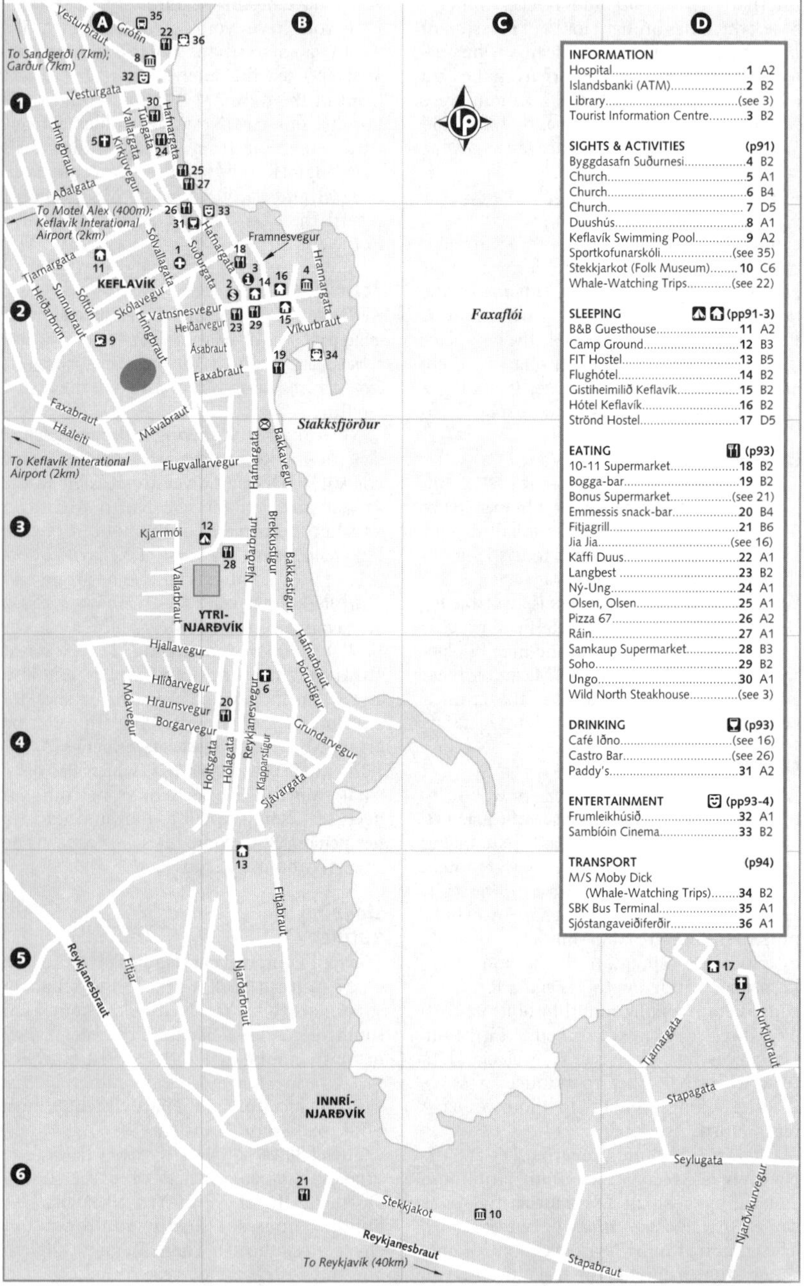

INFORMATION
Hospital ... 1 A2
Islandsbanki (ATM) ... 2 B2
Library ... (see 3)
Tourist Information Centre ... 3 B2

SIGHTS & ACTIVITIES (p91)
Byggdasafn Suðurnesi ... 4 B2
Church ... 5 A1
Church ... 6 B4
Church ... 7 D5
Duushús ... 8 A1
Keflavík Swimming Pool ... 9 A2
Sportkofunarskóli ... (see 35)
Stekkjarkot (Folk Museum) ... 10 C6
Whale-Watching Trips ... (see 22)

SLEEPING (pp91-3)
B&B Guesthouse ... 11 A2
Camp Ground ... 12 B3
FIT Hostel ... 13 B5
Flughótel ... 14 B2
Gistiheimilið Keflavík ... 15 B2
Hótel Keflavík ... 16 B2
Strönd Hostel ... 17 D5

EATING (p93)
10-11 Supermarket ... 18 B2
Bogga-bar ... 19 B2
Bonus Supermarket ... (see 21)
Emmessis snack-bar ... 20 B4
Fitjagrill ... 21 B6
Jia Jia ... (see 16)
Kaffi Duus ... 22 A1
Langbest ... 23 B2
Ný-Ung ... 24 A1
Olsen, Olsen ... 25 A1
Pizza 67 ... 26 A2
Ráin ... 27 A1
Samkaup Supermarket ... 28 B3
Soho ... 29 B2
Ungo ... 30 A1
Wild North Steakhouse ... (see 3)

DRINKING (p93)
Café Iðno ... (see 16)
Castro Bar ... (see 26)
Paddy's ... 31 A2

ENTERTAINMENT (pp93-4)
Frumleikhúsið ... 32 A1
Sambíóin Cinema ... 33 B2

TRANSPORT (p94)
M/S Moby Dick (Whale-Watching Trips) ... 34 B2
SBK Bus Terminal ... 35 A1
Sjóstangaveiðiferðir ... 36 A1

FIT Hostel (☎ 421 8889; www.fithostel.is; Fitjabraut 6; sb/s/d Ikr1700/2800/4800) In an industrial estate just off Route 41, this is the better of the two hostels and has good facilities. You can catch buses to Reykjavík and Keflavík in front of the hostel.

MID-RANGE & TOP END

There are a few standard B&Bs in town.

B&B Guesthouse (☎ 421 8989; Hringbraut 92; s/d Ikr4900/6600) This guesthouse is painted a curious green and yellow, but it's comfortable enough inside. Call from the airport for a free pick-up.

Gistiheimilið Keflavík (☎ 420 7000; www.hotelkeflavik.is; Vatnsnesvegur 9; s/d Ikr7800/9800) Run by Hótel Keflavík, this is a pricey option, but airport transfers are free and you have use of the hotel facilities.

Two places in town claim to be *the* airport hotel and both offer free transfers to and from the airport.

Flughótel (☎ 421 5222; www.icehotel.is; Hafnargata 57; Keflavík; s/d with TV, bathroom & phone from Ikr14,900/19,500) This large custom-built hotel is a fairly typical Icelandair property but rooms are nice and there is a good business centre with free Internet access. There's no point paying extra for the deluxe rooms – the ordinary rooms are just as comfortable. In winter, rates drop by 20%.

Hótel Keflavík (☎ 420 7000; www.hotelkeflavik.is; Vatnsnesvegur 12-14; s/d with TV, bathroom, minibar & phone Ikr17,800/20,800) Almost next door to Flughótel, Hótel Keflavík is friendlier and there's a good restaurant, a fitness centre and a glasshouse bar. The deluxe rooms are worth the extra Ikr2000, and have CD players, large TVs and bathtubs.

Motel Alex (☎ 421 2800; www.alex.is; Aðalgata; s/d Ikr5600/7500) The closest place to the airport is this modernist motel, just off Route 41 close to the airport turn-off. Airport transfers are free and there's a car hire desk and guest kitchen.

Eating

Self-caterers should head to the Samkaup supermarket by the camp site, the Nóatún supermarket on Túngata or the Bonus supermarket on the way to Njarðvík.

For quick eats on the hoof, there are several drive-through snack bars, including **Bogga-bar** (☎ 421 5051; cnr Vikurbraut & Hafnargata) by the harbour and **Ný-Ung** (☎ 421 8000; 12 Hafnargata) and **Ungo** (☎ 421 1544; 6 Hafnargata) on Hafnargata. All serve the usual chips, hot dogs and burgers.

Hafnargata, Keflavík's main street, has numerous places to eat.

Olsen, Olsen (☎ 421 4457; Hafnargata 17; snacks Ikr395-795) Decked out like a 1950s American diner, this little café serves up the usual burger options and pitta sandwiches.

Pizza 67 (☎ 421 4067; Hafnargata 30; meals Ikr1200-2200) Probably the most chilled-out place in town is this new-age pizza parlour on the main street. Delivery is free anywhere in Keflavík or Njarðvík.

Ráin (☎ 421 4601; Hafnargata 19a; mains Ikr1490-4300) Keflavík's finest restaurant serves a familiar menu of Icelandic fish, lamb and beef, in a pleasant dining room overlooking the ocean.

Wild North Steakhouse (☎ 421 5222; Hafnargata 57; mains Ikr900-1800) In the same mall as the library and tourist desk, this place has good-value steaks and grills.

Soho (☎ 421 5600; Hafnargata 61; mains Ikr990-1290) Although it sounds like a Chinese restaurant, this place serves a bit of everything, from noodles to nachos, and prices aren't bad by local standards.

Langbest (☎ 421 4777; Hafnargata 62; snacks Ikr390-1660) Across the road from Soho, this snack bar and canteen is a popular youth hangout and serves burgers, grills and pizzas.

Jia Jia (☎ 420 7011; Hótel Keflavík, Vatnsnesvegur 12-14; dishes Ikr1880-3280) The restaurant at Hótel Keflavík serves up authentic Chinese food and offers kids portions for Ikr680.

Kaffi Duus (☎ 421 7080; Duusgata 10; mains Ikr450-2450) Near the harbour and the bus station, this café has a nice atmosphere and a good selection of snacks and more-substantial meals. You can get fish and chips for around Ikr1900.

In Njarðvík, the only food choices are the drive-through **Emmessis snack bar** or the **Fitjagrill** (☎ 421 3448) at the Orkan petrol station – both are out of town towards Keflavík on Route 41.

Entertainment

As far as bars go, the best spots are the **Castro Bar** (☎ 421 4067; Hafnargata 30), **Paddy's** (☎ 421 7888; Hafnargata) and **Café Iðno** (☎ 420 7011; Vatnsnesvegur 12-14), the glasshouse bar at the Hótel Keflavík.

The large **Sambíóin cinema** (☎ 421 1170; Hafnargata 33) shows imported blockbusters in English nightly.

There are occasional theatrical performances at **Frumleikhúsið** (☎ 421 2540; www.lk.is/frumleikhusid; Vesturbraut 17) – ask at the tourist office for details.

Getting There & Away

AIR

With the exception of flights to Greenland and the Faroe Islands, all of Iceland's international flights arrive into and depart from Keflavík International Airport. For more information see p307.

BUS

There are four or five daily runs between the **BSÍ terminal** (Ikr1020, 1hr) in Reykjavík and Reykjanesbær.

Getting Around

TO/FROM THE AIRPORT

Most of the hotels and guesthouses offer free transfers to and from the airport for their guests. A taxi will cost about Ikr2000 – call ☎ 421 4141 or 421 1515. For information on the Flybus between the airport and Reykjavík, see p82.

BUS

As well as long-distance buses, **SBK** (☎ 420 6000; www.sbk.is) runs local buses (Ikr100) between Keflavík and Njarðvík and around Miðnes – there are services every 30 minutes or so between 7am and 6pm.

WESTERN REYKJANES

The western end of the Reykjanes Peninsula is rugged and exposed, but several fishing villages are clustered around the top of Miðnes and along the west coast.

Garður

If you follow Route 41 on from Keflavík, you'll reach the **Garðskagi lighthouse**, which has been partly converted into a museum. The old lighthouse tower on the sea wall is now a lookout to spot seabirds and an outbuilding at the new lighthouse contains a small **folk museum** (☎ 422 7220; admission Ikr200; 1-5pm May-Aug). The sandbars and skerries offshore are important feeding grounds for migratory birds. There's a tranquil, free **camping area** (☎ 893 8219) by the lighthouse.

Sandgerði

Around the top of Miðnes, this industrious fishing village has the interesting **Nature Centre** (☎ 423 7551; www.sandgerdi.is; Gerðavegur 1; adult/child Ikr300/200; 9am-5pm Jun-Sep) where you can see stuffed and mounted examples of Icelandic creatures and a small aquarium. There are some quite nice beaches on the coast south of Sandgerði, and the surrounding marshes are frequented by more than 170 species of birds. The Nature Centre runs guided nature tours in summer. About 7km south of Sandgerði, you can walk to the ruins of the fishing village **Bátsendar**, which was destroyed by the sea in 1798.

You can get a meal at **Vitinn** (☎ 423 775; Vitatorg 7) or **Mamma Mía** (☎ 423 7377; Hafnargata 5).

Hafnir

Below Miðnes on the edge of vast black lava flows, this fading fishing village has a small **marine aquarium** (☎ 421 6958; Krikjuvogur 13; Ikr300; 2-5.30pm Jun-Aug, noon-4pm Sep-May) where you can see Icelandic fish, crabs and shellfish. Nearby are several decaying sea-shacks and the anchor of the 'ghost ship' *Jamestown*, which drifted ashore mysteriously in 1870 with a full cargo of timber but no crew. About 8km south of Hafnir, a 30-minute walk from the road will take you to the sea cliffs of **Hafnaberg**, an important nesting area for sea birds.

Reykjanesviti

In the far southwest of the peninsula, the landscape breaks down into wild volcanic crags and sea cliffs. The area is an important geothermal field and several factories exploit the natural heat below the surface to produce salt from seawater. At **Valahnjúkur**, a dirt track leads down to the desolate cliffs where you can clamber up to the ruins of the oldest lighthouse in Iceland, built in 1878. It was destroyed in a devastating earthquake and a new lighthouse was built inland in 1908. It's a wonderful, wild spot and well worth a visit. Also interesting is the scalding **hot spring** at Gunnuhver, back on the main road.

The vast lava flows at Reykjanesviti were spewed out by a series of small shield volcanoes, including Skálafell and Eldvarpahraun. The area is criss-crossed by walking tracks that are marked on the *Enjoy More of Reykjanes* map, available from most tourist offices including the offices in Keflavík and at the international airport. However the terrain is tough and not all the paths are clearly marked. One easy detour from the main road is to the so-called **bridge between two continents**, which spans a sand-filled gulf between the North American and European plates.

About 14km off the tip of Reykjanes is the flat-topped rocky crag of **Eldey**, which is home to the world's largest gannet *(Sula bassana)* colony. Some claim the last of the great auk was killed and eaten here, though this is refuted by Faroe islanders, who insist the event occurred at Stóra Dímun. Today, Eldey is protected as a bird reserve but you may be able to visit on a tour – inquire at the tourist office in Keflavík.

Getting There & Away

On weekdays, **SBK** (☎ 420 6000; www.sbk.is) has regular daily buses between Keflavík and Hafnir (Ikr100; 20 minutes), four buses every weekday to Sandgerði (Ikr250; 20 minutes) and two buses every weekday to Garður (Ikr250; 20 minutes). Heading back to Keflavík, you should pre-book with SBK. You'll need a private vehicle to access the area around Reykjanesviti.

BLUE LAGOON

Iceland's most famous tourist attraction is hidden away among tortured black lava flows just off the road between Keflavík and Grindavík. The **Blue Lagoon** (Bláa Lónið; ☎ 420 8800; www.bluelagoon.is; adult/senior/12-15 years/under-12 Ikr1200/900/600/free; 9am-9pm mid-May–Aug, 10am-8pm Sep–mid-May) geothermal spa owes its existence to the nearby Svartsengi geothermal power plant, which is powered by superheated seawater drawn from deep bore holes in the lava. After the steam has passed through the turbines, huge condensers convert it back into water, which is channelled into a huge artificial lagoon that permanently hovers at 37–39°C.

The milky blue waters are rich in blue-green algae (cyanobacteria), mineral salts and fine silica mud which condition and exfoliate the skin – think of it as a beauty spa that men can visit without feeling embarrassed! The lagoon sits in a surreal landscape of black lava and sheets of steam blow across the surface of the water. With the roaring silver steam vents of the power plant as a backdrop, the whole place feels like a set from a sci-fi movie.

The lagoon has been imaginatively landscaped with hot pots, wooden decks and a piping hot waterfall that delivers a powerful hydraulic massage. The water is always hottest near the vents where it emerges and the surface is several degrees warmer than the bottom. The floor of the lagoon is coated with silica mud which many people use as an improvised face-pack. It should go without saying that lounging in the soothing waters is fabulously relaxing.

You can rent towels (Ikr300), swimming costumes (Ikr350) and robes (Ikr700) but the water can corrode silver and gold so leave watches and jewellery in your locker. Be extra careful walking over the wooden bridges in the lagoon – they can be devilishly slippery.

The complex also includes a snack bar, an upmarket **restaurant** (mains Ikr1190-3790) serving lots of Asian-inspired seafood dishes, and a shop selling very pricey health and beauty products made from mineral salts and silica mud. At the attached spa, you can get massages (from Ikr1300 for 10 minutes) and other beauty treatments.

Gjáin

Behind the Blue Lagoon at the geothermal power station, **Gjáin** (the Rift; ☎ 426 8911; adult/12-15 years/under-12 Ikr500/250/free; 10am-5pm mid-May–Aug, 10am-4pm Sep–mid-May) is an interactive museum devoted to geothermal energy, earthquakes, volcanoes, glaciers and geology. The high-tech displays are quite interesting, though the entry fee is a little steep for what you get.

Sleeping & Eating

There's nowhere to stay in the actual Blue Lagoon complex.

Northern Light Inn (☎ 426 8650; www.northernlightinn.is; s/d in summer Ikr10,500/15,000, in winter Ikr8400/10,500; ☒) This large bungalow-style hotel has spacious rooms with fridge, phone, TV and bathroom – it's just across the lava from the power plant and Blue Lagoon. Free transfers are provided to the Blue Lagoon and international airport.

Getting There & Away

The easiest way to get here is with **Þingvallaleið Bus Service** (☎ 511 2600; www.bluelagoonbus.is) from the BSÍ Bus Terminal in Reykjavík, which leaves every few hours from 10am to 6pm. In the opposite direction, the last bus leaves the Blue Lagoon at 9.45pm (8pm in winter). There are also daily buses from the Blue Lagoon to the international airport at 12.40pm, 2.15pm and 4pm (also at 9.45pm in summer). The fare for both these routes is Ikr850.

Alternatively, choose a tour with **Reykjavík Excursions** (☎ 562 1011; www.re.is). Day trips from Reykjavík with entry to the Blue Lagoon cost Ikr3100 and leave at 11am. You can opt to finish up at the international airport. You can also make the Blue Lagoon your first stop when you arrive in Iceland – a bus leaves the airport at 4.30pm and goes to the Blue Lagoon and on to Reykjavík for Ikr2900 including entry fees. Iceland Excursions and Destination Iceland offer similar tours.

GRINDAVÍK

pop 2336

The fishing village of Grindavík is the only settlement on the south coast of Reykjanes. There are some interesting old buildings down by the harbour, but most of Grindavík is made up of modern prefab houses and the centre is looking a little run-down these days. Grindavík's heating and power comes from the Svartsengi geothermal power next to the Blue Lagoon.

Sights

The main attraction here is the museum **Saltfisksetur Íslands** (☎ 420 1190; www.saltfisksetur.is; Hafnargata 12a; 11am-6pm daily; adult/8-16 years/under-8 Ikr500/250/free), dedicated to the fish-salting industry – there's even a pile of salt-fish in the corner to provide the authentic saltfish smell! The same building houses a small **tourist office** (☎ 420 1109; www.grindavik.is; Víkurbraut 62), open the same hours.

There's a good modern **swimming pool** (☎ 426 7555; Austurvegur) and nearby is a rather fanciful reconstruction of a **Viking temple**. The **Hópsnes Peninsula**, just east of Grindavík, has a lighthouse and a 7km-long hiking trail with plaques about local shipwrecks. Longer walks are detailed in the booklet *Enjoy More of Reykjanes* – an interesting 8km walk runs up to the lava cave at **Litla Skógafell**. The horse farm **Víkhestar** (☎ 426 8303; Vesturbraut 15) can arrange riding tours in the local area.

Sleeping & Eating

In summer, you can camp for free at the Austurvegur **camp site** (☎ 420 1190) near the swimming pool, which has toilets, sinks and showers.

Gistiheimilið Fiskanes (☎ 897 6388; Hafnargata 17; sb/s Ikr1700/2700) This large industrial building at the docks has decent rooms, a lounge and a cafeteria.

For reasonably priced meals, you have the choice of the friendly **Sjómannastofan Vör** (☎ 426 8570; Hafnargata 9) by the harbour, the pub **Cactus** (☎ 426 9999; Hafnargata 6), or the pizzeria **Mamma Mía** (☎ 426 7860; Víkurbraut 31) at the Esso petrol station. You can get a meal at any of these places for Ikr750 to Ikr2500.

Sjávarperlan (☎ 426 9700; Stamphólsvegur 2; Ikr1400-3800) Next to the swimming pool, this posh wooden restaurant is recommended for great seafood and meaty grills.

Getting There & Away

In summer, buses between Reykjavík and Grindavík run every few hours from 10am-6pm (Ikr1020), passing the Blue Lagoon. For Keflavík, you'll have to change at the Grindavík junction on Route 41.

VOGAR

The small industrial village of Vogar isn't particularly interesting, but there's a motel, a restaurant and a **swimming pool** (☎ 424 6545) with a small, free camping area. If you follow the small road east along the coast, you'll pass the appealing shingled church at **Kalfatjotn** and the ruins of a circular stone animal enclosure at **Staðarborg**.

Accommodation is available at **Motel Best** (☎ 886 4664; www.motelbest.is; Stapavegur 7; s/d Ikr4900/6900, with bathroom Ikr6900/8900) and you can get meals at **Mamma Mía** (☎ 424 6700; Iðndalur).

REYKJANESFÓLKVANGUR

This 300-sq-km wilderness reserve was established in 1975 to protect the lava formations spewed out from the volcanoes that follow the Reykjanes Ridge. The centrepiece of this scenic area is **Kleifarvatn**, a deep blue lake with submerged hot springs and black-sand beaches, surrounded by eroded lava cliffs. Nearby is the important geothermal zone at **Krísuvík**. The bumpy dirt road discourages a lot of visitors, but you can easily get here in a conventional hire car.

Reykjanesfólkvangur is crossed by dozens of hiking tracks, which are detailed in the pamphlet maps *Walking & Hiking in Krísuvík* (in English) and *Reykjanesfólkvangur* (in Icelandic), available from the tourist office at Keflavík. Popular walks include the loop around lake **Kleifarvatn** and the tracks along the craggy **Sveifluháls** and **Núpshliðarháls** ridges. On the south coast of the peninsula are the remnants of **Selatangar**, an abandoned fishing station with plentiful bird-life, reached by a 2km hike from the dirt road to Grindavík (Route 427). In the opposite direction, unsurfaced Route 42 runs across the lava to Þorlákshöfn, passing through more dramatic volcanic scenery.

For serious hiking, pick up a copy of the park map at the **Náttúruvernd Ríkisins** (Nature Conservation Agency; Map p60) office in Reykjavík (see p44).

Kleifarvatn

This spooky 10-sq-km lake sits in a dramatic volcanic fissure, surrounded by soft lava cliffs that have been sculpted into wild shapes by the wind. There are several black-sand beaches and legend has it that a worm-like monster lurks somewhere in the hidden depths. Steam billows out of the ground from dozens of hot springs at the south end of the lake. A walking trail runs right around the lake offering dramatic views and the eerie crunch of volcanic cinders underfoot.

Krísuvík & Seltún

About 2km south of Kleifarvatn is the geothermal field of Austurengjar, often called **Krísuvík** after the abandoned settlement further south. Even by Icelandic standards, this is a geologically volatile area – the temperature below the surface is 200°C and the water is boiling as it emerges from the ground. A borehole was sunk here to provide energy for Hafnarfjörður during the 1990s, but it exploded without warning in 1999 and the project was abandoned.

The cluster of hot springs and mud pots at **Seltún** has been opened up to the public, and a series of wooden boardwalks weaves between the bubbling pools. The mud around the fumaroles shimmers with opal colours from the strange minerals bubbling up from under the ground. The smell of rotten eggs from the clouds of sulphurous steam will probably stay with you for the rest of the day. Nearby, you can climb up to the rim of the cinder cone **Bleikholl**.

Near the junction of Routes 42 and 427, a dirt track leads down to the coast at **Krísuvíkurberg**, where puffins, guillemots and other sea birds nest in summer. Further west along route 427 is **Krísuvík church**, which was built in 1857 and restored by the National Museum in 1964.

Getting There & Away

There is no public transport to the park, but you can get here by organised tour. Reykjavík Excursions and other tour agents offer six-hour tours through Reykjanesfólkvangur and on to the Salt Fish Museum in Grindavík and the Blue Lagoon. It leaves Reykjavík at 1.30pm and costs Ikr5000, including entry fees.

Otherwise, you'll need a bike or hire car, or you could try hitching or walking from Hafnarfjörður along Route 42.

Southwest Iceland

CONTENTS

Conveniently, many of Iceland's most famous natural wonders are clustered together in the southwest corner of the country. Within a few hours of the capital, you can see live volcanoes, bubbling sulphur springs, spouting geysers and frosty icecaps. Most of these sights can easily be reached from Reykjavík on day trips, so things can get pretty crowded here in summer, but there are plenty of out-of-the-way places where you can enjoy the incredible peace and quiet of the Icelandic landscape without interruption.

East of Reykjavík is the 'Golden Circle', where you'll find Iceland's 'big three' tourist attractions: Þingvellir, Geysir and Gullfoss. The area is packed with day-trippers and the click of camera shutters can be deafening, but it's worth braving the crowds. The national park at Þingvellir is gorgeous, the geyser at Geysir goes off as regularly as clockwork, and the Gullfoss waterfall roars into the gorge like a thundering steam train.

For more tranquillity, visit the tiny fishing villages south of Selfoss or take a horse-riding tour at Hella. Inland from Hella you can climb the brooding volcano Hekla or explore ancient farm ruins in the Þjórsárdalur valley. Continuing southeast, Þórsmörk is one of Iceland's premier hiking destinations, tucked between two towering icecaps. The nearby coast around Skógar and Vík offers fantastic lava formations, waterfalls and Iceland's best folk museum, and just offshore are the charming Vestmannaeyjar (Westman Islands), the scene of a famous volcanic eruption in 1973.

TOP FIVE

- Soaking up Iceland's rich cultural heritage at the folk museum in **Skógar** (p121)
- Waiting for a spout at the famous geyser at **Geysir** (p105)
- Riding an Icelandic horse through the lava fields near **Hella** (p115)
- Walking through the glorious glacial valleys around **Þórsmörk** (p119)
- Admiring the basalt columns and black sand beach at Reynisfjara near **Vík** (p122)

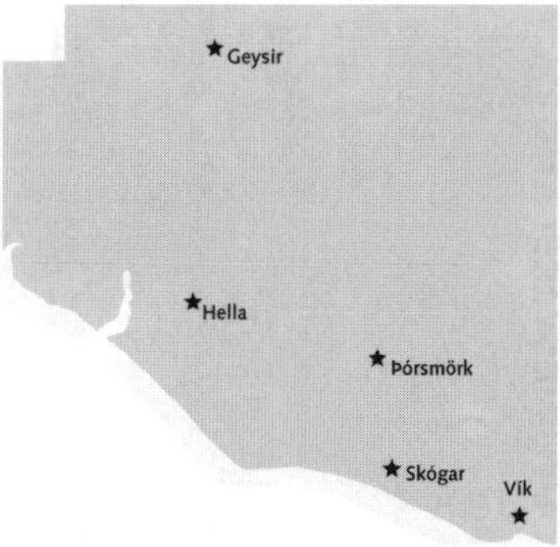

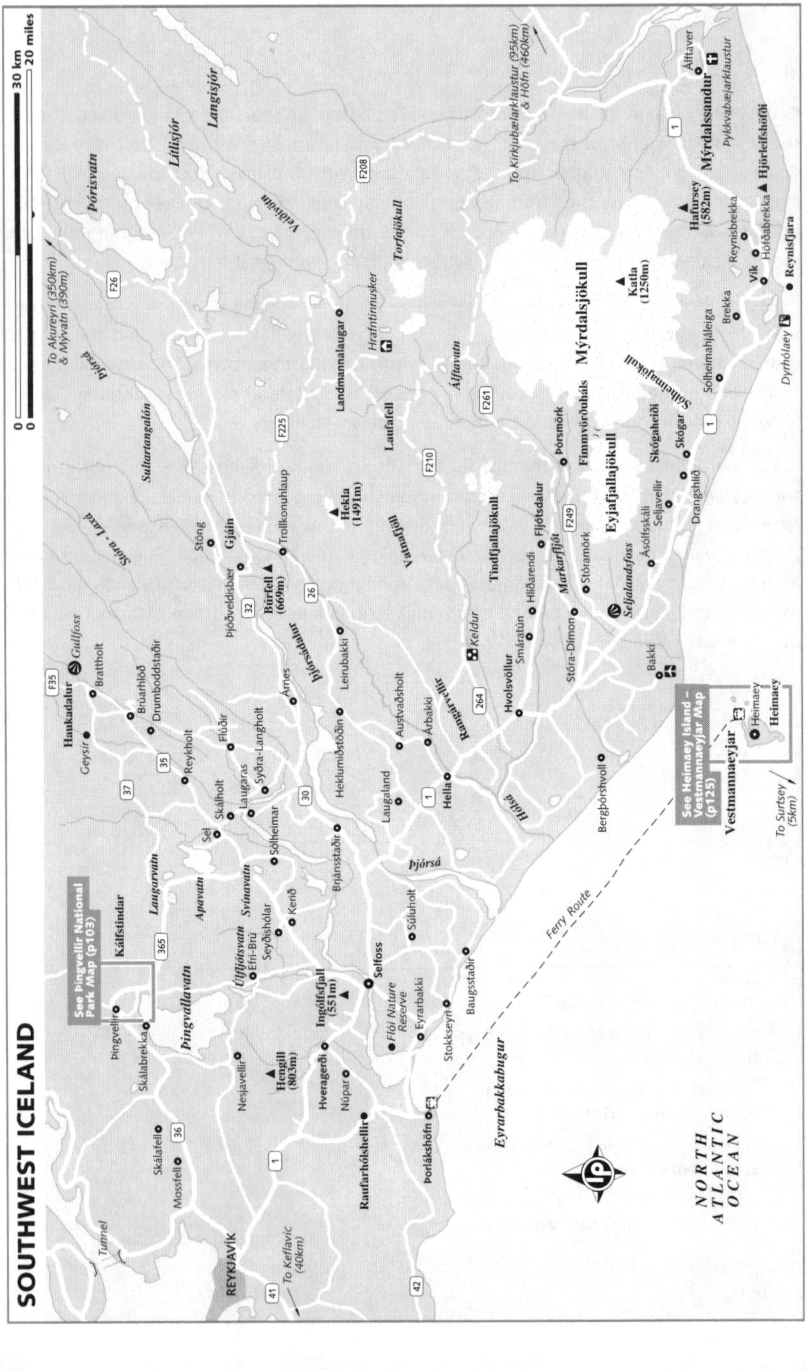
SOUTHWEST ICELAND
0 30 km
0 20 miles
REYKJAVÍK
Tunnel
To Keflavík (40km)
Mosfell
Skálafell
Raufarhólshellir
Hveragerði
Núpar
Hengill (803m)
Nesjavellir
Skálabrekka
Þingvellir
See Þingvellir National Park Map (p103)
Þingvallavatn
Kálfstindar
Úlfljótsvatn
Efri-Brú
Ingólfsfjall (551m)
Selfoss
Flói Nature Reserve
Eyrarbakki
Stokkseyri
Þorlákshöfn
Eyrarbakkabugur
Baugsstaðir
Sűluholt
Seyðishólar
Kerið
Apavatn
Laugarvatn
Svínavatn
Sólheimar
Sel
Skálholt
Laugaras
Reykholt
Syðra-Langholt
Flúðir
Brúarhlöð
Drumboddsstaðir
Haukadalur
Geysir
Gullfoss
Bratthólt
Árnes
Brjánsstaðir
Þjórsá
Heklumiðstöðin
Laugaland
Hella
Austvaðsholt
Árbakki
Rangárvellir
Leirubakki
Þjórsárdalur
Búrfell (669m)
Þjóðveldisbær
Gjáin
Stöng
Trollkonuhlaup
Hekla (1491m)
Stóra - Laxá
Sultartangalón
Þjórsá
To Akureyri (350km) & Mývatn (390m)
Þórisvatn
Veiðivötn
Litlisjór
Langisjór
Landmannalaugar
Hrafntinnusker
Torfajökull
Laufafell
Vatnafjöll
Keldur
Hvolsvöllur
Smáratún
Hlíðarendi
Tindfjallajökull
Fljótsdalur
Markarfljót
Stóramörk
Stóra-Dímon
Seljalandsfoss
Bergþórshvoll
Hólsá
Bakki
Álftavatn
Þórsmörk
Fimmvörðuháls
Eyjafjallajökull
Mýrdalsjökull
Katla (1250m)
Sólheimajökull
Skógaheiði
Skógar
Drangshlíð
Seljavellir
Ásólfsskáli
Sólheimahjáleiga
Brekka
Reynisbrekka
Vík
Höfðabrekka
Hafursey (582m)
Hjörleifshöfði
Mýrdalssandur
Þykkvabæjarklaustur
Álftaver
Reynisfjara
Dyrhólaey
To Kirkjubæjarklaustur (95km) & Höfn (460km)
Vestmannaeyjar
Heimaey
See Heimaey Island – Vestmannaeyjar Map (p125)
To Surtsey (5km)
Ferry Route
NORTH ATLANTIC OCEAN
1
30
32
26
35
36
37
41
42
264
365
F26
F35
F208
F210
F225
F249
F261

GETTING THERE & AROUND

Getting to southwest Iceland from Reykjavík is easy. Regular buses run from the BSÍ Bus Terminal in Reykjavík to most towns in the area, and Vestmannaeyjar is served by daily flights from Reykjavík and ferries from Þorlákshöfn near Hveragerði. Many of the bus routes operate like mini tours – you can break the journey as many times as you want along the route and continue your journey later on the same ticket. Conventional organised tours are also a convenient way to see this area – see p303 for some suggestions. Most roads in the southwest are suitable for a conventional hire car, which can often work out cheaper than an organised tour or public bus.

For information on bus routes and schedules in the southwest, contact **BSÍ** (☎ 591 1000; www.bsi.is) or the bus company **Austurleið-SBS** (☎ 545 1717; www.austurleid.is). If you're heading for Vestmannaeyjar, you have the choice of flying with **Íslandsflug** (☎ 570 8090; www.islandsflug.is) or taking the car ferry **Herjólfur** (☎ 483 3413; www.herjolfur.is) from Þorlákshöfn.

THE GOLDEN CIRCLE

The region immediately east from Reykjavík, popularly known as the 'Golden Circle', is probably the most visited part of Iceland. Here you'll find Iceland's 'big three' tourist destinations: Gullfoss (a wild and roaring waterfall), Geysir (home to the original geyser) and Þingvellir (the original site of the Icelandic parliament). All three sites are mobbed by coach-tour groups throughout the summer but are still well worth visiting for their undeniable natural beauty. If possible, hire a car rather than coming on a tour so that you can detour off the well-trodden path and enjoy some of the other natural highlights of this area. Nearby are several geothermal villages with hot springs and geothermal swimming pools, and you can make a scenic side-trip along the Þjórsárdalur valley for views of the volcano Hekla.

ÞINGVELLIR

This picturesque valley sits in the midst of undulating lava flows about 23km east of Reykjavík and is probably the nation's most important historical site. The Icelandic parliament, the Alþing, convened here for the first time in AD 930. As with many saga sites, there isn't much evidence of Þingvellir's impressive history on the ground, but the surrounding landscape is stunning. The terrain is scarred by rocky fissures, streams trickle between crumpled lava flows and waterfalls tumble into dramatic canyons. The lava plain is cloaked in moss and dwarf birch forest, and the landscape transforms into brilliant reds, oranges and yellows every autumn.

In 1928 the Icelandic government set Þingvellir aside as the country's first *Þjódarðurinn* (national park). The site of the Alþing at the western edge of the park has been developed for tourists, but the remainder of the park is pretty much left to nature. By the turn-off to the lake at Leirar, there's a **visitors centre** (☎ 482 2660; www.thingvellir.is; 8.30am-8pm, closed Oct-Apr) with a café, bookshop and information centre. There's also an **interpretive centre** (admission free; 9am-5pm Apr-Oct) on the ridge above the Almannagjá fault, with multimedia displays about the site.

History

The Icelandic parliament or Alþing was established at Þingvellir in 930 by the descendants of Ingólfur Arnarson, Iceland's first settler. Until 1271 every important decision affecting Iceland was argued out on this plain, from marriages to land contracts and the passing of new laws. It was at Þingvellir that Christianity was accepted as the national religion and where the establishment of the bishoprics at Hólar and Skálholt was agreed. It was at one fateful meeting of the Alþing that Gunnar of Hlíðarendi met Hallgerður Long-Legs. Their sorry tale is recounted in the *Njáls Saga* (see the boxed text p117).

Over the following centuries the Alþing became weakened by infighting, and Norway stepped in to resolve matters. The parliament surrendered to the Norwegian king in 1262, and the Alþing was stripped of its powers in 1271. It continued to function as a strictly judicial body until 1798, when the Alþing was shifted to Austurvöllur in Reykjavík, before being dissolved entirely. The Alþing regained its powers in 1843, but its members elected to meet in Reykjavík rather than return to Þingvellir.

Since then Þingvellir has been the setting for various festivals celebrating important moments in Icelandic history. In 1874 a huge celebration was held here to mark 1000 years of settlement. In 1930 another festival celebrated the 1000th anniversary of the Alþing, and on 17 June 1944 more than 30,000 people turned up to hear the declaration of Iceland's independence. More recently, there were celebrations in 1974 to celebrate the 1100th anniversary of settlement and in 2000, to commemorate 1000 years of Christianity.

Sights

There are various historic sites and natural spectacles on the Þingvellir plain.

THE ALÞING

After its foundation in 930 the Alþing used to convene annually at the **Lögberg** (Law Rock), between the fissures of Flosagjá and Nikulásargjá, in the plain beside the Óxará river. This was where the *lögsögumaður* (law-speaker) recited the law to the assembled parliament each year. After Iceland's conversion to Christianity, the site was shifted to the foot of Almannagjá cliffs, which acted as a natural loudspeaker, broadcasting the voices of the speakers across the assembled crowds. The rock podium has now subsided into a grassy mound, but the site is marked by a flagpole. A path leads down here from the information centre at the top of Almannagjá.

The Lögrétta (Law Council) is thought to have assembled at **Neðrivellir** (Low Fields), the flat area in front of the cliffs. According to the law book *Grágás*, the Lögrétta would meet on three long benches, each accommodating 48 men. The middle bench was reserved for the voting members and the bishops, and the other two were set aside for their advisers.

FISSURES & WATERFALLS

Þingvellir sits on the rift between the North American and European plates, which are moving apart at a rate of 1mm a year. As a result, the plain is scarred by a series of dramatic fissures, including the great rift at **Almannagjá**, which forms a watercourse for the Óxará river before it empties into Þingvallavatn. A broad track follows the fault from the information centre at the top of the cliffs down to the plain below. As it cuts across the fault, the Óxará tumbles in a series of pretty cascades; the most impressive being **Öxaráfoss**, hidden away behind the eastern lip of the fault. A long time ago, the pool **Drekkingarhylur** was used to drown women found guilty of infanticide, adultery or other serious crimes.

There is a smaller fissure system on the east edge of the plain. During the 17th century nine men accused of witchcraft were burned at the stake in **Brennugjá** (the Burning Chasm). Nearby are the fissures of **Flosagjá** and **Nikulásargjá**, which surrounded the original Lögberg. Flosagjá contains an incredibly clear pool that is at least 70m deep, and the southern end of Nikulásargjá is known as **Peningagjá** (the Chasm of Coins) for the thousands of coins tossed into it by visitors.

ÞINGVALLAVATN

Originally known as Ölfusvatn, **Þingvallavatn** sprawls over nearly 84 sq km and is Iceland's largest lake. On the northeastern shore is Vellankatla (the Bubbling Cauldron), a hot spring that emerges from beneath the lava field. Two volcanic craters, Sandey and Nesjaey, form the islands in the western part of the lake. The lake is an important refuelling stop for great northern divers, harlequin ducks and other migratory birds, and is full of trout and char. Anglers can obtain permits from the park service centre for Ikr1000 from 1 May to 15 September.

Boat tours of the lake can be arranged with **Þingvallavatnssiglingar** (☎ 854 7664). Tours leave from the little jetty at Skálabrekka at 11am, 2pm and 5pm on weekends from June to September – call to get the latest rates. Scuba dives to the fissure at the bottom of the lake can be arranged through **Sportkofunarskóli** (☎ 411 7100; www.dive.is) in Keflavík – see p91.

ÞINGVALLABÆR & ÞINGVALLAKIRKJA

The land at Þingvellir originally belonged to a farmer called Þórir Kroppinskeggi, but the plain was appropriated by the Alþing in 930, and subsequent landowners had to put up with hundreds of assembly members tramping over their land every year. The current farmhouse at **Þingvallabær** was built for the 1000th anniversary of the Alþing in 1930 by the state architect Guðjón Samúelsson and extended in 1974. It's now used as a summer home by the Icelandic prime minister. It also houses the park warden's office.

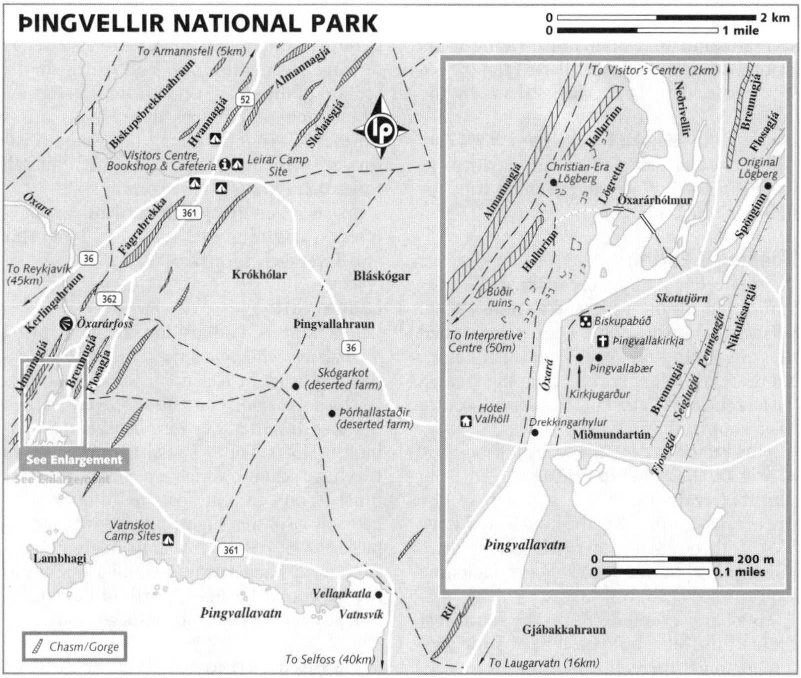

ÞINGVELLIR NATIONAL PARK

Behind the farmhouse is **Þingvallakirkja**, one of Iceland's first churches. The original church was consecrated in the 11th century by the Norwegian bishop Bjarnharður, but the current wooden church only dates from 1859. Inside are several bells from earlier churches, a wooden pulpit from 1683 and a painted altarpiece from 1834. If the doors are locked, contact the national park warden at the Þingvallabær farmhouse. The Independence-era poets Jónas Hallgrímsson and Einar Benediktsson are interred in the small cemetery behind the church.

BÚÐIR

Surrounding the farm at Þingvallabær are the ruins of various *búðir* (booths), which were once owned by the bishops and *goðar* (chieftains) of Iceland. These stone and turf shelters acted as logistical centres for the Alþing, providing ale, writing vellum, weapons, shoes and meals for the assembled crowds, not unlike the stalls at modern rock festivals. Next to Þingvallakirkja, excavations have exposed the ruins of the **Biskupabúð**, which belonged to the bishops of Iceland.

WALKS AROUND ÞINGVELLIR

Various hiking trails cut across the lava fields around Þingvellir, these are marked on the map and booklet *Þingvellir Þjóðarður* (Ikr300), available from the park service centre. Serious walkers should bring the Landmælingar Íslands sheets *Þingvellir* (1:25,000) and *Hengill* (1:100,000). Most trails converge on the abandoned farm at Skógarkot. Southeast lie the ruins of another farm, Þórhallastaðir, where ale was brewed and served to 13th-century Alþing participants. The 5km walk from Þingvellir to the western rim of the continental rift takes a few hours.

Walking trails at the southern end of Lake Þingvallavatn cut south across the slopes of the volcano Hengill (768m) to Hveragerði and the Hengill ski area, just off Route 1. See p110 for more information.

Tours

Various companies offer Golden Circle tours to Þingvellir, Geysir and Gullfoss for around Ikr6100. Try Iceland Excursions, Reykjavík Excursions or Destination Iceland (see p303 for details of operators).

Horse Trekking

Several companies offer horse-riding tours around Þingvellir. **Laxnes Horse Farm** (☎ 566 6179; www.laxnes.is), near Mosfellsbær on the Route 36, offers two- to three-hour rides for Ikr3500. **Íslenskir Freðahestar** (☎ 894 7200; www.centrum.is/travelhorse) offers full-day trips to Þingvellir for Ikr7500 and evening trips (in summer) for Ikr5500.

Sleeping & Eating

There are five camp sites at Þingvellir, administered by the **park service centre** (☎ 482 2660; camp site per person Ikr500). The best-equipped sites are around the service centre at Leirar, but there is another remote camping area on the lakeshore at Vatnskot. The service centre has a shop and snack bar.

Hótel Valhöll (☎ 482 2622; www.hotelthingvellir.is; s/d Ikr10,500/13,900, in winter Ikr5000/8000) This big gabled farmhouse hotel sits across the stream from Þingvallabær. Rooms have TVs, bathrooms and a small lounge area. The dining room serves good Icelandic food from Ikr750 to Ikr3960.

There are several B&Bs on the southwest shore of the lake, but you'll need your own vehicle to get there.

Fosshótel Nesbúð (☎ 482 3415; www.nesbud.is; sb from Ikr2300, s/d Ikr6800/9000, s/d with bathroom Ikr10,000/12,800) This large bungalow guesthouse is just off Route 360 at the foot of Hengill. It offers comfortable rooms and a good restaurant. Hiking tours in the area can be arranged, and room rates drop by 25% in winter.

Getting There & Away

From 25 May to 31 August BSÍ buses run from Reykjavík to Þingvellir (Ikr1020) at 1.30pm daily, returning at 4.45pm. There is no public transport to the south end of Þingvallavatn, but the bus to Þingvellir will get you within 12km and you may be able to hitch the rest. To visit this area during the colourful autumn season, you'll need a hire car, a bike, strong legs or a lucky thumb – or you could just hop on a Golden Circle tour.

AROUND ÞINGVELLIR

Nesjavellir

Near the foot of the volcano Hengill, immediately southwest of Þingvallavatn, is the geothermal field that powers the **Nesjavellir geothermal plant** (☎ 480 2408; 9am-5pm Mon-Sat, 1-6pm Sun Jun-Aug). The water in the 2000m-deep boreholes emerges at temperatures up to 380°C and drives a series of huge steam turbines. You can hear the scream of the steam vents from miles away. The vapour is condensed and ends up as Reykjavík's slightly pongy tap water. Visitors are welcome (June to August) but call to let them know you're coming.

In summer **Reykjavík Excursions** (www.re.is) offers a day tour to Nesjavellir, Þingvellir and Hveragerði for Ikr5000.

Laugarvatn

Laugarvatn is famous for the hot spring Vígðalaug, which was used for early Christian baptisms in Iceland. The bodies of the last bishop of Hólar and his sons were washed in the spring after they were beheaded at Skalhólt in 1550. Today Laugarvatn is home to two huge schools, which are used as summer hotels. You can rent boats to go out on the lake or visit the slightly run-down **natural sauna** (☎ 486 1151). Many short hikes are possible from Laugarvatn, including one up to the viewpoint Hringsjá, north of the village. Ask at your hotel for other suggestions.

SLEEPING & EATING

There's a **camp site** (☎ 486 1155; camp site per person Ikr500) by the highway just outside the village. On summer weekends this is a major Icelandic party venue – if you want peace and quiet, stay elsewhere.

Dalsel Youth Hostel (☎ 486 1215; jbg@ismennt.is; sb member/nonmember Ikr1650/2050, made-up bed Ikr2150/2550, apt Ikr7000) This pleasant hostel midway between the two Edda hotels and is open all year. There's a guest kitchen and hot tub. Laugarvatn has summer hotel accommodation on the lakeshore at **Hótel Edda ML** (☎ 444 4810; www.hoteledda.is; sb Ikr1700, s/d Ikr4300/4500, with bathroom Ikr7300/9100; ⊠) and at **Hótel Edda ÍKÍ** (☎ 444 4820; www.hoteledda.is; s/d with bathroom Ikr7300/9100; ⊠).

Eating options include the grill at the Esso station, **Bláskógar** (☎ 486 8808; snacks Ikr650-2000) on the main road or **Lindin** (☎ 486 1262; pizzas Ikr900-2100) behind the Edda hotels.

GETTING THERE & AWAY

From 1 June to 31 August public buses from Reykjavík to Gullfoss pass through Laugarvatn (Ikr1470, two hours). At other times, you can take a Golden Circle tour and ask to be dropped off.

GEYSIR

Possibly Iceland's most famous tourist attraction, **Geysir** (pronounced GAY-zeer) was the original spouting hot spring – all the others around the world are named after it. The great geyser at Geysir first began spouting in the 14th century, blasting a jet of superheated water up to 80m into the air, but the spring became inactive in the 1960s, after being bunged up by rocks and dirt tossed in by tourists attempting to set the geyser off. The spring occasionally comes back to life after earthquakes, most recently during the rumbles of June 2000. The government used to stage a forced eruption on Icelandic Independence Day by pouring tonnes of soap flakes into the geyser, but this environmentally suspect practice has been discontinued.

Luckily for visitors, Geysir has a back-up, **Strokkur** (the Churn), which spouts up to 35m and erupts every 10 minutes or so throughout the day. This is probably the most reliable geyser in the world – Old Faithful in America's Yellowstone National Park goes off only once an hour. It's easy to get that perfect photo – just find a good shooting position about five minutes after the last eruption and watch for the telltale gurgle at the surface of the water that pre-empts each blast.

Geysers are formed when geothermally heated water becomes trapped in narrow fissures. The water at the surface cools whereas the water below the ground becomes superheated, eventually turning into steam and blasting out the cooler water above it. There's a rope around the spring so you can't get too close, but don't be surprised if you end up a little soggy when the geyser goes off.

Geysir and Strokkur are surrounded by smaller springs, many of them painted psychedelic colours by algae and mineral deposits. Be careful as you walk around the bubbling milky pools and steam vents – the water here emerges from the ground at 100°C. Access to the geothermal area is free, but there's a vast and tacky tourist complex across the road that can soak up any unused money you have in your pockets.

Geysisstofa

Housed in the main tourist complex, **Geysisstofa** (☎ 486 8704; www.geysircenter.com; adult/student, senior, disabled & under-12 Ikr400/200; 🕒 10am-7pm May-Sep) includes a folk museum and an audiovisual exhibition on geysers, volcanoes, glaciers and the northern lights. It opens only in the afternoon in winter. Attached is a vast souvenir emporium selling various items of dubious taste.

Haukadalur

Upstream from the geothermal phenomena at Geysir, Haukadalur (Hawk Valley) was a major centre of learning in Viking times. Ari the Learned (1067–1148) studied here and went on to produce the *Landnámabók* and *Íslendingabók* sagas. As with many saga sites, there isn't a lot to see now, but Haukadalur can be reached via a pleasant stroll up the similarly picturesque Beiná Valley. The area has been planted with thousands of trees by the Icelandic Forestry Commission – there really is one!

Horse Rental

It's possible to rent horses from Hótel Geysir – see Sleeping & Eating following. Rates start at Ikr1950 for a one-hour horse trek.

Sleeping & Eating

The **camp site** (per person adult/child Ikr500/300) is just before the tourist complex and has sinks and toilets. Campers can shower at the Hótel Geysir, where you must pay for camping. The camp site is open from 1 May to 1 October. If you head a few kilometres into the surrounding hills, you can wild-camp for free.

Hótel Geysir (☎ 486 8915; fax 486 8715; dm Ikr1200, sb Ikr2700, s/d Ikr4100/4800, s/d with bathroom from Ikr7300/8900) The original accommodation option at Geysir, this tourist hotel has a good restaurant and a geothermal pool with hot pots (open to non-guests in summer for Ikr200/100 per adult/child). Rooms are in wooden cabins, and all have TVs.

Gistiheimilið Geysir (☎ 486 8733; agustath@visir.is; Haukadalur III; sb Ikr1350-1900, d Ikr3400-4700, breakfast Ikr750) The other place to stay in Geysir is this huge white-and-black bungalow just north of the tourist complex. It has a restaurant, TV lounge and guest kitchen.

For food, you have a choice of the reasonably priced **café** (snacks from Ikr190-790; 🕒 10am-6pm) at the Esso petrol station or the more-expensive **restaurant** (mains Ikr1950-3500) at the Hótel Geysir.

Getting There & Away

There are daily **Austurleið-SBS** (☎ 545 1717; www.austurleid.is) bus services that do a circuit from Reykjavík to Geysir and Gullfoss and back, either via Laugarvatn or via Reykholt. This bus works like a tour, stopping for an hour at Gullfoss and Geysir, and you can leave and rejoin the tour at any point. The return fare for the whole circuit from Reykjavík is Ikr3740 (or Ikr2040 from Selfoss). The one-way fare from Reykjavík to Gullfoss or Geysir is Ikr1870 (2½ hours).

From 1 June to 31 August buses via Laugarvatn leave Reykjavík at 8.30am and reach Gullfoss at 11am and Geysir at 12.10pm. These return to Reykjavík via Reykholt, leaving Gullfoss at noon and Geysir at 2.25pm. On Saturday an extra bus leaves Reykjavík at 5pm and goes as far as Geysir, returning at 7pm. Buses via Reykholt leave Reykjavík at 12.30pm, returning via Laugarvatn at 3.35pm (4.45pm from Geysir).

In the winter buses run only as far as Geysir. Outbound services via Laugarvatn leave Reykjavík at 8.30am on weekdays and at 5pm at weekends, returning at 11am (7pm at weekends). The bus via Reykholt leaves Reykjavík at 3pm on weekdays, returning at 4.45pm.

GULLFOSS

Iceland's most famous waterfall tumbles 32m into a steep-sided canyon about 6km northwest of Geysir, kicking up a sheer wall of spray in the process. Most visitors have already seen pictures of Gullfoss before they arrive, and quite a few people leave feeling that the spectacle is not quite as dramatic in real life. A lot depends on what the weather is like on the day you visit. On sunny days the spray creates shimmering rainbows over the gorge and Gullfoss can seem simply magical. On grey, drizzly days the falls retreat into the mist and can be slightly underwhelming.

The falls came within a hair's breadth of being destroyed forever during the 1920s, when a team of foreign investors suggested that the Hvitá river (white river) should be dammed for a hydro-electric project. The landowner, Tómas Tómasson, refused to sell, but the developers went behind his back and obtained permission directly from the government. To lobby their cause, Tómasson's daughter Sigríður walked all the way to Reykjavík and even threatened to throw herself into the falls if the tribunal decided they were to be destroyed. The government ruled against her, but the investors failed to pay the lease, so the sales agreement was nullified and the falls were saved anyway. Gullfoss was donated to the nation in 1975 and has been preserved as a nature reserve ever since.

Above the falls, there's a small museum, **Sigríðarstofa**, in honour of Sigríður Tómasdóttir, plus a good **café** (☎ 486 8683; admission free; 9am-8pm, 10am-6pm in winter). A tarmac road suitable for wheelchairs leads down to a lookout over the falls. Alternatively you could follow the steps below the café.

With a 4WD, it's possible to continue from Gullfoss to the glacier at Langjökull and other parts of the interior, via mountain road F35.

Sleeping

There is accommodation a few kilometres before the falls at **Hótel Brattholt** (☎ 486 8941; brattholtii@islandia.is; s/d with bathroom Ikr8500/11,300, in winter Ikr5900/7500), a large modern bungalow hotel overlooking the moors. Rooms are fairly standard for this sort of place, and there's a restaurant.

Getting There & Away

See p106 for information on buses to Gullfoss.

GULLFOSS TO SELFOSS

From Gullfoss there are several possible routes back to the main round-Iceland highway (Route 1). Most people follow surfaced Route 35, which passes through Reykholt and meets Route 1 about 2km west of Selfoss. You can detour off this road to the theological centre at Skalhólt. Alternatively, you can follow Route 30, which is partly unsurfaced and passes through Flúðir, meeting Route 1 about 15km east of Selfoss. An interesting detour from this road is along Route 32 through the scenic Þjórsárdalur Valley. From here, you can follow Route 26 past the foothills of the Hekla volcano, emerging on Route 1 about 6km west of Hella.

Reykholt

The rural township of Reykholt – one of several Reykholts around the country – is centred on the hot spring Reykjahver. Several local farms have greenhouses heated by the springs, and there's the inevitable **geothermal swimming pool** (☎ 486 8807). Tourist facilities include a petrol station and grill, a shop, a post office and a bank.

SLEEPING & EATING

Reykholt has a **camp site** (☎ 486 9816) and B&B and sleeping-bag accommodation at the farmhouses of **Húsið** (☎ 486 8680; Bjarkarbraut 26) and **Gilbrún** (☎ 486 8925; Dalbraut 1), both on the main road. There's also farmhouse accommodation (bags and beds) 5km before Reykholt at **Sel** (☎ 486 4441) on the dirt track to Apavatn Lake. For food, you have the choice of the grill at the petrol station or the posher **Kaffi Klettur** (☎ 486 1310).

GETTING THERE & AWAY

The buses described under Skálholt (following) also stop at Reykholt (Reykjavík to Reykholt costs Ikr1470).

Skálholt

Just off Route 35, the historic settlement of Skálholt was one of the two Catholic bishoprics that governed the population of Iceland before the Reformation (the other was at Hólar in north Iceland). Skálholt rose to prominence under Gissur the White, who sat on the Alþing and is widely regarded as the driving force behind the Christianisation of Iceland. The Catholic bishopric lasted until 1550 when the last Catholic bishop, Jón Arason, was executed along with his two sons, on the orders of the Danish king, Christian III. Skalhólt continued as a Lutheran centre until 1797, when the bishopric was shifted to Reykjavík.

Sadly, the original cathedral was dismantled in the 18th century, but a modern theological centre was built here in 1956. During construction the builders discovered the stone sarcophagus of Bishop Páll Jónsson (1196–1211), one of the most powerful bishops of Skalhólt. According to the *Páls Saga*, the earth was wracked by storms and earthquakes when Páll Jónsson died, and, spookily, a huge storm broke at the exact moment that his coffin was reopened. The sarcophagus is now on display in the basement of the modern church. It's the most historic thing here now. The theological centre looks a bit like a conference venue and isn't hugely interesting. In front, you can see the ongoing excavations of the old bishop's residence.

SPECIAL EVENTS

There's an important **classical music festival** (☎ 565 0859; www.skalholt.is) at Skálholt for five weeks each July and August, featuring composers and musicians from all over Iceland and Europe.

SLEEPING & EATING

Visitors can find accommodation and a meal at the theological centre **Skálholtsskóli** (☎ 486 8870; sb Ikr900-2500, s/d from Ikr5950/6800). Rooms are in several buildings at the compound, and rates drop by 20% in winter. There's a nice conservatory restaurant that serves breakfast for Ikr800 and light meals from Ikr1490.

Accommodation is also available beside the suspension bridge over the Hvitá river in Laugarás at **Iðufell** (☎ 486 8600; camp site per person Ikr400 plus Ikr300 per extra person, sb from Ikr1800, s/d 6500/8900), which caters to all budgets and offers meals and a guest kitchen.

GETTING THERE & AWAY

Daily buses from Reykjavík to Geysir and Gullfoss pass Skálholt (Ikr1470, two hours). See p106 for more information.

Sólheimar

At the tiny settlement of Sólheimar, 13km south of Reykholt, you can stay at the comfortable **Gistiheimilið Brekkukot** (☎ 486 4430; www.solheimar.is; s/d with shared bathroom from Ikr3000/4600, ste 9000), an ecologically minded guesthouse overlooking the Hvíta. In Sólheimar there is a small shop and a swimming pool.

Nearby, on Route 35, the café **Gamla Borg** (☎ 485 4550) serves meals throughout the summer.

Kerið & Seyðishólar

Around 10km further south Route 35 passes **Kerið**, a 55m-deep explosion crater with a spooky-looking green lake. About 3km northeast across the road is the red-sided **Seyðishólar** crater group, which produced most of the surrounding lava field. There are lots of sheltered places to camp nearby and a surface stream west of the craters.

FLÚÐIR

About 32km south of Gullfoss along partly unsurfaced Route 30, Flúðir is an alternative base for exploring the Golden Circle, but there isn't much to see. Mushrooms are raised in geothermally heated greenhouses,

SOUTHWEST ICELAND

and there's a **swimming pool** (☎ 486 6790) and a small folk museum at the farm **Gróf** (☎ 486 6634). Tourist facilities include a bank with an ATM, a post office, a shop and a few cafés. Horse rental is available at the nearby farmhouse Syðra-Langholt – see Sleeping & Eating (following).

Sleeping & Eating

The cafeteria **Ferðamiðstoðn** (☎ 486 6535; snacks Ikr350-800) serves snacks and offers camping for Ikr1000 per tent. The other dining option is the pizzeria **Útlaginn** (☎ 486 6425; Ikr900-2000).

Hótel Flúðir (☎ 486 6630; s/d with bathroom Ikr11,200/15,400, in winter Ikr7900/9900) Owned by Icelandair, this modern hotel is quite stylish and has comfortable rooms with TV, phone and minibar.

There's also farmhouse accommodation at **Syðra-Langholt** (☎ 486 6674; sydralangholt@centrum.is; camp site per tent Ikr1000, sb/s/d Ikr1900/2800/5500), 10km south of Flúðir on Route 340. The owners are a lively bunch and the big, white house has all the mod cons, including a hot pot. Horse riding is available for Ikr2000 per hour.

Getting There & Away

From June to August buses leave Reykjavík for Flúðir (Ikr1530, two hours) at 5pm daily, passing 5km from Syðra-Langholt. From Flúðir they leave for Reykjavík at 8.30am and 7.15pm. In winter the afternoon bus leaves Reykjavík at 5.05pm on weekdays and at 7.15pm at weekends. Most Flúðir buses run via Árnes.

ÞJÓRSÁRDALUR

The valley of the Þjórsá (Bull River) winds down to the Atlantic from the glacier Hofsjökull in the centre of Iceland, passing through the lava fields of Hekla, Iceland's best-known volcano. There are hydroelectric plants along the Þjórsá at Búrfell and Bláskógar. Route 32 follows the course of the river and meets up with mountain road F26, which runs across the interior.

Árnes

The tiny settlement of Árnes near the junction of Routes 30 and 32 is a convenient base for exploring Þjórsárdalur.

There's an HI hostel at **Gistiheimilið Nónsteinn** (☎ 486 6048; bergleif@centrum.is; camping Ikr1000, dm member/nonmember Ikr1800/1500, sb Ikr2300/2000), with a licensed restaurant, a guest kitchen and an octagonal outdoor swimming pool.

Most buses between Reykjavík and Flúðir go via Árnes.

Stöng & Þjólðveldisbærinn

The farm of Gaukur Standisson – who gave his name to the Reykjavík pub Gaukur á Stöng – was buried beneath a sheet of lava sand during the devastating eruption of Hekla in 1104, but was uncovered by a team of Scandinavian archaeologists in 1939. The ruins are protected by a wooden shelter at the end of a pitted and bumpy dirt road that branches off Route 32 just before Búrfell. You can still see evidence of stone-lined fire pits and door lintels, made from octagonal basalt columns, and the surrounding lava landscape is impressively desolate.

Probably more interesting is the reconstruction of the farm at **Þjólðveldisbærinn** (☎ 488 7713; admission Ikr300; 🕓 10am-noon, 1-6pm 1 Jun–8 Sep). It was built using traditional materials and techniques, and exactly reproduces the layout of the original building. It's a popular stop for tour groups, and the farmhouses are quite atmospheric. Out of season, you might be able to tag along with a visiting tour group.

Nearby at the Búrfell Hydropower Station is the scenic waterfall **Hjálparfoss**, which tumbles in two chutes over a scarp formed from twisted basalt columns. From Stöng you can hike along a 4WD track to Iceland's second highest waterfall, **Háifoss**, which plunges 122m off the edge of a flat plateau. It takes several hours to hike along the track, but you can get most of the way there by 4WD. Wild camping is possible anywhere in the valley.

SLEEPING

From May to September you can camp in a plantation of fir trees at **Sandártunga** (☎ 893 8889; camp site per person Ikr500) about 7km before Búrfell. Alternatively you could stay at the nearby farm **Asólfsstaðir** (☎ 486 6063; hestur@centrum.is).

GETTING THERE & AWAY

Reykjavík Excursions (www.re.is) runs a Þjórsárdalur tour on Thursday and Saturday from June to September, which visits the Stöng ruins and reconstructed farm, the Gjáin gorge and Hjálparfoss. The nine-hour tour costs Ikr7800 and leaves Reykjavík at 9am.

Otherwise you'll need to walk, hitch or have your own vehicle.

Hekla

The 1491m-high summit of this moody volcano is almost always shrouded in cloud, earning it the name Hekla, 'the Hooded'. The volcano has vented its fury numerous times throughout history, and some historians have identified Hekla as the flaming mountain seen by the 6th-century Irish monk St Brendan on his (probably fantastical) voyage from Ireland to North America.

During the settlement of Iceland, Vikings established farms on the rich volcanic soils around Hekla only to be wiped out by the eruption of 1104, which buried everything within a radius of 50km. Since then the mountain has blown its top 15 times – the 1300 eruption covered more than 83,000 sq km in ash. By the 16th century mainland Europe decided that Hekla was the entrance to hell. Literature of the day reported on its black skies, complete with vultures and ravens, and that the moans of the condemned could be heard crying out from inside.

In 1947, after more than 100 years of inactivity, Hekla belched a mushroom cloud of ash more than 27km into the air. It was followed by another huge eruption in 1970. Since then Hekla has gone off at roughly 10-year intervals, with eruptions in August 1980, April 1981, January 1991 and, most recently, in February 2000. The volcano is still highly active, and seismic teams monitor its activity carefully.

Several walking trails lead up to the summit, but many people are happy just to see Hekla at a distance from Route 26.

HEKLUMIÐSTÖÐIN

This small **museum** (Hekla Centre; ☎ 487 6587; admission Ikr200; 🕑 10am-6pm Jun-Aug) is devoted to Hekla at Brúarlundi; it's along Route 26 near Leirubakki. There are video films, photos and other exhibits relating to the volcano and its effect on the area.

CLIMBING HEKLA

It's possible to climb Hekla, but seek local advice before you set off as it's still an active volcano. Stick to days when the summit is free from heavy cloud, and carry plenty of water. The easiest route to the peak begins along a well-marked walking track on mountain road F225, which branches off Route 26 about 18km northeast of Leirubakki. The track climbs steadily up to the ridge on the northeastern flank of the mountain and then southwest to the summit crater, the scene of the 2000 eruption. Although the peak is often covered in snow, the floor of the crater is still hot to the touch. The round trip takes at least eight hours. The access routes on the west side were damaged during the 1991 eruption and are not recommended.

You can take snowmobile tours to the summit of Hekla with **Toppferðir** (☎ 487 5530; www.mmedia.is/toppbrenna). Tours are possible in summer and winter but you should call for the latest rates and schedule.

WATERFALLS

Close to Hekla on Route 26 are the small waterfalls of **Þjófafoss**, where thieves were once punished with drowning, and **Tröllkonuhlaup**, said to have been created by a lady troll. The falls are sometimes cut off by the hydro plant at Búrfell.

SLEEPING

About 10km from Hekla on Route 26 is the popular **Gistihúsið Leirubakki** (☎ 487 6591; www.leirubakki.is; camp site per adult/child Ikr650/325, sb/s/d Ikr1800/4500/6000). This appealing modern wooden farmhouse has two outdoor hot pots with a front-row view of Hekla. Meals are available, or there's a guest kitchen. Horse rental is available from Ikr2000 per hour, and longer horse tours, lasting from one to seven days, can also be arranged.

Alternatively, you could try the summer hotel and camp site at **Laugaland** (☎ 487 6543), about 23km southwest of Leirubakki.

GETTING THERE & AWAY

From 14 June to 14 September **Austurleið-SBS** (☎ 545 1717; www.austurleid.is) has a daily bus at 8.30am from Reykjavík to Landmannalaugar, which passes Leirubakki (Ikr2070, 2¼ hours) at 10.45am. The return trip passes Leirubakki at 4.15pm.

You can also try a tour. **Mountain Taxi** (www.mountain-taxi.com) runs a Mt Hekla 4WD tour, with a swim in a natural geothermal pool, for Ikr18,000. **Destination Iceland** (www.dice.is) offers a 4WD tour of Landmannalaugar and Mt Hekla at 8.30am daily for Ikr17,140. Tours to Þjórsárdalur (see Getting There & Away, p108) also pass through Leirubakki.

HVERAGERÐI TO VÍK Í MÝRDAL

Southeast of Reykjavík, Route 1 winds southeast along the edge of the coast plain, passing various geothermal fields and hot springs. There are several interesting towns on Route 1 that you can reach easily by public bus, including the geothermal farming centre of Hveragerði and the horse-breeding centre at Hella, a popular starting point for horse-riding tours. Continuing southeast, Hvolsvöllur is the leaping-off point for the Fljótsdalur Valley and Þórsmörk, one of Iceland's most popular hiking destinations. Further east, beneath the Mýrdalsjökull icecap, Skógar is home to one of Iceland's best folk museums, and Vík is surrounded by intriguing glacial and volcanic scenery.

HVERAGERÐI

pop 1864

This friendly little community sits on top of a highly active geothermal field, providing heat for hundreds of greenhouses where fruit, flowers and vegetables are produced throughout the year – the name Hveragerði means 'hot springs garden'. The whole settlement is very tidy and attractive and feels a bit like a planned American suburb. Locally, the town is famous for its horticultural college and naturopathic clinic. You can easily walk from here to Þingvallavatn over the lava plains of the Hengill volcano and to the nearby Gufudalur geothermal valley, which bubbles with hot springs and fissures.

THE CHRISTMAS LADS

The geyser at Hveragerði is named for Grýla, the witch mother of the malevolent *jólasveinarn* (Christmas lads). These vengeful hooligans have names like Ladle-Licker, Sausage-Grabber and Window-Peeper, and they are blamed for all kinds of mischief over the Christmas period. Legend has it that one of the lads plagues the Icelanders each day between Christmas and Þrettandinn (Three Kings Day or 12th Night, which falls on 6 January), when they're all expelled until the following year. Although they form part of the Icelandic Christmas celebrations today, in times past the Christmas Lads were thought to be the children of trolls and were accused of kidnapping the children of Christian families, in protest at the conversion of Iceland.

Information

The friendly and well-informed regional tourist office, **Upplýsingamiðstöð Suðurlands** (☎ 483 4601; www.sudurland.net/info; Breiðamörk 2; 9.15am-4.15pm Mon-Fri, 10am-2pm Sat), is on the main road into town. You can change money and use your ATM card at the Bunaðarbankinn on Breiðamörk. Free Internet access is available at the **library** (Bókasafnið; ☎ 483 4531; Austurmörk 2). Alternatively you could use the machines at the tourist office for Ikr100 per 30 minutes.

Sights

There are a few interesting sights in Hveragerði.

GEOTHERMAL FIELDS

There is a small **geothermal area** (☎ 483 5062; Hveramörk) in the centre of town, with baked earth, small mud pots and several hot springs and pools. In summer there's a small souvenir shop where you can buy rocks and crystals.

Much more interesting is **Gufudalur**, the lovely 'Steam Valley' behind the town. The whole valley explodes with hot springs, geysers, mud pots, fumaroles and steaming vents. The best-known feature is Grýla, a 12m geyser that erupts several times daily. It's near the bridge on the way to the golf course. Some interesting walks lead up the valley from Hveragerði (p111).

EDEN

A geothermal greenhouse has been turned into a tourist attraction at **Eden** (☎ 483 4900; www.eden.smart.is; Austurmörk 32; admission free; 9am-11pm, 9am-7pm in winter) where you can see tropical plants such as bananas and papayas growing close to the Arctic Circle. It's a bit of a tourist trap and exists mainly to steer people through the restaurant and gift shop.

NLFÍ CLINIC

The clinic run by **Náttúrulækningafélag Ísland** (NLFÍ; ☎ 483 0300; www.hnlfi.is; Grænmörk 10) specialises in the naturopathic treatment of rheumatism, stress, arthritis and orthopaedic

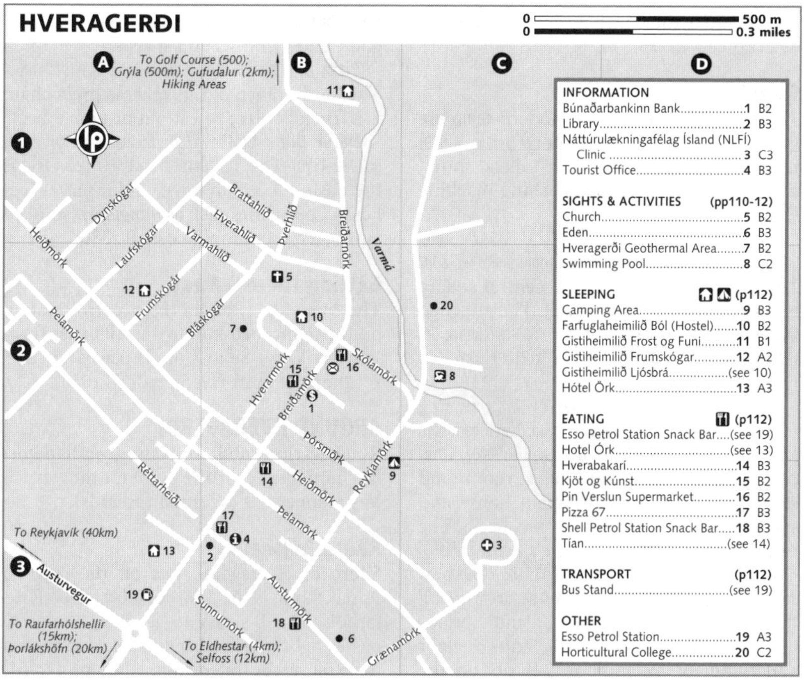

problems. Treatments are based on water and mud from the hot springs. Most patients visit for week-long courses, which involve a strict diet and various naturopathic treatments, but passing visitors can take a mud bath (Ikr2200) if they call ahead.

Activities

HIKING

There are loads of interesting walks around Hveragerði. Bring the Landmælingar Íslands sheet *Hengill* (1:100,000), or ask the tourist office for the map *Hiking Trails in the Hengill Area* (Ikr500). Most of the hiking trails begin at the top of the Gufudalur Valley. From here you can pass along geothermal Reykjadalir Valley to the Dalsel survival hut (3.5km from Hveragerði), where several trails cut across the hills to the shores of Lake Þingvallavatn. The shortest routes run northeast to Úlfljótsvatn (13km) or due north to Ölfusvatnsvík (13.5km).

A longer route will take you over the top of Hengill (768m) to Nesjavellir, where you can stay at the Fosshótel Nesbúð. It's 11.7km to the summit of Hengill and 18.7km to Nesbúð. If you just want to climb Hengill, you can drive as far as the Hengill ski area, about 16km before Hveragerði on Route 1, from where it's 7km to the summit along the ridge to the west, or 6km via the Hengladalir Valley.

SWIMMING

There's a well-designed open-air **thermal swimming pool** (☎ 483 4113; Laugaskarði; adult/child Ikr250/100; 🕑 7am-8.30pm Mon-Fri, 10am-5.30pm Sat & Sun) beside the Varmá river just north of the centre.

GOLF

Hveragerði's **golf course** (☎ 483 5090) is set in the lovely geothermal Gufudalur Valley. It charges green fees of Ikr2000 and Ikr1500 for club hire.

HORSE TOURS

A few kilometres west of Hveragerði, **Eldhestar** (☎ 483 4884; www.eldhestar.is) offers recommended riding tours around Hveragerði. Rates start at Ikr2300 for a one-hour tour, and multiday tours into the interior can also be arranged.

Sleeping

There is an excellent and modern **camp site** (☎ 483 4601; Reykjamörk; camp site per person Ikr500) just east of the centre, with toilets, showers, a cooking area and a washing machine (Ikr200 per load).

Farfuglaheimilið Ból (☎ 483 4198; www.hotelljosbra.is; Hveramörk 14; sb member/nonmember Ikr1800/2150) This tidy hostel by the central square is very popular and often full. The attached **Gistiheimilið Ljósbrá** (☎ 483 4588; Breiðamörk 25; s/d Ikr5700/7100, d with bathroom Ikr8100) is also recommended.

Gistiheimilið Frumskógar (☎ 483 4148; www.frumskogar.is; Frumskógar 3; sb Ikr2000, d with shared bathroom Ikr5500, apt with TV, bathroom & kitchen Ikr9000) This cosy suburban guesthouse offers rooms and sleeping-bag space in the main house and self-catering apartments at the back. The owners are friendly, and there's a hot tub.

Gistiheimilið Frost og Funi (☎ 483 4959; www.frostandfire.is; Hverhamar; s/d with TV & bathroom Ikr7000/10,000, in winter Ikr6500/9000) This splendid building was built for an Icelandic entrepreneur and is full of Icelandic art. It sits on the riverbank surrounded by fumaroles, and there's a pool and an idyllic hot pot overlooking the river.

Hótel Örk (☎ 483 4700; www.www.icelandichotels.is; Breiðamörk 1; s/d with TV, bath & minibar from Ikr12,800/15,100, in winter Ikr8600/10,800) This big custom-built hotel has saunas, tennis courts, a golf course, an excellent swimming pool and a water fun park for kids. Breakfast included.

About 3km west of Hveragerði, **Hótel Eldhestar** (☎ 480 4800; www.eldhestar.is; sb Ikr1800, s/d Ikr8900/12,400, in winter Ikr5700/7800) is attached to the popular riding school. It offers large comfy rooms (some designed to accommodate people who use wheelchairs). The open fire in the lounge is a fine place to relax after a day in the saddle.

Eating

Self-caterers should head for the supermarket **Pin Verslun** (Breiðamörk 27) or the deli **Kjöt og Kúnst** (Breiðamörk 21), which serves food cooked with geothermal steam.

There are several fast-food places in town, including **Tían** (☎ 483 4727; Breiðamörk 10) and the snack bars at the Shell petrol station on Austurmörk and the Esso on Breiðamörk. **Hverabakarí** (☎ 483 4879; Breiðamörk 10) serves good cakes, coffees and snacks.

Pizza 67 (☎ 483 4467; Breiðamörk 2; Ikr900-1900) The local branch of this reliable pizza chain is a friendly place to eat out or grab a beer.

Hótel Örk (☎ 483 4700; Breiðamörk 10; mains Ikr1980-4390) The restaurant at Hótel Örk is the poshest place in town, and it serves Icelandic specialities such as *hangikjöt* (smoked lamb). The set dinner costs Ikr3800.

Getting There & Away

The bus stop is at the Esso petrol station on the main road into town. All buses from Reykjavík to Selfoss and places further southeast stop in Hveragerði (Ikr650).

AROUND HVERAGERÐI

Route 38 runs south from Hveragerði to Þorlákshöfn, the departure point for the ferry to Vestmannaeyjar (Westman Islands).

Raufarhólshellir

South of Hveragerði, just off the road to Þorlákshöfn, is the 1km-long lava tube Raufarhólshellir. It's easy to get to as Route 39 passes right overhead, but you'll need a torch to explore the interesting (and protected) lava formations in the tube. Take care inside as various sections of the roof have caved in over the years. Buses between Reykjavík and Þorlákshöfn pass close to the cave entrance.

Þorlákshöfn

About 20km south of Hveragerði, the rather plain fishing village of Þorlákshöfn has the only viable harbour between Grindavík and Höfn. Most people just come here to catch the vehicle ferry to the Westman Islands, but there's a **camp site** (☎ 483 3631; camp site per person Ikr200 plus Ikr200 per extra person) next to the swimming pool if you need to stay over. Just outside Þorlákshöfn, unsurfaced Route 42 runs west along the bottom of the Reykjanes Peninsula to Krísuvík.

GETTING THERE & AWAY

The buses from Reykjavík to Þorlákshöfn (Ikr850, one hour) are synchronised with the ferry timetable and leave Reykjavík daily at 11am and 5.50pm from Sunday to Friday in summer, returning at 11.10am and 7pm (Sunday to Friday in summer).

For information on the ferry service to Vestmannaeyjar, see p130.

STEVE HUTTON

Þingvellir (p101), Southwest Iceland

WADE EAKLE

Strokkur geyser (p105), Southwest Iceland

RALPH LEE HOPKINS

Þingvellir (p101), Southwest Iceland

Gullfoss (p106), Southwest Iceland

GRAEME CORNWALLIS

STEVE HUTTON

Snæfellsnes (p142), West Iceland

STEVE HUTTON

Snæfellsnes (p142), West Iceland

Bolungarvík (p159), Westfjords

STEVE HU

Bolungarvík (p159), Westfjords

STEVE HU

SELFOSS

pop 6048

Selfoss is the largest town in southern Iceland, and it's growing fast. The land on which the town was built was once 80m under the ocean, but it was thrust upwards by volcanic activity around 12,000 years ago. Today Selfoss is an important centre for the dairy industry. Most things are spread out along the highway, so it doesn't feel as welcoming as some neighbouring towns. You can walk along the Ölfusá river, which flows through the centre, or take longer hikes to the top of **Ingólfsfjall** (551m) just west of Selfoss, said to be the final resting place of Iceland's first settler, Ingólfur Arnarson. The easiest way up here is beside the gravel workings, 3km west of Selfoss on Route 1.

Information

From June to September, there's a **tourist office** (☎ 482 2422; www.arborg.is/tourinfo; Austurvegur 2; 🕑 10am-7pm Mon-Fri & 11am-2pm Sat & Sun) in the town library, close to the roundabout on the main road. Ask for the free map *Árborg*, which is full of tourist information on the area. The library offers Internet access for Ikr100 per 30 minutes.

Landsbanki Íslands, Búnaðarbankinn and Íslandsbanki all have branches with ATMs on Austurvegur.

Activities

Selfoss has a fine geothermal **swimming pool** (☎ 482 1227; Tryggvagata; adult/child Ikr250/120; 🕑 6.45am-9.15pm Mon-Fri, 10am-8pm Sat & Sun) with hot pots, waterslides and a kiddies' play pool.

Mountain Cruiser (☎ 482 2358; Alftarima 30; www.simnet.is/cruiser) offers various mountain tours by 4WD, including trips to Þórsmörk and Landmannalaugar. See their website for details.

Horse rental and tours are available from **Hestakráin** (☎ 486 5616; www.hestakrain.is), 20km east of Selfoss on Route 30; rates start at Ikr2000 for an hour of guided horse riding.

Sleeping

Camping and accommodation in wooden cabins is available at **Gesthús** (☎ 482 3585; www.gesthus.is; Engjavegur; camp site per person Ikr500,

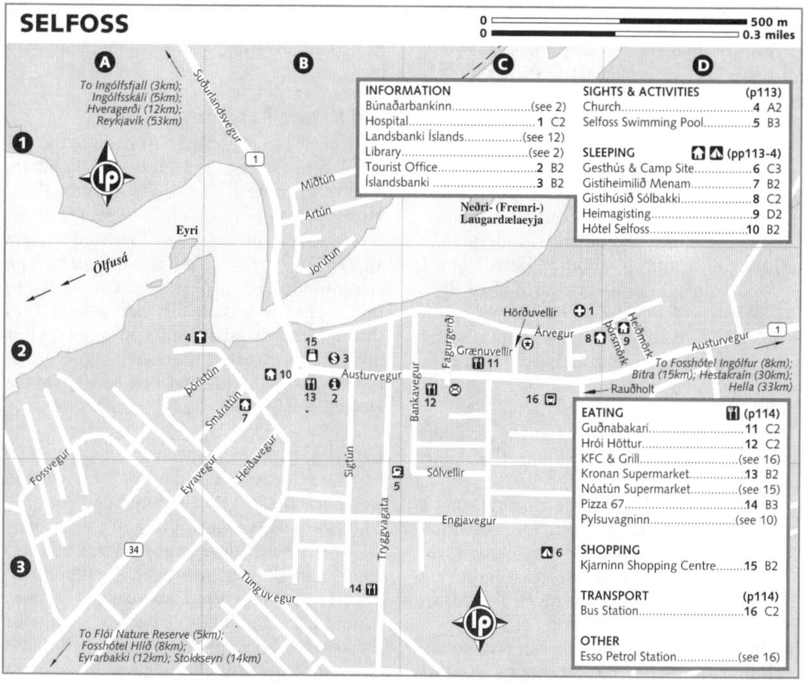

sb Ikr2000, s/d/tr in cabins Ikr6600/8400/9600) by the large park south of the main road. The comfortable cabins have kitchenettes and bathrooms, and there's a hot pot for guests. You can rent mountain bikes for Ikr1200 per day.

Two good guesthouses are just north of the main road at the east end of town.

Heimagisting (☎ 487 6616; Heiðmörk 2a; sb Ikr1500, made-up bed Ikr2500) This red house in a garden full of trees offers simple rooms with quite restrained décor. Breakfast costs Ikr750.

Gistihúsið Sólbakki (☎ 483 4212; fax 483 4012; sb Ikr1500-1700, s/d Ikr2200/3200) This modern guesthouse opposite the hospital has quite lively owners and decent rooms.

Gistiheimilið Menam (☎ 482 4099; www.menam.is; Eyravegur 8; s/d/tr Ikr3900/6200/7300) This Thai restaurant in the town centre has a guesthouse upstairs with nicely furnished, cosy rooms.

Hótel Selfoss (☎ 482 2500; www.icehotel.is; Eyravegur 2; s/d Ikr11,800/17,900, in winter Ikr8700/13,200) Icelandair owns this large institutional hotel near the main roundabout, with similar standards to other Icelandair hotels around the country, ie business-style hotel rooms with good facilities but bland interiors.

There are several large hotel-style guesthouses around Selfoss.

Fosshótel Hlíð (☎ 483 5444; www.hotel-hlid.com; s/d Ikr6800/9000, with bathroom Ikr12,600/16,500) This large bungalow-style place, about 8km south of Selfoss on Route 38, offers the usual high Fosshótel standards.

Fosshótel Ingólfur (☎ 483 5222; Ingólfshvoli; sb/s/d Ikr2300/4200/6400) This large wooden bungalow-style Fosshótel is about 8km west of Selfoss and caters to budget travellers.

Just off Route 1, about 15km east of Selfoss, is the modern white farmhouse **Bitra** (☎ 486 5540; www.bitra.is; sb Ikr1900, s/d with breakfast Ikr3680/4370), which offers tidy rooms, some with private bathrooms, and evening meals.

Eating

Self-caterers should head for the Kronan and Nóatún supermarkets on the main road (Austurvegur).

For fast food, try the drive-through snack bar **Pylsuvagninn** (Ikr200-800) in the Fosshótel car park, or the KFC/grill at the Esso petrol station east of the centre on Austurvegur.

The bakery **Guðnabakarí** (☎ 482 1755; Austurvegi 31b) is good for cakes and coffee.

There are several pizza places in town, including branches of the chains **Pizza 67** (☎ 482 2267; Tryggvagata 40) and **Hrói Höttur** (☎ 482 2899; Austurvegi 22). Both are licensed and offer a familiar range of pizzas for Ikr900 to Ikr2000.

Restaurant Menam (☎ 482 4099; Eyravegur 8; mains Ikr1690-1890) For a break from grills and fish and chips, head for this authentic Thai place on the road to Stokkseyri.

About 3km west of Selfoss, a dirt road (Route 374) leads north to **Ingólfsskáli** (☎ 483 4160; mains Ikr1500-4000; from 6pm), a Viking-theme restaurant in a reconstructed turf-roofed farmhouse. It's all a bit over the top, with waiters in Viking costume and glasses made from sheep's horns, but the food is good and it's worth a look for the unusual building.

Getting There & Away

All buses between Reykjavík and Höfn, Skaftafell, Fjallabak, Þórsmörk, Flúðir, Gullfoss, Laugarvatn and Vík pass through Selfoss, so you'll have numerous options daily. The fare from Reykjavík is Ikr850.

AROUND SELFOSS

Several historic fishing communities are spread along the Selfoss south coast; the nearby Flói Nature Reserve is popular with birdwatchers.

Flói Nature Reserve

Southwest of Selfoss, the east bank of the Ölfusá river has been set aside as the **Flói Nature Reserve** to protect an important marshland visited by migratory birds. Species commonly seen include red-throated divers and various kinds of ducks and geese. The best time to visit is nesting season (May to July). There's a 2km circular hiking trail through the marshes, but you'll need your own transport to get there. For more information, contact the **Icelandic Society for the Protection of Birds** (☎ 562 0477; www.fuglavernd.is).

Eyrarbakki

It's hard to believe today, but Eyrarbakki was once the largest settlement in Iceland. The town was the birthplace of Bjarní Herjólfsson, who made a great sea voyage in AD 985 and might well have been the first European to see America. Unfortunately Bjarní turned back and sold his boat on to Leifur Eiríksson, who went on to discover Vinland and ended up with all the glory.

These days the world seems to have left Eyrarbakki behind, but there are lots of interesting old buildings along the seafront, including **Húsið**, one of Iceland's oldest houses, which was built by Danish traders in 1765. Today this historic building contains the **Árnes Folk Museum** (☎ 483 1504; www.husid.is; Hafnarbrú 3; admission Ikr400; 🕑 11am-5pm Jun-Aug, 2-5pm Apr-May & Sep-Oct), which has displays on the history of the house and the town.

There's also a small maritime museum, **Sjóminjasafnið á Eyrarbakka** (☎ 483 1082; Túngata 59; admission Ikr200; 🕑 11am-5pm Jun-Aug, 2-5pm Sat & Sun Apr-May & Sep-Oct), one street back from the water. The wild, sandy coastline around Eyrarbakki is a fine place to observe migrating birds.

SLEEPING & EATING

There's a rudimentary free camping area by the docks at the west end of the village.

For cheap eats, there's the grill Ás-Inn at the Olis petrol station.

Rauða Húsið (☎ 483 3330; www.raudahusid.is; Buðarstíg 12; mains Ikr1690-3900) Arch rival of the lobster restaurant in Stokkseyri, this upmarket restaurant is housed in a wonderful old red house near the shore. It's a popular lunch stop for tours.

GETTING THERE & AWAY

Buses on the Reykjavík–Þorlákshöfn–Eyrarbakki–Stokkseyri–Selfoss–Reykjavík route run once a day throughout the year (Ikr1080 to Eyrarbakki, 1¼ hours), leaving Reykjavík at 11am and Eyrarbakki at 12.15pm. There are also two daily buses to Selfoss except Saturday (no Saturday and Sunday service in winter).

Stokkseyri

Near the prison on the Eyrarbakki road, a small road runs west along the shore to Stokkseyri, another historic fishing village. A long lava seawall runs along the coast to the mouth of the Ölfulsá lagoon, built during the Básenda (Great Flood) in 1799. Today Stokkseyri is a little faded, but it does have a very fine seafood restaurant.

Next to the grassy square behind the Shell station is **Þuríðarbúð** (☎ 483 1267; admission free; 🕑 always open), a restored turf-roofed fishing hut that once belonged to Þuríður Einarsdóttir (1777–1863), one of the very few female boat captains in Iceland.

About 6km east of Stokkseyri is **Baugsstaðir museum** (☎ 486 3369; admission Ikr200; 🕑 11am-5pm Jun-Aug, 2-5pm Apr-May & Sep-Oct) housed in the last working creamery in Iceland. It ceased operation in 1952, but you can see all the original equipment.

SLEEPING & EATING

There's no official camp site, but you can camp along the beach. For cheap meals, there's a grill at the Shell petrol station.

Við Fjöruborðið (☎ 483 1550; www.fjorubordid.is; Eyrabraut 3a; mains Ikr1020-3500; 🕑 11.30am-10pm, 6-10pm in winter) This little lobster restaurant on the shore has a reputation for serving the best lobster in Iceland. It even played host to the band Foo Fighters when they played in Reykjavík. The legendary lobster soup costs Ikr1450 and is worth every penny.

GETTING THERE & AWAY

Buses from Reykjavík to Eyrarbakki continue to Stokkseyri (from Reykjavík Ikr1080, 1½ hours) and then loop back to Reykjavík via Selfoss.

HELLA

pop 630

This small agricultural community sits on the banks of the Ytri-Rangá river in an important horse-breeding area. In late June Hella holds the **Landsmót**, the world's largest Icelandic horse show – see the website www.landsmot.is/english for more information. On clear days good views of the volcano Hekla can be seen from several places in town. Just west of Hella, near the farm of Áegissíða, are the ruins of 12 artificial **caves**, believed to have been constructed by early Irish hermits, but you'll need local help to find them.

Hella has several places to stay and eat. There are also a supermarket, a **geothermal swimming pool** (☎ 487 5334) and a petrol station with a decent **tourist office** (☎ 487 5165; www.rang.is; 8.30am-12.30pm & 1.30-5.30pm Mon-Fri, 8.30am-1.30pm Sat & Sun, summer only). Ask for the free guide map *Velkomin Í Rangarþing*, which covers the region from Hella to Skógar.

About 8km south of Hella on unsurfaced Route 266, the farm at **Oddi** was the site of an important saga-era monastery. Two of the most important books of Norse mythology – Snorri Sturluson's *Prose Edda* and Sæmundur Sigfússon's *Poetic Edda* – were compiled here

THE EDDAS

The medieval monastery at Oddi was the source of the Norse Eddas, the most important surviving books of Viking poetry. The *Prose Edda* was written by the poet and historian Snorri Sturluson in around 1222. It was intended to be a textbook for poets, with detailed descriptions of the language and metres used by the Norse *skalds* (court poets). It also includes the epic poem *Gylfaginning*, which describes the visit of Gylfi, the king of Sweden, to Ásgard, the citadel of the gods. In the process, the poem reveals Norse myths about the beginning of the world, the adventures of the gods and the fate in store for men at the time of the Ragnarok or 'Twilight of the Gods'.

The *Poetic Edda* was written later in the 13th century by Sæmundur Sigfússon. It is a compilation of works by unknown Viking poets, some predating the settlement of Iceland. The first poem, *Voluspá* (Sibyl's Prophesy), is like a Norse version of the Book of Genesis: it covers the beginning and end of the world. Later poems deal with the story of how Odin discovered the power of runes and the legend of Siegfried and the Nibelungs, recounted in Wagner's *Ring Cycle*. The most popular poem is probably *Thrymskvida*, about the giant Thrym, who stole Thor's hammer and demanded the goddess Freyja in marriage in exchange for its return. To get his hammer back, Thor disguised himself as the bride to be and went to the wedding in her place. Much of the poem is devoted to his appalling table manners at the wedding feast, during which he consumes an entire ox, eight salmon and three skins of mead.

in the 13th century. There's still a church at Oddi, but it isn't of great interest. You'll get more of a sense of Viking history from reading the Eddas themselves.

Horse Riding

If you fancy trotting through the surrounding hills, Hella is surrounded by horse farms, many of which offer horse rental and can arrange riding tours. The largest farm in the area is **Árbakki** (☎ 487 5041; www.vortex.is/arbakki), about 7km northeast of Hella on Route 271. One-hour riding tours around the farm cost Ikr2500, whereas six- to eight-hour tours to Landsveit cost Ikr7900. You can also arrange tours of the stables and farm stays where you help out on the farm.

Other local horse farms include:

Hekluhestar (☎ 487 6598; www.islandia.is/hekluhestar) Route 271, 9km northeast of Hella

Hestheimar (☎ 4876666; www.hestheimar.is) Near Route 26, 7km northwest of Hella

Sleeping & Eating

Most things in Hella are on the main street.

Café Arhús (☎ 487 5577; camp site per person Ikr600, sb Ikr1850, self-catering cabins Ikr5000-10,800; meals Ikr390-1690) Next to the river, Arhús offers a well-equipped camp site and wooden cabins that sleep three to four people, all with bathrooms and kitchenette. The café serves snacks.

Gistiheimilið Brenna (☎ 487 5532; www.mmedia.is/toppbrenna; Þrúðvangur 37; sb Ikr1600) On the road beside the river near the Olis petrol station, this pleasant and pink guesthouse offers hostel-style accommodation and a guest kitchen.

Gistiheimilið Mosfell (☎ 487 5828; fax 487 5004; Þrúðvangur 6; sb Ikr2900, s/d Ikr4100/5300, with bathroom Ikr7700/9200) This large guesthouse is next to the Olis petrol station and tourist office. It has smart, well-kept rooms and plenty of communal spaces.

Hellirinn (☎ 487 5871; hellirinn@simnet.is; Áegissíða; sb Ikr1800, summerhouse with hot pot Ikr6500) This guesthouse on the west side of the river at Áegissíða is good value, but not much English is spoken there.

Hótel Ranga (☎ 487 5700; www.icehotel.is; Suðurlandsvegur; s/d Ikr12,100/18,300, in winter Ikr7900/9900) This huge wooden hotel is about 5km east of Hella. It has bright, wood-panelled rooms, outdoor hot pots and a superior restaurant. Golf, fishing and riding tours can be arranged.

The cheapest place to eat is the grill at the Olis petrol station. Alternatively, there's **Kanslarinn** (☎ 487 5100; meals Ikr750-2690) on the main road or the restaurant **Kristian X** (☎ 487 1515; Ikr400-2500). Both serve the usual burgers, grills and pizzas. Kristian X has another branch on Þrúðvangur.

Getting There & Away

All buses between Reykjavík and Þórsmörk, Vík and Höfn make a brief stop at Hella. In winter the schedule is reduced and there are no buses on Saturday. The fare from Reykjavík is Ikr1340.

HVOLSVÖLLUR

pop 700

This small village is the last settlement of any size before Þórsmörk. The surrounding countryside was the main setting for the events of the *Njáls Saga*, and the farm of **Bergþórshvoll** (Bergþór's Knoll), where saga hero Njál Þorgeirsson and his family were burned to death, is down near the coast, about 21km south of Hvolsvöllur. Hvolsvöllur has a decent supermarket (the last shop before Þórsmörk), a **swimming pool** (☎ 487 8607; Hvolsvegur) and an interesting saga museum. Horse rental can be arranged with **Njálshestar** (☎ 487 8088), about 2km north of Hvolsvöllur at Miðhús.

Sögusetrið

As you might expect, the town museum **Sögusetrið** (Njáls Saga & Viking Exhibition; ☎ 487 8781; Austurvegur 1; admission Ikr400; 9am-5pm Jun-Aug) is devoted to the events of the *Njáls Saga*, which took place in the surrounding hills. There are lots of interesting dioramas about the saga and other aspects of Viking life, labelled in Icelandic, English and German. They also arrange 'Viking feasts' at weekends in July and August; contact the museum for more details.

In summer a seasonal **tourist office** (☎ 487 4878; www.hvolsvollur.is) operates here, open the same hours as the museum.

Sleeping & Eating

There's a small **camp site** (☎ 486 8043; camp site per person Ikr500) opposite the Shell station on Austurvegur; pay at the tourist office. Campers headed for Þórsmörk can pick up last-minute supplies at the 10-11 supermarket on the main road.

Hótel Hvolsvöllur (☎ 487 8187; Hlíðarvegur 7; s/d with TV Ikr4900/6800, with bathroom & TV Ikr9200/12,900) This large hotel in the middle of the village has disabled access, a restaurant and rooftop hot pots. Rooms are large and comfortable, and rates drop by 25% in winter.

Ásgarður (☎ 487 8367; asgardur@immedia.is; sb/s/d Ikr2200/3300/6600) This postcard-perfect wooden house near the church at the start of Route 261 contains a Viking-themed

NJÁLS SAGA

Iceland's most famous legend is a bloodthirsty tale of murder and vengeance, set in the hills around Hvolsvöllur. The saga recounts the story of Gunnar Hámundarson of Hlíðarendi, near Fljótsdalur, and his hot-tempered wife Hallgerður Longlegs. Some time in the 11th century Hallgerður had a falling-out with Bergþóra, wife of Njál Þorgeirsson, who lived at Bergþórshvoll, near Hvolsvöllur. The initial squabble was over some woodland shared by the two farms, but it quickly escalated into a vicious family feud that ended with the death of pretty much every character in the saga.

Gunnar and Njál were friends before the vendetta, but things became increasingly strained as Hallgerður and Bergþóra began murdering each other's clansmen. In one important episode, Hallgerður turned on a local farmer who refused to trade with the family, and Gunnar was then forced to kill the farmer to restore the family honour. He also took some of his anger out on Hallgerður – an act that would later come back to haunt him.

Gunnar was subsequently declared an outlaw, but he couldn't bring himself to leave his beloved farm, and was at home when Gissur the White came looking for revenge. During the siege of the farm at Hlíðarendi, Gunnar snapped his bow string and asked Hallgerður for a lock of her hair to repair it. Remembering her earlier rough treatment, she refused, and Gunnar was killed. For some reason, men laid low by their spouses seem to crop up a lot in Viking stories!

This was not the end of it. The murders continued as Gunnar and Njál's sons and other clan members tried to avenge their slaughtered kin. Njál himself tried to act as a peace-broker, forming treaties and establishing new links between the two families, but in the end it all came to naught. Njál and his wife and sons were trapped in their farm at Bergþóra and, weary of the cycle of violence, they allowed themselves to be burned alive.

The only survivor of the fire was Njál's son-in-law Kári, who launched a legal case against the arsonists, committed a bit of extrajudicial killing himself and was finally reconciled with his arch enemy Flosi, who ordered the burning of the Njál family. The story is incredibly convoluted and it can be hard to keep track of whose cousin or step-brother is murdering whom, but it's certainly epic. Read an online translation of the saga on the website www.sunsite.berkeley.edu/omacl/njal.

steakhouse restaurant. It offers good-value accommodation in the main house and in wooden cabins in the garden. Meals cost Ikr990 to Ikr2350.

For cheap meals, you have the roadhouse-style **Hlíðarendi** (Ikr350-8197) at the Esso petrol station on the main road, which also has a Vin Búd liquor store, or the grill at the Shell petrol station down the road.

Nuddhúsið (☎ 487 8440; Hvolsvegur 29; Ikr900-1900) The town pizzeria, one street back from the main road, also serves burgers, sandwiches and grills.

Getting There & Away

Buses stop at the Shell station on the main road. Public transport to Hvolsvöllur is identical to that going to Selfoss or Hella; the fare from Reykjavík is Ikr1540. In summer buses to Þórsmörk (Ikr1650, 1¼ hours) leave Hvolsvöllur at 10.30am daily, returning at 3.30pm. On weekdays from 15 June to 15 August, a second service leaves Hvolsvöllur at 7pm. In the reverse direction, it leaves Þórsmörk at 7.20am.

Charter flights to Vestmannaeyjar leave from the airstrip at Bakki, about 27km south of Hvolsvöllur. See p130 for details.

AROUND HVOLSVÖLLUR

Keldur

About 5km west of Hvolsvöllur, an unsurfaced road (Route 264) winds north along the Rangárvellir valley to the medieval farm at **Keldur** (☎ 487 8452). This historic farm once belonged to Ingjaldur Holksuldsson, a character in the *Njáls Saga*, and was occupied until 1946 when it was turned into a museum. It closed in 2000 after being damaged by earthquakes, but it's still worth visiting to see the multi-gabled turf building.

Stokkalækur (☎ 487 8780; www.stokkalaekur.is; s/d Ikr10,000/13,000, in winter Ikr7000/9000) Meals and good rooms with bathrooms are available at this white bungalow-style guesthouse, about 2km before Keldur.

There is no public transport along Route 264, but the 12km walk to Keldur is pleasant enough.

Hvolsvöllur to Fljótsdalur

East of Hvolsvöllur, Route 261 follows the edge of the Fljótshlíð hills, offering great views over the floodplain of the Markarfljót river and the Eyjafjallajökull glacier. There are several B&Bs along the surfaced section of the road, which terminates near the farm and church at **Hlíðarendi**, once the home of Gunnar Hámundarson of *Njáls Saga* fame. Although it seems tantalisingly close, Þórsmörk can be reached only by 4WD via mountain road F249, on the far side of the Markarfljót bridge on Route 1.

About 8km after the tarmac ends, Route 261 passes the turf-roofed youth hostel at **Fljótsdalur**. This is a very popular place to stay, and there are great walks in the surrounding countryside, including the 10km trek northeast to the icecap at **Tindfjallajökull** (1462m). With a 4WD, you can continue along mountain road F261 and up to the glacier Mýrdalsjökull.

SLEEPING & EATING

There are several places to stay along Route 261.

Breiðabólstaður (☎ 487 8101; onundur@simnet.is; sb Ikr1800, linen hire Ikr800) This friendly farm is owned by the minister of the church next door. It has a bright and comfortable wooden bunkhouse with a kitchen, TV lounge and indoor barbecue area.

In summer, **Kaffi Langbrók** (☎ 487 8333; Kirkjulæk III) has a coffee shop, Internet café and camp site.

Húsið (☎ 487 8448; husidha@simnet.is; sb Ikr1500, made-up bed Ikr2600) This smart blue-and-white house opposite the village school has sparklingly clean rooms and a kitchen for guests.

Smáratún (☎ 487 8471; www.smaratun.has.it; sb Ikr1700, made-up bed Ikr2400, summer house Ikr8900) This attractive white farm with a blue tin roof has horses, sleeping bag spaces, B&B rooms and a summer house that sleeps six people.

Fljótsdalur Youth Hostel (☎ 487 8498; www.hostel.is; sb member/non-member Ikr1600/1950) This cosy turf-roofed farmhouse is a great place to relax, and it has a good library. However, advance booking is strongly advised. Other HI hostels in Iceland can tell you when Fljótsdalur is booked out by groups. The nearest shop is 27km away, so bring all the supplies you need with you.

GETTING THERE & AWAY

In summer, Austurleid-SBS buses from Reykjavík to Hólaskjól pass through Fljótsdalur (Ikr2150, three hours), or you could try hitching from Hvolsvöllur.

Hvolsvöllur to Þórsmörk

The road to Þórsmörk (Route 249/F249) begins at just east of the Markarfljót river on Route 1. Although it quickly turns into a 4WD-only road, there are a few interesting sights at the start of the road that can be reached by conventional vehicle.

From the highway, you can see the beautiful high falls at **Seljalandsfoss**, which tumble over a rocky scarp into a deep, green splash pool. This wonderful waterfall routinely creates rainbows in the afternoon sunshine, and you can walk around behind the tumbling water on a slippery, eroded path. Buses on the Höfn–Reykjavík run often wait here for the Þórsmörk bus, giving you time to take a few quick photos.

A few hundred metres further down the Þórsmörk road, in the grounds of the farm Hamragarðar, is the spooky waterfall **Gljúfurárfoss** (Canyon River Falls), which gushes down into a hidden canyon. To catch a glimpse of the falls, you'll either have to wade up the stream beside the farm or climb up the steep rock wall that hides the falls.

SLEEPING

Right next to the hidden waterfall at Gljúfurárfoss, you can camp at the farm **Hamragarðar** (☎ 487 8920; camp site per person Ikr500).

About 5km closer to Þórsmörk, there's farmhouse accommodation at **Stóra-Mörk III** (☎ 487 8903; frontpage.simnet.is/storamork; sb Ikr1500, made-up bed Ikr2300) on Route 249.

RAFTING IN SOUTHWEST ICELAND

The rivers running down from the interior of Iceland provide great opportunities for white-water rafting. The most popular is the Þjórsá river between Hekla and Selfoss, which has rapids ranging from grade 2 to grade 3 – bumpy enough to be exciting but gentle enough for anyone to be able to give it a go. More serious white water can be found on the Markarfljót near Þórsmörk and on the Hólmsá on the east side of Mýrdalsjökull. Most rafting trips are run as day tours from Reykjavík, and costs range from Ikr5900 to Ikr8900 for the day, including transfers and lunch. For more information, contact **Highlanders** (☎ 568 3030; www.hl.is), **This is Iceland** (☎ 561 6010; www.this.is/iceland) or the **Activity Group** (☎ 580 9900; www.activity.is).

Nearby, on Route 1, the school at **Heimaland** (☎ 487 8920) has sleeping bag spaces and a camp site in summer.

ÞÓRSMÖRK

The valley of Þórsmörk (the Woods of Thor) was created by glacial streams running off from underneath the icecaps of Eyjafjallajökull and Mýrdalsjökull. It's undeniably one of the most beautiful locations in Iceland: tongues of ice extend down from the glaciers towards the valley floor and the meltwater streams converge into the Markarfljót river, which empties into the sea near Skógar, depositing huge sandbars of black volcanic sand.

Beautiful as it is, Þórsmörk is extremely popular. Since 1921 the valley has been protected as a recreational reserve, and on summer weekends it can be more crowded here than in central Reykjavík, particularly in July, when students from around Iceland descend on the valley for a huge party. It's all good-natured fun, but if you want to take your place among the intoxicated revellers and duelling car stereos, you should make a booking months in advance. If peace and tranquillity are more your thing, you don't have to go far off the beaten track to find a bit of solitude, and if you're feeling a little more adventurous, the icecaps await.

The main accommodation area is at Húsadalur, where the Austurleið-SBS bus from Reykjavík terminates. On the hill behind the hut is the cave **Sönghellir** (one of several 'singing caves' in Iceland), from where a maze of walking trails leads through scrubby dwarf birch forests to the Þórsmörk hut, about 3km further up the valley. The summit of **Valahnúkur** (458m), immediately west of Þórsmörk hut, has a view disc that identifies all the surrounding mountains. Allow about an hour to get there from either Húsadalur or Þórsmörk.

The higher reaches of the valley are known as **Goðaland** (Land of the Gods) and are full of bizarre hoodoo formations. There's a mountain hut at Básar, on the far bank of the Krossá river, which marks the start of the popular trek over Fimmvörðuháls Pass to Skógar. The trail passes right between Eyjafjallajökull and Mýrdalsjökull, and the pass itself makes an easy day trek from either Þórsmörk or Básar. To get to Básar from further down the valley, you must cross the pedestrian bridge over the Krossá, just downstream from the Þórsmörk hut. Experienced four-wheel-drivers might be able to ford the river in a high-clearance 4WD vehicle.

Trekking

Loads of treks are possible in the mountains around Þórsmörk, and most can be undertaken independently without any special equipment, but be sure to carry plenty of water and a compass. The relevant topographic sheet is the Landmælingar Íslands *Þórsmörk/Landmannalaugar* (1:100,000). As well as local hikes, you can continue inland to Landmannalaugar (see p254). Alternatively, you could head down to the coast at Skógar via Fimmvörðuháls Pass – see later in this section.

If you'd rather be guided over the difficult terrain, the travel agency **Útivist** (☎ 562 1000; www.utivist.is; Laugavegur 178, IS-101 Reykjavík) runs guided treks in the valley every weekend from mid June to late August. Útivist also owns the Básar and Fimmvörðuskáli huts. Similar tours are available through **Ferðafélag Íslands** (☎ 568 2533; www.fi.is; Mörkin 6, IS-108 Reykjavík), which runs the Þórsmörk hut and the mountain huts along the Landmannalaugar-Þórsmörk trail.

SHORT TREKS

From Route F249, you can easily hike up to **Steinholtsjökull**, a tongue of ice extending off the north side of Eyjafjallajökull. The ice has carved a sheer-sided, 100m-deep gorge, and the short river Stakksholtsá flows out from under it and winds down to Markarfljót. Further west the larger glacial tongue of **Gígjökull** descends into a small lagoon right beside Route F249 and fills it with carved icebergs. To explore the main icecaps at Eyjafjallajökull and Mýrdalsjökull you'll need proper equipment – including ropes, crampons and ice-axes – and ideally a GPS device. Several companies offer hiking trips on Sólheimajókull, a tongue extending down from Mýrdalsjökull near Skógar – see p122 for details.

ÞÓRSMÖRK TO SKÓGAR TREK

The dramatic and popular trek from Þórsmörk to Skógar passes between the glaciers of Eyjafjallajökull and Mýrdalsjökull and will get you right up among the snow and ice. The trek can be done in a long day, but it's more enjoyable to break the journey at Fimmvörðuháls Pass (1093m), which has a mountain hut run by Útivist (see Sleeping following). Although the glaciers seem close enough to touch, this walk is fairly easy and you won't need any special gear. However, you should keep an eye on the weather – it can change rapidly up here.

The trek starts about 1.5km east of the Básar hut at Goðaland and then climbs steadily to **Mornisheiði**, which has dramatic views over Mýrdalsjökull, and Eyjafjallajökull. From here, you face a steep ascent to the ridge at **Heljarkambur**. The next stage takes you across tundra and snowfields to **Fimmvörðuháls Pass** itself, with Mýrdalsjökull on the left and Eyjafjallajökull on the right. The Fimmvörðuskáli mountain hut is a short walk off the main track, near a small lake.

The following day, you can begin the trek down to Skógar. The main trail is clear and well trodden, but an interesting alternative is to leave the track at the footbridge and follow the stream Skógá down to the waterfall **Skógafoss**, about 1km west of Skógar village. Both routes are marked on the Landmælingar Íslands map *Landmannalaugar-Þórsmörk*. Owing to snow the trek is best attempted from mid-July to early September.

Destination Iceland (www.dice.is) in Reykjavík overs a package with bus transfers and accommodation in the mountain huts at Fimmvörðuháls Pass and Húsadalur for Ikr10,900.

Sleeping

There are three huts in the Þórsmörk area – at Þórsmörk, Básar and Húsadalur – and another at the top of the Fimmvörðuháls Pass. All have cooking facilities, showers and running water, but they tend to be packed with Icelanders at weekends. You'll need to bring your own food and sleeping bag, and it wouldn't hurt to bring your own stove, to avoid waiting for the crowded facilities. To preserve the pristine environment, wild camping is prohibited, but all of the huts at Þórsmörk have camping areas.

To book spaces at the Þórsmörk huts, contact the organisations listed following.

HÚSADALUR

The Húsadalur hut **Austurleiðarskáli** (camp site per person Ikr500, sb Ikr1400-1600, 5-person cottages

Ikr5900) is almost a tourist village. You can book through the bus company **Austurleið-SBS** (☎ 482 3400; www.austurleid.is).

ÞÓRSMÖRK HUT

The Þórsmörk hut **Skagfjörðskáli** (camp site per person Ikr500, sb member/non-member Ikr1100/1700) can sleep 75 and may be booked through **Ferðafélag Íslands** (☎ 568 2533; www.fi.is; Mörkin 6, IS-108 Reykjavík). This organisation can also take bookings for any of the huts along the Landmannalaugar–Þórsmörk track.

BÁSAR HUT & FIMMVÖRÐUHÁLS PASS

There is space for 80 people in the hut at **Básar** (camp site per person Ikr500, sb Ikr1300), which is booked through **Útivist** (☎ 562 1000; www.utivist.is; Laugavegur 178, IS-101 Reykjavík).

The 23-bed hut at **Fimmvörðuskáli** (sb Ikr1300), on the pass between Eyjafjallajökull and Mýrdalsjökull, is also booked through Útivist. It lies 600m west of the main trail, so it's easy to miss in poor weather. The hut is very comfortable, but Útivist tour groups have priority here, so it's often booked out.

Getting There & Away

BUS

From 1 June to 14 September buses leave Reykjavík for Þórsmörk (Ikr3200, 3½ hours) at 8.30am daily, reaching Húsadalur around noon and returning at 3.30pm. On weekdays from 15 June to 15 August a second service leaves Reykjavík at 5pm; in the reverse direction, the extra bus leaves Þórsmörk at 7.20am.

Numerous organised tours come up here in summer. Destination Iceland and others offer day trips to Þórsmörk from Reykjavík for around Ikr6400. See p303 for further information.

CAR & BIKE

Don't even think about attempting the mountain road to Þórsmörk (Route F249) with a conventional vehicle. To get all the way to Þórsmörk, you'll need a 4WD with decent clearance – a 4WD car probably won't make it over the bumps. Plenty of pedal cyclists fight their way up to Þórsmörk, but it's a long hard slog. You can shave a few kilometres off the journey by leaving Route 1 near the farm Vorsabær and taking the old bridge over the Markarfljót, which is now closed to cars.

HIKING

You can walk to Þórsmörk from Landmannalaugar (three or four days), Skógar (one or two days) or along Routes 249 and F249 from Seljaland (one long day). The Skógar trek is covered in more detail on p120, and the Landmannalaugar to Þórsmörk trek is covered in the Central Iceland chapter (p256).

SKÓGAR

The tiny settlement of Skógar is about 1km off Route 1 beneath the brooding mass of the Eyjafjallajökull icecap. The dramatic Skógafoss waterfall tumbles down a moss-encrusted cliff just outside Skógar, and the village is the start – or the end point – of the trek over the Fimmvörðuháls Pass to Þórsmörk. This is covered in detail in the Þórsmörk section (p120). Skógar is mainly a summer resort and is pretty quiet out of season, but it boasts one of Iceland's best museums and there are hotels, a camp site and a bank.

Folk Museum

The highlight of Skógar – indeed of this whole stretch of coast – is the wonderful **Skógar Folk Museum** (☎ 487 8845; www.skogasafn.is; adult/under-16 Ikr600/free; 9am-6.30pm Jun-Aug, 10am-5pm May & Sep), which covers all aspects of Icelandic life. The vast collection was put together by 82-year-old Þórður Tómasson, who began collecting when he was just 14. This is one of the best museums in the country, and you might be lucky enough to meet Þórður in person – he often comes in to play traditional songs for visitors on an old church organ. As well as the main museum, there are various restored farmhouses in the grounds, and a new hangar-like building at the back houses an interesting museum devoted to transport in Iceland.

Skógafoss

A short walk west of the Edda hotel is thundering **Skógafoss**, which tumbles 62m over a rocky scarp, kicking up vast sheets of mist. The falls are very dramatic, and the camp site here is the starting point for one of the trekking routes up to Fimmvörðuháls Pass. Legend has it that a settler named Þrasi hid a chest of booty behind the falls, but no-one has yet been able to find it.

Sólheimajókull

This tongue-like projection off the main icecap at Mýrdalsjökull is visible from the main road, and a small dirt track leads to within a few hundred yards of the ice. It's easy to scramble up on top of the glacier, but be careful if you come up here, and keep an eye out for fissures and crevasses. The sand and gravel deposited by the rivulets running out of the end of the glacier are a definite no-go area because of quicksand.

Activities

The most popular walk in the area is the two-day trek over Fimmvörðuháls Pass to Þórsmörk – see p120 for details. However, you can also take a morning trek up to the pass and return to Skógar the same day. The trail starts on the 4WD track to Skógarheiði behind the village. The return trip should take about seven hours.

Icelandic Mountain Guides (☎ 587 9999; www.mountainguide.is) runs ice-trekking tours to Sólheimajókull from Reykjavík, with about four hour's walking with crampons on the ice and the opportunity for some proper ice-climbing (Ikr14,900).

For more icy shenanigans, **Arcanum Adventure Tours** (☎ 487 1500; www.snow.is) offers ski-doo trips on Sólheimajókull and Mýrdalsjökull glaciers. Prices start at Ikr7200 for one hour, and pick up from Skógar is Ikr2000.

Horse-riding trips can be arranged through the farm **Skálakot** (☎ 487 8953), 10km west of Skógar. Rates start at Ikr2300 for one hour.

Sleeping & Eating

The Skógar **camp site** (☎ 487 8843) beside the waterfall is free, but a contribution is requested. There are toilets and sinks, and Skógafoss provides a soothing backdrop while you sleep.

Edda Hotel (☎ 487 8830; www.hoteledda.is; sb Ikr1100-2000, s/d with shared bathroom Ikr5000/6400; ☒) From May to September you can stay at this modern and comfortable summer hotel on the road to the museum. The two buildings share a pool, hot pot and restaurant.

Hótel Skógar (☎ 487 8988; www.hotelskogar.is; s/d/tr 9500/14,000/18,000, in winter Ikr8000/10,000/12,500) This architecturally interesting hotel has a decent restaurant and tasteful rooms with TV, phone, shower and flagstone floors.

Drangshlíð I (☎ 487 8868; drangshlid@islandia.is; s/d Ikr6300/10,200) This modern white farmhouse is about 2km west of Skógar and at the foot of a green cliff full of nesting birds. It has large guest rooms and a big bright dining room for meals. Look out for the barns built into caves in the surrounding fields.

Nearby is **Hótel Edinborg** (☎ 487 8011; www.islandia.is/thorn; sb/s/d Ikr1800/6000/9000), a tall tin-clad house with inviting wooden rooms. Further uphill is the farm **Seljavellir** (☎ 487 8810; camp site per person Ikr500), which has a lovely camp site with a geothermal pool and hot pots.

Further west a small dirt road loops north off Route 1 passing the upmarket **Country Hotel Anna** (Moldnúpur; ☎ 487 8950; www.simnet.is/moldnupur; s/d with bathroom Ikr9900/13,500), and the cheaper **Skálakot** (☎ 487 8953; skalakot@simnet.is; sb Ikr1700), which also offers horse rental.

Heading east from Skógar, inexpensive farmhouse accommodation is available at **Sólheimahjáleiga** (☎ 487 1320; eyrunfb@simnet.is; sb Ikr1650, s/d Ikr3500/5000).

For information on the huts at Fimmvörðuháls Pass, see p120.

Getting There & Away

All buses from Reykjavík to Höfn or Vík stop at the Edda Hotel in Skógar (Ikr2230, three hours).

VÍK Í MÝRDAL

pop 310

This tiny trading community sits beneath a brooding ridge on a broad black-sand beach, close to the start of the Mýrdalssandur sand plains. The name Vík í Mýrdal means 'Bay of the Marshy Valley', but it's usually shortened to just Vík. Despite being the rainiest spot in Iceland, Vík is a welcoming little place, and the surrounding countryside is full of natural wonders, including the sea stacks at Reynisdrangur and the glacier Mýrdalsjökull. The village started life as a fishing outpost, but a cooperative society was formed here in 1906 and is still Vík's biggest employer.

Information

The **tourist office** (☎ 487 1395; www.vik.is; Víkurbraut 28; ⏰ 10am-noon & 1-5pm May-Sep) is housed in the historic building Brydebúð. The Búnaðarbankinn has an ATM and a foreign exchange desk.

Sights

The tin-clad house **Brydebúð** was built in Vestmannaeyjar in 1831 and moved to Vík in 1895. Today it houses the tourist office, the Halldórskaffi restaurant and a small **fishing museum** (☎ adult/under-16 Ikr250/free; 🕑 11am-9pm).

The most famous sight in the area is the cluster of sea stacks at **Reynisdrangur**, which rise from the ocean at the west end of Vík's black-sand beach like sinister rocky fingers. The highest stack is 66m tall, and the cliffs on the shore here are good for puffin watching. A nice short walk west from Vík takes you up to the top of the ridge **Reynisfjall** (340m), which offers great views along the coast. You can continue over the top of the ridge to Reyniskirkja and down to the wonderful volcanic beach at Reynisfjara. The track up here turns off Route 1 by the first house in Vík.

You can rent horses at the farm **Vellir** (☎ 487 1312) about 6km west of Vík on Route 219. Rates start at Ikr2500 for one hour.

Tours

Destination Iceland (www.dice.is) runs a 10-hour tour from Reykjavík that takes in Eyrarbakki, Seljalandsfoss, Skógafoss, Dyrhólaey, Sólheimajókull and Vík. It operates on Monday, Wednesday, Friday and Sunday from May to October (Tuesday and Saturday in winter) and costs Ikr6600 per person.

Sleeping & Eating

The Vík **camp site** (☎ 487 1345; camp site per person Ikr500) sits under a grassy ridge at the east end of the village, just beyond the Edda Hótel. There's an octagonal building with cooking facilities, toilets and showers. Six-person farmhouse-style cottages are also available.

Norður-Vík (☎ 487 1106; www.hostel.is; Suðurvikurvegur; sb Ikr1400/1750) Vík's friendly youth hostel is housed in a beige house on the hill behind the village. It has clean rooms and a guest lounge and kitchen.

Gistihús Ársalir (☎ 487 1400; simon@ismennt.is; Austurvegur 7; sb/s/d Ikr1750/4300/5000) This welcoming white house on the outskirts of the village has spacious rooms with shared bathrooms (some with balconies) and a kitchen for guests. Guests can hire mountain bikes in summer.

Hótel Lundi (☎ 487 1212; www.hotelpuffin.is; Víkurbraut 26a; s/d with bathroom Ikr7200/9800) This small family-run hotel is near Brydebúð. It has rooms with telephones and bathrooms and a respectable restaurant. Attached is the cheaper **Guesthouse Puffin** (Víkurbraut 24a; sb Ikr1900, s/d with shared bathroom Ikr3200/5500), which has a guest kitchen and lounge.

Edda Hótel Vík Í Mýrdal (☎ 444 4840; www.hoteledda.is; s/d with bathroom Ikr8500/10,700) This smart modern hotel sits at the east end of the village. It has a restaurant and breakfast room facing the ocean.

For self-caterers, there's a large Kjaroval supermarket near Brydebúð.

Diners have the choice of the restaurants at the Edda Hótel and Hótel Lundi or the recommended **Halldórskaffi** (Austurvegur 18; mains Ikr400-1800) in the same building as the tourist office. It serves pizzas, burgers, sandwiches, grills and beers in an old-world wooden dining room.

For cheap eats, head to the **Víkurgrill** (snacks Ikr750-1580) at the Esso petrol station, which also has a Vin Búd liquor shop.

Getting There & Away

Vík lies on the main bus route between Höfn and Reykjavík, and buses stop at the Esso petrol station. In summer there are at least two daily buses from Reykjavík as far as Vík (Ikr2750, four hours) leaving at 8.30am and 5pm and returning from Vík at 7.30am and 1.45pm. In winter Reykjavík–Höfn buses leave Reykjavík at 12.30pm, returning from Vík at 4pm.

AROUND VÍK

Reynisfjara

On the west side of Reynisfjall, the high ridge above Vík, a dirt road leads down to the black volcanic beach at Reynisfjara, which is backed by an incredible stack of **basalt columns**, like a giant church organ. The surrounding cliffs are full of caves formed from twisted and tortured basalt, and puffin chicks belly-flop off the cliffs here every summer. Immediately offshore are the sea stacks of **Reynisdrangur**. There are fabulous views west along the beach to the rock arch at **Dyrhólaey**.

You can stay at the friendly **Garðar** (☎ 487 1260; sb Ikr2000, made-up beds Ikr3000) just behind the beach, but there are only four beds, so book well in advance, especially in the puffin season. Wild camping is also possible at the wild western end of the beach, by the Dyrhólaós lagoon.

Dyrhólaey

About 10km west of Vík, unsurfaced Route 218 runs southeast to the rocky plateau at Dyrhólaey, which rises dramatically from the surrounding plain. According to the *Njáls Saga*, Kári – the only survivor of the fire that wiped out the Njáls clan – had his farm here. The rocky spur is protected as a bird reserve for eider ducks and arctic terns, and it is closed to visitors during the nesting season. At the eastern end of the spur is a vast rock arch, which is best seen from the long sandy beach at Reynisfjara. You can take a tour through the arch in an amphibious vehicle with **Dyrhólaeyjarferðir** (☎ 487 8500; www.dyrholaey.com; tours Ikr1900/2900 per adult/child). In Vík, the hostel Norður-Vík runs sunset tours to Dyrhólaey in summer for Ikr800. Just before the causeway to Dyrhólaey, a track leads to the cave **Loftsalahellir**, which was used for council meetings in saga times.

SLEEPING

Camping is prohibited on Dyrhólaey itself, but you can camp on the long beach at Reynisfjara – see p123 for details.

Hótel Dyrhólaey (☎ 487 1333; dyrholaey@islandia.is; s/d/tr Ikr8900/11,700/16,000) About 10km west of Vík at the farm Brekkur I, this large, green guesthouse has the usual big rooms that you find in all modern bungalow hotels in Iceland – and there's a restaurant.

Mýrdalsjökull

Looming above Vík, Mýrdalsjökull is Iceland's fourth-largest icecap. It covers 700 sq km. The glacier rises to 1480m at its highest point and reaches a maximum thickness of more than 1000m. The volcano Katla snoozes beneath the icecap and periodically blasts up through the ice, drowning the coastal plain with meltwater, sand and tephra. It has been estimated that the material slewing off the volcano moves at an incredible 70,000 cubic metres per second – a rate five times the bore of the Amazon River. The most recent eruption was in 1918, but there may have been another small eruption under the ice in 1955, and scientists predict that another eruption is due some time during the noughties. With the right equipment, treks are possible on the main icecap and on the finger-like projection Sólheimajökull, close to Skógar. See p122 for details.

Destination Iceland (www.dice.is) runs a tour from Reykjavík to Mýrdalsjökull, with a snowmobile ride on the ice, a beach drive and photo stops at Seljalandsfoss and Skógafoss, but it costs Ikr20,900. Jeep tours to Þórsmörk and Mýrdalsjökull are run by **Highlanders** (☎ 568 3030; www.hl.is) for Ikr17,500. From May to August, **Dog Steam Tours** (☎ 487 5412; www.dogsledding.is) offers one-hour dog-sledding trips on the glacier for Ikr6900, including transfers by mountain bus and snowscooter.

Mælifell

About 5km east of Vík, a dirt road (Route 214) leads 14km to the ridge at Mælifell (642m) on the edge of Mýrdalsjökull. The simple camp site at **Þakgil** (☎ 853 4889; camp site per person Ikr500) is high in the hills and makes a convenient base from which to explore the icecap.

Hótel Höfðabrekka (☎ 487 1208; hotel-hokabrekka@isholf.is; s/d with bathroom 9000/12,000, in winter Ikr5000/7800), at the start of Route 214, is reputedly haunted. It offers tasteful wood-panelled rooms.

Mýrdalssandur

Just east of Vík are the vast black lava sand flats of Mýrdalssandur, formed from material washed out from underneath the glacier Mýrdalsjökull. The 700-sq-km sands are bleak and apparently lifeless, but arctic foxes (which have a black coat in summer) and seabirds are common here. South of Route 1, the small peak of **Hjörleifshöfði** (231m high) rises above the sands and offers good views towards the Westman Islands. On the other side of Route 1, the green hill of **Hafursey** (582m) is another possible destination for walks from Vík. As you head east towards Höfn, look out for the stone cairns constructed by early travellers to mark safe routes across the sands.

At the eastern end of the strands, near the estuary of the Kúdafljót, there is sleeping bag accommodation at the farm **Herjólfsstaðir** (☎ 487 1390; sb Ikr1500). It's on Route 211, in a small green area in the middle of the black sand fields.

VESTMANNAEYJAR

Vestmannaeyjar (the Westman Islands) takes its name from the Irish slaves (West Men) who fled to the islands from the mainland during the 11th century. Most of the 16 islands in the group were formed by submarine volcanoes 5000 to 10,000 years ago, but tiny Surtsey, created by an undersea eruption in 1963, is one of the world's youngest islands.

All of Vestmannaeyjar's human population lives on the largest island, Heimaey, which rises from a flat central plain to almost perpendicular cliffs along the north coast. Several other islands have temporary huts used by puffin hunters and egg collectors. The economic mainstay of Vestmannaeyjar is fishing, and the islands supply around 15% of Iceland's catch of halibut, cod, sole, haddock, ocean perch, lobster, herring, catfish and pollock.

Perhaps because of its relative isolation, Vestmannaeyjar is one of the friendliest places in Iceland, and the settlement on Heimaey is lively and self-sufficient. There are daily flights here from Reykjavík, and charter flights come here from Selfoss and Bakki (near Hvolsvöllur). The ferry *Herjólfur* provides daily connections to Þorlákshöfn on the mainland. Heimaey is small enough to explore on foot, and there are some excellent places to stay and eat. The island became

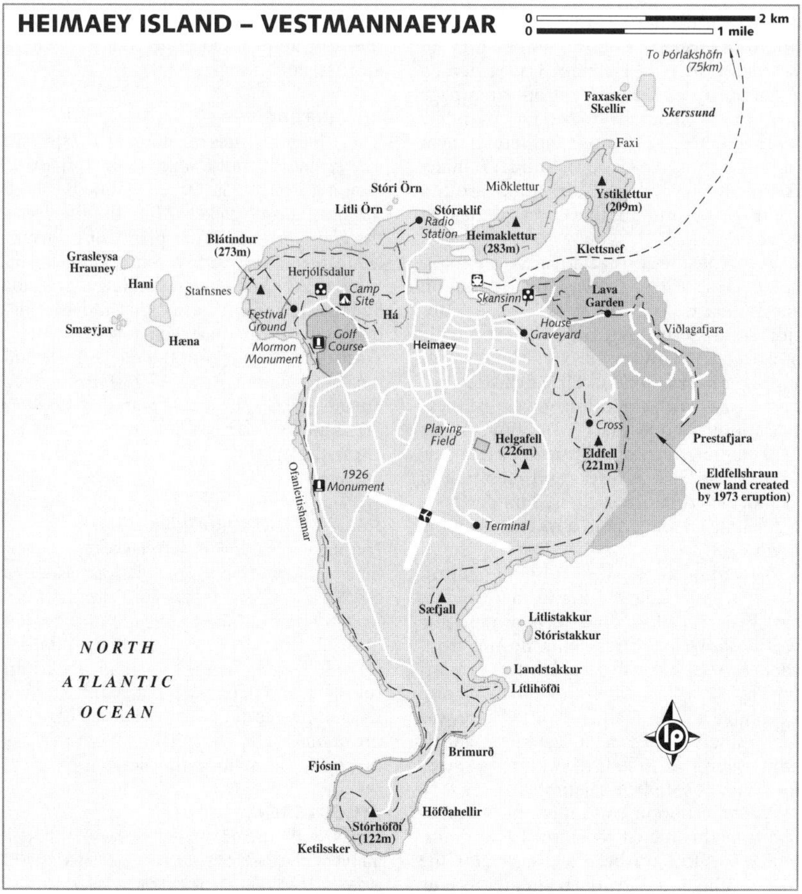

famous around the world in 1973 when the town was almost obliterated by the eruption of the volcano Eldfell.

History

According to the *Landnámabók*, Heimaey was first settled by Irish slaves (Westmen) belonging to Hjörleifur, blood-brother of Ingólfur Arnarson. After murdering their master, they fled to the rugged islands off the coast, but were quickly hunted down and killed. The first permanent settler was Herjólfur Barðursson, who settled in the Herjólfsdalur valley on Heimaey.

In the following centuries Heimaey was attacked numerous times by marauding ships. First came the English, who used Heimaey as their North Atlantic headquarters throughout the 15th century, building Iceland's only stone fort at Skansinn. In 1627 Heimaey was raided by Algerian pirates, who went on a rampage around the island, murdering 40 islanders and kidnapping 242 more and selling them into slavery. To escape the raiders, many islanders scaled the cliff walls around Heimaey or hid in the caves along the west coast.

The volcanoes that formed Heimaey came close to destroying the island on several occasions. The most famous eruption of modern times began unexpectedly at 2am on 23 January 1973. Without warning the eastern slope of Helgafell was torn apart by a vast explosion. Over the next five months more than 30 million tonnes of lava spewed over the town of Heimaey, destroying 360 houses and creating a brand-new mountain, the red cinder cone Eldfell, just a few hundred metres from the town centre.

A third of the town was buried beneath the lava flow, and the island increased in size by 2.5 sq km. Newsreels around the world showed the residents fleeing from their homes against a backdrop of fountaining lava. All 5000 inhabitants were evacuated to the mainland, and there was just a single fatality: an alleged drug addict who attempted to loot the town pharmacy and died of smoke inhalation.

As the eruption continued, the advancing lava threatened to close the harbour, which would have been a disaster for the local fishing industry. In an attempt to slow the lava down, firefighters hosed the flows with cold seawater, which seemed to work, as the lava halted just 175m short of the harbour mouth. In the event, the harbour facilities were actually improved by the increased shelter gained from the flow.

In September 1998 Keiko the killer whale (who starred in the Hollywood movie *Free Willy*) was released into the North Atlantic ocean off Vestmannaeyjar.

HEIMAEY

pop 4558

The village of Heimaey occupies most of the northern half of the island of the same name, and it has better tourist facilities than many towns on the mainland. Heimaey enjoys a spectacular setting, squeezed between a series of dramatic *klettur* (escarpments) to the west and the volcanic cones of Eldfell and Helgafell to the east.

Information

The helpful **tourist office** (☎ 481 3555; www.eyjar.is/eyjar; Skildingavegur; 🕑 8am-5pm Mon-Fri, 10am-4pm Sat, 1-5pm Sun May-Sep) is in the same building as the ticket office for the ferry, the *Herjólfur*, and it has plenty of information on the Vestmannaeyjar region. If you need an ATM or foreign exchange, head for Sparisjóðurinn on Bárustigur and Íslandsbanki on Vestmannabraut.

Internet access is available for Ikr200 per hour at the Pizza 67 restaurant (see Eating, p130) or the **library** (☎ 481 1194; Ráðhústræti; 🕑 11am-7pm Mon-Thu, 11am-5pm Fri, 1-4pm Sat & Sun).

Sights

FISKA-OG NÁTTÚRÚGRIPASAFN

Heimaey's **natural history museum** (Fiska-og Nattúrugripasafn; ☎ 481 1997; Heiðarvegur; adult/child Ikr300/free; 🕑 11am-5pm May-Aug, 3-5pm Sat & Sun Sep-Apr) was founded in 1964, and it has an interesting collection of stuffed and preserved wildlife. There's a small aquarium full of weird Icelandic fish, and a video link to the nearby puffin nesting cliffs. The museum acts as a hospital for puffin chicks during the annual nesting season.

BYGGÐASAFN

Housed in the Heimaey library, this **folk museum** (Byggðasafn; ☎ 481 1194; Ráðhústræti; adult/under-14 Ikr 300/100; 🕑 11am-5pm mid-May–mid-Aug,

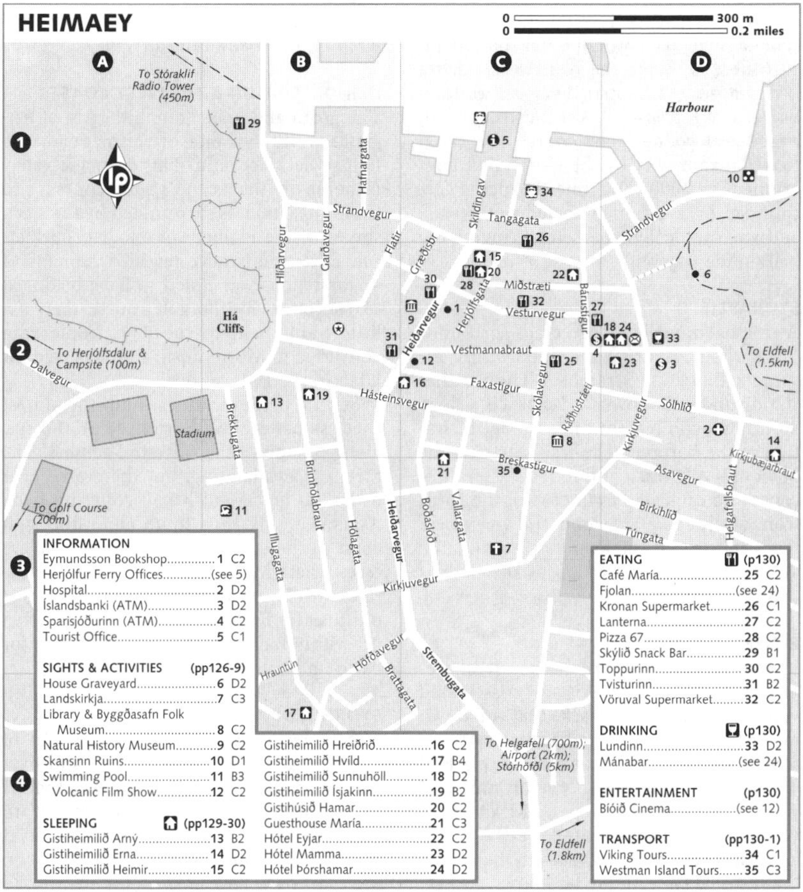

3-5pm Sat & Sun at other times) has loads of interesting displays on local history, including a large section on the 1973 eruption. Note the cabinet of Nazi regalia, from Vestmannaeyjar's short-lived branch of the Nazi Party. The movement fizzled out once WWII started, and the items on display were deposited anonymously in a plastic bag in front of the museum in the middle of the night!

VOLCANIC FILM SHOW

The tumultuous events of the 1973 eruption and the creation of Surtsey in 1963 are relived daily at the **Volcanic Film Show** (☎ 481 3366; Heiðarvegur; Ikr600). There are five other documentaries on offer, including shows on whales, puffins and various Vestmannaeyjar traditions. The shows last 55 minutes, starting at 11am, 2pm, 3.30pm and 9pm in English. The shows at 11am, 3.30pm and 9pm are also in German, and the 2pm show is also in French.

SKANSINN

This historical complex at the edge of the 1973 lava flows preserves the walls of the old stone fortress, built by the English in the 15th century to protect their trade interests in the Atlantic. You can also see the remains of the old town water tanks, which crumpled under the weight of lava. The small museum **Landlyst** (adult/child Ikr300/100; 11am-5pm mid-May–mid-Sep) is housed in the old town maternity hospital, built in 1847. It has a small display of medical equipment. Also here is the so-called **Norwegian church** (admission free; 🕒 11am-5pm mid-May–mid-Sep, 11am-5pm Sat & Sun at other times), a reconstruction of a medieval wooden stave church, presented to Vestmannaeyjar by the Norwegian government in 2000. The inner chapel is surrounded by a bitumen-coated outer wall, and you can deafen yourself by ringing the bell on the way out.

STÓRAKLIF

A ring of strangely eroded crags surrounds the harbour, offering the opportunity for some exhilarating scrambles. The weather station and radio tower at **Stóraklif** is a steep 40-minute climb from the Esso petrol station at the harbour. The trail starts on the obvious 4WD track and follows a series of ropes and cables up to the top of the cliffs, from where there are wonderful views over the whole island and over to the mainland. Take care on your way up as the path is badly eroded.

ELDFELLSHRAUN

Known as Eldfellshraun, the new land created by the 1973 lava flow is now crisscrossed with a maze of hiking tracks that run down to the fort at Skansinn and a small **memorial garden**, which provides a welcome splash of colour in this other-worldly environment. If you climb the wooden steps on Kirkjuvegur, you'll reach a curious **'house graveyard'**, where locals have erected memorials to the houses that now lie beneath the lava flows.

ELDFELL & HELGAFELL

The 221m-high volcanic cone of **Eldfell** appeared from nowhere in the early hours of 23 January 1973. Eldfell makes an easy climb from Heimaey, with the best route to the rim climbing the collapsed northern wall of the crater, where a cross was erected on 3 June 1993 to commemorate the 20th anniversary of the eruption. The summit still steams slightly, and the ground is still hot enough in places to bake bread or char wood.

With difficulty you can descend over the cinders to the base of 226m **Helgafell**, the 5000-year-old cone that formed most of central Heimaey. The cinders are grassed over today, and you can scramble up here without much difficulty from the football pitch on the road to the airport.

HERJÓLFSDALUR & THE WEST COAST

The green and grassy amphitheatre of **Herjólfsdalur** was the home of Vestmannaeyjar's first settler, Herjólfur. This dramatic valley is home to the island's golf course and camp site, and it is surrounded by the steep slopes of the extinct volcano Norðurklettur. Excavations have revealed remains of a Norse house, assumed to have belonged to Herjólfur. By the golf course there's a little monument to the 200 people who converted to Mormonism and departed for Utah in the 19th century.

Several perilous tracks climb the almost sheer slopes around Herjólfsdalur and run along the top of the ridge to **Stafnsnes**. The ascent is exhilarating, but there are sheer drops, so be careful if you come up here. A gentler walk runs south along the west coast of the island, passing numerous **lava caves** where local people hid from the pirates in 1627. At **Ofanleitishamar** hundreds of puffins nest in the cliffs, and you can often get within metres of the cheeky scamps for close-up photos.

STÓRHÖFÐI

The rocky peninsula at the south end of Heimaey is linked to the main island by a narrow isthmus, and there are good views from the 122m summit. It's possible to scramble down to the boulder beach at **Brimurð** and continue along the cliffs on the east coast, returning by the main road just before the airport. From June to August the sea cliffs at **Lítlihöfði** are a good place to watch puffins.

LANDSKIRKJA

The lava stopped just short of the stone Landskirkja church in the middle of town. It's worth a visit to see the carved wooden doors, which feature scenes from Vestmannaeyjar's history.

Activities

Heimaey's **swimming pool** (adult/child Ikr200/100; 🕒 7am-9pm Mon-Fri, 9am-5pm Sat & Sun) is open from 25 May to 1 October. Golfers can hire clubs at the 18-hole **golf course** (☎ 481 2363; www.eyjar.is/golf) in the Herjólfsdalur valley; green fees are Ikr1500. Horse rental is available through **Hestaleiga Gunnars** (☎ 481 1478) at the farm Lukka, near the airport. Kayaks can be rented from **Kayakferðir** (☎ 861 3090).

In summer you can see locals practising the ancient art of cliff-scaling – an essential skill for egg-collectors and puffin-hunters – on the cliffs between the harbour and Herjólfsdalur.

Tours

The main tour operator at Vestmannaeyjar is **Viking Tours** (☎ 488 4884; www.boattours.is), which offers boat tours around the island that visit various caves and bird-nesting cliffs at 10.30am and 3.30pm (Ikr2000). Their whale-watching tours depart at 5pm (Ikr3500). **Westman Island Tours** (☎ 481 1909) offers various bus and boat tours of the islands.

Festivals & Events

The three-day Þjóðhátíð (People's Feast) is held at the festival ground at Herjólfsdalur over the first weekend in August to commemorate Iceland's first constitution, proclaimed on 1 July 1874. Bad weather prevented Vestmannaeyjar people from joining the mainland celebration, so they held their own festival at home a month later, and it's been an annual tradition ever since. The festivities are centred on Herjólfsdalur, and include music, singing, dancing, a big bonfire and lots of drinking. Upwards of 11,000 people attend the festival. Extra flights are laid on from Reykjavík, but you should still book your transport to Heimaey and accommodation well in advance. Admission costs Ikr7500 for three days or Ikr3000 for Sunday only.

Over the course of Whitsunday weekend in May, the island plays host to a three-day jazz festival and Sjóstangaveiðimót, a deep-sea fishing competition. On 3 June the church organises a march up to the cross beneath the volcano Eldfell to pray and give thanks for being spared even greater damage in the 1973 eruptions.

Sleeping

Heimaey has a camp site, several hotels and loads of guesthouses. Most places drop their rates by around 20% in winter.

CAMPING

The popular Herjólfsdalur **camp site** (☎ 481 2075; camp site per person Ikr500) is surrounded by sheer grassy slopes. It has hot showers and a hut with cooking facilities.

GUESTHOUSES

Gistiheimilið Hreiðrið (☎ 481 1045; eyjamyndir@isholf.is; Faxastígur 22; sb/s/d Ikr1700/3400/5600) The best budget option is this friendly guesthouse run by the owners of the cinema and volcano show. Just look for the orca mural on the wall and the whalebones in the garden. There's a kitchen and guest lounge.

Gistiheimilið Heimir (☎ 481 2929; fax 481 2912; Heiðarvegur 1; s/d with shared bathroom Ikr4000/7000) This little guesthouse above some shops is handy for the ferry terminal.

Gistihúsið Hamar (☎ 481 3400; Herjólfsgata 4; http://hotel.eyjar.is; s/d/tr Ikr6900/9200/11,700) Owned by the Hótel Þórshamar, this red-and-grey guesthouse has large modern rooms with bathrooms, TV and phone.

Gistiheimilið Sunnuhöll (☎ 481 2900; hotel.eyjar.is; Vestmannabraut 28b) Sunnuhöll is tucked away behind Hótel Þórshamar, which acts as the reception for the guesthouse.

Hótel Mamma (☎ 481 2900; Vestmannabraut 25; s/d/tr Ikr4900/7000/9500) Across the road from

PUFFIN FOR TEA?

Around eight million puffins visit Vestmannaeyjar every summer, and the tiny birds have been an important source of food in the islands since Viking times. Puffins are still harvested here in the traditional way: either by climbing the cliffs or from the ground using a long net called a *hafur*. The harvest is regulated so that only nonbreeding birds are taken, and most restaurants in town feature puffin on the menu, either roasted or smoked. It's actually very tasty, although some people might be a little traumatised by the idea of chowing down on these clown-faced little characters.

Of course, not all the locals regard puffins as free lunch. Every August during the annual flight of the pufflings, Heimaey is bombarded by puffin chicks making their first fumbling attempts at flight, and many locals rescue the chicks and release them by hand at the water's edge. If you're here at the right time, you'll probably be invited to help out.

Hótel Þórshamar, this place offers spacious rooms with shared bathrooms, TVs and video players. There are two guest kitchens and a washing machine. Reception is at Hótel Þórshamar.

Gistiheimilið Erna (☎ 481 2112; www.simnet.is/hvild; Kirkjubæjarbraut 15; sb Ikr1800, made-up bed Ikr2700, apt Ikr10,000) A huge white house on the edge of the 1973 lava flows, Gistiheimilið Erna is a great budget choice. Rooms have TVs, and there's a shared kitchen, bathroom and laundry. There's also an apartment for eight people.

Gistiheimilið Hvíld (☎ 481 1230; www.simnet.is/hvild; Höfðavegur 16; sb Ikr2000, s/d Ikr2800/5200) This large green family house has big rooms with shared bathroom and a TV lounge but no cooking facilities.

Other options include **Guesthouse María** (☎ 481 2744; fax 481 2745; Brekastígur 37), **Gistiheimilið Árny** (☎/fax 481 2082; Illugagata 7) and **Gistiheimilið Ísjakinn** (☎ 481 2920; fax 481 2951; Brimhólabraut 1).

HOTELS

Hótel Þórshamar (☎ 481 2900; http://hotel.eyjar.is; Vestmannabraut 28; s/d/ste Ikr8400/11,900/16,500) Vestmannaeyjar's best hotel, the Þórshamar has rooms with TVs, phones, minibars and bathrooms. Some rooms have great views towards the harbour.

Hótel Eyjar (☎ 481 3636; www.hoteleyjar.eyjar.is; Bárustigur 2; s/d Ikr5800/8800, in winter Ikr4800/6800) This hotel on the corner of Strandvegur offers huge and comfortable apartment-style rooms with bathrooms, kitchens and lounges – they are basically suites at room prices!

Eating

There are loads of places to eat in Heimaey.

Self-caterers should head for the Kronan supermarket on Strandvegur or the igloo-shaped Vöruval on Vesturvegur. The local Vin Búd liquor shop is on Strandvegur. There are several bakeries in town where you can get bread, cakes and coffee.

Heimaey has several cheap drive-through grills, including **Tvisturinn** (☎ 481 3410; Heiðarvegur 10), **Topurinn** (☎ 481 3410; Heiðarvegur) and **Skýlið** (☎ 481 1445) at the Esso petrol station by the harbour. You can get a meal at any of these places for Ikr300 to Ikr2000.

Pizza 67 (☎ 481 1567; Heiðarvegur 5; Ikr900-2000) This reliable pizza chain has a branch on the main road with an Internet café. It's also a cheerful place to sink a cold beer.

Prófasturinn (☎ 481 3700; Heiðarvegur 3; mains Ikr750-3200) For a break from the pizzas, grills and puffins, this restaurant serves Chinese and Thai dishes, as well as the usual Icelandic offerings.

Lanterna (☎ 481 3393; Bárustígur 11; mains Ikr1300–3100) As well as Icelandic staples, this friendly place offers all sorts of dishes from the Balkans. You can also get cooked puffins, either plain (Ikr1300) or smoked (Ikr1500).

Fjolan (☎ 481 3663; Vestmannabraut 28; Ikr890-2650) This posh restaurant at Hótel Þórshamar serves the best food for miles. Weekday lunch specials are top value at Ikr850.

Café María (☎ 481 3160; Skólavegur 1; mains Ikr980-3150) A little further from the centre, this friendly café serves crepes, sandwiches and hearty Icelandic food, including puffin.

Entertainment

The cinema **Bíóið** (☎ 481 3366) shows conventional films, as well as the Volcano Show. The pub **Lundinn** (☎ 481 1426; Kirkjuvegur 21) often has live music at weekends, and you can see big-screen football at **Mánabar** (the bar at Hótel Þórshamar).

Getting There & Away

AIR

The Vestmannaeyjar airport is about 3km from Heimaey – a **taxi** (☎ 698 2038) will cost Ikr800. You could walk it in about 20 minutes if you don't have much luggage.

Scheduled flights to Heimaey are offered by **Íslandsflug** (☎ 570 3030; www.islandsflug.is), which flies two or three times daily from Reykjavík's domestic airport. The flight lasts 30 minutes, and the fare is Ik6900 for a full-price one-way ticket or Ikr3785 if you book online using the Íslandsflug website.

Alternatively, you could get here on a charter flight with **Flugfélag Vestmannaeyja** (☎ 481 3255; www.eyjaflug.is), which flies to the small airstrips at Bakki (south of Hvolsvöllur) and Selfoss. Most flights require a minimum of five persons.

FERRY

The car ferry **Herjólfur** (☎ 483 3413; www.herjolfur.is) sails between Þorlákshöfn and Heimaey daily throughout the year, but few people bother to bring their cars as Heimaey is tiny. From May to August, the ferry sails from

Þorlákshöfn to Heimaey at noon and 7.30pm (noon only on Saturday); the crossing takes 2¾ hours. The boat returns from Heimaey at 8.15am and 4pm (8.15am only on Saturday). There is a reduced schedule at other times of year (see the website for details). Passenger fares are Ikr1700 (Ikr850 for 12- to 15-year-olds, seniors and the disabled; free for under 12s). Motorbikes/cars cost an additional Ikr1100/1700.

Getting Around

Heimaey is small and the whole island can be comfortably explored on foot. The local taxi service is **Eyjataxi** (☎ 698 2038).

SURTSEY

Surtsey, 18km from Heimaey, was named for the Norse god Surtur, who has the duty of setting fire to the earth at the end of the world. People around the globe watched the creation of this island live on television during the volcanic eruptions in 1963. The island has provided scientists with a unique insight into the way plants and animals colonise new territory and consequently it's off-limits to visitors. You can get a vicarious view of Surtsey by visiting the Volcano Show in Reykjavík or take a charter flight over the islands with Flugfélag Vestmannaeyja (see p130) – call for prices.

West Iceland

CONTENTS

Heading north from Reykjavík, the jagged west coast of Iceland is made up of alternating fjords and peninsulas, running up to the edge of the Westfjords. The most significant place in the region is the Snæfellsnes peninsula, home to the icecap Snæfellsjökull, which you can see from Reykjavík on a clear day. A series of friendly fishing communities is strung out along the north coast of the peninsula, including Stykkishólmur, where the ferry *Baldur* departs for Brjánslækur in the Westfjords.

In the south is the village of Akranes – which has a good museum – and there is impressive scenery around Hvalfjörður. The largest town in the area is Borgarnes, which has a youth hostel and several large supermarkets where you can stock up on provisions before heading inland to the dramatic scenery of upper Borgarfjörður. At the top of the region is the stubby Klofningsnes Peninsula and the fjord Hvammsfjörður, which is partially blocked by the islands of Breiðafjörður.

The authors of the *Laxdæla Saga* and *Egils Saga* lived in the region around Borgarnes and many farms in the area have some kind of saga link. However, the Viking farms have vanished long ago, and most of the saga sites aren't really that exciting today. However, it's still worth reading the sagas before you come, to help you put the area into some kind of historical perspective. The glacial landscape along the coast is striking and the lava flows around Húsafell in Upper Borgarfjörður have sculpted some impressive lava caves and waterfalls.

TOP FIVE

- Journeying to the centre of the earth in the lava caves of **Viðgelmir, Surtshellir** and **Stefánshellir** (p140)
- Lapping up the sand, surf and silence at **Skarðsvík beach** (p149) in the Öndverðarnes peninsula
- Getting adventurous among the lava flows at the recreation centre at **Húsafell** (p140)
- Exploring the wild volcanic landscapes at the west end of **Snæfellsnes** (p149)
- Tramping up among the ice floes on the glacier **Snæfellsjökull** (p147)

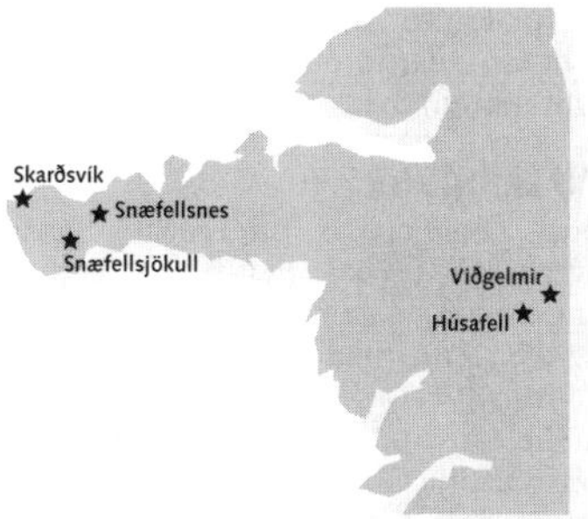

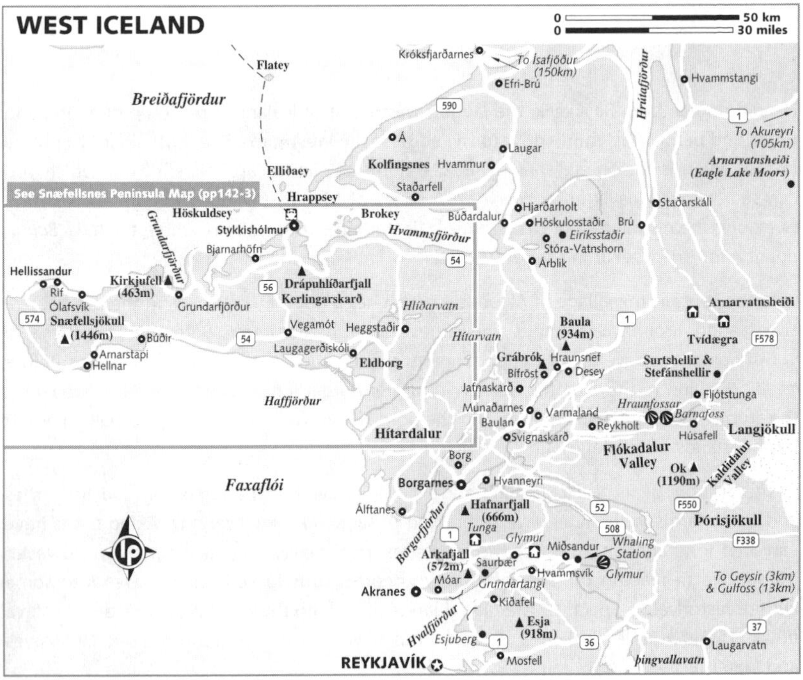

GETTING THERE & AROUND

It's easy to get around West Iceland by scheduled bus. There are regular services from Reykjavík to Akranes, Borgarnes, Reykholt and Búðardalur, as well as daily buses to the Snæfellsnes peninsula. Buses between Reykjavík and towns in Snæfellsnes stop at the petrol station Vegamót, by the junction of Route 54 and Route 56, connecting with buses to Stykkishólmur and Grundarfjörður or to Ólafsvík and Hellissandur-Rif. In summer, there's also a service from Grundarfjörður to Ólafsvík and a bus right around the glacier Snæfellsjökull.

HVALFJÖRÐUR

Most people pass underneath beautiful Hvalfjörður (Whale Fjord), via the 5.7km-long tunnel on Route 1, but it's worth taking the scenic road around the fjord for the moorland views. Many whale species frolic in the fjord – a little ironic as the fjord was once the site of Iceland's main whale-processing plant. At the mouth of the fjord is the Grundartangi ferro-silicon smelter, which produces iron from Norwegian ore.

Sights

On the south side of the fjord, the dramatic peak of **Mt Esja** (909m) offers lots of wilderness hiking. You can hike up to the summit from the old farm Esjuberg, site of Iceland's first church, via the 850m spur Krehólakambur and 830m Kistufell. To get here, turn off Route 1 just north of Mosfell.

At the head of the fjord, a 5km trail runs up the valley Botnsdalur to Iceland's highest waterfall, 198m-high **Glymur**. It's at its best after heavy rain or snow-melt – in a dry period, there may be little to see.

On the north shore, the church at **Saurbær** contains beautiful stained-glass work and was built in memory of Hallgrímur Pétursson, who composed Iceland's most widely known religious work, *50 Passion Hymns* – Reykjavík's Hallgrímskirkja is named after him.

Whaling Station

The Miðsandur NATO Fuel Depot on the northern shore of Hvalfjörður was the main whale-processing plant in Iceland until 1989, when protesters sunk two of Iceland's

TO WHALE OR NOT TO WHALE?

In August 2003, Iceland stunned the world by announcing that it intended to resume whaling. The International Whaling Commission (IWC) introduced a worldwide ban on commercial whaling in 1986, but Iceland continued, killing 90 cetaceans for so-called 'scientific purposes' until 1989. Quite where the science came in was never fully explained, as the whale meat was sold to restaurants in Iceland and Japan, and the carcasses were rendered down to make pet food, vitamins, chicken feed, bouillon cubes and lubricating oil – all of which had cheaper and more environmentally sound substitutes.

Icelandic whaling was finally closed down in 1989 by international pressure and direct action by conservationists against the Icelandic whaling fleet. Iceland quit the IWC in protest in 1992. Ten years later, Iceland rejoined the IWC, but this turned out to be a ruse to try and push through a proposal to slaughter 100 minke whales, 100 fin whales and 50 sei whales (the most commonly seen species on whale-watching tours) as part of a so-called 'feasibility study' to study the effect of whales on the marine environment. With aid from Norway and Japan – the only other whaling nations – Iceland passed the motion by one vote in August 2003.

It was obvious from the proposals that this was simply a precursor to a full resumption of commercial whaling and the IWC issued a formal protest, backed by members of the international scientific community. They were joined by members of Iceland's tourism industry, who anticipated a massive tourist backlash if hunting was resumed. Many feared that hunting would devastate the whale-watching industry, which attracted more than 62,000 visitors to Iceland in 2002, bringing in more than US$16 million to the Icelandic economy.

Since then, conservationists from around the world have joined the anti-whaling campaign: the Greenpeace boat *Rainbow Warrior* recently completed a tour around the country to draw attention to the hunt. As a compromise, the Icelandic government announced that it would reduce the kill to 38 minke whales, and promised that all would be caught outside of whale-watching areas. So much for promises – when the hunt began in September 2003, the first whale to be killed was caught in the main whale-watching area south of Reykjavík!

Whaling is a hugely political issue in Iceland. Although Icelanders have only been hunting whales since the 1950s, around 70% of the population support the resumption of whaling. The core issue for most Icelanders is job creation and the traditional Icelandic resistance to being pushed around by other nations. The Icelandic fishing industry is in crisis and the recent calls for an end to cod fishing in the North Atlantic have created panic among Icelandic fishermen. One of the main pro-whaling arguments is that the growing population of minke whales is having a negative affect on cod stocks in the region.

However, pro-whaling groups have also insisted that the hunt would not affect the minke-whale population – if this is true, then the hunt would also have no benefits for the cod! Whaling is also unlikely to do much for the Icelandic economy. During the 1980s, when there was a global market for whale meat, the industry only brought in US$3 million a year, less than a fifth of the income currently provided by whale-watching tours. Marine biologists have also attacked the scientific validity of the hunt, pointing out that the same data can easily be obtained by non-lethal biopsies.

Since the resumption of whaling, the UK, Germany and France have issued formal protests and the United States is considering imposing trade sanctions against Iceland. Conservation organisations are calling on tourists to boycott Iceland and avoid buying Icelandic goods. Recently, unexpected support for the anti-whaling lobby has come from Japanese consumer groups, who are concerned that Icelandic whale meat may be unfit for human consumption due to heavy-metal pollution. There is very little demand for whale products inside Iceland and without a Japanese market, the industry is unlikely to be commercially viable. So, ironically, it may be pollution that ultimately saves the Icelandic whale!

For the latest on this controversial issue, visit the following websites:

- **International Whaling Commission** www.iwcoffice.org
- **Greenpeace** http://whales.greenpeace.org
- **Ocean Alliance** www.oceanalliance.org
- **Whale & Dolphin Conservation Society** www.wdcs.org

whaling boats and sabotaged the plant, forcing Iceland to finally submit to the international moratorium on whaling. You can see grisly pictures of the operations at the plant in the snack bar at the Olís petrol station at Fertikkiskáli, 4km west of the whaling station. There are chances that the station could be revived, however, after Iceland returned to scientific whaling in 2003 – see the boxed text (p135) for more information on this thorny issue.

Sleeping & Eating

There's a camp site, golf course and kayak hire at the recreation centre **Hvammsvík** (☎ 566 7023; www.hvammsvik.is; camping per person Ikr500). It's located on the southern shore of the Hvalfjörður.

On the other side of the fjord, farmhouse accommodation is available at **Tunga** (☎ 433 8956; camping per person/sb Ikr400/1000), which also offers horse riding.

Hótel Glymur (☎ 430 3100; www.hotelglymur.is; s/d/tr Ikr11,900/14,900/16,900) This recommended hotel sits on the north shore of Hvalfjörður and has a lovely relaxed atmosphere. There's a huge open-plan restaurant, library and lounge and two outdoor hot pots looking out over the fjord.

Getting There & Away

Buses along the west coast bypass the area, but with a private vehicle you can drive around the fjord on Route 47. Destination Iceland visits Hvalfjörður as part of its six-hour tours of Kaldidalur and upper Borgarfjörður from Reykjavík (Ikr7000).

If you take the tunnel on Route 1, the toll is currently Ikr1000/400 per car/motorcycle. Cyclists aren't permitted to use the tunnel.

AKRANES

pop 5520

Akranes (Field Peninsula) lies at the tip of the peninsula separating Hvalfjörður from Borgarfjörður. According to the *Landnámabók*, the town was settled in around 880 by a group of Irish hermits, but fishing quickly became the main industry. There's a decent beach and a good museum, but the town is basically a dormitory for the huge fish-processing plants and cement factory near the end of the peninsula. The town is backed by the concave plateau Akrafjall (572m) which is a pleasant destination for walks.

Information

The hospitable **tourist office** (☎ 431 3327; www.akranes.is; 1-6pm, 10am-6pm mid-May–mid-Sep) is based at the folk museum. There are branches of Landsbankinn and Íslandsbanki with ATMs plus a post office on Kirkjubraut, the main street through the old part of town.

Akranes Museum Centre

This interesting and above-average **folk museum** (☎ 431 5566; www.museum.is in Icelandic; adult/child & senior Ikr700/400; 1-6pm, 10am-6pm mid-May–mid-Sep) is about 1km east of the centre, just off Graðagrund. It's full of nautical relics and there's a huge display of crystals and fossils, and a museum of sporting heroes – check out the bike bent into a ball by an Icelandic weightlifter! There are several fishing boats on blocks in front of the museum and a restored church and other old houses in the grounds.

Other Attractions

The 1km-long sandy beach at **Langisandur** is quite attractive on sunny days, though it can be windy and exposed. Nearby is the town's **geothermal swimming pool** (☎ 433 1100). The 572m peak **Akrafjall**, which dominates Akranes, can be easily climbed in a day via the Berry Valley, which splits the plateau in two.

Sleeping

Akranes' **camp site** (☎ 431 5100; camping per tent/person Ikr350/300; 15 May-15 Sep) is on the shore on the way into town, just off Kalmansbraut. There are sweeping views over the fjord to Snæfellsjökull on clear days.

Hótel Barbró (☎ 431 4240; www.barbro.is; Kirkjubraut 11; sb/s/d Ikr2500/6500/9500, s without bathroom Ikr5500) This friendly family-run hotel is on the main road in the old part of Akranes. Rooms are chintzy but comfortable and there's a good restaurant.

Just off Route 1 near Akranesvegamót, 4km east of Akranes, is the friendly, modern farmhouse **Móar** (☎ 431 1389; sb/made-up bed Ikr2000/3000).

Eating

For self-caterers, there are several supermarkets near the town centre, a bakery on Kirkjubraut, and a branch of Vin Búd on Þjóðbraut 13.

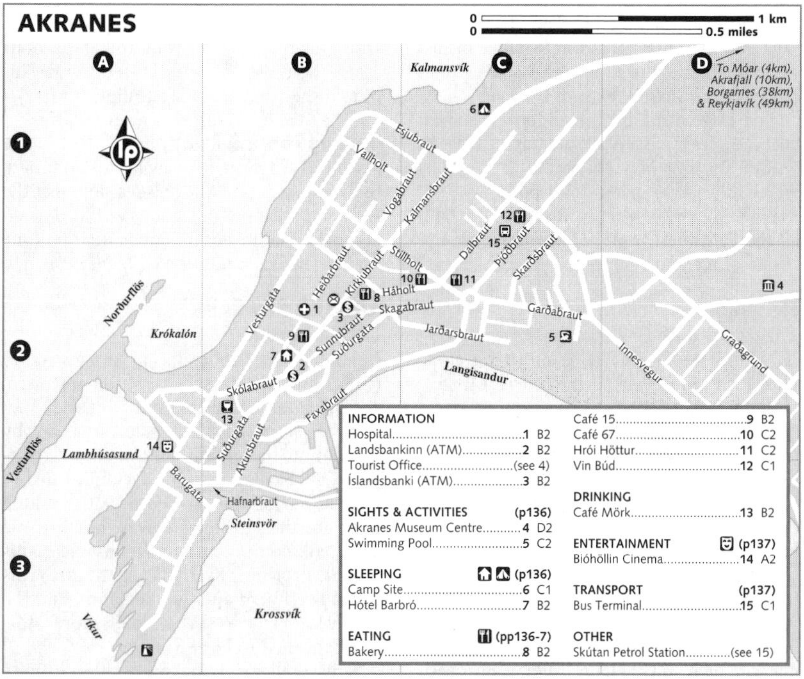

The usual hot dogs, soft drinks and other inexpensive snacks are served up at several petrol stations, including the bus-station grill **Skútan** (☎ 431 2061; Þjóðbraut 9).

Café 15 (☎ 431 3515; Kirkjubraut 15; mains Ikr600-1800) In a historic, corrugated-iron house, this place serves light meals, coffees and beers.

Hótel Barbró (☎ 431 4240; www.barbro.is; Kirkjubraut 11; mains Ikr400-2500) This quite cosy family restaurant serves pizzas, grills and burgers.

In the new part of town are the pizzerias **Hrói Höttur** (☎ 431 1200; Stillholti 23) and **Café 67** (☎ 4301 4767; Garðabraut2), whose pizzas cost from Ikr800 to Ikr800.

Entertainment

The cinema **Bíóhollin** (☎ 431 1100; Vesturgata 27) shows films several times weekly. The best spot for a drink is the trendy **Café Mörk** (☎ 431 5030; Skólabraut 14).

Getting There & Away

There are five daily buses between Reykjavík and Akranes daily on weekdays and two at weekends (Ikr850, 30 minutes).

BORGARNES

pop 1217

Many people just see the cluster of petrol stations, cafeterias and supermarkets at Borgarnes as they pass through on Route 1, but there's also a small village set back from the highway, overlooking Borgarfjörður. As the district headquarters, there are good facilities for tourists, and you can stock up on supplies here before heading off into the rugged interior of Upper Borgarfjörður.

Information

The main tourist office for West Iceland, **Vesturland** (☎ 437 2214; www.west.is; 9am-7pm Mon-Fri & 9am-3pm Sat & Sun, 9am-5pm Mon-Fri & 10am-2pm Sat mid-May–mid-Sep), is in the Hyrnan complex by the Esso petrol station. Ask for the free *Welcome to West Iceland guide* and *History & Heritage* map. There's a Sparisjoðurinn bank with ATM and a post office on Brákarbraut.

Sights

In summer, you can see art, natural history and folk exhibits at the **Borgarfjörður Museum** (☎ 430 7200; Bjarnarbraut 4-6; admission free; 1-6pm daily & 1-8pm Tue & Thu). The village has several saga monuments, including a **burial mound** said to contain the father and son of poet Egill Skallagrímsson, hero of the *Egils Saga*.

The huge outdoor and indoor **swimming pool** (437 1444; Þorsteinsgata; adult/child Ikr280/140; 7am-10pm Mon-Fri & 9am-6pm Sat & Sun) has water slides, a sauna and hot pots.

North of the centre on Route 1, the **Golfklúbbur Borgarness** (☎ 437 1663; www.gbborgarnes.net) is one of Iceland's popular golf courses.

Sleeping

The **camp site** (☎ 437 2214; camping Ikr500 per person) is behind the Hyrnu Torg shopping complex, off Route 1. Pay at the tourist office.

Hostel Hamar (☎ 437 1663; www.gbborgarnes.net; sb members/nonmembers Ikr1950/2300) About 3km north of town on Route 1, the hostel is in a huge gabled house at the Hamar Golf Club. It's a bit strange being upstairs from a golf club but the hostel is well equipped with a kitchen, café and TV lounge.

Hótel Borgarnes (☎ 437 1119; hotelbo@centrum.is; Egilsgata 14; s/d Ikr8900/10,900) In the main village near the western end of the peninsula, this large, modern hotel is the most upmarket place in town and has large bright rooms with TV. Rates drop by 40% in winter. The same owners provide summer accommodation at the **Hotel Hvanneyri** (s/d Ikr6800/8900, without bathroom Ikr4500/5900), about 16km east of Borgarnes at the Hvanneyri agricultural college.

Bjarg (☎ 437 1925; bjarg@simnet.is; sb/made-up bed/apt Ikr1900/2700/3500) North of the centre, just off Route 1, this attractive gabled farmhouse has wood-panelled rooms with TV and a small self-catering apartment with four beds.

Mótel Venus (☎ 437 2345; www.motelvenus.net; 311 Borgarnes; sb/s/d without bathroom/d Ikr750/3600/5700/7300) East across the fjord, beside Route 1, this large motel has a good restaurant, a lakefront camping area and a branch of the Hrói Hröttur pizza chain. Rates fall by 30% in winter.

Eating

Self-caterers should head to the supermarket at the Hyrnu Torg centre on the main road (which also has a branch of Vin Búd).

There are recommended canteens in the Hyrnan complex by the Esso petrol station, and at the nearby Shell petrol station. Both are licensed and offer grills, burgers and hearty homestyle canteen meals from Ikr700 between 8am and 11pm daily.

Matstofan (☎ 437 2017; Brákarbraut 3; mains Ikr350-1250) This place on the way to the harbour serves home-style Icelandic food and Filipino dishes such as *adobo* (Filipino curry).

Getting There & Away

All buses between Reykjavík and Akureyri, the Westfjords and Snæfellsnes stop near the Esso and Shell petrol stations at the Hyrnan complex. The Reykjavík fare is Ikr1600 (one hour). There is a **taxi service** (☎ 892 7029).

AROUND BORGARNES

Borg á Mýrum

Iceland's most famous farm, Borg á Mýrum ('Rock in the Marshes'), is the historical equivalent of George Washington's Mt Vernon. The farm site was selected, in a way, by Kveldúlfur, the grandfather of the warrior-poet Egill Skallagrímsson. Kveldúlfur fled to Iceland during the 9th century after falling out with the king of Norway, but became gravely ill on the journey. He instructed his son, Skallagrímur Kveldúlfsson, to throw his coffin overboard after he died and build the family farm wherever it washed ashore – this just happened to be at Borg.

Egill Skallagrímsson was a bloodthirsty individual who killed his first adversary at the age of seven and went on to carry out numerous raids on the coast of England. The story of the family is told in the *Egils Saga*, believed to have been written by the historian Snorri Sturluson, who married into the family in 1197. Snorri lived briefly at Borg, but the marriage broke down and he moved inland to Reykholt.

There isn't much here now but you can still see the large rock that gave the place its name; there's also a wooden church and a modernist sculpture by Ásmundur Sveinsson. In case you were wondering, the Icelandic beer Egil's is named after Egill Skallagrímsson.

UPPER BORGARFJÖRÐUR

Varmaland

About 17km northeast of Borgarnes, the summer hotel at Varmaland is a possible base for walks along the Hvítá and Norðura rivers – a free walking map is available from the tourist office in Borgarnes. The summer hotel **Varmaland** (☎ 430 1516; kof@ismennt.is; camping per person/sb/s/d Ikr500/1650/3050/6100; 15 Jun-15 Aug) has a restaurant and **geothermal swimming pool** (adult/child Ikr280/120). The hotel is about 6km from Route 1 – take Route 50, then Route 527.

There's a grill at the nearby **Baulan** (☎ 435 1440) petrol station complex, near the junction of Route 1 and Route 50.

Bifröst

The next settlement north is Bifröst, which has a vast school complex that functions as a hotel from June to August. Just north along Route 1 are the 3000-year-old cinder cones of **Grábrók** and **Grábrókarfell**, which belched out the surrounding lava field. A well-worn track leads up through the moss, lichen and dwarf birch to the lip off **Grábrók** (173m) which offers great views, but be careful of the wind up here. Nearby, **Grábrókarfell** has been rather disfigured by gravel extraction.

SLEEPING & EATING

Hótel Bifröst (☎ 435 0005; www.bifrost.is; sb from Ikr2300, s/d Ikr10,000/12,800, without bathroom Ikr6800/900) is at the school but is run by the Fosshótel group. It offers rooms, meals and petrol and has a small coffee shop and supermarket.

Beside the Grábrók crater, **Hreðavatnskáli** (☎ 435 0011; topas@mmedia.is; sb/summerhouses Ikr1500/5000) offers sleeping-bag space, summerhouses sleeping four people and a good range of snack foods.

GETTING THERE & AWAY

Bifröst lies on the main bus route between Reykjavík and Akureyri; the fare from Reykjavík is Ikr2400.

Deildartunguhver

The powerful hot spring Deildartunguhver is close to Route 50 at the Reykjadalsá crossing, about 21km from Reykholt. The water here bubbles up out of the ground at a rate of 180L per second and provides the region with its boiling hot water. A 64km-long pipeline supplies Borgarnes and Akranes with hot tap water.

Reykholt

The Viking historian Snorri Sturluson composed many of his most famous works at Reykholt, about 40km northeast of Borgarnes. In 1241 he was assassinated here by his political enemy, Gissur Þorvaldsson – see the boxed text below for more on Snorri Sturluson. Today, the village is home to a huge religious centre and the interesting museum **Snorrstofa** (Heimskringla; ☎ 435 1491; www.reykholt.is; Ikr300; 🕙 10am-6pm Jun-25 Aug), devoted of course to Snorri Sturluson. If you stroll down beside the school house, you'll come to **Snorralaug** ('Snorri's pool'), a circular, stone-lined pool about 4m in diameter, fed by a hot spring. It looks a little like a stone Jacuzzi, but no-one bathes here today. Behind the pool is a passage believed to lead to the cellar where Snorri Sturluson was murdered.

SLEEPING & EATING

Hótel Reykholt (☎ 435 1260; www.reykholt.is; sb Ikr1850; s/d Ikr7865/10,150, without bathroom Ikr4829/6215) is housed in the modern block behind the religious centre and offers tasteful and

SNORRI STURLUSON

The chieftain and historian Snorri Sturluson is one of the most important figures in medieval Norse history – partly because he wrote a lot of it down himself. Snorri was born at Hvammur near Búðardalur, but was raised and educated at the theological centre of Oddi near Hella and later married the heir to the farm Borg near Borgarnes. For reasons not fully revealed, he abandoned his family at Borg and retreated to the isolated farm at Reykholt where he wrote the famous *Prose Edda* (a textbook to medieval Norse poetry) and *Heimskringla* (a history of the kings of Norway). Snorri is also widely believed to be the hand behind the *Egils Saga*, a family history of the Viking *skald* (court poet), Egill Skallagrímsson.

At the age of 36 Snorri was appointed *lögsögumaður* (lawspeaker) of the Alþing (Icelandic parliament), but during a trip to Norway, he allowed himself to be persuaded to promote Norwegian interests at the parliament. He soon became so busy with his writing that he stopped showing up to meetings of the Alþing altogether and the Norwegian king Hakon issued a warrant for his capture – dead or alive. The ambitious *jarl* (earl) Gíssur Þorvaldsson, who had his eye on the governorship of Iceland, visited Reykholt with 70 armed men on the night of 23 September 1241 and hacked the historian to death in the basement of his home at Reykholt. Today Reykholt has a museum devoted to Snorri and you can see the hot spring where he used to bathe.

well-appointed rooms and a decent restaurant. Rates drop by 30% in winter.

There's a **camp site** (☎ 435 1182; Ikr500 per person) at the tiny geothermal centre of Kleppjárnsreykir on Route 50 about 6km west of Reykholt, where you'll also find a pleasant **geothermal swimming pool**.

About 11km down the valley on Route 50, the red-and yellow farm **Brennistaðir** (☎ 435 1193; brennist@islandia.is; sb/made-up bed/summerhouse Ikr1500/3000/6000) is run by a jolly old farmer.

GETTING THERE & AWAY

During the summer, there is a bus from Reykjavík to Borgarnes and on to Hvanneyri and Reykholt at 5pm on Friday and Sunday (Ikr1650, two hours). In the opposite direction it leaves Reykholt at 7.15pm.

Húsafell

On the edge of the desolate lava fields at Hallmundarhraun, Húsafell is a popular outdoor retreat for Reykjavík residents, tucked in among dense thickets of dwarf birch on the edge of the river Kaldá. The leisure complex **Ferðaþjónustan Húsafelli** (☎ 435 1550; www.husafell.is) includes a camp site, a petrol station and snack bar, a huge complex of wooden guest cabins and a lovely outdoor **geothermal swimming pool** (adult/child Ikr350/200).

Various adventure and team-building activities can be arranged through the **Activity Group** (☎ 580 9900; www.activity.is), including snowmobile tours on Langjökull (Ikr7200 per person), white-water rafting on the river Hvítá (Ikr5900 per person), dogsledding on Langjökull (Ikr6900 per person) and quad-bike rides (Ikr6200 per person).

SLEEPING & EATING

The complex at **Ferðaþjónustan Húsafelli** (☎ 435 1550; www.husafell.is; camping per person/sb Ikr600/1400-1600, d with/without bathroom Ikr7400/8400) includes a camp site, wooden cabins with sleeping-bag space and a farmhouse with double rooms, a kitchen and hot pots.

Beyond Húsafell, Route 518 loops around and passes **Fljótstunga** (☎ 435 1198; www.fljotstunga.is; sb/s/d Ikr1700/4900/8200), which runs guided tours of the lava tube at Viðgelmir.

GETTING THERE & AWAY

No buses run to Húsafell, but twice a week you can get as far as Reykholt by bus from Reykjavík or Borgarnes – see p107 for details.

Reykjavík Excursions' (see p304) 'Organised tours to Kaldidalur' tour also passes through Húsafell – see the following section.

Around Húsafell

HRAUNFOSSAR & BARNAFOSS

Four kilometres west of Húsafell is **Hraunfossar**, a series of trickling cascades that emerge as if by magic from beneath the lava flow. From here, a short trail leads upstream to the **Barnafoss** (Children's Waterfall), where the river Hvítá roars through a cauldron-like gorge. There used to be a rock arch here, but two children were swept off it to their deaths – hence the name – and the arch was destroyed.

LAVA TUBES

The vast, barren lava flows around Hallmundarhraun contain some gigantic lava tubes, formed by flows of molten lava beneath the solidified lava crust. They look like they've been created by a hellish giant serpent.

About 2km southeast of the farm **Fljótstunga**, on the looping road from Húsafell, the lava tube **Viðgelmir** is 1.5km long. A track leads from the access road across the lava to where a section of the roof has caved in, creating a huge rock arch and two forbidding black chasms descending into the earth. If you want to explore further, you must arrange a tour at Fljótstunga (Ikr4000 per person with a minimum of four people).

Even more dramatic are the tubes of **Surtshellir** and **Stefánshellir**, which together cover more than 3.5km. To reach the caverns, you must leave Route 518 midway between Fljótstunga and Húsafell and continue 8km on mountain road F578. The tube roof has collapsed in three places and you can enter the tube at the far end and scramble back toward the road along the tube floor, exiting via a cairn of stones in the first chasm. The floor of the tube is covered in slippery boulders so don't attempt this without a torch.

It's possible to continue along Route F578 to the lakes of **Arnarvatnsheiði** (Eagle Lake moors) and on to Hvammstangi.

KALDIDALUR

Southeast of Húsafell, the Kaldidalur valley skirts the edge of the **glacier** (1450m) offering tremendous views over a series of high-altitude icecaps. On fine days, you can see the snows of Langjökull, Eiríksjökull, Okjökull and Þórisjökull. Unsurfaced Route 550 runs south along the valley from Húsafell to Þingvellir, cresting at Langihryggur (727m).

Reykjavík Excursions (see p304) and other companies run scheduled coach tours to Kaldidalur via Þingvellir, which loop round via Húsafell and Reykholt for around Ikr7000. Snowmobile and snow-scooter excursions are available on the Langjökull Icecap with the Activity Group, based at Húsafell – see p140 for details.

LAXDÆLA SAGA COUNTRY

Laxárdalur (Salmon River Valley) served as the setting for *Laxdæla Saga*, the most popular of the Icelandic sagas. The story revolves around a love triangle between Guðrun Ósvífursdóttir, said to be the most beautiful woman in Iceland, and the foster-brothers Kjartan Ólafsson and Bolli Þorleiksson, who both took a shine to her. In a fairly typical saga tale, Guðrun had both men wrapped around her little finger and schemed and connived until both of them were dead – Kjartan at the hands of Bolli, and Bolli at the hands of Kjartan's brothers. Most Icelanders know the stories and characters by heart, but unless you have read the saga, all the names rather blend into one.

Búðardalur

pop 260

Búðardalur looks out over Hvammsfjörður, at the mouth of the Laxá river. It was founded as a cargo depot and boat shed in saga times, but today it's a fairly nondescript fish-processing village. There's a petrol station and a **tourist office** (☎ 434 1410; 🕓 10am-6pm Mon-Sat Jun-Aug) at the handicraft shop on the way through town.

SLEEPING & EATING

You can camp at the pleasant, free official **camp site** (☎ 434 1132) behind the school or 13km south of the village (by Route 60) at the **Árblik Community Centre** (☎ 434 1366; per person Ikr500).

The guesthouse and restaurant **Bjarg** (☎ 434 1644; www.aknet.is/bjarg; Dalbraut 2; sb/s/d Ikr1500/3000/5000) offers good-value meals and decent rooms upstairs. It's a pleasant place for a meal or a beer and there's a net café in summer.

For food, there's also **Grillið** (mains Ikr250-990) at the Esso petrol station.

GETTING THERE & AWAY

Four buses run between Reykjavík and Búðardalur daily except on Wednesday and Saturday (Ikr2550; 2½ hours). Except on Friday, buses continue to Króksfjarðarnes. Tuesday and Sunday services also continue to Reykholar in the Westfjords.

Eiríksstaðir

The farm Eiríksstaðir, across the Haukadalsá from Stóra-Vatnshorn church, was the home of Eiríkur Rauðe, father of Leifur Eiríksson, believed by many to be the first European to visit America. The ruins are hard to discern, but there's an impressive **reconstruction of the farm** (☎ 434 1132; adult/senior/child under 14 Ikr500/400/free; 10am-6pm Jun-Sep) built using only the tools and materials available at the time. Guides dressed in Viking garb show people around in summer.

The huge farmhouse at **Stóra-Vatnshorn** (☎ 434 1342; storavatnshorn@islandia.is; sb/made-up beds/summerhouse Ikr1500/2300/5000) offers good-value rooms and a self-catering wooden summerhouse.

Saga Farms

Various farms in the area crop up in the Icelandic sagas, but all have been replaced by modern farmhouses today and there's not much to see on the ground. About 4km up the Laxá river from Búðardalur, **Höskuldsstaðir** was the birthplace of Hallgerður Longlegs, wife of Gunnar of Hlíðarendi, who starred in *Njáls Saga*. Other important descendants of the family include Bolli and his foster brother Kjartan from the *Laxdæla Saga*.

Across the river from Höskuldsstaðir is **Hjarðarholt**, the one-time home of Kjartan and his father Ólafur Peacock. The Viking farm was said to be one of the wonders of the Norse world, with scenes from the sagas carved into the walls and a huge dining hall that could seat 1100 guests, but no trace of it remains today.

Further north, the farm at **Hvammur** in Dalur produced a whole line of prominent Icelanders, including Snorri Sturluson of *Prose Edda* fame. It was settled in around 895 by Auður the Deep-Minded, the wife of the Irish king Olaf Godfraidh, who has a guest role in the *Laxdæla Saga*. By coincidence, Árni Magnússon, who rescued most of the Icelandic sagas from the 1728 fire in Copenhagen, was born at Hvammur.

About 1km north of Hvammur on Route 1, the geothermal village of **Laugar** was the birthplace of the *Laxdæla Saga* beauty Guðrun Ósvífursdóttir.

SLEEPING

The Laugar resort has a camp site and an **Edda Hotel** (☎ 444 4930; www.hoteledda.is; camping per person/sb Ikr500/2000; s/d Ikr8500/10,700, without bathroom 5000/6400) in the usual schoolhouse setting. There's a restaurant and naturally heated swimming pool and a small folk museum.

Getting There & Away

The only public access to the Laxárdalur area is by the Reykjavík–Búðardalur–Króksfjarðarnes bus – see p141 for details.

SNÆFELLSNES

Jutting into the Atlantic Ocean between Faxaflói and Breiðafjörður, the 100km-long Snæfellsnes Peninsula is dominated by the icecap Snæfellsjökull, immortalised in Jules Verne's fantasy tale *Journey to the Centre of the Earth*. It was a lot more remote in Jules Vernes' day – these days a dirt-and-tarmac road runs right around the peninsula. Most of Snæfellsnes's inhabitants live on the rugged and mountainous north coast, in the towns of Stykkishólmur, Grundarfjörður, Ólafsvík and Hellissandur-Rif. Because of its orientation, Snæfellsnes gets a bit of a hammering from the weather and it can be windy and rainy here while it's sunny and bright in Borgarnes and the Westfjords. When the rain comes in horizontally, you'll appreciate the warm petrol station restaurants at the bus stops around the peninsula.

STYKKISHÓLMUR

pop 1239

The largest town on Snæfellsnes, Stykkishólmur sits at the end of the Þórsnes Peninsula and benefits from an excellent natural harbour formed by the basalt island Súgandisey, which sits at the north end of the peninsula. It's a friendly little place and you can stroll out onto the island for grand views over Breiðafjörður. Stykkishólmur is also the departure point for the *Baldur* ferry

SNÆFELLSNES PENINSULA

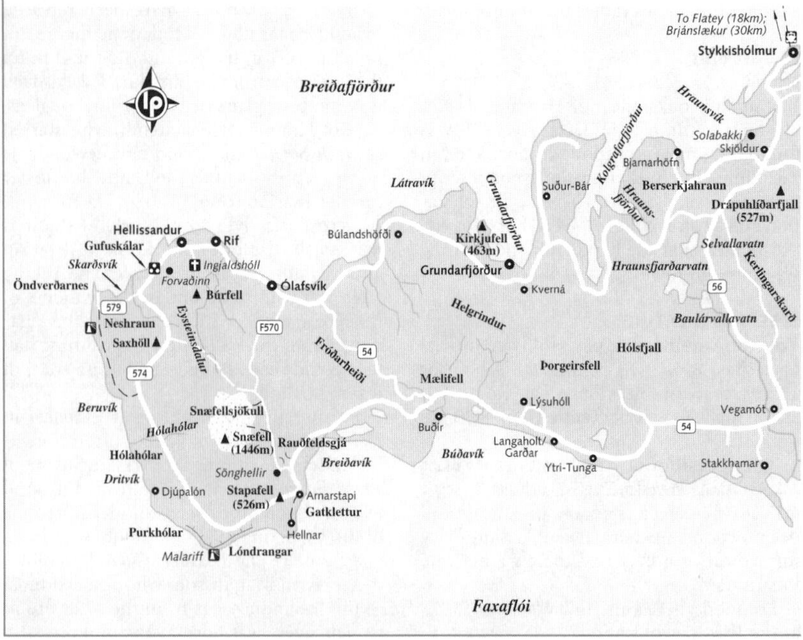

to the island Flatey and Brjánslækur in the Westfjords.

Information

Tourist information is available at the **sports centre** (☎ 438 1150; efling@islandia.is; Borgarbraut; 🕑 10am-6pm 4 Jun-25 Aug), but may move to the red house opposite the restaurant Narfeyrarstofa. The Búnaðarbanki bank and post office are on Aðalgata. Internet access is available for Ikr100 per 30 minutes at the town **library** (☎ 438 1281; Bókhlöðustígur; 🕑 3-5pm Mon-Thu, 1-5pm Fri), one road west of the hostel.

Norska Húsið

Behind the Ráðhús (town hall), the municipal **museum** (☎ 438 1640; Hafnargata 5; adult/child & senior Ikr400/100; 🕑 11am-5pm) is housed in the Norska Húsið (Norwegian House) built by trader Árni Þorlacius in 1832. It has been skilfully restored and there's a wonderful eclectic attic full of farm equipment, butter churns, sewing machines, saddles, wooden skis and other salvaged items of local history.

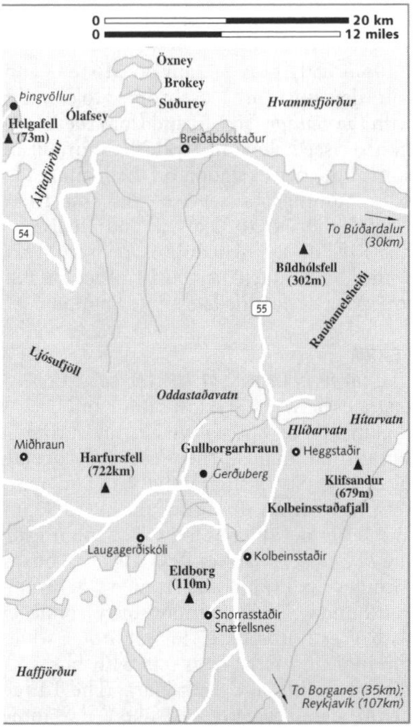

Other Attractions

Stykkishólmur's futuristic **Stykkishólmskirkja** looks a little like a space ship and has a huge modern painting of the Virgin Mary and Jesus floating in the night sky. On the rocky hill between the church and camp site is a **view disk** which identifies the features around Breiðafjörður. The basalt island of **Súgandisey** is accessible via a stone causeway from the harbour and offers good views across Breiðafjörður.

Tours & Activities

As well as operating the ferry *Baldur*, **Sæferðir** (☎ 438 1450; www.saeferdir.is; Aðalgata 2) runs a variety of boat tours, including popular nature-watching cruises to the islands of Breiðafjörður, where you can see seals, puffins and eagles (Ikr3600, 2¼ hours). Sæferðir also runs whale-watching trips from Ólafsvík (see p147).

Kayak tours around the islands of Breiðafjörður can be arranged through **Sagan Kayakferðir** (☎ 690 3877; www.kayak.vef.is) – see p145.

The village also has a **swimming pool** (☎ 438 1372) with water slides and hot pots and a **golf course**.

Sleeping

The **camp site** (☎ 438 1150; camping per person Ikr500), near the pool and golf course, has toilets and sinks.

Sjónarhóll Hostel (☎ 438 1095; www.hostel.is; Höfðagata 1; sb members/non-members Ikr1600/1950; 🕑 1 May-30 Sep) Housed in one of the town's oldest buildings, this spic-and-span hostel is very popular. It can squeeze in up to 50 people in two- and four-bed dormitory rooms and it's open from 1 May to 30 September.

Heimagisting María Bæringsdóttir (☎ 438 1258; Höfðagata 11; s/d Ikr4000/5800) Set back from the waterfront in a residential street, this is a simple but welcoming B&B.

Hótel Stykkishólmur (☎ 430 2100; fax 430 2101; Borgarbraut; s/d Ikr9460/11550) Out of the centre on Borgarbraut, this modern hotel has a posh dining room and a great view. Off-season discounts are available.

Eating

There's a good **bakery** (Nesvegur 1) on the main road out of town, where you can buy *ástarpungar* (fried balls of dough and raisins). Near the pool and sports centre is a 10-11

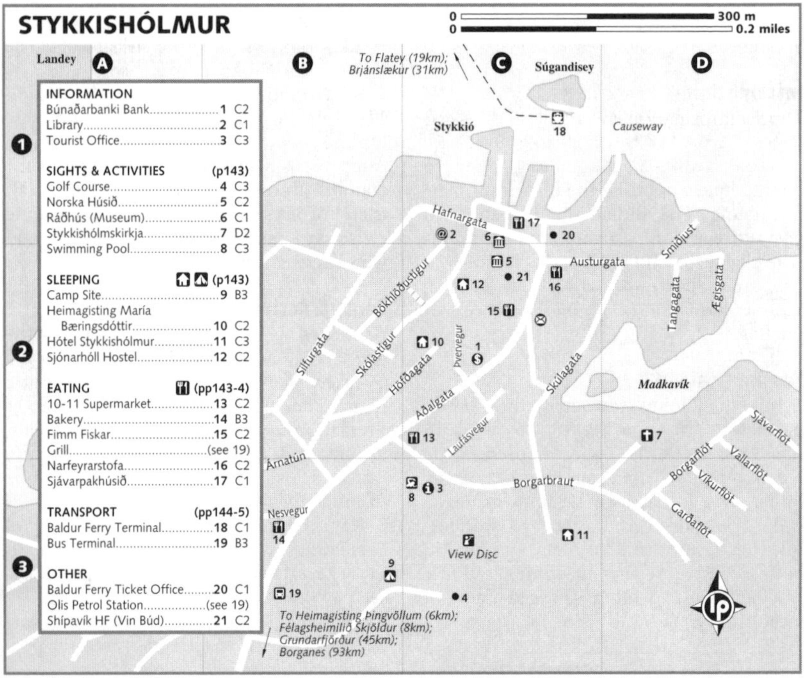

supermarket. The local Vin Búd is at the hardware store Shípavík HF, behind the Norska Húsið.

There's a cheap grill at the Olís petrol station and bus stand.

Narfeyrarstofa (☎ 438 1119; Aðalgata 3; mains Ikr450-2350) In an old house, this bar and restaurant serves good-value homestyle meals, coffee, cakes and even locally brewed beer.

Fimm Fiskar (☎ 436 1600; Frúarstígur 1; mains Ikr650-2550) Over the road, this place has pizzas, grills and a good range of seafood dishes, including local monkfish and scallops.

Sjávarpakkhúsið (☎ 438 1001; Hafnargata 2a; mains from Ikr1250) If you fancy supping on a hearty bowl of lamb or fish soup, head to this wooden house down by the harbour.

Getting There & Away

BUS

Buses run from Reykjavík to Stykkishólmur (Ikr2450, 2½ hours) at 8.30am Monday to Friday and at 1pm on Saturday and Sunday, with a second bus at 5pm on Friday and Sunday. All continue to Grundarfjörður. From Stykkishólmur to Reykjavík, they leave at 6.20pm daily plus 8.15am on Monday and Saturday. Buses are loosely timed to connect with the *Baldur* ferry to and from the Westfjords – see below. In Stykkishólmur, buses stop at the petrol station on the main road.

In summer, a service runs on from Grundarfjörður to Ólafsvík and Hellissandur-Rif but the schedule is revised every winter so contact the tourist office or BSÍ in Reykjavík for the latest information.

FERRY

The car ferry **Baldur** (☎ 438 1120; www.saeferdir.is) operates between Stykkishólmur and Brjánslækur (three hours), via Flatey. From 1 June to 30 August, there are daily departures from Stykkishólmur at 9am and 4pm, returning from Brjánslækur at 12.30pm and 7.30pm – the bus to Stykkishólmur for the *Baldur* ferry leaves Reykjavík at 8.30am Monday to Friday and 1pm on Saturday and Sunday. The afternoon ferry connects with Westfjords buses to Ísafjörður, while the morning ferry connects with buses to the bird cliffs and Látrabjarg. The Látrabjarg busses can be used like a day tour, returning to Brjánslækur for the 7.30pm boat to Stykkishólmur. Buses from Ísafjörður also connect with the 7.30pm ferry.

Fares to Brjánslækur and Flatey are Ikr1650 and Ikr1200 (Ikr825/Ikr610/free for seniors/children 12-15/children under 11). Vehicles up to 5m long cost Ikr1650 and motorcycles cost Ikr825.

AROUND STYKKISHÓLMUR

Helgafell

About 5km south of Stykkishólmur is the holy mountain Helgafell (73m) which was once venerated by worshippers of the god Þór. The first Icelandic *þing*, or legislative assembly, met here in the 9th century, but it was later moved to the flat promontory Þingvöllur after assembly members defiled the sacred mountain with their toilet ablutions – this triggered several bloody battles in saga times. A Christian church was built here in the late 10th century by Snorri Goði, a Þór worshipper who converted to Christianity, and the nearby farm at Helgafell was where the conniving Guðrun Ósvífursdóttir of the *Laxdæla Saga* spent her lonely old age.

You can stay nearby at the farm **Þingvellir** (Ból og Biti; ☎/fax 438 1051; sb/made-up beds Ikr1800/3500), close to the former site of the assembly.

About 10km south of Stykkishólmur, near the intersection of Route 57, you'll find sleeping-bag accommodation at the community centre **Félagsheimilið Skjöldur** (☎ 438 1535; sb Ikr1300).

Breiðafjörður

The entrance to Hvammsfjörður is almost entirely blocked by thousands of tiny islands – current estimates place the number at 2700 – which spill out into Breiðafjörður. The islands have such an effect on the tidal flow in the fjord that the water level inside Hvammsfjörður is sometimes 1m higher than the rest of Breiðafjörður. According to legend, the islands were created by trolls from the Westfjords – see the boxed text p167. The low, rocky islets are rich in bird life including kittiwakes, fulmars, gulls, guillemots, puffins, cormorants and eagles. Seals are also commonly seen on low-lying skerries. There are also interesting basalt features on Þórishólmur and Purkey. The only inhabited island is Flatey, on the ferry route to Brjánsláekur.

FLATEY

The low-lying island of Flatey, or 'Flat Island', has a tiny village full of historical buildings and a church with paintings by the Spanish-Icelandic artist, Baltasar. In the 11th century it was the site of a literary monastery, and in modern times it was the location of the film *Nonni & Manny*.

Ferðiþjónustan Grænigarður (☎ 438 1451; camping per person Ikr500; 15 Jun-15 Sep), 300m from the ferry dock, offers camping with decent facilities.

Alternatively, there's the pleasant **Gistiheimilið Vogur** (☎ 438 1413; fax 438 1093; sb/s/d Ikr2500/3500/6800). Meals and drinks are available and breakfast is always included in the price. Advance bookings are strongly recommended.

TOURS

Daily boat tours of Breiðafjörður are offered by **Sæferdir** (☎ 438 1450; www.sæferdir.is) in Stykkishólmur, from 1 May to 30 September. The 2½-hour trip winds through the southern islands, and costs Ikr3600, including a chance to try fresh oysters and sea urchin roe. These tours are also available as part of coach trips from Reykjavík with Reykjavík Excursions (Ikr10,000). Sæferdir also offers transfers to Flatey – see p144.

Sagan Kayakferðir (☎ 690 3877; www.kayak.vef.is) in Stykkishólmur offers kayaking trips around Breiðafjörður – a three-hour tour around the islands costs Ikr4000 per person, while day trips cost Ikr8000.

Berserkjahraun

The lava field Berserkjahraun (Berserks Lava), 15km west of the intersection of the Stykkishólmur road and Route 57, was named after a tale from the *Eyrbyggja Saga* – see the boxed text p146. You can detour to the farm **Bjarnarhöfn** (☎ 438 1581) to see the traditional production of the Icelandic delicacy *hákarl* (putrid shark meat) – call ahead to make sure someone is in. The farm is at the end of a dirt track, signposted off Route 54.

Kerlingarskarð

About 25km south of Stykkishólmur, **Kerlingarskarð** (Witch Pass) was named after a female witch or troll, who was turned into the stone pillar at the northwestern foot of Kerlingarfjall, the mountain east of the pass.

GONE BERSERK

The wild lava flows southwest of Stykkishólmur were named for an unusual tale from *Eyrbyggja Saga*. Apparently, the farmer of Hraun was frustrated with having to walk around these ragged flows to visit his brother at the farm Bjarnarhöfn. On one voyage to Norway, he brought back two berserkers, insanely violent fighters who were employed as hired thugs in Viking times, but to his dismay, one of the berserkers took a liking to his daughter. He turned to the local chieftain, Snorri Goði, for advice, but Snorri had his eye on the farmer's daughter himself and he recommen ded setting the berserker an impossible task. The farmer decided to promise the amorous berserker his daughter's hand in marriage if he was able to clear a passage through the troublesome lava field – surely impossible for a normal man.

To the horror of both Snorri and the farmer, the two berserkers set to work and soon managed to rip a passage straight through the lava flow. Rather than honouring the promise, the farmer trapped the beserkers in a sauna and then murdered them, and Snorri went on to marry the farmer's daughter. The moral of the tale isn't really clear, but the passage through the lava between Hraun and Bjarnarhöfn can still be seen and a grave was discovered here containing the remains of two large men.

Nearby lake **Baulárvallavatn** is reputed to be the home of a Nessie-style lake monster. Buses between Reykjavík and Stykkishólmur pass the lake, but the pass itself is reached via a long track, which branches off Route 54 just east of the junction with Route 56.

GRUNDARFJÖRÐUR

pop 956

The next town along the coast, Grundarfjörður gets battered by the wind and rain, but the setting is spectacular – the sugarloaf-shaped peak of Kirkjufell (463m) looms over the harbour and behind the town is the forbidding ridge of Helgrindur (986m). It's a fairly typical prefab Icelandic fishing community, but some interesting tours can be arranged through **Detours** (☎ 562 6533; detours@grundafjordur.com), including kayaking trips and scree climbs. There's a shop, bank and a library with Internet access.

Sleeping & Eating

Near the church, the **Grundarfjörður Hostel** (☎ 562 6533; Hlíðarvegur; sb member/non-member Ikr1600/1950) has a guest kitchen and lounge and offers bike hire for Ikr1200 per day. Lots of tours can be arranged.

Hótel Framnes (☎ 438 6893; www.hotel-framnes.is; Nesvegur 8-10; sb/s/d Ikr2000/6900/8000) Housed in an anonymous building at the docks, this place is warm and cosy inside and has a decent restaurant. Local walking tours are laid on for guests.

Apart from the hotel, there's a snack bar at the Olís petrol station. There are two similar restaurants serving grills, pizzas and fish and chips towards the west end of the village. **Kaffi 59** (☎ 438 6988, Grundargata 59) and **Krákan** (☎ 438 6999, Sæbol 13) both offer meals for Ikr900 to Ikr1600.

About 1km outside Grundarfjörður, is the cosy farm **Kverná** (☎ 438 6813; kverna@simnet.is; camping per person/sb/made-up bed Ikr500/1800/2500), which offers loads of outdoor activities, including fishing trips, horseback tours around Snæfellsjökull, boat tours on Breiðafjörður and walking tours to Kirkjufell.

Alternatively, there's **Suður-Bár** (☎ 438 6815; www.sudurbar.sveit.is; s/d Ikr7500/10,200, without bathroom Ikr6200/8800), 8km north along the peninsula east of Grundarfjörður. It's run by an enthusiastic family and there's a golf course and horse riding from Ikr 2500 per hour.

Just down the road is **Setbérg** (☎ 438 6817; camping per person/sb/made-up bed Ikr500/2000/3000), a modern wooden farmhouse with views of Kirkjufell.

Getting There & Away

Buses from Reykjavík to Stykkishólmur continue on to Grundarfjörður. The direct fare from Reykjavík is Ikr2650 (3¼ hours). In summer, a service runs along the coast to Ólafsvík and Hellissandur-Rif but the schedule is revised every winter – contact BSÍ in Reykjavík for the the most up-to-date information.

SNÆFELLSJÖKULL

The mighty icecap Snæfellsjökull is famous around the world courtesy of the French fantasy writer Jules Verne, who used it as the setting for his famous *Journey to the Centre of the Earth*. In the book, a German geologist and his nephew embark on an epic journey into the crater of Snæfells, guided by a 16th-century Icelandic text with the following advice:

> Descend into the crater of Yocul of Sneffels, Which the shade of Scartaris caresses, Before the kalends of July, audacious traveller, And you will reach the centre of the earth. I did it.
>
> *Arne Saknussemm*

It's easy to see why Jules Verne selected Snæfells – the dramatic peak was torn apart when the volcano beneath the icecap exploded and the volcano subsequently collapsed into its own magma chamber, forming a huge caldera. Among certain New Age groups, Snæfellsjökull is considered one of the world's great 'power centres' and it definitely has a brooding presence.

Today, the crater is filled in with ice and makes a popular hiking destination in summer. There are several routes to the summit. The shortest trails start on mountain road Route 570, which cuts across the peninsula from Arnarstapi to Ólafsvík. A longer and more interesting route climbs the west slope along Móðulækur, passing the red scoria craters of Rauðhólar and the waterfall Klukkufoss.

On any of these routes, you should be prepared for harsh weather conditions, and carry food and water as well as a map and compass. If you want to reach the summit, you'll need crampons and ice axes. With a 4WD, you can drive some of the way along all of these routes. From either Ólafsvík or Arnarstapi allow at least five hours for the ascent and another three hours to get down. The western approach takes considerably longer and will require an overnight stay on the mountain.

Organised Tours

Snowmobile tours on the glacier are run by **Ferðaþjónustan Snjófell** (☎ 435 6783; www.snjofell.is) at Arnarstapi. In summer, snowcat tours of the glacier cost Ikr5200 per person or there's a tour by snowmobile for Ikr3500 per person (minimum six). Midnight sun tours are also available. If you just want a lift as far as the snow line, it will cost you Ikr900 each way.

ÓLAFSVÍK

pop 1100

The village of Ólafsvík was the first place in Iceland to be issued a trading licence, granted in 1687; the famous ship *Swan of Ólafsvík* called here for 116 years until it ran onto an offshore reef in 1893. The modern village is tidy and quite prosperous, with a good hotel, a small museum and a swimming pool and you can pick up the 'round glacier' bus here in summer.

Gamla Pakkhúsið

The old packing house **Gamla Pakkhúsið** (☎ 436 1543; Ólafsbraut; 9am-7pm Jun-27 Aug) was constructed in 1841 by the Clausen family, which owned Ólafsvík's leading trading firm and now houses the tourist office and a decent folk museum. There's also a maritime museum, **Sjávarsafnið Ólafsvík** (☎ 436 6961; 10am-6pm), down by the harbour.

Ólafsvík is also a potential starting point for hikes up Snæfellsjökull; the difficult trail begins 1km east of the camp site. Allow four hours to reach the edge of the ice and bring crampons and ice axes if you intend to go out onto the icecap.

The local **swimming pool** (☎ 436 1199) is on Ennisbraut.

Tours

Sæferdir (☎ 438 1450; www.saeferdir.is) offers whale-watching trips in Breiðafjörður at 10am daily in summer (Ikr7950, four to seven hours). Various species of whales are commonly seen, including orcas, minke whales, humpback whales and occasionally blue whales; dolphins are spotted on most trips. These trips are also offered as part of coach tours from Reykjavík with Reykjavík Excursions (Ikr14,900, including transfers).

Sleeping

The **camp site** (☎ 436 1543; camping per person Ikr300) is by the road 1km east of town, near the beached fishing boat.

Hótel Ólafsvík (☎ 436 1650; hotelo@simnet.is; Ólafsbraut 19; s/d Ikr11,450/14,070) Right in the middle of the village, this large hotel offers neat, tiled rooms with TVs, phones and showers. The hotel also offers simpler rooms in the attached **guesthouse** (s/d without bathroom Ikr6510/8820). Breakfast is Ikr700 extra.

Other options include **Gistiheimili Ólafsvíkur** (☎ 436 1300; Ólafsbraut 19) and **H-Hus** (☎ 436 6925, Ólafsbraut), but check first to see if they are still open.

Eating

For self-caterers, there's a large Pin-Verslun supermarket by the harbour, a bakery opposite the hotel and a Vin Búd liquor store on Mýrarholt, uphill from the main street.

For fast food, you have the choice of **Prinsinn** (☎ 436 1362; Ólafsbraut) in the main shopping arcade or the snack bar at the town petrol station.

The **restaurant** (mains Ikr790-2750; lunch & dinner) at Hótel Ólafsvík serves high-quality Icelandic meals and is recommended for both the food and atmosphere.

Getting There & Away

Buses from Reykjavík to Ólafsvík connect through Vegamót, leaving Reykjavík at 8.30am Monday to Friday and at 1pm on Saturday and Sunday, with a second bus at 5pm on Friday and Sunday (Ikr2650, 2¼ hours). All buses continue on to Hellissandur (Ikr100, 15 minutes). In the opposite direction, buses leave the petrol station in Ólafsvík at 6pm daily, and also at 7.45am on Monday and Saturday.

A summer service runs on from Grundarfjörður to Ólafsvík and Hellissandur-Rif but the schedule is revised in winter – contact the tourist office or BSÍ in Reykjavík for the latest information.

Ólafsvík is also a departure point for the round glacier bus – see the boxed text below.

HELLISSANDUR-RIF

pop 580

The twin towns of Hellissandur-Rif are about 1km apart near the end of the Snæfellsnes peninsula. Hellissandur was the original fishing village, while Rif is a modern creation built up around the modern concrete town harbour. Hellissandur makes a good bases from which to explore some of the interesting sights around the western tip of Snæfellsnes and there's a guesthouse and Edda Hótel.

On the western edge of Hellissandur is **Sjómannagarður** (☎ 436 6784; admission Ikr200; 9am-6pm Thu-Tue Jun-Aug), a maritime museum in an old turf-roofed sea shanty. There's a set of lifting stones (used to test the strength of prospective fishermen) and lots of old photos and bits of fishing memorabilia.

About 2km inland from Hellissandur is the church at **Ingjaldshóll**, the first concrete church in Iceland. If the doors are open, you can see some ancient heraldic tombstones and painted wooden altarpieces inside.

Sleeping & Eating

Hellissandur has a free **camp site** (☎ 436 1543) with sinks and toilets, across the road from the Edda Hótel.

There are two formal places to stay in Hellissandur.

Gistiheimilið Gimli (☎ 436 6825; Keflavíkurgata 4; sb/made-up bed Ikr2000/3700) On the winding shorefront road in Hellissandur, this friendly red house has bright, homely rooms and a guest kitchen. Reception is at the Edda Hotel.

Edda Hótel (☎ 444 4940; Klettsbúd; s/d Ikr8300/10,400; May-Sep) This comfortable and well-run modern hotel is just off the main road There's a good restaurant with Icelandic main courses from Ikr1850 to Ikr2450.

Svörtuloft (☎ 436 6855; Hellisandsbraut 20; mains Ikr590-2050) West along the waterfront in

THE ROUND GLACIER BUS

During summer, a special 'round glacier' bus leaves from Hellissandur at 1pm from Monday to Friday, and does a complete loop around Snæfellsjökull. The bus passes through Ólafsvík at 1.15pm and then runs south and west around the icecap, stopping at Arnarstapi, where passengers disembark and walk along the sea cliffs to Hellnar. Here, everyone reboards and the bus continues to Djúpalón beach and then completes the run around the west coast to Hellissandur. The entire circuit costs Ikr2000 and you can get off and reboard anywhere along the route. It's a handy option if you want to stop and explore the rugged southwest tip of the peninsula and you can use the same ticket to get back to civilisation the next day.

Hellissandur, this jolly little place functions as the village pub and restaurant.

There's a supermarket in the Esso petrol station at Hellissandur.

Getting There & Away

All buses from Reykjavík to Ólafsvík continue to Hellissandur, stopping at the Esso petrol station. The fare from Reykjavík is Ikr2750 (three hours). In summer there's also a bus along the north coast of Snæfellsnes to Grundarfjörður, but the schedule changes regularly so contact the tourist office or **BSÍ** (☎ 591 1000) in Reykjavík for the latest times.

SOUTHWEST SNÆFELLSNES

Continuing southwest from Hellissandur, Route 574 skirts the rugged western slopes of Snæfellsjökull, known as Forvaðinn, offering eerie views of spurs of lava sticking up through the scree. On misty days, when the clouds swirl among the peaks, you can easily see where the legends about trolls came from. Beyond the glacier, the road passes the villages of Arnarstapi and Hellnar, which are surrounded by interesting sea-sculpted rock formations, and continues east along the broad southern coastal plain, passing the huge sandy bays at Breiðavík and Búðavík.

Gufuskálar

About 2km west of Hellissandur, the huge radar mast of the US Loran Station is the tallest structure in Iceland. Nearby is the small ruined **Írskibrunnur** (Irish Well), which has a whale skull as a lintel and was built by Irish monks before the Norse settlement. On the opposite side of Route 574 is a vast lava field with the ruins of hundreds of **fiskbyrgi** (stone fish-drying sheds) constructed by medieval Viking fishermen. A trail leads between the huts marked with red posts.

Öndverðarnes

At the westernmost tip of Snæfellsnes, Route 527 cuts south, while a tiny bumpy track heads west across an ancient lava flow to the tip of the Öndverðarnes peninsula. This desolate area contains hidden wonders, most notably **Skarðsvík**, a perfect golden sandy beach lapped by blue waters and hidden by black lava cliffs. A Viking grave was discovered here in the 1960s – you can see why he chose this wonderful, wild spot as his final resting place. A walking track leads from Skarðsvík across the lava flows to the imposing volcanic crater **Vatnsborg**.

Beyond Skarðsvík, the road bumps along to the **lighthouse** at the tip of the cape, passing the abandoned stone well **Fálkí**. On foot, you can continue around the south edge of the cape, where seals laze on the skerries and the cliffs are carved into dramatic sea arches and caves by the constant pounding of Atlantic breakers.

Southwest of the Öndverðarnes turn-off, the road passes the start of the steep 4WD track to Snæfellsjökull and the roadside scoria crater, **Saxhóll**, which can be climbed in a few minutes for views northwest over the Neshraun lava flows.

Hólahólar

About 5km further south, the volcanic craters of **Hólahólar** are clustered about 150m west of the road. A track passes through the wall of the largest, **Berudalur**, and into a natural amphitheatre inside the cone.

Dritvík & Djúpalón

About 4km further along Route 574, a dirt road leads down to the wild black-sand beach at **Djúpalónssandur**. A series of dramatic rocky stacks emerge from the ocean and on the beach sit four 'lifting stones' where fishing boat crews would test the strength of aspiring fishermen. The smallest stone is Amloði (bungler) at 23kg; followed by Hálfdrættingur (weak) at 54kg; Hálfsterkur (half-strong) at 100kg; and the largest, Fullsterker (fully strong), at 154kg. Hálfdrættingur marked the frontier of wimphood and any man who couldn't heft it was deemed unsuitable for a life at sea. Mysteriously, there now appear to be five stones...

If you tramp up over the craggy headland you'll reach the similar black-sand beach at **Dritvík**, where around 60 fishing boats were stationed from the 16th to the 19th century. The black sands are covered in pieces of rusted metal from the English trawler *Eding*, which was wrecked here in 1948 with the loss of 14 of her 19 crew. There are the remains of a **maze** next to the path and close to the car park are several freshwater pools and the rocky arch **Gatklettur**.

About 2km south of Djúpalón, a track leads down to the rocket-shaped **lighthouse** at Malariff, from where you can walk along the cliffs to the rock pillars at **Lóndrangar**, which surge up into the air like a frozen splash of lava. Locals claim that elves use the lava formations as a church. The surrounding area is preserved as a national park.

Hellnar & Arnarstapi

On the south coast of Snæfellsnes, the fishing villages of Hellnar and Arnarstapi are linked by a scenic 2.5km coastal path which passes lava flows which have been eroded into weird and wonderful shapes by the crashing waves. On the shore at Hellnar is the cave, **Baðstofa**, which is chock-a-block with nesting birds. Between Hellnar and the highway is the pool **Bárðarlaug**, supposedly the bathing pool of Bárður Snæfellsás, the guardian spirit of Snæfells – the weird rock slab sculpture at Arnarstapi is meant to represent Bárður. The round glacier bus stops at Arnarstapi and passengers walk along to Hellnar.

STAPAFELL

The 526m-high mountain behind Arnarstapi, **Stapafell**, is another reputed home of little people and is the starting point for mountain road F570, which provides access to the upper slopes of Snæfells. About 1.5km along the road, a collapsed crater has created a series of strange lava caves. The largest is **Sönghellir**, which is full of 18th-century graffiti and is rumoured to resound with the songs of dwarfs (or wind in the lava, if you aren't occult minded). Bring a torch and look for the smallest cave entrance along the ridge.

West of the junction along Route 527 is a small monument to **Guðríður Þorbjarnardóttir**, the first European woman to give birth on American soil. Technically she was the first European to give birth on the soil of Vinland; history is still out on whether the Vikings actually discovered North America.

Heading east from Stapafell, a small track branches off Route 527 to **Rauðfeldsgjá**, a steep and narrow cleft that disappears mysteriously into the cliff wall beside the road. A stream runs along the bottom of the gorge, and you can scramble up between the sheer walls for quite a distance.

TOURS

Walking tours in the area can be arranged with **Guiding Lights Tours** (☎ 435 6754), based at ECO-Guesthouse Brekkubær in Hellnar, including trips to the cliffs at **Lóndrangar** (per person Ikr1000).

SLEEPING & EATING

Near the church at Hellnar, the recommended **ECO-Guesthouse Brekkubær** (☎ 435 6754; www.hellnar.is; s/d with shared bathroom Ikr7150/8950, with private bathroom Ikr8750/10900) is a cluster of smart wooden houses run by a New Age–oriented couple. Various health and spiritual retreats are available and there's a lounge overlooking an area of ocean frequented by orcas.

Fjöruhúsið (☎ 435 6844; snacks Ikr200-1000), by the harbour in Hellnar, is a small but good café that serves quiche, soup and coffee.

At Arnarstapi, **Ferðaþjónustan Snjófell** (☎ 435 6783; www.snjofell.is; camping/sb/made-up bed Ikr500/1900/2450) is a petrol station, restaurant (meals from Ikr580 to Ikr1590) and guesthouse. Snjófell also runs snowmobile and snow-cat tours on the glacier – see p147 for details.

Breiðavík & Búðavík

East of Hellnar and Arnarstapi, Route 527 skirts the edges of the long sandy bays at Breiðavík and Búðavík. These windswept beaches are covered in yellow-grey sand and are wonderfully peaceful places to walk. At Búðavík, the abandoned fishing village of Búðir is now home to one of Iceland's best country hotels. From the hotel, a walking trail leads across the elf-infested Buðahraun lava field to the crater, **Buðaklettur**. According to local legend, a lava tube beneath Buðahraun is said to lead all the way to Surtshellir in Borgarfjörður, paved with gold and precious stones. It takes about three hours to walk to the crater and back.

SLEEPING & EATING

The lonely and very romantic **Hótel Búðir** (☎ 435 6700; www.budir.is; s/d from Ikr12,500/15,900) is a strong contender for the title of Iceland's best hotel. The huge twin-gabled farmhouse has wood-floored lounges with open fireplaces, extensive libraries, a very refined restaurant and luxurious rooms with flagstone bathrooms and elegant furnishings. Every room is different – best is No 23 with its huge freestanding bathtub, separated from the bedroom by a wooden screen. Winter rates drop by 30%.

About 10km east of Búðir and 1.5km off the main road, **Gistiheimilið Lysuhóll** (☎ 435 6716; lysuholl@islandia.is; summerhouses Ikr6900) has cosy wooden cottages that sleep up to four, and offers home-cooked meals. They also offer horse-riding tours in the surrounding hills and along the beach (from Ikr2000 per hour) and there's also a **geothermal swimming pool** (10am-10pm Jun-Aug).

Further to the east is **Gistiheimilið Langaholt** (435 6789; langaholt@langaholt.is; camping/sb Ikr500/2000; s/d Ikr4900/7300, without bathroom Ikr4300/6100), which offers everything from camping to B&B.

Also worth a look is the wooden B&B **Ytri-Tunga** (435 6698; gudmsig@ismennt.is; r per person with/without bathroom Ikr4500/3500) and the turf-roofed **Gistiheimilið Hof** (435 6802, 846 3897; sb/made-up bed/apt Ikr1700/2500/12,000).

Eldborg

Immediately southeast of Snæfellsnes, the prominent egg cup–shaped volcano, **Eldborg**, rises 100m above the desolate Eldborgarhraun plain. It's a 4km walk from Kolbeinsstaðir, which lies on the main road from Borgarnes to Ólafsvík (Route 54). Almost opposite the turn-off to the Hótel Eldborg, a dirt road leads northeast to **Gerðuberg**, a long escarpment formed from ruler-straight basalt columns.

SLEEPING

From 5 June to 25 August, you can stay at **Hótel Eldborg** (435 6602; http://this.is/eldborg; camping per person/sb Ikr500/1250-2100; s/d Ikr7000/8000, without bathroom Ikr4400/6200) in the Laugagerðiskóli school, west of the crater on Route 567 and 4km from the main road. There's also a toasty geothermal swimming pool.

Three kilometres from Eldborg and 2km from the main road is the cosy horse farm **Snorrastaðir** (435 6628; snorrastadir@simnet.is; camping per tent/sb/cabins Ikr1000/1900/8500), with sleeping-bag space and wooden cottages. Horse rides along the beach cost from Ikr2000 per hour.

GETTING THERE & AWAY

There's no public transport to either Hótel Eldborg or Snorrastaðir, but buses between Reykjavík and Stykkishólmur can drop you at the junction on the main road.

The Westfjords

CONTENTS

The Westfjords peninsula in the far northwest of the country looks like a giant amoeba that is struggling to break off from the rest of Iceland and escape into the North Atlantic. This fantastically rugged and remote region is linked to the mainland by a narrow isthmus, and the landscape is truly humbling, with soaring mountains and unfathomably deep and silent fjords. The Westfjords were created by the creeping action of ice sheets over the Thulean plateau, which rose between Europe and Greenland when the continents drifted apart. Today the only surviving icecap is 176-sq-km Drangajökull (925m) in the far north of the region.

The Westfjords is currently home to around 8000 people, most of whom live in the built-up area around Ísafjörður. Most people still make their living from fishing, but the population of the Westfjords has been falling for decades as people have left looking for work elsewhere in Iceland. Apart from Ísafjörður, the settlements here are generally faded little places – the main attraction of the Westfjords is the surrounding landscape.

The remote Hornstrandir peninsula in the far north of the Westfjords was abandoned in the 1950s, and it's now a popular summer hiking destination. The landscape at the south-west end of the Westfjords is less dramatic, but there are some good beaches and several small fishing communities are strung out along the coast. The small spit of Látrabjarg is Iceland's westernmost point, and it's mobbed by nesting birds in summer. In the south of the Westfjords, the ferry *Baldur* runs between Brjánslækur and Stykkishólmur on the Snæfellsnes peninsula.

Tourist offices in the region provide invaluable free *Vestfirdir* pamphlets, which list all the tourist facilities in the area. The green guide covers the east of the region, the red guide covers the central Westfjords and the blue guide covers the southwest. More information about the Westfjords can be found on the Internet at www.westfjords.is and www.nat.is.

TOP FIVE

- Gazing out across the fjords from the historic town of **Ísafjörður** (p154)
- Taking in the views at the rugged **Þingeyri Peninsula** (p161)
- Hiking up to the waterfall at **Djúpavík** (p168) on the rugged Strandir Coast
- Playing with puffins on the bird cliffs at **Látrabjarg** (p164)
- Soaking up the silence on the remote peninsula at **Hornstrandir** (p168)

GETTING THERE & AWAY

There are year-round flights between Reykjavík and Ísafjörður and the airstrips at Gjógur and Bíldudalur with **Íslandsflug** (☎ 570 8090; www.islandsflug.is). There's also a limited bus service around the peninsula from 1 June to 31 August. Buses connect with the ferry *Baldur*, which goes to Stykkishólmur, at Brjánslækur and with the Reykjavík–Akureyri bus at Staðarskáli, near Brú. Boat transfers to the remote Hornstrandir region can be arranged from Ísafjörður and Drangsnes from June to August.

From September to May, you can get around with a conventional hire car on most of the main roads, but not on the smaller tracks and mountain routes. Roads in the Westfjords are mostly unsurfaced and hug the deeply indented coastline, winding in and out of fjords and around headlands, so driving here can be slow. Watch for dangerous *blindhæð* (blind rises) and *einbreið brú* (single-lane bridges), and be prepared to give way to speeding 4WDs on single-track roads. Petrol stations are few and far between.

CENTRAL WESTFJORDS

ÍSAFJÖRÐUR

pop 4182

The pleasant and prosperous town of Ísafjörður is the commercial centre of the Westfjords and is home to more than half

the population. It's an attractive place, with lots of old tin-clad wooden houses spread out along a gravel spit that extends out into Skutulsfjörður (Harpoon Fjord). Parts of the old town centre have barely changed since the 18th century, when the harbour was full of tall ships and Norwegian whaling crews. The town is hemmed in on all sides by towering peaks, and the waters of the fjord are eerily dark and still.

Despite its relative isolation, Ísafjörður is surprisingly cosmopolitan, with numerous places to eat and stay, even a small cinema. There are good walks in the surrounding hills, and in summer regular boats ferry hikers across to the remote Hornstrandir peninsula. The only problem is getting here – reaching Ísafjörður will involve either a long drive or a bus ride over bumpy gravel roads, or a hair-raising flight into the tiny airstrip on the opposite side of the fjord.

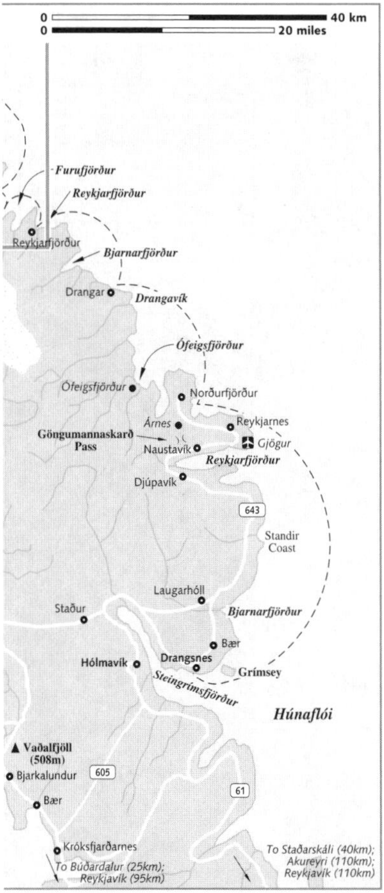

History

The first inhabitants of the Skutulsfjörður area were Norwegian and Icelandic traders who set up temporary summer trading camps on the gravel spit. They were joined later by German and English trading firms. There's mention of a Hanseatic League trading post as early as 1569. Under the Danish Trade Monopoly of 1602, the Danish took over the whole enterprise, and Ísafjörður developed as a fishing and trading centre.

In the following centuries Ísafjörður became a logistical centre for Norwegian whaling ships, although the Icelanders themselves took up commercial whaling only in the 1950s. Ísafjörður was the setting for some of the battles between whalers and environmental campaigners that eventually led to the world-wide ban on commercial whaling in 1989. The recent decision by the Icelandic government to resume limited whaling has brought Ísafjörður back into the media spotlight – see the boxed text on p135 for more information.

In 1991 a tunnel was constructed that links Ísafjörður and the nearby towns of Suðureyri and Flateyri. The three towns and nearby Þingeyri were amalgamated into a single administrative unit called Ísafjarðarbær in 1996.

Information

The friendly Vesturfirðir **tourist office** (☎ 456 5121; www.isafjordur.is; Aðalstræti 7; 🕑 8am-6pm Mon-Fri, 10am-3pm Sat & Sun, in winter 10am-5.30pm Mon-Fri) is down by the harbour in the Edinborgarhús, built in 1781. Also here is the tour company **Vesturferðir** (☎ 456 5111; Aðalstræti 7; www.vesturferdir.is), which offers a huge range of tours in the surrounding area. You can also rent bikes here – see p159.

For foreign exchange, Íslandsbanki and Sparisjóðurinn have branches with ATMs on Hafnarstræti. Internet access is available at the town **library** (☎ 456 3296; Eyrartúni; 🕑 3-7pm Mon-Fri, 3-5pm Sat & Sun) for Ikr100 per hour. The post office is at Aðalstræti 18.

The bookshop **Bókhlaðan Penninn** (☎ 456 3123; Hafnarstræti 2) is well stocked and has maps and books in English.

For laundry services and dry cleaning, go to **Efnalaugin Albert** (☎ 456 4670; Póllgata).

Westfjords Maritime Museum

Housed in a cluster of ancient wooden buildings by the harbour, the **Westfjords Maritime Museum** (☎ 456 3293; 10am-5pm Mon-Fri, also 1-5pm Sat & Sun May-Jun & 10am-5pm Sat & Sun Jul-Aug) is highly recommended. The main museum is housed in the tall **Turnhús**, which was built in 1784 as a warehouse. It's full of fishing and nautical exhibits, including relics from the whaling days. There's a nice wooden café in the **Tjöruhús** (1781), open from June to August. Other old houses in the compound include **Krambúd** (1757), now a private house, and the **Faktorhús**, built in 1765 to house the manager of the village shop.

Slunkariki Gallery

The art gallery **Slunkariki** (☎ 456 4418; Aðalstræti 22; admission free; 4-6pm Thu-Sun) has regularly changing displays of modern art. There's also an informal gallery on the top floor of the town library.

Town Park & Church

The park in the centre of town has a **whalebone arch** made from a whale's jawbone. Nearby are Ísafjörður's interesting **seamen's memorial** and the modernist town **church**, which looks a lot like an old-fashioned press camera with a flash on top.

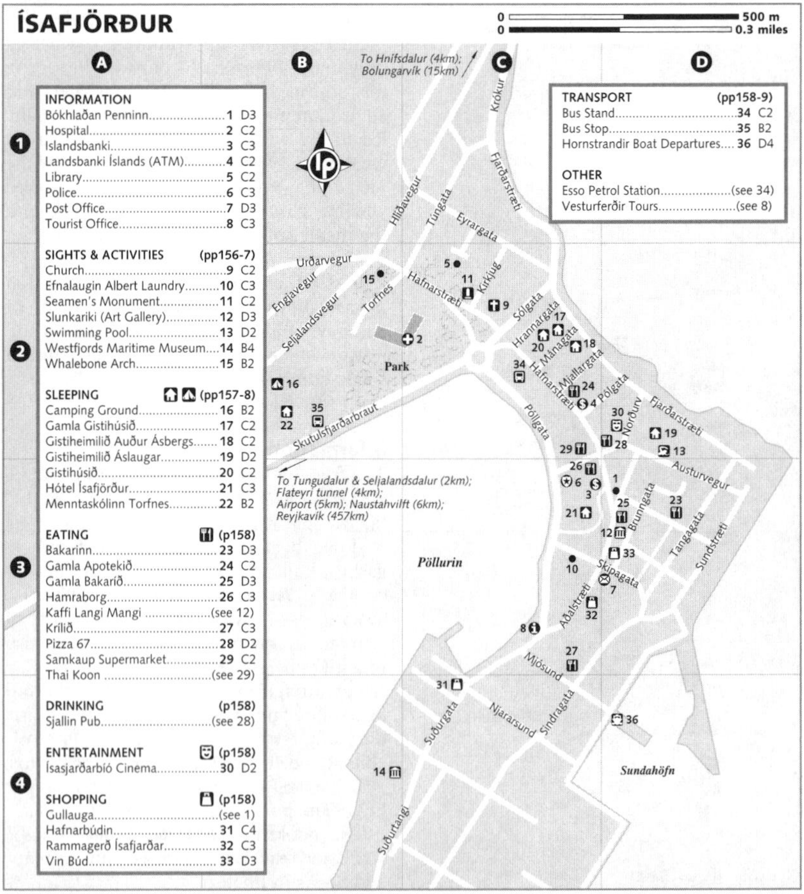

Tungudalur & Seljalandsdalur

These glacial valleys about 2km west of Ísafjörður, at the head of the fjord, offer some interesting hiking routes into the surrounding mountains. **Tungudalur** is lined with waterfalls and scrub birch forest, and it also has a wonderful, secluded camp site and a scenic **golf course** (☎ 456 5081; green fees Ikr1000, club hire Ikr1500). One pleasant walk is the 1.2km trail beside the waterfall to the viewpoint at Siggakofi.

There also pleasant walks along the river valley **Seljalandsdalur**, which is lined with small lakes and leads up to the desolate moors around Breiðafell (724m). You can link up with the popular Hnífsdalur to Bolungarvík trek. In winter both valleys are good for skiing – see 'Westfjords in Winter' opposite.

Hnífsdalur

The village of Hnífsdalur sits in a deep fjord 4km north of Ísafjörður and is locally famous for producing *harðfiskur* (dried haddock) and *hákarl* (rotten shark). The hills around town are dotted with smelly fish-drying sheds. There are uplifting walks in the surrounding hills, including the recommended 8km trek along the Hnífsdalur valley and over the ridge to lake Syðridalsvatn, by the Redihjallavirkjun power plant at Bolungarvík.

Activities

The town **swimming pool** (☎ 456 3200; Austurvegur 9; adult/child Ikr220/100; 🕑 7am-4pm & 6-9pm Mon-Fri, 10am-4pm Sat & Sun) is pretty plain by Icelandic standards but the water is warm. In summer, sea-kayaking tours of Jökulfirðir can be arranged through **Vestfirskar Ævintýraferðir** (☎ 456 3574; www.vestfirdir.is/kayak). Skiing is also possible here in winter – see the boxed text 'Westfjords in Winter', opposite.

There are loads of walking trails around Ísafjörður, most of which are covered in the pamphlet map *Gönguleiðir Í Nágrenni Ísafjardar* (Ikr200), available from the tourist office. One of the more unusual and shorter walks is up to the truncated valley of **Naustahvilft** – about 1km above the airport – which offers fantastic views over the fjord. Several other trails start near the road bridge at the head of Skutulsfjörður, where the last wizards in Iceland were burned at the stake in 1656.

WESTFJORDS IN WINTER

Visiting the remotest part of Iceland in the depths of winter might sound extreme, but the mountains around Ísafjörður are a popular destination for Icelandic skiers. The season runs from January to Easter, and there are daily flights from Reykjavík timed to fit in with the limited daylight hours. The main ski areas are the Tungudalur and Seljalandsdalur valleys at the head of Skutulsfjörður. Tungudalur has illuminated slopes and a cosy ski chalet with a café, ski hire and three ski lifts. Passes are available at the nearby petrol station or the chalet for Ikr1100/500 per adult/child per day or Ikr5000/2000 per week. Nearby, Seljalandsdalur has no ski lifts, but the gentle slopes and level terrain are great for cross-country skiing, and there's a heated chalet. Snows permitting, there is a ski festival here during the week after Easter. In May, cross-country skiers from around Iceland head to Ísafjörður for the 50km Fossavatn Ski Race (www.snerpa.is/sfi/fossavatn). More information on skiing at Ísafjörður is available on the website www.isafjordur.is/ski. The chalets are basically warm rooms with toilets for skiers rather than places to stay, and the one at Seljalandsdalur is unstaffed.

Tours

Vesturferðir (☎ 456 5111; www.vesturferdir.is) is based at the tourist office, and it offers a huge range of excursions from Ísafjörður. As well as tours of Ísafjörður and Bolungarvík, the company offers popular cruises to the island of Vigur (Ikr3700) in Ísafjarðardjúp – see p162 for details. Vesturferðir also offers various tours to Hornstrandir – see p169.

Sleeping

The town **camping ground** (☎ 456 4485; camp site per person Ikr550) is beside the Menntaskólinn Torfnes summer hotel on Skutulsfjarðarbraut. It's open from June to August. There's also a tranquil **camp site** (☎ 456 5081; camp site per person Ikr750) near the waterfall in Tungudalur.

Gistiheimilið Áslaugar (☎ 456 3868; gistias@snerpa.is; Austurvegur 7; sb/s/d from Ikr1800/3800/5400) This grey pebble-dash house near the pool has a nice restaurant in an old wooden house and comfortable rooms in the main building. Breakfast is Ikr900.

Gistihúsið (☎ 456 4200; bilvest@snerpa.is; Hrannagata 8a; sb Ikr1500, made-up bed Ikr2500) This silver tin-clad house in the old part of town has simple rooms and a handy central location.

Gamla Gistihúsið (Old Guesthouse; ☎ 456 4146; www.gistihus.is; Mánagata 5; sb Ikr1600, s/d with breakfast Ikr2600/5200) Housed in another old wooden fisherman's house, the cheerful and intimate Gamla has a guest kitchen and TVs.

Gistiheimilið Auður Ásbergs (☎ 456 4263; Mánagata 6; sb/s/d Ikr1800/3000/5500) Across the road, beside the Salvation Army headquarters, this small townhouse offers both sleeping-bag space and made-up beds.

Hótel Ísafjörður (☎ 456 4111; www.hotelisafjordur.is; Silfurtorg 2; s/d from 12,300/14,800, ste Ikr20,000) This hotel on the main shopping street looks a little like an upended ice-cube tray. Rooms have TVs, bathrooms, phones, minibars and views over the sea or town square. The suites on the top floor are particularly sumptuous. Rates drop by 25% in winter.

From mid-May to mid-August, the same owners run a summer hotel, **Menntaskólinn Torfnes** (☎ 456 4485; sb Ikr1100, s/d with own bedding Ikr3300/4400, made-up s/d Ikr6100/8800) at the school west of the town centre.

Eating

Self-caterers should head for the Samkaup supermarket on Austurvegur. The Vin Búd liquor store is at Aðalstræti 20.

For cakes, *snuður* (glazed buns), fresh baked bread and coffee, head to **Gamla Bakaríð** (☎ 456 3226; Aðalstræti) or **Bakarinn** (☎ 456 4770; Silfurgata 11).

There's a drive-through grill at **Krilið** (Sindragata) near the harbour.

Thai Koon (☎ 456 0123; Hafnarstræti 9; mains Ikr590-990; ⏰ 11.30am-9pm, from 5pm Sun) at the Samkaup supermarket serves up canteen-style Thai meals.

Hamraborg (☎ 456 3166; Hafnarstræti 7; snacks Ikr200-900) This shop/kiosk sells sandwiches and burgers.

Pizza 67 (☎ 456 3367; Hafnarstræti 12; Ikr600-1900) The cosiest eatery in town is this pizzeria and pub on the main drag. It's also the best place in town for a beer.

Kaffi Langi Mangi (☎ 456 3022; Aðalstræti 22; Ikr190-750) This friendly little café sells sandwiches, soup, pancakes and crepes, as well as decent espresso.

Gamla Apótekið (☎ 456 7000; Hafnarstræti 18; meals Ikr90-1800) Isafjordur's young people hang out at this youth centre and café on the main drag, and you can get a cold beer here in the evening.

The **Hótel Ísafjörður** dining room (mains Ikr980-2650) is worth the splurge. The menu features the usual Icelandic lamb and fish dishes, and lunch is cheaper than dinner.

Entertainment

Although weekdays are pretty quiet, the pub **Sjallinn** (☎ 456 3367; Hafnarstræti 12) at Pizza 67 becomes pretty lively at weekends and opens until 3am. The town cinema **Ísasjarðarbíó** (☎ 456 3202; Austurvegur) shows films several nights a week at 8pm.

Shopping

If you are heading for Hornstrandir, you can buy outdoor clothing and camping equipment at **Hafnarbúdin** (☎ 456 3245; Suðurgata). **Rammagerð Ísafjarðar** (☎ 456 3041; Aðalstræti 16) sells quality glassware and other crafts, and **Gullauga** (☎ 456 3460; Hafnarstræti 4) is good for gold jewellery.

Getting There & Away

AIR

Flights into Ísafjörður sweep along the fjord and offer spectacular views. **Air Iceland** (☎ 456 3000; www.airiceland.is) is based at the airport and flies to/from Reykjavík two or three times daily from 29 May to 10 September. The winter schedule is reduced, and flight times vary, depending on the available daylight. Flights to Akureyri connect through Reykjavík but cost less than buying one ticket to Reykjavík and another ticket on to Akureyri. The cheapest online-booked fare from Reykjavík to Ísafjörður is Ikr4885.

A special bus service runs to the airport about 45 minutes before departure for Ikr400. It starts in Bolungarvík and stops near the Hótel Ísafjörður.

BUS & BOAT

Buses stop at the Esso petrol station on Hafnarstræti. Local council buses (☎ 456 4258) run twice daily from Ísafjörður to Flateyri and Þingeyri and three times daily to Suðureyri. The fare to all these places is Ikr200. Buses to Bolungarvík are described on p159.

From 1 June to 31 August there are also daily services to Staðarskáli (where you can change to buses for Reykjavík and Akureyri) and Brjánslækur, where you can catch the **Baldur ferry** (☎ 438 1120; wwwsaeferdir.is) to Stykkishólmur.

Buses leave from Reykjavík for Stykkishólmur on Monday and Wednesday at 8.30am and on Saturday at 1pm, connecting with the 4pm ferry to Brjánslækur, and then the 7pm bus to Ísafjörður. In the reverse direction, buses leave Ísafjörður at 9am, connecting with the 12.30pm ferry to Stykkishólmur, and the 6.20pm bus to Reykjavík. The combined bus and ferry fare from Reykjavík to Ísafjörður is Ikr6900. The Ísafjörður–Brjánslækur buses continue to Patreksfjörður, Breiðavík and Látrabjarg.

On Sunday, Tuesday and Friday, the 8.30am Reykjavík to Akureyri bus connects with buses to Hólmavík and Ísafjörður at Staðarskáli, near Brú. The 9.30am bus from Akureyri to Reykjavík should also connect with this service, but check to make sure. In the opposite direction, the 11.30am bus from Ísafjörður connects with the 8.40pm bus from Staðarskáli to Reykjavík and the 8.15pm bus to Akureyri. From Reykjavík to Ísafjörður the total bus fare is Ikr8700; from Akureyri, it's Ikr8900.

In summer, ferries to Hornstrandir depart from the Sundahöfn docks on the east side of the isthmus – see p170 for more information.

Getting Around

City buses operate from 7am to 7pm on weekdays (until 10.30pm in winter) and connect the town centre with Hnífsdalur and Tungudalur (Ikr200, 15 minutes). The tourist office rents out mountain bikes for Ikr1000 for six hours or Ikr2500 for 24 hours. For a taxi, call ☎ 456 3518.

BOLUNGARVÍK

pop 958

Cowering below the peak of Traðarhyna (636m) in a gorgeous fjord, Bolungarvík is the Westfjords' second largest town. A surfaced road runs around the headlands from Ísafjörður, lined with tunnels and steel nets to catch falling boulders. The village has two good museums, and a pleasant 8km hike starts from the Redihjallavirkjun power plant above Bolungarvík and heads over the ridge to Hnífsdalur.

Museums

In the main shopping arcade in the middle of the village, the **History Museum** (☎ 456 7207; Aðalstræti 21; adult/child Ikr300/free; 🕑 9am-noon & 1-5pm Mon-Fri, 1-5pm Sat & Sun Jun-Sep) contains stuffed animals and birds – including a polar bear killed by fishermen just off the Hornstrandir coast in July 1993.

Housed in an old turf and stone fishing shack on the way into town, the interesting **Ósvör Maritime Museum** (☎ 456 7172; adult/child Ikr200/free; 🕑 daylight hours) is set up to look as if the fishermen have just set off to sea to bring back the day's catch. The buildings here are full of interesting fishing relics, and there's a fish-salting shed – it's full of eye-wateringly stinky salt fish. On a ridge across the road is a **view disc** describing the surrounding landscape.

Activities

As well as the walk to Hnífsdalur, there are interesting hikes to the remote coastal valley at Skálavík, 12km from Bolungarvík along a steep mountain road. About halfway along, you can detour 3.5km to the radar station at Bolafjall (638m), but be careful as some of this land is off limits to walkers.

Bolungarvík also has a **swimming pool** (☎ 456 7381) and a **golf course** (☎ 456 7072), and you can rent horses from the farm **Hraun** (☎ 456 7450).

Sleeping & Eating

The **camping ground** (☎ 456 7381; camp site per person Ikr400) is beside the swimming pool.

Gistiheimilið Finnabær (☎ 456 7254; Vitastígur 1; sb/made-up bed Ikr2000/3200) On the corner of the main shopping arcade is this large restaurant and pub with comfortable rooms upstairs. Grills, burgers and sandwiches cost from Ikr380 to Ikr1650.

As well as the restaurant at Finnabær, there's also a snack bar at the Shell petrol station and a Sparakaup supermarket on the main road.

Getting There & Away

From June to August, there are two or three buses between Ísafjörður and Bolungarvík (Ikr200) from Monday to Friday. See p158 for information on the airport bus.

SUÐUREYRI

pop 330

The isolated fishing community of Suðureyri sits on 13km-long Súgandafjörður, which is linked to Ísafjörður by a 5km tunnel. The setting is aesthetically pleasing, with sweeping views across the fjord, but there's not much here apart from a **monument** to the Icelandic poet Magnús Magnússon (1873–1916) – not to be confused with the TV *Mastermind* host – and the village **swimming pool** (☎ 456 6121; Túngata 8).

Sleeping & Eating

You can stay at **VEG-Gisting** (☎ 456 6666; Aðalgata 14; s/d 3200/5500) on the main road through town. For meals, there's a snack bar at the Esso petrol station.

Getting There & Away

From Monday to Friday, there are three daily local council buses between Ísafjörður and Suðureyri (Ikr200, 20 minutes).

FLATEYRI

pop 300

Like Ísafjörður, Flateyri is built on a gravel spit sticking out into the broad fjord of Önundarfjörður. It was once a support base for Norwegian whalers, but the whaling station burned down in 1901. You can see the chimney and boiler from another abandoned whaling station at Hóll, near the head of the fjord. The vast earth chute above the village was built to defend the town from avalanches after a devastating avalanche in 1995. The popular Kirkjubol youth hostel is 10km south of Flateyri at the head of Önundarfjörður.

Activities

Sea kayaks and guides can be rented from **Ferðaþónustan Grænhöfði** (☎ 456 7762; jens@snerpa.is). There is also a **swimming pool** (☎ 456 7738). There are lots of good hiking opportunities in the hills and valleys around the Kirkjuból HI Hostel – ask the warden for some recommendations.

Sleeping & Eating

The free **camping ground** (☎ 456 7738) is next to the avalanche defences on the edge of the village. The nearby Esso petrol station has a cheap grill.

Ferðaþónustan Grænhöfði (☎ 456 7762; jens@snerpa.is) has three six- to 10-person chalets in Flateyri for Ikr4500 to Ikr6000 per day or Ikr24,000 to Ikr30,000 per week.

On the street in town, **Vagninn Restaurant** (☎ 456 7751; Hafnarstræti 19; mains Ikr650-1900) offers meals and snacks. It also serves as the town pub.

The popular and cosy **Korpudalur Kirkjuból** (Önundarfjörður Hostel; ☎ 456 7808; www.superhighway.is/travel/korpudalur; camp site per tent Ikr400 plus Ikr160 per person, sb member/nonmember Ikr1950/1600) is housed in a little white cottage at the bottom of the broad valley at the head of the fjord, about 10km south of Flateyri.

Getting There & Away

On weekdays, there are two daily buses between Ísafjörður and Flateyri (Ikr200, 30 minutes). You must book ahead (☎ 456 4258); otherwise the bus might not drive into the village.

ÞINGEYRI

pop 340

This tiny village was the first trading station in the Westfjords, but these days the world seems to have passed Þingeyri by. The surrounding hills look like something from *The Lord of the Rings* and there are some dramatic walks in the area, including the short hike up to **Sandfell**, the 367m ridge behind the village, which begins just south of the village on Route 60.

In summer there's a **tourist office** (☎ 456 8304; www.thingeyri.com; Hafnarstræti; 🕑 10am-6pm) on the main road. The village has the inevitable **swimming pool** (☎ 456 8375), and you can rent horses from **Kristín Elíasdóttir** (☎ 456 8107) and at the farm **Hraun** (☎ 456 7450) on Route 624 near Núpur.

Sleeping & Eating

The official **camping ground** (☎ 456 8285; camp site per person Ikr500) is behind the swimming pool.

Við Fjörðinn (☎ 456 8172; vidfjordinn@vestfirdir.is; Aðalstræti 26; sb/made-up bed Ikr1800/3000) This simple guesthouse on the main road through Þingeyri has a guest kitchen and TV lounge.

Alternatively, there's **Gistiheimilið Vera** (☎ 456 8232; Hlíðargata 22).

The village has a small supermarket, and there's a snack bar at the Esso station or the town restaurant **Tókí Munkur** (☎ 456 8466; Hafnarstræti 1; mains Ikr650-1800), which serves the usual burgers, fish and grills.

Getting There & Away

Þingeyri has an airstrip, although no flights are currently operating. Local council **buses** (☎ 456 4258) run twice every weekday between Þingeyri and Ísafjörður (Ikr500, 30 minutes).

AROUND ÞINGEYRI

Þingeyri Peninsula

The Þingeyri Peninsula's dramatic northern peaks have been dubbed the 'Northwestern Alps', and the region offers some excellent remote trekking. The mountains are partly volcanic in origin, and the peaks are made up of rock and scree – a marked contrast to the green valleys elsewhere in the Westfjords. A dirt road runs northwest along the eastern edge of the peninsula to the scenic valley at **Haukadalur**.

If the road isn't blocked by landslides, you can continue right around the peninsula with a 4WD, passing bird cliffs and the remote lighthouse at **Svalvogar**. The highest peak in the Westfjords, **Kaldbakur** (998m), lies in the rugged heart of the Northwestern Alps. You can hike up to the summit on a steep trail that begins on the road from Þingeyri to Kirkjuból. For more information on trekking in the Þingeyri Peninsula, click on the British flag on the website www.thingeyri.com.

Over on the south side of the Þingeyri Peninsula, **Hrafnseyri** was the birthplace of Jón Sigurðsson, the architect of Iceland's independence, which took place on 17 June 1811. The small Hrafnseyri **museum** (☎ 456 8260; www.hrafnseyri.is; 10am-8pm; 17 Jun–1 Sep) outlines aspects of his life. There's a wooden church that dates from 1886.

Mýrar & Núpur

On Dýrafjörður's north shore is a series of gorgeous broad valleys. At the start of the valley is a delightful weatherboard church and the charming garden at **Skrúður** (free admission; daylight hours), established in 1905. This peaceful glade of trees and ornamental shrubs is reached through a whale-bone arch and has benches looking out across the fjord. The surrounding wilderness is an important eider-duck breeding ground.

Nearby to the gardens is the somewhat industrial-looking **Edda Hotel Núpur** (☎ 444 4950; www.eddahotel.is; sb/s/d Ikr2000/5000/6400), which has a restaurant and a large indoor swimming pool. It's the huge white building with the red roof and tall chimney, just off Route 624.

Just past the Edda Hotel at Núpur, **Alviðra** (☎ 456 8229; alvidra@snerpa.is; sb in schoolhouse/farmhouse Ikr1100/1700, s/d with breakfast Ikr4000/6200, summerhouse from Ikr7000) has accommodation in a variety of buildings, including farmhouses and a large modern schoolhouse.

There's no public transport to Núpur, but Ísafjörður–Þingeyri buses can drop you by the junction of Route 624, 2km from the Edda Hotel and 8km from Alviðra.

Dynjandi

Sometimes known as Fjallfoss, the broad waterfall at Dynjandi is the best known and most dramatic waterfall in the Westfjords. It tumbles like a white curtain over a rocky scarp at the head of Dynjandivogur, just off Route 60. The surrounding area is protected as a nature reserve, and there's a free camp site right by the falls. Nearby is the Mjólkárvirkjun (Milk River) hydroelectric power station. Buses between Brjánslækur and Ísafjörður take a 10-minute break here to appreciate the falls.

Beyond Dynjandi, Route 60 cuts across the desolate moonscape of the Gláma moors, which are covered in coarse tundra vegetation and mirror-like pools of standing water. It's possible to hike across this bleak moorland up to the ridge at **Sjónfrið** (920m) in a long, damp day.

ÍSAFJARÐARDJÚP

The largest of the fjords in the region, 75-km-long Ísafjarðardjúp (Ice Fjord Deep) nearly chops the Westfjords in two. Most people just pass by on the winding road from Hólmavík to Ísafjörður (Route 61).

Súðavík

pop 170

The fishing community of Súðavík sits in the next fjord east from Ísafjörður, facing out on to Ísafjarðardjúp. After a massive avalanche rumbled into Súðavík in 1995, killing 14 people, a series of new avalanche defences were constructed on the ridge above town. At Langeyri, 2km south along Álftafjörður, are the remains of a Norwegian **whaling station** that was used until the 1900s.

There's an camp site near the river, or you could stay in a series of summerhouses with self-catering , rented through **Sumarbyggð í Súðavík** (☎ 456 4986; www.sudavik.is/sumarbyggd; sb Ikr1700, summerhouses Ikr4000/6800).

There's a good grill at the Shell petrol station, and the restaurant **Þjónustuhúsið** (☎ 456 4981; mains Ikr600-1800) serves meals.

GETTING THERE & AWAY

A good tarmac road runs between Ísafjörður and Súðavík, and there is at least one daily bus (Ikr800, 20 minutes) from Monday to Saturday year-round (more often in summer). On Sunday, Tuesday and Friday, buses between Ísafjörður and Hólmavík also pass through the village.

Vigur

The tiny island of Vigur, at the mouth of Hestfjörður, is a haven for seabirds, including eider ducks, Arctic terns, guillemots and puffins. The farm here has a small windmill and a display of antique farming paraphernalia. **Vesturferðir** (☎ 456 5111; www.vesturferdir.is) in Ísafjörður runs three-hour excursions to Vigur at 2pm daily from 10 June to 31 August; the cost is Ikr3700, including refreshments. On Tuesdays in June and July, there's an evening tour at 6pm with dinner at the farmhouse (Ikr5500).

Ögur

These days, Ögur is mainly notable as a wrecking yard for thousands of old cars, but the **church** contains some interesting historical relics and you can stay at the **Ögur farm** (☎ 456 4804; sb Ikr1500). Further west on the edge of Skötufjörður, the road passes the unusual stone farmhouse of **Litlibær**, built in 1895.

Mjóifjörður, Vatnsfjörður & Reykjarfjörður

These three slender fjords lie off the main Hólmavík to Ísafjörður road on Route 633.

At the head of Mjóifjörður, the farm **Heydalur** (☎ 456 4824; www.heydalur.is; camp site per person Ikr500, sb from Ikr1500, s/d Ikr5000/7000) is peaceful and secluded. It offers horse rental for Ikr1500 per hour and kayaks for Ikr1000 per hour or Ikr6000 per day.

Vatnsfjörður, around the headland to the east, has the ruins of turf farmhouses and fish-drying racks dating from the 9th century.

At the end of tiny Reykjarfjörður is the friendly but well-weathered **Hótel Reykjanes** (☎ 456 4844; www.rnes.is; camp site per tent Ikr1000, sb/s/d Ikr1800/3850/7000), housed in the huge white district school. Meals are available, and there's a swimming pool (Ikr200).

Snæfjallaströnd

On the east shore of Ísafjarðardjúp, unsurfaced Route 635 leads north to **Kaldalón**, the beautiful green valley running up to the receding Drangajökull icecap. It's an easy walk up to the snowline, but watch out for crevasses if you venture out on to the ice. Further north, **Snæfjallaströnd** (Snowy Mountain Coast) was abandoned in 1995, but adventurous hikers can walk from the church at Unaðsdalur along the coast to the bunkhouse at Grunnavík, from where you can catch boats to Ísafjörður and Hesteyri.

Just before the church at Unaðsdalur, **Félagsheimilið Dalbær** (☎ 456 1818; inkjar@eldhorn.is; camp site per person Ikr500, sb from Ikr1600, made-up bed Ikr3500) is a good place to get a last meal and warm night's sleep before you head off into the wilderness.

Getting There & Away

Buses between Ísafjörður and Hólmavík wind in and out of the fjords along Ísafjarðardjúp, providing access to most of the area.

SOUTHWEST PENINSULA

This trident-shaped peninsula between in the far west of the Westfjords is scenic and sparsely populated. This is the westernmost point in Europe, and the beaches are the finest in Iceland, with golden sand from hidden sandbars offshore and shimmering blue water. The highlight here is Latrabjarg, a 12km stretch of towering sea cliffs with unbelievable numbers of nesting seabirds in summer. There are several small villages on the north side of the peninsula but only isolated guesthouses in the far south and west.

BÍLDUDALUR & AROUND

pop 240

Bíldudalur looks out over Aranfjörður towards the Þingeyri Peninsula's wild south coast. Founded in the 16th century, today the village is a major supplier of shrimp, which might explain the fishy smell in the air. For tourists, Bíldudalur has a camp site, a guesthouse, a bank and a petrol station.

About 26km northwest of Bíldudalur, at Selárdalur is a small **museum** (☎ 456 2186; admission free; ⌚ 1-5pm 17 Jun–10 Sep), dedicated to the local singer Jóns Ólafsson. Right at the end of this road (Route 216) is the ruined wooden **farmhouse** of eccentric Icelandic artist Samúel Jónsson (1884–1969), which is full of wacky statues of people and horses.

Fossdalur Walk

There's a roaring falls and a small farm with its own little hydroelectric power plant at **Foss**, which is the start of the long, dramatic 15km hike along the Fossdalur valley to Tungamúli or Krossholt on the south coast road (Route 62). The next fjord east from Fossfjörður (Reykjarfjörður) has a rundown **geothermal swimming pool**.

Sleeping

There's a free camp site beside the golf course on the outskirts of town, and the village has a small supermarket.

Gistiheimilið Fjalli (☎ 456 2328; hmk@snerpa.is; Hafnarbraut 2; sb/s/d Ikr1500/3200/6000) This guesthouse near the docks has an attached restaurant and a guest kitchen and TV lounge. Meals cost from Ikr350 to Ikr1690.

You can also get meals at the grill **Vegamót** (☎ 456 2232; mains Ikr395-1550) by the petrol station.

Getting There & Away

Íslandsflug (☎ 456 2151; www.islandsflug.is) flies daily except Saturday from Reykjavík to the airstrip at Foss (Bíldudalur). The cheapest online-booked one-way ticket costs Ikr4785, and the flight takes 40 minutes. Buses from Patreksfjörður via Tálknafjörður run by request (☎ 855 3665 or 863 0990) to connect with flights.

TÁLKNAFJÖRÐUR

pop 340

Tálknafjörður is surrounded by rolling green hills and sits on the edge of a bubbling geothermal field. There's a decent outdoor **swimming pool** (☎ 456 2639; admission adult/child Ikr250/100; ⌚ 9am-9pm Mon-Fri, 9am-6pm Sat-Sun), and nearby is a sparkling yellow sand beach. In summer, a **tourist office** (☎ 456 2639; www.talknafjordur.is; ⌚ 9am-9pm Mon-Fri, 9am-6pm Sat-Sun) operates at the pool. There's also a bank, post office and supermarket.

Sleeping & Eating

The **camping ground** (☎ 456 2639; camp site per person Ikr800; sb Ikr1200-1500) is beside the swimming pool, which also operates a bunkhouse in summer. There's a laundry and cooking facilities for guests.

Close to each other on Strandgata in the centre of the village are the pleasant guesthouses **Gistiheimilið Hamrarborg** (☎ 456 2514; fax 456 2694) and **Skrúðhamar** (☎ 456 2604; hopid@centrum.is), both of which offer sleeping-bag space for around Ikr1500 and made-up beds for Ikr3000.

There's a snack bar and supermarket at the Esso petrol station.

The town restaurant **Posthúsið** (☎ 456 2500; Strandgata 32; mains Ikr450-1600) serves burgers, pizzas and grills.

For drinks, head for the pub **Hópið** (☎ 456 2631; Hrafnardalsvegur), which sometimes has bands playing at weekends.

Getting There & Away

Buses will run from Patreksfjörður to Bíldudalur on request (☎ 855 3665 or 863 0990) to meet flights, passing through Tálknafjörður.

PATREKSFJÖRÐUR & AROUND

pop 771

The largest village in this part of the Westfjords, Patreksfjörður sits on a long gravel spit that extends into the fjord of the same name. The town was named for St Patrick of Ireland, who was the spiritual guide of Örlygur Hrappson, the first settler in the area. In 1983 part of Patreksfjörður was buried by a mudslide, but the town has bounced back. Today there are quite good facilities for tourists, including a **swimming pool** (☎ 456 1523; Eyrargata), a tiny cinema on Aðalstræti and a bank with an ATM.

Sleeping & Eating

There's a rather exposed camp site behind the Esso petrol station. Alternatively, you could stay at the friendly **Stekkaból** (☎ 456 1675; stekkabol@snerpa.is; Stekkar 19; sb/made-up beds Ikr1700/3000) behind the Þorpið restaurant in the middle of the village.

The Esso petrol station on the main road has a grill.

For full meals, try **Rabba Barinn** (☎ 456 1667; Aðalstræti 89; mains Ikr350-1600) or **Þorpið** (☎ 456 1295; Aðalstræti 73), both on the main street.

There are several supermarkets and a Vin Búd liquor store on Þórsgata.

Getting There & Away

Patreksfjörður has an airstrip, which is across the fjord from the village, but there are no flights here at present.

On Monday, Wednesday and Saturday from 1 June to 31 August, there are buses between Patreksfjörður and Brjánslækur/Baldur ferry (Ikr1900, 1¼ hours), Látrabjarg (Ikr1200, two hours) and Ísafjörður (Ikr3400, two hours).

Buses also run by request (☎ 855 3665 or 863 0990) from Patreksfjörður to meet flights into Bíldudalur.

LÁTRABJARG PENINSULA

Southwest of Patreksfjörður, Route 62 cuts across the ridge at Kleifaheiði to the south coast, whereas Route 612 runs west to the end of the Latrabjarg peninsula. Near the head of the fjord on Route 612 is the rusting hulk of the fishing boat *Garðar*, and there are empty, golden beaches around the airstrip at Sauðlauksdalur.

Hnjótur

The entertaining **Egill Ólafsson Folk Museum** (☎ 456 1569; admission adult/concession Ikr500/free; 10am-6pm 1 Jun-16 Sep) has an eclectic collection of exhibits, including salvaged fishing boats, old aircraft and displays on the history of the region. The museum sprawls over several hangars, and behind it is a circle of stones commemorating the many fishing ships lost at sea off the tip of the peninsula.

Breiðavík

The farm at Breiðavík sits behind an idyllic golden sand beach framed by rocky cliffs. It's a lovely spot, and you can camp or stay in rooms at the **Gistiheimilið Breiðavík** (☎ 456 1575; breidavi@li.is; camp site per person Ikr600, sb from Ikr1800, evening meals Ikr2500). Between Breiðavík and Látrabjarg there's another golden sand beach at Hvallátur, a gorgeous spot for wild camping.

Rauðisandur

Rauðisandur (Red Sands) is a long gorgeous pink beach with pounding surf, backed by a huge lagoon. A bumpy 10km dirt road runs across to Rauðisandur from the main road at Patreksfjörður, providing access to some wonderful wild camping areas.

Látrabjarg

The dramatic cliffs at Látrabjarg range from 40m to 400m high and extend for 12km along the coast from the western tip of the westernmost peninsula in the Westfjords. The Bjargtangar lighthouse is actually Europe's westernmost point. The area is incredible for bird-watching, and unbelievable numbers of puffins, razorbills, guillemots, cormorants, fulmars, gulls and kittiwakes nest here during the summer. The puffins in particular are incredibly tame, and you can often get within a few feet of the birds for photos. On calm days, seals are often seen basking on the skerries around the lighthouse.

Getting There & Away

From 1 June to 31 August, buses leave Ísafjörður at 9am on Monday, Wednesday and Saturday, and pass through Brjánslækur (noon) and Patreksfjörður (1.10pm), reaching Látrabjarg at 2.10pm. They return from Látrabjarg at 3.30pm and connect with the *Baldur* ferry to Stykkishólmur at Brjánslækur. If you want to stay longer, you'll have to camp overnight or hike 11km to the guesthouse at Breiðavík. You can also reach the cliffs by hiking 5km east from Hvallátur.

DÉJÀ VU

Icelanders have scaled the Latrabjarg cliffs to collect eggs and bird chicks since Viking times, and these skills came in handy in the winter of 1947, when the British trawler *Dhoon* foundered off the cliffs in high seas. The residents of Hvallátur descended the cliffs on ropes and hauled 12 crew members to safety. Many of the rescued men were suffering from exposure, so hot soup was lowered to sustain them until they reached the top of the cliffs. The following year a film crew visited to make a documentary about the rescue. As they were setting up a re-enactment of the scene, they encountered another British trawler that had crashed into the rocks at Patreksfjörður and were able to film the rescue live, with no need for a re-enactment. The documentary was later released as *Rescue Deed at Látrabjarg*.

SOUTH COAST

Because of the ferry connection to Stykkishólmur on the Snaefellsnes peninsula, the south coast gets plenty of tourist traffic, but it isn't as dramatic as the wilderness areas further north and west. There are no towns in the area – the largest settlement is the tiny cluster of farms around the jetty for the *Baldur* ferry – but there are several small guesthouses dotted along the coast. The south coast fjords are shorter and shallower than their northern counterparts, so driving around the area is less of a winding ordeal.

REYKHÓLAR & DJÚPADALUR

The kidney-shaped peninsula of Reykjanes is a minor geothermal area. Steam rises spontaneously from the ground around the village of **Reykhólar** (Smoke Hills), which has the inevitable **geothermal swimming pool** (☎ 434 7738). The village also has a **tourist office** (☎ 434 7830; 10am-noon & 2-6pm Jun-Aug). The hiking map *Gönguleiðir Reykhólasveit* (Ikr200) covers a number of walks in the region.

The tiny village of Bjarkalundur on Route 60 near the start of the peninsula is the starting point for hikes to the peak of Vaðalfjöll (508m). At the head of Djúpafjörður, 20km west of Bjarkalundur, are the hot springs and steaming vents of the Djúpadalur geothermal field, where there's an indoor **thermal swimming pool** (☎ 434 7853; adult/child Ikr200/50).

Sleeping & Eating

In Reykhólar, there's a **camping ground** (☎ 434 7738; camp site per person Ikr500) by the swimming pool.

Gistiheimilið Álftaland (☎ 434 7878; bjornsam@centrum.is; sb/s/d Ikr2750/5700/72000) This is the only option in the village itself. It's a bungalow-style guesthouse with a sauna and hot pots.

Miðjanes (☎ 434 7787; sb Ikr1500) Sleeping-bag accommodation is available at this little wooden farmhouse about 4km west of Reykhólar.

The only food option is the supermarket and snack bar **Árnhóll** (☎ 434 7890; Ikr300-900).

At Bjarkalundur, the only option is **Hótel Bjarkalundur** (☎ 434 7762; www.bjarkalundur.is; sb Ikr2000; s/d with breakfast Ikr4900/7100), a large tin farmhouse with a petrol station, a cafeteria and reasonably priced rooms.

Djúpadalur has the welcoming **Guesthouse Djúpadalur** (☎ 434 7853; sb/made-up bed Ikr1500/2100). About 8km west at Gufudalur is the friendly blue farm **Fremi-Gufudalur** (☎ 434 7855; rani@vortex.is; camp site per person Ikr700, sb/summerhouse Ikr1500/7000), which offers horse riding for Ikr2000 per hour.

Getting There & Away

Buses run between Reykjavík and Reykhólar (Ikr3650, four hours), via Króksfjarðarnes on Tuesday and Sunday year-round. There's no bus service between Bjarkalundur and Brjánslækur.

FLÓKALUNDUR

The village of Flókalundur was named for the Viking explorer Hrafna-Flóki Vilgerðarson, who gave Iceland its name in 860 AD. Down the road at Flókalaug is a **thermal swimming pool** (☎ 456 2011; adult/child Ikr200/100) managed by the hotel. The most interesting thing in the area is the **Vatnsfjörður Nature Reserve**, established to protect the area around Lake Vatnsdalsvatn, a nesting site for harlequin ducks and red-throated and great northern divers (loons). Various hiking trails run around the lake and into the hills beyond.

Sleeping & Eating

Hótel Flókalundur (☎ 456 2011; www.flokalundur.is; camp site per tent Ikr1000, s/d with breakfast Ikr8000/10,500, meals Ikr550-2400) This cosy wooden bungalow-style hotel is close to the junction of the Patreksfjörður and Ísafjörður roads. It has a petrol station, a decent restaurant and homely rooms with bathrooms, and it's open from May to September.

BRJÁNSLAEKUR

There is nothing much at Brjánslækur except the terminal for the *Baldur* ferry to Stykkishólmur and Flatey. If you're killing time here, there are some turf-covered 9th-century ruins south of the terminal.

Sleeping & Eating

Across the road from the ferry landing on Route 62, the ferry office has a basic **camp site** (☎ 456 2020; camp site per tent Ikr600).

About 8km west of Brjánslækur on Route 62, you can stay at **Gistihúsið Rauðsdal** (☎ 456 2041; raudsdal@vortex.is; sb/made-up bed Ikr1900/2500). A few kilometres west is the similar farm **Hvammar** (☎ 456 2032; valgeird@isholf.is; sb from Ikr1800), which offers sleeping-bag accommodation and a guest kitchen.

At Krossholt, 14km west of Brjánslækur, you'll find **Gistiheimilið Bjarkarholt** (☎ 456 2025; torfis@simnet.is; sb/made-up bed Ikr1500/2500). Accommodation is also available at **Birkimelur** (☎ 456 2080; sb Ikr1200) next door, which runs the geothermal pool on the shore.

Getting There & Away

Bus schedules are timed to connect with the **Baldur ferry** (☎ 438 1450; www.islandia.is/~eyjaferdir) to Stykkishólmur. For details, see p144.

On Monday, Wednesday and Saturday from 1 June to 31 August, buses run from Brjánslækur to Ísafjörður (Ikr2800, two hours) at 7pm. In the reverse direction, buses leave Ísafjörður at 9am reaching Brjánslækur at noon. The same bus continues to Patreksfjörður (Ikr600, 1¼ hours) and Látrabjarg (Ikr2500, two hours), returning from Látrabjarg at 3.30pm after an hour-long stop to admire the birdlife.

STRANDIR COAST

The east coast of the Westfjords is very sparsely populated, and the shoreline is indented by a series of broad fjords, the most important being Steingrímsfjörður. The only settlement of any size is Hólmavík, near the head of the fjord. From here, Route 61 turns inland towards Ísafjörður, and a rough dirt road runs north along the east coast to the tiny village of Norðurfjörður. This is one of the most dramatic and mountainous parts of the Westfjords, and the sense of peace and quiet is magnificent. You can walk from Norðurfjörður to the Drangajökull icecap and Hornstrandir. There are buses along the coast as far as Hólmavík and Drangsnes, but you'll need your own vehicle to get further.

BRÚ TO HÓLMAVÍK

Heading north from Brú, Route 61 passes through a landscape of gently rolling hills, with small farmhouses and churches dotted around the hills. At the head of Bitrufjörður is the horse farm **Snartartunga** (☎ 451 3362; snartartunga@bigfoot.com; sb Ikr1500, made-up bed s/d Ikr3300/4070), which offers horse riding for Ikr1500 per hour. A trail from Snartartunga leads 10km across to Kleifar on the opposite side of the peninsula.

In summer camping and sleeping-bag accommodation is available at the **Broddanesskóli** (☎ 451 3347) about 8km further north on the little fjord of Kollafjörður.

HÓLMAVÍK

pop 370

The fishing village of Hólmavík on the southern shore of Steingrímsfjörður is the only settlement of any size on the Strandir coast. It offers sweeping views over the still waters of the fjord, and there's a fantastic witchcraft museum, plus a shop, petrol station, post office and a bank with an ATM. You can rent horses through **Strandahestar** (☎ 451 3196).

Information

The **tourist office** (☎ 451 3465; www.holmavik.is/info; 9am-8pm 10 Jun–20 Aug) is inside the modern community centre near the Esso petrol station. Ask for a copy of the hiking brochure *Gönguleiðir í Strandasýslu*, which has maps of local hikes (Ikr200).

Sights & Activities

Down by the harbour, the popular **Exhibition of Witchcraft & Sorcery** (☎ 451 3525; www.vestfirdir.is/galdrasyning; admission Ikr500; 10am-6pm Jun-Aug) tells the macabre but fascinating story of 17 men and women who were burned at the stake for witchcraft in the Westfjords during the 17th century. Most of the occult practices they were accused of were simply old Viking traditions, but looking at the displays in the exhibition, you can see why the witch-hunters were suspicious! Be sure to check out the 16th-century grimoires (magic books), which are full of sinister incantations.

There is some good **hiking** in the area. An easy short hike follows the coast north

THE WRONG TROUSERS?

One particularly gruesome display at the Hólmavík witchcraft museum deals with the legend of *necropants* – unspeakable trousers made from the skin off the legs and groin of a dead man. It was believed that the necropants would spontaneously produce money when worn, as long as the donor corpse had been stolen from a graveyard at the dead of night and a magic rune and a coin stolen from a poor widow were placed in the dead man's scrotum!

to the farm at Ós, then cuts back to Hólmvík along the Stakkar ridge further inland. Another walk that is quite easy on the legs is the 4km circuit of Lake Þiðriksvallavatn from the Þverárvirkjun hydroelectric plant, 2km south of Hólmavík.

The wooden church at **Staður**, 14km northwest of Hólmavík at the head of Steingrímsfjörður, has a pulpit that dates back to 1731.

Sleeping & Eating

The official **camping ground** (☎ 451 3111; camp site per person Ikr500) is beside the community centre and tourist office. It has toilets, showers and a laundry.

Gistiheimilið Borgarbraut (☎ 451 3136; fax 451 3413; Borgarbraut 4; sb/made-up bed Ikr1700/2500) Run by a high-spirited local family, this place has welcoming rooms, a guest kitchen and a TV lounge. It's uphill from the seafront, near the church.

About 8km south of Hólmavík and right by the seashore is the big and comfortable white and red painted farmhouse **Kirkjubol** (☎ 451 3474; www.strandir.is/kirkjubol; sb/s/d Ikr1700/2900/4800).

For cheap eats, head for the grill at the Esso petrol station in Hólmavík.

Café Riis (☎ 451 3567; www.caferiis.is; Hafnarbraut 39; mains Ikr900-1900), the town pub and restaurant, is in a historic wooden building that dates from 1897. It's a fine place to chill out with a pizza or a beer, and there's a lounge with sofas on the top floor.

Getting There & Away

The summer bus service between Reykjavík and Ísafjörður involves a change of buses at Hólmavík. Buses run only on Sunday, Tuesday and Friday, and you'll pay Ikr4800 from Reykjavík to Hólmavík (6½ hours) and Ikr3900 from Hólmavík to Ísafjörður (four hours). The Ísafjörður-bound bus leaves Hólmavík at 3pm, and the Staðarskáli bus – for Reykjavík and Akureyri – leaves at 3.15pm. On Friday only, there is also a bus to Drangsnes.

DRANGSNES

Across the fjord from Hólmavík, Drangsnes is a remote little colony with views across to north Iceland and the small uninhabited island of **Grímsey**, which has a large puffin colony. Local fisherman **Ásbjörn Magnússon** (☎ 451 3238) runs boat trips to Grímsey on request. Legend has it that the rocky stack **Kerling** by the shore is a petrified troll – see 'The Grímsey Trolls' following. Several walking trails in the area lead up to scenic lakes on the Bjarnarfjarðarháls ridge.

The coast north of Bjarnarfjörður is backed by dramatic crumbling escarpments and offers fine views across to the Skagi peninsula in north Iceland.

THE GRÍMSEY TROLLS

According to legend, the stone stack at Drangsnes was once one of the Grímsey trolls. These unpleasant creatures decided one night to dig a trench right across the peninsula and sever the Westfjords from the mainland. In the process they created a number of new islands, including Grímsey and the many islands of Breiðafjörður. Unfortunately, the trolls were so wrapped up in their endeavour that they failed to notice the rising sun. As the first rays broke over the horizon, the two trolls working at the west end of the trench were transformed into standing stones at Kollafjörður. The female troll at the east end of the trench nearly escaped, but as she was turning to flee, she realised that she had marooned her cow on the newly created island of Grímsey. She was petrified in that position, forever gazing towards her lost cow. A rock in the shape of a cow can still be seen down by the waterline at the north end of Grímsey island.

Sleeping & Eating

There's a small **camp site** (☎ 451 3238) with a toilet block and showers on the foreshore at Drangsnes.

Three kilometres north of Drangsnes, you can stay at the farm **Bær III** (☎ 451 3241; fax 451 3274; sb/made-up bed Ikr1100/2200). A trail to Bjarnarfjarðarháls starts just behind the farm, and the owners can arrange fishing and bird-hunting trips. It closes from October to May.

Further north at the head of Bjarnarfjörður, **Hótel Laugarhóll** (☎ 451 3380; www.strandir.is/lauargholl; camp site per person Ikr300; sb from Ikr1000, s/d Ikr3400/4700, with bathroom Ikr6700/8800) is a large modern white building in a cluster of farms overlooking the coast. There's also a restaurant and geothermal pool. You can buy supplies at the resort's small supermarket. A trail behind the hotel leads up to the 451m peak Hólsfjall.

Getting There & Away

The Friday buses from Staðarskáli to Hólmavík continue to Drangsnes (20 minutes) at 3pm, returning at 4pm. No buses run north of Drangsnes, so you'll need a vehicle to reach Laugarhóll or anywhere further north. **Ásbjörn Magnússon** (☎ 451 3238) offers boat transfers up to the east coast of Hornstrandir – call for the current rates.

DRANGSNES TO REYKJARFJÖRÐUR

North of Drangsnes, the road winds around a series of gorgeous and dramatic fjords that are excellent for walking and wild camping. However, there is no public transport north of Drangsnes. The broad fjord at **Kaldbaksvík** has a small fishing lake that reflects the surrounding mountains. A 4km trail just beyond the lake runs up to the summit of Lambatindur (854m).

Tucked in beneath a looming rock wall at Reykjarfjörður, the herring-processing village of Djúpavík is mostly abandoned. However, the owners of the small and friendly **Hótel Djúpavík** (☎ 451 4037; www.djupavik.com; sb/s/d Ikr1800/4600/5800) are hanging in there. They serve tasty home-cooked food, and their friendly dog often accompanies walkers on treks into the hills. A spectacular glittering **waterfall** tumbles over the sheer scarp behind the village – you can walk up here in about 30 minutes for stunning views of the fjord. The scramble up to the foot of the falls begins by the stream, behind the ruins of the old fishing station.

Longer walks are possible at the head of the fjord, along the Reykjarfjörðardalur valley. On the north side of the fjord, a marked trail runs up over the headline from Naustvík to Árnes. Just beyond the airstrip at Gjögur, a 2km trail leads from a small radar station to the towering sea cliffs at **Reykjaneshryna**.

NORÐURFJÖRÐUR & AROUND

The road along the Strandir coast ends just beyond the little fishing village of Norðurfjörður, which has a shop and petrol station and a few guesthouses. This is the last village before Hornstrandir, and trekkers should stock up on supplies here. About 2km beyond Norðurfjörður is the hamlet Krossnes, which has an open-air **geothermal swimming pool** (☎ 451 4048; adult/child Ikr200/100) on a wild black pebble-beach with some dramatic sea stacks.

About 6km before Norðurfjörður at Árnes is the small museum **Kört** (☎ 451 4025; admission Ikr250; 🕑 11am–6pm), which has displays on fishing and farming. Note the two eye-catching churches in Árnes. From here, a scenic hiking trail crosses the Reykjanes Peninsula to Naustavík on Reykjarfjörður (the southern fjord of this name).

Sleeping & Eating

At Norðurfjörður is the recommended green **Ferðafélag Íslands' hut** (☎ 568 2533; www.fi.is; camp site per person Ikr600, sb members/non-members Ikr1200/1700; open May-Sep). Down at the harbour, **Gistiheimilið Árneshreppi** (☎ 451 4060; arneshreppur@simnet.is) has sleeping-bag accommodation, plus a shop and petrol station.

At Árnes, the village school **Finnbogastaðaskóli** (☎ 451 4031; camp site per person Ikr500, sb Ikr1600) offers sleeping-bag accommodation and camping in summer.

Heading north along the coastal walking trail towards Hornstrandir, you'll come across a basic camp site at **Ófeigsfjörður** (☎ 554 4341), with toilets but no kitchen facilities or showers.

Getting There & Away

No buses run to Norðurfjörður, but Íslandsflug flies on Monday and Thursday between Reykjavík and the airstrip at Gjögur, 16km southeast of Norðurfjörður. Fares start at Ikr4785 one way (50 minutes).

HORNSTRANDIR

The wonderful empty peninsula at the north end of the Westfjords is a fantastic destination for wild hiking. Hornstrandir covers 580 sq km of grassland and tundra, and the coast is indented by dozens of deep fjords, which are ringed by craggy mountains and precarious sea cliffs. Walkers often see arctic foxes here – they're black in summer and white in winter – and seals and whales are commonly spotted offshore. A handful of hardy farmers lived up here until the 1950s, but the peninsula is uninhabited today, and

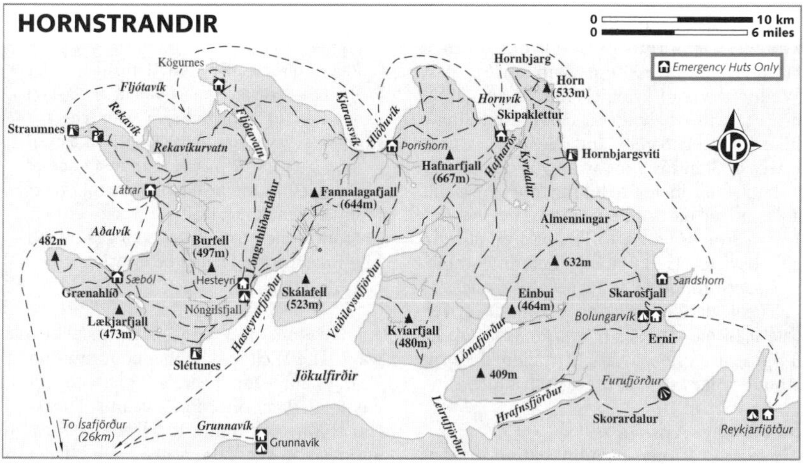

in 1975 it was set aside as a national monument and nature reserve.

Hornstrandir is a popular destination for hikers in summer, and accommodation is available at Hesteyri, Grunnavík, Reykjarfjörður and Bolungarvík. Boats run to Hornstrandir from Ísafjörður or Drangsnes between June and August, or you can walk here from Norðurfjörður on the Strandir coast or Unaðsdalur on the Snæfjallaströnd coast.

TREKKING AT HORNSTRANDIR

The most popular starting point for hikes is the semi-abandoned village of **Sæból** in Aðalvík. Boats run to Sæbol several times a week from Ísafjörður, and you can hike from here south along the coast and over the ridge to the former Norwegian whaling station of **Hesteyri** in about six hours. Hesteyri has a mountain hut, and you can catch a boat back to Ísafjörður the following day or continue north along the Lönguhlíðardalur and Grúmsdalur valleys to pretty lake **Fljótavatn** (seven hours). After a night of camping, continue over the headland westwards to the lagoon at **Rekavík** (three hours) or the clifftop lighthouse at **Straumnes** (four hours). It's then an easy three hours or so back to Aðalvík. The complete circuit will take three days. You can also start the loop at Hesteyri.

Another popular route is from the head of Veiðileysufjörður north across the isthmus to **Hornvík** and the towering 534m sea cliffs at **Hornbjarg**. Over on the east coast, boats can drop you near the mountain huts at **Reykjarfjörður** or **Bolungarvík**, or the hot spring and abandoned church at Furufjörður, the start of the trail to Hrafnfjörður. You can make the crossing in a day and be picked up by the Ísafjörður boat on the far side.

Outside the reserve but similarly remote is the mountainous spur at **Grunnavík**, bound by the fjords Ísafjarðardjúp and Jökulfirðir. Boats run from Ísafjörður to the mountain hut here, and you can hike to dramatic sea cliffs along **Snæfjallaströnd** or walk up to the glacier **Drangajökull** along the **Kaladalón** valley.

Note that the trails in Hornstrandir are crude and pass over some very rough terrain. Always get local advice before you set off as some routes might be impassable after the winter and many trails are negotiable only at low tide. The tourist office in Ísafjörður has a tide table to help you plan your journey. Bring the Landmælingar Íslands topographic sheet *Hornstrandir* (1:100,000) and a compass, as well as adequate food and water for your trip.

If you don't feel like going it alone, the tourist office in Ísafjörður can recommend local guides. Alternatively you could come on a guided trek – see Tours (following) for details.

Tours

It's easy enough to organise your own transport and accommodation at Hornstrandir and then hike independently, but several organisations offer organised trips.

Based in Ísafjörður, **Vesturferðir** (☎ 456 5111; www.vesturferdir.is) runs five-hour day tours to Hesteyri for Ikr3900 at 2pm on Sunday, Wednesday and Friday. There is also a 12-hour trip to Aðalvík (Ikr8500), including a hike between Sæból and Hesteyri, which leaves at 8am on Sunday and Wednesday.

Longer all-inclusive hiking tours are available on set dates in summer. The five-day circuit from Aðalvík to Hesteyri, Fljótavatn and back costs Ikr44,900 including transport, accommodation, meals and guides.

The Icelandic trekking organisation **Ferðafélag Íslands** (☎ 568 2533; www.fi.is; Mörkin 6, IS-108 Reykjavík) also offers a variety of guided Hornstrandir hikes several times each summer.

Sleeping

There are various accommodation options along the coast, accessible on foot or by boat from Ísafjörður or Drangsnes. Expect to pay Ikr500 for camping and Ikr1000 to Ikr1500 for sleeping-bag space. All the following places have guest kitchens, and Grunnavík and Hestryri have basic snack bars.

On the east coast, camping and sleeping-bag accommodation is available at **Reykjarfjörður** (☎ 456 7215, 853 1615; reykjarf@mis.is) and **Bolungarvík** (☎ 456 7192, 852 8267), which can be reached by chartered boat from Drangsnes on the Strandir coast.

On the west coast, camping and sleeping-bag accommodation is provided at **Hesteyri** (☎ 456 7183, 853 6953) and **Grunnavík** (☎ 456 4664, 848 0511; www.grunnavik.it.is). Both can be reached by boat from Ísafjörður.

Bright orange emergency huts with radios and heaters are provided at remote locations throughout Hornstrandir for use in case of sudden blizzards or storms.

Getting There & Away

BOAT

Most people come to Hornstrandir via the boat service from Ísafjörður, which can be booked either directly with the boat companies or through the tour company **Vesturferðir** (☎ 456 5111; www.vesturferdir.is). Boats run only from June to August, and different boats stop running at different times, so check the latest schedules before you arrive. Most services require a minimum of four people.

Sjóferðir Hafsteinn og Kiddýjar (☎ 456 3879; www.sjoferdir.is) sails from Ísafjörður to Hesteyri at 2pm on Wednesday, Friday and Sunday and at 6pm on Wednesday (Ikr2900 one way). The Wednesday boat continues on to Veiðileysufjörður. There are boats to Grunnavík at 9am on Monday and Thursday (Ikr3100), continuing to Hrafnfjörður. On Sunday and Wednesday at 8am, a boat runs to Sæból in Aðalvík (Ikr3100, one way).

Hornstrandir EHF (☎ 456 5111; www.hornstrandir.is) runs boats to/from Ísafjörður to Aðalvík (Ikr3000) at 10am on Monday, Tuesday and Friday. There's a second boat at 6pm from 12 June until 1 August. Another service runs from Ísafjörður to Hornvík (Ikr4500) at 10am on Monday and Friday (also on Wednesdays from 9 July to 6 August). If advance arrangements are made, it can drop off or pick up in Aðalvík, Fljótavík and Hlöðuvík. On Monday there's a 6pm boat to Grunnavík (Ikr2500) and Hesteyri (Ikr3000).

On the east coast, you can charter a boat from Drangsnes to Reykjarfjörður, Bolungarvík or a number of uninhabited coves along the east coast. For details contact **Ásbjörn Magnússon** (☎ 451 3238) in Drangsnes.

WARNING

Before disembarking on Hornstrandir, let the boat operator know where and when you want to be picked up. If your schedule changes while you are walking, pass a message back to the mainland through one of the guesthouses or through another hiker to let them know that you won't be there to meet the boat; otherwise a search and rescue operation might be launched.

BUS, PLANE & TREKKING

The closest you can get to Hornstrandir by bus is Ísafjörður, which has regular boat services to the peninsula. Alternatively, take the bus to Drangsnes and then a boat on to Hornstrandir.

If you'd rather make the journey on foot, you can save yourself some time by flying from Reykjavík to Gjögur (north of Hólmavík) with **Íslandsflug** (☎ 570 8030; www.islandsflug.is) and then walking from there. Another possible access route for trekkers is to take the Ísafjörður bus as far as the junction of Route 61 and Route 635 and then walk north along Route 635 to the guesthouse at Dalbær. From here, you can head up the Snæfjallaströnd coast to Grunnavík.

Northwest Iceland

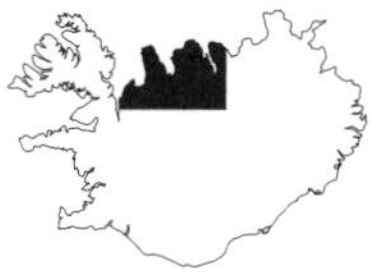

CONTENTS

Snuggled between the Westfjords and Eyjafjördur, Northwest Iceland consists of three rugged peninsulas jutting into the Arctic Ocean, separated by bays and braided river deltas, and punctuated by rather unremarkable fjords, with the exception of the beautiful Eyjafjörður, Iceland's longest fjord. Glancing at the map, most travellers between Reykjavík and Akureyri won't see much of interest in this part of the central north, and might consider it a region to be passed through quickly.

It's true that there's not a great deal of interest along the Ring Road between Brú and Akureyri, but for travellers prepared to abandon the main highway and seek out the remote corners, there's plenty to recommend it. Tourists are refreshingly thin on the ground, and the region is specked with some truly spectacular sites – from wildlife-rich Vatnsnes to historic Hólar, the lonely islands and headlands of Skagafjörður, and the remote, enchanting fishing village of Siglufjörður.

Another attraction here is year-round activities. This is one of the best places in Iceland for white-water rafting and horse riding, and opportunities for hiking, fishing, bird-watching and winter skiing abound.

Akureyri, beautifully situated on Eyjafjörður, offers the best of urban Iceland – a clean, green and lively town that makes a perfect base or starting point for all of northern Iceland's attractions.

TOP FIVE

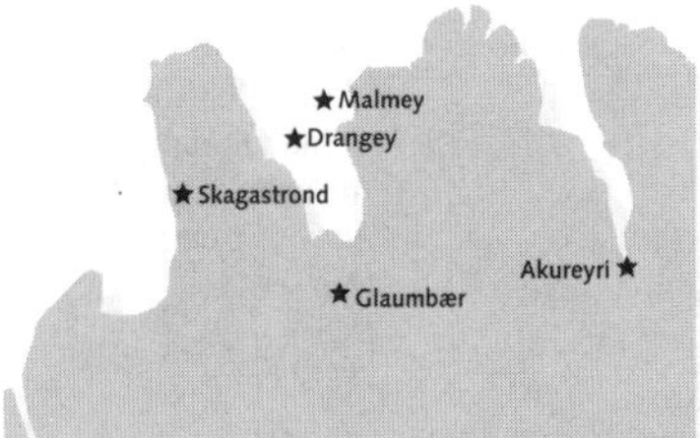

- Sitting down to a good meal in **Akureyri**, before a night out at the lively cafés and bars (p192)
- Exploring the folk museum at **Glaumbær**, the best of Iceland's restored turf-roofed farmhouses (p178)
- Joining a riding tour in Iceland's premier horse-breeding country, or experiencing the white-water thrills of the **Austari Jökulsá** (East Glacial River) (p177)
- Learning everything there is to know about herring fishing in the spectacularly situated **Siglufjörður** (p183)
- Taking a boat trip out to the bird-rich islands of Drangey and Málmey in **Skagafjörður** (p180)

GETTING THERE & AWAY

Air

Air Iceland (☎ 570 3030; www.airiceland.is) has several daily flights between Reykjavík and Akureyri (from Ikr5990 one way, 45 minutes) and at least once daily to Sauðárkrókur (Ikr6135, 40 minutes) and Grímsey (Ikr 7765, 85 minutes).

Bus

From 15 June to 31 August, **BSÍ/SBA-Norðurleið** (☎ 551 1145 Reykjavík, 462 3510 Akureyri; www.bsi.is) operates two buses a day between Reykjavík and Akureyri (Ikr5700, six hours), via Brú (Ikr2800), Hvammstangi (Ikr3100), Blönduós (Ikr3800) and Varmahlíð (Ikr4500). They depart Reykjavík at 8.30am and 5.30pm, arriving in Akureyri at 2.30pm and 11.20pm. From Akureyri, they depart at 9.30am and 5pm. There's a reduced service the rest of the year but still at least one bus daily.

Heading east, there are daily buses from Akureyri to Mývatn (Ikr2000, 1½ hours), Húsavík (Ikr1800, 70 minutes) and Egilsstaðir (Ikr4900, four hours).

GETTING AROUND

Away from the Ring Road, getting around this area can be frustrating without your own transport. In summer there's a daily bus between Varmahlíð and Sauðárkrókur, and a bus three times a week between Varmahlíð and Siglufjörður. There's also a weekday bus from Akureyri to Ólafsfjörður, via Dalvík.

EASTERN HÚNAFLÓI

HRÚTAFJÖRÐUR

Húnaflói (Bear Bay – after the many Greenland bears that have come ashore there) is the first bay to the east of the Westfjords, and Hrútafjörður, the long narrow fjord extending south from it, is the first stretch of water you'll reach if coming from the south. The fjord is surrounded by low, treeless hills and provides a nesting site for wild swans, ptarmigans, divers and golden plovers, but there's not much here aside from a few tiny settlements and farms.

Brú & Staðarskáli

The tiny junction of Brú acts mainly as a connection point for buses between Reykjavík, Akureyri and Hólmavík. The name means 'bridge', and that fairly sums up the extent of the place – scarcely anyone lives here.

About 5km north along the Ring Road, **Staðarskáli** (☎ 451 1150) is a small tourist centre with a petrol station, ATM, accommodation, restaurant and information office. Among the activities here is the two-day return **hike** to the Hrútafjarðarháls highlands southeast of Staðarskáli, where you can see Iceland's largest colony of great northern divers.

Gistihús Brú (☎ 451 1122; sb/s/d Ikr1800/2900/5000) This austere-looking building at the highway junction is an option for weary cyclists.

Staðarskáli (☎ 451 1150; fax 451 1107; s/d Ikr5900/8400) Comfortable hotel-standard rooms with bathroom are available in the complex across from the tourist centre. There's also a free camp site down by the river.

The **restaurant** at Staðarskáli serves up breakfast, the usual hamburgers, hot dogs and chips from around Ikr700, and meat and fish dishes from Ikr1190.

Reykir & Byggðasafu Museum

At Reykir, an active geothermal field 12km north of Staðarskáli, you'll find the **Byggðasafu museum** (☎ 451 0040; admission Ikr400; 🕒 10am-6pm, Jun-Aug). This local folk exhibition features an array of household and agricultural implements from early Iceland, with an emphasis on the local black magic practised in early medieval times. Highlights are the well-reconstructed interior of a 19th-century homestead and the fantastic old shark-fishing boat *Ófeigur*, built from driftwood in 1875 and used until 1915.

Sæberg HI Hostel (☎ 451 0015; saeberg@isholf.is; dm members/nonmembers Ikr1550/1900, d per person Ikr2100; ♿) A few hundred metres from the folk museum at Reykir, this is a good place to break up the trip between Reykjavík and Akureyri. It's a cosy, well-equipped little hostel with a geothermally heated swimming pool and hot tubs.

HVAMMSTANGI & AROUND

pop 593

Hvammstangi, on the eastern shore of Miðfjörður, is the biggest speck of civilisation in this area, but it's one of those forlorn fishing towns that looks as if it has seen better days. A licensed trading centre since 1895, it continues to struggle along on shrimp and mollusc fishing. Being 6km off

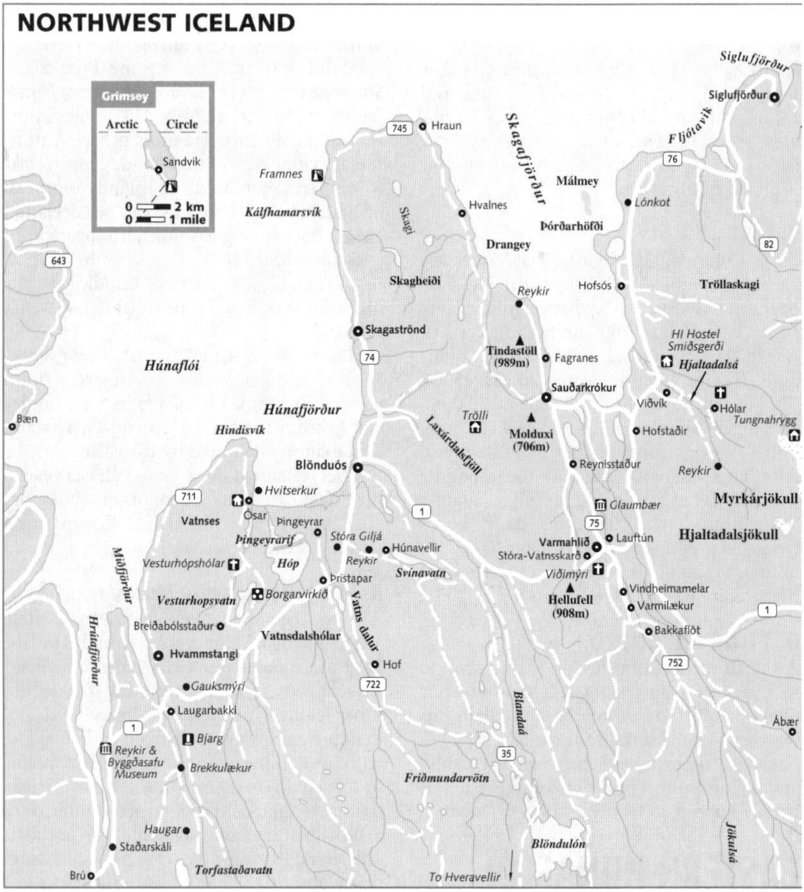

the Ring Road, the main likelihood of travellers wanting to pass through here is if you're taking the long route around the Vatnsnes Peninsula (Route 711). It's a narrow gravel road that can be rough in places, but it takes in a few points of interest.

There are some excellent opportunities for **horse riding** around Hvammstangi. The highly professional outfit **Gauksmýri** (☎ 451 2927; www.gauksmyri.is; 1hr tours Ikr2000; s/d Ikr3100/5400), on the Ring Road about 10km south of Hvammstangi, offers horse rental, tuition and regular one-hour horse shows. Adventure day tours (six hours; Ikr7000 per person) are held daily in summer. Longer tours, from four to eight days, including a sheep roundup, can also be arranged. At the farm **Brekkulækur** (☎ 451 2938; brekka@nett.is), 9km south of the Ring Road, Arinbjörn Jóhannsson organises adventurous and highly acclaimed eight- to 14-day horse-riding and hiking tours around Arnarvatnsheiði and upper Borgarfjörður. Both places also offer accommodation and meals.

Sleeping & Eating

Gistiheimili Hönnu Siggu (☎ 451 2407; Garðavegur 26; sb/r per person Ikr1750/2500) This neat family-run guesthouse in Hvammstangi has a guest lounge, kitchen and breakfast (Ikr750).

Gunnukaffi Gistihus (☎ 451 2630; Norðurbraut 1; sb/s/d Ikr2000/5600/7900) This guesthouse on the main road through town has comfortable rooms with TV and bathroom. It also has

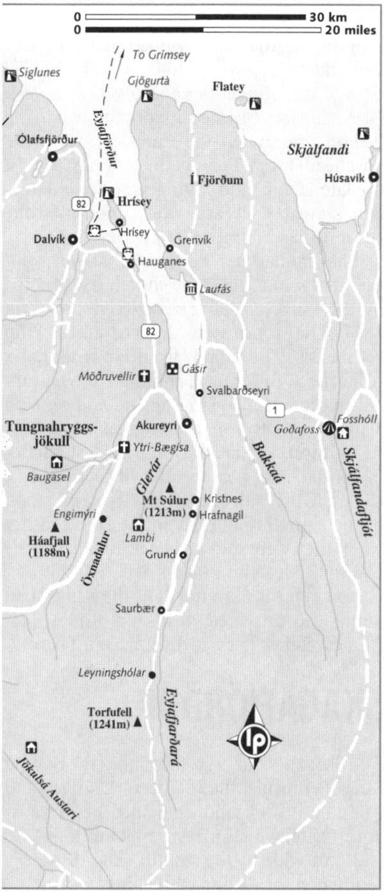

the town's only restaurant and a pub that gets lively on Friday and Saturday nights.

There's a well-stocked **supermarket** by the harbour.

VATNSNES PENINSULA

The stubby peninsula of Vatnsnes, poking out into Húnaflói, has a stark beauty, a colony of seals living off its northern tip and the endearing Ósar Youth Hostel.

Iceland's largest readily accessible seal colony and breeding ground is at **Hindisvík**, on Route 711, 10km north of Ósar. Another colony lives near the partially enclosed Sigriðarstaða lagoon just below the hostel.

A short walk from here, and accessible from a parking area near the road, is the bizarre 15m-high sea stack **Hvítserkur**. Wave action has eroded the rock into a strange and whimsical formation. Legend has it that Hvítserkur was a troll caught by the sunrise while attempting to destroy the Christian monastery at Þingeyrar. As with all trolls caught by the sunrise, he was turned to stone. Opinions on what became of the troll range from a grazing Brahman bull, an American bison, a dinosaur, or an Asian elephant with a howdah on its back, to – perhaps most apparent of all – a large Alaskan moose dredging pond weeds from the bottom of a lake.

Sleeping

Ósar Youth Hostel (☎ 451 2678; osar@simnet.is; dm members/nonmembers Ikr1600/1950, d Ikr4000, linen Ikr500) This renovated farmhouse is one of Iceland's nicest hostels, thanks to friendly management, good views and the nearby seals and bird life. The hostel is on a working dairy farm, and the owner indulges his hobby of building more rooms and welcoming guests. Bring your own food as there are no shops out here.

There are no buses to Ósar, but if you ring the hostel in advance someone can pick you up at the Viðihlíð petrol station on the Ring Road for Ikr2000 return. It's 30km from the Ring Road by the most direct route.

BLÖNDUÓS

pop 619

Blönduós is a trading centre and a shrimp and shellfishing community at the mouth of the river Blandá, but its lack of harbour facilities inhibits prosperity. It's popular with visiting salmon anglers in summer and is the closest town to the northern end of the Kjölur Route through the Interior, so it's a welcome stop for hikers and cyclists.

The nearby river Laxá offers some of Iceland's best salmon fishing, but a one-day licence costs from Ikr15,000 to a staggering Ikr200,000, so don't forget to bring your platinum hooks and 24-carat gold sinkers!

There's a small **tourist office** (☎ 452 4520; 9am-9pm 1 Jun-26 Aug;) at the camp site, just off the main road north of the river.

Sight & Activities

The islet of **Hrutey**, just upstream from the Blandá Bridge, is a nature reserve and the site of a reforestation project. Access is via a footbridge from near the camp site.

The small **Textiles Museum** (Heimilisiðnaðarsafnið; ☎ 452 4067; www.simnet.is/textile; Árbraut 29; adult/child Ikr400/100; 10am-5pm Jun-Aug), in the modern building on the north bank of the Blandá, displays local textile work, handicrafts and early Icelandic costumes. Part of the museum is devoted to Halldorá Bjarnadóttir, a local teacher, craftswoman and advocate of women's rights.

The **swimming pool** (admission Ikr200; 8.30am-9pm Mon-Fri, 10am-5pm Sat & Sun) is just below the prominent but ugly Blönduós **church**.

Sleeping & Eating

The **camp site** (☎ 452 4520; per person Ikr500) occupies a lovely setting near the river.

Glaðheimar (☎ 452 4403, 898 1832; www.gladheimar.is; 3-person cabin weekday/weekend Ikr5300/6500, 4-person Ikr7000/8000) Beside the camp site are several comfortable three- to eight-person self-contained cabins, some with hot tub and sauna (luxury!). Glaðheimar also runs a slick **guesthouse** (☎ 452 4403; Blöndubyggð 10; sb/s/d Ikr2000/4500/6500) in the former post-office building. It has nine clean rooms sharing three bathrooms and two kitchens.

Hótel Blandá (☎ 452 4205; arnibald@lax-a.is; Aðalgata 6; s/d Ikr10,300/12,400) South of the river, this is the top hotel in town. It's popular with visiting anglers so it's often full on summer weekends. The **restaurant** (mains Ikr1200-2700; noon-2pm & 7-10pm) has good local fish and lamb dishes, a plush dining room and a full bar that's the local pub on weekends.

The closest farm accommodation is **Stóra Giljá** (☎ 452 4294; giljan@binet.is; sb/s/d Ikr1800/4000/6000), 13km south on the Ring Road, with cottages and a hot tub.

Við Árbakkann (☎ 452 4678; Húnabraut 2; light meals Ikr500-750) This fine country-style café north of the river serves coffee, waffles, cakes, baguettes, bagels and salads. Not a burger in sight! There's also a bar and summer terrace.

AROUND BLÖNDUÓS

Þingeyrar

Sitting alongside the 44-sq-km lagoon Hóp, 20km south of Blönduós, Þingeyrar is one of Iceland's great historical sites but, as with many such places, the only remaining evidence is a small church. It was the site of a district assembly (Alþing) and where Jón Ögmundarson, the original Bishop of Hólar, founded Iceland's first monastery in 1112.

Hoping to ease some of the famine and crop failure that had plagued northern Iceland, the bishop vowed to build a church. He cleared the foundations and, less than a week later, the soil regained its productivity. The bishop interpreted the miracle as a divine go-ahead for a Benedictine monastery. In the late 12th century, Þingeyrar became Iceland's greatest library, where monks wrote, compiled and copied histories and sagas.

The monastery no longer stands, but there's a wonderful stone church constructed by the Þingeyrar farmer between 1864 and 1877. The stones were dragged across Hóp on the ice. The pulpit, from Holland, dates from the 17th century, and the 15th-century altarpiece was made in England and set with alabaster reliefs from the original monastery. Most impressive are the replica oak statuettes of Christ and the apostles. The originals, carved in the 16th century in Germany, stood in the church until early in the 20th century when they were sold and later donated to the National Museum in Reykjavík.

Þingeyrar is 6km north of the Ring Road along the unsealed dead-end Route 721. The caretaker lives at the adjacent farm.

SKAGAFJÖRÐUR

The Skagafjörður region includes the remote Skagi Peninsula, the islands of Drangey and Málmey in Skagafjörður, and the Héraðsvötn Delta, which measures 40km long and is 30km wide at the mouth. The district is renowned for its horse breeding.

SKAGASTRÖND

pop 650

Skagaströnd is one of northern Iceland's oldest trading centres, first established as a German and English merchant town in the 16th century. These days it's a fishing village with a busy fish processing plant that at first glance looks typically boring but is actually the 'country-music capital' of Iceland!

The main reason to venture the 20km north of the Ring Road is to pop into Iceland's only country-music bar, **Kántrýbær** (☎ 453 2950; www.kantry.is). Upstairs is a small museum of country-music memorabilia and a working radio station, where you'll most likely find Iceland's original cowboy spinning a few tunes. See the boxed text on p177.

ICELANDIC COWBOY

Hallbjön Hjartason, the 'Icelandic Cowboy', fell in love with country-and-western music while working on the American base at Keflavík in the 1960s. Even after moving back to the remote fishing community at Skagaströnd, he continued to indulge his passion for playing and recording country music (he released his first record in 1975). He organised Iceland's first country-music festival there in 1984. The four-day event is now held annually on the first weekend in August and attracts fans from all over Iceland.

Sleeping & Eating

The **camp site** (per person Ikr500), just west of the town centre at the end of Holabraut, has a flashy new pine kitchen and toilet block.

Guesthouse Soffia (☎ 452 2625; Holabraut 25; sb/made-up beds Ikr1700/3400) This family home near the camp site has just two rooms.

Hotel Dagsbrún (☎ 452 2730; Turnbraut 1-3; beds per person Ikr3900) A standard hotel in a multistorey block of offices in the town centre. If no-one is here, inquire at Kántrýbær.

Kántrýbær (☎ 453 2950; Holanesvegur; mains Ikr450-1800; 11.30am-10pm) With its rustic 'Wild West saloon' atmosphere, booth seating, check tablecloths and the constant twang of country music, a meal or a beer here is a must. The menu is mostly hamburgers, pizzas, nachos and pies. The bar, open until 3am on Friday and Saturday, becomes pretty crowded with locals and country-music enthusiasts, and there's occasional live music.

VARMAHLÍÐ

pop 130

Varmahlíð (Warm Slope), named after nearby geothermal sites, lies at the intersection of the Ring Road and the Sauðárkrókur road, Route 75. Not quite a town, Varmahlíð has developed into another Ring Road service centre with the requisite bank, swimming pool, supermarket and tourist facilities.

The main reason to spend any time here is to organise activities – this is an excellent base for rafting, hiking, horse riding and boat trips on the fjord.

There's a hiking trail (one hour) to the summit of 111m **Reykjahóll**, which affords a broad view over the surrounding green countryside as far as the fjord Skagafjörður.

The **Varmahlíð tourist office** (☎ 455 6161; www.northwest.is; 9am-9pm Jun–mid-Aug, 9am-6pm mid-Aug–Sep;) is in the little turf-roofed cottage beside the Esso petrol station. It's a helpful place with free Internet access and coffee.

For an unusual souvenir, check out **Ash** (☎ 453 8031), the workshop of Anna Hróðmarsdóttir, who produces fine ceramics from volcanic ash.

Activities

WHITE-WATER RAFTING

Between May and September the area around Varmahlíð is the best in northern Iceland for white-water rafting. **Activity Tours** (☎ 453 8383; www.rafting.is) is a professional outfit with a base about 2km west of Varmahlíð that specialises in rafting trips from three to six hours on three varied rivers, as well as a multiday safari. Day trips include: the Vestari Jökulsá (West Glacial River; four to five hours; Ikr5400), with grade II–III rapids passing through an impressive gorge; an easy paddle on the Blandá (three to four hours; adult/child Ikr4900/2700) with grade I—II rapids; and the exciting Austari Jökulsá (East Glacial River; six to seven hours; Ikr8800), where you can tackle grade III–IV+ rapids. The ultimate rafting adventure is the three-day 'River Rush' (Ikr44,000), which starts in the Sprengisandur desert and follows the Austari Jökulsá back to the coast over two days.

South along Route 752, in Tungusveit, the farm **Bakkaflöt** (☎ 453 8245, fax 453 8837, www.bakkaflot.com) also offers rafting (one to five persons) from Ikr4400 to Ikr7400 per person and boat trips on Skagafjörd to the islands Drangey and Málmey.

HORSE RIDING

One of Iceland's most respected riding outfits, **Hestasport** (☎ 453 8383; www.riding.is), offers one-hour horse rides for Ikr2000 and full-day rides for Ikr7900. Multiday horse-riding tours and visits to the September *réttir* (roundups) are scheduled in summer, and there's a 'winter' tour in April. Nine- or 10-day trips cost from Ikr146,000 (Kjölur) to Ikr185,000 (Sprengisandur–Mývatn). The six-day *réttir* costs Ikr115,000.

For casual visitors, Hestasport also runs one-hour shows about the Icelandic horse at the Vindheimamelar racing grounds

10km south of Varmahlíð. Admission costs Ikr1700, including coffee and Icelandic refreshments. Call ahead to book.

The farm **Lýtingsstaðir** (☎ 453 8064; www.lythorse.com), 20km south of Varmahlíð on Route 752, offers a similar program of tours, including one/two-hour rides (Ikr1500/2500) and a 'stop and ride' package that includes accommodation, breakfast, dinner and a two-hour ride for Ikr7300. Longer tours are usually on scheduled dates and are cheaper than Hestasport – check the website.

Sleeping & Eating

There's a **camp site** (☎ 453 8230; per person Ikr400) on the south side of the Ring Road opposite the service station.

Adventure Cottages (☎ 453 8383; www.rafting.is; 4-person cottages Ikr13,000) This brand-new group of self-contained timber cottages is perched on the hill above Varmahlíð (follow the gravel road past Hótel Varmahlíð). It's beautifully located with good views and has a very inviting stone hot pool.

Hótel Varmahlíð (☎ 453 8170; fax 453 8870; s/d Ikr9900/13,800) This big, white hotel dominates the community and has spacious rooms. Its **restaurant** (mains Ikr1500-2500; 🕑 noon-2pm & 7-9.30pm) is the best place for a decent meal, with good local trout and lamb dishes. There's also a Ikr1500 soup and fish lunch menu.

There are plenty of farmhouse options in the area – the tourist office has a list. **Lauftún** (☎ 453 8133; sb/made-up beds per person Ikr1500/2300) is closest to Varmahlíð, only 500m east along the Ring Road, with rooms in a cosy farmhouse and camping (per person Ikr400).

Stóra Vatnsskarð (☎ 453 8152; sb/made-up beds per person Ikr1800/2600) On the Ring Road 10km west of Varmahlíð, this is a small, four-room guesthouse with cooking facilities on a sheep and cattle farm.

Bakkaflöt (☎ 453 8245; www.bakkaflot.com; camp sites per person/sb/s/d Ikr600/2200/4300/6500, 4/6-person cottages Ikr7300/8500) On Route 752, 10km south of Varmahlíð, this is as much an activity centre as farmhouse accommodation. It's well set up with cooking facilities, a restaurant and hot tubs.

The Esso petrol station in Varmahlíð has a busy **cafeteria** (mains Ikr500-1350) that serves lamb chops, fish dishes and hamburger meals, and there's a **supermarket** attached.

Getting There & Away

All buses between Reykjavík (Ikr4500, 4¾ hours) and Akureyri (Ikr1500, 1¼ hours) stop at the terminal at the Hótel Varmahlíð. Suðurleiðir buses to Siglufjörður (Ikr1000) leave on Sunday, Tuesday and Thursday at 1.25pm, returning on Monday, Wednesday and Friday at 8.30am.

AROUND VARMAHLÍÐ

At **Vatnsskarð** (Lake Pass), about 12km east of Varmahlíð, the Ring Road crosses the Húnafjörður–Skagafjörður watershed. At the eastern foot of the pass there's the hill **Arnarstapi**, which bears a view disc and a monument to the Icelandic-Canadian poet Stephan G Stephansson, the 'Rocky Mountain Bard'.

About 3km west of Varmahlíð and signposted just off the Ring Road, the old chieftain's residence, **Víðimýri**, has a lovely turf-covered church. It was completed in 1834 and is still in use, and there's an altarpiece that dates from 1616. It's open from 9am to 6pm daily, June to August (Ikr100).

Glaumbær

The 18th-century turf farm at Glaumbær, 8km north of Varmahlíð on Route 75, features some of the finest remaining examples of early Icelandic building techniques you'll see. It's the best museum of its type in northern Iceland – don't miss it if you're in the area.

Snorri Þorfinnsson, the first European born in North America (in 1003), is buried at Glaumbær, where he lived after his parents returned to their native Iceland.

The farm buildings themselves date from the 18th and 19th centuries. They've been beautifully restored to house the **folk museum** (☎ 453 6173; www.krokur.is/glaumb; adult/child Ik400/200; 🕑 9am-6pm 1 Jun-20 Sep). The main farm buildings comprise 12 rooms linked by a narrow passage. The low ceilings, cramped living space and preserved furniture and utensils give a real sense of this bygone era. Items on display include household furniture, textiles, costumes, instruments including a *fiddla* (a two-stringed instrument played with a bow), blacksmith tools and kitchen utensils. The only drawback is that the tiny rooms can get pretty crowded with tourists! Staff in period costume can offer free guided tours to groups.

The adjacent **church** dates from 1926 but has interesting Dutch pulpit paintings (1685) from a previous church on the site and an organ made entirely of pinewood: pipes, keys and all.

Also on the site are two 19th-century timber houses, both examples of early types of homes that replaced the turf dwellings. Áshús, moved here in 1991, has a small historical and craft exhibition and a lovely café.

Áskaffi (☎ 453 8855; 9am-6pm Jun-Aug) is a quaint little tearoom in Áshús where you can sample home-made Icelandic sweets such as *kleinur* (pancakes), tarts, *skyr* (a bit like yoghurt), rye bread and coffee.

Buses between Varmahlíð and Sauðárkrókur pass Glambær daily in summer.

SAUÐÁRKRÓKUR

pop 2600

Although it's the second-largest town in northern Iceland, not many tourists venture up to Sauðárkrókur, 23km north of the Ring Road on the shores of Skagafjörður. However, there are a few things to see and do in the area, and this is the jumping-off point for boat tours to Drangey and Málmey islands. The town also boasts one of the best hotels in northern Iceland.

Economically, Sauðárkrókur is dependent on fishing, trading and wool tanning at the tongue-torturing Gönguskarðsárvirkjun ('trail pass river hydroelectric power station') and fish-leather tanning at Sjávarleður.

The nearest tourist office is at Varmahlíð, but you can also obtain information from local hotels. Other services include banks, a library, a laundry, a swimming pool and horse rental.

Sights & Activities

It doesn't take long to see all that Sauðárkrókur has to offer, although it's pleasant just to wander around the old part of town around Aðalgata. Many of the old houses have been restored and bear plaques showing when they were built. At the northern end of Aðalgata, **Villa Nova** (1903) is a former hotel and merchant's residence currently being restored.

The town museum, **Minjahúsið** (☎ 453 6870; Aðalgata 16b; admission Ikr400; 2-6pm Jun-Aug), at the harbour, houses a stone collection and various displays relating to local crafts and industry: blacksmiths, carpenters, saddlers and watchmakers.

The **Blacksmith's Workshop** (☎ 453 5020; Suðurgata 5; admission free), in the small blue-and-white building south of the church, remains as it was when the last blacksmith downed tools in the mid-20th century. It's open on request.

A fine day hike will take you to the summit of 706m **Molduxi** for a broad view over all of Skagafjörður. The walk starts just past Fosshotel Áning. There's also a nine-hole **golf course**, on the hillside above town (follow Hlíðarstígur).

Sleeping

The free **camp site** (☎ 453 8860), beside the swimming pool and football pitch, has toilets, hot water and power.

Gistiheimilið Mikligarður (☎ 453 6880; banani@simnet.is; Kirkjutorg 3; sb/s/d Ikr2000/4000/6000) This welcoming place in the blue building by the post office (across from the church) has comfortable double rooms, a modern kitchen and TV lounge.

Hótel Tindastóll (☎ 453 5002; www.hoteltindastoll.com; Lindargata 3; s/d Ikr11,900/16,300) It might come as a surprise way up here to find one of the best boutique hotels in Iceland, but this is it: a charming four-star hotel in a traditional building dating from 1884. The rooms are brimming with character and furnished with antiques, but have low-key modern touches such as TV, minibar, bathrobe and slippers, and Internet connections. Marlene Dietrich stayed here in 1941 in the room now called Guðriður Þorbjarnadottír (rooms are named after famous Icelanders). Outside is an irresistible stone hot tub, and in the basement is one of the cosiest bars you'll ever find.

Fosshotel Áning (☎ 453 6717; aning@fosshotel.is; s/d without bathroom Ikr6500/8700, with bathroom Ikr9600/12,300) The district boarding school becomes a hotel from June to August. It's an option if everything else is full.

Eating & Drinking

Most of the eating and entertainment is on Aðalgata, between the church and Hótel Tindastóll.

Sauðárkróks Bakari (☎ 455 5000; Hólavegi 16; 7am-6pm) The best place for breakfast is this bakery and country-style café where you can pick up fresh bread, filled rolls and a plethora of rich cakes and buns.

Kaffi Krókur (☎ 453 6299; Aðalgata 16; mains Ikr900-3500) This cosy café-pub looks simple enough, but the menu covers everything from burgers and fish and lamb dishes to fillet of horse (Ikr3290), shellfish soup (Ikr950) and authentic pasta (Ikr890–1550). The food is good, and there's a buffet salad bar for Ikr990. The bar fires up on weekend nights, and there's a pleasant summer terrace.

Ólafshús (☎ 453 6454; www.olafshus.is, Aðalgata 15; mains Ikr2200-3300, pizzas Ikr950-2600) Almost across the road from Kaffi Krókur, this is a good restaurant for a splurge. Pizzas are served all day, and Icelandic specialities, such as fish and lamb, are available as small portions or full meals. There's also a bar open until 3am Friday and Saturday.

For a drink, don't miss the rustic **bar** at Hótel Tindastóll.

The **Skagfirðingabúð supermarket** is on Skagfirðingabraut and the **Vín Búð** liquor store is at Smáragrund 2.

Getting There & Away

In summer, two buses run daily between Varmahlíð and Sauðárkrókur (Ikr500), connecting with the Ring Road buses to Reykjavík and Akureyri. They leave from the store opposite Hotel Tindastóll.

AROUND SKAGAFJÖRÐUR

Tindastóll

North of Sauðárkrókur, Tindastóll (989m) is a prominent Skagafjörður landmark, extending for 18km along the coast north of Sauðárkrókur. The mountain and its caves are believed to be inhabited by an array of sea monsters, trolls and giants, one of which kidnapped the daughter of an early bishop of Hólar.

The summit affords a spectacular view across all of Skagafjörður. The easiest way to the top, now a marked trail, starts from the high ground along Route 745 west of the mountain. At the mountain's northern end is a geothermal area, Reykir, which was mentioned in *Grettis Saga*. Grettir supposedly swam ashore from the island of Drangey in Skagafjörður, and one of the hot springs at Reykir is named Grettislaug, or 'Grettir's bath'.

From the farm Tunga, at the southwestern foot of Tindastóll, it's an 8km climb to the **Trölli mountain hut**. The hut has 18 beds but no cooking facilities. To book, contact **Ferðafélags Skagafirðinga** (☎ 453 5718) in Sauðárkrókur or the tourist office in Varmahlíð.

Drangey & Málmey Islands

The uninhabited islands of Drangey and Málmey guard the mouth of the fjord and are both saturated with nesting sea birds. In summer, boat trips can take you to both islands.

The tiny rocky islet of **Drangey**, in the middle of Skagafjörður, is a flat-topped mass of tuff rising abruptly 170m above the water. The cliffs serve as nesting sites for around a million sea birds, and have been used throughout Iceland's history for egg collection and bird netting. *Grettis Saga* recounts that both Grettir and his brother Illugi lived on the island for three years and were slain there.

From the landing place, a steep path leads to the summit. Icelanders maintain that a prayer is necessary before ascending since only part of the island was blessed by the early priests and the northeastern section remains an abode of evil. Locals will collect birds or eggs only from the parts that have been stamped with the greater powers' official seal of approval.

Some 30,000 eggs were collected annually, but now the collection has dropped to around 5000. A turf-roofed hut on the island still serves as shelter for egg-collectors.

The 2.5-sq-km island **Málmey**, known mainly for its abundance of sea birds, isn't as foreboding as Drangey. It rises to just over 150m. Nevertheless it has been uninhabited since 1951.

Recommended five-hour boat trips to Drangey, including a hike to the summit, can be arranged directly with the Fagranes farmer **Jón Eiríksson** (☎ 453 6503). Alternatively, book through hotels in Sauðárkrókur or the tourist office in Varmahlíð. The trips cost Ikr4000 and depart daily on request from the farm Fagranes, 7km north of Sauðárkrókur.

Adventure Tours (☎ 855 5000, 453 8245) also has boat trips to Drangey and Málmey from Sauðárkrókur and Hofsós. Five-hour tours to either island cost Ikr5200, and a three-hour tour of the fjord costs Ikr4500.

You can travel to Málmey by private boat from the opposite side of the fjord at Lónkot – see p182.

TRÖLLASKAGI

This rugged peninsula, which lies between Skagafjörður and northern Iceland's longest fjord, Eyjafjörður, is a maze of mountains, rivers and even a number of mini glaciers. This is ideal hiking country, and parts of the peninsula, especially around Ólafsfjörður and Siglufjörður, are reminiscent of the Westfjords.

Tröllaskagi's best-known historical attraction is **Hólar**, medieval Iceland's northern bishopric. In the far north, at the very end of a spectacular drive along Route 76, is the scenic fishing village and one-time herring capital of Iceland, **Siglufjörður**.

This section follows Route 76 from the Ring Road up to Siglufjörður. For information on the villages of Ólafsfjörður and Dalvík, on the eastern side of Tröllaskagi, see p197 and p196.

HÓLAR Í HJALTADALUR

With its prominent red stone church dwarfed by a looming mountain backdrop, the tiny settlement of Hólar makes an interesting historical detour from the Ring Road. Although the church itself is the only specific attraction, it's an important one as the northern bishopric of Hólar was the ecumenical and educational capital of northern Iceland between 1106 and the Reformation. It continued as a religious centre and the home of the northern bishops until 1798, when the bishop's seat was abolished.

Hólar then became a vicarage until 1861, when the vicarage was shifted to Viðvík. In 1882 the present agricultural school was established, and in 1952 the vicarage returned to Hólar. The agricultural college now offers two-year degrees in animal husbandry, fish farming and rural tourism. The small **aquarium** (☎ 453 6300; admission Ikr200; 9am-5pm Jun-Aug), opposite the church, is part of the aquaculture research at the college. It contains local freshwater species such as arctic char and salmon.

Hólar Cathedral

The red stone cathedral was built out of sandstone taken from Hólabyrða, the prominent mountain in Hólar's backdrop. The church was financed by donations from Lutheran congregations all over Scandinavia and was completed in 1763. The extraordinary carved altarpiece was made in Germany around 1500 and was donated by the last Catholic bishop of Hólar, Jón Arason, in 1522. After he and his son were executed at Skálholt for opposition to the Danish Reformation, his remains were brought to Hólar and entombed in the bell tower. The present church tower was built in 1950 as a memorial. It contains a mosaic of the good reverend, a chapel and his tomb.

THE BISHOP'S LAW

The first bishop at Hólar, Jón Ögmundarson, who served from 1106 to 1121, took the strict moral code of his religion very seriously.

Bishop Jón established a successful school at Hólar, where church attendance and memorisation of sacred recitations were obligatory and the only books permitted were those the bishop himself judged to be edifying. He abolished all merriment and mischief, which he thought would detract from students' and parishioners' moral values. Public dances, love songs, celebrations and anything that could be construed as paganism or sorcery were forbidden within his jurisdiction. He even changed the names of weekdays named after Norse gods (those still used in English!) to the more mundane ones used in Icelandic today. In short, Bishop Jón's word was law in northern Iceland.

The bishop was nominated for sainthood by his Icelandic constituency, and although the canonisation was never recognised by Rome, a monk at the monastery of Þingeyrar entitled his biography *Jóns Saga Helga*, or the 'Saga of St John'.

The first timber cathedral at Hólar, which replaced a small turf church, was constructed by Bishop Jón using Norwegian wood. Until 1135, when the Skálholt cathedral was completed, it was the world's largest wooden church.

Other influential bishops at Hólar included Guðbrandur Þorláksson (1571–1627), who was the first person to translate the Bible into Icelandic (in 1584) and the first to produce a map of Iceland, and the last Catholic bishop, Jón Arason, who was beheaded in 1550.

The church is open from 9am to 6pm daily from June to August (or on request). It's brimming with historical works of art, including a baptismal font carved from a piece of soapstone that washed in from Greenland on an ice floe. A guided tour costs Ikr300. A church leaflet (Ikr50), a historical trail brochure (free) and a brochure outlining other Hólar sites (Ikr100) are available from the information desk in the adjacent hotel.

Sleeping & Eating

Ferðaþjónustan Holum Hjaltadal (☎ 453 6300; fax 453 6301; sb/made-up beds per person Ikr 1900/3550; 💻 🏊) Right beside the church, this college building opens its dormitories to travellers as a summer hotel, and it's the only place to stay in Hólar. There's a **restaurant** and a heated swimming pool. Nearby is a small **camp site** (per person Ikr400) amid the trees.

HI Hostel Smiðsgerði (☎ /fax 453 7483; jas@ismennt.is; dm members/nonmembers Ikr1550/1900) This converted farmhouse, about 12km from Hólar, off Route 76 and just north of the junction with Route 769, has dorm beds and a kitchen.

HOFSÓS

pop 170

This tiny village on the eastern shore of Skagafjörður has been a trading centre since the 1500s. There's an attractive little harbour at the mouth of the Hofsá, but these days the main attraction is the Icelandic Emigration Center, where the families of Canadian and American emigrants seek their Icelandic roots. The Siglufjörður bus passes through Hofsós.

Icelandic Emigration Center

Vesturfarasafnið (Icelandic Emigration Center; ☎ 453 7935; www.hofsos.is; admission all exhibits Ikr900; 🕐 11am-6pm 1 Jun-15 Sep) has a display on Icelandic emigration to North America, and it's the office for the Icelandic-American Emigration Center. The exhibitions are well presented and fascinating even if you're not a descendant of Icelandic emigrants.

The centre is housed in three old buildings down by the harbour. The main building contains the exhibition 'New Land, New Life', which follows the lives of emigrating Icelanders in photographs, letters and displays. 'The Road to Zion' and 'Prairies Wide and Free' tell the story of Icelandic settlers in Utah and North Dakota, respectively. A ticket to visit all exhibitions is Ikr900; separate admission to each costs Ikr400.

Also at the harbour is the historic, black-tarred **Pakkhúsið**, a log warehouse built in 1777 by the Danish Royal Greenland Company. It's one of the oldest timber buildings in Iceland.

Other Attractions

South of town are some unusual hexagonal **basalt formations**. They're on the shore almost directly opposite the village church. Near Grafarós, the mouth of the River Grafará, are the remains of a 19th-century **trading post**.

The farm Gröf, 3km south of the river, has an old **turf-roofed church** surrounded by a circular turf wall. The church was built in the late 17th century but renovated and reconsecrated in 1953. If the key isn't in the door, ask at the farm.

Sleeping & Eating

Gistiheimilið Sunnuberg (☎ 453 7434, 853 0220; Sudurbraut; s/d Ikr4500/6000) Opposite the petrol station and post office, this is an old-fashioned place with the air of Grandma's house. There are five double rooms with bathroom, some of which overlook the water. If there's no-one here enquire at the Emigration Center.

Prestbakki and **Kárastígur 9** are two simple cottages in the village offering made-up beds for Ikr2200 and sleeping-bag accommodation for Ikr1800. Again, enquire at the Emigration Center.

Sigtún (☎ 453 7393) Next door to Gistiheimilið Sunnuberg, this restaurant serves coffee, burgers and tasty Icelandic meat and fish dishes. There's also a small but atmospheric bar.

Sólvík (☎ 453 7930; snacks Ikr250-400, mains around Ikr1350; 🕐 10am-9pm in summer) Down at the small harbour among the museum buildings, this pleasant country-style café has a summer veranda where you can recharge with coffee, cakes and pancakes. The evening menu includes pasta, salted cod, marinated trout and other fish and lamb dishes.

AROUND HOFSÓS

Lónkot

If you have your own vehicle, it's worth continuing 11km north of Hofsós to the farm **Lónkot** (☎ 453 7432; fax 453 7492; sb/d per person Ikr1900/2900). Clearly visible from the road is a marquee (used for group functions and occasional concerts), but continue down to the farmhouse where there's an innovative gourmet restaurant with attached accommodation. There's no set menu, but a changing four-course meal (around Ikr3900) is served nightly in summer. It usually features fish, such as trout or perch, or lamb and sometimes birds, such as puffin. You can ask for just one or two courses, and light lunches, coffee and cakes are available all day. There's also a sunken barbecue pit, nine-hole golf course and fishing pond stocked with trout.

The super sea views include Málmey (ask here about private boat trips) and the bizarre promontory **Þórðarhöfði**, which is tethered to the mainland by a delicate spit.

SIGLUFJÖRÐUR

pop 1065

Siglufjörður was once one of Iceland's boom towns. When the herring industry was in full swing this place was heaving with fishing boats and workers from all over Iceland and abroad. After the herring abruptly disappeared from Iceland's north coast in the late 1960s, Siglufjörður declined and has never fully recovered. However, the town enjoys a dramatic setting beside the small fjord of the same name, and it still retains a sense of pride in its past. It's the sort of place that in any other country (and perhaps if it weren't so remote!) might develop into a trendy seaside art colony.

The historic architecture, the colourful rooftops of the upper town, the harbour and the inspiring backdrop are all postcard material on a fine day, but you won't see busloads of tourists here, even in midsummer.

The precarious but stunning route into Siglufjörður winds its way around the northwest of Tröllaskagi and is one of northern Iceland's most scenic coastal routes. The road is sealed all the way in, and just before town you pass through an 800m single-lane tunnel.

There's a small but helpful **tourist office** (☎ 465 1555; Aðalgata; 🕓 9am-noon & 1-5pm Jun-Aug) with Internet access (Ikr300 for 30 minutes including free coffee). More information, including hiking routes, can be found on the town website at www.siglo.is.

Síldarminjasafn

The big attraction in town is the **Herring Adventure Museum** (Síldarminjasafn; ☎ 467 1604; adult/child Ikr500/250; 🕓 10am-6pm Jun-Aug, 1-5pm or by request other times). It is quite a touching link between the town's glory days – roughly between 1903 and 1968, when the herring industry started and collapsed – and its future as a fishing village. The museum has grown into three separate houses: the first is the rust-coloured, Norwegian-built salting house and workers' accommodation, with photographs, displays and a classic piece of nostalgic 1930s film to bring early Siglufjörður to life; Next door is a re-creation of the reducing plant where the majority of herrings were separated into oil (a valuable commodity) and meal (used for fertiliser); The third, and newest, building is a re-creation of harbour life with actual trawler boats, models and equipment based on life on the busy pier during the boom days. Anything you can't find out about herring fishing here isn't worth knowing!

If you can manage to be here at 3pm on a Saturday, from 8 July to 3 August, you can watch **herring-salting demonstrations**, accompanied by lively traditional concertina music and songs. It's quite a show, and the cost of Ikr700 includes admission to the museum.

Other Attractions

Bjarnarstofa (☎ 460 5615; admission free; 🕓 2-5.30pm Tue-Fri) is a small memorial museum dedicated to the priest and musician Bjarní Þorsteinsson. It's in the library section of the town hall building near the harbour.

Siglufjörður has developed a reputation as a folk-music centre. An **Icelandic Folk Music Museum**, just behind the tourist office, was in the making at the time of writing and should be worth checking out.

Activities

The old route over 630m to Siglufjarðarskarð, between Siglufjörður and Fljótavík, was once thought to be haunted, but in 1735 it was consecrated by a Christian priest. In more recent years the greatest dangers have been from avalanches. Since the opening of the 800m-long tunnel Strákagöng through the mountain Strákar, the road has been abandoned, but from early July to late August, it's open to **hikers**. The route up to the pass and north along the ridge to Strákar (above the tunnel) affords some wonderful views.

North along the western shore of Siglufjörður, it's a short walk to the abandoned herring factory, which was destroyed in an avalanche in 1919. Longer hikes will take you over the passes Hólskarð and Hestskarð to the wild, beautiful and uninhabited Héðinsfjörður, the next fjord to the east.

In winter a **ski lift** operates in Skarðsdalur above the head of the fjord. From there, it's a lovely day walk over Hólsfjall to the abandoned valley above Héðinsfjörður. In summer you can opt for a nine-hole round of **golf** at the Hóll sports centre.

Festivals & Events

Despite the utter demise of the herring industry, Siglufjörður still considers itself a herring fishery capital – or at least pines for those days – and, over the bank holiday in early August, the town stages a **herring festival** with much singing, dancing, drinking, feasting and fish cleaning. It's a lot of fun and is one of Iceland's most enjoyable local festivals.

An annual Icelandic and foreign **folk-music festival** is staged over five days in mid-July, with workshops and several concerts every evening.

Sleeping

There's a free **camp site** (☎ 460 5600) right in the middle of town near the harbour and town square, and another **camp site** at the sports centre (take the road past the harbour and museum and follow Lanjeranegar). Also here is **Iþróttamiðstöðin Hóll** (☎ 467 1817, 895 2214; sb Ikr1200), where you can get basic beds in three- to six-person rooms, with cooking facilities in the local sports hall.

Gistiheimilið Hvanneyri (☎ 467 1378, 864 1822; Aðalgata 10; sb/s/d Ikr1800/3500/6000) This is the best option in Siglufjörður. The grey 1930s building looks a bit drab, but the three floors of this guesthouse have clean and comfortable rooms, spotless bathrooms and TV lounges.

Eating

Aðalbakari (☎ 467 1720; Aðalgata 30; 🕑 7am-5pm) This bakery and small café is the place to start the day, with fresh bread, cakes, pastries, filled rolls and endless cups of self-service coffee. Try the cheese rolls (Ikr300) or the Icelandic speciality *ástar pungur* (love balls) – deep-fried spiced balls, a bit like donuts (Ikr60).

Nýja Bíó (☎ 467 1790; Aðalgata 30; mains Ikr300-1800) This cinema-inspired diner is the only genuine restaurant in town. It's a great place to mix with locals, and the quirky menu has a list of pizzas named after Hollywood movies. You can also get hamburgers, hot dogs, and fish and lamb specials (around Ikr1700). The small bar is open until 1am.

There's an **Úrval supermarket** across from the harbour and a **Vín Búð** liquor shop on Tungata. **Fiskbuð Siglufjörður**, opposite Nýja Bíó on Aðalgata, is a fishmonger selling fresh fish, such as catfish, haddock and halibut.

Getting There & Away

From 29 May to 30 September **Suðurkiðir** (☎ 453 6806, 894 4331) runs three buses a week between Siglufjörður and Varmahlíð (Ikr1000), connecting with the Akureyri–Reykjavík buses. They depart on Monday, Wednesday and Friday at 8.30am, and from Varmahlíð on Tuesday, Thursday and Sunday at 1.30pm.

If you're heading east toward Akureyri in your own car, it's possible to take a short cut across Tröllaskagi on Route 82 to Ólafsfjörður. From the turn-off to Varmahlíð it's 37km along a narrow gravel road. Although a scenic route, it's usually closed in winter, so check beforehand. A planned tunnel through the mountain will cut the journey between Siglufjörður and Ólafsfjörður to only 15km, but it's not expected to be finished until 2008.

ÖXNADALUR

Back on the Ring Road between Varmahlíð and Akureyri, travellers passing through the valley Öxnadalur at the base of the Tröllaskagi are treated to some the finest scenery between Reykjavík and Akureyri. The Ring Road follows a narrow valley for more than 30km and reaches its highest point at an altitude of 540m.

The imposing 1075m spire of **Hraundrangi** and the surrounding peaks of **Háafjall** are probably the most dramatic in Iceland. Early settlers considered the summit of Hraundrangi inaccessible and perpetuated legends of a hidden cache of gold that awaited the first climber to reach the top. It was finally climbed in 1956, but the treasure seemed to have already gone.

AKUREYRI

pop 15,139

With its superb setting spread across the head of a long fjord, sunny summer climate and bustling town centre, Akureyri ('meadow sand-spit') offers the best of urban Iceland.

Snowcapped peaks rise above the town and provide the best winter skiing in northern Iceland, while Akureyri's spring and summer climate supports diverse vegetation, and locals put lots of effort into planting trees and gardens to maintain the town's lovely appearance. Along the streets, in flower boxes and in private gardens grow some colourful blooms, and the clear air is saturated with the fresh scent of sticky birch sap. On a fine day, you'd never guess you were just a stone's throw from the Arctic Circle.

Although Akureyri is Iceland's second-biggest town, it comes a long way behind Reykjavík. It has just a single pedestrian shopping street and a compact knot of cafés, bars, museums and shops just west of a busy commercial harbour. Still, it has some quality restaurants and guesthouses and a relaxed small-town air, and it's the natural base for exploring Eyjafjörður and further east to Mývatn.

HISTORY

The first permanent inhabitant of Eyjafjörður was Norse-Irish settler Helgi Magri

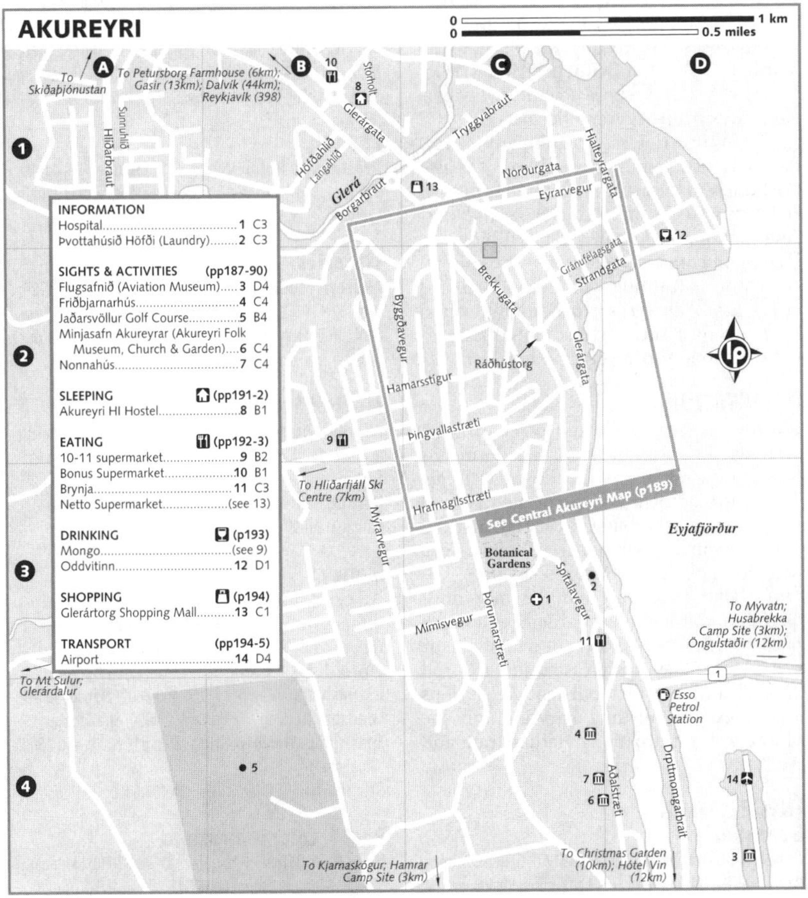

(Helgi the Lean), so named because of an unfortunate nutritional deficiency during his youth in the Orkneys. Although Helgi worshipped Þór and tossed his high-seat pillars overboard to sanction his homestead site (they washed up 7km south of present-day Akureyri), he hedged his bets by naming his farm Kristnes (Christ's Peninsula).

Akureyri began as a trading centre just before the Danish Trade Monopoly of 1602 came into effect. The town was used for commercial enterprises, but no-one lived there as all the settlers maintained rural farms and homesteads.

By the late 18th century the town had accumulated a whopping 10 residents, all Danish traders. By 1900 Akureyri numbered 1370 people. The original cooperative Gránufélagsins had begun to decline and, in 1906, was replaced by Kaupfélagið Eyjafirdinga Akureyrar (KEA; the Akureyri Cooperative Society), whose ubiquitous insignia still graces many Akureyri businesses.

The Akureyri Fishing Company is Iceland's largest, and the city's shipyard is also the busiest in the country. Before the decline in herring stocks off northern Iceland, herring salting was the town's largest industry. Fishing remains important, but the emphasis is now on trawling, canning and freezing larger fish. Akureyri's expanding industrial base includes such diverse enterprises as brewing, food processing and tourism.

ORIENTATION

Akureyri is small and easy to see on foot, although its location on a hillside means you'll do a bit of up and down walking. The centre of town is concentrated around the pedestrian shopping street Hafnarstræti with the small town square Raðhús Torg (actually a circle) at its northern end.

A walking tour around the museums, churches and botanical gardens will easily occupy a day, but Akureyri certainly justifies a longer stay. It's pleasant just to stroll around and see the well-tended gardens and trees, the bustling harbour and the oldest part of town along Hafnarstræti and Aðalstræti.

INFORMATION

Bookshops

Penninn Bókval (Map p189; ☎ 461 5050; Hafnarstræti 91-93; 🕑 9am-10pm) Excellent bookshop with souvenir books in English, French and German, Icelandic titles, popular foreign-language paperbacks, videos, DVDs and CDs.

Fróði (Map p189; Kaupvangsstræti) Second-hand bookshop next to Karolína Café, full of books in several languages.

Emergency

Fire and ambulance (☎ 112 or 462 2222)

Police (☎ 462 3222; Þórunnarstræti 140)

Internet Access

Akureyri Centrum (Map p189; ☎ 461 2968; Hafnarstræti 94; Ikr300 for 15 min, Ikr750 per hour; 🕑 10am-10pm Mon-Sat) Internet café, booking centre and bar.

Akureyri Municipal Library (Map p185; ☎ 462 4141; Brekkugata 17; 🕑 10am-7pm Mon-Fri) Free Internet access for 20-minute slots. Must be booked.

Café Paris (Blaá Kannan; Map p185; ☎ 461 4600; Hafnarstræti 96; Ikr150 for 15 min; 🕑 8.30am-11pm) Popular café with one Internet terminal.

Tourist Office (Map p185; ☎ 462 7733; Hafnarstræti 82; Ikr150 for 15 min; 🕑 7.30am-7pm Mon-Fri, 8am-5pm Sat & Sun) One Internet terminal.

Laundry

Þvottahúsið Höfði (Map p185; Hafnarstræti 34; Ikr600/900 for 5/8kg load; 🕑 8am-5pm Mon-Sat) Service laundry. Laundries also at camp site and youth hostel.

Libraries

Akureyri Municipal Library & Archives (Map p189; ☎ 462 4141; Brekkugata 17; 🕑 10am-7pm Mon-Fri) Books in English (including novels) and extensive historical archives; book loan is free and available to travellers.

Medical Services

Akureyri Hospital (Map p185; ☎ 463 0100; Spítalavegur) Just south of the botanical gardens. Doctors on call around the clock (☎ 852 3221).

Heilsugæslustöðin Clinic (Map p189; ☎ 462 2311; Hafnarstræti 99)

Money

All central bank branches (🕑 9.15am-4pm) offer commission-free foreign exchange and have 24-hour ATMs. After hours, ask at Hótel KEA.

Íslandsbanki (Map p189; ☎ 460 7800; Skipagata 14)

Landsbanki (Map p189; ☎ 460 4000; Strandgata 1)

Sparisjóður Norðlendinga (Map p189; ☎ 460 2500; Skipagata 9)

Búnaðarbanki (Map p189; ☎ 460 5400; Geislagata 5)

Post & Communications

Main Post Office (Map p185; ☎ 460 2600; Skipagata 10; 🕑 8.30am-4.30pm Mon-Fri)

Telephone office (Map p185; off Hafnarstræti mall; 9am-6pm Mon-Fri & 10am-2pm Sat)

Tourist Offices

Akureyri Tourist Office (Map p189; ☎ 462 7733; www.eyjafjordur.is; Hafnarstræti 82; 7.30am-7pm Mon-Fri, 8am-5pm Sat & Sun) In the BSÍ bus terminal. Internet access, toilets and helpful staff. Open from 7.30am to 5pm weekdays in off season.

Ferðafélag Akureyrar (Map p185; ☎ 462 2720; fax 462 7240; www.ffa.est.is; Strandgata 23; 4-7pm Mon-Fri Jun-Aug) Local branch of the Icelandic Touring Association. Good for maps and hiking information.

Travel Agencies

Akureyri Centrum (Map p185; ☎ 461 2968; www.sporttours.is; Hafnarstræti 94) Agent for whale-watching, horse-riding, rafting and super-jeep tours.

Nonni Travel (Map p189; ☎ 461 1841; www.nonnitravel.is; Brekkugata 5; 8am-6pm) Day trips, excursions, car rentals and flights. See p190.

Ferðaskristofa Akureyrar (Map p189; ☎ 460 0600; Raðhústorg 3) Domestic and international flights and ferries.

SIGHTS

Churches

The 'geological' theme common to modern Icelandic church architecture hasn't been lost on **Akureyrarkirkja** (Map p189; open 10am-noon & 2-5pm daily, services 11am & 8.30pm Sun), the prominent church that sits above the town centre. It was designed by Gudjón Samúelsson, the architect responsible for Reykjavík's Hallgrímskirkja, but Akureyrarkirkja is less blatantly 'basalt' and its interior is more traditional.

Built in 1940, Akureyrarkirkja contains a large and beautiful 3200-pipe organ and a series of rather untraditional reliefs of the life of Christ. There's also an unusual interpretation of the crucifixion, and the centre window in the chancel originally graced Coventry Cathedral in England (it miraculously survived the WWII bombing that destroyed the old cathedral). The ship hanging from the ceiling reflects an old Nordic tradition of votive offerings for the protection of loved ones at sea.

The **Catholic church** in Akureyri is an attractive old house at Eyrarlandsvegur 26. It was built in 1912 and acquired by the church in 1952. On the nearby roundabout is Einar Jónsson's sculpture *Útlaginn* (The Outlaw).

Museums

Akureyri has several low-key museums, many of them homes of 'local boys made good'. It's to Iceland's credit that it remembers its artists, poets and authors rather than generals and politicians, but unless you're an Icelander or have a particular admiration for a specific artist's work, some museums might be of limited interest.

MINJASAFN AKUREYRAR

The **Akureyri Folk Museum** (Map p185; ☎ 462 4162; www.akmus.is; Aðalstræti 58; adult/child Ikr400/free; 11am-5pm daily 1 Jun-15 Sep, 2-4pm Sat rest of the year) houses an interesting collection of art and practical items from the Settlement era to the present day. Among the displays are fish-drying racks, farming tools, photographs and re-creations of early Icelandic homes, and themed exhibitions are mounted each summer.

The **church** outside the folk museum is constructed in typical 19th-century Icelandic style. It was originally built at Svalbarðseyri on the eastern shore of Eyjafjörður and moved to its present site in 1970. The **museum garden** became the first place in Iceland to cultivate trees when a nursery was planted in 1899.

NONNAHÚS

The most interesting of the artists' homes, **Nonnahús** (Map p185; ☎ 462 3555; www.nonni.is; Aðalstræti 54; adult/child Ikr350/free; 10am-5pm Jun-Sep), was the childhood home of the Reverend Jón Sveinsson (Nonni), who lived from 1857 to 1944 (see the boxed text on p188). The cosy old house, built in 1850, is a fine example of an early village dwelling. Perhaps its most interesting features are its cramped, lived-in atmosphere and simple furnishings, which reveal much about life in 19th-century Iceland. Photographs and an original collection of Nonni books complete the museum, and you can buy books in English and Icelandic here.

MATTHÍAS JOCHUMSSON MEMORIAL MUSEUM

Also known as Sigurhæðir, the **Matthías Jochumsson Memorial Museum** (Map p189; ☎ 462 6648; Eyrarlandsvegur 3; adult/child Ikr300/free; 1.30-3.30pm Mon-Fri, 1 Jun-13 Aug), situated beside the Akureyrarkirkja stairs, honours the former Icelandic poet laureate and dramatist

REVEREND JÓN SVEINSSON

Jón Sveinsson (nicknamed Nonni) is one of Iceland's best-loved children's authors, so it's ironic that only his early childhood years were spent in Iceland. He was born in 1857 at Möðruvellir and moved south to Akureyri at the age of eight. When his father died four years later, he was sent to France to attend the Latin School.

On a visit to Denmark he converted to Roman Catholicism, and in 1878 he joined the Jesuit order. He continued his theological education around Western Europe before accepting a teaching post in Ordrup, Denmark, in 1883. After several years he went to England and was ordained a priest before returning to Denmark. There he taught in Catholic schools for 20 years until ill health forced him to retire to a more sedate literary life.

It was during his later years that Nonni wrote his best-known works, the *Nonni & Manni* children's adventures about his early life in Iceland with his brother (who had died at the age of only 23). He wrote 12 Nonni books and travelled the world lecturing on his works and his homeland, which made him something of a local hero in Iceland. Originally written in German, the books have been translated into 40 languages, including Icelandic, and many of the original copies as well as numerous illustrations are now displayed in the Nonnahús museum. Nonni died in Germany in 1944.

Matthías Jochumsson. Born in 1835, he wrote the noted play *The Outlaws* in 1861 and the Icelandic national anthem, *Iceland's 1000 Years*, in 1874. He also translated Byron, Shakespeare and German poetic works into Icelandic.

The house was built in 1902, and Jochumsson lived there until his death in 1920. The museum houses his collection of works and his personal property.

FRIÐBJARNARHÚS

Unless you're especially interested in the International Organisation of Good Templars (a remnant of the 11th- to 13th-century Christian Crusades in the Middle East), **Friðbjarnarhús** (Map p185; ☎ 462 2035; Aðalstræti 46; admission free; 2-5pm Sat & Sun Jul & Aug) won't be of much interest. It commemorates the founding of Iceland's first chapter on 10 January 1884, and most of the items displayed relate to their activities.

DAVÍÐSHÚS

In a forlorn-looking house northwest of the centre, **Davíðshús** (Map p189; ☎ 462 2874; Bjarkarstígur 6; admission Ikr100; 4-5pm Sat & Sun, 10 Jun-20 Aug) was built in 1944 by the poet, novelist and playwright Davíð Stefánsson, who became an Icelandic poet laureate. His most notable work was *Black Feathers*, published in 1919, and his most famous play was *The Golden Gate*.

The museum was created upon the artist's death in 1964, and his books and belongings remain exactly as he left them.

LISTASAFN (AKUREYRI ART MUSEUM)

The **Akureyri Art Museum** (Map p189; ☎ 462 2610; Kaupvangsstræti 12; admission Ikr350; noon-5pm Tue-Sun), opposite Karolína Café, was opened in 1993. It has gathered works of art that were previously scattered around town. It's in the complex known as Listagil, which also holds studios, commercial galleries and an art school. Exhibitions by local contemporary artists are sometimes held here.

FLUGSAFNIÐ (AVIATION MUSEUM)

The **Aviation Museum** (Map p185; ☎ 863 2835; admission Ikr400; 2-5pm Thu-Sat Jun-Aug, 2-5pm Sat Sep-May), in a hangar at Akureyri Airport, was opened in 2000. It charts the history of aviation in Iceland from the first flight in 1919 and first passenger flight in 1928 to the present. Photographs, memorabilia, gliders and small aircraft make up the display.

SAFNASAFNIÐ

The **Safnasafnið** (☎ 461 4066; adult/child Ikr400/free; 10am-6pm Jun–mid-Sep), or Icelandic Folk Art Museum, is 12km from Akureyri at Svalbarðseyri. It contains an exhibition of amateur art.

Botanical Gardens

Akureyri is proud of its moderate microclimate, and locals boast that plants from New Zealand, Spain and Tanzania grow just a few kilometres south of the Arctic Circle. See it at the small botanical gardens, **Lystigarður Akureyrar** (Map p185; ☎ 462 7487; 8am-10pm Mon-Fri & 9am-10pm Sat & Sun 1 Jun-31 Oct).

The gardens were first opened in 1912, two years after a local women's group founded the Akureyri Park Society to provide a green place for family recreation. The municipality took over management of the park in 1955, and two years later it bought a private collection of Icelandic plants to create a botanical garden. It now has examples of every species native to Iceland, as well as an extensive collection of high-latitude and high-altitude plants from around the world, all meticulously labelled with scientific names and countries of origin.

The lawns are sheltered from the wind and make a nice place to crash in the sun. Around the gardens are statues of the poet Matthías Jochumsson and Margrethe Schiöth, who voluntarily managed the gardens for 30 years, along with local contemporary art and sculptures.

Helgi the Lean Statue

On the hill northeast of Klapparstígur, a five-minute walk from the city centre, is a **statue of Helgi the Lean** (Map p189), the first settler in the Akureyri area. There's also a **view disc**, but the view, of shops and office buildings obscuring the fjord, isn't brilliant.

Kjarnaskógur

About 3km south of town is Iceland's most visited 'forest', the Kjarnaskógur woods (Map p185). This bushland area has a 2km-long athletic course, walking tracks, picnic tables,

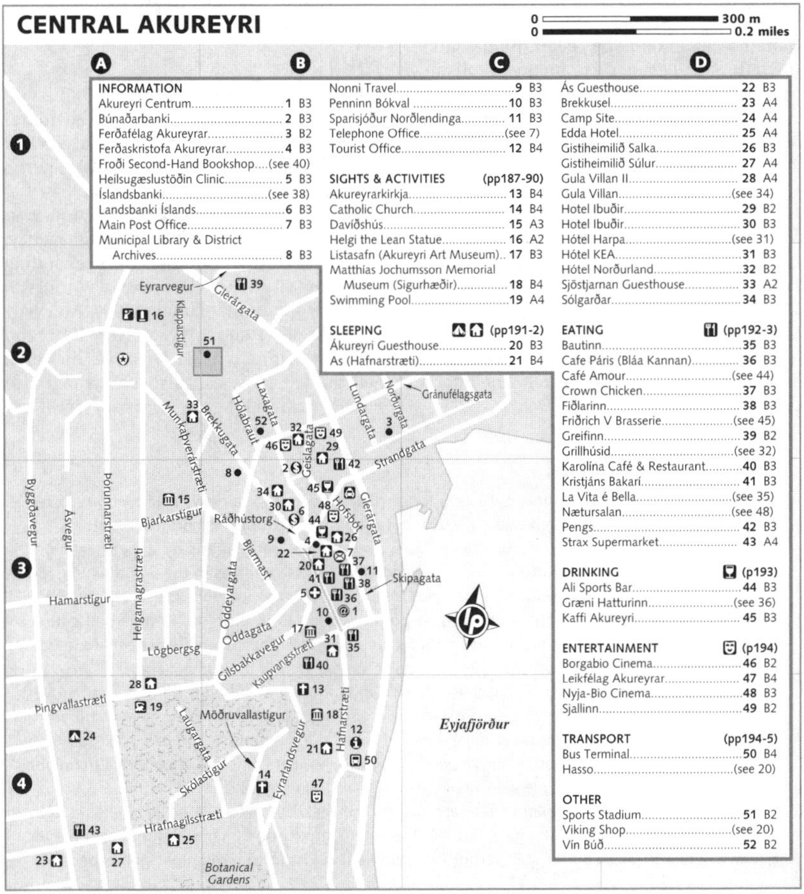

an amusing children's playground and some novel fitness-testing devices. It's great for a few hours on a sunny day, and there's camping at Hamrar. Check out the amusing log sundial designed by Icelandic Scouts.

Glerárdalur & Mt Súlur Hikes

A pleasant but demanding day hike is up the Glerá Valley to the summit of Mt Súlur (1144m; Map p185). Begin by walking west on Þingvallastræti, and turn left just before the Glerá Bridge. It's about an hour from town to the rubbish dump, then 2½ hours to the summit and a total of three hours back to town.

With two days, you can continue up the valley to the beautifully situated Lambi mountain hut, which accommodates up to six people. From the Hlíðarfjall ski resort, there's a challenging but beautiful day hike up to the small glacier Vindheimajökull and the 1456m peak Strýta.

For more information, contact **Ferðafélag Akureyrar** (Map p185; ☎ 462 2720; fax 462 7240; www.ffa.est.is; Strandgata 23).

ACTIVITIES

Swimming

The superb **swimming pool** (Map p189; ☎ 461 4455; admission Ikr290, with sauna Ikr500; 7am-9pm Mon-Fri, 8am-6.30pm Sat & Sun), near the camp site, is one of Iceland's finest. It has three heated pools, hot pots, water slides, saunas, a steam bath and a solarium – perfect for relaxing after a day hike up Mt Súlur.

Skiing

The **Hlíðarfjall ski centre** (Map p185; ☎ 462 2930), 7km up Glerárdalur, is probably Iceland's premier downhill ski slope, partly because of the excellent snow cover here most winters (2003 being a notable exception). The longest run is 2.5km long with a vertical drop of about 500m, and 20km of cross-country ski routes are open whenever snow cover is sufficient.

Between January and May, the chairlift and ski tows operate most days, but hours vary so you should check locally. In the long hours of winter darkness, the downhill runs are floodlit. In season, buses connect the site with Akureyri three times daily.

The ski lodge has a restaurant, and a ski school offers individual and group instruction and equipment hire.

TOURS

BSÍ runs year-round sightseeing tours to Mývatn (Ikr6400, 10 hours), departing at 8.15am daily from the airport and 8.30am from the bus terminal (Map p189). There's a 5% discount for bus-pass holders.

Nonni Travel (Map p189; ☎ 461 1841; www.nonnitravel.is; Brekkugata 5) is the main tour agency, running a host of summer tours, including two-hour city tours (Ikr3900), day tours to Ólafsfjörður and Hólar (Ikr6400), Aldeyjarfoss (Ikr7000) and Mývatn (Ikr6400), and whale-watching trips at Húsavík (Ikr7400). Self-guided trips can also be arranged to Hrísey (Ikr2000) and Grímsey by ferry

TEEING OFF AT MIDNIGHT

The sun hangs low on the horizon, casting long shadows over the fairway. You're about to tee off on the first hole. Your watch says 11.30pm, but it doesn't matter how long this round takes – you've got all night. For anyone who loves golf, there's something strangely appealing about playing 'midnight golf' – and there are only a handful of 18-hole courses in the world where you can do it. At a few degrees south of the Arctic Circle, Akureyri's hillside golf course, **Jaðarsvöllur** (Map p185; ☎ 462 2974; gagolf@nett.is), claims to be the world's northernmost 18-hole golf course (although the one in Kangerlussuaq, Greenland, is actually further north, and the Green Zone Golf Course at Tornio-Haparanda on the Finnish-Swedish border makes the same claim).

The par 71 course, which boasts Jack Nicklaus as an honorary member, is home to the annual 36-hole Arctic Open, a golf tournament played here overnight in late June (from around 8pm to 5am). During the perpetual summer daylight from June to early August, you can play golf here around the clock. The pro shop officially closes at 10pm, but you can book ahead for a midnight tee-off. Alternatively, if you have your own clubs, just walk on anyway.

Icelandic golf is not cheap. Green fees are Ikr2500 on weekdays before 2pm, Ikr2800 after 2pm and Ikr3500 on weekends. Club hire is Ikr1500. The most famous sportsman rumoured to come for a round here was basketballer Michael Jordan, who flew in just for the midnight golf experience.

(Ikr4200) or flight and ferry (Ik9400), as well as rafting, horse-riding and jeep trips.

Horse tours and hire are available from outlying farms. The best known is **Pólar Hestar** (☎ 463 3179; www.polarhestar.is), at Grýtubakka (p198), which offers wilderness trips. Other operators include **Hestaleigan Kátur** (☎ 862 2600; 1/2/3hr tours Ikr2800/3600/4800); **Engimýri** (☎ 462 6838), in Öxnadalur, 36km to the west of Akureyri, and **Sportferðir** (☎ 466 1982), at Ytri-Vík on Árskógsströnd and in Akureyri (☎ 461 2968).

Sporttours (☎ 862 2600, www.sporttours.is) runs horse-riding tours for Ikr2200/3500/4500 for one/two/three hours from the Kaupangar farm on Route 829 just south of Akureyri, and other activities, including white-water rafting and snowmobiling.

FESTIVALS & EVENTS

The annual summer-long **arts festival** runs from 20 June to late August and attracts artists and musicians from around Iceland. There's free jazz at 9pm on Thursday, and it culminates in a weekend street party and parade. For details on events and exhibitions, contact the tourist office.

SLEEPING

Budget

The town **camp site** (Map p189; ☎ 462 3379, 862 2279; Þórunnarstræti; per person Ikr600), a grassy lawn across from the swimming pool, has a kitchen, toilet and shower block, and a washer and dryer.

Húsabrekka camp site (Map p185; ☎ 462 4921; per person Ikr500) On the eastern shore of Eyjafjörður, 6km away, this site is quieter and offers similar facilities, including five-person cottages from Ikr5000 per night.

Akureyri HI Hostel (Map 185; ☎ 462 3657; storholt@nett.is; Stórholt 1; sb Ikr2100-3100, s/d/tr Ikr4000/6200/7800) This friendly, well-equipped hostel is a 15-minute walk north of the city centre. The owner keeps the place in mint condition, and there are three kitchens, lounge areas and a barbecue deck. You'll meet travellers from all over the place here – advance bookings are essential in summer.

Mid-Range

Akureyri's best accommodation can be found in its guesthouses, which range from simple family homes to four-storey warrens. It pays to book ahead in summer.

Gistiheimilið Salka (Map p189; ☎ 461 2340; salka@nett.is; Skipagata 1; sb double/triple Ikr4400/6000, s/d Ikr4600/6000) For cosiness and friendliness, this is the pick of the central guesthouses. It has just three large, comfortable and well-furnished rooms, so book ahead. There's a kitchen, and sleeping-bag space is possible for two or more people.

Ás Guesthouse (Map p189; ☎ 461 2248; fax 461 1073; Skipagata 4; s/d with bathroom Ikr5200/8100, without bathroom Ikr4300/5800) Across the road, this place is less welcoming but has a lot more rooms, including some with bathroom. There are no kitchen facilities here, but they have another summer-only guesthouse at Hafnarstræti 77 with the same rates and cooking facilities.

Sólgarðar (Map p189; ☎/fax 461 1133; Brekkugata 6; sb/s/d Ikr2000/3500/5000) In a quiet but central location, this is a friendly place with three nicely furnished rooms (book ahead) and a kitchen.

Akureyri Guesthouse (Map p189; ☎ 462 5588; www.nett.is/guest; Hafnarstræti 104; sb Ikr2200, s/d with bathroom Ikr6900/9400, without bathroom Ikr4900/6900) Very central and an excellent choice, falling somewhere between a hotel and a family-run guesthouse. Rooms are compact but spotless, all with TV and sink. There's a guest kitchen, and the bright top-floor dining room is great, with a balcony overlooking the pedestrian shopping street.

Gula Villan (Map p189; ☎ 461 2860, 896 8464; Brekkugata 8; s/d Ikr4600/5800, sb Ikr2900/4400) A stylish, stark-white place close to the centre. They have another, slightly older, guesthouse at Þingvallastræti 14, with the same rates, as well as cooking facilities.

Sjöstjarnan Guesthouse (Map p189; ☎ 462 1285, 692 7278; fjola@brudarkjolar.is; Brekkugata 27a; s/d Ikr5350/8500) A cut above most of Akureyri's guesthouses, this heritage home has a variety of rooms (some with balcony) and a lounge and formal dining room.

Brekkusel (Map p189; ☎ 462 3961; Hrafnagilsstræti 23; sb/s/d Ikr2500/4000/5500) A pleasant family home that has spartan but clean rooms with shared bathroom.

Gistiheimilið Súlur (Map p189; ☎ 461 1160; sulur@islandia.is; Þórunnarstræti 93; s/d/tr Ikr4600/6200/7800, sb Ikr3100/4400/6000) Across from the swimming pool, this is a more formal summer guesthouse (open from 1 June to 31 August). It's clean and comfortable enough and has a small kitchen.

Hotel Íbuðir (Map p189; ☎ 462 3727, 892 9838; www.hotelibudir.is; Brekkugata 4; s/d Ikr5500/7500, with bathroom Ikr7900/9900, apt Ikr12,000-19,500) Íbuðir has three locations: a guesthouse and two sets of furnished apartments that suit families or longer stays. A good choice.

FARMHOUSE ACCOMMODATION

Pétursborg (Map p185; ☎ 461 1811; www.petursborg.com; s/d Ikr3700/5400, d with bath Ikr6900, f Ikr9200) This place is 6km north of the city centre and 1.5km off the Ring Road. It's close enough to Akureyri to be convenient but has a pleasant rural setting on the edge of the fjord. There's an outdoor hot pot, cooking facilities, a relaxing lounge and dining room, and a boat for sea fishing.

Öngulstaðir (Map p185; ☎ 463 1380; johannes@est.is; s/d Ikr4500/6250, s/d/tr with bathroom Ikr5600/7600/9500) On Route 829, 12km south of Akureyri (cross to the eastern side of the fjord before heading south), this farm also has a gallery, a souvenir shop and a restaurant.

Top End

Hótel KEA (Map p189; ☎ 460 2000; www.hotelkea.is; Hafnarstræti 87-89; s/d Ikr13,900/17,800) In the thick of the action, this is Akureyri's flashest hotel, although it's a bit sterile and looking decidedly threadbare. Some rooms have harbour views. There's a bar, café and the swanky Rósagardúrinn restaurant.

Hotel Harpa (Map p189; ☎ 460 2000; www.hotelkea.is; Hafnarstræti 87-89; s/d Ikr11,900/15,100) Located in the same building as Hotel KEA, this is a cheaper alternative with simpler rooms, but it's perfectly comfortable and shares the same facilities as KEA.

Hótel Norðurland (Map p189; ☎ 462 2600, fax 462 7962, Geislagata 7; s/d Ikr11,900/15,100) The other upmarket business-class hotel in the centre. Clean, modern rooms with attached bath and TV.

Edda Hotel (Map p189; ☎ 461 1434; fax 461 1423; Eyrarlandsvegur 28; sb Ikr2000, s/d without bathroom Ikr4900/6200, with bathroom Ikr9100/11,400) There's a brand-new wing in this summer hotel which has large modern rooms (like an Ikea display home), while the older wing still has some rooms with shared facilities. Comfortable but bland.

EATING

Akureyri has Iceland's best range of cafés and restaurants outside Reykjavík. If you can manage only one dining splurge on the long trip around the country, this is a good place to do it. Along with a handful of ethnic restaurants, there are some good-value places serving up Icelandic fish and meat dishes.

Cafés

Karolína Café (Map p189; ☎ 461 2755; 11.30am-1am Mon-Thu, until 3am Fri & Sat, 2pm-1am Sun) Akureyri's most bohemian café, on 'artists' alley'. Karolína is popular with the theatre and arts crowd, but with its relaxed atmosphere, great coffee and cakes, and leather couches, it's a great spot to linger on a rainy day.

Café Paris (Map p189; ☎ 461 4600; Hafnarstræti 96; 8am-10pm, ☒) Also called Blaá Kannan, this is a great spot for breakfast or for watching the world go by from the tables on the pedestrian mall. There are sweet and savoury cakes and a great salad buffet.

Quick Eats

On the pedestrian shopping mall are several small **kiosks** selling hot dogs, chips, burgers, sandwiches and soft drinks. The most popular fast-food place with the late-night crowd is **Nætursalan** on Strandgata (near the Nyja-Bio cinema; Map p189). It's open until at least 3am on Friday and Saturday nights, which is precisely when an Icelandic hot dog tastes best. Join the queue.

Brynja (Map p189; Aðalstræti 3; 9am-11.30pm) Legendary sweet shop that locals claim makes Iceland's best ice cream.

Crown Chicken (Map p189; ☎ 461 3010; Skipagata 12; meals Ikr550-1200; 11am-11.30pm) Fried chicken makes a change from burgers, but they have those too, along with pitta sandwiches and chips, eat in or takeaway.

Kristjáns Bakarí (Map p189; Hafnarstræti; 9am-6pm Mon-Sat, 10am-2pm Sun) Fresh bread, cakes and pastries are available at this excellent bakery on the pedestrian mall.

Restaurants

Bautinn (Map p189; ☎ 462 1818; Hafnarstræti 92; mains Ikr900-3500) A good choice for a filling meal in casual surroundings, Bautinn is popular with locals and visitors alike. It has a smart glassed-in dining area at the side. There's an all-you-can-eat soup and salad bar for Ikr1090, and with any main course the salad bar is included, so you can really fill up. Daily specials, which are posted at the door, include creatively prepared fish, lamb, beef and vegetarian dishes as well as puffin, horse and other Icelandic delicacies.

Greifinn (Map p189; ☎ 460 1600; www.greifinn.is; Glerárgata 20; mains Ikr750-2200; 🕑 11.30am-10.30pm Sun-Thu, 11.30am-11.30pm Fri & Sat) Near the sports stadium, this is one of the most popular family places locally, and it's legendary for its pizza. Daily special dishes cost Ikr1290, and the bar prices are cheaper than most pubs.

La Vita é Bella (Map p189; ☎ 462 5858; Hafnarstræti 92; mains Ikr850-2500; 🕑 from 6pm) Next to Bautinn, this is definitely the place to indulge your desire for pasta and all things Mediterranean. Italian salads, risottos and pasta, including lasagne and ravioli, stand out on the menu. Prices are reasonable, and half-serves are available. There's a nice bar upstairs.

Karolína Restaurant (Map p189; ☎ 461 2755; www.karolina.is; Kaupvangsstræti 23; mains Ikr2500-3950) This fashionable old-world restaurant is an Akureyri institution. It mixes Icelandic and international culinary ideas well, with dishes like cod with couscous, pepper steak and *skyr* cake.

Grillhúsið (Map p189; ☎ 462 6006; Geislagata 7; dishes Ikr390-2350) An unpretentious American-style grill with a vast menu of pizzas (from Ikr1100), hamburgers, Tex-Mex (nachos Ikr390), and fish and meat dishes. Some of the meals are priced as high as at the fancy restaurants. The decking at the side is good in summer.

Friðrich V Brasserie (Map p189; ☎ 461 5775; Strandgata 7; mains Ikr2200-3500; 🕑 6-10pm) One of Akureyri's newest gourmet restaurants, this place has a stiff, silver-service décor and a platinum menu of Icelandic delicacies, including lobster tails, *carpaccio* and lamb. There's also a four-course gourmet meal for Ikr5950! Good for an intimate splurge. It's above Kaffi Akureyri.

Fiðlarinn (Map p189; ☎ 462 7100; www.fidlarinn.is; Skipagata 14; mains Ikr2400-4300, specials from Ikr1650) The last word in fine dining in Akureyri, this atmospheric top-floor restaurant has a fine view over the harbour and fjord. It's small and elegant with a brief menu that includes pan-fried lobster tails (Ikr1900) for starters and main courses of salmon, lamb fillet and roasted quail. Although it's one of Akureyri's more expensive restaurants, the daily specials in summer make it an affordable place to splurge. We had delicious Icelandic trout for Ikr1650. Wine is available by the glass (Ikr750) and bottle (Ikr3600–5200).

Pengs (Map p189; ☎ 466 3800; Strandgata 13; mains Ikr990-2000; 🕑 11.30am-1.30pm & 5-10pm Mon-Sat, 3-10pm Sun) Probably the only Chinese restaurant outside Reykjavík, Pengs is authentically 'Euro-Asian' and quite cheap – the multicourse set menu is Ikr2090 per person.

Self-Catering

Akureyri has a wealth of supermarkets, all well stocked and convenient. The biggest is the huge **Netto supermarket** (Map p185; 🕑 10am-7pm Mon-Fri, 10am-6pm Sat, noon-5pm Sun) in the new Glerártorg shopping mall on Glerárgata, north of town.

Strax supermarket (Map p189; Byggðavegi; 🕑 10am-11pm) and **10-11 supermarket** (Map p185; Þingvallastræti; 🕑 10am-11pm) are both near the camping ground west of the centre.

Vín Búð (Map p189; ☎ 462 1655; Hólabraut 16; 🕑 11am-6pm Mon-Thu, 11am-7pm Fri, 11am-4pm Sat), the government liquor store, is near the Borgabio cinema.

DRINKING

Café Amour (Map p189; ☎ 461 2222; Radhustorg 9; 🕑 10am-midnight Sun-Thu, until 3am Fri & Sat) Euro-style café and bar where the cool crowd hangs out at all hours. By day it's a popular place for coffee, light meals such as bagels, focaccia and crepes (Ikr750–900), or just sitting around reading the paper. At night it's a popular wine bar with a lengthy cocktail list (Ikr1100–1400). The cream furniture spells sophistication, and the mirrored wall makes it look bigger than it really is. Upstairs is a small nightclub.

Oddvitinn (Map p185; ☎ 462 6020; Strandgata 53) Down by the harbour, Oddvitinn is the sort of pub you don't often see in Iceland. It's in an historic building (with reputedly the longest bar in Iceland), is popular with a mature drinking crowd and has regular karaoke.

Kaffi Akureyri (Map p189; ☎ 461 3999; Strandgata 7; 🕑 3pm-1am Sun-Thu, 3pm-4am Fri & Sat) Stylish, modern café-bar and one of Akureyri's best live-music venues. Packed on Friday and Saturday nights.

Other recommended places for a drink include **Karolína Café** and **Café Paris** (see Cafés, p192).

ENTERTAINMENT

Pubs & Clubs

Several pubs and discos in the town centre are quite popular with youth, but the intensity of Akureyri's nocturnal scene doesn't compare with Reykjavík's. With numerous strip clubs, Akureyri reputedly has the dubious distinction of having the greatest number of such places per head of population in the world!

Sjallinn (Map p189; ☎ 462 2770; Geislagata 14) This is the most popular nightclub in town with Akureyri's youth. It has two pubs, Góði Dátinn and Kjallarinn. At weekends, there's live music and dancing, which winds down at 3 am.

Kaffi Akureyri (Map p189; ☎ 461 3999; Strandgata 7; 🕑 3pm-1am Sun-Thu, 3pm-4am Fri & Sat) Another big live-music venue with local and visiting bands on Friday and Saturday nights.

Græni Hatturinn (Map p189; Hafnarstræti 96) The 'Green Hat', down a lane behind Café Paris, is a popular English-style pub with music and dancing on weekends.

There are two sports bars in Akureyri, which are invariably packed when big football matches are on. **Ali Sports Bar** (Map p189), next to Café Amour, is a central place with a big screen and pool tables upstairs. **Mongó** (Map p185; ☎ 461 3141; Kaupangar), up near the camp site, is a bit rough around the edges, but it's a heaving local drinking hole.

Cinema

There are two cinemas in the town centre: **Borgabio** (Map p185; ☎ 462 3599; Hólabraut 12) and **Nyja-Bio** (Map p185; ☎ 461 4666; Strandgata 2), just around the corner from the town square. Both show latest-release mainstream films in the original language (usually English) with subtitles. You can see what's playing from the advertising on the windows, and check times at the box office.

THE AKUREYRI RUNTUR

Reykjavík has its famous *runtur* ('round tour') – bar-hopping on foot around the hotspots of downtown 101. With fewer bars and lots of bored teenagers, Akureyri has its own form of weekend *runtur*. From around 8pm you'll see a procession of cars, bumper to bumper, driving round and round in circles on a loop along Skipagata, Strandgata and Glerárgata. The speed rarely rises above 5km/h, horns blare and kids scream out to each other. It goes on for hours and is quite a scene.

Theatre

As in most Nordic countries, Akureyri's theatre season runs from September to June, rather than during summer. The main theatre venue is **Leikfélag Akureyrar** (Map p189; ☎ 462 1400; www.leikfelag.is; Hafnarstræti 57). It hosts theatre, dance and opera. For information and coming performances, check the website or ask at the tourist office.

SHOPPING

On the Hafnarstræti pedestrian strip, several shops offer woollens and souvenirs on the 'tax-free' scheme. They include the **Viking Shop** (Map p189; ☎ 461 5551; Hafnarstræti 104), which has Icelandic knitted jumpers from Ikr8000 to Ikr10,000, and **Pennings Bookshop** (Map p185; ☎ 461 5050; Hafnarstræti 91-93; 🕑 9am-10pm), which has books, calendars and souvenirs.

Fold-Anna (Map p185; ☎ 461 1167; Hafnarstræti 85; 🕑 9am-7pm Mon-Fri, 10am-2pm Sat) is the Álafoss woollens factory outlet, where jumpers and other woollen goods can be purchased at factory prices. That's the theory, anyway. The jumpers, hats, gloves and other garments are marginally cheaper than anywhere else, but it's fun to see the staff knitting behind the counter.

About 10km south of Akureyri, the **Christmas Garden** (Map p185; ☎ 463 1433; 🕑 10am-10pm) is a kitsch, bright red house and garden packed with Christmas cheer: trees, decorations, cards, elves, sweets and traditional Icelandic Christmas foods and gifts. It's free to visit and is great for kids.

GETTING THERE & AWAY

Air

Air Iceland (☎ 460 7000) flies daily between Akureyri and Reykjavík (Ikr9775), and to Grímsey (Ikr7330), Vopnafjörður (Ikr9230) and Þórshöfn (Ikr9230). Other domestic (and international) flights are via Reykjavík. The airport (Map p185) is 2km south of town.

Bus

The bus terminal is at the tourist office on Hafnarstræti (Map p189). Buses that run between Akureyri and Reykjavík depart at 9.30am and 5pm daily (Ikr5700, six hours). From 24 June to 31 August, there's also a daily service over the Kjölur route, departing from Reykjavík and Akureyri at 9am (Ikr7400, eight hours).

Buses to/from Egilsstaðir (Ikr4900, four hours) run once daily from 1 June to 31 August. All Egilsstaðir buses pass through Reykjahlíð and Skútustaðir, at Mývatn. In summer up to three additional buses run to Mývatn (Ikr2000, 1½ hours).

To Húsavík (Ikr1800, 70 minutes), buses run one to four times daily all year. There are also buses to Asbýrgi and to Þórshöfn via Húsavík.

Buses to Árskógssandur and Dalvík (for the Grímsey and Hrísey ferries) and Ólafsfjörður leave three times a day from Monday to Friday.

Car Rental

Akureyri has several rental agencies, and rates here are slightly cheaper than in Reykjavík. The cheapest is **Hasso** (Map p185; ☎ 464 1030; hasso@kaupa.is, Hafnarstræti 99-101), which has small cars from Ikr3900 per day, or Ikr7600 with unlimited kilometres and insurance. Four-wheel drive Explorers cost from Ikr10,900 per day. **Avis** (Map p185; ☎ 461 2428, Draupnisgata 4) is also recommended. For an extra fee of around Ikr4000, most companies will let you pick up a car in Akureyri and drop it off in Reykjavík or vice versa.

GETTING AROUND

Bus

Akureyri is easy to get around on foot, but there's a regular town bus service (Ikr150, 6.20am–11.30pm daily). Unfortunately it doesn't go where most tourists want to go: the airport.

Taxi

The **BSO Taxi stand** (Map p185; ☎ 461 1010) is on the corner of Strandgata and Hofsbót. Taxis may be booked 24 hours a day.

Bicycle

Once you've sweated up the steep slope onto the bluff, cycling around Akureyri is a breeze, and traffic in town is light. **Skíðaþjónustan** (Map p185; ☎ 462 1713; Fjölnisgata 4b) hires bicycles for around Ikr1200 per day.

AROUND AKUREYRI

Iceland's longest fjord, Eyjafjörður, is home to a number of small fishing communities, particularly along its western shore. Route 82 north of Akureyri is a mostly sealed road following the fjord through Dalvík to isolated Ólafsfjörður. West of here are some excellent hiking opportunities in Tröllaskagi.

A drive along either side of the fjord is worth at least a day trip from Akureyri, if only for the stunning views along the way. In summer there are three buses each weekday between Akureyri and Ólafsfjörður (at 7.30am, 12.30pm and 6pm), but there's no bus service beyond the Ring Road turn-off on the eastern side of the fjord.

ÁRSKÓGSSTRÖND

pop 561

Between the Ring Road and Dalvík, Route 82 runs along the western shore of Eyjafjörður through a rich agricultural area known as Árskógsströnd. There are a few farms with accommodation, but the main points of interest are the ferries to Hrísey island and whale-watching trips from Hauganes.

The former medieval trading post of **Gásir** lies on the fjord side of Route 816, south of the Hörgá estuary. Dating from the Saga Age it was once the largest port in northern Iceland. The protected ruins here are part of an archaeological site with **guided tours** (www.gasir.is; admission Ikr300; 🕒 1pm, 2pm & 3.30pm Mon-Fri, 11.30am, 1pm, 2pm & 3.30pm Sat, Jul & Aug). Jewellery, coins and implements have been unearthed, and recent evidence suggests that there was commercial trading here until the 16th century. Tangible sites include the foundations of a medieval church, a graveyard and some grass-covered outlines where port trading offices once stood, but you really need to take the tour to bring the remains to life. To get there, head 7km north from Akureyri along the Ring Road, turn east on Route 816 (signposted), then continue another 6km along a gravel road to the site.

North of the Hörgá River is the large farm **Möðruvellir**. It was the site of a monastery founded in 1296 and the birthplace of the author Jón Sveinsson (Nonni). The present church at Möðruvellir, built in 1868, is attractive inside and has a blue ceiling covered with stars.

Whale-watching trips depart daily in summer from **Hauganes**, a tiny village 2km off the Ring Road and about 14km south of Dalvík. Trips aboard the former fishing boat **Niels Jonsson** (☎ 867 0000; www.niels.is; 3hr trips Ikr3500 per person) boast a high cetacean-spotting record and include a stop at Hrísey island.

HRÍSEY

pop 210

The peaceful, low-lying island of Hrísey sits in the middle of Eyjafjörður and is easily reached from the mainland at Árskógssandur. At about 7km by 2.5km, it's the second-largest island off the Icelandic coast (after Heimaey), but you can easily explore its charms in a leisurely half-day.

Hrísey is especially noted as a breeding ground and protected area for the ptarmigan (a bird that is often hunted for the dinner table elsewhere in Iceland, but will happily wander through the village streets here!), as well as the eider duck and an enormous colony of arctic terns.

During WWII the island was a posting for five unarmed British Army personnel whose job was to guard the entrance to Eyjafjörður and check passing trawlers for suspicious cargo or activities. These days Iceland's quarantine station for pets is based here.

There's a small **information office** (☎ 695 0077; 1-6pm mid-Jun–Aug) in the Pearl Gallery craft shop by the harbour. You can pick up the handy Hrísey brochure here or in Akureyri. The island also has a **bank** and **post office** on the main street of the village.

Sights & Activities

The picturesque **village** at the island's southern end is a quiet, almost traffic-free community, with a harbour, cobbled streets, a few shops and a striking red-and-white church. The island's cliff-girt northeastern coast is indented by **sea caves**, and the bush areas have reverted to a natural state, having been free of sheep for many years.

Most of the northern part of Hrísey is a private ptarmigan and eider duck sanctuary, but there are three marked **nature trails** on the southeastern part of the island that will take you to some good cliff-top viewpoints. These walks can be covered in two hours. For a guided sightseeing trip around the island by tractor, contact local farmer **Ásgeir Halldórsson** (☎ 466 1079; Ikr400 per person, minimum Ikr1500).

Sleeping & Eating

Campers must stay at the **camp site** (☎ 466 1769; 1 Jun-15 Sep; per person Ikr800), near the community centre.

Gistiheimilið Brekka (☎ 466 1751; fax 466 3051; sb Ikr1800; d Ikr5400-6000) You can't miss the bright yellow Brekka, and as the only hotel on the island it's understandably very popular during summer, so book ahead. Rooms are above the restaurant, and some have harbour views.

Another option is the private **summer chalets**. Call ☎ 466 1079 for bookings and information.

Brekka Restaurant (mains Ikr950-4900; 10am-11pm) Brekka is an unassuming restaurant and bar that overlooks the village and harbour and has an amazing gourmet menu. Along with the usual burgers, pizza, pasta and salads, it specialises in beef steaks (Ikr3400–4900). Lamb, local fish and seafood, and even snails also make an appearance.

Þorpið, the nearby village store, has a small café and supermarket.

Getting There & Away

In summer (15 June to 15 August) the ferry **Sævar** (☎ 462 7733; fax 461 1817; Ikr600 return, 15 minutes) leaves Hrísey daily at 9am and 11am, then on the hour from 1pm to 7pm, and again at 9pm and 11pm. It returns from Árskógssandur 30 minutes later. There's a reduced schedule after 15 August. Buses from Akureyri (Ikr550) connect with the ferries three times daily from Monday to Friday.

The ferry **Sæfari** (☎ 466 1444; www.samskip.is) sails between Dalvík and Hrísey at 1.15pm on Tuesday and Thursday.

Nonni Travel in Akureyri has six-hour tours to Hrísey by bus and ferry (Ikr2600) from Monday to Friday; see p190.

DALVÍK

pop 1479

Dalvík nestles in a spectacular spot between Eyjafjörður and the hills of Svarfaðardalur. The town became a population centre only in the 20th century, and its excellent harbour has naturally meant that its economic emphasis is on fishing. Ferries also leave from here for Grímsey island (see p199).

In 1934, an earthquake measuring 6.3 destroyed or damaged 77 homes, leaving nearly half the inhabitants homeless.

There's **tourist information** (☎ 466 3233) at the swimming pool on Svarfaðarbraut. A good place to find information about Dalvík on the Internet is www.islandia.is/~juljul.

Sights & Activities

Byggðasafnið Hvoll (☎ 466 1497; Karlsbraut; adult/child Ikr400/100; 🕑 11am-6pm Jun-Sep), in the red-and-yellow building just back from the main street, is a bit quirkier than most small-town folk museums. Along with the usual array of art and natural exhibits, including a stuffed polar bear, there's a room dedicated to local giant Jóhan Pétursson who, at 2.34m (almost 7ft 7in), was Iceland's tallest man. There are photos and personal effects, many from his days as a circus act. Another room is dedicated to another local, Kristjárn Eldjárn, who became president of Iceland.

In summer you can play a round of **golf** (☎ 466 1204) at the nine-hole Arnarholt golf course in the Svarfaðalur valley about 8km northwest of the town. In winter there's a **ski tow** on Böggvisstaðafjall, the prominent ridge above Dalvík. With a group you can go on a half-day horseback ride through the valley, then canoe back along the Svarfaðardalsá river (around Ikr6000 per person). Inquire at the Árgerði Guesthouse (see p197).

Dalvík has a good little **swimming pool** (admission Ikr250; 🕑 6.45am-8pm Mon-Fri, 10am-7pm Sat & Sun) with hot pots, steam bath and solarium.

A popular hike or horseback tour from Dalvík is over **Heljardalsheiði**. It begins at the end of Route 805, 20km up Svarfaðardalur, and traverses the Tröllaskagi peninsula to Hólar. However, there's no public transport from Hólar.

This unmarked backpacking route passes through some of Iceland's best mountain scenery. Allow at least two days for the walk. For hut and map information, contact Ferðafélag Akureyrar in Akureyri (p187).

Sleeping & Eating

There's free **camping** (☎ 466 3233) behind the summer hotel. The camp site has basic facilities – campers can't use the hotel.

Summerhotellet (☎ 466 3395; fax 466 1661; Skíðabraut 4; sb/s/d Ikr1700/4300/5800) Dalvík's summer hotel, open from June to the end of August, is typically austere, but there's a small café and TV lounge.

Árgerði Guesthouse (☎/fax 555 4212; www.argerdi.com; s/d Ikr4700/6000) On the Svarfaðardalsá river about 1km out on the Akureyri road, Árgerði is easily the nicest place to stay in Dalvík. This welcoming family-run guesthouse has 12 rooms – ask for the huge upstairs room with balcony. There's a summer deck with barbecue, and guests can use bicycles and canoes for a paddle on the river.

Eating-out options are slim in Dalvík. For breakfast, drop into **Bakari Axis**, a bakery and coffee shop on Hafnarbraut that serves coffee, pastries, cakes, filled rolls and fresh bread. In summer there are tables out the front so that you can fully appreciate Dalvík's pungent fishy air.

Kaffihúsid Sogn (☎ 466 3330; Goðabraut 3; mains Ikr600-2200; 🕑 11am-9pm Mon-Thu, 11am-11pm Fri, 3-11pm Sat, 3-9pm Sun) This café-bar opposite the town hall is the best choice. As well as coffee and cakes, you can get filled Icelandic pancakes (Ikr600), tacos and tortillas (Ikr700), and fish and lamb dishes (Ikr1800–2200).

Tomman (☎ 466 1559; Hafnarbraut; pizzas Ikr800-2000; 🕑 6-11pm) This popular takeaway pizza joint occupies a tin shed on the main street.

There's an **Úrval supermarket** in the small shopping complex opposite the harbour.

Getting There & Away

In summer **Sæfari** (☎ 466 1444; www.samskip.is; Ránarbraut 2b) runs ferries to Grímsey at 9am on Monday, Wednesday and Friday, with bus connections from Akureyri. The return fare is Ikr3500 (Ikr4000 including a bus to/from Akureyri that leaves at 7.30am), and the one-way journey takes 3½ hours.

ÓLAFSFJÖRÐUR

pop 1020

The fishing town of Ólafsfjörður is beautifully situated beneath snowcapped 1200m-high peaks. It makes an ideal day trip from Akureyri, if only to see how an isolated community lives. To get here you pass through a 3km-long tunnel bored through the mountain.

In the valley south of town is the large lake Ólafsfjarðarvatn, which is connected to the fjord Ólafsfjörður by a short tidal channel. The valley was an exclusively agricultural area until the 1890s, when a village grew up around the harbour. Ólafsfjörður was granted trading rights in 1905 and became a municipality in 1944.

There's no tourist office, but you can get information from the helpful owners of the Brimnes Hotel.

Sights & Activities

Náttúrugripsafnið (☎ 848 4071; Aðalgata; admission Ikr300; 2-5pm Tue-Sun Jun-Aug), on the 3rd floor above the post office, is a small natural-history museum with a collection of stuffed animals. There are as many stuffed birds (every species found in the region) as you're likely to find in a local museum.

One of the highlights of Ólafsfjörður is **hiking** in the hills that enclose and dwarf this little fishing village. For several weeks around the end of June, the beautiful 400m-high headland **Ólafsfjarðarmúli** will allow you to see beyond the Arctic Circle and experience the real midnight sun. Unfortunately, there's no easy route up; the scree slopes are steep and rather hazardous to climb, so most people do their viewing from the high point along the rough coast road.

Ólafsfjörður receives good snow coverage. In winter there's downhill **skiing** on the slopes above town and **snowmobile excursions** (around Ikr5000 for two to three hours). It's possible to ride cross-country from Ólafsfjörður to Siglufjörður in about half an hour. Brimnes Hotel can help organise such activities as horse rental, free lake and sea fishing, ice fishing (in winter), rowing boats and winter snowmobile excursions.

Ólafsfjörður competes with Siglufjörður for the title of Iceland's northernmost **golf course**. The nine-hole course is in a lush geothermal area just north of the town.

Sleeping & Eating

There's a basic, free **camp site** (with toilets) beside the swimming pool, just below the mini ski jump.

Brimnes Hotel & Cabins (☎ 466 2400, 466 2660; www.brimnes.is; Bylgjubyggð 2; s/d Ikr6500/8500, cabins Ikr8500-12,000) The only real accommodation in Ólafsfjörður is fortunately very good. Brimnes' 11 hotel rooms are bland but adequate; however, it's really the Scandinavian-style log cabins on the lake shore that you should head for. All have an outdoor hot tub built into the veranda, and they're superb value for groups.

Glaumbær Café (☎ 466 2449; Ægisgata; mains Ikr800-2300; 10am-11pm) This is the pick of the places to eat in Ólafsfjörður. There's nothing flash about it, but there's a courtyard at the side for summer dining, a bar that stays open until 3am on Friday and Saturday, and a menu that runs from pizzas to fish and lamb dishes (Ikr1650), hamburgers and submarine sandwiches.

The glassed-in restaurant at **Brimnes Hotel** is also good. Again, you can expect pizza (Ikr700–2200) and daily specials of fish and lamb (Ikr1500–2000). The owner specialises in superb home-made Icelandic sweets and desserts, so ask about the pancakes even if they're not on the menu.

GRENIVÍK

pop 269

Tiny Grenivík at the end of Route 83 is the last stop on the eastern shore of Eyjafjörður. Established in 1910, the harbour and fish-freezing plant have kept the town going, and there's a supermarket, camp site and petrol station. Most visitors are interested in the nearby Laufás museum or the local horse tours. There's no public transport to Grenivík.

Laufás Farm Museum

Laufás (☎ 463 3196; admission Ikr400; 10am-6pm 15 May-15 Sep), 11km south of Grenivík, originally served as a manor farm and vicarage. The gabled, turf-roofed farmhouse dates from 1850 and contains the usual household and agricultural implements used by the gentry during that period and earlier. The vicarage was home not only for the vicar but also for his many farm hands and, at any one time, up to 30 people were occupying the building. The church, with a typical barrel-shaped ceiling, was built in 1865 and is dedicated to St Peter.

If you haven't seen one of these old farmhouses before, it's well worth the trip from Akureyri. The setting, on the edge of Eyjafjördur, is particularly beautiful, and there are numerous eider duck nesting sites nearby.

Attached to the farmhouse is a lovely country-style **café** where you can get coffee, cakes and traditional Icelandic dishes.

Tours

Pólar Hestar (☎ 463 3179; www.polarhestar.is) runs seven- to nine-day horseback tours from the farm Grýtubakki II, about 4km south of Grenivík. Destinations include Goðafoss,

Mývatn and Krafla, and the valleys and mountains of Northeast Iceland. Prices range from Ikr72,000 to Ikr140,000 and include accommodation and meals. Full-day rides are available on request for around Ikr7200.

Sleeping & Eating

Gistiheimilið Miðgarðar (☎ 463 3223; hladir@nett.is, Miðgarður 4; sb/s/d Ikr1500/3500/6000) The only guesthouse in town with five rooms in a comfortable building. The **café-bar** next door serves Icelandic dishes, coffee and cakes.

GRÍMSEY

pop 95

The northern tip of the 5.3-sq-km island of Grímsey, 41km north of the mainland, constitutes Iceland's only real bit of Arctic territory. Yes, Grímsey is dissected by the Arctic Circle, and here you'll see the real midnight sun in Iceland (of course, you'll have to stay here overnight to see it). Although the attention span of most tourists falters there, the island's 100m-high cliffs harbour extensive bird colonies, which accommodate at least 60 different species. Of these, 36 nest on the island: kittiwakes, puffins, razorbills, fulmars, guillemots, arctic terns etc. Historically, Grímsey provided an abundant supply of birds and fresh eggs, and its waters were some of Iceland's richest in fish.

Grímsey is a flat-topped island with some dramatic cliffs and basalt formations plunging into the sea. Sandvík is the island's only settlement. Services are limited to a church, swimming pool, guesthouse and community centre.

Tours

Nonni Travel in Akureyri (p190) runs Grímsey tours on Monday, Wednesday and Friday in summer, flying both ways (Ikr14,100), by flight and ferry (Ikr10,850) or by ferry both ways (Ikr4900). The last is a 12-hour day tour. Participants receive a certificate stating that they have crossed the Arctic Circle. For longer stays, you can leave the tour on the island and return to Akureyri later.

Sleeping & Eating

You can **camp** nearly anywhere away from the village.

Gistiheimilið Básar (☎ 467 3103; ljosbud@nett.is; sb/s/d Ikr1800/3200/5000) Beside the airfield, this is the island's original guesthouse, and it's still the only place to get a proper meal. Breakfast/dinner costs Ikr800/1900, and snacks are available during the day.

Gallerí Sól (☎ 467 3114; sb/s/d Ikr1400/2200/4400) A slightly cheaper and more basic alternative with six rooms and cooking facilities. It's attached to a local handicrafts shop.

Getting There & Away

AIR

From 9 June to 17 August **Air Iceland** (☎ 460 7000, 467 3148) flies daily except Saturday to/from Akureyri. From March to early June and from mid-August to October, flights are on Tuesday, Thursday and Saturday only. The 25-minute flights, usually in a tiny Piper Chieftain or Otter aircraft, are an experience in themselves, and they take in the full length of Eyjafjörður. The cheapest one-way/return fare is Ikr4790/9580.

GRÍMSEY'S CHECKMATE

Grímsey is known as the home of Iceland's most avid chess players and, historically, many a poor performance at this sacred pastime resulted in messy dives from the sea cliffs; on Grímsey, failure at chess was equated with failure in life. Enthusiasm for the game might have dampened in the past two generations, but everyone on the island knows the story of its rather unconventional American benefactor, Daniel Willard Fiske.

During the late 1870s Fiske, a millionaire journalist and chess champion, set himself up as the island's protector after hearing about its passion for the game. He sent badly needed firewood (as well as chess supplies!), financed the island's tiny library and bequeathed part of his estate to the community without ever making a visit.

In the library at the community centre, you can see a portrait of Fiske and some of his donations. Grímsey celebrates his birthday on 11 November. For more on the amusing Fiske story, read Lawrence Millman's account of a visit to the island in his book *Last Places: A Journey in the North.*

BOAT

In summer the **Sæfari ferry** (☎ 464 0000, 466 1444; www.samskip.is) departs Dalvík for Grímsey at 9am on Monday, Wednesday and Friday, returning from Grímsey at 4pm. If you're coming from Akureyri, a bus leaves at 7.30am to connect with the ferry. The return trip costs Ikr3500 (Ikr4000 including buses to/from Akureyri), and the one-way journey takes 3½ hours.

UPPER EYJAFJÖRÐUR

Heading south from Akureyri, Route 821 follows Eyjafjörður to its head, passing several historical sites and farms. If you have a vehicle and some spare time, it's worth an afternoon's excursion from Akureyri – if only to leave behind the Ring Road traffic between Mývatn and Akureyri – and there are some good opportunities for uncluttered hiking in the south.

About 10km south of Akureyri, **Kristnes** was the original Eyjafjörður settlement. At Pollurinn (The Puddle), near the head of the fjord, Helgi the Lean found his high-seat temple pillars and hedged his bets religion-wise by naming his farm 'Christ's Peninsula'.

A further 2km south is **Hrafnagil** (Raven's Ravine), which was the historic home of Bishop Jón Arason of Hólar. Today there's accommodation at **Hótel Vin** (☎ 463 1333; fax 463 1399; sb Ikr1200-1800, s/d Ikr4100/5200;), with a café, greenhouse, summer camp site and geothermally heated pool.

The odd little onion-domed church at **Grund**, about 5km past Hrafnagil, was built by the farmer Magnús Sigurðsson in 1905. Its neo-Romanesque style seems anomalous in Iceland, but early in the 20th century it was one of the country's most impressive churches. Ask for a key at the farmhouse.

The farm **Saurbær**, 28km south of Akureyri on Route 821, has an interesting turf-and-stone church that dates from 1838 and is now under national protection. It was constructed on the site of a church that had existed there since the 11th century.

The eccentric **Museum of Small Exhibits** (☎ 463 1261; admission Ikr400; 1-6pm 15 May-15 Sep) is at Sólgarður near Saurbær. It's the lifelong private collection of Sverrir Hermannsson, a local character who clearly doesn't like to throw anything away.

Torfufell, at the end of Route 821, offers good hiking, including a climb up Torfufell mountain (1241m) and a walk up the Torfufellsá canyon.

GOÐAFOSS

One of Iceland's most recognisable and easily accessible major waterfalls is Goðafoss (Waterfall of the Gods). It's right beside the Ring Road. It was formed by the glacial waters of the river Skjálfandafljót, which cut through the 8000-year-old Bárðardalur lava field (from the Trölladyngja crater near Vatnajökull).

The falls' romantic name wasn't aesthetically derived. At the Alþing in the year 1000, the *lögsögumaður* (law-speaker), Þorgeir, spent 24 hours meditating on the issue of a national religion. His cerebral pondering resulted in a public declaration that Iceland would thenceforth be a Christian nation and would forbid the open practice of paganism. On his way home to Ljósavatn, he passed the familiar horseshoe-shaped waterfall near his farm Djúpá (Deep River) and tossed in his carvings of the Norse gods, thus bestowing the falls' present name.

Sleeping & Eating

Fosshóll (☎ 464 3108; fax 464 3318; sb Ikr2100, d without/with bathroom Ikr8350/10,350) Beside the falls, this hotel is open from May to September and has camping for Ikr400 per person. There's a nice **restaurant** that serves burgers and meat and fish dishes for lunch and dinner daily.

The adjacent **petrol station** has a café and information office, and sells basic groceries.

Northeast Iceland

CONTENTS

The northeastern corner of Iceland is the undisputed gem of the north. In spite of the high latitude, the climate and weather here are generally better than in the west, and some of Iceland's most inspiring attractions are neatly contained in a small area.

The obvious highlights are the lake Mývatn and the surrounding lava fields and bubbling hot spots of Krafla, the pretty fishing village of Húsavík – Iceland's whale-watching capital – and the spectacular waterfalls, canyons and rock formations of Jökulsárgljúfur National Park.

Away from this popular circuit is a large area of practically uninhabited upland moors, wild coastal country and barren desert. Since the Ring Road takes a great short cut across the desertlike interior between Mývatn and Egilsstaðir, fewer visitors make it out into the remote northeastern corner, but intrepid travellers with time and/or their own transport will find a rugged and strangely captivating coastline teeming with bird life and punctuated by a handful of sleep-inducing fishing villages. The Langanes peninsula is as remote as it gets, but travellers interested in off-the-beaten-track hiking and getting away from the Ring Road 'crowds' need look no further.

TOP FIVE

- Cycling around Mývatn Lake before relaxing in the local '**Blue Lagoon**' (p206)
- Experiencing one of the great wonders of nature on a whale-watching cruise from **Húsavík** (p217)
- Standing on the edge of **Dettifoss** – Europe's most powerful waterfall (p223)
- Hiking from Dettifoss to Ásbyrgi through the spectacular **Jökulsárgljúfur National Park** (p220)
- Marvelling at the lava fields and volcanic mayhem caused by **Krafla** (p212)

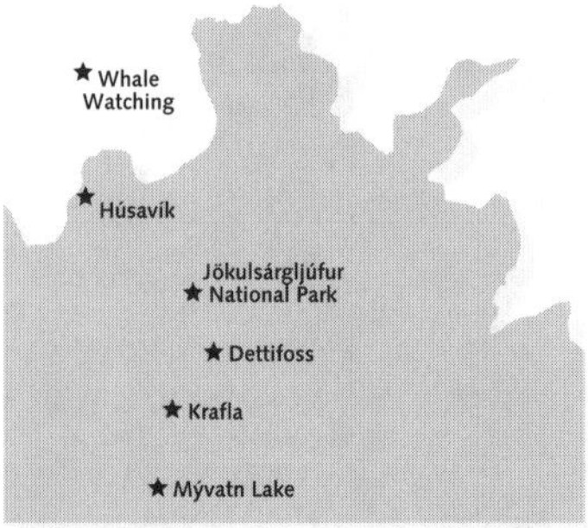

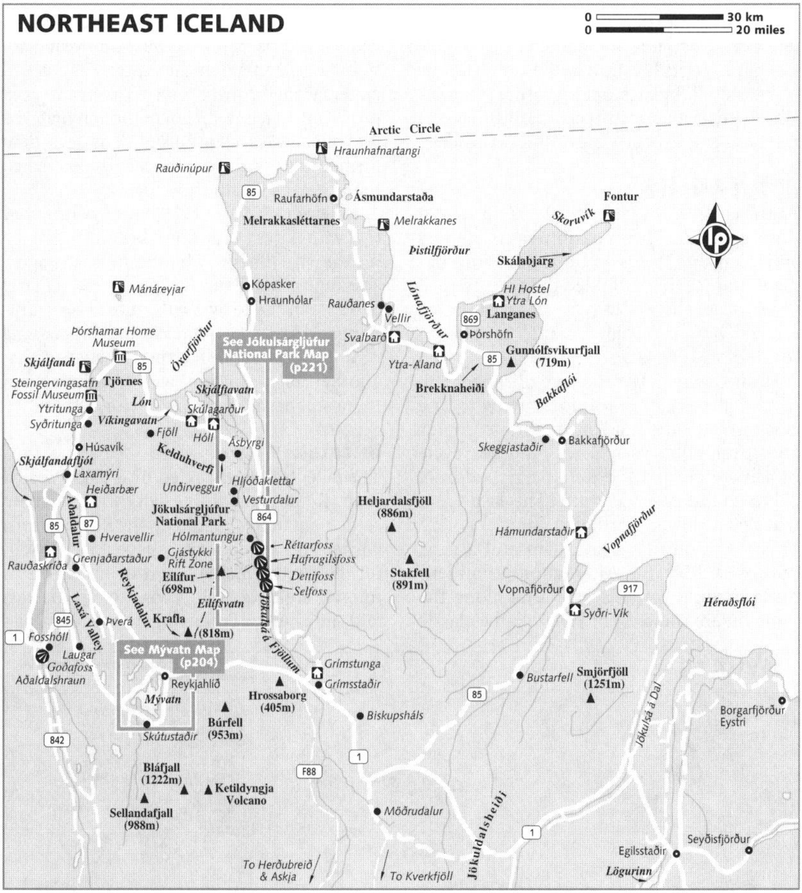

MÝVATN & KRAFLA

Mývatn (which ominously means 'midge lake') is more than merely a lake – it's the centrepiece of a rich volcanic area of lava flows, geothermal activity, craters and rock formations that epitomise Iceland's violent geological character. This type of landscape can be found elsewhere in Iceland, but it's the stark beauty and accessibility of Mývatn-Krafla that makes it so alluring. Mývatn is a place to savour, where you can settle in for a week of sightseeing, touring and relaxing and not become bored.

In 1974 the region was set aside as the Mývatn-Laxá special conservation area, and the pseudocrater field at Skútustaðir, at the southern end of the lake, is preserved as a national natural monument.

The Mývatn basin sits squarely on the Mid-Atlantic Ridge. Although most of the interesting sights are volcanic or geothermal features, the 37-sq-km lake Mývatn itself, which averages a depth of only 2.5m, has plenty to offer. Algae thrive in the fertile water, providing a perfect breeding ground for the notorious midge and blackfly larvae, which in turn attract prolific bird life.

The lake is nearly bisected by the peninsula Neslandatangi, which separates Ytriflói or 'Outer Gulf' from the larger Syðriflói or 'Southern Gulf', and it contains more than 50 islands and islets, mostly pseudocraters formed by gas explosions caused when molten lava flowed into the water.

Thanks to its location in the rain shadow of the Vatnajökull icecap, Mývatn is statistically the driest spot in Iceland and in summer you can expect a bit of fine weather.

History & Geology

At the close of the last glacial period 10,000 years ago, the Mývatn basin was covered by an icecap, and it was volcanic eruptions beneath this ice that moulded the symmetrical *móberg* peaks (flat-topped mountains formed by subglacial volcanic eruptions) south of today's lake.

Immediately after the ice disappeared, so did the lake. Volcanic activity to the east formed the Lúdent tephra complex and, over 6000 years later, another cycle of activity created the Ketildyngja volcano, 25km southeast of Mývatn. The lava from that crater flowed northwest along the Laxá Valley, and created a lava dam and a new, improved Mývatn. After another millennium or so, a volcanic explosion along the same fissure spewed out Hverfell, the classic tephra crater that dominates the modern lake landscape. Over the next 200 years, activity escalated along the eastern shore and craters were thrown up across a wide region, providing a steady stream of molten material flowing toward Öxarfjörður. The lava dam formed during the end of this cycle created the present Mývatn shoreline.

Between 1724 and 1729, the Mývatnseldar (Mývatn Fires) eruptions began at Krafla, northeast of the lake. This dramatic and sporadically active fissure erupted spectacularly in 1984. In the early 1990s, subsurface rumblings were on the increase and the magma chamber had refilled; experts believed that another big eruption was imminent but there still hasn't been any major activity.

Orientation

The lake itself is encircled by a 37km sealed road (Route 1 and Route 848), with the main settlement of Reykjahlíð on the northeastern corner and a secondary village, Skútustaðir, on the southern side. Most of the sights of interest are close to this road, or to the east and northeast. Following the Ring Road

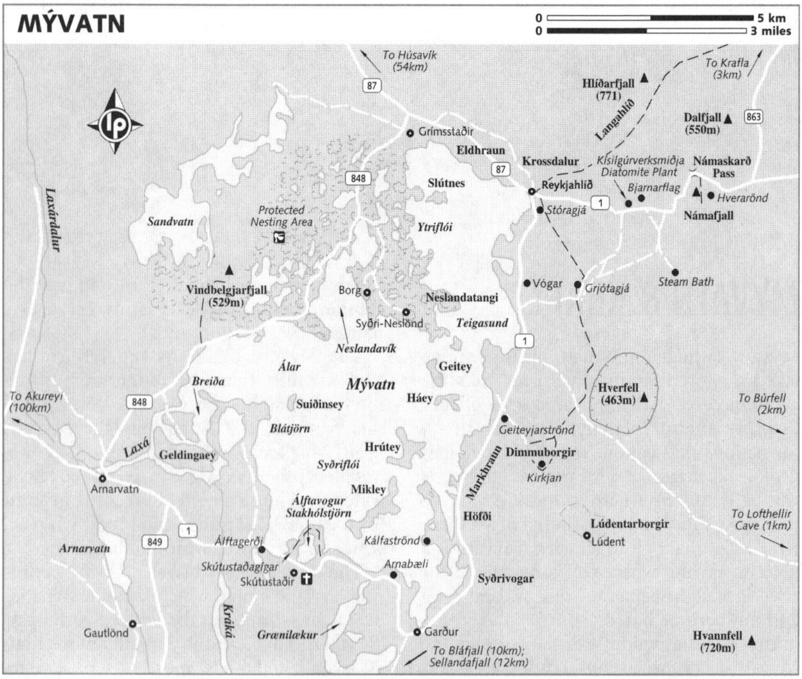

INTO THE MADDING SWARMS

If you're being driven to distraction by swirling swarms of Mývatn's eponymous midges and you're wondering why nice creatures like pandas are almost extinct when species like this are left to run rampant, take a moment to consider the adversary.

First of all, Mývatn has two species of midges, both of which are apparently attracted to carbon dioxide (emitted when people exhale, hence the clouds of them that gather around your face). The small, skinny, mosquito-like ones are called *mýflugur* or *rikmý*. Although they invade your eyes, ears, nose and mouth – and occasionally make a kamikaze dive for your lungs – they're chironomids, an insect family of nonbiting midges.

The other species is the *bitmý* (blackfly), fatter and even more pesky. They don't bite, but they do seem to be particularly fond of thick hair, where they can curl up and imitate chainsaws – it's a real buzz, but not a particularly pleasant one. They are, however, a vital food source for wildlife. Their larvae are eaten by brown trout and both the harlequin duck and Barrow's goldeneye subsist on them during the nesting season.

About all you can do for relief is wear a head net, which you can buy for around Ikr500 at Eldá (p206), or pray for a good wind, which will send the nasty little buggers diving for shelter amid the vegetation.

(Route 1) east from Reykjahlíð takes you over the Námaskarð pass to the Hveraröndd geothermal area, then a turn-off to the north (Route 863) leads to Krafla, 14km from Reykjahlíð.

With your own vehicle, this whole area can be explored in a single day, but if you're using the bus or a bicycle allow two days. If you want to hike and explore more distant mountains and lava fields, allow at least three.

Getting There & Away

Mývatn's main long-distance bus terminal is at the Hótel Reynihlíð in Reykjahlíð, although buses to/from Akureyri also stop at Skútustaðir. SBA-Norðurleið runs daily buses between Akureyri and Mývatn (Ikr2000, 1½ hours). In summer there are four buses a day in either direction.

To/from Egilsstaðir (Ikr2000, two hours) there's at least one Mývatn bus a day. From Húsavík (Ikr1400, 45 minutes), buses run two to four times daily in either direction.

Getting Around

Without a car or bicycle, you may find getting around Mývatn a bit frustrating. Hitchers invariably find themselves walking anyway. Most of the vehicles travelling around the lake belong to tourists and tour companies, neither of which are disposed to picking up dust-covered hitchers!

There are a few hiking trails, but they won't take you to all the points of interest, so you must sometimes walk along the road. Allow about three hours to walk between Reykjahlíð and Skútustaðir.

CAR

You can hire a car from **Hótel Reynihlíð** (☎ 464 4170; www.reynihlid.is). The cheapest vehicle will cost you Ikr6700 per day with 100km free, but for a 4WD vehicle it's Ikr17,900 per day with 200km free.

BICYCLE

If you have calm wind and weather, the best option is to hire a mountain bike. In Reykjahlíð, you can rent bikes from Hótel Reynihlíð (Ikr1200 per day), Eldá (Ikr1000/1500 for six/12 hours) and Hlíð Camping Ground (from Ikr1000). In Skútustaðir go to Sel-Hótel Mývatn (Ikr1200).

The 37km ride around the lake can be easily done in a day, allowing time for sightseeing at all the major stops.

REYKJAHLÍÐ

pop 452

Sitting on the northeastern shore of the lake, Reykjahlíð is the main village and the obvious base for trips around the lake and to Krafla. According to the *Landnámabók*, the first settler was the farmer Arnór Þorgrímsson.

Today, Reykjahlíð's livelihood revolves mainly around the nearby diatomite plant, the Krafla power station and the tourism industry.

Information

The small **information desk** (☎ 464 4390) inside the supermarket is staffed in summer.

A better bet for information, especially on tours, is **Ferðaþjónustan Eldá** (Eldá Travel Services; ☎ 464 4220; www.elda.is). It's open long hours and can book tours, onward transport or accommodation, or arrange horse riding. Pick up a copy of the map *Lake Mývatn & the River Laxá* (Ikr100) from here.

The **post office** (Helluhraun; 9am-4pm Mon-Fri) is on the street behind the supermarket. Inside is the local bank, **Sparisjóður Mývetninga**, with foreign exchange and a 24-hour ATM.

Internet is available at Hotel Reynihlíð (Ikr500 for 30 minutes, free to hotel guests).

Sights & Activities

REYKJAHLÍÐ CHURCH

During the huge Krafla eruption of 1727, the Leirhnjúkur crater, 11km northeast of Reykjahlíð, kicked off a two-year period of volcanic activity, sending streams of lava along old glacial moraines and past Reykjahlíð to the lakeshore. On 27 August 1729 the flow ploughed through the village, destroying farms and buildings, but, amazingly, the well-placed wooden church, which sat on a low rise, was spared – some say miraculously – when the flow parted and missed it by only a few metres. It was rebuilt on its original foundation in 1876. You can still see remnants of the original Reykjahlíð farm, which was destroyed by the lava.

In 1972 the original church was demolished and reconstructed on the same site. The interior of the present church is filled with carvings, paintings and batik-style art. The wooden carving on the pulpit is a representation of the church that survived the lava.

SWIMMING

A stormy day in Reykjahlíð is well spent at the 25m **outdoor swimming pool and hot tub** (adult/child Ikr250/120; 9am-10pm Jun-Aug, 9am-8pm Sep-May), 1km east of the village. It also has a sauna, solarium and gym (Ikr500).

Even better for a dip is Reykjahlíð's own 'Blue Lagoon', the steaming turquoise pool of bore water from the diatomite plant. It's right beside the Ring Road about 1.5km east

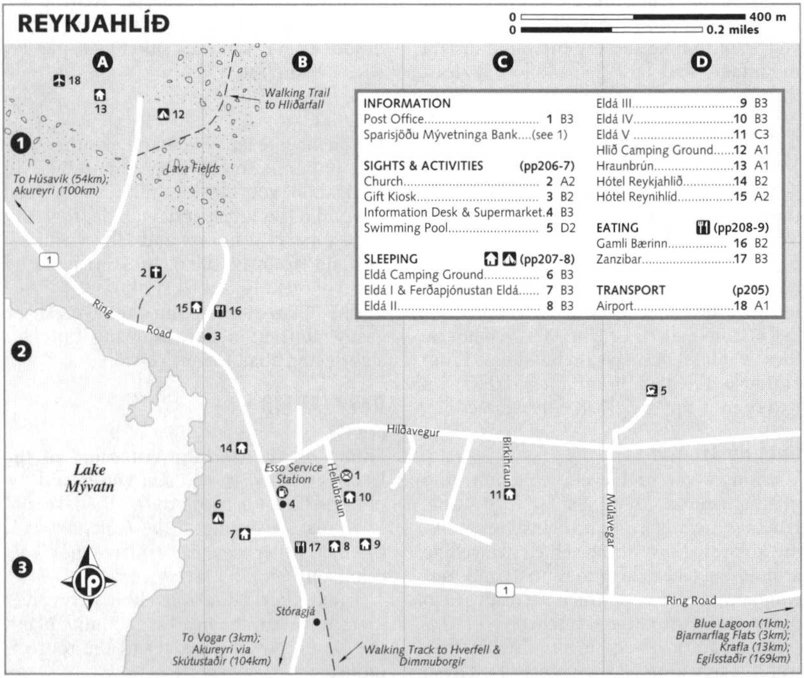

of the village and has none of the sanitised swimming pool atmosphere of the more famous Blue Lagoon near Reykjavík – plus swimming here is free.

A new geothermally heated complex – more along the lines of the Reykjavík Blue Lagoon – is proposed for an area near Vogar, 3km southeast of Reykjavík.

BOATING & FISHING

There are no regular boat trips on Mývatn, but you can hire rowing boats and kayaks (and obtain fishing permits and gear) from Eldá for Ikr1000/1500 for one/two hours.

Tours

Tourism with a capital 'T' reigns at Reykjahlíð and, fortunately for travellers without private transport, numerous Mývatn-area tours are run by Ferðaþjónustan Eldá and the bus company SBA-Norðurleiðar. Children aged four to 11 pay half price. Tours can get extremely crowded in summer, so book at least a day before departure.

HORSE RIDING

Horse-riding tours around the lake are available through **Bangahestar** (☎ 464 4103; Ik2200/3500 for one/two hours) – book at Hlíð Camping (see p208).

MÝVATN

SBA runs a 10-hour tour of the Mývatn-Krafla area from Akureyri (Ikr6400). A 2½-hour whirlwind sightseeing tour around the lake (Ikr3300) departs from Hótel Reynihlíð at 1pm daily and from Skútustaðir at 11.10am daily (May to September), allowing a fleeting glimpse of the main sights.

DETTIFOSS & JÖKULSÁRGLJÚFUR

Eldá offers the recommended 11-hour Super Dettifoss Tour (Ikr6500). The tour heads up to the western bank of the Jökulsá á Fjöllum and the waterfalls Selfoss, Dettifoss and Hafragilsfoss, then makes stops at Hólmatungur, Hljóð-aklettar, Ásbyrgi, Tjörnes and Húsavík. Departures from Eldá are at 8.15am on Monday, Wednesday and Friday from 18 June to 31 August.

GJÁSTYKKI

Another Eldá 4WD tour runs from Mývatn to Krafla and the colourful Gjástykki rift zone, which erupted vast amounts of lava in 1984 – the terrain here will remind you more of the moon than anywhere on Earth. The six- to seven-hour trip costs Ikr6000 and operates on request (minimum four people).

LOFTHELLIR CAVE

The five-hour tour to the Lofthellir cave, east of Hvannfell and 13km southeast of Reykjahlíð, runs via the Hverfell crater and the Lúdentarborgir crater row. The lava cave, which contains magnificent natural ice sculptures, was discovered in 1989. Departures in a 4WD truck are from Eldá at 9am on Tuesday, Thursday and Saturday, from 25 June to 31 August, or by request. The tour costs Ikr6000, including all necessary equipment.

HERÐUBREIÐ & ASKJA

Mývatn Tours (☎ 464 4196; myvatntours@isholf.is; tours 8am Mon, Wed & Fri 15 Jun-14 Jul & 16-31 Aug, daily 15 Jul-15 Aug, snow conditions permitting) runs long but rewarding day tours to Herðubreið and the Askja caldera, deep in the Interior. These tours last from 11 to 13 hours and cost a well-spent Ikr7500.

AIR SIGHTSEEING

Mýflug Air (☎ 464 4400; www.myflug.is) operates flight-seeing on request. The cost is from Ikr4500 per person for 20 minutes over Mývatn and Krafla, Ikr10,000 for an hour including Askja, or Ikr12,000 for 1½ hours including Kverkfjöll.

Festivals & Events

In late June, there is an annual **Mývatn marathon** which follows a circuit around the lake, as well as 3km and 10km fun runs. For information, contact the tourist office or the organisers (www.myvatn.is).

There's also a **music festival** lasting several days in mid-June, which includes a classical concert held in Kirkjan at Dimmuborgir. The new **Marimo Festival** is held at Skútustaðir in September – see the boxed text on p210.

Sleeping

Most Mývatn accommodation is in or near Reykjahlíð, and there are a few more places in Skútustaðir (see p211).

BUDGET

Camping outside the reserve is difficult due to the lack of surface water, and wild camping inside the reserve is prohibited so you might be hit with a fine.

Hlíð Camping Ground (☎ 464 4103; hlid@isholf.is; camp sites Ikr600; cabins per person Ikr1800, sb Ikr1800) About 300m uphill from the church and surrounded by lava, this is the largest camp ground. It has showers, toilets, drying sheds and, in summer, a kitchen tent. There's also a laundry service (Ikr500 per wash and Ikr500 to dry). Next to the camping ground are half-a-dozen basic cabins sleeping four.

Hraunbrún (☎ 464 4103; sb Ikr1800) This 'summerhouse' (although it's open all year), in the red building just past Hlíð Camping Ground, has no-frills kitchen facilities and a shower block. Check in at the camp site.

Eldá (☎ 464 4220; camp sites Ikr625) This smaller site has a better location on the lakeshore. There's a common area with cooking facilities in a large tent.

MID-RANGE & TOP END

The best chance of a cheap bed is at **Eldá** (☎ 464 4220; www.elda.is; sb Sep-May only Ikr2000, s/d Ikr5500/7700). This friendly and recommended guesthouse is spread over five locations around town, but all guests should check in at Eldá I (Bjarg) on the main road. All four houses are very clean and comfortable, but Eldá IV, near the post office, has cooking facilities and a TV lounge. The main house also has cooking facilities. An impressive buffet breakfast, included in the rates for all guests, is served at Eldá V on Birkihraun.

Vogar (☎ 464 4399; www.vogarholidays.is in Icelandic; camping/sb/d Ikr550/3000/8000) This quiet farm, on the lake road about 2.5km south of Reykjahlíð, has comfortable rooms with shared bathroom, cooking facilities and a lounge. Rates include breakfast in the Cowshed Café across the road. There's also a good camp site.

Hótel Reykjahlíð (☎ 464 4142; www.reykjahlid.is; s/d Ikr7900/10,800) A cute, nine-room hotel with a lovely position right on the lakeshore. The rooms are spacious and well furnished and the front rooms have superb lake views. There's a TV lounge, dining room (breakfast is included) and a video library bigger than some of Iceland's video stores. The atmosphere here is more guesthouse than hotel.

Hótel Reynihlíð (☎ 464 4170; www.reynihlid.is; s/d Ikr14,400/16,900; 💻) Mývatn's up-market, business-class option is the hub of the village. All rooms have satellite TV and some have good lake views. There's a good restaurant here and a small bar. A buffet breakfast is included in the rates.

Both hotels substantially reduce their rates outside the summer high season – by up to 50%.

Eating & Drinking

Don't miss trying the gooey, cakelike *hverabrauð* (hot spring bread); it's full of molasses and is slow-baked underground in the Bjarnarflag flats geothermal area east of town. Once you've started with a loaf and a stick of butter, it's difficult to stop. If the supermarket runs out, you'll also find it at the gift kiosk near the Hótel Reynihlíð, and it's served at local restaurants.

Gamli Bærinn (☎ 464 4170; 🕑 8am-10pm; mains Ikr900-1800) This cosy, country-style pub-café beside Hótel Reynihlíð is the best place for a meal in town. Try the Icelandic char soup (Ikr900), or the smoked char with *hverabrauð* (Ikr450). Pan-fried lamb (Ikr1800) is also good and there's a grill and carvery. Desserts include cakes, *skyr* (a kind of yoghurt) and apple pie. In the evening the bar is a great place to unwind with a drink.

Zanzibar (☎ 464 2910; 🕑 11am-1am, till 3am Fri & Sat; mains Ikr300-700) A more casual burger and pizza bar with a good view of the lake from its large front windows, Zanzibar is reasonably cheap and cheerful. The soup and bread (Ikr500) is good and the bar is popular with locals on Friday and Saturday.

Hótel Reykjahlíð (☎ 464 4170; 2/3 courses from Ikr3000/3500) The fanciest restaurant in town specialises in set-course menus of Icelandic specialities. The 'house special' of hot spring bread, poached arctic char and *skyr* with blueberries (Ikr3700) is one of half-a-dozen choices. There's also a lunch menu and buffet breakfast but the ambience here is a bit dull.

Vogafjós Cowshed (☎ 464 4303; snacks Ikr400-900; 🕑 10am-10pm Jun-Sep) A slightly bizarre café in a dairy shed in Vogar, 2.5km south of Reykjahlíð. Glass walls allow you to watch the cows being milked (mechanically, of course) while you sip your coffee, and you can try fresh milk straight from the cow. Milking times are 5.30pm to 9pm, but at any time the café has a certain country charm, and it gets going as a bar on summer evenings. There's a good range of snacks, including crepes, waffles, sandwiches, smoked trout and local hot spring bread.

STEVE HUTTON

Akureyrarkirkja (p187), Akureyri, Northwest Iceland

Akureyri (p185), Northwest Iceland

GRAEME CORNWALLIS

GRAEME CORNWALLIS

Skagafjörður (p176), Northwest Iceland

Glaumbær (p178), Northwest Iceland

PAUL HARDING

GRANT DIXON

Dettifoss (p223), Northeast Iceland

GRANT DIXON

Húsavík (p215), Northeast Iceland

Mývatn (p203), Northeast Iceland

GRAEME CORNW

Námafjall (p212), Northeast Iceland

STEVE HUTTON

Strax supermarket (10am-8pm) at the Esso petrol station is well stocked and has a hot-dog grill.

AROUND THE LAKE

By car or bicycle, Mývatn is 37km around by the shortest route. There are walks and side trips away from the main roads so, even with a vehicle, allow at least a day to explore the sites, and two days if you want to hike the Hverfell-Dimmuborgir trail system. Sites not to be missed along the way include **Dimmuborgir**, **Hverfell**, **Höfði**, the **pseudocraters** and the view from **Vindbelgjarfjall**.

This section is organised in a clockwise direction from Reykjahlíð and includes Skútustaðir.

Hverfell & Dimmuborgir Trail

In a day, you can walk the well-marked track from Reykjahlíð to Dimmuborgir and back (four hours), and explore the sites of interest along the way. Start by walking southeast from the intersection of the Ring Road and the round-the-lake route. After a few minutes, the trail reaches a dead end at a pipeline. Here you should turn left and walk several hundred metres to the point where the track continues south toward Hverfell.

STÓRAGJÁ & GRJÓTAGJÁ

These two rather eerie, watery fissures have traditionally been popular spots among locals for bathing and partying, but changing temperatures have made them less appealing. **Stóragjá** is just 100m southeast of the Reykjahlíð intersection of the Ring Road and the round-the-lake route. The 28°C hot spring, which is reached by a ladder and rope, has been cooling down and the water temperature fosters the growth of potentially harmful algae. It's still OK to have a dip (check you don't have any cuts) and it's much cleaner in spring than later in the season when – as locals like to point out – only tourists and drunken Icelanders take advantage of its charms.

In a gaping fissure along the walking track between Reykjahlíð and Hverfell, the beautiful hot spring **Grjótagjá** is now too hot for comfort. In the late 1980s it heated up to 60°C and is currently about 50°C – still too hot to soak in – but it periodically cools, so it's worth investigating and is well worth a look anyway. When the sun is shining, the steam, underground pools and light filtering through cracks in the roof create a mesmerising otherworldly effect. It's accessible via the Hverfell footpath or on the drivable track that turns off the Ring Road about 1km east of Reykjahlíð.

HVERFELL

The classic tephra ring Hverfell stands prominently, 463m above the lava fields east of the lake. It appeared 2500 years ago in a cataclysmic eruption of the existing Lúdent complex. The 1040m-wide crater serves as a Mývatn landmark and is surely one of Iceland's most interesting mountains.

The crater is comprised of loose gravel and resembles a mound of ball bearings. If you want to hike to the top, follow the ready-made tracks, where you're least likely to damage the feature. The track ascends the northern slope, then circles around the western rim of the crater to a lookout at the southern end before descending steeply towards Dimmuborgir.

Because of damage to the formation, the crater floor is now closed to hikers.

DIMMUBORGIR

The jumbled 'black castles' of Dimmuborgir are good for hours of imagination-invoking exploration. It's believed that the oddly shaped pillars and crags were created 2000 years ago by lava from the Þrengslaborgir and Lúdentarborgir crater rows (which originally erupted 9000 years ago). The lava flowed across older Hverfell lava fields and was dammed into a fiery lake in the Dimmuborgir basin. When the surface of this lake cooled, a domed roof formed over the still-molten material below. It was supported by pillars of older igneous material welded by the heat of the lava lake. When the dam finally broke, the molten lava drained in stages and the odd pillars of Dimmuborgir remained, marked with terraces at various surface levels.

The remaining formations contain natural arches, caves and zoomorphic features. Perhaps the most interesting is a large lava cave known as Kirkjan (the Church), because its interior resembles a vaulted Gothic cathedral. Concerts are held here in mid-June (see Special Events, p207).

In order to prevent erosion, vandalism and injury, specific walking routes have been roped off and colour-coded. Especially if you're walking with children, beware of the small and innocent-looking cracks that run throughout the area. Many are deep and dangerous fissures with no bottom in sight.

Höfði

The forested lava headland Höfði is covered with wildflowers and birch and spruce trees. In spring the fresh scent of the vegetation is very pleasant and its rambling footpaths can be easily covered in an hour. Listen to the wild and chilling cries of the great northern divers on the lake and observe the many small caves and *klasar* (lava pillars) along the shore.

The **Kálfaströnd** coastline, on the southern shore of the Höfði peninsula, has some of the most interesting *klasar* formations on the lake. It's also a nesting site for great northern divers.

Pseudocraters

The pseudocrater 'swarms' that formed most of Mývatn's islands, as well as the small hills around the southern, western and southeastern shores, were formed as molten lava from the craters east of the lake flowed across existing lava fields and into the water. Trapped subsurface water boiled and exploded in steam eruptions through the lava surface, forming small scoria cones and craters. The largest of these, which measure more than 300m across, are east of Vindbelgjarfjall on the western shore of Mývatn. The smallest ones – the islets and those south of the lake – are just a couple of metres wide. They're most impressive from the air (as seen in the postcards).

SKÚTUSTAÐAGÍGAR

The most accessible pseudocrater swarm is Skútustaðagígar, near Skútustaðir on the southern lakeshore. This field, which surrounds the lovely pond Stakhólstjörn, was designated a national natural monument in 1973. The pond and surrounding boggy marshland are havens for nesting waterfowl. HSiking trails, starting near the camp site at Skútustaðir, lead around and over the craters; a complete circuit of Stakhólstjörn takes about an hour at a leisurely pace. The features are rather delicate, so hikers must remain on the marked tracks.

MARIMO BALLS

Marimo balls *(Cladophora aegagropila)* are bizarre little spheres of green algae that are thought to grow naturally in only two places in the world – Mývatn and Japan (specifically Lake Akan). The tiny balls grow slowly, to about the size of a golf ball, and have a mind of their own, rising to the surface of the water in the morning to photosynthesise (when there's enough sunlight) and sinking to the bottom at night.

The balls have been honoured with a festival in Japan for some years (the name is Japanese for 'algae ball'), so Mývatn locals decided to do the same and in late September 2003 the first **Marimo Festival** was held at Skútustaðir. The festival takes some cues from the Japanese version, with a symbolic gathering of *marimo* balls which are displayed at the Skjölbrekka community centre for the weekend before being returned to the lake. Fireworks, plenty of partying, traditional costumes and demonstrations of glíma (Icelandic wrestling) give it an Icelandic touch.

Skútustaðir

The settlement of Skútustaðir serves as Mývatn's secondary base. During saga times, it was owned by the notorious Vigaskúta (Killer Skúta), who was known for his ruthlessness and was marked for assassination by his neighbours. He was clever though and, more often than not, turned the tables on those who threatened him.

The **church**, just east of the village, contains a painting of the Last Supper and makes a quiet and shady vantage point. The local museum was closed in 2003 – so the collection is busy gathering dust – but may reopen in the future.

TOURS

To complement the summer tours run out of Reynihlíð, Sel-Hótel Mývatn offers a program of **winter tours** from September to May, including snowmobiling, 4WD tours, ice fishing and cross-country skiing. Snowmobiling costs from Ikr6500 for a half-hour tour around Mývatn to Ikr32,000 for a six-hour trip to Dettifoss.

Horse riding is available at Arngrímes Farm (☎ 464 4203; Ikr2000/3800 for one/two hours).

SLEEPING & EATING

The **camping ground** (☎ 464 4212; per person Ikr500) is at the roadside opposite Sel-Hótel Mývatn.

Skjölbrekka (☎ 464 4202; sb Ikr1800) Basic bedding is available in this local community centre during summer.

Skútustaðir (☎ 464 4212; sb/d Ikr2000/7500) Friendly farmhouse accommodation right on the lake road next door to Sel-Hótel Mývatn.

Sel-Hótel Mývatn (☎ 464 4164; www.myvatn.is; s/d Ikr12,500/15,500; 💻) This is Skútustaðir's number one hotel, and unlike a lot of up-market hotels in Iceland it has a bit of class and sophistication, with polished floorboards, elegant furniture, decent-sized TVs and Internet connections in the rooms. There's a hot pot, sauna and a lounge area downstairs. The hotel **cafeteria** serves burgers and pizzas, and the **restaurant** offers traditional hot and cold lunch and dinner buffets (Ikr1090 and Ikr2100, respectively).

Hótel Gigur (☎ 464 4455; gigur@keahotels.is; s/d Ikr11,900/15,100; 💻) With claustrophobic rooms, this is well overpriced compared with its neighbour, but you can't beat the location right on the lake. The **restaurant** – if you can ignore the sickening green décor – is in a perfect position, with a glassed-in section overlooking the lake and a lovely outdoor patio.

Laxá

One of the many Icelandic rivers called 'Salmon River', the beautiful Laxá flows toward Skjálfandi from the western end of Mývatn and is one of the best – and most expensive – salmon-fishing spots in the country. The clear and turbulent stream rolls across the tundra and past numerous midchannel islets. More affordable brown trout fishing is also available. Permits are available from Eldá in Reykjahlíð.

Vindbelgjarfjall

The easy climb up 529m-high Vindbelgjarfjall (the Windbag), west of the lake, takes about half an hour up and 15 minutes down. Since it's so close to the lake, the summit offers one of the best views across the water, the pseudocraters and the protected wetlands along the northwestern shore.

Protected Nesting Area

The bogs, marshes, ponds and wet tundra along the northwestern shore of Mývatn are a high-density waterfowl nesting zone. Off-road entry is restricted between 15 May and 20 July (when the chicks hatch), but overland travel on this soggy ground would be challenging at any time.

Most species of waterfowl present in Iceland are found here in great numbers – including nearly 10,000 breeding pairs of ducks, representing 15 species – and the area is world-famous among bird-watchers. Three duck species – the scoter, the gadwall and Barrow's goldeneye – breed nowhere else in Iceland. Also present are incredible numbers of eider ducks, harlequin ducks, red-breasted mergansers, mallards, long-tailed ducks, pintail ducks, tufted ducks, wigeons, goosanders, teals, shovellers, whooper swans, horned grebes, great northern divers (loons), red-throated divers, black-headed gulls, ptarmigans, arctic terns, great skuas, several species of geese, ravens, gyrfalcons, golden plovers, snipe, whimbrels, wheatears, and lots of other species.

Mink and arctic foxes, which take advantage of the abundant avian prey, are also occasionally seen.

Eldhraun

The lava field along the northern lakeshore, Eldhraun (Fire Lava), includes the flow that nearly engulfed the Reykjahlíð church. It was belched out of Leirhnjúkur during the Mývatnseldar in 1729 and flowed down the channel Eldá (Fire River). With some slow scrambling, it can be explored on foot from Reykjahlíð.

Hlíðarfjall

The prominent 771m-high rhyolite mountain Hlíðarfjall, 5km northeast of Reykjahlíð, is sometimes called Reykjahlíðarfjall. It makes a pleasant day hike from the village, affording spectacular views over the lake on one side and over the Krafla lava fields on the other.

BJARNARFLAG

The Bjarnarflag flats, 3km east of Reykjahlíð, overlie an active geothermal area, and during the 20th century they have been the site of several economic ventures. Early on, farmers tried growing potatoes but, unfortunately, they often emerged from the ground already boiled (silly, but true!). In the early 1950s, attempts to extract sulphur from the solfataras that dot the area proved to be uneconomical and were abandoned.

A cinder-brick factory has been set up to manufacture building materials from the volcanic ash deposits, and nearby is the underground bread oven where *hverabrauð* is packed into milk cartons and slowly baked over 22 hours into delicious cakelike loaves. Look for the small, round glass doors that open into the ground, but don't disturb the bread.

In the late 1960s, 25 test holes were bored at Bjarnarflag to ascertain the feasibility of a proposed geothermal power station. One, which lies just southeast of the 'bakery', is 2300m deep and the steam roars out of the pipe at 200°C.

Kísilgúrverksmiðja (Diatomite Plant)

The most prominent and unusual Bjarnarflag enterprise is the geothermal diatomite plant. Diatoms are tiny microfossils, the skeletal remains of a type of single-celled algae. Although they are only approximately 1/20,000th the size of a sand grain, the 15m-thick deposits on the floor of Mývatn are steadily thickening at a rate of 1mm annually. Near the northern end of the lake, a barge gathers sediment from the lakebed and pipes it to the shore, where it's strained and channelled into holding ponds to settle. It's then transported to the plant and treated with fire and steam to remove any further impurities before it's exported. Diatomite is used as a filler in fertilisers, paints, toothpaste and plastics and also as a filtering agent for oil, pharmaceuticals, aviation fuel, beer and wine.

Unfortunately, the environmental impact of diatomite extraction is not yet fully known. The collection barge may infringe on the waterfowl breeding grounds, increasing the water's depth and preventing some bird and fish species from obtaining food from the lakebed. Furthermore, if the extraction of diatomite continues at its present annual rate of 25,000 tonnes, supplies from the northern lakebed will be exhausted within a decade and operations will be forced to move into unspoilt areas in order to supply the plant.

Námafjall

Produced by a fissure eruption, the pastel-coloured Námafjall ridge lies south of the Ring Road, 6km east of Reykjahlíð. It sits squarely on the spreading zone of the Mid-Atlantic Ridge and is dotted with steaming vents. A walking trail leads from the highway at Namaskarð pass to a view disc at the summit. This 30-minute climb provides a grand vista over the steamy surroundings. North of the pass is another ridge, Dalfjall, which sports a large and growing notch – dramatic evidence that the mountain is slowly being split in two by tectonic spreading.

Hveraröndi

Hveraröndi, the geothermal field immediately to the east of Námafjall, is full of mudpots, steam vents, sulphur deposits, boiling springs and fumaroles, some of which are real dynamos. Boardwalks have been erected and some of the more active features have been roped off, but that doesn't seem to stop people going for a closer look. To avoid risk of serious injury and damage to the natural features, avoid the lighter-coloured soil and respect the ropes.

KRAFLA

Technically, Krafla is just an 818m-high mountain 7km north of the Ring Road, but the name is now used for the entire volcanic region as well as a geothermal power station and the series of eruptions that created Iceland's most awesome lava field.

The heart of volcanic activity is known as the Krafla central volcano, but it bears little resemblance to the popular image of a volcano. Rather than a cone-shaped peak, Krafla is a largely level system of north–south trending fissures underlaid by a great magma chamber. Activity is normally characterised by fissuring and gradual surface swells followed by abrupt subsidence, which triggers eruptions. At present, the ground surface is rising, indicating possible activity in the future. Details of the most recent eruptions are on the Internet at www.norvol.hi.is, the site of the Nordic Volcanological Institute.

Kröflustöð (Power Station)

The idea of constructing a geothermal power station at Krafla was conceived in 1973, and preliminary work commenced with the drilling of 24 test holes to determine project

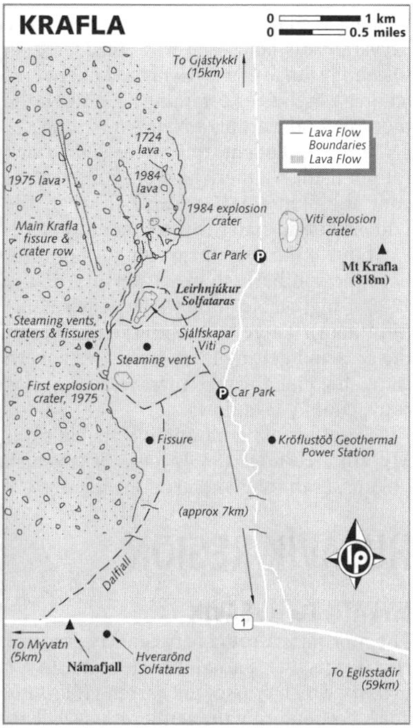

feasibility and provide steam sources should the plan be given the green light.

On 20 December 1975, however, after a rest of several hundred years, the Krafla fissure burst into activity with the first in a series of nine eruptions and 20 cases of surface subsidence. This considerably lowered the site's projected geothermal potential and nearly deactivated one of the primary steam sources, but the project went ahead and was completed in 1978. The present operation utilises only one of its two 30-megawatt generators and 17 of the boreholes. The power plant is open every afternoon (free).

Viti

The name of this impressive 320m-wide explosion crater means 'hell'. It's only one of many vents along the Krafla central volcano, where the destructive Mývatnseldar began in 1724. The series of eruptions that built it lasted for five years, and although activity has continued in spurts to the present day, Viti is now considered inactive.

Behind the crater are the 'twin lakes', boiling mud springs which aren't included in the guided tours. During the Mývatnseldar, they spurted mud 10m into the air, but they're now down to a mere simmer.

Leirhnjúkur & Krafla Caldera

The horrendous red warning sign that once forbade visitors entering the Leirhnjúkur and Krafla Caldera area has now been removed, so tourists can no longer photograph it with a backdrop of tour groups, cyclists, grandparents and young children streaming in as if it were a funfair. This is one of Iceland's most impressive – albeit potentially risky – attractions and no-one is going to keep the tourists out!

To be safe, avoid the lighter-coloured soil around the mudpots, snowfields that may overlie hidden fissures, sharp lava chunks and scoria slopes. Since Krafla is expected to erupt again within the next few years, a visit will naturally involve some risk. (At the first sign of an eruption, you can expect half the population of Iceland to descend on the place rather than follow official advice and clear out!)

LEIRHNJÚKUR

The big attraction at Krafla is the colourful Leirhnjúkur crater, which originally appeared in August 1727. It started out as a lava fountain, and spouted molten material for two years before subsiding. After a minor burp in 1746, it became the menacing sulphur-encrusted mud hole that tourists love today.

A well-defined track leads northwest to Leirhnjúkur from the Krafla parking area. Along the way, note the steaming vents on

HOME-MADE HELL

The impressive crater known as Sjálfskapar Viti, or 'home-made hell', near the Krafla car park, isn't like other craters in the area. When teams were drilling the Krafla boreholes, one was so powerful that when they hit the steam chamber it exploded. A huge crater was created and bits of the drilling rig were discovered up to 3km away. Miraculously, no-one was killed. Had the project been successful, this one borehole would have been sufficient to power the entire Krafla power station. Now, the same work is done by 17 boreholes!

the pastel-coloured rhyolite mountain to the west. The Leirhnjúkur crater lies just north of this mountain.

KRAFLA CALDERA

The source of the lava layers in the Krafla Caldera is a north–south tending fissure that bisects it. From the rim above Leirhnjúkur, you can look out across flows from the original Mývatnseldar, as well as from the 1975 eruptions, which are all overlaid in places by 1984 lava. Some areas west of Leirhnjúkur are still fairly hot. In 1975, the small grass-filled crater on the western slope of the rhyolite mountain, south of Leirhnjúkur, set off a series of explosive eruptions known as the Kröflueldar (Krafla Fires); these eruptions were a continuation of the Mývatnseldar of the early 18th century.

GJÁSTYKKI

Continuing on the 4WD track beyond the Viti parking area brings you to Gjástykki, the remote 'rift zone' at the northernmost end of the Krafla fissure swarm. This was the source of the first 1724 eruptions, and was activated when Leirhnjúkur went off in the 1975 eruptions. However, the current Gjástykki lava fields were created by the Krafla central volcano between 1981 and 1984. The best-known Gjástykki landmark is a red mountain that protrudes from the 1984 lava.

Getting There & Away

In summer Krafla can be reached on the daily bus (Ikr800, 15 minutes), which leaves at 8am and 11.45am from Hótel Reynihlíð and returns at 8.15am and 3.30pm. The Mývatn–Dettifoss excursion bus also runs via Krafla daily.

From Reykjahlíð, it's also a wonderful day hike to Leirhnjúkur. The marked footpath strikes off to the northeast from near the airport, along Langahlíð. Another walking route leads from Namaskarð along the Dalfjall ridge to Leirhnjúkur.

SOUTHEAST OF MÝVATN

With lots of time and an inclination to walk long distances over rugged terrain, you can explore the scattered mountains and geological features in the deserts south and east of the main lake area.

The **Lúdentarborgir** crater row, east of Mývatn, is part of the 8km **Þrengslaborgir** fissure, which lies 5km due east of southern lake Mývatn. This landscape was considered so uncannily lunar that in 1968 the Lúdent crater area was used as a training ground for the moon-bound astronaut Neil Armstrong.

To get to Lúdent, follow the light track rounding the southern base of Hverfell, then continue 5km southeastward through the Lúdentsborgir crater row to Lúdent itself.

About 13km southeast of Grænavatn, near the southern shore of Mývatn, is the 1222m-high table mountain **Bláfjall** (Blue Mountain). There are no marked routes in the area and getting there from Grænavatn is tough going, through marshes and across ropy, chunky lava flows.

Two other table mountains visible from Mývatn are **Búrfell** (953m) and **Sellandafjall** (988m), both long and arduous hikes.

HÚSAVÍK REGION

MÝVATN TO HÚSAVÍK

The most direct route between Mývatn and Húsavík is the partially sealed Route 87 (54km), which crosses the barren Hólarsandur before entering the gentle, grassy valleys of the Laxá and Skjálfandafljót that belie the area's substantial geothermal activity. With a vehicle, this whole area can be explored as a day trip from Húsavík or Mývatn.

Turning off either Route 85 or 87, the wealthy old farm **Grenjaðarstaður** served as a church and vicarage during the 19th century, but in the churchyard is a stone with runes dating from medieval times. The turf-roofed farmhouse, constructed in 1865, is one of only three left in the district and now houses a simple **folk museum** (☎ 464 3545; adult/child Ikr400/150; 🕑 10am-6pm Jun-Aug) similar to Laufás near Akureyri (p198). Grenjaðarstaður is 5km from public transport routes, so if you don't have your own transport it's hardly worth the effort.

The geothermal site **Hveravellir** on Route 87, about 26km south of Húsavík, provides some of Húsavík's hot water supply. The farm sells fresh vegetables from its geothermally heated greenhouses.

The alternative road from Mývatn or Akureyri to Húsavík starts on the Ring Road before turning north on Route 845 at **Laugar** (Hot Springs), the main village in this area. The school here was built in 1924 and the following year received Iceland's first indoor swimming pool. It operates as a summer hotel, **Fosshótel Laugar** (☎ 464 6300; bokun@fosshotel.is; s/d without shower Ikr6500/8700, with shower Ikr13,100/16,900; ⏲ 10 Jun-26 Aug). Other facilities include a snack bar, kiosk, petrol station and camping ground. There's not much reason to stop here unless you're cycling or if accommodation at Mývatn is booked out.

HÚSAVÍK

pop 2500

With its colourful houses tumbling down to the picturesque harbour and snowcapped peaks of Viknafjöll across the bay, Húsavík could easily win the title of 'most typical Icelandic town', and it's certainly the prettiest fishing town on the northeast coast. Although fishing and fish processing have traditionally been the main bastions of the local economy, tourism is playing an increasing role – Húsavík is *the* place to experience the magic of whale watching in northern Iceland.

Along with regular cruises in search of marine life, Húsavík has two fine museums, horse riding and some good local walks.

History

Although the honours normally go to Reykjavík and Ingólfur Arnarson, Húsavík was the real site of the first Nordic settlement in Iceland. Garðar Svavarsson, a Swedish Viking who set off around 850 for the mysterious Thule or Snæland (Snowland), was actually responsible for the island's first permanent human settlement.

After a brief stop off at Hornafjörður in the south, Garðar arrived at Skjálfandi (Shivering Gulf) on the north coast and built a settlement which he called Húsavík (Bay of Houses). Modestly renaming the country Garðarshólmur (Garðar's Island), he dug in for the winter. At the advent of spring, he prepared to depart, but some of his slaves were inadvertently left behind. In effect, these castaways were Iceland's first real settlers, but history hasn't credited them because their settlement was probably unintentional.

The historic Kaupfélag Þingeyinga was one of the first cooperatives in Iceland, but it went bankrupt in 1999. Despite the town's early roots and economic importance, it received municipal status only in 1950.

Information

The **Húsavík Information Centre** (☎ 464 4300; www.husavik.is; Garðarsbraut 5; ⏲ 9am-7pm Jun-Aug) is inside the Strax supermarket on the main

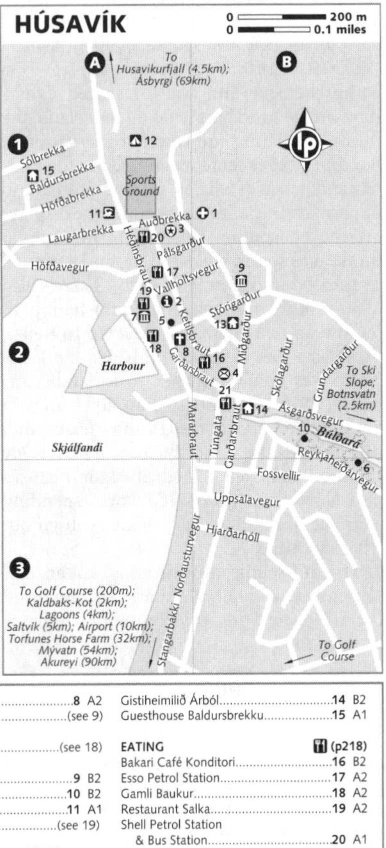

INFORMATION
- Hospital ... 1 B1
- Húsavík Information Centre ... 2 A2
- Police ... 3 A1
- Post Office ... 4 B2
- Íslandsbanki ... (see 5)
- Þórarins Stefánssonar Bookshop ... 5 A2

SIGHTS & ACTIVITIES (pp216-8)
- Arholt ... 6 B3
- Hvalaferði ... (see 19)
- Húsavík Whale Centre ... 7 A2
- Húsavíkurkirkja ... 8 A2
- Library ... (see 9)
- Norður Sigling (Whale Watching) ... (see 18)
- Safnahúsið á Húsavík (Húsavík Museum) ... 9 B2
- Skrúðgardin ... 10 B2
- Swimming Pool ... 11 A1
- Whale Watching Tours ... (see 19)

SLEEPING (p218)
- Camping Ground ... 12 A1
- Fosshótel Húsavík ... 13 B2
- Gistiheimilið Árból ... 14 B2
- Guesthouse Baldursbrekku ... 15 A1

EATING (p218)
- Bakari Café Konditori ... 16 B2
- Esso Petrol Station ... 17 A2
- Gamli Baukur ... 18 A2
- Restaurant Salka ... 19 A2
- Shell Petrol Station & Bus Station ... 20 A1
- Strax Supermarket ... (see 2)
- Túnberg Restaurant ... (see 13)
- Vín Búð Liquor Store ... 21 B2

street. Staff behind the boat-shaped counter can book tours and provide information on accommodation in private homes and farmhouses in the region.

Húsavík has car hire, banks, a post office and other facilities. The **Íslandsbanki bank** (Stórigarður 1) is opposite the church and has an ATM. There's Internet access at the **library** (Ikr5 per min; 10am-7pm Mon-Fri) or at **Fosshótel Húsavík** (Ikr300 for 15 min).

Þórarins Stefánssonar Bookshop (464 1234; Garðarsbraut 9), beside the bank, sells a good range of souvenirs, maps, books and novels in English and German.

Sights & Activities

HÚSAVÍK WHALE CENTRE

The excellent **Húsavík Whale Centre** (Hvalamiðstöðin; 464 2520; www.icewhale.is; adult/child Ikr400/150; 9am-9pm Jun-Aug, 10am-5pm May-Sep) is a comprehensive and well-presented exhibition on the history of whaling in Iceland, the future of whaling and whale conservation (a hot topic if ever there was one), and the ecology and habits of whales, orcas, dolphins and other marine mammals. Among the displays are the enormous skeletons of humpback, minke and sperm whales (all found stranded or trapped in fishermen's nets). There's also a 30-minute film chronicling whaling in Iceland and an exhibition devoted to Keiko, the killer whale captured off Iceland in 1979. Keiko was finally returned to Icelandic waters in 1998 after spells in an aquarium, in amusement parks in the US and Mexico and, of course, as the star of the movie *Free Willy* (in late 2003, Keiko died of natural causes in a Norwegian fjord). It's worth spending a couple of hours in here before you go out whale spotting.

The museum, now housed in an old slaughterhouse at the harbour, received the UN award for environmental tourism in June 2000.

SAFNAHÚSIÐ Á HÚSAVÍK

The town museum, **Safnahúsið á Húsavík** (464 1860; www.husmus.is; Stórigarður 17; adult/child Ikr400/150; 10am-6pm Jun-Aug, 9am-noon & 1-5pm Mon-Fri Sep-May) is one of the best local museums you'll find in Iceland, especially if you're lucky enough to get shown around by the passionate curator. The museum is in three sections – the 1st and 3rd floor of the main building (the town library is on the 2nd floor) and an annexe containing a maritime museum. The 3rd floor has a relatively small collection of folk history exhibits, including art and traditional costumes. The natural-history display on the 1st floor has an array of stuffed animals, including arctic foxes, a frightening-looking hooded seal, and the town's pride and joy – a stuffed polar bear, which was welcomed to the island of Grímsey in 1969 with both barrels after a long cruise from Greenland on an ice floe. There's also a healthy collection of 16th-century weapons, photographs, paintings and books – including a copy of a Bible printed in 1584 – and a re-creation of an early farmhouse. If you're interested, ask the curator to show you the carefully catalogued collection of more than 100,000 beer-bottle labels from around the world!

In a new building, the excellent maritime section has preserved fishing boats, a pungent fish-drying shed, and lots of memorabilia and displays relating to the fishing industry.

HÚSAVÍKURKIRKJA

The cross-shaped church in Húsavík is unique in Iceland. Constructed in 1907 from Norwegian timber, it's a bit like a gingerbread house. The altarpiece depicts the resurrection of Lazarus, but the Middle Eastern architecture sits in a lovely, green Icelandic backdrop. Also note the carving on the font, the murals and the candlesticks, which date from 1600.

SKRÚÐGARDIN

The small **town park** is a lovely little piece of nature running in a narrow strip along the south bank of the Buðará river through town. The main entrance is off Fossvellir, where you'll find a small waterfall and a basin filled with mallard ducks. It's a relaxing spot for a walk and there are several heritage houses scattered around, including one of Húsavík's original homes, **Arholt**. The park was established in 1975 and was planted with more than 50 species of trees and shrubs.

LUNDEY & FLATEY

The small islands of Lundey and Flatey lie anchored in Skjálfandi, near Húsavík. Lundey (Puffin Island) is a breeding ground for puffins, fulmars and other sea birds. It rises dramatically from the sea in a series of

WHALE WATCHING IN HÚSAVÍK

Húsavík is known as Iceland's premier whale-watching venue. The area is a veritable cetacean paradise and you'll almost certainly see whales during the May–September high season.

The most commonly spotted species is the minke whale, but on a good day you might also be lucky enough to see humpbacks, orcas, fin, sei or pilot whales, and the 'big one' – blue whales. Remember though, that this is nature – although whale-watching tours report 95% success rates, whales don't appear on cue. The thrill of the 'chase' is a big part of the boat cruises. Boats sail for about an hour to prime feeding grounds, then the crew and tour participants get busy looking out for telltale signs or a surfacing whale. When something is spotted, a 'clock' system is used to pinpoint it, with the stern of the boat at 12 o'clock. A crew member will yell out 'eight o'clock' or 'three o'clock', and all eyes will swing to the relevant side of the boat.

Different whales have different habits and identifying features. The minke whale surfaces two or three times in quick succession before executing a deep dive. Humpback whales breach and sometimes roll over, holding an enormous flipper in the air. Some are curious and will approach the boat (such as minke whales); others remain distant.

Most whales arrive in Icelandic waters in spring (around May) and stay to feed until September, when they return to warmer southern waters for breeding. It's thought that the waters of Skálfjandi around Húsavík attract large numbers of whales because of the rich feeding grounds stirred up by two rivers that converge in the bay. Baleen whales eat mostly plankton and krill; toothed whales feed on fish and squid.

Two whale-watching tours operate from Húsavík harbour. The original operator is **Norður Sigling** (Northern Sailing; ☎ 464 2350; www.nordursigling.is; 3hr trips adult/child Ikr3800/1900), which started whale watching here in 1994. They have four boats, including the 20-tonne oak fishing boat *Knörrinn* and an old whaling boat. Trips run up to four times daily from 1 May to 20 September. The same company also runs daily combination whale- and puffin-watching tours to Lundey and Flatey, for groups on request.

Hvalaferði (☎ 464 2551; www.hvalaferdi.is; 3hr trips Ikr3300/1700) is the other operator, with a 20-tonne oak fishing boat, *Faldur*, and a similar sighting success rate. From July to mid-August there are up to four departures daily.

Early and late in the season both operators may have only one departure daily, so check in advance. If there are no sightings, you can usually get on another trip for free.

high, nest-covered cliffs. Flatey (Flat Island) lives up to its name, rising only a couple of metres above sea level. It's now abandoned, but as recently as 1942 it had a population of more than 100. To arrange boat trips to either island, contact Norður Sigling (see the boxed text above).

HIKING

It's a steep hike of a couple of hours (4.9km from town) to the summit of 417m-high **Húsavíkurfjall**. The view from the summit, alongside the communication antennae, is fine – on exceptionally clear days you can see the Vatnajökull icecap. The path starts on the main road just 1.8km north of town. You can also drive to the top with a 4WD vehicle – it's a steep and rough road.

Another walk takes you to the lake **Botnsvatn**, in a hollow behind the village, where reafforestation projects are greening the landscape. It's a 5.2km walk around the lake. Campers are welcome around the lake but there are no facilities.

HORSE RIDING

Kaldbaks-Kot (☎ 892 1744; www.cottages.is) has short horse-riding tours along the coast daily at 5pm for Ikr2500 per person.

Saltvík Horse Farm (☎ 847 9515; www.saltvik.7p.com), 5km south of Húsavík, has short guided riding tours from one to three hours, midnight-sun rides from 15 June to 20 July, and a highly recommended eight-day highland tour taking in Mývatn and Jökulsárgljúfur (Ikr128,000).

Torfunes (☎ 4643622; www.torfunes.com), at Ljósavatnshreppur, 32km south of Húsavík on the road to Akureyri, is another established farm offering three-hour horse rides from May to September (minimum four persons), as well as six- to eight-day trips in July.

OTHER ACTIVITIES

Northeast of town, one **ski lift** operates during winter. There's also a **swimming pool** (☎ 464 1144; Laugarbrekka 2; 7am-9pm Mon-Fri, 10am-6pm Sat) with hot pots and water slides for kids, and a challenging, undulating, nine-hole **golf course** (☎ 464 1000) at the southern edge of town.

About 4km south of town are two **lagoons**. The smaller of the two, which receives excess water from the power plant, is warm enough for bathing (20° to 30°C), and there's free trout fishing in the larger one.

Tours

The SBA-Norðurleið bus picks up at Húsavík at 10am daily in summer, and does a return eight-hour excursion to Jökulsárgljúfur National Park and Dettifoss (Ikr5600), stopping at the main sights.

Three-day tours to Kverkfjöll and Askja with **Ice & Fire Expeditions** (☎ 464 2200; www.sba.is; Ikr18,200) also pick up in Húsavík. In July and August, tours depart from the Shell petrol station at 9.45am on Monday.

Highland Expedition Tours (☎ 464 3940; www.fjallasyn.is; Hrísateigur 5), run by Rúnar Óskarsson, has Super Jeep tours year-round in the Northeast region.

Sleeping

The **camping ground** (☎ 464 2299; sites Ikr600), next to the sports ground at the north end of town, is lovingly run and has such luxuries as heated toilets and laundry and cooking facilities.

Gistiheimilið Árból (☎ 464 2220; guest.hus@isl.is; Ásgarðsvegur 2; s/d Ikr5700/8600) Housed in a 100-year-old building that once belonged to the governor of the region, this is a charming and hospitable guesthouse. The rooms are spacious and furnished in that appealing old-fashioned way, and there are two cute attic rooms with polished timber beams. There's a garden by the river and an outdoor barbecue deck, and breakfast is included.

Guesthouse Baldursbrekku (☎ 464 1005; mariam@simnet.is; Baldursbrekku 20; sb/s/d Ikr1800/3200/6000) A handful of rooms in the friendly family home of Aðalbjög Birgisdóttir.

Fosshótel Húsavík (☎ 464 1220; fax 464 2161; Ketilsbraut 22; s/d Ikr13,100/16,900; 💻) The only standard hotel in town is welcoming and comfortable, though the rooms, with TV and attached bathroom, are fairly pokey.

Kaldbaks-Kot (☎ 892 1744; www.cottages.is; cabins Ikr8900-11,900) Beautifully situated timber cottages on a farm above the coast about 2km south of Húsavík. The cottages are fully self-contained and attractively furnished, and have verandas overlooking the bay. Cheaper than a hotel room, this is the best place to stay in Húsavík. There's an outdoor hot pot and horse riding is available for Ikr2500 per person for a short tour.

Eating & Drinking

Gamli Baukur (☎ 464 2442; www.gamlibaukur.is; 11am-midnight Sun-Thu, 11am-1am Fri & Sat; starters Ikr590-980, mains Ikr1590-3990) In the rustic timber building down by the harbour, this is a good fish restaurant with a small menu of soups and seafood for starters, and catfish, cod, char and tuna steak for main courses. It has a dose of nautical atmosphere, a terrace facing the harbour and a cosy little lounge bar upstairs.

Restaurant Salka (☎ 464 2551; Garðarsbraut; mains Ikr800-2400; 11am-11pm) Across from the supermarket on the main street, this is another inviting, rustic place. Again, seafood is the speciality and you can try smoked puffin or lobster tails, but there's also an extensive pizza menu and bar.

Túnberg restaurant (mains Ikr1200-3200; 7-9am, 12-2pm, 6-10pm) At Fosshotel Húsavík, this cosy dining room serves standard pizza, pasta, beef and lamb dishes, along with puffin and local fish specialities.

Bakari Café Konditori (Garðarsbraut; 8am-5pm) The town bakery has fresh bread, sandwiches and a good range of sweets and cakes.

Both the Esso and Shell petrol stations have **cafés** selling the usual fast-food fare.

For self-caterers, the **Strax supermarket** (Garðarsbraut 5; 9am-8pm) is well stocked, with excellent meat and fish counters and locally grown vegetables. There's a **Vín Búð** at Túngata 1.

Getting There & Away

The bus terminal is at the Shell petrol station. There are five buses a day in summer and at least one year-round between Akureyri and Húsavík (Ikr1800, 70 minutes), and weekday connections from Húsavík to Ásbyrgi (Ikr1400, 1½ hours) at 9am and 10am. On weekdays buses run from Húsavík to Raufarhöfn (Ikr2400, 2¼ hours) and Þórshöfn (Ikr3000, 3½ hours)

Between Húsavík and Mývatn (Ikr1400, 45 minutes) there are two or three buses daily in summer.

TJÖRNES

The stubby peninsula Tjörnes, along Route 85 north of Húsavík, separates **Skjálfandi** from **Öxarfjörður**. In summer colonies of puffins and other sea birds nest on the 50m-high cliffs along the eastern coast. Near the northern end is a **lighthouse**, from which clear weather allows a good view of Grímsey in the Arctic Circle.

Buses between Húsavík and Ásbyrgi follow the route around the Tjörnes peninsula, but it's not practical to explore without your own transport.

Ytritunga Fossils

Turning off at Ytritunga farm, about 10km north of Húsavík, a track leads down the coastal cliffs on either side of the Hallbjarnarstaðaá river mouth, which contains alternating layers of fossil shells and lignite. The oldest layers, which were laid down about two million years ago, are at about the 12m level. The present water temperature along Iceland's Arctic Ocean coast is around 4°C, yet the creatures that inhabited the shells are now found only in waters of 12°C or warmer, an indication that the sea has cooled over the past two to three million years.

If you're interested in learning more, drop into the **Steingervingasafn fossil museum** (☎ 464 1968; ⏲ 10am-6pm summer only), about 2km further up Route 85 at the farm Hallbjarnarstaðir. It displays interesting finds from the area, including plant and animal fossils from the Pleistocene era.

Þórshamar Home Museum

At the farm Mánárbakki, on the river Máná about 23km north of Húsavík, the **Þórshamar Home Museum** (☎ 464 1957; adult/child Ikr300/free; ⏲ 10am-7pm Jun-Aug or by request) is one of those quirky Icelandic collections in the middle of nowhere. The museum is the pride of a local farmer and contains objects dating all the way back to the Settlement era. The house, in its original state, is packed with crockery, photographs, homewares, an interesting Icelandic Christmas tree (in the absence of actual trees they had to improvise!), Viking-age jewellery and the owners' personal matchbox and tobacco tin collection.

KELDUHVERFI

Like Þingvellir, low-lying Kelduhverfi reveals some of the most visible evidence that Iceland is spreading from the centre. Beside the drowned estuary of the Jökulsá á Fjöllum, the Mid-Atlantic Ridge enters the Arctic Ocean in a series of odd cracks, fissures and grabens up to 7m deep. Most of those you see today were formed by earthquakes and dramatic fissuring and subsidence during the Krafla eruption of 1975. The locals were literally rattled, but you can imagine their surprise to discover that their farms had actually increased in size overnight!

Near the estuarine lake **Víkingavatn**, north of the highway at Kelduhverfi, is a farm of the same name that has been occupied by the descendants of the original farmer for nearly four centuries. Between Víkingavatn and **Lón**, the lagoon to the west, look out for a large and interesting tree. Anything relating to a large tree would be notable in Iceland, but this one appears to be devouring a house.

East of Víkingavatn is **Skjálftavatn** (Shivering Lake), recently formed by surface subsidence. It's now used for freshwater fish farming.

Sleeping & Eating

There are several farmhouses along Route 85 between the Tjörnes peninsula and Ásbyrgi, which can make a good base for visits to Jökulsárgljúfur National Park. The rivers, inlets and lakes here also offer abundant bird life and opportunities for fishing.

Keldunes (☎ 465 2275; keldunes@isl.is; s/d Ikr4900/7000) The best of the farmhouse accommodation along here is only about 10km west of Ásbyrgi. The brand-new six-room pine guesthouse has a superb kitchen, tidy double and twin rooms and a TV lounge to curl up and die for, and there's an enclosed hot-pot spa just outside. There's even a telescope for viewing the bird life on Skjálftavatn. There's no sleeping-bag accommodation.

Hóll (☎ 465 2270; hrunda@ismennt.is; sb/made-up beds Ikr1800/2500) Even closer to the national park, this farm has four simple twin rooms in the main house, and a summerhouse about 1km away with cooking facilities. Groups can rent the summerhouse for Ikr9000 per night. Breakfast (Ikr800) and dinner (Ikr1800) are available. This is also a horse farm and riding tours are available for Ikr2000 per hour.

Skúlagarður (☎ 465 2280; skulagardur@simnet.is; sb/s/d Ikr1850/5000/7800) More of a hotel set up, this place has plenty of rooms, a restaurant, a bar and common areas.

JÖKULSÁRGLJÚFUR NATIONAL PARK

The formidable name of this fabulous national park means 'glacial river canyon', and it's often described as 'Iceland's Grand Canyon', in reference to the narrow 30km gorge carved out by Iceland's second-longest river, the **Jökulsá á Fjöllum** (Glacial River from the Mountains). The river starts in the Vatnajökull icecap almost 200km away and flows to the Arctic Ocean at Öxarfjörður. The canyon through Jökulsárgljúfur National Park was formed by *jökulhlaups* (flooding from volcanic eruptions beneath the icecap) – minor ones an average of every 10 years and a major one once or twice in a century.

Unless you're planning on hiking right through the canyon (see the boxed text p223), the key points of interest for visitors are the **waterfalls** at the southern end of the park and the horseshoe-shaped **Ásbyrgi canyon** at the northern end. Between them are diverse birch forests, striking rock formations, lush valleys and commanding perpendicular cliffs. In the south is **Dettifoss**, Europe's greatest waterfall, which is somewhate predictably touted as the 'Niagara of Europe'. Fortunately, you won't find any kitsch souvenir stalls, restrictive barriers or coloured floodlights here – just nature at its most spectacular. At the heart of the park is the 30km canyon **Jökulsárgljúfur**, which averages 100m deep and 500m wide.

After Mývatn and Krafla, one of the things that surprises visitors is the remote feel to such an important attraction. Access on either side of the canyon is along rough gravel roads – the western approach (Route F862) isn't really suitable for a 2WD vehicle in places. Unless you're using public transport, the main points of interest – Dettifoss, Ásbyrgi canyon and Vesturdalur – can be visited in a leisurely day, but allow more time if you want to explore further into the park.

History

Most of the land that is now protected within Jökulsárgljúfur historically belonged to the Ás estate, one of Iceland's largest private holdings, which extended from Dettifoss to Öxarfjörður. Until the early 19th century, there was a church at Ás, near the highway on the northern end, but it has now gone and only remnants of the cemetery are visible.

Ásbyrgi has long been considered prime farmland and in medieval times the living was good due to the anomalous profusion of trees – that was until *jökulhlaup* floods tore through in the 17th and 18th centuries.

The national park was established in 1973, initially including only the farm Svínadalur, part of Vesturdalur and a small portion of Ásheiði. In 1974 the huge Ás estate was added, and in 1978 Ásbyrgi came under national park protection. Jökulsárgljúfur now contains 120 sq km and extends 28km from south to north.

Orientation

The park's southern anchor is Dettifoss and 8km to the north are the springs and luxuriant vegetation of Hólmatungur. Right in the heart of the park is Vesturdalur, with lots of caves and Iceland's most interesting basalt formations. Near the northern end is Ásbyrgi, a verdant, forested plain enclosed by vertical canyon walls. From Dettifoss to Ásbyrgi on Route 864 is 25km, about half an hour's drive.

Information

Park information is available at the main ranger station in **Ásbyrgi** (☎ 465 2195, 893 6059; 8am-11pm Jun & Jul, shorter hrs May & Sep) and at Vesturdalur. Both stations have toilets and a car park.

The best hiking map is the *Dettifoss* 1:100,000 sheet, but if you also want to hike at Mývatn, it's worth purchasing the thematic *Húsavík-Mývatn* 1:100,000 map, which includes both areas. The park brochure (Ikr200), available at the ranger stations and some tourist offices, shows the main hiking routes and is adequate for most hikes. A number of self-guided trail brochures are available free from the Ásbyrgi ranger station.

Although the park is open all year, snowfalls can make the roads impassable between October and May.

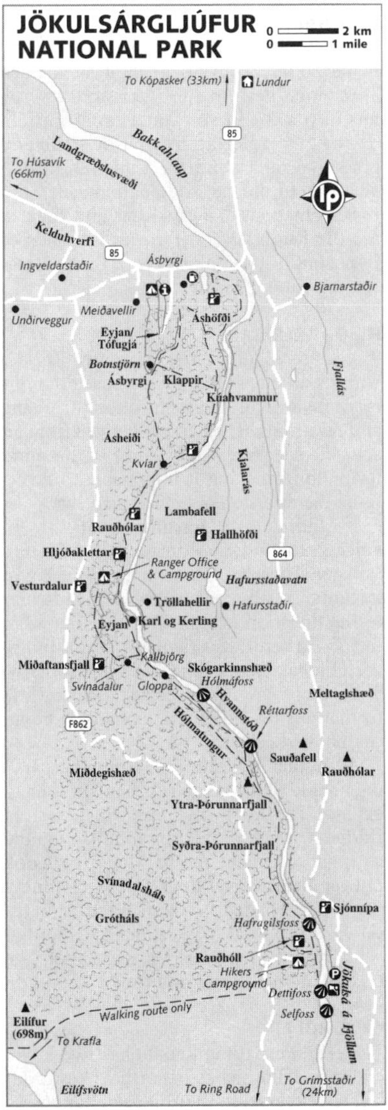

Tours

Several companies offer tours of Jökulsárgljúfur from Mývatn, Akureyri and Húsavík – see Tours under those sections for details. The tours are good value if you're in a hurry and don't have private transport. You can usually leave any of these tours at any time and rejoin later, with advance arrangements.

Sleeping & Eating

Camping inside the park boundaries is limited to the official **camping grounds** at Ásbyrgi, Vesturdalur and Dettifoss. Sites at Ásbyrgi and Vesturdalur cost Ikr600 per person.

As the only camping ground in the park between Dettifoss and Ásbyrgi, Vesturdalur is the usual overnight stop for hikers. The basic facilities don't really merit the fee, but the setting is pleasant. The free hikers' camping ground at Dettifoss has only a freshwater tank. Note that motorists aren't permitted to stay here.

If you're expecting fancy hotels close to the park, think again. The nearest formal accommodation is **Lundur** (☎ 465 2247, 863 4311; lundur@dettifoss.is; sb/s/d Ikr1800/3500/6200), 8km northeast of Ásbyrgi on Route 85. What it lacks in style it makes up for in homeliness – the home-cooked meals are superb (Ikr800/1200 for breakfast/dinner). There are kitchen facilities and across the road is a heated swimming pool.

See also the farmhouse options under Kelduhverfi, p219.

The closest place to eat or buy supplies is the **café** at the Ásbyrgi petrol station on Route 85, 1km from the camping ground. It also has a small selection of groceries at high prices – if you're hiking, bring food with you.

Getting There & Away

SBA-Norðurleið buses operate between Akureyri and Ásbyrgi (Ikr3000) daily from 18 June to 31 August, via Húsavík (Ikr1400 from Ásbyrgi). This bus conveniently continues to the main sites on the western side of the park: Hljóðaklettar, Hólmatungur, Dettifoss and back. At Dettifoss it connects with a bus to Mývatn. The daily Akureyri–Þórshöfn bus also passes through Húsavík and Ásbyrgi.

Coming from the south, there's a daily bus from Mývatn to Dettifoss via Krafla (Ikr1800, 30 minutes).

The main access roads to the park are Route 864 off the Ring Road from the south (28km to Dettifoss along a gravel road), or the sealed Route 85 from Húsavík to Ásbyrgi, joining up with Route 864. This covers the eastern side of the canyon. The alternative, for the west side, is the more rugged Route F862, either from the south (turning off the Ring Road) or from the north, just before Ásbyrgi.

Hitching isn't recommended along the lightly travelled route (F862) between the Ring Road and Dettifoss (west bank), unless you're prepared for a 20km road walk before you get onto the park trail system.

JÖKULSÁRGLJÚFUR

Ásbyrgi

Just south of Route 85 is the lush, horseshoe-shaped Ásbyrgi canyon, which extends 3.5km from north to south, averages 1km in width and reaches 100m in depth at its head. Near the centre of the canyon is the prominent outcrop **Eyjan** ('island'). Thanks to protection from grazing sheep and the windbreak provided by the canyon walls, Ásbyrgi is remarkably well forested, with birch trees up to 8m high.

There are two stories about the creation of Ásbyrgi. The early Norse settlers believed that Óðinn's normally airborne horse, Slættur (known in literature as Sleipnir), accidentally touched down on earth and left one hell of a hoof print to prove it. The other theory, though more scientific, is equally incredible. Geologists believe that the canyon was created apocalyptically by an eruption of the Grímsvötn caldera beneath distant Vatnajökull. It released an immense *jökulhlaup*, which ploughed northward down the Jökulsá á Fjöllum and gouged out the canyon in three days or less. After flowing through Ásbyrgi for 100 years or so, the river shifted eastward to its present course.

HIKING

From the car park near the end of the road, several short tracks lead through the forest. The eastern track leads to a spring near the canyon wall, the western one climbs to a good view across the valley floor, and the boardwalk leading straight ahead ends at a small lake (Botnstjörn) at the head of Ásbyrgi. Full of moss-covered boulders, it has a vaguely primeval feel.

You can also climb to the summit of **Eyjan** (2km, 45 minutes return) or ascend the cliffs at **Tófugjá**. From there, a loop track leads around **Áshöfði** past the gorges. Alternatively, follow the rim right around to **Klappir**, above the canyon head, from where you can head south to Kvíar (or head east to Kúahvammur) and return via the river (the route via Kvíar will take up to four hours return).

Vesturdalur

The diversity of Vesturdalur (West Valley) makes it a favourite off-the-beaten-track attraction. Vesturdalur is crisscrossed by lots of tracks and you could easily spend a day or two exploring. The bushy scrub and grassy lawns around the camping ground give way to the cave-riddled pinnacles and rock formations of **Hljóðaklettar**, and you can see the **Rauðhólar** crater row, the ponds of **Eyjan** (not to be confused with the Eyjan at Ásbyrgi) and the canyon itself.

HLJÓÐAKLETTAR

A visit to Hljóðaklettar (Echoing Rocks), with its unique swirls, spirals, rosettes, honeycombs and columns of basalt, is surprising and rewarding. The name is derived from an acoustic effect created by some of the spiral formations, making it impossible to determine the direction of the roaring river.

It's difficult to imagine what sort of volcanic activity produced Hljóðaklettar. Polygonal basalt columns normally form in instantaneously cooled lava perpendicular to the direction of flow. Because they were formed in vertically oriented volcanic plugs, the Hljóðaklettar columns lie horizontally. Still, there are some bizarre concertina formations for which there seems to be no rhyme or reason.

A circular walking trail from the parking area (2.5km) takes less than an hour to explore. The best formations, which are also riddled with lava caves, are found along the river, northeast of the parking area. Look out for **Trollið** (Troll Rock), with its honeycomb pattern, **Kirkjan** (the Church), a natural cave in a grassy pit about 15 minutes' walk from the parking area, and **Kastali** (the Castle), a huge basalt outcrop.

RAUÐHÓLAR

The eruptions at the Rauðhólar (Red Hills) crater row, immediately north of Vesturdalur, were related to the Hljóðaklettar basalt. The craters can be explored on foot, but they're a two-hour return walk from the parking area. You could also take the excursion bus from Ásbyrgi to Vesturdalur and walk back to Ásbyrgi (three to four hours).

KARL OG KERLING

Karl og Kerling (the Man and the Witch), on the west bank of the river, can be accessed in an hour from the Vesturdalur car park. Across the river is **Tröllahellir**, the largest cave in the gorge, but it's reached only on a 5km cross-country trek from Route 864 on the east side.

EYJAN

From Karl og Kerling, you can return to Vesturdalur in about three hours by walking around Eyjan, a mesalike 'island' covered with low scrubby forests and small ponds. Follow the river south to Kallbjörg then turn west along the track to the abandoned site of Svínadalur, where the canyon widens into a broad valley, and follow the western base of the Eyjan cliffs back to the Vesturdalur parking area.

Hólmatungur

The real attraction of the lush Hólmatungur area is its peaceful greenery, and in fine weather, it's surely one of Iceland's most beautiful spots. At the mouth of the spring-fed Hólmá, the harsh lines of the canyon soften and produce several nice waterfalls – **Hólmáfoss** on the Hólmá and **Réttarfoss** on the Jökulsá á Fjöllum. For the best overall view of Hólmatungur walk to the hill Ytra-Þórunnarfjall, just 1km south of the car park.

The most popular walking route is the 3km loop from the parking area to Jökulsá á Fjöllum, north to Hólmáfoss and then back along the Hólmá toward the Hólmatungur parking area.

Hólmatungur is accessible by car, otherwise it's three hours on foot south of Vesturdalur and four hours north of Dettifoss. Camping is prohibited here but it's a great spot for a picnic lunch on the first day of the Dettifoss to Ásbyrgi hike.

Dettifoss

With the greatest volume of any waterfall in Europe, Dettifoss is a veritable powerhouse. At only 44m in height, and with its milky, dishwater-grey glacial water, it's not Iceland's prettiest waterfall, but up to 500 cu metres of water per second thunders over the edge, sending up a plume of spray that can be seen 1km away and forming brilliant double rainbows above the canyon.

DETTIFOSS TO ÁSBYRGI HIKE

The most popular hike in Jökulsárgljúfur National Park – and justifiably so – is the two-day trip (34km) from the western side of Dettifoss to Ásbyrgi, which takes in all of the canyon's major sights. To get to the start of the hike by public transport, take the scheduled bus (Monday to Friday) from Akureyri or Húsavík to Dettifoss, then walk north and pick it up again in Ásbyrgi.

From Dettifoss, head north along Sandadalur until you begin seeing yellow trail markers. If you go left up the hill, it will lead you fairly easily around the rim of Hafragil. Go right and you'll descend steeply into the canyon, to re-emerge on the rim beyond Hafragilsfoss. With a heavy pack, this will be difficult as it involves some serious scrambling and climbing.

From Hafragilsfoss, the route leads north along the canyon rim to beautiful Hólmatungur. You'll cross the Hólmá on two bridges, then descend past Hólmáfoss. The trail then joins a lateral moraine beneath towering basalt cliffs and crumbled basalt columns, and follows the *yazoo* (parallel) river Stallá, which eventually must be forded. After the ford, the trail climbs back to the canyon rim for a beautiful walk over the moors.

At unassuming Kallbjörg, it's a 100m detour to an overlook perched on a rock column with sheer drops on three sides. You don't realise the drama until you're right on top of it. Another short detour will take you to Gloppa, a basalt amphitheatre that ominously resembles the maw of a hellishly large shark.

The requisite first-night camp site is at the **Vesturdalur camping ground** (per person Ikr600). The next day, the trail winds through beautiful Hljóðaklettar and Rauðhólar to the Kvíar trail junction, where you must decide whether to shoot across the moorland to the incredible view from Klappir into the Ásbyrgi canyon or continue following the main canyon rim. Both are equally worthwhile, although the former gets a bit soggy in places. There's also the Kúahvammur–Klappir trail, which takes an hour longer. The Klappir options rejoin the main canyon route at the head of Tófugjá, a challenging descent into Ásbyrgi with the aid of a fixed rope – or you can continue easily northwards to Ásbyrgi petrol station.

The Super Dettifoss Tour from Mývatn and the SBA bus from Ásbyrgi visit the western bank, while other tours and most tourists in private vehicles stop at the more accessible eastern bank. It's hard to say which is the better vantage point; most people who've seen the western bank cast a vote in its favour because the entire face of Dettifoss is visible, as opposed to just a side view. The car park on the western bank is a 20-minute walk from the viewpoints.

If you have a 2WD vehicle, stick with the eastern bank as it's a rough ride coming from the south to the western bank (the road is better coming from the north) – either way it's a long drive around if you want to see both sides. From the carpark on the eastern bank it's a five-minute walk down to the lookout, but you can continue on to the edge of the waterfall for an even better view.

Continuing for another 20 minutes south over the boulders brings you to **Selfoss**. It's only 11m high but it's much broader and quite a striking waterfall.

Hafragilsfoss

In one of the deepest parts of the canyon, 2km downstream from Dettifoss, the 27m-high Hafragilsfoss cuts through the Raudhóll crater row to expose the volcanic dyke that formed it. From the eastern bank, the best view is down the canyon from the small hill just north of the Hafragilsfoss parking area. In the same area are numerous red scoria cones and craters.

The overlook on the western bank affords a marginal view of the falls, but the view down Jökulsárgljúfur is one of the best available. You can climb down to the river from the vantage point, but near the bottom you must lower yourself down a challenging vertical wall on fixed ropes.

NORTHEASTERN CIRCUIT

For travellers with a bit of time and imagination (and preferably a vehicle), the wild, sparsely populated coastal route around Iceland's northeastern tip is a spectacular alternative to the direct but dreary Mývatn–Egilsstaðir Ring Road journey.

Route 85 takes you from Kópasker on a mostly gravel road around the Melrakkaslèttarnes peninsula to within a few kilometres of the Arctic Circle, before following the coast down to Þórshöfn and Vopnafjörður. The mountain pass from here to the Héraðssandur in East Iceland is one of the most spectacular drives in the whole of the country. The highlights of this northeastern jaunt are nature – the coast is rich in bird life – and the sheer isolation, without the desolation.

The road has improved dramatically in recent years and is easily tackled in a 2WD vehicle – several sections have even been sealed. A scheduled SBA-Norðurleið bus runs on weekdays all year round from Akureyri to Þórshöfn (Ikr4600) and back via Húsavík, Ásbyrgi (Ikr3100), Kópasker (Ikr3400) and Raufarhöfn (Ikr4000). Surprisingly, that's where the bus service stops – there's currently no bus to or from Vopnafjörður.

KÓPASKER

pop 150

Kópasker, a tiny village on the eastern shore of Öxarfjörður, 33km north of Ásbyrgi, is the first place you pass through before disappearing into the expansive wilds of Iceland's far northeast. An international trading port since 1879, today it relies on agricultural trade and the shrimp industry.

On 13 January 1976, Kópasker suffered a severe earthquake that destroyed several buildings and cracked the harbour wall. Rockslides and fissuring were violent and evidence of seismic activity can still be seen at **Hraunhólar** near Presthólar, about 5km south of Kópasker.

About 500m before the village itself, you'll see the red-roofed **church** beside the road. The building next to it is the old school, which now houses the town **Folk Museum & Library** (☎ 465 2171; adult/child Ikr300/free; 1-5pm Tue, Thu, Sat & Sun Jun-Sep). The prized exhibits in an otherwise unremarkable collection are the locally made textiles, some dating back to 1860, and traditional costumes, including a white wedding dress (black was customary at the time). Other interesting exhibits include an elaborately carved cabinet from 1726 and a horse-drawn fire engine with sled attachments.

Alongside the church is **Snartarstaðir**, an early district assembly site.

Sleeping & Eating

There's a free **camping ground** in the village.

HI Hostel Kópasker (☎ 465 2314, 861 2314; fax 476 2314; Akurgerði 7; sb members/nonmembers Ikr1850/1500, made-up beds per person Ikr2000) This simple five-room hostel and guesthouse has a lounge, good kitchen and spotless bathrooms.

There's a small **café** on the left as you enter the village, serving the usual burgers, hot dogs, soup and fish dishes. The village supermarket, **Verslunin Bakki**, is well stocked.

MELRAKKASLÉTTARNES

The Melrakkasléttarnes peninsula, between Öxarfjörður and Þistilfjörður, is characterised by low-lying flatlands, ponds and marshes, which provide nesting grounds for eider ducks, curlew and dunlin. In its far northwestern corner is the extinct 73m crater **Rauðinúpur**, a cliff-girt headland occupied by nesting sea birds and a lonely lighthouse. A rough 5km track turns off to Rauðinúpur from Route 85, 18km north of Kópasker. It's a remote and scarcely visited place, and can be reached only on foot or in a private vehicle.

Heading east through more fertile farmland, you approach the remote peninsula **Hraunhafnartangi**, the northernmost point of the Icelandic mainland. If it were just 2.5km further north, it would lie within the Arctic Circle and would probably be one of Iceland's biggest attractions! Even so, the latitudinal hype can't be avoided, and guests at the Hótel Norðurljós in Raufarhöfn still receive a certificate stating they've approached the magic line!

Even without the Arctic Circle looming out to sea, Hraunhafnartangi wouldn't lack interest. As well as another lonely lighthouse, this was a Saga Age landing site and home to the burial mound of saga character Þorgeir Hávarsson, who killed 14 enemies before being struck down in battle. If you blink you might miss the turn-off as it's not well signposted – look out for the lighthouse. It's possible to set up camp anywhere on this remote headland.

RAUFARHÖFN

pop 165

The harbour of Raufarhöfn is aesthetically one of the finest in all of northeastern Iceland, formed not by a sheltered fjord as with many other Icelandic ports, but by the small **Ásmundarstaða Islands**, just offshore.

The port has functioned since the Saga Age, but the town's economic peak came early in the 20th century during the herring boom, when it was second to Siglufjörður in volume. The village itself isn't too pretty, with rows of dull prefab housing and storage tanks, but the harbour is colourful and the flat surrounding farmland is dotted with more than 29 lakes, all teeming with bird life. Hótel Norðurljós rents **kayaks** for paddling on the lakes.

The free **camping ground** (☎ 465 1151; 🕑 Jun-Aug) is located beside the swimming pool at the south end of the village.

Hótel Norðurljós (☎ 465 1233; ebt@vortex.is; Aðalbraut 2; sb/s/d Ikr1800/5500/8000) The town's only hotel, right on the harbour, doesn't look like much from the outside, but the spacious, spruced-up rooms with attached bathroom are fine. There's also a good **restaurant** here with a bar, a bright dining area and a terrace overlooking the harbour. The menu mainly consists of a fish or meat dish of the day (Ikr1800–2000) and a few light courses.

The other options for a meal or quick snack are the **Esso petrol station** (☎ 465 1256) or the **Hafnarkjör supermarket** and snack bar, by the main road.

ÞÓRSHÖFN & AROUND

pop 414

From Raufarhöfn, Route 85 continues south past some scenic coastal landscapes to the port of Þórshöfn, the jumping-off point for the eerily remote Langanes peninsula and a base for the interesting hike to Rauðanes. Although it has served as a busy port since saga times, Þórshöfn didn't kick on until a herring-salting station was established in the early 20th century.

Tourist information is available at the architecturally interesting and well-equipped **swimming pool** (☎ 468 1515; 🕑 8am-8.30pm Mon-Fri, 11am-4pm Sat & Sun) on the Langanes road. There's also a bank with an ATM in town.

The annual 'Happy Days' festival is held over a weekend in July, with markets, sporting events, dances and a bonfire.

Rauðanes

About 26km west of Þórshöfn, on the road back to Raufarhöfn, a 4WD track heads north from Route 85 to Rauðanes (Point Red). This small and scenic peninsula is endowed with steep cliffs full of nesting birds, caves, offshore sea stacks and an exposed rock face, Stakkatorfa, where a great chunk of land collapsed into the sea. It's an excellent area for hiking, with marked paths leading to bizarre rock formations, caves, puffin colonies and secluded beaches.

There's a parking area about 1km in from the Ring Road, but from there it's a 4km walk to the bridge before the farm Vellir, then another 3km northeast to the cape.

Sleeping & Eating

The free **camping ground**, off Hálsvegur, is just east of the centre.

Guesthouse Lyngholt (☎ 468 1253, 897 5064; karenrut@simnet.is; Langanesvegur 12; sb/s/d Ikr2000/4000/6000) Next to the swimming pool, this spotless guesthouse is the cosiest place to stay in Þórshöfn.

Hótel Jórvík (☎ 468 1149; jorvik@netfang.com; Langanesvegur 31; sb/s/d Ikr1800/3500/5000) It looks more like a brightly painted home than a hotel, but there are some nice sea views and a dining room serving meals in summer.

Ytra-Aland (☎ 468 1290; ytra-aland@simnet.is; r Ikr3400-4200, sb Ikr1900, summerhouse Ikr9000) About 18km west of Þórshöfn, this is a beautifully located horse farm with top-quality accommodation, including a self-contained cottage. Meals are available, as are horse-riding tours.

Hafnarbar-Inn (☎ 468 1338; Eyravegur 3; mains Ikr750-2500; 🕙 11am-11pm Sun-Thu, 11am-3am Fri & Sat) At the harbour, this is the local pub, café, pool hall, restaurant and meeting place. It serves up pizza, burgers, meat and fish.

The alternative is the diner-style **café** at the Esso petrol station, and self-caterers can stock up at the **Lónið supermarket** (closed Sunday).

LANGANES

Shaped like a goose with a very large head, the foggy Langanes peninsula is one of the loneliest corners of Iceland. Route 869 ends only 17km along the 50km peninsula, and although it's possible to continue along the track to the tip at Fontur in a 2WD vehicle, it's a pretty rough road.

Most of the flat or undulating part of Langanes, which is riddled with abandoned farms, is rich in marshland as well as arctic and alpine flora. The moors at the base of Langanes form a tundra plain of lakes, marshes and low hills. It's pleasant and unchallenging walking country. The tallest peak of mountainous southern Langanes, **Gunnólfsvíkurfjall**, rises to 719m and the easternmost coasts are characterised by cliffs up to 130m high.

Drinking water is plentiful, but there are no facilities beyond Þórshöfn, so carry everything you'll need. Hikers should allow a week for the return trip from Þórshöfn to Fontur.

After the turn-off to the youth hostel, the road gets a little rougher but is still OK for 2WD vehicles. At Skoruvík, towards the end of the peninsula, there's a long bay that provides a major breeding ground for the peripatetic arctic tern. The fog-bound cliffs at the northeastern tip of Langanes have long proved dangerous to passing ships. The **Fontur lighthouse** at the cape dates from 1910 and there's a monument to the shipwrecked English sailors who died of hypothermia after ascending the ravine there. It's now called **Engelskagjá** (English Gorge).

From the western end of Skoruvík a rough track leads across the peninsula to **Skálabjarg**, a long and formidable bird cliff on the wild south coast of Langanes. At the turn of the century, the ruined farm of Skálar, northeast of the cliff, was a prosperous fishing village.

If you're not camping, the best base from which to explore the Langanes peninsula is

LANGANES EGG COLLECTORS

Every year from around 15 May to 10 June, Þórshöfn's 'egg gathering club' heads up to the wild and rocky cliffs on the Langanes peninsula to collect eggs from the colonies of black gulls, a tradition stretching back many years. The collection involves cliff-climbing and abseiling using professional equipment.

The local club welcomes visitors to join in the two- to three-day tours, which include camping out, meals, bird-watching guides and cliff-climbing instruction. For information contact **Halldór** (☎ 468 1192; fontur@isl.is).

Ytra Lón HI Hostel (☎ 468 1242; ytralon@mmedia.is; sb members/nonmembers Ikr1550/1900, s/d Ikr3600/5200), 14km northeast of Þórshöfn and just off Route 869. It's part of a working farm run by a young family, and the renovated 16-bed hostel provides plenty of comfort in this remote outpost. Phone in advance to arrange pick-up from the bus stop in Þórshöfn.

BAKKAFJÖRÐUR

pop 150

Bakkafjörður is a tiny fishing settlement on the southern shore of Bakkaflói with a view to Gunnólfsvíkurfjall, the highest point on Langanes. Since the village has no accommodation and is 5km off Route 85, few travellers will venture in here.

The church at the estate farm, **Skeggjastaðir**, 6km west of Bakkafjörður, is worth a stop though. It was originally built of wood in 1845, but has since been radically renovated. With permission from the proprietor, you can camp at Skeggjastaðir and visit the church.

VOPNAFJÖRÐUR

pop 608

Another 30km on, Vopnafjörður is the last village on the road around the northeastern circuit. From here you can cut down to the Ring Road and west to Mývatn and Akureyri, or take the truly spectacular mountain drive over Hellisheiði and down to the east coast – either way, getting to or from Vopnafjörður is half the fun. The latter road, which may be impassable in bad weather, climbs up a series of switchbacks and hairpin bends before dropping down to the striking glacial river deltas on the Héraðssandur. The views on both sides are superb.

The town proudly lays claim to being the home of a former Miss World (even if it was 15 years ago!) and the choice of some of Prince Charles' angling holidays. Icelanders also claim that Father Christmas makes his home on 1251m-high **Smjörfjöll** (Butter Mountain), south of town. Otherwise, it's a typical modern harbour town in a typically pretty fjord setting.

The **tourist office** (☎ 473 1331; 10am-5pm Jun-Aug), in the big yellow building down by the harbour (across from the supermarket), has information and a small local history display.

Unusually, Vopnafjörður decided to build its **swimming pool** (☎ 473 1499) way out of town – 12km north then 3km west of Route 85 via a dirt road. It's a very natural geothermally heated location by the Séla river and there are outdoor hot pots – worth a stop if you're passing by and desperate for a soak.

Bustarfell

Heading south along Route 85, you'll pass the farm Bustarfell, at the foot of the mountain of the same name, 20km west of Vopnafjörður. The **folk museum** (☎ 473 1466; adult/child Ikr400/150; 10am-6pm 15 Jun-5 Sep), in an 18th-century, gabled, turf-roofed farmhouse, provides an interesting look at rural life two centuries ago. There's a festival here on the second Sunday in July.

Sleeping & Eating

There's a good free **camping ground** – follow Miðbraut north of town and turn left at the school.

Hótel Tangi (☎ 473 1224; fax 473 1146; Hafnarbyggð 17; s/d Ikr5100/6700) The only formal accommodation in the village looks like a tin shed from the outside but has been renovated within so the rooms are comfortable. You may be able to arrange cruises on the fjord here.

Skjól (☎ 473 1332; Vatnsdalsgerði; sb/made-up beds Ikr2000/2500) This small guesthouse, at a typical farm 4km south of town, has simple rooms, kitchen facilities and camping (Ikr700). It's perched up on a hill with great views across to the Krossavík mountains and the fjord.

Syðri-Vík (☎ 473 1199; budargerdi@fel.rvk.is; sb Ikr1000-1700, made-up beds Ikr2500) Across the fjord 8km south of Vopnafjörður, this place has farmhouse accommodation as well as five- to eight-person cottages from Ikr6000 to Ikr8500. Horse-riding tours are Ikr1400 and fishing permits are available for the trout-filled Hofsá river.

The only **restaurant** is the dining room at the Hotel Tangi, which serves up pizzas and burgers, as well as local fish and meat dishes from Ikr1800. The **Esso petrol station** (☎ 473 1204), on the main road south of town, has a café, and the **Kauptún supermarket**, by the hotel, has groceries. **Verður Barinn** is a pub attached to Hotel Tangi and is open late on Friday and Saturday nights.

NORTHEAST INTERIOR

Heading between Mývatn and Egilsstaðir, the Ring Road takes a drastic short cut inland across the stark and barren highlands of the northeast interior. There's little to lure travellers off the bus, but the loneliness can be an attraction in itself in this eerie and otherworldly place of endless vistas.

If you won't be travelling into the interior, you'll catch a glimpse of it here. The land is dotted with small lakes caused by melting snowfields; streams and rivers wander aimlessly and disappear into gravel beds. In summer the grey landscape seems unimaginably dull, where even a sprig of grass would considerably liven the scene, but in spring the land is spattered with clumps of tiny purple blooms which somehow gain root in the gravelly volcanic surface.

Grímsstaðir is a remote farm near the intersection of the Ring Road and Route 864, 3km from the Jökulsá á Fjöllum. Before the river was bridged, it was crossed by ferry. The old **ferryman's hut**, built in 1880, can still be seen on the western bank, 2km downstream from the Ring Road bridge. It's reputedly haunted.

If you get stuck, the nearby farm **Grímstunga** (☎ 464 4294; sb/s/d Ikr12003850/5400) has basic accommodation with kitchen facilities. There's also a **camp site** at Grímsstaðir.

Isolated **Möðrudalur**, an oasis in the barren desert amid an entanglement of streams, is the highest farm in Iceland at 470m. The bus between Egilsstaðir and Mývatn stops for half an hour at the Fjalla-kaffi snack bar. Across the road is a church with an interesting altarpiece.

The vast **Jökuldalsheiði** moorland, along the Ring Road between Jökuldalur and Möðrudalur, is quite verdant and was farmed until 1875, when the cataclysmic explosion of the Askja caldera displaced its inhabitants.

East Iceland

CONTENTS

East Iceland – particularly the Eastfjords – comes as a charming surprise. It may lack any obvious star attractions, but the dramatic mountain backdrops as you descend into the fjords, the isolated fishing villages that seem to materialise from nowhere, and the peaceful charm of the intermittent farmland combine to give a powerful sense of rural Iceland at work. The Ring Road itself bypasses the best of the fjords and heads inland, so this is the time to leave it and follow the convoluted, occasionally precipitous (but mostly sealed) road along the coast.

Away from the coast, East Iceland can boast the country's largest forest – a source of great pride for tree-starved Icelanders! – and its longest lake, stretching southwest from Egilsstaðir.

Since it's away from the spreading zone along the Mid-Atlantic Ridge, the east is one of Iceland's oldest and most geologically stable regions, and is largely protected from the worst of the North Atlantic weather from the west; in summer it's often cool but clear and locals are fond of saying that if it's raining in Reykjavík it will be fine in Egilsstaðir.

For all its rugged beauty, many travellers pass quickly through East Iceland, eager to get to Mývatn or Skaftafell without having appreciated the appeal of this largely tourist-free corner of the country. Of course, that's what makes it largely tourist-free.

The scenery of the region can be digested in a quick drive through, but if the weather is fine, several days spent exploring, hiking or kayaking in the fjords may be some of your most memorable in Iceland.

Some pretty dramatic changes are about to take place in East Iceland, both environmentally and socially, with the controversial go-ahead for a dam and hydroelectricity plant in the highlands, and an aluminium smelter on Reyðarfjörður – see the boxed text on p245.

TOP FIVE

- Arriving by ferry or descending the spectacular road into **Seyðisfjörður** (p240), East Iceland's most beautiful fjord and friendliest village
- Taking to the calm waters of **Seyðisfjörður** (p242) or **Norðfjörður** (p246) on a guided midnight kayaking trip
- Marvelling at the mineral collection of Petra Sveinsdóttir in **Stöðvarfjörður** (p247)
- Stopping for a meal at cosy Café Margret near **Breiðdalsvík** (p248)
- Bird-watching along the coast and offshore islands – a haven for sea birds such as puffins and kittiwakes; top spots include **Borgarfjörður** (p238), **Skálanes** (p243) and **Norðfjörður** (p246)

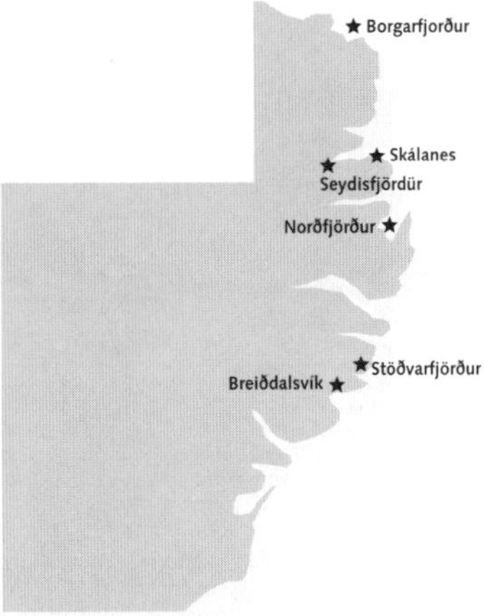

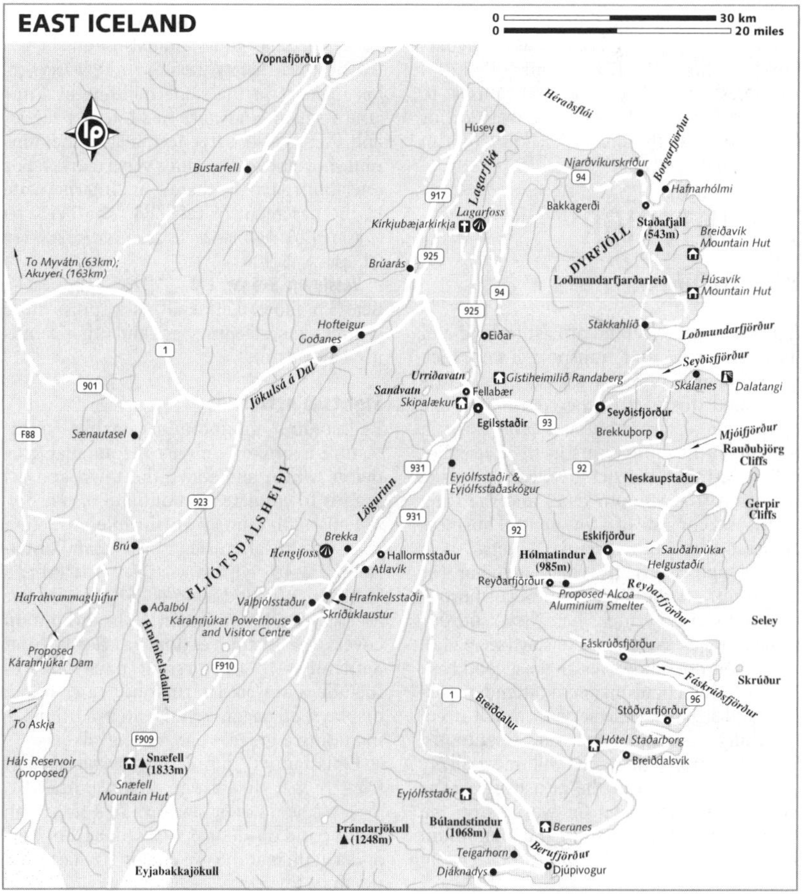

GETTING THERE & AROUND

AIR

In summer **Air Iceland** (☎ 471 1210; www.airiceland.is) flies up to four times daily between Reykjavík and Egilsstaðir (from Ikr6575 one way, one hour), and once or twice a day to/from Akureyri (Ikr6575, 40 minutes). The airport is about 1km north of Egilsstaðir.

BUS

Egilsstaðir is one of the four Ring Road cornerstones, so all buses passes through here. From Akureyri to Egilsstaðir, SBA Norðurleið has a daily bus at 8.30am (Ikr4900, four hours). The return bus to Akureyri via Mývatn (Ikr2000, three hours) departs at 2pm.

From 1 June to 31 August, Austurleið buses run daily from Egilsstaðir to Höfn (Ikr4790, four hours) via Breiðdalsvík (Ikr1950, 2½ hours). Southbound from Egilsstaðir they depart at 2pm; northbound from Höfn they leave at 8.30am. For Seyðisfjörður (Ikr800, 30 minutes), there's a bus from Egilsstaðir at 9.15am weekdays and in summer there's an additional bus on Wednesday, Thursday, Saturday and Sunday at 2.20pm. Coming from Seyðisfjörður it departs at 8.20am weekdays, and in summer at 1.30pm and 4.30pm on Wednesday, Thursday, Saturday and Sunday. Buses connect with the Norröna ferry.

For villages around the fjords, **Austfjarðaleið** (East Iceland Bus Company; ☎ 477 1713;

www.austfjardaleid.is) runs buses daily (except Sunday) between Egilsstaðir and Reyðarfjörður (Ikr720), Eskifjörður (Ikr1200) and Neskaupstaður (Ikr1500). Buses to Fáskrúðsfjörður (Ikr1440), Stöðvarfjörður (Ikr1920) and Breiðdalsvík (Ikr1950) run on weekdays only.

THE INTERIOR

EGILSSTAÐIR

pop 1637

Egilsstaðir is the capital of East Iceland and its commercial and transport hub, which gives you an immediate idea of how lightly populated this part of the country is. The town, which started out as a large farm in the late 19th century, sits in the Lagarfljót valley farming district between the lake Lögurinn (the Smooth One) and the Ring Road, and consists of a tiny central business area and a grid of residential streets.

Although many travellers arriving (or departing) on the ferry from Seyðisfjörður choose to spend a night here, Seyðisfjörður is the more pleasant place to stay (see p242). Egilsstaðir does, however, make a good base for exploring Lögurinn and its attendant forests, and it has all the services you'll need, including a bar and some good restaurants. What's more, Egilsstaðir will most likely undergo a boom over the next five years as the main service town for workers on the hydroelectric power station and aluminium smelter.

Orientation & Information

Egilsstaðir has a twin, **Fellabær**, separated from it by the lake. There are a few places to stay in Fellabær but it's mostly industrial and residential. Once you cross the bridge into Egilsstaðir you'll find the tourist complex, with a petrol station, cafeteria, bus terminal, Landsbanki Íslands bank (with ATM), supermarket and camp site, neatly located in a square block on the Ring Road.

The **tourist office** (Upplýsingamiðstöð; ☎ 471 2320; www.east.is; 🕑 9am-5pm May-Sep except 8am-10pm mid-Jun–mid-Aug) is conveniently central at the camp site and bus terminal. Staff are helpful and there's a display on the Kárahnjúkar hydropower plant, including a film explaining the project and a relief model of the dam site.

The post office is just up the hill on the corner of Selás and Fagradalsbraut.

The town **library** (Laufskógar 1; 🕑 2-7pm Mon-Fri), upstairs in the same building as Minjasafn Austurlands, has free Internet access, and there's also a free terminal in the Simmin shop above the Bonus supermarket. For after-hours email, there's an Internet café in the basement of **Café KHB** (☎ 471 2220; per 15 mins Ikr300; 🕑 8am-1am Thu, 8am-3am Fri, 2pm-3am Sat, 2pm-1am Sun).

Verslunin Skógar (☎ 471 1230; Dynskógum 4), near Fosshótel Valaskjálf, is a sports store selling tents, sleeping bags and other camping equipment.

Sights & Activities

Egilsstaðir's monotonous boxlike architecture is broken only by the angular grey **church**, which sits above the town and attempts to emulate its mountain backdrop.

Egilsstaðir's most worthwhile attraction is the cultural museum, **Minjasafn Austurlands** (☎ 471 1412; www.minjasafn.is in Icelandic; Laufskógar 1; adult/child Ikr400/150; 🕑 11am-5pm Jun-Aug, 1-5pm Mon-Fri Sep-May). The exhibition covers the history of the Eastfjords from Settlement to the present day. Features include a restored farmhouse re-creation, displays of pagan relics and traditions – including a grave – and Viking silver.

Egilsstaðir's impressive **swimming pool** (☎ 471 1866; Tjarnarbraut; adult/child Ikr250/120; 🕑 7am-8.30pm Mon-Fri, 10am-5pm Sat & Sun), with indoor and outdoor pools, saunas, hot pots and a gym, is at the top end of Tjarnarbraut, north of town.

Tours

For horse tours through the spectacular Eastfjords, **Gæðinga Tours** (☎ 471 1727; www.gaedingatours.is), 7km south of Egilsstaðir at Útnyrðingsstaðir, runs a variety of tours, including short rides and a seven-day tour of East Iceland.

Tanni Travel (☎ 476 1399; www.tannitravel.is), based in Eskifjörður, runs a 10-hour tour to Snæfell on Wednesday and Saturday in July and August (Ikr6000 per person without lunch). It includes stops at Hallormsstaður and the hot pool at Laugarvellir, and about a 45-minute stop at Snæfell itself. It also offers hikers transport to and from Snæfell or other areas for groups of five or more with advance notice.

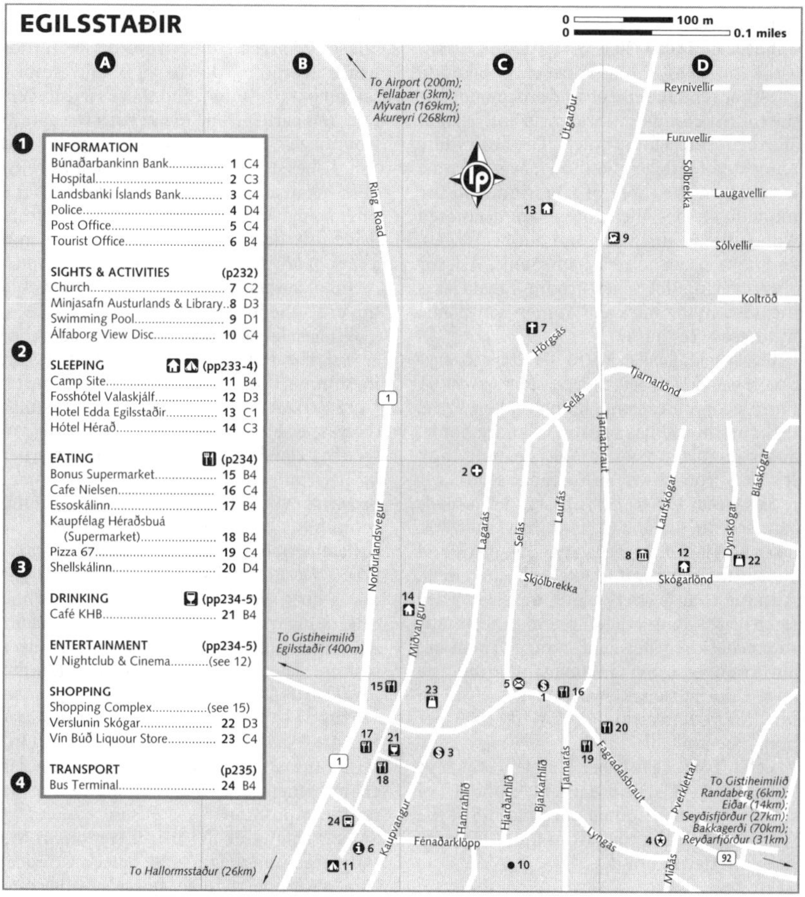

LAKE CRUISES

In summer, the 110-passenger cruise ship **Lagarfljótsormurinn** (☎ 471 2900) sails on the narrow lake Lögurinn. Although there's a terminus for the ferry at the bridge in Fellabær, at the time of writing there were scheduled cruises only from the camp site at Atlavík, 3km south of Hallormsstaður, at 2.30pm and 8.30pm daily. Check with the tourist office to see if scheduled cruises have resumed from Egilsstaðir.

Festivals & Events

Egilsstaðir's annual jazz festival, **Djasshátíð Egilsstaða**, which attracts mainly Icelandic musicians, takes place at Fosshótel Valaskjálf in mid-June. In Eiðar, 14km north, the East Iceland Opera Company hosts **Bright Nights in June**, a two-week series of operas, and classical and choral performances.

Sleeping

BUDGET

Egilsstaðir has no hostel, so most budget travellers wind up at the **camp site** (☎ 471 2320; tent sites per person Ikr550, sb Ikr1500, 5-person hut Ikr6500; all year), which also has a dormitory building. Tent sites are well sheltered and there are cooking facilities.

Skipalækur (☎ 471 1324; per person Ikr550), over the bridge in Fellabær about 4km from Egilsstaðir, also has camping. Showers, the use of a hot pot and cooking facilities are available.

MID-RANGE

Gistiheimilið Egilsstaðir (☎ 471 1114; Egilsstaðir@isholf.is; s/d Ikr8200/12,100) This leafy, lakeside guesthouse, at the end of a side road opposite the tourist complex, oozes style and is a cut above most Icelandic hotels. The beautifully renovated heritage guesthouse has a serene location on the shore of Lögurinn, and the individually designed rooms are decorated with antique furniture and timber floors, and have TVs and new bathrooms. Ask for a west-facing (lake-view) room. Breakfast is included in the rates and dinner is available in the cosy restaurant.

Gistiheimilið Randaberg (☎ 471 1288; randaberg@binet.is; sb/d Ikr2200/6500, cabin per person Ikr1700) A more economical and homely alternative, this guesthouse has beds in a family home, and a couple of basic cabins sleeping four. It's 5km from town on the Eiðar road.

Skipalækur (☎ 471 1324; fax 471 2413; sb/made-up beds per person Ikr1700/2700, d with bathroom Ikr9000, chalets Ikr6800-8500) In Fellabær, this is a good choice for the comfortable, self-contained, A-frame chalets overlooking the lake. They sleep three to six people and have bathroom, basic kitchen and lounge. There are also cramped rooms in the main farmhouse and a no-nonsense owner to keep you in line. Short horse-riding trips (Ikr1500 per hour) are available.

Hotel Edda Egilsstaðir (☎ 444 4880; sb/s/d Ikr2000/8300/10,400) The usual Edda standard of rooms (with bathroom) can be found at the school, across the road from the swimming pool off Tjarnarbraut.

TOP END

Hótel Hérað (☎ 471 1500; herad@icehotel.is; Miðvangur 5; s/d Ikr10,800/15,000) This Icelandair three-star hotel is the plushest in town. Rooms are pretty standard, modern fare with satellite TV, bathroom and buffet breakfast included. There's a small cocktail bar and a flash restaurant.

Fosshótel Valaskjálf (☎ 471 1000; fax 471 1001; Skógarlönd 3; s/d with bathroom Ikr12,100/15,900, without bathroom Ikr6500/8700) Valaskjálf is a slightly decrepit, overpriced summer hotel – an option only if everything else is full.

Eating

Café Nielsen (☎ 471 2626; Tjarnarbraut 1; light meals Ikr650-990, mains Ikr1190-2500; 🕑 11.30am-11pm Sun-Thu, 11.30am-2am Fri & Sat) This great, renovated café-restaurant is in Egilsstaðir's oldest house. It merges somewhere between old-world tearoom (downstairs) and smoky saloon bar (upstairs), and there's a leafy terrace and garden. The menu runs the gamut from bagels, sandwiches, crepes, pasta and fish dishes, to traditional fare such as reindeer meatball casserole (Ikr1990) and the interesting 'Viking Special' (smoked lamb, dried fish, herring, rye bread, potatoes and a shot of *brennivín*; Ikr1950). There's even a menu of authentic Chinese food – probably the only one in East Iceland.

Gistiheimilið Egilsstaðir (☎ 471 1114; Egilsstaðir@isholf.is) The restaurant here is worth a visit in summer for its Icelandic dinner buffet (Ikr2900). At other times it has a regular daily special on the menu, and you can try that classic Icelandic stomach-churner *hákarl* (putrid shark meat) and a shot of *brennivín* (Ikr650) here. The bright dining room has a lovely view over the lake.

Hótel Hérað (☎ 471 1500; Miðvangur 5; mains Ikr2450-2750) A stylish licensed restaurant and a good place for a splurge, with some interesting traditional dishes such as foal fillets, lamb ribs, reindeer steak and reindeer sashimi. There's also a huge breakfast buffet for Ikr850. Ask about daily specials.

Pizza 67 (☎ 471 2424; Lyngás 3; pizzas Ikr700-2000; 🕑 5-11pm Mon-Fri & noon-midnight Sat & Sun) Opposite the Shell petrol station, this popular chain restaurant has a good view from its top-floor position.

Essoskálinn, at the petrol station in the tourist complex, is a dull but economical choice with hearty daily specials of fish and meat dishes (around Ikr1800) as well as the usual fast food.

Self-caterers can rely on the well-stocked Kaupfélag Héraðsbúa (KHB) supermarket in the tourist complex, and the Bonus supermarket in the shopping complex across the road. Both are open daily.

The Vin Buð liquor store is on the ground floor of the office building opposite Bonus supermarket.

Entertainment

Egilsstaðir doesn't have a thriving nightlife, but more places are likely to open to cater for the influx of workers (Icelandic and foreign) on the Kárahnjúkar power project.

Café KHB (☎ 471 2220; Kaupvangi 2; 🕑 8am-1am Thu, 8am-3am Fri, 2pm-3am Sat, 2pm-1am Sun) In the cramped basement of the building opposite the tourist complex, this is the only dedicated bar in town. It doubles as a sports bar when football matches are on (there's a big screen), and as an Internet café. It's a noisy drinking hole on Friday and Saturday nights.

Café Nielsen (471 2626; Tjarnarbraut 1; 11.30am-11pm Sun-Thu, 11.30am-2am Fri & Sat) The 1st-floor lounge here is a good place for a drink.

V is a tatty, darkened nightclub and disco attached to the Fosshótel Valaskjálf, which attracts the youth of Egilsstaðir on summer weekends. There's also a cinema here.

Getting There & Away

Egilsstaðir is the transport hub of East Iceland, with an airport (1km north of town) and all bus services passing through here (see p231).

The Ring Road naturally passes through Egilsstaðir, but if you want to explore the Eastfjords you need to leave it here. Route 94 takes you north to Borgarfjörður, Route 93 goes east to Seyðisfjörður, and Route 92 goes south to Reyðarfjörður and the rest of the fjord towns.

Getting Around

Car rental is available from **Europcar** (471 3171; Laugarbraut 4) in Fellabær, and from **Avis** (861 9043; Miðás 23). Both have agents at the airport. You can hire bicycles at the tourist office for Ikr600/1000/1500 per six/12/24 hours.

LAGARFLJÓT

The 'Smooth River', Lagarfljót, starts its journey in the Vatnajökull icecap and flows north to the Arctic Ocean. For much of its length, it widens into the 38km-long narrow lake **Lögurinn**. Like Loch Ness, Lögurinn is reputed to harbour its very own resident monster, Lagarfljótsormurinn ('serpent of Lagarfljót'), which is said to put in an occasional appearance.

From Egilsstaðir a sealed road (Route 931) follows the lake southwards to a bridge crossing. A mostly gravel road then heads northeast along the western shore to Fellabær. Using this route you can make an interesting 56km circuit of the lake in an afternoon. There's no regular public transport along here and traffic is very light on the western shore if you're planning on hitching. On the eastern side of the lake you'll notice it's pretty woolly with birch and fir trees – this is East Iceland's forest belt and that alone is a big attraction for Icelanders.

Eyjólfsstaðaskógur

This small forested area lies just east of the Ring Road, 11km south of Egilsstaðir. As forests go, it's pretty comical – more like a patch of oversized Christmas trees. Still, there's a picnic site and 3.5km of leafy walking tracks to a couple of nice waterfalls. About 1km north of the forest turn-off, on the lake side of the road, **Eyjólfsstaðir** (471 1732; eyjolf@isholf.is; sb/s/d Ikr1900/4000/5900) has spacious rooms in two farmhouse buildings.

Hallormsstaður

When Icelanders talk longingly of their forest, this is what they mean. Believe it or not, Iceland has a forestry commission and Hallormsstaður, on the eastern shore of Lögurinn, is its showcase. In addition to protecting the native dwarf birch and mountain ash, it has planted many species, including Alaskan poplar and Siberian larch. Much of the forest is laid out in neatly ordered rows, but tree-starved Icelanders still flock to it and everyone appreciates the leafy reprieve. Don't miss Iceland's oldest tree, Guttormslundur, 2.5km south of Fosshótel Hallormsstaður, which was planted in 1938 and has now attained the whopping height of nearly 20m!

Formerly a large farm, Hallormsstaður encompasses 800 hectares. It was once the home of Guðmundur Magnússon, Iceland's prominent 18th-century publisher and translator.

You can hire pedal boats, rowing boats or canoes or arrange horse-riding tours from **Fljótsbátar** (471 1763; 10am-10pm Jun-Aug) at Atlavík.

Down the hill, close to the lakeshore at Atlavík, is a beautiful **camp site** (per person Ikr550), which is very popular with Icelanders during summer and is often the scene of raucous parties on summer weekends.

Skriðuklaustur

About 5km south of the bridge across the lake, **Skriðuklaustur** (471 2990; www.austurland.is/skriduklaustur; adult/child Ikr500/free; 10am-6pm, 10am-10pm Wed in July) was the site of a monastery from 1493 until the Reformation, when it was demolished by order of the Danish king, and a church until 1792. The unusual, turf-roofed stone building you see now was built in 1939 by Icelandic writer Gunnar Gunnarsson. It's now used as a cultural and research centre on Gunnarsson and his works.

Even if you don't find time to visit the museum and cultural centre, the downstairs Klausturkaffi serves wonderful lunches, including a superb coffee-and-cake buffet (Ikr890) on weekends, with all-you-can-eat sweet and savoury cakes. The lunch buffet is Ikr1290.

Valþjófsstaður

The unassuming church at Valþjófsstaður, at the head of Lögurinn and 7km south of the first bridge across the lake, is worth a look. The door, depicting an ancient battle scene, is a replica of the famous original, which was carved at Valþjófsstaður around 1200 and is displayed at the National Museum in Reykjavík.

Hengifoss

Hengifoss (Hanging Falls) is Iceland's third-highest waterfall, and once you've made the climb up and into the canyon, you'll experience the sound this unforgettable dynamo makes, it's like a Boeing 747 taking off as the water plummets 120m into a brown-and-red–striped boulder-strewn gorge.

To get to Hengifoss requires a return walk of about 1½ hours. From the parking area on Route 933, about 200m south of the bridge across the lake, a well-defined path leads up the hillside – Hengifoss is soon visible in the distance. It's a steep climb up in places, but flattens out as you enter the gorge. Halfway up is a smaller waterfall, **Lítlanesfoss**, which is surrounded by spectacular vertical basalt columns in a honeycomb formation.

NORTH OF EGILSSTAÐIR

From Egilsstaðir/Fellabær, Lagarfljót flows northwards before joining up with Jökulsá á Dal and emptying into the ocean at the bight Héraðsflói in a series of delta streams across the *sandur* (black sand deltas). There's not as much to see here as there is south of Egilsstaðir; the roads are rougher, and unless you're heading up to Borgarfjörður or the youth hostel at Husey, most travellers will give this region a miss. If you do have time to explore, there's some good scenery at the northern end, where the broad *sandur*, sandwiched between the mountains, forms an intriguing landscape of sand dunes, basalt outcrops, river deltas and marshes.

There's no regular public transport here, but with your own vehicle you could do a loop drive along routes 94 and 925.

Eiðar

Eiðar, 14km north of Egilsstaðir, was the farm of Helgi Ásbjarnarson, grandson of Hrafnkell Freysgoði. The **church**, built in 1887, contains an interesting statue of Christ that washed up on the shore at Héraðssandur, north of Eiðar. Its location beside a popular trout lake, Eiðavatn, makes it especially appealing for anglers.

Hotel Edda Eiðar (☎ 444 4870; sb Ikr1500-2000, s/d Ikr4900/6200) In the local school just off the Egilsstaðir–Borgarfjörður road, this summer hotel has a swimming pool and licensed restaurant.

Lagarfoss

The Lagarfoss falls are actually a long, turbulent chute along a small tributary of Lagarfljót, where a power plant is fed by a 6m drop in one small channel. The main point of interest is the fish ladder, where jumping salmon may be seen from late July to late August. The falls are close to the road on Route 944.

Kirkjubæjarkirkja

Kirkjubæjarkirkja, 3km west of Lagarfoss, is one of the oldest wooden churches in Iceland, built in 1851 and restored to its original condition in 1980. It has the oldest pulpit in the country (dating from around 1590), and also contains beautiful paintings of biblical figures, including St Peter and King David.

Húsey

The only reason to venture out to the isolated farm at Húsey, near the shores of Héraðsflói, is to stay at the friendly **Húsey HI Hostel** (☎ 471 3010; husey@binet.is; dm members/nonmembers Ikr1500/1950). Apart from the sheer isolation and the stark but beautiful surroundings, this is a great spot to observe geese, wading birds and seals (the farmers hunt, tan and eat them) – more than 30 bird species breed at Húsey. If you don't have a vehicle, the wardens might pick up pre-booked guests (for a fee) from Egilsstaðir or the Brúarás bridge. There are cooking facilities at the hostel but nowhere to buy food, so bring supplies.

JÖKULSÁ Á DAL

The name of this 150km-long river means 'Glacial River of the Valley', and each hour this silty and turbulent watercourse deposits in Héraðsflói nearly one tonne of Icelandic real estate for each kilometre of its length.

For part of its journey from the Vatnajökull icecap to the sea it follows the Ring Road, and this stretch is said to be haunted by mischievous leprechauns and bloodthirsty Norse deities.

The outcrop called **Goðanes**, about 3km west of the farm Hofteigur, was the site of an ancient pagan temple where some ruins are still visible. The iron-stained spring **Blóðkelda** (Blood Spring) carries an apocryphal legend that the blood of both human and animal sacrifices once flowed into it.

Beside the lake Sænautavatn, 32km west of Hofteigur and 3.5km south of the Ring Road via Route 907, is the reconstructed turf farmhouse **Sænautasel** (☎ 855 5399, 471 1086), which dates from 1843. It's open daily to the public.

The tributary valley of **Hrafnkelsdalur**, south of the Jökulsá á Dal, is bursting with Saga Age ruins, though you'd have to be a real saga buff to venture out here. The farm **Aðalból** was the home of Hrafnkell Hallfreðarson Freysgoði, the priest of Freyr and hero of the popular *Hrafnkels Saga* (see the boxed text below). The 4WD track (F910) past Aðalból offers an alternative route to Snæfell.

EAST ICELAND

HRAFNKELS SAGA

The saga of Hrafnkell, a priest of the god Freyr, is one of Iceland's most popular sagas. The story is particularly interesting because its premises seem to derail any modern notions of right, wrong and justice served.

The main character, Hrafnkell, was a religious fanatic who built a temple to Freyr on the farm Aðalból in Hrafnkelsdalur. Hrafnkell's prized stallion, Freyfaxi ('the mane of Freyr'), was his treasured possession, and he swore to the gods to strike down anyone who dared ride him without permission. As might be expected, someone did. It seems the stallion himself tempted one of Hrafnkell's shepherds into riding him to find a herd of lost sheep. Discovering this, Hrafnkell wasted no time taking his axe to the errant youth.

In a moment of belated conscience, he offered the boy's father, Þorbjörn, compensation for the loss of his son in the form of foodstuffs and financial help. Proudly, the man refused, and the characters were launched into a court battle that ultimately led to Hrafnkell being declared an outlaw, but he chose to ignore the sentence and return home.

He didn't have long to wait before Þorbjörn's nephew Sámur Bjarnason took the matter into his own hands. Hrafnkell was summarily subjected to the particularly painful and humiliating Norse custom of stringing enemies up by their Achilles tendons until they were prepared to make enough concessions to their torturers.

Hrafnkell gave up his estates and his priestly authority as a result of the experience. His temple was destroyed and the hapless Freyfaxi was weighted with stones, thrown over a cliff and drowned in the water below. Hrafnkell, by now convinced that his favourite god didn't give two hoots about his predicament, renounced his beliefs and relocated to a new farm beside Lagarfljót, which he called Hrafnkelsstaðir. He vowed to reform his vengeful character and become a kind and simple farmer. So great was his success with the new farm, however, that he gained even more wealth and power than he'd had at Aðalból and it appeared as though history was fated to repeat itself.

One day, Sámur and his brother Eyvindur came by en route to Aðalból. As they passed Hrafnkelsstaðir, Hrafnkell's maid saw them and reminded her employer of his responsibility to take his revenge. Something snapped in Hrafnkell. Abandoning his vow to reform, he set out in pursuit of the troublesome brothers and made quick work of dispatching Eyvindur before tackling Sámur and forcing him to flee the ill-gotten Aðalból. Hrafnkell thus regained his former estates and, as far as anyone knows, lived there happily ever after.

SNÆFELL

The 1833m-high extinct volcano Snæfell (Snow Mountain) is Iceland's highest peak outside the Vatnajökull massif, and its relative accessibility makes it popular with hikers and mountaineers. Snæfell looms over the southern end of Fljótsdalsheiði (River Valley Moors), an expanse of spongy tussocks of wet tundra, boulder fields, perennial snow patches and alpine lakes, stretching westwards from Lögurinn into the interior.

Access to Snæfell is strictly by 4WD, and only for two months at the height of summer. Along the way, watch for wild – albeit introduced – reindeer. At the base of the peak, at 800m elevation, is the **Snæfell mountain hut**, accommodating up to 62 people. Beds and use of cooking facilities cost Ikr1200/1700 for Ferðafélag Íslands members/nonmembers.

Although climbing the mountain itself is not difficult for experienced, well-prepared hikers, weather can be a concern and technical equipment is required.

Tanni Travel (☎ 476 1399; www.tannitravel.is) runs a 10-hour tour to Snæfell on Wednesday and Saturday in July and August (Ikr6000 per person without lunch). It includes a 45-minute stop at Snæfell itself. The tour leaves from Egilsstaðir camp site at 9.30am.

Snæfell–Lónsöræfi Trek

One of Iceland's most challenging and rewarding treks takes you from Snæfell to the Lónsöræfi district in Southeast Iceland. The five-day route begins at the Snæfell hut and heads across the glacier Eyjabakkajökull (an arm of Vatnajökull) to Geldingafell, Egilssel and Múlaskáli huts before dropping down to the coast at Stafafell.

This route should not be approached lightly – it's for experienced trekkers only. You'll need good route-finding skills and, for the glacier crossing, you must be able to use a compass and have a rope, crampons and ice axe. If you're unsure of your skills, you'd be much wiser doing the trip commercially with Ferðafélag Íslands.

Advance hut bookings are advised for July and August. Contact **Ferðafélag Íslands** (☎ 568 2533; www.fi.is; Mörkin 6, IS-108 Reykjavík).

You'll need the following topo sheets for walking in this region: *Hornafjörður* 1:100,000 (1986), *Hamarsfjörður* 1:100,000 (1987) and *Snæfell* 1:100,000 (1988).

THE EASTFJORDS

The convoluted Eastfjords are the highlight of this corner of Iceland. Although not as wide nor as rugged as their counterparts in Northwest Iceland, the surrounding mountains loom higher, offering dramatic views, and good roads make them easily accessible. Small fishing villages provide the base for hiking and kayaking, and thousands of sea birds nest along the cliffs and offshore islands.

Most travellers stick to the route between Egilsstaðir and Höfn, which takes in a handful of southern fjords, but the most dramatic scenery is in the north. Try not to miss Seyðisfjörður and Neskaupstaður, both reached by spectacular mountain roads.

The following section is organised from north to south.

BORGARFJÖRÐUR EYSTRI

pop 146

The most northerly of the Eastfjords, Borgarfjörður Eystri (the tiny village itself is also known as Bakkagerði) is a stunning location, framed by a backdrop of rugged rhyolite peaks on one side and the spectacular Dyrfjöll mountains on the other. Half the fun is getting here, with Route 94 winding steeply over the Vatnsskarð mountains before dropping down to the coast. The main reason to come here is to hike in the surrounding hills – there's very little in the village itself.

There's **tourist information** (☎ 472 9977; alfasteinn@alfasteinn.is) at the Álfasteinn rock shop.

Sights & Activities

The touristy rock shop **Álfasteinn** (Elf Stone; www.alfasteinn.is in Icelandic; 🕑 10am-6pm Jun-Aug, 11am-5pm Sep-May) does a booming business collecting semiprecious stones, polishing them up, gluing them into kitsch shapes and selling them at premium prices. However, there's a reasonable local mineral collection, including petrified wood from Loðmundarfjörður. Out the front is a 2250kg piece of raw jasper, the biggest found in Iceland.

Iceland's best-known artist, Jóhannes S Kjarval, who lived at the nearby farm Geitavík, took much of his inspiration from Borgarfjörður Eystri. The **Kjarval Room** (☎ 472 9950; www.kjarvalsstofa.is; adult/child Ikr500/

free; ⏰ noon-6pm Jun-Aug), next to Fjarðarborg, is an exhibition of some of his works and a collection of bits and pieces associated with his life. A source of pride in the village is the beautiful altarpiece in its small **church** – a Kjarval painting depicting the Sermon on the Mount with Dyrfjöll in the background and a typically Icelandic sky above.

Also in the village, you can't help but notice the bright red, turf-covered home **Lindarbakki**. The original building dates from 1899 but has been restored and is now used as a private home during summer, so it's not open to the public.

Álfaborg (Elf Rock), the small mound and nature reserve near the camp site, is the 'borg' that gave Borgarfjörður Eystri its name. From the view disc on top, there's a fabulous vista of the surrounding fields, which, in summer, turn white with blooming arctic cotton. Locals believe that the queen of Icelandic elves lived here. Borgarfjörður Eystri's main festival, **Elf Dance**, held on the weekend nearest 6 January, involves a bonfire and candle-lit procession led by the elf king and queen (with attendants), singing traditional elf songs.

At the end of the road, 5km northeast of Borgarfjörður Eystri, is the small boat harbour and the islet **Hafnarhólmi** (connected to the mainland by causeway), which has a puffin colony with 10,000 pairs. There are also kittiwakes, fulmars and eiders. The viewing platform is open from 10am to 7pm daily in June and July (free) and at all times in August. Back in the village there's a small **bird-watching hide** behind the general store.

Tours

Skúli Sveinsson at **Borg Travel Services** (☎ 472 9870, 854 4470; gisting-borg@visir.is) runs 4WD tours and transports hikers and luggage to trail heads.

Sleeping & Eating

There's not much choice in remote Borgarfjörður Eystri. The free **camp site** is beside the church.

Borg (☎ 472 9870, 854 4470; gisting-borg@visir.is; sb/s/d Ikr1900/3500/6000) This is the best bet for accommodation since the owner has rooms in three houses in the village. The houses are OK, with cooking and lounge facilities – it's just that the dead insect problem is really off-putting!

Fjarðarborg community centre (☎ 472 9920; bergrunj@mi.is; sb Ikr1800) In summer, there's basic sleeping-bag accommodation here. There's also a simple restaurant at Fjarðarborg, but otherwise self-catering is the only way to avoid starvation. The KHB general store by the pier sells groceries.

Getting There & Away

The only public transport to Borgarfjörður Eystri is the **postal van** (☎ 472 9805) from Egilsstaðir on weekdays except Wednesday. About half of the 70km road (Route 94) from Egilsstaðir is sealed, and gravel sections, including the climb up and over the mountain, are in good condition.

AROUND BORGARFJÖRÐUR EYSTRI

There are lots of mountain walks within easy reach. For a short scramble amid rhyolite peaks, walk around the estuary to Geitfell and Svartfell. However, in nonvegetated areas, note that the unconsolidated material makes for an experience akin to walking on thousands of tiny ball bearings.

The colourful rhyolite peak **Staðarfjall** (543m) rises 8km southeast of Borgarfjörður Eystri and makes a nice day walk. The best access is up the ridge from Desjamýri farm, across the estuary from Borgarfjörður Eystri.

Dyrfjöll

One of Iceland's most dramatic ranges, the Dyrfjöll mountains rise precipitously to an altitude of 1136m between the Lagarfljót Valley and Borgarfjörður Eystri. The name means 'Door Mountain' and is due to the large and conspicuous notch in the highest peak – an Icelandic counterpart to Sweden's famous Lapporten. There are two walking tracks crossing the range, allowing day hikes or longer routes from Borgarfjörður Eystri.

Stórurð (the name means 'big area covered with boulders'), on the western flank of Dyrfjöll, is an extraordinary place scattered with huge rocks and small glacial ponds. It can be reached in 2½ hours from just west of the pass on the road to Egilsstaðir (Route 94).

Njarðvíkurskriður

Njarðvíkurskriður, a dangerous scree slope along Route 94 near Njarðvík, was a habitual site of accidents in ancient times. All the tragedies were blamed on a nuisance creature (half man, half beast), Naddi, who dwelt in a sea-level cave beneath the slope.

In the early 1300s, Naddi was exorcised by the proper religious authorities, and in 1306 a cross was erected on the site bearing the inscription 'Effigiem Christi qui transis pronus honora, Anno MCCCVI' – 'You who are hurrying past, honour the image of Christ – AD 1306'. The idea was that travellers would repeat a prayer when passing the danger zone and therefore be protected from malevolent powers. The cross has been replaced several times since, but the current one still bears the original prayer.

LOÐMUNDARFJARÐARLEIÐ

The relatively little-known mountain route between Borgarfjörður Eystri and Loðmundarfjörður is one of those obscure hikes that is sure to increase in popularity in coming years. It follows a 4WD track up over the pass and opens up lots of opportunities to explore the pristine surroundings. The required topo sheet is *Dyrfjöll* (1:100,000 1986). For 4WD transport to the trail heads or huts, contact Skúli Sveinsson at Borg Travel Services (see p239).

The route begins at the farm Hvannstöð, 7km south of Borgarfjörður Eystri, and continues for 20km over Húsavíkurheiði (477m). You can either descend along the side track to the small bay of Húsavík or continue south to the deserted fjord, Loðmundarfjörður. From there, the route follows the historic 20km bridle path up Hjálmárdalur and across Hjalmardalsheiði to Seyðisfjörður.

A more direct route leads due south from Hvannstöð, across the mountains to Loðmundarfjörður, via the strange **Álfakirkjan** (Elf Church), a huge, house-shaped rock.

The shallow bay **Breiðavík** has a deep valley and a Ferðafélag Íslands hut, reached by 4WD track from the head of Borgarfjörður or a hiking trail from Húsavíkurheiði. The valley isn't on the direct Loðmundarfjarðarleið route, but it makes a fine side trip.

At the **Neshals pass**, between Víkurá and Loðmundarfjörður, the track reaches an altitude of 435m. Just west is the peak **Skælingur** (832m), sometimes called the 'Chinese temple'.

Loðmundarfjörður

This short but beautiful fjord was once well settled, and at least six farms occupied the upper basin. However, after the coastal supply boats stopped running, construction of all-season roads into such sparsely populated outposts became uneconomical and the region was finally abandoned in 1973.

The entire valley is now deserted except for the friendly farm **Stakkahlíð** (☎ 472 1510; fax 472 1590; sb/made-up beds Ikr1800/2500), at the head of Loðmundarfjörður. If you've hiked this far, the warm welcome, hot showers and cooking facilities cannot be overestimated! There's also a **camp site** (per person Ikr500).

From Loðmundarfjarðarleið it's a six- to eight-hour walk south to Seyðisfjörður, where there are plenty of facilities and buses back to Egilsstaðir.

SEYÐISFJÖRÐUR

pop 804

If you visit only one town in the Eastfjords, this should be it. The village, at the head of a deep, 16km-long fjord and wedged in on three sides by imposing mountains, is the most historically and architecturally interesting in East Iceland. It's also a friendly place with a gregarious and bohemian community of artists, musicians and craftspeople.

Sadly for Seyðisfjörður, the fish-processing plant – a significant part of the local economy – closed in 2003. Since this is the terminal for the Smyril Line ferry from the European mainland, a steady flow of travellers passes through here, and tourism is a growing industry.

The road from Egilsstaðir into Seyðisfjörður is a scenic drive, following the river Fjarðará, which has 25 large waterfalls. The town website is www.sfk.is (in Icelandic).

History

Seyðisfjörður started around 1848 as a trading centre and later a herring fishery and, thanks to its sheltering fjord, grew over the following decades into East Iceland's largest settlement. During this period of prosperity, most of its beautiful and unique wooden buildings were constructed by Norwegian settlers, who came for fishing opportunities.

During WWII, Seyðisfjörður was used as a base for British and American forces, but the only attack was upon the oil tanker *Grillo*, which was bombed by three German warplanes. The bombs missed their target, but one exploded so near that the ship sank to the bottom, where it remains to this day.

GRANT DIXON

Seyðisfjörður–Vestdalur hike (p242), East Iceland

GRANT DIXON

Skeiðarársandur (p263), Southeast Iceland

GRAEME CORNWALLIS

St Nicholas church (p263), Núpsstaður farm, Southeast Iceland

Jökulsárlón (p269), Southeast Iceland

GRANT DIXON

GRA

Landmannalaugar–Þórsmörk trek (p256), Southeast Iceland

Askja caldera (p286), Interior

DEANNA SWANEY

GRAEME CORNWALLIS

Kverkfjöll ice caves (p288), Interior

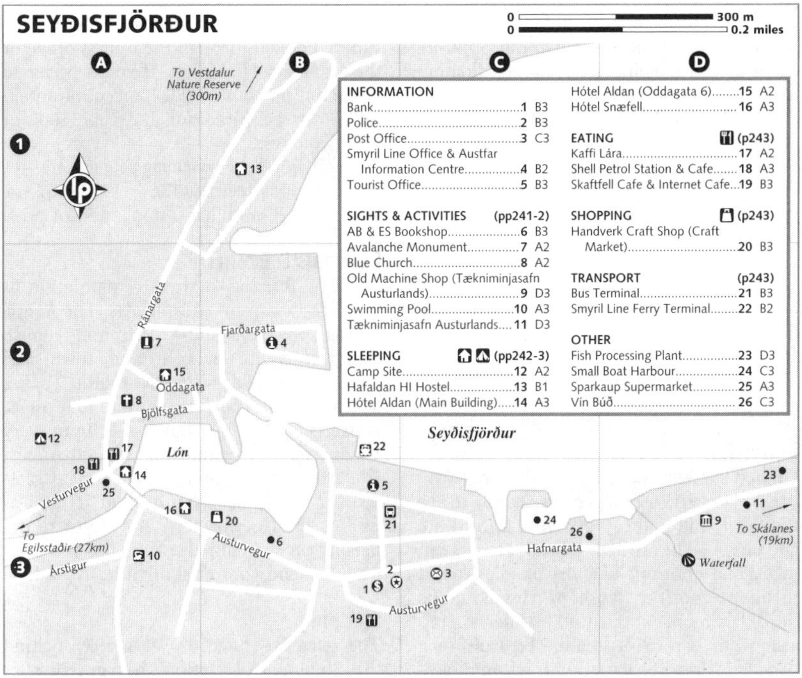

Seyðisfjörður's steep-sided valley has made it prone to avalanches. In 1885 an avalanche from Mt Bjólfur killed 24 people, pushing several houses straight into the fjord. A more recent avalanche in 1996 flattened a local factory but no lives were lost. The **avalanche monument** near the church is made from twisted girders from the factory, painted white and erected as they were found.

Information

The **tourist office** (☎ 472 1119; 8am-noon & 1-5pm Mon-Fri), in the modern ferry terminal building, sells bus passes and books onward accommodation, and the **Austfar Information Centre** (☎ 472 1111), in the old Smyril Line building at the ferry dock, also has information for the benefit of arriving ferry passengers.

The **bank** (9.15am-12.30pm & 1.30-4pm Mon-Fri) can get crowded when the ferry arrives, but there's also an ATM at the Shell petrol station.

There's Internet access at the **Skaftafell Cultural Centre** (☎ 472 1632; Austurvegur 42; Ikr150 for 30 min). AB & ES Bookshop, on Austurvegur, sells books, maps and postcards.

Sights

Seyðisfjörður is crammed with historic timber **buildings**, most dating from the late 19th century and brought here in kit form from Norway by merchants, traders and fishermen. The excellent brochure *Historic Seyðisfjörður* (Ikr300), available from the tourist office, provides a detailed walk through the town.

The town's cluttered historical museum is **Tækniminjasafn Austurlands** (☎ 472 1596; Hafnargata 44; adult/child Ikr400/free; 11am-6pm Jun–mid-Sep), housed in two buildings a short distance apart on Hafnargata: the impressive 1894 home of ship-owner Otto Wathne (also home to the municipal offices), and the old machine shop, built in 1907. Seyðisfjörður was very much at the cutting edge of Iceland's technology, workmanship and telecommunications in the 19th century – the first submarine telephone cable linking Iceland with Europe was brought ashore here in 1906 (incidentally, the new fibre-optic cable arrived here in 2003). The museum charts this history with displays of old machinery, photographs, and a re-creation of the original telegraph station, foundry and machine shop. An old fishing boat in the harbour opposite the museum is being restored as a floating addition to the collection.

The **Skaftafell Cultural Centre** (☎ 472 1632; Austurvegur 42) is the place to 'hang out' in Seyðisfjörður. It's a meeting place for local artists and musicians with a very bohemian vibe. Upstairs is a spacious gallery of changing exhibitions, and occasional concerts and poetry readings are held here.

Upriver from the town centre, 15 minutes on foot, is the **Fjarðarsel hydroelectric power station**. This remnant of modern technology 1913-style is one of the oldest in the world still in use. Free guided tours are available on request – contact the tourist office.

Activities

Guided **kayaking trips** (☎ 865 3741; ferdamenning@skf.is; ½hr trips Ikr1500/2500) are a great way to see the fjord, and you can get close to bird life and possibly the resident seals. Beginners can take a one-hour introductory paddle around the *lón* (lagoon) or two-hour trips along the fjord. For more experienced paddlers there's also a day trip to Austdalur (Ikr8500) or a two-day trip to Skálanes with accommodation and meals included (Ikr17,000).

Guided **mountain-bike tours** (2hr, Ikr2000) with the same guide (Hlynur Oddssen) are also available in summer. These trips can be booked through the tourist office or the Hafaldan HI Hostel. If you'd prefer to strike out on your own, 24-speed mountain bikes can be hired for Ikr2500/3400 for one/two days.

Seyðisfjörður's **swimming pool** (☎ 472 1414; Suðurgata 5; adult/child Ikr260/130; 🕒 7-9.30am & 2-9pm Mon-Fri, 11am-4pm Sat) has a pool and hot pots.

Festivals & Events

Seyðisfjörður has a growing reputation as a centre for music and the arts. The **Á Seyði festival** runs from mid-June to mid-August. Exhibitions are held around town and concerts are held in the **Blue Church**. There's also a series of classical, jazz and folk-music concerts in the Blue Church at 8.30pm every Wednesday from mid-June to mid-August (Ikr1000). This popular program attracts visiting musicians from around Iceland as well as local performers, and if you're departing on the Thursday ferry this is a great way to spend your final night in Iceland.

Sleeping

The **camp site** (☎ 861 3097; sites Ikr500), behind the Shell petrol station, has grassy sites separated by neat shrubs. Note that camping isn't permitted in Vestdalur or anywhere along the roads.

SEYÐISFJÖRÐUR–VESTDALUR HIKE

A wonderful introduction to hiking in Iceland will take you up through the **Vestdalur Nature Reserve** and around Mt Bjólfur down to the Seyðisfjörður–Egilsstaðir road.

Start by walking up the road past the HI hostel to where a rough 4WD track takes off up the glacial valley to your left. The track peters out after a few hundred metres, but keep walking uphill, along the left side of the Vestdalsá river. After a couple of hours and several tiers of glorious waterfalls, you'll arrive at a small lake, **Vestdalsvatn**, which remains frozen most of the year. Here you'll see **Mt Bjólfur** to your left.

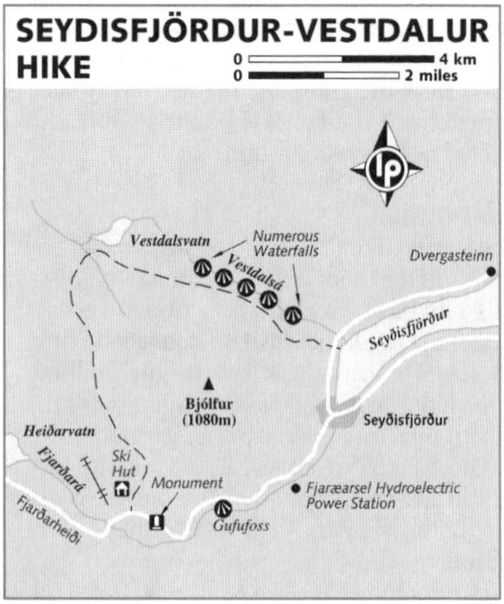

From the lake, bear left and make your way westwards over the tundra, through the snowfields and past a small ski hut to the highway. From there, hitch to either Seyðisfjörður or Egilsstaðir. If you do hitch, please take the usual precautions; see p314 for more details. The trip can also be done in the opposite direction – and more easily because most of it is downhill.

Hafaldan HI Hostel (☎ 472 1410; thorag@simnet.is; Ránargata 9; dm members/nonmembers Ikr1550/1900, s/d Ikr2800/4800) This clean, cosy hostel is the best place to relax and meet other travellers. The bright common room catches the morning sun and overlooks the harbour, and there's a well-equipped kitchen, a laundry and a TV room with videos. Book ahead if you're arriving on Wednesday when the ferry comes in.

Hótel Aldan (☎ 472 1277, 472 1610; hotelaldan@simnet.is; Norðurgata 2 & Oddagata 6; s/d with bathroom Ikr11,800/15,800, without bathroom Ikr6500/8700) Probably the best heritage hotel in East Iceland, friendly Aldan is a boutique guesthouse in two historic buildings. The main building, with the reception and café, has five simple, compact rooms with shared bathroom, but the best rooms are in the former bank (dating from 1887) at Oddagata 6. The exotic rooms here are spacious and furnished with antiques, bedspreads and rugs from India. Modern touches include minibars and TVs with DVD players, but it's the little things like stained floorboards and alcoves with Rajasthani cushions that stand out.

Hótel Snæfell (☎ 472 1460; fax 472 1570; Austurvegur 2; sb/s/d Ikr2000/6000/8000) This hotel, built in 1908, may have once been grand, but these days it's run-down and neglected. There's a good restaurant overlooking the lagoon.

Eating & Drinking

Skaftafell Café (☎ 472 1632; Austurvegur 42; light meals Ikr450-1100, mains Ikr2000-3500; 🕑 11am-10pm, till 1am Fri & Sat; 💻) The bistro-bar is a great place to dine or to linger over coffee and a good book. The seafood soup (Ikr900) is something special and there's a great range of seafood, including local mussels, tuna and lobster. Light meals include toast with caviar, omelette, and waffles and cream.

Hótel Aldan (☎ 472 1277; Norðurgata 2; mains Ikr800-3000; 🕑 7am-9.30pm) The chic restaurant-bar offers a mix of casual and stylish dining. There's a spectacular breakfast buffet here served from 7am (Ikr1100), with home-baked bread and fresh fruit along with the usual breakfast fare. Coffee, cakes, sandwiches and desserts such as blueberry *skyr* (a kind of yoghurt) are served all day and there are fish and meat specials for dinner.

Kaffi Lára (☎ 472 1703; Norðgata 3) Opposite the Shell petrol station, this cooperative gift shop serves coffee, tea, cakes and snacks in quaint, doily-covered surroundings.

If all else fails, the snack bar at the Shell petrol station does hot dogs, sandwiches and other quick eats.

The **Sparakaup supermarket** (🕑 Mon-Sat) is opposite the petrol station and there's a Vín Búð liquor store on Hafnargata.

Shopping

An art and craft market that began as a twice-weekly event for ferry passengers is now held every weekday in summer from 1pm to 6pm and 8am to 6pm on Thursday. It's held at the Handverk craft shop.

Getting There & Away

BUS

There's at least one bus to/from Egilsstaðir (Ikr800, 30 minutes) daily in summer. The bus from Seyðisfjörður departs at 8.20am weekdays, and in summer at 1.30pm and 4.30pm on Wednesday, Thursday, Saturday and Sunday. From Egilsstaðir it departs at 9.15am weekdays, and in summer there's an additional bus on Wednesday, Thursday, Saturday and Sunday at 2.20pm.

BOAT

From May to early September, the Smyril Line ferry *Norröna* arrives from Esbjerg (Denmark), Tórshavn (the Faroe Islands), Lerwick (Shetland) and Bergen (Norway) at 8am on Thursday and departs for Tórshavn and Esbjerg at noon. For more information see p308, or check the website www.smyril-line.fo.

AROUND SEYÐISFJÖRÐUR

Skálanes

About 19km east of Seyðisfjörður, **Skálanes** (☎ 868 9058; camping/sb Ikr500/1900; 🕑 Jun-early Sep) is a remote farm on the edge of the fjord that now operates as a summer guesthouse. It can be used as a staging point for the long hike around to Mjóifjörður, but the main attraction is the abundance of bird life and isolated location. Meals can be arranged and there are cooking facilities if you bring your own food.

To get here, walk the 9km from Seyðisfjörður along Hafnargata to where the road ends. From there it's another 10km hike along a 4WD track to Skálanes. With a 4WD vehicle you can drive the whole way. Another option is the kayak or mountain-bike trips offered by Hlynur Oddssen (see p242). It's another 19km (five- to six-hour hike) around to the farm Sólbrekka in Mjóifjörður.

MJÓIFJÖRÐUR

pop 35

The next fjord south of Seyðisfjörður, Mjóifjörður (Narrow Fjord), flanked on both sides by spectacular **cliffs**, lies well off the worn tourist circuit. The several abandoned **turf farmsteads** (hard to find), the site of the early-20th-century **Norwegian whaling station** at Asknes and the 19th-century **wooden church** at Brekkuþorp are worth visiting, but the best-known attraction is the ruin of the **Dalatangi light**, Iceland's first lighthouse. The new lighthouse and the nearby vegetable and flower gardens are also of interest.

Sólbrekka (☎ 476 0007; fax 476 0019; sb/s/d Ikr1900/4000/6000; 🕑 1 Jun-25 Aug) At Brekkuþorp, this is the one and only place to stay around here and it comes as a welcome sight for hikers. There's also a camp site out back, but you can camp almost anywhere along the fjord.

REYÐARFJÖRÐUR

pop 650

Back on the sealed road (Route 92 from Egilsstaðir), Reyðarfjörður sits at the head of the largest fjord on the east coast. It's a relatively new settlement, having become a trading port early in the 20th century, and is not as pretty as some fjord towns. During WWII it was one of several Allied bases in Iceland, evidence of which remains today. Its current claim to fame – or notoriety – is that it's the site for the controversial Alcoa aluminium smelter, to be built on the fjord about 3km northeast of the village, starting in 2005.

Sights & Activities

Above the fjord, 2km east of Reyðarfjörður, is a **view disc** accompanied by a commanding vista. The very energetic can make the 985m climb up **Hólmatindur**, which rises east of the village and separates it from Eskifjörður.

The **Iceland Wartime Museum** (☎ 470 9095; Spítalakampur; adult/child Ikr400/200; 🕑 1-6pm Jun-Aug) is the town's main cultural attraction. It holds relics from the WWII era and reconstructions of barracks life. There are a lot of photographs and dummies wearing costumes, but it provides a good background to Iceland's wartime involvement. Around 3000 Allied soldiers were based in Reyðarfjörður from 1940 to 1945 – about 10 times the local population. The museum is behind a rusting old set of army barracks (follow Heiðarvegur to its end), which were built as a hospital camp in 1943 but never used for that purpose.

Sleeping & Eating

Campers can head to the free **camp site** on the main road into town. Also here is a set of three tiny **cabins** (☎ 474 1111; per cabin Ikr2500), like children's playhouses, which sleep three. The adjoining pond is popular with salmon anglers.

Fosshótel Reyðarfjörður (☎ 474 1600; bokun@fosshotel.is; Búðareyri 6; s/d Ikr12,100/15,900) This is the only hotel in Reyðarfjörður and is open all year. It's a comfortable enough place with spacious rooms (some with facilities for disabled people).

The **restaurant** (mains Ikr1190-2900) at Fosshótel Reyðarfjörður is open for breakfast, lunch and dinner. You can get light meals during the day and meat and fish dishes for dinner, including flounder and trout. The only other choices are burgers, pizzas and snacks at the Shell or Olís petrol stations. There's a **KHB supermarket** (🕑 9am-6pm Mon-Sat) next to the church just off the main road.

ESKIFJÖRÐUR

pop 1006

Stretched along a short side-fjord of Reyðarfjörður, the friendly village of Eskifjörður looks over the water to the majestic, 985m-high peak of Hólmatindur. Eskifjörður's setting is as dramatic as any of the fjord towns and the drive from here to Neskaupstaður crosses the highest highway pass in Iceland. Although there are few facilities town, if you're the sort who likes to hike, fish, explore and experience things for yourself, this is a rewarding place.

Eskifjörður was recognised as a trading centre as early as the late 18th century and its herring fishery reached its height in the late 19th century, but the village didn't receive municipal status until 1974. Take a look inside the freezing plant (almost opposite the museum), whose walls are graced with murals by the Spanish-Icelandic artist Baltasar.

Eskifjörður is one of the least expensive places to fish for salmon in Iceland – it's free on the river Eskifjarðará (but most fish are trout).

KÁRAHNJÚKAR – OPENING THE FLOODGATES

Hydroelectric power schemes are nothing new in Iceland – 90% of the country's energy is derived from them – but the latest and biggest project to get the green light has created a river of controversy and divided the community. The Kárahnjúkar hydroelectric project aims to dam two glacial rivers, Jökulsá á Dal and Jökulsá í Fljótsdal, flooding a remote part of the Eastern Highlands west of Snæfell and creating the 57-sq-km reservoir Hálsón. The energy from this project will be used solely to power the proposed Alcoa aluminium smelter, to be built on Reyðarfjörður in the Eastfjords and expected to be completed in 2007.

As far as environmentalists are concerned, that's two disasters for the price of one. Opponents, including the Iceland Conservation Association (INCA), say the scale of the dam and flooding will cause irreparable damage to one of Europe's largest and most pristine wilderness areas, as well as damaging the ecology of the rivers and wetlands below the dam. They're also sceptical about Alcoa's claims that the smelter will be among the most environmentally friendly in the world.

The idea of building large-scale industry in the Eastfjords has been on the cards for more than 30 years, but it was only when Alcoa joined forces with Landsirkjun, Iceland's national power company, that the project became viable. Ultimately it's a case of ecology versus economy. The project will provide around 1000 jobs and boost the economy in a part of the country where people are leaving in droves because there's no work outside the fishing industry. Landsirkjun also points out that new access roads to be built will open up parts of the previously inaccessible Eastern Highlands to tourism. A **visitors centre** (☎ 471 2044) has been set up at Végarður in the Fljótsdalur valley, where you can learn more about the project while it's still being built.

Information

For tourist information visit the souvenir shop **Verkstæði Kötu** (☎ 476 1745; Strandgata 29), just off the main street. The Landsbanki Íslands bank has an ATM.

Sights & Activities

The **East Iceland Maritime Museum** (Sjóminjasafn Austurlands; ☎ 476 1179, 476 1605; Strandgata 39b; adult/child Ikr400/150; 🕒 2-5pm Jun-Aug), in the black timber warehouse 'Gamla Buð', dating from 1816, illustrates two centuries of the east coast's historic herring and shark fisheries and whaling industry. It's a jumble of fishing boats, nets, tools and other paraphernalia central to Iceland's maritime history. There's also a model of Eskifjörður as it was in the 1920s and a re-creation of a general store.

The remains of the world's largest *silfurberg* (Iceland spar) mine can be found at **Helgustaðir**, 9km east of Eskifjörður. It began operating in the 17th century but is now abandoned. The largest specimen taken from Helgustaðir weighed 230kg and is displayed in the British Museum. Geology buffs may want to have a look, but note that the mines are a national preserve, so absconding with anything of interest is an official no no.

Plans to open the mine as a tourist attraction are yet to happen, and at present it's poorly signposted and reached via a rough dirt road then an uphill walk from the coast.

HIKING

Although it's a beautiful mountain peak, **Hólmatindur**, looming over the southwest of the fjord, is also a nuisance because it cuts out all sunlight to the village from September to April. The four rivers tumbling down its slopes also pose landslide threats. The southern shore of the **Hólmanes peninsula**, below Hólmatindur, has been designated a nature reserve. Hiking in the area offers superb maritime views, as well as the chance to observe the protected vegetation and bird life.

In addition to Hólmanes, you'll find longer hiking routes: Oddsskarð, Helgustaðarsveit, Hellisfjörður, Vindháls and the mountain areas around the end of the peninsula, where you may even see reindeer. The main routes are marked on the map *Gönguleiðir á Austurlandi II* (Ikr500; available from tourist offices).

SKIING

From January to May, daily skiing is possible on slopes near Oddsskarð. The longest run is 327m and floodlighting is available. Oddsskarð, the pass leading over to Neskaupstaður, has a ski slope and a basic ski hut, **Skíðaskáli** (☎ 476 1465; skidam@itn.is).

Sleeping & Eating

If you don't have a tent, there's nowhere to stay. The decaying **Hotel Askja** (☎ 476 1261; fax 476 1561; Hólsvegur 4) was closed in 2003 and showed no signs of reopening.

The free camp site is near the river at the western end of town, but good wild camping is possible just up the valley.

The Shell petrol station, along the main drag, has a grill and snack bar. The Sparakaup supermarket is on the same street.

NESKAUPSTAÐUR

pop 1534

Sometimes called Norðfjörður (after the fjord it sits on), Neskaupstaður is the largest and most industrious settlement in the Eastfjords. Dominated by the Síldarvinnslan (SNV) fish-processing plant – the biggest in East Iceland – the harbour is a modern-day bustle of workers and fishing boats.

As with most coastal towns, Neskaupstaður began as a trading centre when the first merchants arrived in 1882. It prospered during the herring boom in the early 20th century, but then lapsed into obscurity before being revived with the current fish-processing and freezing plant that employs more than 250 people.

The highway approach to Neskaupstaður passes underneath **Oddsskarð**, the highest highway pass in Iceland at 632m, via a single lane 630m-long tunnel. Its lovely position does have drawbacks; backed by steep slopes, it's prone to avalanches, and in 1974 a large one tumbled down and killed 12 residents.

There's no tourist office in Neskaupstaður, but there's information at Café Nesbær, on Egilsbraut (opposite the harbour). The library (with Internet access) is in part of the defunct Hotel Egilsbúð on Hafnarbraut.

Sight & Activities

NATURAL HISTORY MUSEUM

In the village centre, **Náttúrugripasafnið í Neskaupstað** (☎ 477 1606; Miðstræti 1; adult/child Ikr400/150; ⏲ 1-5pm 17 Jun-31 Aug) has a big collection of local stones, including zeolites, spar from the Helgustaðir mine and crystal quartz. On the lower floor is a dull array of stuffed animals, birds, fish and pinned insects.

TRYGGVI GALLERY

This small **gallery** (☎ 861 4747; Hafnarbraut 2; adult/child Ikr400/200; ⏲ 2-5pm Jun-Aug) showcases a collection of paintings by prominent modern artist Tryggvi Ólafsson. Tryggvi was born in Neskaupstaður and studied art in Reykjavík and Copenhagen. His colourful abstracts, some of which hang in national galleries in Reykjavík, Sweden and Denmark, depict Icelandic scenes and are visually quite striking.

HIKING

A rewarding hike will take you up **Goðaborg** (1132m) from the farm Kirkjuból, 8km west of town. From the summit, you can also descend into Mjóifjörður, the next fjord to the north; allow two days and, due to late snows at higher altitudes, attempt it only at the height of summer.

A more difficult walk is from **Oddsskarð** along the ridges eastward to the deserted fjords Hellisfjörður and Viðfjörður. The dramatic Gerpir cliffs, Iceland's easternmost point, can be reached with difficulty, but the only way to visit this beautiful place is on foot. For route-finding, use the *Gerpir* (1:100,000; 1986) topo sheet or the map *Gönguleiðir á Austurlandi II.*

KAYAKING

There's no better way to explore the fjords than in a kayak. **Kaj Kayak Club** (☎ 863 9939; ariben@honnun.is; 3hr trips Ikr2500) offers guided kayaking trips around Norðfjörður, exploring sea caves and resident bird life. Trips are on request; in midsummer, midnight kayaking is possible.

Sleeping

The excellent free **camp site** (☎ 470 9000), with laundry and hot showers, is at the end of the main road on the eastern edge of town, 2km from the harbour.

Gistiheimilið Tröllanaust (☎ 477 1800; Hafnarbraut 2; sb/made-up beds Ikr2000/3600) This guesthouse, on the main road near the harbour and in the same building as the Tryggvi Gallery, is the best budget option, although the owners have plans to turn it into something else. It has 10 neat rooms and cooking facilities.

Hotel Capitano (☎ 477 1800; island@islandia.is; Hafnarbraut 50; s/d Ikr5600/8900) This is a real bargain. The bright-blue corrugated iron building doesn't look like much, but all rooms have attached bathrooms and some of the doubles are spacious and well appointed. Modern art by celebrated local artist Tryggvi Ólafsson adorns the walls.

Hotel Edda Nes (☎ 444 4850; Nesgata 40; s/d Ikr8300/10,400) On the waterfront at the eastern end of town, Nes provides a summer alternative, but there's no sleeping-bag accommodation and the overpriced rooms (all with bathroom) are predictably staid.

Eating

Bakari Neskaupstaður (☎ 477 1306; Hólgata; 7am-5pm Mon-Fri) For breakfast, cakes or pastries, the local bakery, just off Hafnarbraut, is the place. There are a few tables and chairs inside and coffee is only Ikr100.

Hotel Capitano (☎ 477 1800; Hafnarbraut 50; mains Ikr1200-2500) The hotel restaurant has an easy, informal atmosphere and is as good a place as any for a meal during summer. The small bar and lounge are also inviting.

Pizza 67 (☎ 477 1321; in the former Hotel Egilsbúð, Hafnarbraut; 10am-11pm Mon-Thu, 10am-2am Fri & Sat; mains Ikr620-1800) Serves up pizza, pitta sandwiches, Chinese, vegetarian, burgers and full steak and seafood meals, and at weekends there's a lively bar with live music.

Café Nesbær (1-5pm Mon-Fri, 11am-5pm Sat) is a good spot to stop by for coffee and cake. For fast-food grills and hot dogs, there's the **Olís petrol station** (☎ 477 1476; Hafnarbraut). Sparakaup supermarket, on Hafnarbraut opposite the harbour, is open daily.

Getting There & Away

There are two buses every weekday to/from Egilsstaðir (Ikr1500), via Reyðarfjörður and Eskifjörður, and one on Saturday morning. In addition there's at least one weekday bus from Reyðarfjörður to Neskaupstaður (Ikr800).

FÁSKRÚÐSFJÖRÐUR

pop 580

The village of Fáskrúðsfjörður, sometimes known as Búðir ('booths'), was originally settled by French seamen who came to fish the Icelandic coast during the late 1800s. The French left in 1914 and the population continues to decline. Down on the shore on the western approach to the village is a small cemetery and monument commemorating the French seamen who died here, and, in a gesture to the French heritage, street signs are in both Icelandic and French.

The full story on the French seamen in Fáskrúðsfjörður can be found at **Fransmenn á Íslandi** (☎ 475 1525; Búðvegur 8; admission Ikr300; 10am-5pm Jun-Aug), in the blue building on the main road near the harbour. The museum features pictures and historical displays. Otherwise, there's little to do in Fáskrúðsfjörður and it's among the least appealing of the Eastfjords villages.

For hiking, head up to Dalir, above the head of the fjord, where you can hike the old route up over Stuðlaheiði to Reyðarfjörður. Near the mouth of the fjord are two islets. **Andey** (Duck Island) has a large colony of eider ducks, and the green island **Skrúður** is home to a colony of gannets and a large cave which is believed to shelter a giant. Hótel Bjarg (see below) may be able to organise boats to Skrúður in summer.

Above the southern shore of Fáskrúðsfjörður is the laccolithic mountain **Sandfell**, part of the volcanic system that dominated the Eastfjords during the Tertiary geological period. It's one of the world's most impressive visible examples of this sort of igneous intrusion.

Sleeping & Eating

The free camp site is on the slope just west of the village.

Hótel Bjarg (☎ 475 1466; fax 475 1476; Skólavegur 49; s/d with bathroom Ikr5200/6800, without bathroom Ikr4200/5800) In the upper part of the village overlooking the fjord, this is an ageing, old-fashioned sort of place, but it's comfortable enough, has good facilities and is the only hotel in town.

The restaurant at the Hótel Bjarg is your best chance a decent sit-down meal. It's open for breakfast, lunch and dinner and has a reasonable range of Icelandic meat and fish dishes. For hamburgers and hot dogs, try the Esso petrol station.

Getting There & Away

In summer there's one bus every weekday between Egilsstaðir and Breiðdalsvík, stopping at Fáskrúðsfjörður and Stöðvarfjörður. In winter it runs daily except Monday.

STÖÐVARFJÖRÐUR

pop 277

This tiny village, on the fjord of the same name, is sometimes called Kirkjuból. It's pretty somnolent and naturally derives most of its income from fishing.

The best thing in Stöðvarfjörður is the eye-popping rock collection of **Steinasafn**

Petru (☎ 475 8834; Fjarðarbraut 21; adult/child Ikr300/free; 9am-7pm). This diverse exhibit of stones and minerals has been assembled as a 70-year lifelong labour of love by resident Petra Sveinsdóttir. The stones are collected not because they're especially rare or valuable, but for their beauty or interest, and include a huge number of jasper, agate, amethyst and other crystal pieces, along with zeolite and spar. The most enticing pieces are inside, carefully laid out from floor to ceiling, but it's also worth having a look around the garden, which is awash with rocks interspersed with a mishmash of interesting junk. Some of the rocks are for sale, either in raw form, polished up or mounted onto ornaments – it's hard to resist buying a memento from this place! Petra doesn't speak much English, but she's happy to show you around.

The owners of Kirkjubær (see below) organise boat trips from the harbour in an old six-tonne fishing boat. Trips out into the fjord, following the coast from Gerpir to Eystrahorn, cost around Ikr1500 per person for two hours, and you can try a bit of fishing.

Sleeping & Eating

The free camp site is just east of the village.

One of the most unusual places to stay in the Eastfjords is the tiny old church **Kirkjubær** (☎ 475 8819, 892 3319; sb/made-up beds per person Ikr1700/2500) on the hill above Fjarðarbraut. The church dates from 1925 but is now in private hands and has been renovated into a sort of one-room hostel. It's quite cute inside: the pulpit and altar are still there and some of the pews are now part of the furniture. There's a full kitchen and bathroom, and the beds (mostly just mattresses) are on the upper mezzanine level. It supposedly sleeps 10, but that would be pretty cosy! The owners live in the yellow house just below the church at Skolúbraut 1.

Kutterin Restaurant (☎ 475 8852; Fjarðarbraut 44; mains Ikr600-1800) This nautical-theme restaurant-pub on the harbour looks and feels like the sort of place you might rub shoulders with salty old seadogs, and that may just happen on weekend evenings. It serves the usual daily specials, burgers and pizzas, and is the only sit-down place to eat other than the Esso petrol station.

BREIÐDALSVÍK

pop 186

Continuing south from Stöðvarfjörður, the Ring Road joins Route 96 at the young fishing village of Breiðdalsvík, beautifully situated in the lowland valley of the same name. Its most recent claim to fame is that it was attacked by a German bomber in 1942.

Apart from walking in nearby hills and fishing in fish-rich rivers and lakes, the only thing to do here is take a cruise on the bay in summer. **Eastern Adventures** (☎ 475 6646, 864 0246) runs one-hour cruises (Ikr2000) and four-hour trips to Skrúður island (Ikr4000). The prime attraction is the bird life but you may also see seals and whales. Trips leave from the harbour when there are enough passengers.

Sleeping & Eating

Café Margret (☎ 475 6625; s/d Ikr5500/7900) Across the mouth of the fjord from Breiðdalsvík and dwarfed by the mountains behind it, German-run Café Margret is best known for its food, but it's also a beautiful boutique guesthouse with four spacious rooms (three doubles and a small single) above the café. Built from Finnish pine and full of antique German furniture and Persian rugs, this place is a delight.

Even if you're not staying, the **café** (mains Ikr800-2700; 10am-11pm) is like a beacon of light to hungry East Iceland travellers tired of soggy hamburgers. The menu includes German specialities such as pork schnitzel (Ikr1450) and sausage platter (Ikr1500), as well as Icelandic meat and fish dishes – the pan-fried lobster tails are a steal at Ikr1600. There's also a good range of open sandwiches (Ikr600–850), desserts (Ikr400–600), coffee, beer and wine.

Hótel Bláfell (☎ 475 6770; blafell@simnet.is; Sólvellir 14; sb/s/d Ikr1700/6800/8900) This cosy timber hotel by the harbour is popular with visiting anglers. The lounge, with open fire and leather couches, is a great place to unwind, and there's a sauna and solarium. Its restaurant is worth checking out. The camp site is behind the hotel.

AROUND BREIÐDALSVÍK

Breiðdalur & Norðurdalur

As the Ring Road returns to the coast it passes through the lovely Breiðdalur valley, nestled beneath colourful rhyolite peaks. Near the head of the valley you may see reindeer. At the abandoned farm Jórvík, a forestry reserve harbours native birch and aspen.

Hótel Staðarborg (☎ 475 6760, www.stadarborg.is; sb/s/d Ikr1600/7100/9700) is 6km west of Breiðdalsvík on the Ring Road, near the turn-off to Route 964. Breakfast is included with made-up beds, and dinner is available, as is horse rental.

Berunes & Berufjörður

South of Breiðdalur along the Ring Road is Berufjörður, a longish, steep-sided fjord flanked by rhyolite peaks. The southwestern shore is dominated by the obtrusive, pyramid-shaped mountain **Búlandstindur**, which rises 1068m above the water. The westernmost ridge is known as Goðaborg or 'God's rock'. When Iceland officially converted to Christianity in 1000, locals supposedly carried their pagan images to the top of this mountain and threw them over the cliff.

Around Berufjörður are several historical walking routes through the steeply rugged terrain. The best-known of these climbs from Berufjörður, the farm at the head of the fjord, and crosses the 700m Berufjarðarskarð into Breiðdalur.

On the farm **Teigarhorn**, 4km from Djúpivogur, is the historic Weyvadts House. It was constructed in the early 1880s and the trading office has been preserved just as it was left in 1883. The National Museum of Iceland has plans to turn the building into a museum and photographic gallery. Incidentally, Iceland's highest temperature, 30.6°C, was recorded here in 1939.

The farm also has the finest deposits of zeolite in Iceland. Don't get any ideas about collecting, however, as the geology is officially protected. The **mineral museum and shop** (☎ 478 8905; admission Ikr200; 9am-8pm Jun-Aug) has a small display of minerals collected from the area, but it's got nothing on Petra's collection in Stöðvarfjörður (p247)!

SLEEPING & EATING

Berunes HI Hostel (☎ 478 8988; berunes@simnet.is; beds members/nonmembers Ikr1550/1900, s/d Ikr3200/5800, cottages Ikr7000-8000; May-Oct) On the farm of the same name 25km along the Ring Road south of Breiðdalsvík, this is a great little hostel and guesthouse. The building dates from 1907 and the neighbouring church was used in the 19th century. There are rooms, kitchen and lounge in the old farmhouse, plus two self-contained family apartments and a separate cottage. A new addition is the bright dining room where you can join the owners for breakfast (Ikr800), including delicious homemade pancakes, and dinner on request (Ikr1500-1650). There's also camping (Ikr500).

Hamraborg (☎ 476 1348; mains Ikr800-1900; 10am-10pm Jun-Aug) About 1km past Berunes HI Hostel, this is a unique café-restaurant specialising in local game and small 'gourmet' courses. Special dishes include locally caught fish, puffin, reindeer and wild goose. Many of the dishes are served cold and entrée-sized, such as 'graved reindeer with blueberry sauce', where the reindeer is marinated in herbs rather than cooked. If your tastes aren't quite so exotic, there are salads, home-baked bread, omelettes, coffee and cakes, and a well-stocked bar. Definitely worth a stop.

Eyjólfsstaðir (☎ 478 8137; camping/sb Ikr400/1500) This farm, tucked away 2km off the Ring Road near the southwestern shore of Berufjörður, has a beautiful, secluded location in the valley of the river Fossá. The self-contained accommodation has kitchen facilities, bathroom, lounge and basic rooms.

DJÚPIVOGUR

pop 386

Djúpivogur is a quiet, unassuming fishing village at the mouth of Berufjörður. It's the oldest trading centre in the Eastfjords, serving as a commercial port since the 16th century. German merchants were trading here as early as 1589 and the port thrived through the inception and heyday of the Danish Trade Monopoly, despite a small hiccup in 1627 when, according to local history, pirates from North Africa rowed ashore at Djúpivogur, plundering the village and nearby farms and carrying away dozens of slaves.

These days the village merits a brief look around for its historic buildings and small, colourful harbour, but the main reason to visit is to take a boat trip to Papey island (p250).

The **tourist office** (☎ 478 8220; 10am-6pm Jun-early Sep) is in the historic rust-coloured building, Langbúð, alongside the harbour. The village also has a bank (there's an ATM in Við Voginn café), post office and swimming pool.

Sights & Activities

Some of the town's lovely wooden **buildings** date from the late 19th century. The oldest building, **Langbúð**, is a harbourside log warehouse dating from 1790, which now houses the tourist office, a coffee shop and an unusual local **museum** (☎ 478 8220; adult/child Ikr400/200; ⏲ 10am-6pm 1 Jun-5 Sep) and cultural centre. Along with displays relating to local history and trade, there's a section devoted to renowned woodcarver Ríkharður Jónsson, and a small art and craft gallery.

The Djúpivogur peninsula is compact and ideal for short hikes from town. A particularly nice walk is to **Álfkirkja** (Elf Church) on the rock formation Rakkaberg, north of town. The **swimming pool** (☎ 478 8863; Varða 4; admission Ikr200), up behind Hótel Framtíð, is a good place to unwind after hiking.

Sleeping & Eating

The official **camp site** (☎ 478 8887; per person Ikr500), just behind the Við Voginn shop, has showers and cooking facilities.

Hótel Framtíð (☎ 478 8887; framtid@simnet.is; Vogaland 4; s/d with bathroom Ikr7900/10,100, without bathroom Ikr5100/6500, s/d sb Ikr2200/3800) This friendly hotel by the harbour is impressive for a village of this size. Although it's been around for a while (the building was brought in pieces from Copenhagen in 1905), a new wing of modern rooms gives it a nice mix of history and freshness. As well as a flash new à la carte **restaurant** (mains Ikr1250-2800) specialising in local fish, the hotel has a café in the original building, where you can get sandwiches, soup and waffles from Ikr400 to Ikr650.

The **Langabúð coffee shop** (⏲ 10am-6pm, till 11.30pm Fri & Sat in summer) has a suitably old-world atmosphere and serves cakes, soup and bread with a view over the harbour.

Við Voginn (☎ 478 8860; Vogaland 2; mains Ikr400-1800; ⏲ 9am-11pm) is a lively meeting place for locals and serves a big range of fast food, such as hamburgers and pizzas, along with fish dishes. On the main road into town is a **Kjarval supermarket** (Búland 2) with a Vin Buð liquor store attached.

AROUND DJÚPIVOGUR

Papey

The name of the lovely offshore island of Papey (Friars' Island) suggests it was once a hermitage for the Irish monks who inhabited Iceland before the arrival of the Norse. It's thought that they fled in the face of Nordic settlement. This small and tranquil island was once a farm, but it's presently inhabited only by seals and nesting sea birds. In the early summer, the dramatic, 45m-high cliffs are crowded with nests. Other highlights include the **Hellisbjarg lighthouse**, which dates from 1922; Iceland's oldest and smallest **wooden church**, built in 1805; and the remains of an **apartment house** from the early 20th century. There's no formal accommodation, but camping is allowed by prior arrangement.

Getting to Papey is easy enough in summer. From 1 June to 15 September (weather and numbers permitting), four-hour tours to the island leave from Djúpivogur harbour daily at 1pm aboard **Gislí Papey** (☎ 478 8183; adult/child Ikr3000/1500). In fine weather this tour is truly magical. Make sure you bring good footwear, as a visit will involve some hiking.

EAST ICELAND

Southeast Iceland

CONTENTS

Iceland's southeastern quarter is dominated by the vast Vatnajökull icecap, the world's third largest after those of Antarctica and Greenland. Even the casual traveller passing by on the Ring Road will be in awe of the huge glacier tongues reaching through steep-sided valleys towards the sea, icebergs floating in a natural lagoon and the blackboard-flat sandy plains of glacial detritus known as the *sandur*.

Here nature reigns supreme, as is evident in the 30km-long Lakagígar (Laki) fissure, Iceland's most destructive volcano, which caused famine and destruction across the country in the late 18th century. Similarly, beneath Vatnajökull lie Grímsvötn and Öræfi, volcanoes which cause more damage locked beneath the ice than they would if allowed to spout. Eruptions cause glacial melting, and pressure from the heat and steam actually lifts the icecap, releasing devastating floods (the most recent of which occurred in late 1996) that spread out across surrounding lowlands.

Few travellers in Southeast Iceland miss Skaftafell National Park, a pristine enclave between Vatnajökull's southernmost extremes. Although it's a popular holiday spot, you can easily escape the crowds by striking out on foot. Also an obvious attraction, the Vatnajökull icecap itself is popular with skiers and climbers as well as casual visitors, who can easily join glacier walks or snowmobiling tours.

Although technically part of the interior, we've included Fjallabak Nature Reserve and Landmannalaugar in this section, an area with mesmerising landscape and superb hiking. This 'back road' between the southeast and southwest should not be missed.

Even by Icelandic standards, the narrow southeastern strip between the icecap and the sea is thinly populated. Most people live in the small towns of Höfn and Kirkjubæjarklaustur, or on a few farms strung out along Vatnajökull's southern flank.

TOP FIVE

- Bathing in steaming thermal pools at **Landmannalaugar** (p254), or finishing the challenging **Landmannalaugar to Þórsmörk Trek** – one of the world's great walks (p256)
- Imagining you're in Antarctica or Greenland at the beautiful iceberg-filled lagoon at **Jökulsárlón** (p269)
- Hiking in **Skaftafell National Park** and staring out over the vast *sandur* (sand deltas) (p264)
- Snowmobiling on **Vatnajökull icecap** at Jöklasel (p270)
- Reaching the summit of **Hvannadalshnúkur** on a guided climb (p268)

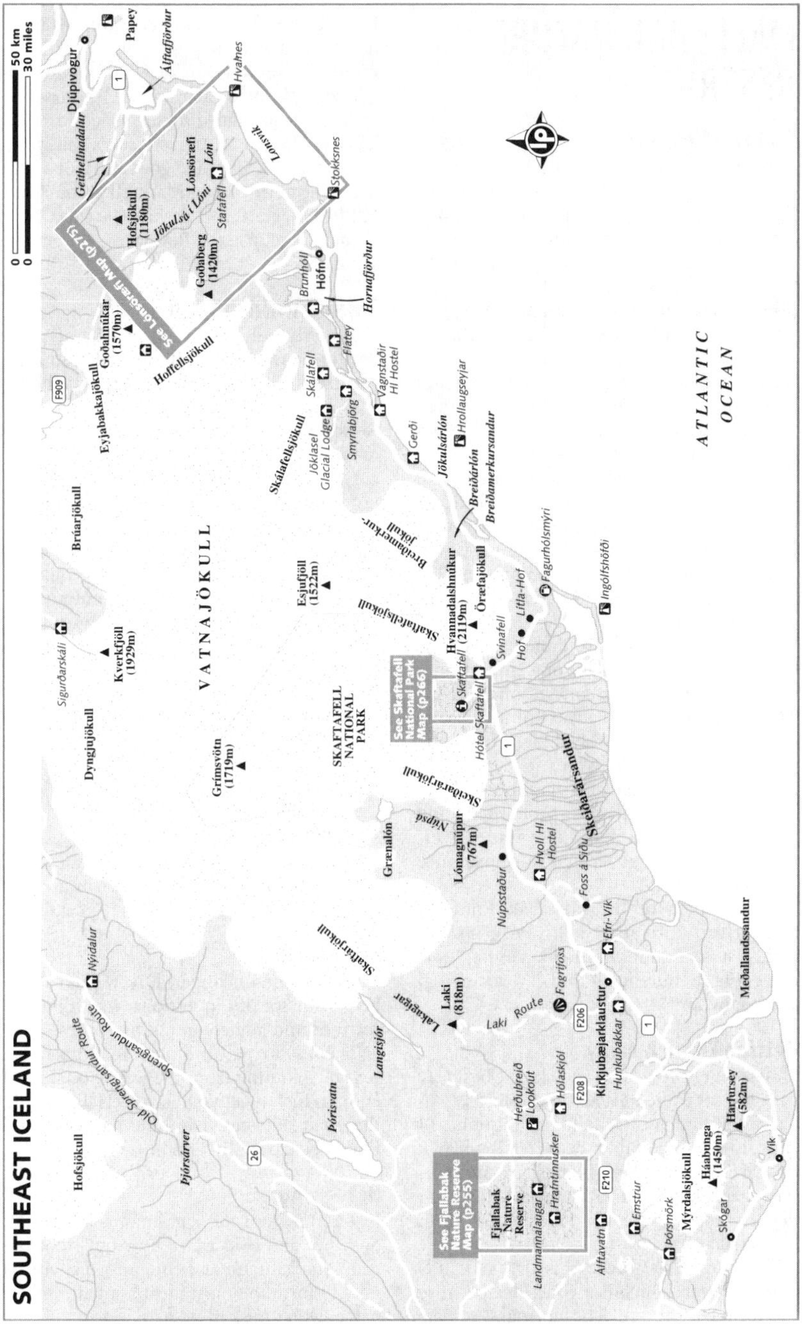
SOUTHEAST ICELAND
0 50 km
0 30 miles
Djúpivogur
Papey
Álftafjörður
Geithellnadalur
Hvalnes
Lónsvík
Lónsöræfi
Lón
Stafafell
Jökulsá í Lóni
Hofsjökull (1180m)
Goðaberg (1420m)
See Lónsöræfi Map (p275)
Stokksnes
Höfn
Brunhóll
Hornafjörður
Goðahnúkar (1570m)
Hoffellsjökull
Flatey
Skálafell
Vagnstaðir HI Hostel
Smyrlabjörg
Jöklasel Glacial Lodge
Skálafellsjökull
Eyjabakkajökull
F909
Gerði
Hrollaugseyjar
Jökulsárlón
Breiðárlón
Breiðamerkursandur
Brúarjökull
VATNAJÖKULL
Breiðamerkurjökull
Esjufjöll (1522m)
Hvannadalshnúkur (2119m)
Öræfajökull
Fagurhólsmýri
Ingólfshöfði
Litla-Hof
Hof
Svínafell
Skaftafellsjökull
Kverkfjöll (1929m)
Sigurðarskáli
Skaftafell
Hótel Skaftafell
See Skaftafell National Park Map (p266)
SKAFTAFELL NATIONAL PARK
Dyngjujökull
Grímsvötn (1719m)
Skeiðarárjökull
Skeiðarársandur
Núpsá
Grænalón
Lómagnúpur (767m)
Núpsstaður
Hvoll HI Hostel
Foss á Síðu
Efri-Vík
Skaftárjökull
Nýidalur
Laki (818m)
Lakagígar
Laki Route
Fagrifoss
F206
Kirkjubæjarklaustur
Hunkubakkar
Meðallandssandur
Sprengisandur Route
Old Sprengisandur Route
Langisjór
Hólaskjól
F208
Herðubreið Lookout
Hofsjökull
Þjórsárver
Þórisvatn
26
See Fjallabak Nature Reserve Map (p255)
Fjallabak Nature Reserve
Landmannalaugar
Hrafntinnusker
F210
Álftavatn
Emstrur
Þórsmörk
Mýrdalsjökull
Háabunga (1450m)
Hafursey (582m)
Vík
Skógar
ATLANTIC OCEAN

FJALLABAK NATURE RESERVE

FJALLABAK ROUTE

Although part of Iceland's foreboding interior, the Fjallabak (Behind the Mountains) Route (F208), north of the Mýrdalsjökull massif, is a spectacular alternative to the coast road between Hella and Kirkjubæjarklaustur. It begins near the Sigölduvirkjun power plant on the Tungnaá river and passes through the scenic Fjallabak Nature Reserve to Landmannalaugar. From there, it continues east past the Kirkjufell marshes and enters Jökuldalur, then along a riverbed for 10km before climbing to the Herðubreið lookout and descending to Eldgjá.

For the next 40km the road is fairly good, but there are a couple of river fords, so conventional vehicles going to Eldgjá from the east may have difficulties during high water. At Búland, the route joins Route 208 and emerges at the Ring Road southwest of Kirkjubæjarklaustur.

A non-4WD vehicle wouldn't have a hope of completing the through route. In summer, if the rivers are low, a conventional vehicle can reach Landmannalaugar from the west (F208 only) and possibly Eldgjá from the east, but the route between the two would be impassable under any conditions. Note that hire-car companies prohibit taking 2WD vehicles on any of these routes, so if something should go wrong, your insurance would be void.

Since much of the Fjallabak Route is along rivers (or rather in rivers!), it's not ideally suited to mountain bikes either. Lots of people do attempt it, but it's not casual cycling by any stretch.

Getting There & Away

Unless you have a 4WD vehicle, the best way in is the scheduled **BSÍ/Austurleið-SBS** (☎ 545 1717) bus which runs daily from around 14 June to 14 September between Reykjavík and Skaftafell via Selfoss, Hella, Landmannalaugar, Eldgjá and Kirkjubæjarklaustur. It departs from Reykjavík at 8.30am and from Skaftafell at 8am.

Most travellers break this trip at Landmannalaugar, which is a good idea because there's plenty to see. The normal one-way fare (Reykjavík to Skaftafell) is Ikr6900 (11 hours) and it's unquestionably worth the money. From Reykjavík to Landmannalaugar costs Ikr3950 each way (5½ hours).

Another scheduled route to southern Fjallabak (15 July to 20 August) leaves daily from Reykjavík at 8.30am and goes via Hvölsvollur along the north side of Markarfl jót on Route F261 to Eldgjá and Hólaskjól (Ikr8900, eight hours). It returns to Reykjavík at 3pm the same day.

LANDMANNALAUGAR

The eerily colourful landscape, hot pools and great walking around Landmannalaugar make this a favourite among travellers – if you're thinking of taking the bus from Reykjavík to Skaftafell in a single day (or making a day return trip to Landmannalaugar), you'll wind up kicking yourself for not allowing more time. The magnificent rhyolite peaks, rambling lava flows, blue mountain lakes and soothing hot springs should hold anyone captive for several days, especially if the weather is cooperating.

Landmannalaugar (600m above sea level) comprises the largest geothermal field in Iceland outside the Grímsvötn caldera in Vatnajökull. The variegated peaks of Landmannalaugar are composed of rhyolite, a mix of minerals metamorphosed by geothermal and volcanic activity believed to have been centred on the Torfajökull caldera.

Although Landmannalaugar gets quite chilly, the weather is generally more stable than in coastal areas, and when it does rain, it's more of a wind-driven horizontal mist than a drenching downpour.

Information

The Landmannalaugar hut wardens can help with specific questions, including directions and advice on hiking routes.

There's no petrol at Landmannalaugar. If you're coming from the west, you'll need enough fuel to get you back to Hella should the road between Landmannalaugar and Eldgjá be closed by flooding.

Hot Springs

Just 200m from the Landmannalaugar hut, both hot and cold water flow out from beneath Laugahraun and combine in a natural pool to form the most ideal hot bath imaginable. Don't miss it!

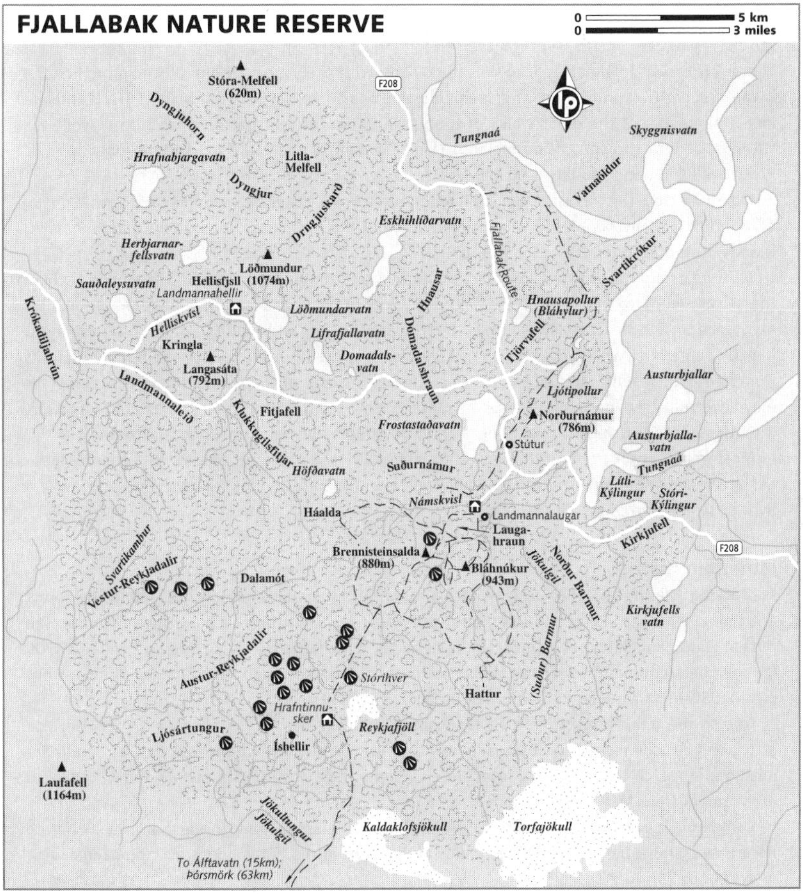

Hiking

Laugahraun, the convoluted lava field behind Landmannalaugar hut, offers vast scope for exploration. Across it, the slopes of the rainbow-streaked mountain **Brennisteinsalda** (Burning Stones Crest) are punctuated by steaming vents and sulphur deposits. Climb to the summit for a good view across the rugged and variegated landscape.

From Brennisteinsalda, it's another 90 minutes along the Landmannalaugar to Þórsmörk route to the impressive **Stórihver** geothermal field.

The blue lake **Frostastaðavatn** lies behind the rhyolite ridge immediately north of the Landmannalaugar hut. A walk over the ridge will be rewarded with far-ranging views as well as close-ups of the interesting rock formations and moss-covered lava flows flanking the lake. If you walk at least one way on the road and spend some time exploring around the lake, the return trip takes two to three hours.

The incredible red crater lake **Ljótipollur** (Ugly Pond) makes a fine day hike from Landmannalaugar and affords vistas of many types of terrain, from tephra desert and lava flow to marsh and braided glacial valley. Technically, Ljótipollur is a maar lake (one which has been created in a volcanic explosion). Oddly enough, it's rich in trout. To get there you can climb over the 786m-high peak **Norðurnámur** (well worthwhile) or just traverse along its western base to emerge

LANDMANNALAUGAR TO ÞÓRSMÖRK TREK

The trek from Landmannalaugar to Þórsmörk – known as the Laugarvegurinn (Hot Spring Road) – is the premier walk in Iceland, and seems destined to some day join the Milford Track and the Inca Trail as one of the great walks of the world. Strap on your backpack and do it while it's still relatively unknown outside Iceland. The best map of the route is Landmælingar Íslands' Þórsmörk/Landmannalaugar 1:100,000.

In high season, the trek can be completed in three or four days by anyone in reasonable physical condition. Many people do it independently, but the tour companies Útivist and Ferðafélag Íslands both offer organised trips (see p303).

Most years, the track is passable for casual trekkers from mid-July to mid-September. Early in the season (early to mid-July), there's normally lots of snow and you may need an ice axe for assistance on the steeper slopes. It positively bustles in July and August, so consider walking it in early September when you'll have crisp weather and the chance to watch the Northern Lights from near-empty huts. That late in the year, however, some of the snow bridges across ravines may have collapsed, necessitating detours. At any time the trek is not to be taken lightly though. It requires river crossings, all-weather gear, sturdy boots and sufficient food and water.

Most trekkers walk from north to south to take advantage of the net altitude loss and the facilities at the Þórsmörk hut. You can also continue along the Þórsmörk to Skógar track and make a five- or six-day trip of it.

Mountain Huts

Ferðafélag Íslands (☎ 568 2533; www.fi.is) owns and maintains several huts along the route: at Landmannalaugar, Hrafntinnusker, Álftavatn (two huts), Emstrur (two huts) and Þórsmörk. The huts at Landmannalaugar, Þórsmörk and Emstrur, and the larger Álftavatn hut, cost Ikr1200/1700 for members/nonmembers of Ferðafélag Íslands. Hrafntinnusker and the smaller Álftavatn hut cost Ikr850/1110. All offer camping (Ikr500/600).

Due to the trek's popularity, it's wise to book and pay hut fees in advance. Otherwise, you can take your chances on space availability and just turn up. There are wardens at Landmannalaugar in March and April and from June to September, at Álftavatn in July and August and at Þórsmörk from May to September.

Camping is permitted around any of the huts, but wilderness camping inside the Fjallabak Nature Reserve requires a permit (Ikr500 per night) available from the hut wardens at Landmannalaugar or Þórsmörk.

Landmannalaugar to Hrafntinnusker (12km, 4–5 hours)

The route begins behind the hut at Landmannalaugar and crosses the Laugahraun lava flow before climbing into the rhyolite peaks and steaming vents at Brennisteinsalda. It then climbs over some high and lonesome rhyolite hills before descending to the field of steaming vents at **Stórihver**. Near the track is a sinister round hole – like the mouth of hell – which belches forth a roaring spume of riotously boiling water.

Beyond Stórihver, the route climbs through fields of shiny chunks of glinting obsidian and crosses high and perpetually snow-covered moors. After the crest of the pass, **Hrafntinnusker hut** comes into view. Some trekkers stay the night here but others reckon it's too cold and forbidding, and there are no showers, so it's possible to make the first day a longer walk to Álftavatn.

Hrafntinnusker to Álftavatn (12km, 4–5 hours)

From Hrafntinnusker, the track descends to cross a stream then bounces over parallel rhyolite ridges and snow bridges before ascending steeply to a ridge studded with hot springs and fumaroles.

A pleasant side trip in this section heads east from the main route and ascends to the summit of **Háskerðingur** (1278m), across the northern spur of **Kaldaklofsfjöll** icecap. On a clear day, the views are indescribable.

The route then rolls up and down over ridges of descending altitude before dropping steeply from the Jökultungur Ridge into the **Álftavatn** Valley. Here you'll have a glorious view of Tindfjallajökull, Eyjafjallajökull and Mýrdalsjökull, as well as the many volcanic formations spread out below.

After a stream crossing at the bottom of the slope, the route levels out and joins a 4WD track across a grassy plain to Álftavatn, where there are two **huts**.

A pleasant afternoon hike from Álftavatn is the 5km track to **Torfahlaup**, where the mighty Markarfljót is constricted and forced through a 15m-wide canyon. Looming above, the velvety, emerald-green peak of **Stóra Grænafell** is visible for many kilometres in all directions.

Álftavatn to Emstrur (15km, 6–7 hours)

Six kilometres south of Álftavatn, the track joins up with the F210 4WD track and follows it on and off for 10km. About 1.5km from the hut, there's a foot-numbing stream crossing, but it's the least of several you'll encounter on this stage. From here, the road climbs steadily for several kilometres before dropping into the pleasant oasis of **Hvanngil**, where you cross a stream on two small footbridges. You'll find two huts and a camp site here.

After rejoining the road, you cross the raging **Kaldaklofskvísl** on a footbridge. At the intersection on the southern bank, follow the route posted 'Emstrur/Fljótshlíð'. The left turning, which is the Fjallabak Syðra Route, goes to Mælifellssanður. Several hundred metres south of the intersection, you'll have to ford the knee-deep **Bláfjallakvísl**.

The track then enters a lonely and surreal 5km stretch of black sand and pumice desert, skirting the obtrusive pyramid-shaped peak Stórasúla. The next barrier is the murky river **Innri-Emstruá**. The glacial torrent portion is bridged, but at times of high water – after rains or warm sunny periods – you'll still have to ford a knee-deep side channel.

Across the bridge, continue up the other side of the gully and, at the crest, watch on your left for the signpost which reads 'FÍ Skáli'. Here the track strikes off across the desert through some Sahara-like passes and desolate hills. After 1½ to two hours, you'll reach the **Emstrur huts**.

A rewarding and requisite 2km side trip southwest from the Emstrur huts will take you to the **Markarfljótgljúfor gorge**. Just as impressive as better known Jökulsárgljúfur in Northeast Iceland, this gaping green canyon will take your breath away.

Emstrur to Þórsmörk (15km, 6–7 hours)

From the Emstrur huts, the track crosses a small heath then drops steeply to cross the roiling Fremri-Emstruá on a small footbridge, just below the **Entujökull** glacier tongue. The next landmark is the **Ljósá** (River of Light), which is crossed on a footbridge at a point where the river squeezes through a 2m-wide fissure. The view down to the water can be quite mesmerising.

Over the next hill is the unbridged river **Þrongá**, which must be forded. The onward route on the opposite bank isn't obvious; look for a V-shaped ravine just west of the marked crossing point. There the track enters the grassy birch- and mushroom-studded Þórsmörk woodland and, at this point, you're less than an hour from trail's end. When you reach a junction, the right fork leads to **Húsadalur hut** and the left fork to **Þórsmörk Hut**. Note that the bus to Reykjavík stops at Húsadalur, so if you're not staying overnight in Þórsmörk, head there.

For more on Þórsmörk or the continuing route to Skógar, see the Southwest Iceland chapter (p120).

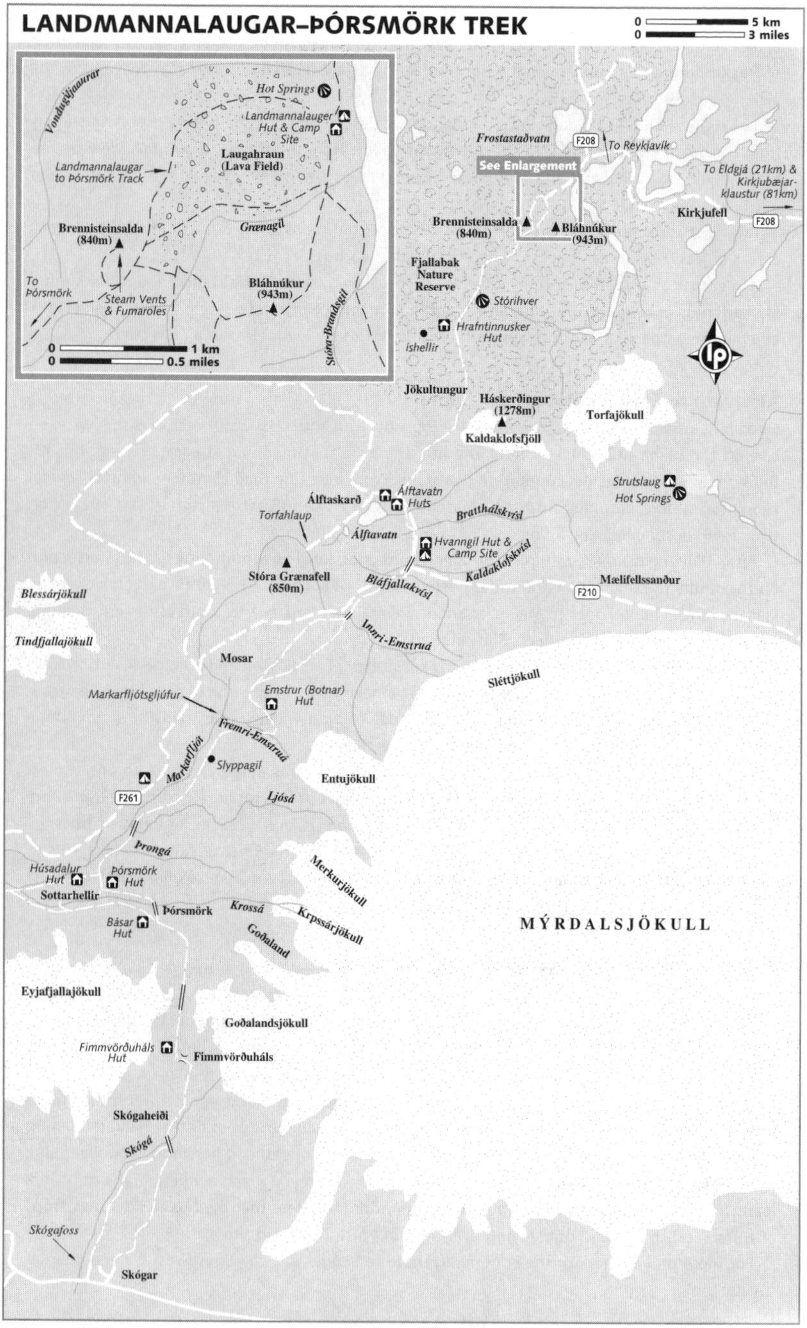
LANDMANNALAUGAR–ÞÓRSMÖRK TREK
0 5 km
0 3 miles
Vondugiljaaurar
Hot Springs
Landmannalauger
Hut & Camp
Site
Laugahraun
(Lava Field)
Landmannalaugar
to Þórsmörk Track
Brennisteinsalda
(840m)
Grænagil
To
Þórsmörk
Steam Vents
& Fumaroles
Bláhnúkur
(943m)
Stóra-Brandsgil
0 1 km
0 0.5 miles
Frostastaðvatn
F208
To Reykjavík
See Enlargement
To Eldgjá (21km) &
Kirkjubæjar-
klaustur (81km)
Kirkjufell
F208
Brennisteinsalda
(840m)
Bláhnúkur
(943m)
Fjallabak
Nature
Reserve
Stórihver
Hrafntinnusker
Hut
Íshellir
Jökultungur
Háskerðingur
(1278m)
Kaldaklofsfjöll
Torfajökull
Strutslaug
Hot Springs
Álftaskarð
Álftavatn
Huts
Torfahlaup
Bratthálskvísl
Álftavatn
Hvanngil Hut &
Camp Site
Kaldaklofskvísl
Stóra Grænafell
(850m)
Bláfjallakvísl
Mælifellssandur
F210
Blessárjökull
Tindfjallajökull
Innri-Emstruá
Mosar
Sléttjökull
Markarfljótsgljúfur
Emstrur (Botnar)
Hut
Fremri-Emstruá
Markarfljót
Slyppagil
Entujökull
F261
Ljósá
Þrongá
Merkurjökull
Húsadalur
Hut
Þórsmörk
Hut
Sottarhellir
Þórsmörk
Krossá
Krossárjökull
Básar
Hut
Goðaland
MÝRDALSJÖKULL
Eyjafjallajökull
Goðalandsjökull
Fimmvörðuháls
Hut
Fimmvörðuháls
Skógaheiði
Skógá
Skógafoss
Skógar

on the Ljótipollur road. A number of routes ascend to the crater rim, but the most interesting is probably the footpath which climbs its southernmost slope. If you walk all the way around the crater rim, it's an 18km hike which takes the better part of a day.

Another good day walk from Landmannalaugar is around the peak **Tjörvafell** and the crater lake **Hnausapollur** (also known as Bláhylur).

Sleeping

The Ferðafélag Íslands **hut** at Landmannalaugar accommodates 115 people on a first-come, first-served basis, but in July and August it's often booked out by tour groups and club members. Fees are Ikr1200/1700 per night for members/nonmembers. There's a **camp site** (Ikr600 per person) nearby.

Southeast of Torfajökull, there's excellent **wild camping** at Strútslaug hot springs.

LANDMANNALAUGAR TO ELDGJÁ

East of Landmannalaugar, the F208 leaves Fjallabak Reserve and skirts the river Tungnaá as it flows past the Norðurnámshraun lava field.

After dropping into Jökuldalur, the road deteriorates into a valley route along a riverbed and effectively becomes a 10km-long ford interspersed with jaunts across the odd sandbar or late snowfield. When it climbs out of the valley, it ascends the tuff mountain **Herðubreið**, which affords a far-ranging vista across the lowlands to the south.

Just west of the Herðubreið lookout a rough 4WD road heads 25km northeast to the blue lake **Langisjór**. On the far side of the lake lie the astonishing green mountains of **Fögrufjöll** (1090m), and beyond them is the black-sand outwash plain of the glacial river Skaftá.

ELDGJÁ

Eldgjá (Fire Gorge) is a volcanic rift stretching 40km from Mýrdalsjökull to the peak Gjátindur. At its northeastern end, Eldgjá is 200m deep and 600m across, with odd, reddish walls that recall the fire after which it's named.

Although it's not as outwardly spectacular as you may expect, Eldgjá is quite intriguing and the name alone conjures up images of a malevolently mysterious and powerful place.

In the green and fertile **Hánípufit** area, 8km south of the Eldgjá turn-off, the river Skaftá widens into an entanglement of cascades and waterfalls measuring 500m across in places. It's unusual and quite beautiful.

At Lambaskarðshólar, west of the F208 road near Syðrifærá, 5km south of the Eldgjá turn-off, there's the mountain hut **Hólaskjól** (☎ 854 9977; per person Ikr1700) where you'll find sleeping-bag accommodation, hot showers and a camp site. It's a great place to hole up for a couple of days.

SOUTHERN VATNAJÖKULL

Vatnajökull (Water Glacier), far and away Iceland's greatest icecap, rests on top of 8400 sq km of otherwise rugged territory and is almost 1km thick in places. Scores of smaller valley glaciers slide down from the central icecap in crevasse-ridden rivers of sculpted ice. The best known of these is probably Skaftafellsjökull, a relatively small glacier that ends within 1.5km of the Skaftafell camp site. Two much larger valley glaciers, Skeiðarárjökull and Breiðamerkurjökull, flow down to the *sandur* plains in broad, spreading sheets and are plainly visible from the Ring Road.

The mind-blowing drive from Kirkjubæjarklaustur to Höfn takes you across the *sandur*, past farms, mountains, glacier tongues and ice-filled lagoons – the only thing you won't pass is a town.

KIRKJUBÆJARKLAUSTUR

pop 170

Many a foreign tongue has been tied in knots trying to wrap itself around Kirkjubæjarklaustur. It might help if you break it into bits: *Kirkju* (church), *bæjar* (farm) and *klaustur* (convent). Otherwise, just do as the locals do and call it 'Klausturs' (pronounced more or less like 'cloisters').

Klausturs is a tiny place, even by Icelandic standards, but it is the gateway to the southeast if you're coming from the west and more or less a crossroads for the routes to Fjallabak, Landmannalaugar and Laki. It's the only real service town between Vik and Höfn, and there are enough sights here to merit a quick stop.

History

Originally, the village was known as Kirkjubær; the 'klaustur' bit was added in 1186 when a convent of Benedictine nuns was established. Although it was abandoned with the Reformation in 1550, the name stuck. According to the *Landnámabók*, this tranquil place between the cliffs and the river Skaftá was first settled by *papar*, Irish monks who used Iceland as a retreat before the Norse arrived.

The first Icelander here was an early Christian, Ketill Fíflski or Ketill the Foolish, who, despite his name, had an impressive genealogy. He was the nephew of Auður the Deep-Minded (Unnur) of *Laxdæla Saga*, the son of Jórunn Wisdom-Slope and grandson of the renowned Ketill Flatnose. He was called 'the Foolish' because his pagan peers saw his religious deviation as decidedly foolhardy, given that the gods might be displeased.

During the devastating Laki eruptions of the late 18th century, this area suffered greatly and, west of Kirkjubæjarklaustur, you can see ruins of farms abandoned or destroyed by the lava stream. The lava field, Eldhraun (Fire Lava), averages 12m thick. It contains over 12 cubic km of lava and covers an area of 565 sq km, making it the largest recorded lava flow from a single eruption.

Information

The **tourist office** (☎ 487 4620; www.south.is/klaustur.html; Klausturvegur; 9am-5pm Jun-Sep) is in the community centre opposite the chapel. Diagonally opposite is a complex containing the **bank, post office** and **supermarket**.

Sights & Activities

Steingrímsson Memorial Chapel, the triangular, distinctly atypical wood and stone chapel on Klausturvegur, was consecrated in 1974. It commemorates Jón Steingrímsson's Eldmessa (Fire Sermon), which saved the town from the lava on 20 July 1783. (See the boxed text on p261).

Although it's completely natural, it's easy to see why early settlers named **Kirkjugólf** (church floor), perhaps assuming that it had once served as the floor of a church. The 80-sq-metre, honeycombed plane is actually the smoothed top surface of vertical basalt columns. It lies in a field about 400m northwest of the Skaftárskáli petrol station just off Route 203.

Religious connections are strong in this area and the prominent rock pillar **Systrastapi** (Sisters' Pillar), near the line of cliffs west of town, provides a good example. The local legend goes that two unruly nuns were executed and buried atop the rock. One was allegedly guilty of slandering the pope and the other was accused of all sorts of heinous crimes, including fraternising with the devil, sleeping with parishioners and desecrating the communion host. After the Reformation, it was said that flowers bloomed for the first time on Systrastapi.

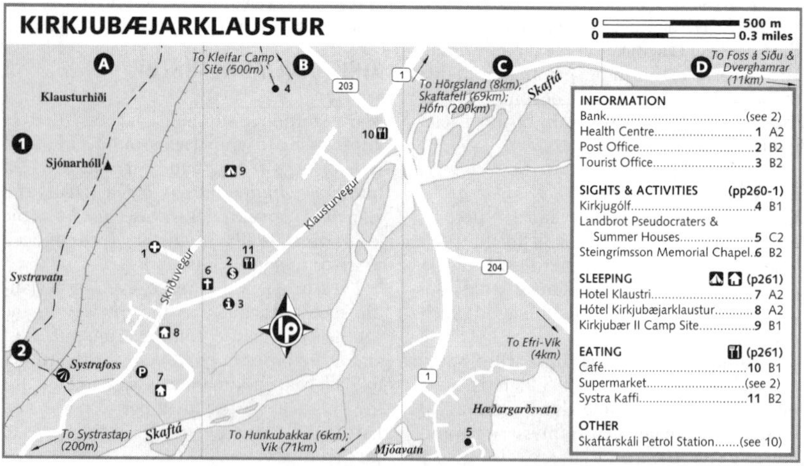

HELLFIRE & BRIMSTONE

The eruptions of the volcano Laki, in the late 18th century, brought death and devastation to much of southeastern Iceland, especially to nearby Kirkjubæjarklaustur. On 20 July 1783, a particularly insidious flow of chunk-ridden lava bore down on the town, and residents feared for their lives and property. As the stream threatened to engulf the town, the pastor Jón Steingrímsson gathered his parishioners into the church and delivered a passionate hellfire and brimstone sermon while some appropriate special effects smoked and steamed just outside. By the time the oratory ended, the flow had stopped at a rock promontory (now called Eldmessutangi, 'Fire Sermon Point') just short of the town, and the grateful residents credited their good reverend with some particularly effective string-pulling on their behalf.

The prominent waterfall that tumbles down the cliffs via the Bæjargil ravine is known as **Systrafoss**. The **Systravatn** lake above the falls was reputedly a bathing place for the nuns. The lake is a short and pleasant walk up the cliffs from the village.

South of the Ring Road, the vast pseudocrater field known as **Landbrot**, formed during the Laki eruptions of 1783 by steam explosions in the lava-heated marshes, is now a repository for Icelandic summer houses.

On the farm **Foss á Siðu**, 11km east of Kirkjubæjarklaustur, is an attractive waterfall which normally tumbles down from the cliffs. During especially strong sea winds, however, it actually goes straight up! Opposite Foss á Siðu is the outcrop **Dverghamrar** (Dwarf Cliffs), which contains some classic basalt columns.

Sleeping

Kirkjubær II camp site (☎ 487 4612; per person Ikr500) This site is right in town and has pretty good facilities including kitchen, hot showers and laundry. The **Kleifar camp site** (☎ 487 4675; per person Ikr500) is 1km northwest of the Skaftárskáli petrol station.

Hotel Klaustri (☎ 487 4838; fax 487 4827; Klausturvegur 4; sb Ikr1500-2000, s/d Ikr4900/6200;) This summer-only hotel, in the school at the end of the main road through the village, has simple rooms, cooking facilities and a swimming pool. Sleeping-bag accommodation is either in private rooms or dormitory-style in the classrooms.

Hótel Kirkjubæjarklaustur (☎ 487 4799; klaustur@icehotel.is; Klausturvegur 6; s/d Ikr10,800/15,000, superior rooms Ikr11,200/17,300) This is a surprisingly plush hotel for a village of this size. Like most business hotels it has functional rooms with bathroom and satellite TV, as well as a bar, restaurant and spa/sauna.

Hörgsland (☎ 487 6655; www.horgsland.is; sb Ikr1800, made-up beds Ikr2500, cottages from Ikr6000) This new place, on the Ring Road about 8km northeast of Kirkjubæjarklaustur, is like a minivillage of very spacious and comfortable self-contained cottages. The two-bedroom timber cabins sleep at least six and have kitchen, lounge and veranda. There are a couple of outdoor hot pots here, as well as a café, and you can arrange fishing permits.

There's quite a bit of farmhouse accommodation in the area – the tourist office has a full list.

Efri-Vík (☎ 487 4694; efrivik@simnet.is; sb Ikr2000, s/d Ikr4000/6000) A good choice is this farm 5km from Kirkjubæjarklaustur on Route 204. As well as beds in comfortable cottages, it has a lovely nine-hole golf course, boat rental and lake fishing.

Hunkubakkar (☎ 478 4681; hunka@mmedia.is; s/d Ikr4000/6000; Laki Rd) This farm, 7km from Klausturs, has rooms, cottages and horse hire.

Eating

Systra Kaffi (☎ 487 4848; Klausturvegur; light meals Ikr350-1100, mains Ikr950-2500; 10am-midnight, 10am-2am Fri & Sat) This ambient little café and bar has soft music and a menu ranging from deep-fried cheese bars, hamburgers and pizzas to reasonably priced Icelandic fish and meat dishes. It's the most atmospheric place for a meal in tiny Kirkjubæjarklaustur.

Hótel Kirkjubæjarklaustur (☎ 487 4799; Klausturvegur 6; mains Ikr1900-3900) For fine dining in stiff surroundings, the restaurant here has an à la carte menu with typical meat and fish courses and some unusual starters such as *escargot* (snails) and caesar salad. The bar also holds up a few patrons and locals on Friday and Saturday nights.

For cheap burgers, hot dogs and pizzas, the **Skaftárskáli** (☎ 487 4628) petrol station has a café.

Getting There & Away

Buses between Reykjavík and Höfn stop at Hótel Kirkjubæjarklaustur. In summer they run daily from Reykjavík (Ikr3830) at 8.30am and arrive in Kirkjubæjarklaustur at 1.15pm, continuing on to Skaftafell (Ikr1940). Westbound buses depart from Höfn (Ikr2790) at 8.30am and arrive at 12.40pm, then continue on to Reykjavík. The bus runs daily from 1 June to 14 September and on Tuesday, Friday and Saturday the rest of the year.

The Fjallabak bus between Reykjavík and Skaftafell passes around 6.30pm eastbound and 9am westbound daily from 18 June to 5 September. The entire route costs Ikr6900.

LAKAGÍGAR

The Laki eruptions of 1783 were among the most catastrophic volcanic events in human history and were by far the most devastating Iceland has yet known. The main period of activity, which started in the spring of 1783 and lasted for 10 months, was known as the Skaftáreldar (Shaft River Fires). Fountains of molten lava spouted up to around 1000m above ground level, usually from four or five craters at once, lighting up the night sky in Kirkjubæjarklaustur.

Of all the misfortunes to befall Iceland during the Norwegian and Danish regimes, the Skaftáreldar brought the most suffering. During the Skaftáreldar, the Laki fissure spewed more than 30 billion tonnes of lava and 90 million tonnes of sulphuric acid. Across Iceland, farms and fields were devastated and well over half the livestock died from starvation and poisoning. Some 9000 people – 20% of Iceland's population – were killed and the remainder faced the Moðuharðindi (Haze Famine) that followed.

Although Laki is extinct and hasn't erupted at all in modern times, it has loaned its name to the volatile, 25km-long Lakagígar crater row which stretches southwestward from its base. Laki itself can be climbed in less than an hour from the parking area, and yields a fantastic view of the active fissure. The easiest route lies to the left of the crest leading up to the first plateau.

Usually the 50km 4WD road (F206) west of Kirkjubæjarklaustur to the Lakagígar crater row is passable from mid-July. There are still puddles and some rivers to ford so, after rain, the route may forestall low-clearance vehicles. Don't think about it in a 2WD.

Lakagígar Crater Row

The Lakagígar crater row is fascinating to explore, particularly the crater nearest Laki itself, which contains an interesting lava cave. Another cave, two hours' walk south of the parking area, shelters a mysterious lake. The area is also riddled with black-sand dunes and lava tubes, many of which contain tiny stalactites. Nowadays the lava field belies the apocalypse that spawned it just over 200 years ago and the sharp, black boulders are overgrown with soft and spongy moss.

Lakagígar Road

There are a few interesting things to see along the road to Lakagígar. **Fjarðrárgljúfur**, a peculiar, picturesque canyon, carved by the river Fjarðrá, is lined with steep rock walls and chunky promontories. It's only 3.5km north of the Ring Road and a walking track begins at the mouth of the canyon and follows the southern rim for a couple of kilometres. Around the nearby Holt farm is the small **Holtsborg Nature Reserve**. This is the only place in Iceland where wild roses grow naturally.

The surprising and relatively little-known **Fagrifoss** ('beautiful falls') is on the Geirlandsá river east of the Laki road, hidden from view by a low rise. Look for the turn-off about 22km north of the Ring Road.

Not far from Fagrifoss is a very deep **hole** in a small slump crater about 200m east of the Laki road. It doesn't seem to have a particular name but locals will jokingly tell you it's the back door to hell (Hekla is the front door). In

TRUE GRIT

When driving on the *sandur* in high winds, there's no avoiding the sandblasting a vehicle will suffer, but it will help to rinse the car with water (don't wipe it) once you're across. Car-wash hoses are free of charge at most Icelandic petrol stations.

For cyclists, the *sandur* becomes a nightmare when the wind blows. The fine sand and talcum-like glacial flour whip up into abrasive clouds, drift across the road and reduce visibility. Cyclists tell tales of being blown off the road and into sand drifts with no shelter from the stinging clouds. Be prepared to pitch a tent in the bleakest of surroundings and wait out the weather.

1989, an impromptu French expedition, the Groupe Speleo Gaillard, descended into the hole and ran out of rope at 45m with lots of hole left beneath them. The entrance to this unassuming cavern is just 35cm across and hidden in a cleft in the rocks, so it's unlikely you'll find it without a guide.

Tours

You can get to the Lakagígar area on the worthwhile 10-hour **BSÍ/Austurleið-SBS** (☎ 545 1717) bus from Skaftafell or Kirkjubæjarklaustur. It departs daily, from 1 July to 31 August, at 8am from Skaftafell (Ikr6500) and at 9am from Kirkjubæjarklaustur (Ikr4500). Tours can be booked at the tourist office or hotel in Kirkjubæjarklaustur. If you're staying at the camp site or one of the farmhouses, ring in advance for a pick-up.

THE SANDUR

The broad, desert expanse that sprawls along Iceland's southeastern coast is known as the *sandur*, which is another Icelandic word that's come into general international usage to describe a topographic phenomenon. In this case, it's the deposits of silt, sand and gravel scraped from the high peaks by glaciers and carried down in *jökulhlaups* and braided glacial rivers.

Skeiðarársandur, the most visible and dramatic of this phenomena, stretches some 40km between icecap and coast from Núpsstaður to Öræfi. Here you'll encounter a flat expanse of grey-black sands, some fierce winds and fast-flowing glacial rivers the colour of used dishwater.

Meðallandssandur

Meðallandssandur spreads across the Meðalland district south of Eldhraun and east of the river Kúðafljót. This sandy desert is so flat and featureless that a number of ships have run aground on its coast, apparently unaware they were nearing land. Shipwrecked sailors have died in quicksand while trying to get ashore. There are now several small lighthouses along the coast.

Skeiðarársandur

Impressive Skeiðarárjökull, 'the wandering river glacier', is Iceland's (and Europe's) largest valley glacier and covers an area of 1600 sq km. Its relentless scouring action, combined with the many Grímsvötn *jökulhlaups*, is responsible for this 600-sq-km glacial delta, the largest of Iceland's *sandur*.

Since Settlement, Skeiðarársandur has swallowed a considerable amount of farmland and it continues to grow. The area was relatively well populated (for Iceland, anyway), but in 1362 the volcano Öræfi beneath Öræfajökull erupted and the subsequent *jökulhlaup* laid waste the entire district.

The Ring Road across Skeiðarársandur, built in 1974, was the last bit of the National Highway to be constructed. Long gravel dykes have been strategically positioned to channel floodwaters away from this highly susceptible artery. They did little good, however, when in late 1996 three Ring Road bridges were washed away like matchsticks by the massive *jökulhlaup* released by the Grímsvötn (or Gjálp) eruption (see the boxed text on p264). There's a memorial of twisted bridge girders and an information board along the Ring Road just west of Skaftafell National Park.

Núpsstaður & Núpsstaðarskógar

Beneath the western cliffs of Lómagnúpur (Loon Peak; 767m) sits the Núpsstaður (Peak Stead) farm, which is towered over by bizarrely eroded cliffs and pinnacles. The farm buildings date back as far as the early 19th century and the small turf-roofed church, which is dedicated to St Nicholas, was mentioned in church records as early as 1200. It was renovated in 1657 by Einar Jónsson and the current building has been restored again by the National Museum. This is one of the last turf churches in Iceland to remain in general use.

Inland from Lómagnúpur is **Núpsstaðarskógar**, a beautiful woodland area on the slopes of the mountain Eystrafjall. This area is best explored on a tour run by the Hvoll HI Hostel (see Tours, p264).

About 10km southwest of Núpsstaður, **Hvoll HI Hostel** (☎ 487 4785; www.simnet.is/nupsstadarskogur; dm members/nonmembers Ikr1750/2150, s/d Ikr3100/5200; 🕑 Jun-Sep) is 3km off the Ring Road via a gravel road, which gives it a pretty remote feel. The hostel is in two buildings with kitchen, lounge and dining facilities. It's a little less homely than some smaller hostels but it's an excellent base for exploring Skaftafell, Núpsstaðarskógar and the surrounding *sandur*. Call ahead and the owners will pick you up from Núpsstaður.

JÖKULHLAUP!

In late 1996, the devastating Grímsvötn eruption – Iceland's fourth largest of the 20th century, after Katla in 1918, Hekla in 1947 and Surtsey in 1963 – shook Southeast Iceland and caused an awesome *jökulhlaup* (glacial flood) across Skeiðarársandur. The events leading up to it are a sobering reminder of the power of Iceland's volatile 'fire and ice' combination.

On the morning of 29 September 1996, a magnitude 5.0 earthquake shook the Vatnajökull icecap. Magma from a new volcano, in the Grímsvötn region beneath Vatnajökull, had made its way through the earth's crust and into the ice, causing the eruption of a 4km-long, subsurface fissure known as 'Gjálp'. The following day, the eruption burst through the surface, ejecting a column of steam that rose 10km into the sky and inspiring impressive aerial photography which was televised worldwide.

Scientists' concerns lay not so much with the ejecta itself, but with the fact that the subglacial lake in the Grímsvötn caldera was filling with water from ice melted by the heat of the eruption. Initial predictions on 3 October were that the ice would lift and the lake would give way within 48 hours and spill out across Skeiðarársandur, threatening the Ring Road and its bridges, which serve as vital links between eastern and western Iceland. In the hope of diverting floodwaters away from the bridges, massive dyke-building projects were organised on Skeiðarársandur.

On 5 November, over a month after the eruption started, the ice lifted and the Grímsvötn reservoir drained in a massive *jökulhlaup*, releasing up to 3000 billion cubic litres of water within a few hours. The floodwaters – dragging along icebergs the size of three-storey buildings – destroyed the 375m-long Gigja Bridge and the 900m-long Skeiðarár Bridge, both on the Skeiðarársandur, as well as another 50m-long bridge nearby. See video footage of the eruption and enormous multitonne blocks of ice being hurled across Skeiðarársandur at the Skaftafell visitor centre.

Grænalón

From the southern end of Núpsstaðarskógar, a good two- or three-day hike will take you over the ridges and valleys west of immense Skeiðarárjökull to Grænalón (Green Lagoon). This ice-dammed lake is best-known for its ability to drain like a bathtub. The 'plug' is the western edge of Skeiðarárjökull and, when the water pressure builds to breaking point, the glacier is lifted and the lake lets go. It has been known to release up to 2.7 million cu metres of water at 5000 cu metres per second in a single burst.

To get started, you'll have to join the Núpsstaðarskógar tour (see below), as it's impossible to cross the Núpsá and Súlaá rivers on foot. The topo sheet to use is Lómagnúpur 1:100,000 (1986).

Tours

One of Iceland's most rewarding day tours – especially when the sun is shining – is the eight- to nine-hour Núpsstaðarskógar tour run by **Hannes Jónsson** (☎ 487 4785; www.simnet.is/nupsstadarskogur; Ikr4100, children under 16 half-price) at Hvoll HI Hostel.

After a short ride to the eastern slopes of Lómagnúpur, you travel on foot to the Núpsá river, where you're pulled across on a raft and then driven to Núpsstaðarskógar. From there, a couple of hours' walk brings you to the confluence of the Núpsá and Hvitá, which spill over two spectacular turquoise-coloured waterfalls to converge in a dramatic canyon. The tours run from 9am to 6pm daily, from 1 July to 28 August, depending on demand, from the Núpsstaður farm. It's possible to connect with the morning bus from Skaftafell or arrive by your own transport. If you're coming from the other direction by bus, it's more convenient to stay the night at Hvoll HI Hostel and go from there.

Mountain Guides (☎ 587 9999, 899 9982; www.mountainguide.is) has a guided three-day hike through Núpsstaðarskógar and across the Hvítárdalur valley to the Björninn mountain ridge and back down to Núpsstaður. The trip costs Ikr20,900 with food, camping gear and transport from Skaftafell included.

SKAFTAFELL NATIONAL PARK

Iceland's largest and best-loved national park, Skaftafell offers unparalleled access to the stunning scenery of Southeast Iceland, where icecap and glaciers strive to meet the coast. Nowhere else can you so easily approach a glacier, see such lovely natural vegetation, enjoy such stunning panoramas of ice and ice-scoured rock, or gaze across a tangled web of braided rivers as they slice across the *sandur*.

Skaftafell merits its reputation and few Icelanders – even those who shun the great outdoors and leave Reykjavík only once in a summer – can resist it either. On long summer weekends you may be looking at a mob scene, with tent-fly-to-caravan-door camping conditions, a cacophony of boom-box stereo systems and raucous all-night parties. It can be lots of fun but may prove disappointing if you've come to camp and commune with nature. However, the Icelandic attitude of 'camping-means-party' is gradually changing, and nature-lovers and families are creating a more serene environment at Skaftafell. And if you're prepared to get out on the more remote trails and take advantage of the fabulous day hiking on the heath and beyond, you'll leave the crowds far behind.

The main drawback, for those without a tent or private transport, is that there's not much accommodation close to the park, so you may be limited to a few short hikes in between bus connections.

History

The historical Skaftafell was a large farm at the foot of the hills west of the present camp site, but a build-up of the *sandur* forced the farm to shift to a more suitable site, on the heath 100m above the *sandur*. The district came to be known as Hérað Milli Sandur (Land Between the Sands), but after all the farms were annihilated by the Öræfi eruptions of 1362, the district became the 'land under the sands' and was renamed Öræfi (Waste Land). Once the vegetation returned, however, the Skaftafell farm was rebuilt in its former location on the moor.

The modern park was jointly founded in 1967 by the Icelandic government and the World Wildlife Fund (now the World Wide Fund For Nature). It originally contained only the area cradled between Skeiðarárjökull and Skaftafellsjökull, and included Skaftafellsheiði (Shaft Mountain Heath), the Morsárdalur valley and the Skaftafellsfjöll range. In June 1984, the park was expanded to about 20% of the Vatnajökull icecap. Sheltered by mountains, Skaftafell enjoys better weather conditions than its surroundings, but the wind can still get very fierce, especially outside the summer months.

Information

The **Skaftafell visitor centre** (☎ 478 1627; 🕑 8am-9pm Jun-Aug, 8am-6pm May & Sep) has a useful information desk that hands out brochures and sell maps, a free exhibition with a video showing the Grímsvötn eruption and subsequent *jökulhlaup*, and informative displays on the Öræfi area, including geology, glaciers, flora, fauna and history.

All flora, fauna and natural features of the park are protected, open fires are prohibited and rubbish must be carried out. In the high-use area around Skaftafellsheiði, stick to the tracks to avoiding damaging delicate plant life.

Of course, advice not to approach or climb on glaciers without proper equipment and training should apply doubly here. The average ice block calving off Skaftafellsjökull would crush anyone within a few metres of the face.

Landmælingar Íslands publishes a thematic map of Skaftafell National Park showing the nonglacial area of the park at 1:25,000 and the Öræfi district at 1:100,000 (2002). It's available at the Skaftafell visitor centre (Ikr715) and in bookshops and tourist offices elsewhere in Iceland. You can also use the Öræfajökull 1:100,000 (1986) topo sheet.

Sel

This traditional farmhouse museum, built in Burstir style in 1912, has the typical appearance of several turf-roofed buildings attached by their side walls. Although there's not much inside – mostly bare floors with a few old bits of furniture and farmhouse equipment – it's worth a look around and is always open (free). The hill just above offers a good photo opportunity of the farmhouse and the grey *sandur* stretching out to the coast.

Hiking

Skaftafell is ideal for day hikes and also offers longer treks through its wilderness regions. Most of Skaftafell's visitors keep to the popular routes on Skaftafellsheiði. Hiking in other accessible areas, such as upper Morsárdalur and Kjós, requires more time, motivation and effort.

Wilderness camping permits are available from the information centre (Ikr600) and are compulsory. Also inquire about river crossings along your intended route. Without a permit, camping is forbidden

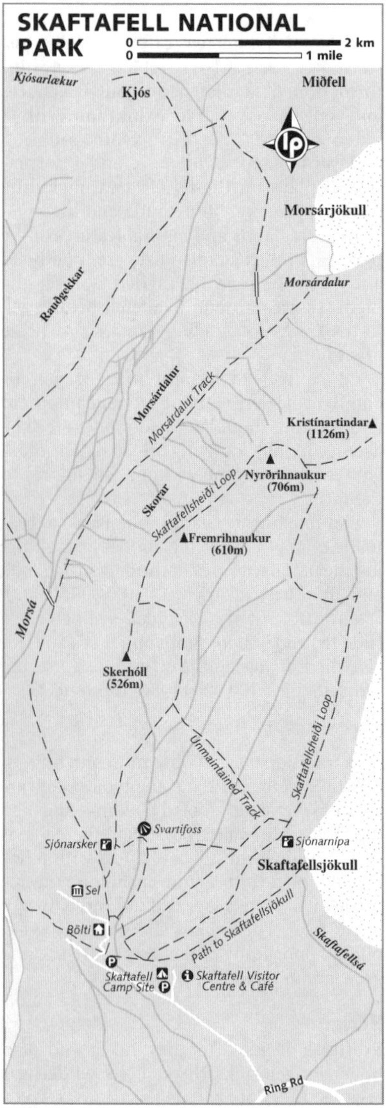

anywhere in the park outside the official camp site, including on the icecap!

SKAFTAFELLSJÖKULL

The park's most popular trail is the easy one-hour return walk to the glacier Skaftafellsjökull. The sealed track begins at the visitor centre and leads to the glacier face, where you can experience first-hand evidence of glacial activity – bumps, groans and flowing water – although the glacier is pretty dirty and ugly here. The glacier has been receding in recent years and over the past 50 years has lost nearly 1km of its length.

SVARTIFOSS

If Skaftafell has an identifying and much-photographed feature, it's Svartifoss, a lovely waterfall flanked by unusual overhanging basalt columns. It's reached by another easy and well-trodden track leading up from the camp site. Plan on 1½ hours for the return trip, although from the parking area above the camp site it's only about 45 minutes. From Svartifoss, it's worth continuing west up the short track to **Sjónarsker**, where there's a view disc and a memorable view across Skeiðarársandur.

SKAFTAFELLSHEIÐI LOOP

On a fine day, the five- to six-hour walk around Skaftafellsheiði is a hiker's dream. It begins by climbing from the camp site past Svartifoss and Sjónarsker, continuing across the moor to 610m-high **Fremrihnaukur**. From there it follows the edge of the plateau to the next rise, **Nyrðrihnaukur** (706m), which affords a superb view of Morsárdalur, Morsárjökull and the iceberg-choked lagoon at its base. Note Morsárjökull's perfect example of a medial moraine.

At this point, the track turns southeast to a point on the cliff above Skaftafellsjökull (Gláma). There you can begin to fathom the size of this relatively small river of ice!

For the best view of Skaftafellsjökull, Morsárdalur and the Skeiðarársandur, it's worth following one of the several possible routes to the summit of **Kristínartindar** (1126m). The easiest way follows a well-marked route up the prominent valley southeast of the Nyrðrihnaukur lookout.

MORSÁRDALUR & BÆJARSTAÐARSKÓGUR

The seven-hour hike from the camp site to the glacial lake in Morsárdalur is ordinary but enjoyable. There's a footbridge across the lake outlet, and from there you can continue to **Kjós**. Alternatively, cross the Morsá on the footbridge near the point where the Kambgil ravine comes down from Skaftafellsheiði and make your way across the gravel riverbed to the birch woods at **Bæjarstaðarskógur**.

The trees here reach a whopping (for Iceland) 12m and 80°C springs flow into the tiny but heavenly Heitulækir (Hot Stream) to the west in Vestragil. The return walk to Bæjarstaðarskógur takes about six hours; add an hour to visit Heitulækir.

OTHER HIKES

Other possibilities include the long day trip beyond Bæjarstaðarskógur into the rugged Skaftafellsfjöll. A recommended destination is the 965m-high summit of the **Jökulfell ridge**, which affords a commanding view of the vast expanses of Skeiðarárjökull. Even better is a three-day excursion into the **Kjós** region. When you reach Kjós, a very difficult hike leads to the base of Þumall ('the thumb'), then west along the glacier edge, around the valley rim, and southward down to your starting point.

Grímsvötn

Historically, Grímsvötn has been known to blow its top and release apocalyptic *jökulhlaups*, and it was Grímsvötn which caused the cataclysmic flood that carved out the Ásbyrgi canyon in just a few days (see p222). In 1934 it had a fit of temper which released a *jökulhlaup* of 40,000 cu metres per second, which swelled the river Skeiðará to 9km in width and laid waste large areas of farmland. Until October 1996, it remained deceptively inconspicuous, quietly rumbling away beneath a mantle of Vatnajökull ice – see the boxed text on p264.

Grímsvötn erupted again from 18 to 28 December 1998. A plume rose 10km into the air from a spot 10km south of the 1996 eruption, but there was no *jökulhlaup*. There's more information available at www.hi.is/~mmh/gos.

Tours

Mountain Guides (☎ 587 9999, 899 9982; www.mountainguide.is) is a professional outfit with a summer base at the Skaftafell camp site, but most of its organised hikes are outside the national park itself. Longer backpack hikes include the challenging four-day route from Núpsstaðarskógar, up the Núpsá canyon to Grænalón and over Skeiðarárjökull to Skaftafell (Ikr28,900, six to 12 people), and the epic nine-day trek from Laki to Skaftafell (Ikr62,900). The cost includes all food, tent camping, guides, equipment and transport.

Mountain Guides also offers two-day hikes and glacier walks in the Vatnajökull region – see the website for details.

Sleeping & Eating

Since Skaftafell is a national park, most people planning on staying here bring a tent and wind up at the **camp site** (☎ 478 1627; sites per person Ikr600, showers Ikr100 for 5 minutes) at park headquarters. The **café** at the visitor centre is the only place to eat here, with a range of snacks, sandwiches, burgers and hot meals, as well as a limited supply of groceries.

A fine alternative is the farm **Bölti** (☎ 478 1626; fax 478 2426; sb Ikr2000, s/d Ikr5000/6500), on Skaftafellsheiði above the western end of the camp site. There are rooms with made-up beds and views out over the *sandur* in the main farmhouse, and small cottages with cooking facilities. Book ahead in summer. Breakfast is Ikr900 and dinner is also available by advance request.

The nearest **hotel** is at Freysnes (see p268), about 5km east of the national park entrance, and there's more farmhouse accommodation (both sleeping bag and cabins) at the **Hof** and **Lítla-Hof** farms, 23km away.

Getting There & Away

From 1 June to 14 September, BSÍ/Austurleið-SBS buses run daily between Reykjavík and Höfn, leaving each end at 8.30am and passing Skaftafell at 2.35pm eastbound and 11.10am westbound. From 18 June to 5 September, there's another bus direct from Reykjavik to Skaftafell via the scenic inland route through Landmannalaugar and Eldgjá, departing daily from Reykjavík at 8.30am and arriving at Skaftafell at 7.30pm (Ikr5000). Westbound it departs from Skaftafell at 8am.

In winter the Reykjavík–Höfn bus runs on Tuesday, Friday and Sunday and departs at 12.30pm.

SKAFTAFELL TO HÖFN

From Skaftafell the Ring Road heads northeast, passing more visible valley glaciers and eventually leaving the *sandur* behind. The premier stop for tourists along here is the iceberg-filled Jökulsárlón, but there are also opportunities for glacier walks, tours on the Vatnajökull icecap, horse riding and several farms with accommodation. It's 130km from Skaftafell to Höfn.

Svínafell & Svínafellsjökull

The farm Svínafell, 8km southeast of Skaftafell, was the home of Flosi Þórðarson, the character who burned out Njál and his family in *Njáls Saga*. It was also the site where Flosi and Njál's family were finally reconciled, thus ending one of the bloodiest feuds in Icelandic history (see p117).

In the 17th century, the glacier Svínafellsjökull nearly engulfed the farm, but it has since retreated. From the road it's a short walk over the prominent terminal moraine to the snout of the glacier. There's not much to this tiny settlement now, but you can go swimming at **Flosalaug** (☎ 478 1765; 🕑 1-9pm), a complex with a pool, Jacuzzis, showers and camp sites.

ICE CLIMBING & GLACIER WALKS

You can get up onto Svínafellsjökull on a two- to three-hour glacier walk with **Mountain Guides** (☎ 587 9999, 899 9982; www.mountainguide.is; Ikr2990), based at Skaftafell National Park, and **Öræfaferðir** (☎ 478 2382, 854 0894; www.hofsnes.com; Ikr4000), based at the farm Hofsnes. The trips offer an introduction to ice climbing and include crampons and ice axes, but no technical experience is required. Mountain Guides also has a more difficult five-hour glacier walk (Ikr4990), and three-hour ice-climbing expeditions using ice walls on the glacier (Ikr4400).

SLEEPING & EATING

Hótel Skaftafell (☎ 478 1945; www.hotelskaftafell.is; sb Ikr2000, s/d Ikr10,500/13,900) This modern place on the Ring Road at Freysnes is the closest hotel accommodation to Skaftafell National Park. Rooms are bright and spacious, with TV and attached bathroom, and there's more basic sleeping-bag accommodation in the older wing. Lunch and dinner are available in the hotel **restaurant**. As locations go, it's pretty spectacular, with towering glaciers behind and the *sandur* and glacial rivers in front.

Flosi (☎ 478 1765; sb Ikr1800) At the swimming pool at Svínafell, this place has six basic cabins, each with four bunks, and a simple amenities block. If you have your own vehicle, it's an alternative to the camp site at Skaftafell.

Öræfajökull & Hvannadalshnúkur

Öræfajökull, the southernmost spur of Vatnajökull, forms a separate icecap over the immense Öræfi caldera. The volcanic eruption here in 1362 is thought to be the biggest tephra eruption in Iceland's recorded history. The nunatak (mountain peak) protruding above Öræfi's crater rim is known as **Hvannadalshnúkur**, which at 2119m is the highest point in Iceland.

The best access for climbing Hvannadalshnúkur is from Sandfellsheiði, above the abandoned farm Sandfell, about 12km southeast of Skaftafell. Climbers should be well versed in glacier travel, and although most guided expeditions manage the trip in a very long and taxing day (see Tours, following), independent climbers should carry enough supplies and gear for several days.

TOURS

Local companies **Öræfaferðir** (☎ 478 2382, 854 0894; www.hofsnes.com) and **Mountain Guides** (☎ 587 9999, 899 9982; www.mountainguide.is) run guided 10- to 15-hour ascents of Hvannadalshnúkur. The day trips costs Ikr10,000 per person (minimum of three people), including transport, guide and use of equipment. If you're fit and looking for a challenge, this is certainly one of the best deals in Iceland.

Transport is provided up to the snow line, where you transfer to snowshoes for the ascent to the 1820m-high crater rim. After walking across the crater, you make the final summit ascent with crampons and ice axe. You need to bring warm clothing, and your own food and water. Trips run on request, generally from June to August. It makes sense to book in advance and allow yourself extra days in case the weather causes a cancellation.

Hof

At the Hof (Temple) farm is a peat-brick and wooden church on the 1343 foundations of a previous church and a Viking temple dedicated to Þór. It was reconstructed in 1883 and now sits pleasantly in a thicket of birch and ash with flowers growing on the grassy roof.

Frost & Fire Guesthouse (☎ 478 1669; www.frostogfuni.is; sb Ikr1900, s/d Ikr5000/7000, d with bath Ikr8000) At the Hof farm, and beautifully situated beneath the Öræfajökull glacier, this guesthouse has a variety of rooms in the main farmhouses and chalets. A separate farm building has a kitchen, lounge and sleeping-bag accommodation. This is a good base for glacier tours to Öræfajökull. Nearby is another farm, **Lítla-Hof** (☎ 478 1670), with similarly priced rooms.

The nearest shop and snack bar is at the lonely **Esso petrol station** at Fagurhólsmýri, 5km east along the Ring Road.

Ingólfshöfði

The Ingólfshöfði promontory rises 76m above a sandy barrier island, about 8km across a shallow, tidal lagoon from the mainland coast. It was here that Ingólfur Arnarson, Iceland's first settler, stayed the winter on his original foray in Iceland in 874, and a monument on the cape marks the event. In the summer it's rife with nesting puffins and other sea birds, and you'll often see seals and whales offshore.

A 4WD track connects Ingólfshöfði to the Fagurhólsmýri farm, but even on foot or with a 4WD, it's a rough route across wet tidal flats, and it's easy to get bogged. Fortunately, farmer Sigurður Bjarnason runs three-hour tractor-and-haywagon tours daily in summer for Ikr1200 per person (minimum Ikr7200) from Fagurhólsmýri. The tours depart at 1.30pm from 20 June to 20 August, and there's an extra tour at 9.30am from 10 July to 10 August. The emphasis is on birdwatching and the trip includes a walk to the best viewing spot. Book through **Öræfaferðir** (☎ 478 2382, 854 0894; www.hofsnes.com).

Breiðamerkursandur

The easternmost of the big *sandurs*, Breiðamerkursandur is the home and main breeding ground of Iceland's largest colony of great skuas, the original dive bombers, which nest in grassy tufts atop low mounds. Thanks to this rich, easy-to-catch bounty, there's also a growing population of arctic foxes. If you want to see the birds, you can avoid painful aerial attacks by wearing a hat or carrying a stick above head level. At the western end of the *sandur*, **Kvíájökull glacier** snakes down to the Kvíá river and is easily accessible from the Ring Road via a short, signposted sideroad then an easy walk.

Above the *sandur* you'll see an expansive panorama of the glacier-capped mountains fronted by deep lagoons. The 742m-high **Breiðamerkurfjall** was once a nunatak enclosed by Breiðamerkurjökull and Fjallsjökull, but the glaciers have since retreated and freed it. At the foot of the peak is the glacial lagoon **Breiðárlón**, and the smaller Fjallsárlón, which are crowded with icebergs calved from Fjallsjökull. The scene here is similar to Jökulsárlón, but since it's some way back from the Ring Road and not immediately obvious, there are very few tourists here. It's worth the short drive (over a rough gravel road) or 20-minute walk from the highway to see it.

Breiðamerkursandur also figures in *Njáls Saga*, which ends with the remaining protagonist, Kári Sölmundarson, arriving in this idyllic spot to 'live happily ever after'.

Jökulsárlón

It's not every day you see luminous blue icebergs floating in a lake right beside a national highway, but that's the scene that confronts you as you sweep around a bend in the Ring Road, slowing to approach a small suspension bridge, and Jökulsárlón (Glacial River Lagoon) suddenly materialises.

The 200m-deep Jökulsárlón is an obligatory photo stop for travellers between Skaftafell and Höfn, and if possible it's worth spending a couple of hours here,

SOUTHEAST ICELAND

ICEBERGS ON FILM

Given the right lens treatment, Jökulsárlón presents a convincing enough Arctic scene to have attracted quite a few film and TV location teams to shoot here. A number of TV commercials, from Iceland and abroad, have used it as a backdrop, and in 1985 the opening scenes from the James Bond film *A View to a Kill* were shot here.

In 2002 the Bond crew were back to film scenes from *Die Another Day*. Bond (Pierce Brosnan) himself wasn't required – only his stunt double showed up – but they still reportedly managed to wreck six Aston Martins on set. The production crew even froze the lagoon over (in March) by blocking the river's passage to the sea. The remaining heavier salt water sunk to the bottom and the fresh water, which has a lower freezing temperature, froze over.

The following year, Lara Croft (Angelina Jolie) swapped Cambodia for Iceland for a brief scene in *Lara Croft: Tomb Raider* that was supposed to represent Siberia. The amphibious boats used to carry tourists were even painted grey and used as Russian ships.

exploring the various angles, looking for seals and taking an amphibious boat trip among the bergs. The lagoon, with a small river mouth flowing into the nearby ocean, is crammed with icebergs calved from the glacier Breiðamerkurjökull and, taken out of context, it makes a classic Arctic scene.

Breiðamerkurjökull seems to advance and retreat with some frequency, and in the restaurant near the lagoon there are aerial photos taken in 1945, 1982, 1990 and 1998, which show the changing patterns. In 1932 the glacier reached as far as the present Ring Road but, with around 100m of ice breaking off each year, it has retreated considerably since 1990 – over the past few years, the lagoon appears to have doubled in size.

A small colony of seals has made a home at the river mouth and individuals often come into the lagoon itself. If you can't spot any in the lagoon, wander over the Ring Road for a look.

BOAT TRIPS

The best way to get among the icebergs is to take the 40-minute spin in the novel, wheeled (amphibious) boats (Ikr1900). In summer cruises leave regularly from just outside the café, trundling off like a tour bus before splashing into the water. There's a guide on board so you can learn some useful information about the formation of the icebergs and why some of them appear so blue.

SLEEPING & EATING

The **Jökulsárlón café** (☎ 478 2122; www.jokulsarlon.is; 9am-7pm Jun–mid-Aug, shorter hours May & Sep) beside the lagoon is a good pit stop for information and some of Southeast Iceland's best seafood soup (Ikr750). You can also get coffee, fast food and sticky snacks from 9am to 8pm daily in summer.

It's possible to **camp** away from the Ring Road. The nearest farmhouse accommodation is at **Gerði** (☎ 846 0641; sb Ikr2000, made-up

RIDING ON THE VATNAJÖKULL ICECAP

For most travellers with any sense of adventure, seeing the glaciers of the Vatnajökull icecap from the Ring Road isn't enough – they have to get up there! There are a number of routes onto the icecap, but by far the easiest is up the F985 4WD road to the broad glacial spur, Skálafellsjökull (don't take 2WD cars up this road – you'll end up with a huge rescue bill).

At the top is the **Jöklasel glacier lodge** (☎ 478 1703; sb Ikr1800) and a beautifully situated **restaurant**, and from here Vatnajökull presents a clean, white slate. On a clear, fine day you can see 10km across the icecap to towering snowcapped peaks and south towards the ocean. Of course, it's one thing to get up here. In summer, there's a daily bus from Höfn leaving at 9am. It goes up to Jöklasel and back, then on to Jökulsárlón, then straight back to Höfn. But unless you're set up for a real polar-style expedition, exploration on Vatnajökull is limited to commercial tours – that's where snowmobiling comes in. Without a guide, or technical gear and expertise, hikers must not wander past the red poles planted in the ice about 1km from the hut. Beyond here are lots of snow-bridged crevasses and the danger is extreme. Even lower down, avoid any linear depressions in the snow. White-out conditions may also be a problem.

A quick and painless way to get above the valley glaciers and onto the icecap is with the daily Vatnajökull tour from Smyrlabjargarárvirkjun car park on the Ring Road. It follows the twisting, 16km 4WD road to the Jöklasel glacier lodge at the edge of Skálafellsjökull. There you're kitted out with overalls, boots and gloves and taken by glacier buggy to the snowmobiles. A one-hour Skidoo ride playing follow-the-leader gives you the briefest introduction to glacier travel. This tour costs Ikr7200 per person for the snowmobile ride from Jöklasel, or Ikr8900 if you include the super-jeep ride up. It's also possible to do a 2½-hour snowmobile trip to Brókarjökull, as well as cross-country skiing tours on the icecap (Ikr16,900). Most tours depart daily in summer and start to wind down around early September, but there's also a program of winter trips.

From Jöklasel, you can arrange day excursions by glacier buggy to Brókarjökull (2½ hours, Ikr14,000), Hvannadalshnúkur (eight to 11 hours, Ikr30,000), Kverkfjöll (eight to 10 hours, Ikr30,000), Grímsvötn (eight to 10 hours, Ikr30,000) or Goðahnúkur (eight to 10 hours, Ikr30,000).

The main tour operators on Vatnajökull are **Glacier Jeeps** (☎ 478 1000; www.glacierjeeps.is) and **Arctic Ice** (☎ 893 6024; www.arctic-ice.is). Coming from Höfn or Skaftafell, scheduled buses can drop you at the car park to link up with tours, or you may be able to arrange a pick-up.

beds Ikr2700), about 13km east along the Ring Road. This sprawling farm has a guesthouse with cooking and lounge facilities.

Suðursveit & Mýrar

East of Jökulsárlón, the Ring Road passes more farmland with mountainous backdrops split by occasional valley glaciers, then crosses the lovely **Mýrar**, a region of wetlands surrounding the deltas of Hornafjarðarfljót and Kolgrímaá, home to lots of water birds.

About 35km on is Route F985 to Jöklasel, the start for most tours on the Vatnajökull icecap – see the boxed text on p270.

The prominent and colourful mountain **Ketillaugarfjall** rises 670m above the Hornafjarðarfljót delta near Bjarnarnes. Its name derives from a legend about a woman named Ketillaug, who carried a pot of gold into the mountain and never returned. A brilliantly coloured alluvial fan at its base is visible from the road.

There are several good farmhouse accommodation options and a youth hostel in this area west of Höfn.

Vagnstaðir HI Hostel (☎ 478 1048; glacierjeeps@simnet.is; camping Ikr500, dm members/nonmembers Ikr1550/1900) As the home of the Vatnajökull Glacier Jeep outfit, this is the obvious place to stay the night before or after a tour. The hostel itself, by the Ring Road 50km west of Höfn, is a simple, purpose-built house in the shadow of some imposing mountains.

Smyrlabjörg (☎ 478 1074; smyrlabjorg@eldhorn.is; s/d Ikr6200/11,400) More like a hotel than a farm property, Smyrlabjörg has 48 modern rooms, all with satellite TV and attached bathroom. There's a restaurant which serves an Icelandic buffet (Ikr3100) for dinner in summer, and a bar. If you're after mod cons rather than a rural farmstay experience, this is the place.

Skálafell (☎ 478 1041; skalafell@isholf.is; sb Ikr2200, d Ikr7500-10,000) At the foot of the Skálafell glacier, this friendly working farm has a couple of rooms in the quaint family farmhouse, and three two-bedroom cabins. There are no cooking facilities but breakfast and dinner are available. The owners offer guided walking trips to the glacier.

Flatey (☎ 478 1036; flatey1@mmedia.is; sb Ikr2100, s/d without bathroom Ikr4000/6300, with bathroom Ikr4900/8100) With a pair of glacier tongues backing up to the property, Flatey has a great location and a variety of rooms in the family farmhouse or in a separate guesthouse with lounge and kitchen facilities.

Brunhóll (☎ 478 1029; brunnhol@eldhorn.is; s/d without bathroom Ikr5700/8500, with bathroom Ikr7200/10,900) A gorgeous farm property 30km from Höfn on the south side of the Ring Road, Brunhóll has a cosy, nine-room guesthouse and a bright, glassed-in dining room where breakfast is served.

HÖFN

pop 1783

The main town and harbour of the southeast, tiny Höfn almost appears as something of a 'metropolis' after the long drive from Vík or down the east coast from Egilsstaðir. Sprawling across a sandy spit in the lagoon Hornafjörður, it's a fairly modern fishing and fish-processing town set amid stunning surroundings – if you're coming from the northeast it offers your first view of Vatnajökull and its valley glaciers. As well as the typical fish catch, Höfn's port is known for lobster and prawns.

Since the completion of the Ring Road brought it within a day's drive of Reykjavík (until 1974, Höfnites had to drive to Reykjavík via Akureyri!), the population has grown significantly and the town has plenty of services, accommodation and a few good restaurants. As it's one of the cornerstones of the Ring Road, bus travellers will have to stay overnight here and most travellers stop in for the night anyway, so it pays to book accommodation in summer.

The town's name, which simply means 'harbour', is pronounced like an unexpected hiccup; if you're not prone to hiccups, just say 'hup' while inhaling.

Information

The useful **tourist office** (☎ 478 1500; www.east.is; Hafnarbraut 52; ⌚ 8am-8pm mid-Jun–mid-Sep; 💻) is at the camp site complex where the buses pull in. There's an Internet terminal here (Ikr250 for 30 minutes). In the off season information and Internet access can be found at the **library** (☎ 470 8050; Litlabrú; ⌚ 9am-7pm Mon-Thu, 11am-5pm Fri, 1-5pm Sat; 💻), in the community centre opposite the supermarket.

Landsbanki Íslands and Sparisjóðurinn banks, both on Hafnarbraut, handle foreign exchange from 9.15am to 4pm. The latter has a 24-hour ATM and you'll also

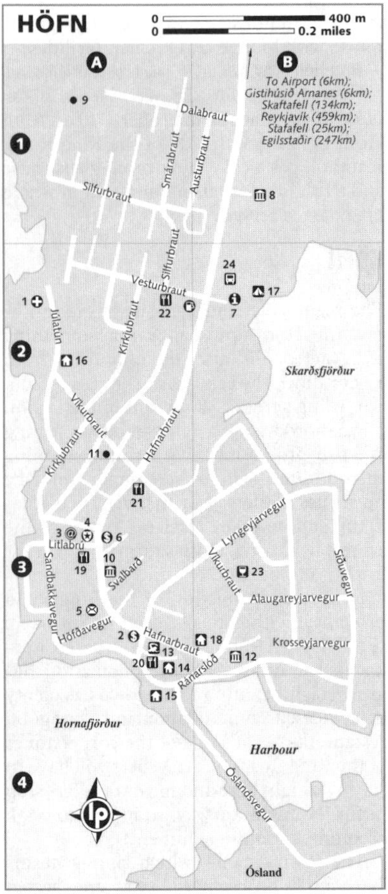

INFORMATION		
Hospital	1	A2
Landsbanki Íslands Bank	2	A3
Library (Internet Access)	3	A3
Police	4	A3
Post Office	5	A3
Sparisjóðurinn Bank (ATM)	6	A3
Tourist Office	7	B2
SIGHTS & ACTIVITIES	(pp272-3)	
Gamlabúð (Regional Folk Museum)	8	B1
Golf Course	9	A1
Jölasýning Glacier Exhibition	10	A3
Müsteridð	11	A2
Pakkhúsuð (Maritime Museum)	12	B3
Swimming Pool	13	A3
SLEEPING	(p273)	
Gistiheimilið Hvammur	14	A3
Gistiheimilið Ásgarður	15	A4
Hótel Höfn	16	A2
Höfn Camp Site	17	B2
Nýibær HI Hostel	18	B3
EATING	(p273)	
11-11 Supermarket	19	A3
Hafnarbúðin Snack Bar	20	A3
Kaffi Hornið	21	A3
Kronan Supermarket	22	A2
DRINKING	(p273)	
Víkinn Pub	23	B3
TRANSPORT	(p274)	
Bus Terminal	24	B2

find an ATM in the 11-11 supermarket on Hafnarbraut.

Sights

JÖKLASÝNING GLACIER EXHIBITION

Everything you need to know about Vatnajökull and glaciers in general should become clear at the **Glacier Exhibition** (☎ 478 2665; adult/child Ikr500/free; 1-6pm & 8-10pm Jun-early Sep). The collection of exhibits relating to glacier expeditions – including a tent, clothing, an old *pulka* (boat-shaped sled), crampons and snowshoes – is pretty sparse, but informative panels and photographs explain glacial action, *jökulhlaups*, current changes in the icecap, and research and expeditions. Your first port of call should be the 10-minute video of the 1996 Grímsvötn eruption and other cataclysmic Vatnajökull activity.

Lectures about Vatnajökull are given at 8pm every second Tuesday of the month.

MUSEUMS

Höfn has two local museums, which are worth a look, not least because they're both free. The regional folk museum **Gamlabúd** (☎ 478 1833; 1-6pm Jun-Sep), near the tourist office and camp site, is housed in an 1864 trade warehouse, which was moved to Höfn from Papaós, further east. It has agricultural displays as well as small natural history and marine life exhibits. A collection of farm machinery stands out the front.

Pakkhúsið (☎ 478 1540; Krosseyjarvegur; 1-6pm), the local maritime museum near the harbour, displays old fishing equipment, boats, tools and photographs. There's also an art and craft gallery here with local handicrafts and textiles for sale.

Activities

The **swimming pool** (☎ 478 1157; Hafnarbraut 11; Ikr200; 7am-8.30pm Mon-Fri, 9am-6pm Sat & Sun) has an outdoor heated pool and hot pots. If you feel like a bit of pampering, **Müsterið** (☎ 478 2380; Víkurbraut) is a private spa, sauna and massage centre.

Höfn has a nine-hole **golf course** at the end of Dalabraut at the north end of town.

Horse rental is available at the farm Árnanes (☎ 478 1550; www.arnanes.is), 6km west of Höfn (see Sleeping, below).

Tours

For information on Vatnajökull tours, see the boxed text on p270.

Festivals & Events

Höfn hosts an annual tourist-oriented festival, **Humarhátið** (lobster party), in July, in honour of the lowly lobster, which is a renowned local catch. It takes place around the first or second week in July with a fun fair, flea markets, dancing, music, ice sculpture competitions (yes, in July!), lots of alcohol and even a few lobsters.

Sleeping

Lots of travellers stay at Höfn's hilly **camp site** (☎ 478 1500; Hafnarbraut 52; camp sites Ikr600 per person, sb Ikr2000, 6-person cabins Ikr6500) on the main road into town. As well as camping there are four log cabins, but there are no cooking or bathroom facilities inside.

Nýibær HI Hostel (☎ 478 1736; nyibaer@simnet.is; Hafnarbraut 8; dm members/nonmembers Ikr1650/2000, s/d Ikr1000 extra, d with bathroom members/nonmembers Ikr5600/6400) Höfn's best budget option is usually bustling with travellers in summer (it's open all year). It's in an old but cosy house with a separate kitchen and a dining room that doubles as the common area (where many a glacier tour and long-distance hike has been dissected!).

Gistiheimilið Hvammur (☎ 478 1503; hvammur3@simnet.is; Ránarslóð 2; sb Ikr2000, s/d Ikr5500/6900; 💻) One of two decent guesthouses down by the harbour, Hvammur has 13 clean, spacious rooms with shared bathroom and satellite TV. There's a dining area, guest kitchen and Internet access.

Gistiheimilið Ásgarður (☎ 478 1365; asgardur@eldhorn.is; Ránarslóð 3; s/d Ikr7600/9200) Harbourside Ásgarður is more like a hotel than a guesthouse. All rooms have attached bathroom and small TV, and some have good glacier or (less inspiring) harbour views. It's all a bit drab but the location is good and the management friendly. Breakfast costs Ikr850.

Hótel Höfn (☎ 478 1240; www.hotelhofn.is; Vikurbraut; s/d/ste Ikr10,900/15,100-12,700/18,100) Höfn's business-class hotel is often busy with tour groups in summer, but still manages to be a welcoming place. It's a bit frayed around the edges and even the deluxe rooms are not flash. All rooms have attached bathroom and TV and breakfast is included, plus there are a couple of decent restaurants here.

Gistihúsið Árnanes (☎ 478 1550; www.arnanes.is; sb Ikr2300, s/d Ikr5700/7200, with bathroom Ikr7500/9900) Back on the Ring Road 6km west of Höfn, this rural place is an excellent choice for cosy guesthouse accommodation in cottages or budget rooms. There's also a very ambient dining room and gallery (the owner is the artist) serving set meat and fish courses every evening (from Ikr1500).

Eating & Drinking

Kaffi Hornið (☎ 478 2600; Hafnarbraut; 🕑 10am-11.30pm, 10am-3am Fri & Sat; light meals Ikr600-1920, mains Ikr1550-2990) In the timber house as you enter town, this is a bit of a gem – a relaxed, unpretentious restaurant and bar with first-rate food. Light meals and lunches such as crepes, baguettes and sandwiches are reasonably priced and there's a self-service salad bar (Ikr600). For dinner there's local lobster, fish and superb lamb dishes. There's even a couple of vegetarian options, such as the interesting 'vegetable steak with estragon sauce'. The bar and side lounge (with open fire) is a good place for an evening drink.

Ósinn (☎ 478 2200; 🕑 9am-10 pm; mains Ikr490-2690) In the Hotel Höfn, Ósinn specialises in pizza and pasta, but also has a full complement of burgers, grill snacks, soup, and fish and lamb dishes. It's a pleasant family sort of restaurant, open year-round. The 1st-floor **hotel dining room** (☎ 478 1240; 🕑 summer only; mains Ikr1990-3900) is a good place for a splurge. Try lobster and other local fish dishes, as well as puffin and lamb. There's also a cocktail bar and views across to the glacier.

Víkinn Pub (☎ 478 2300; Víkurbraut) This pub-restaurant and pizza bar lacks much in character, but it's a popular drinking hole and nightclub, open till 3am on Friday and Saturday nights.

Hafnarbúðin (☎ 478 1095; snacks Ikr160-600) This snack bar on Ránarslóð near the harbour does a brisk trade in hot dogs, burgers and submarine sandwiches.

The **11-11** supermarket is conveniently located opposite the town hall and police station on Hafnarbraut, while **Kronan**, on Vesturbraut, is close to the camp site.

Getting There & Away

AIR

Höfn's airport is about 6km northwest of town. From May to August **Air Iceland** flies daily (except Tuesday and Saturday) between Reykjavík and Höfn (Hornafjörður; Ikr6575 one way).

BUS

Buses arrive and depart at the tourist office and camp site, which is a 10-minute walk from the town centre. From 1 June to 14 September, there are daily buses between Reykjavík and Höfn, leaving from both ends at 8.30am and arriving at 5pm. At other times of year, they run on Tuesday, Friday and Sunday only, departing at 12.30pm. Fares from Höfn include: Jökulsárlón (Ikr1110, 1½ hours), Skaftafell (Ikr1930, 2½ hours), Kirkjubæjarklaustur (Ikr2790, four hours), Vík (Ikr3870, 5¼ hours), Hella (Ikr5280, 6½ hours), Reykjavík (Ikr6620, 8½ hours). From June to the end of August there's an additional bus from Höfn to Jökulsárlón and back at 9am.

To Egilsstaðir, buses leave daily at 8.30am from 1 June to 31 August (Monday, Wednesday and Friday only in May and September); from Egilsstaðir, they leave at 2pm. Fares include: Stafafell (Ikr520, 30 minutes), Djúpivogur (Ikr1710, 1 hour 40 minutes), Berunes (Ikr2260, two hours) and Egilsstaðir (Ikr4790, four hours).

LÓNSÖRÆFI

East of Höfn the Ring Road passes Lónsöræfi (Lagoon Wilderness), a protected nature reserve taking in the vast farm Stafafell and the Stafafellsfjöll mountains. The spectacularly colourful rhyolite scenery and countless hiking options will keep you occupied for days, but it's also a friendly and relaxing spot to settle in and enjoy the facilities and hospitality of the Stafafell youth hostel.

Numerous day hikes can be done using Stafafell as a base, but it's also possible to camp at sites in the reserve, and there are mountain huts along the Lónsöræfi–Snæfell hike, which begins (or ends) at the Illikambur parking area. The only road in the reserve is the rough 4WD track which ends at Illikambur. There's nowhere to eat or buy food here, so bring supplies from Höfn or Djúpivogur.

STAFAFELL

Nestled between the rainbow-hued Lónsöræfi peaks and Lónssandur, the delta of Jökulsá í Lóni, Stafafell functioned as a remote parsonage until 1920 and the present church contains some lovely artefacts, including an original altarpiece. Stafafell is not a village – merely a farm – and the only facilities here are at the youth hostel. This is the obvious base for exploring Lónsöræfi, and tours and hikers' transport can be organised here.

Stafafell HI Hostel (☎ 478 1717; www.eldhorn.is/stafafell; sb member/nonmembers Ikr1500/1800, s/d Ikr4500/6000, with bathroom Ikr5400/7500) Stafafell is one of the friendliest hostels in Iceland, thanks to the efforts of Mr Bergsveinn Ólafsson. Accommodation is in either the 19th-century farmhouse or two cottages, all with access to cooking facilities. The farmhouse is in varying states of repair, but is cosy enough. The cottages, with their own kitchen, lounge and TV, are good for groups or families. Camping is Ikr500 and breakfast is available for Ikr800. Although dinner can be arranged with advance notice during summer, it's best to bring your own food – the nearest store is 25km away in Höfn.

LÓN

The name 'Lón', which is pronounced 'lone' and means 'lagoon', fairly sums up the nature of this shallow bay enclosed by two long spits between the Austurhorn and Vesturhorn. To the northwest is the delta of **Jökulsá í Lóni**, a breeding ground for swans. Boat tours can be arranged through the Stafafell hostel. Don't miss seeing the enormous colony of swans which nests at the eastern end of Lón in spring and autumn.

As with most other peaks in the region, the batholithic peak **Austurhorn**, at the eastern end of Lón, was formed as an igneous intrusion beneath the surface and was then thrust up and revealed through erosion of the overlying material. This is the best access for strolls on the Fjörur sandspit, which encloses the eastern portion of Lón.

At the western end of Lón, the commanding 575m-high peak **Vesturhorn** and its companion **Brunnhorn** form a cape between Skarðsfjörður and Papafjörður. Ruins of the fishing settlement Syðri-Fjórður, which was abandoned in 1899, are still visible, and just south of it are the more intriguing ruins of Papatóttir.

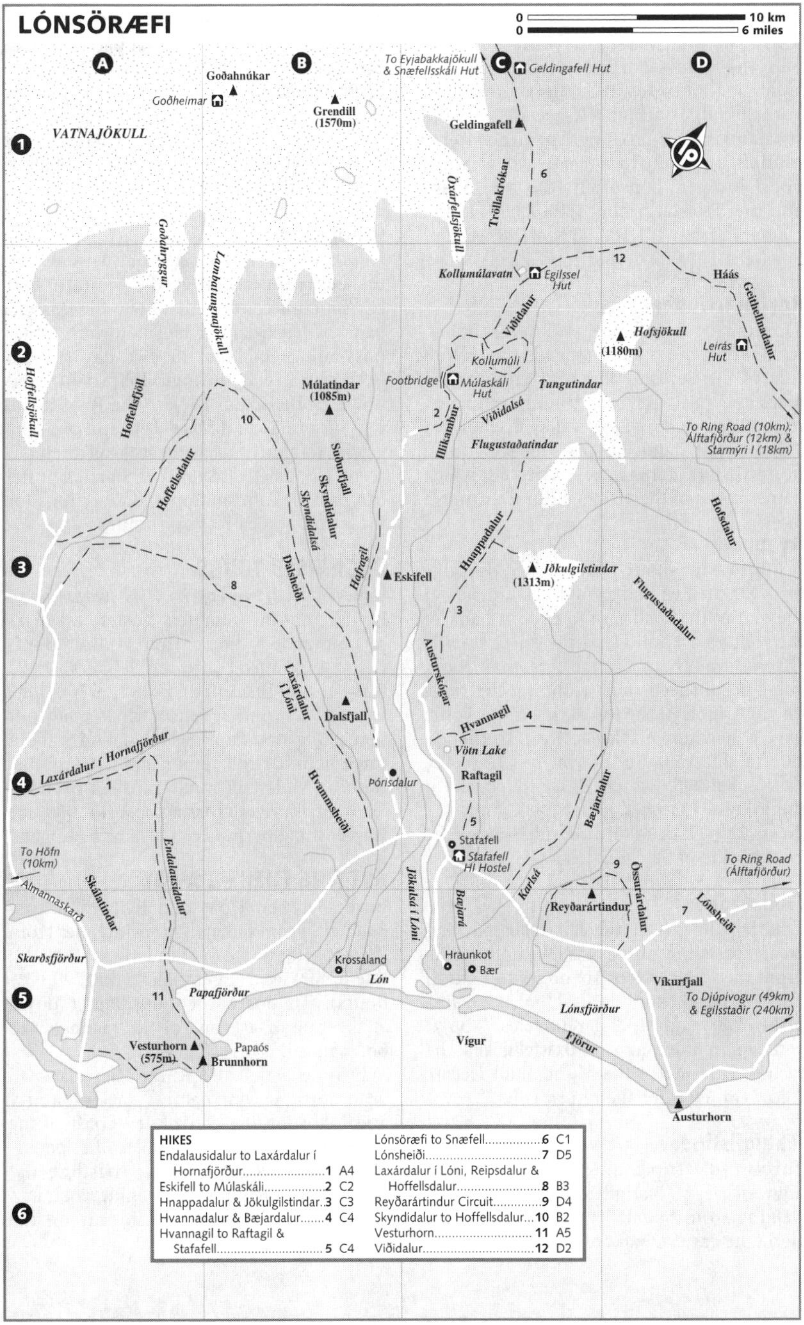
LÓNSÖRÆFI
0 10 km
0 6 miles
VATNAJÖKULL
Goðahnúkar
Goðheimar
Grendill
(1570m)
To Eyjabakkajökull & Snæfellsskáli Hut
Geldingafell Hut
Geldingafell
Öxárfellsjökull
Tröllakrókar
Goðahryggur
Lambatungnajökull
Kollumúlavatn
Egilssel Hut
Háás
Geithellnadalur
Víðidalur
Kollumúli
Hofsjökull
(1180m)
Leirás Hut
Hoffellsjökull
Hoffellsfjöll
Múlatindar
(1085m)
Footbridge
Múlaskáli Hut
Tungutindar
Víðidalsá
Illikambur
Flugustaðatindar
To Ring Road (10km); Álftafjörður (12km) & Starmýri I (18km)
Hoffellsdalur
Suðurfjall
Skyndidalur
Skyndidalsá
Hofsdalur
Hnappadalur
Dalsheiði
Hafragil
Eskifell
Jökulgilstindar
(1313m)
Flugustaðadalur
Austurskógar
Laxárdalur í Lóni
Dalsfjall
Hvannagil
Vötn Lake
Raftagil
Laxárdalur í Hornafjörður
Þórisdalur
Hvammsheiði
Bæjardalur
Stafafell
Stafafell HI Hostel
To Höfn (10km)
Endalausidalur
Jökulsá í Lóni
Bæjará
Karlsá
Össurárdalur
To Ring Road (Álftafjörður)
Almannaskarð
Skálatindar
Reyðarártindur
Lónsheiði
Skarðsfjörður
Krossaland
Lón
Hraunkot
Bær
Víkurfjall
Papafjörður
To Djúpivogur (49km) & Egilsstaðir (240km)
Lónsfjörður
Vesturhorn
(575m)
Papaós
Brunnhorn
Vígur
Fjörur
Austurhorn
HIKES
Endalausidalur to Laxárdalur í Hornafjörður 1 A4
Eskifell to Múlaskáli 2 C2
Hnappadalur & Jökulgilstindar 3 C3
Hvannadalur & Bæjardalur 4 C4
Hvannagil to Raftagil & Stafafell 5 C4
Lónsöræfi to Snæfell 6 C1
Lónsheiði 7 D5
Laxárdalur í Lóni, Reipsdalur & Hoffellsdalur 8 B3
Reyðarártindur Circuit 9 D4
Skyndidalur to Hoffellsdalur 10 B2
Vesturhorn 11 A5
Víðidalur 12 D2

HIKING

There are many easy day hikes in the hills and valleys north of Stafafell, as well as longer hikes towards the southeast of Vatnajökull. Some of these walks require substantial river crossings, so use extreme caution, especially in warm or wet weather. For hiking in Lónsöræfi, the best maps are the Hornafjörður 1:100,000 (1986), Hamarsfjörður 1:100,000 (1987) and Snæfell 1:100,000 (1988) topo sheets.

Reyðarártindur

This four-hour walk begins 7km east of Stafafell. From the road, it ascends the eastern side of the **Reyðará Valley** and circumnavigates the peak Reyðarártindur, returning to the Ring Road via the valley **Ossurardalur**, 11km east of Stafafell. Across the Ring Road near the start of this walk is a **view disc** which names some of the visible natural features.

Hvannagil

A four- or five-hour, well-marked day hike from Stafafell will take you to Hvannagil, at the end of the road on the eastern bank of the Jökulsá í Lóni. Head up this dramatic rhyolite valley and, after less than 1km, you'll see a sheep track climbing the ridge on your right. At the top of this ridge, you'll have a view down **Seldalur**. Keep to the left side of this valley until you pass the side valley, **Raftagil**, which descends back to the Jökulsá í Lóni. You can pick your way down Raftagil or follow the ridge above the eastern side of Seldalur.

Tröllakrókur

This trip begins at the **Illikambur** parking area, accessible along 4WD Route F980. From there, it's five or six hours to Egilssel hut at Tröllakrókur (Trolls' Hooks), an area of bizarre wind-eroded pinnacles. Above, you can see the tongue of **Öxárfellsjökull**, the eastern extreme of the Vatnajökull icecap. Allow two days for the return trip.

Jökulgilstindar

This two-day trip climbs up to the 1313m-high icecap Jökulgilstindar. Begin by walking from Stafafell up the 4WD track along the eastern bank of **Jökulsá í Lóni**, then continue up the valley through the Austurskógar woods toward Hnappadalur. You can either continue up to the headwaters of **Hnappadalur** or climb steeply to Jökulgilstindar from a short way up the valley. The top has a glacier and hikers should be experienced with glacier travel before venturing onto the ice.

Other Routes

Another hike is the one- or two-day trip up **Endalausidalur**, from the western foot of Almannaskarð, and down the eastern bank of Laxárdalur í Hornafjörður. Other possibilities include the two-day trip up **Laxárdalur í Lóni**, through Reipsdalur and down Hoffellsdalur back to the Ring Road. Or you can ascend **Skyndidalur** and skirt the glacier tongue of **Lambatungnajökull** then descend along **Hoffellsdalur**. The Stafafell hostel can provide information and directions for these and other hikes and routes.

ORGANISED TOURS

Lónsöræfaferðir (☎ 478 1717; www.eldhorn.is/stafafell), at the Stafafell hostel, arranges recommended horse tours and 4WD excursions into Lónsöræfi. Hikers' 4WD transfers to Illikambur cost Ikr2500/4000 one way/return. The return trip is a day tour (departing at 9.30am), which includes about three hours at Illikambur and a 45-minute walk to Múlaskáli hut. Transfers over the Skyndidalsá river crossing cost Ikr1000 one way. Fishing permits can also be arranged.

GETTING THERE & AWAY

Buses between Höfn and Egilsstaðir pass Stafafell. From Stafafell fares include: Höfn (Ikr520, 30 minutes), Djúpivogur (Ikr1710, one hour) and Egilsstaðir (Ikr4790, 3½ hours). To board the bus, flag it down at the gate or ask one of the managers to book ahead.

From Stafafell the Ring Road starts to head north, leaving behind glacier country and following the convoluted coast of the Eastfjords. The stretch from Hvalnes peninsula to Djúpivogur hugs the coastline and passes beneath some frightening rock and shale mountain faces that appear on the verge of a landslide!

The Interior

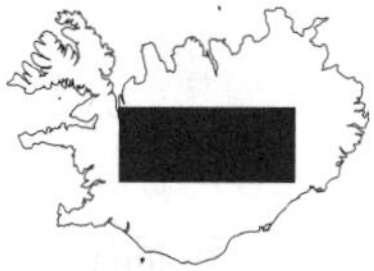

CONTENTS

Iceland's vast, lunarlike Interior comprises one of Europe's greatest wilderness areas, and although it isn't a true desert – it receives far too much precipitation for that – it's as close as you'll get anywhere in Europe. Historically, Interior routes were used during summer months as short cuts between the northern and southern coasts. It was a region which existed only as a barrier between where one was and where one wanted to go, and early travellers put it behind them as quickly as possible. Outlaws fled to the central highlands and those that survived gained legendary, superhuman status.

Even today, travelling in Iceland's uninhabited centre isn't like travelling anywhere else in the country. There are practically no services, accommodation, hot-dog stands, bridges, mobile-phone signals or guarantees should something go wrong. In some cases, there isn't even a road. Gazing across the expanses, you could imagine yourself in Tibet, Mongolia or, as many people have noted, on the moon. The Apollo astronauts even held exercises here in preparation for their lunar landing. Some travellers find the Interior routes disappointing, bleak and just plain hard work. Others find the isolation and desolation exhilarating and the satisfaction of completing a tough cross-country crossing rewarding in itself.

Weather is always a concern. Conditions can be fickle and snow isn't uncommon, even in the summer months of July and August. Good warm clothing and protection for the face and eyes from gritty, wind-driven sand are particularly important.

TOP FIVE

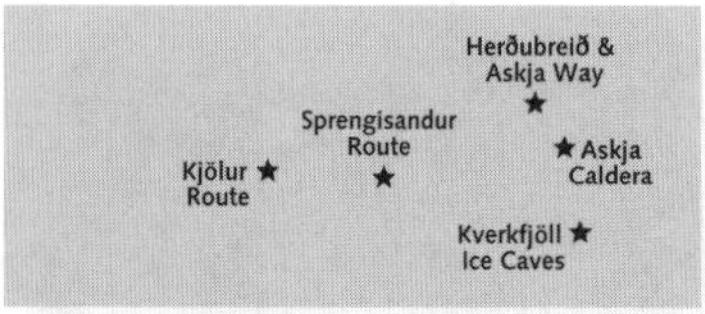

- Bathing in the turquoise waters of the Viti crater at the **Askja caldera** (p286)
- Driving or taking the bus along the **Kjölur Route**, Iceland's most accessible inland route (p280)
- Seeing where that 'fire and ice' tag comes from at the hot-spring-filled **Kverkfjöll ice caves** (p288)
- Experiencing the sheer isolation of crossing central Iceland on the **Sprengisandur Route** (p282).
- Hiking around **Herðubreið** (p284) and the lava fields of **Askja** (p286)

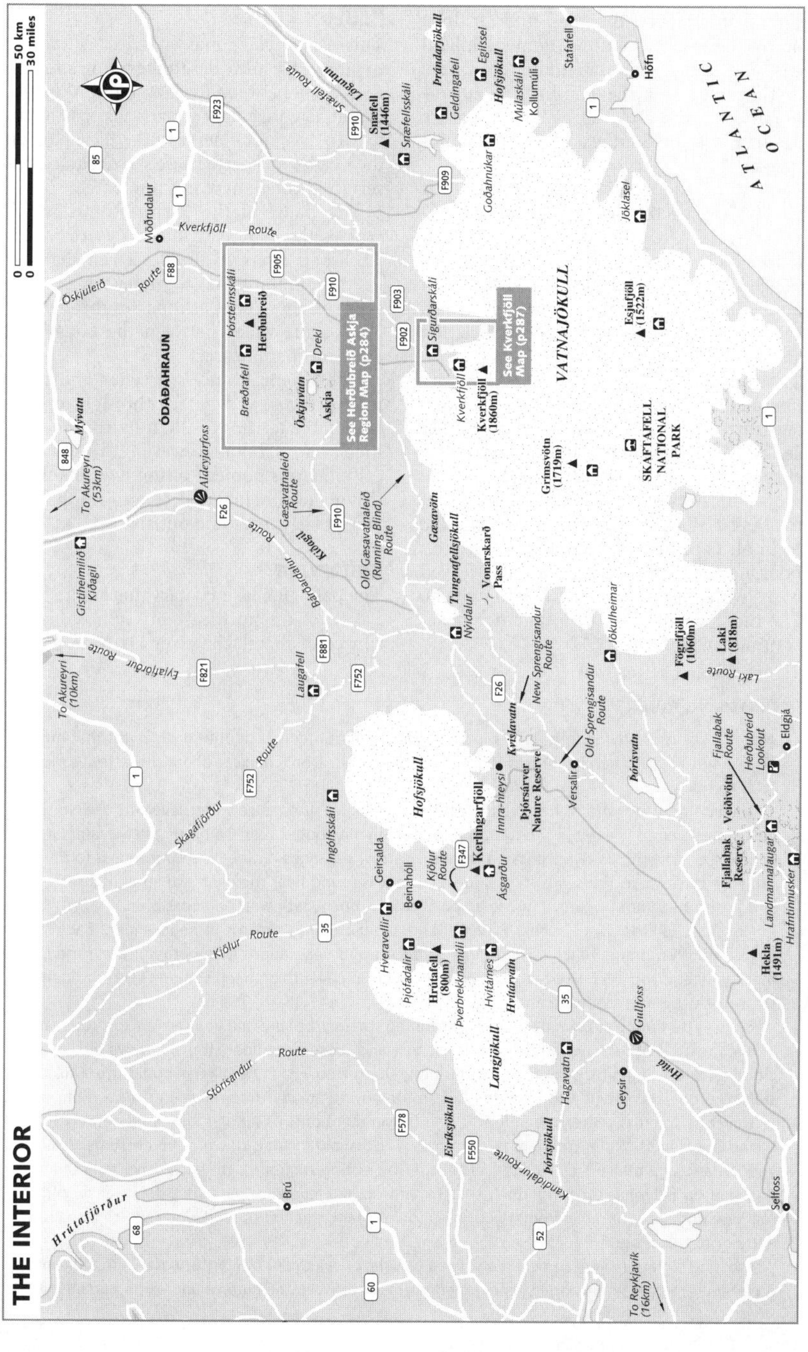
THE INTERIOR
0 50 km
0 30 miles
ATLANTIC OCEAN
VATNAJÖKULL
SKAFTAFELL NATIONAL PARK
ÓDÁÐAHRAUN
Hofsjökull
Langjökull
Eiríksjökull
Þórisjökull
Tungnafellsjökull
Hofsjökull
Þrándarjökull
See Herðubreið Askja Region Map (p284)
See Kverkfjöll Map (p287)
Herðubreið
Herðubreið
Þorsteinsskáli
Bræðrafell
Dreki
Öskjuvatn
Askja
Kverkfjöll
Kverkfjöll (1860m)
Sigurðarskáli
Snæfell (1446m)
Snæfellsskáli
Snæfell Route
Lögurinn
Geldingafell
Egilssel
Múlaskáli
Kollumúli
Goðahnúkar
Stafafell
Höfn
Jöklasel
Esjufjöll (1522m)
Grímsvötn (1719m)
Gæsavötn
Vonarskarð Pass
Nýidalur
Jökulheimar
Fögrifjöll (1060m)
Laki (818m)
Laki Route
Eldgjá
Herðubreid Lookout
Fjallabak Route
Fjallabak Reserve
Veiðivötn
Landmannalaugar
Hrafntinnusker
Hekla (1491m)
Þórisvatn
Versalir
Old Sprengisandur Route
New Sprengisandur Route
Kvíslavatn
Þjórsárver Nature Reserve
Innra-hreysi
Kerlingarfjöll
Ásgarður
Kjölur Route
Hveravellir
Beinahóll
Geirsalda
Ingólfsskáli
Þjófadalir
Hrútafell (800m)
Þverbrekknamúli
Hvítárnes
Hvítárvatn
Hagavatn
Gullfoss
Geysir
Hvítá
Selfoss
To Reykjavík (16km)
Kaldidalur Route
Stórisandur Route
Brú
Hrútafjörður
Skagafjörður Route
Eyjafjörður Route
To Akureyri (10km)
To Akureyri (53km)
Laugafell
Bárðardalur Route
Kiðagil
Gistiheimilið Kiðagil
Aldeyjarfoss
Gæsavatnaleið Route
Old Gæsavatnaleið (Running Blind) Route
Mývatn
Öskjuleið Route
Möðrudalur
Kverkfjöll Route
1
35
52
60
68
85
848
F26
F88
F347
F550
F578
F752
F821
F881
F902
F903
F905
F909
F910
F923

This chapter covers the main Interior driving routes and attractions. Popular inland trekking routes can be found elsewhere in this book: for the Landmannalaugar–Þórsmörk Trek and the Fjallabak Nature Reserve, see the Southeast Iceland chapter (p251).

Most of the routes described in this chapter are strictly for high-clearance 4WD vehicles. If you're driving, it's recommended that vehicles travel in pairs, so if one gets bogged, the other can drag it out or fetch help. Carry lots of supplies, especially if you can scarcely afford to take one vehicle, let alone two!

Almost all mountain huts in Iceland are operated by **Ferðafélag Íslands** (Iceland's Touring Association; ☎ 568 2533; www.fi.is; Mörkin 6, IS-108 Reykjavík). The **Ferðafélag Akureyrar** (Touring Club of Akureyri; ☎ 472 2720; www.ffa.est.is) operates all the mountain huts and most camp sites along the Askja Way. In summer it is advisable to book your accommodation in advance; bookings are on a first-come-first-served basis, with cheaper rates for club members. For more details about mountain hut accommodation see p292.

KJÖLUR ROUTE

This is a popular route with visitors wanting to sample Iceland's desertlike centre and take a short cut between Reykjavík and Akureyri. Route 35 conveniently starts just past Gullfoss (p106) and emerges near Blönduós on the northwest coast. There's a scheduled bus service through here in summer.

The name of the Kjölur Route, which crosses the central highland desert, means 'keel' and refers to the perceived shape of the topography. At its highest point, the track reaches 700m as it passes through the 30km-wide valley between the Langjökull and Hofsjökull icecaps.

The Kjölur Route is greener and more interesting – and passes through less inhospitable territory – than its counterpart, the Sprengisandur. However, it was historically the less popular of the two, thanks to the general belief that it was infested by particularly fearsome outlaws.

Hvítárvatn

The pale-blue lake Hvítárvatn (White River Lake), 45km northeast of Gullfoss, is the source of the glacial river Hvítá. A glacier

CROSSING RIVERS

While trekking or driving in Iceland's Interior, you'll undoubtedly face unbridged rivers that must be crossed – a frightening prospect for the uninitiated. Don't panic – there are a few simple rules to follow.

The sun and heat of the day melt snow and glacial ice and cause water levels to rise, so the best time to cross is early in the morning, preferably no sooner than 24 hours after a rainstorm. Remember, constricted rivers passing through narrow passages run deep, so the widest ford will likely be shallowest. The swiftest, strongest current is found near the centre of straight stretches and at the outside of bends. Choose a spot with as much slack water as possible.

Never try to cross just above a waterfall and avoid crossing streams in flood – identifiable by dirty, smooth-running water carrying lots of debris and vegetation. A smooth surface suggests that the river is too deep to be crossed on foot. Anything over thigh deep shouldn't be considered crossable without experience and extra equipment.

Before attempting to cross deep or swift-running streams, be sure that you can jettison your pack in midstream if necessary. Unhitch the waist belt and loosen shoulder straps, remove any bulky clothing that will inhibit swimming, and remove long trousers. Lone hikers should use a hiking staff to probe the river bottom for the best route and to steady themselves in the current.

Never try to cross a stream barefoot (a pair of wet-suit boots or sandals will avoid getting your hiking boots wet). While crossing, face upstream and avoid looking down or you may risk losing your balance. Two hikers can steady each other by resting their arms on each other's shoulders.

If you do fall while crossing, don't try to stand up. Remove your pack (but don't let go of it), roll over onto your back, and point your feet downstream, then try to work your way to a shallow eddy or to the shore.

Crossing a glacial river can be a hazard in a vehicle. Check the depth of the water if possible and drive slowly across in a wedge shape, entering the water with the current and exiting against it.

tongue of Iceland's second largest icecap, Langjökull, calves into the lake and creates icebergs, adding to the beauty of this spot.

In the marshy grasslands northeast of Hvítárvatn is the 30-bed Hvítárnes hut, with cooking facilities. Built in 1930, it was Ferðafélag Íslands' first hut. Oddly, the hut is another Kjölur site believed to be haunted, this time by the innocuous spirit of a young woman. If a female camper sleeps in one particular bed, it is said she will dream of the ghost carrying two pails of water. From the Kjölur road, where the bus will drop you, it's an 8km walk along the 4WD track to the hut.

Hrútafell

This relatively tiny 10-sq-km icecap rises 800m above the surrounding landscape and sits atop Hrútafell (Ram's Mountain), which is a *móberg* peak (birthday-cake-shaped resulting from subglacial volcanic eruptions). From the Kjölur Route, as soon as Hrútafell comes into view, look on the eastern side of the road for a cairn shaped exactly like a Hershey's Kiss!

Kerlingarfjöll

Kerlingarfjöll (Witch Mountains), 12km southeast of Route 35 on Route F347, is considered the most 'alpine' of all Iceland's ranges, and the highest peak, Snækollur, rises to 1477m. Until around the 1850s, Icelanders believed that these peaks harboured the vilest sort of outlaws and that in the heart of the range existed a deep, isolated, Shangri-la-type valley where these loathsome characters operated a clandestine, outlaw society. People were so frightened by the prospect of encountering them that Kerlingarfjöll wasn't explored until the mid-19th century.

There's a **guesthouse** (☎ 852 4223; www.kerlingarfjoll.is; camping/sb Ikr750/Ikr1850-2000), camp site and snack bar at Ásgarður.

Hveravellir

Hveravellir, the 'hub' of the Kjölur Route 30km north of the Kerlingarfjöll turn-off, is an enticing geothermal area of fumaroles and multicoloured hot pools. Among them are Bláhver, a brilliant blue pool; Öskurhólhver, Hveravellir's largest hot spring; and Eyvindarhver, named after the outlaw Fjalla-Eyvindar. Hveravellir is reputedly one of the many hideouts of this ubiquitous character who spent much of his life outrunning pursuers across the Icelandic Interior. On a small mound near the geothermal area are the ruins of a shelter where he is believed to have holed up with his wife, Halla, and their family during one 18th-century winter.

Services at Hveravellir are limited to a 66-person Ferðafélag Íslands hut with cooking facilities. This makes an excellent stop on a Kjölur crossing and is the end of the Kjölurvegur Trek (see the boxed text above).

KJÖLURVEGUR TREK

A good preparation for more challenging Interior trekking routes is the easy and scenic Kjölurvegur trek from Hvítárvatn to Hveravellir. The trail follows the original horseback Kjölur Route (west of the present road), via the Hvítárnes, Þverbrekknamúli and Þjófadalir mountain huts.

From the Hvítárvatn turn-off, it's 8km along the 4WD track to Hvítárnes hut. From there you follow the Fúlakvisl river (14km) to Þverbrekknamúli hut. Continue between the river and Kjalhraun lava field to Þjófadalir hut (14km). A possible detour here is across the lava field to Beinahóll (Bone Hill). The final day is a 12km walk to Hveravellir, where you can soak in hot springs. Overall, the marked route is easy to follow and huts are four to six hours apart.

The route can be done in three days at a leisurely pace. Access is via the Kjölur bus, but remember to reserve a seat for the day you want to be picked up.

Hofsjökull

The 995-sq-km Hofsjökull icecap, east of the Kjölur Pass, is the third largest icecap in the country. A caldera, or collapsed magma chamber, lies beneath it.

Sleeping

Ferðafélag Íslands maintains mountain huts at Hvítárnes, Hveravellir, Þverbrekknamúli (8km west of Innri-Skúti hill), Þjófadalir (12km southwest of Hveravellir) and Hagavatn (near the southern end of Langjökull and about 15km off the Kjölur Route by 4WD track). All of these huts have outdoor pit toilets, but Hagavatn and Þjófadalir don't have running water.

THERE'S BONES IN THAT THAR HILL

At the edge of the Kjalhraun lava flow near Kjafell (the highest point on the Kjölur Route), about 4km west of the road, is a small lava hill called Beinahóll (Bone Hill). The spooky name is the cue for another of those eerie and tragic Icelandic legends. The story goes that in October 1780, a party of four men and a flock of sheep were returning across Kjölur to Skagafjörður. They realised their journey would be difficult so late in the year, but decided to have a go anyway. When a blizzard set in, they decided to hole up until it passed, but it was three weeks before there was any change and by then all had perished. Even more eerily, although the victims were discovered, when authorities returned later to pick up the bodies, two had disappeared.

Icelanders believe that Beinahóll is haunted by the victims of this unfortunate incident (this presumably includes the sheep), and that to remove any of the bones or disturb the site is to invite permanent bad luck. If you should hear ominous bleating in the night...

Getting There & Away

The public transport option is the scheduled bus run by **BSÍ** (www.bsi.is; Akureyri ☎ 462 4442, Reykjavík ☎ 591 1000) between Reykjavík and Akureyri (Ikr7400, eight hours) from 24 June to 31 August. In either direction the buses make brief stops at Geysir and Gullfoss, and a lunch stop at Hveravellir. The buses leave at 9am from both ends.

In summer, 2WD vehicles may be able to travel on this route but it's not recommended. There are rivers to ford and in a hire car your insurance will probably be void if anything goes wrong. Drivers with 4WD vehicles will have no problems.

Of all the Interior routes, Kjölur is probably the best suited to cycling and hiking. For a humorous account of a cycling trip on the Kjölur Route, read Tim Moore's *Frost on My Moustache* (see p11 for details).

SPRENGISANDUR ROUTE

The Sprengisandur Route (F26) crosses the pass between Tungnafellsjökull and Hofsjökull at over 800m elevation. The name Sprengisandur refers to the desert moors that lie around the northern end of this 20km saddle. It may be less interesting than Kjölur, but does offer some wonderful views of Vatnajökull, Tungnafellsjökull and Hofsjökull, as well as Askja and Herðubreið from the western perspective.

Sprengisandur is to Icelanders what the Santa Fe Trail is to Americans, and the name conjures up cowboy images of outlaws and long sheep drives across the barren wastes. The historical route, which is now abandoned, lies a few kilometres west of the current route.

Skagafjörður Approach

The 81km Skagafjörður access (F752) to the Sprengisandur Route connects southern Skagafjörður (the nearest town is Varmahlíð on the Ring Road) with the F26, near the lake Fjórðungsvatn, 20km east of Hofsjökull.

Its main site of interest is Laugafell, an 879m-high mountain with some nice hot springs bubbling on its northwestern slopes. There are three Ferðafélag Íslands huts (a total of 35 beds, no kitchen) and a beautiful geothermally heated pool. Some stone ruins near the springs are reputed to have housed escapees from the Black Death.

Eyjafjörður Approach

The road from southern Eyjafjörður (F821), south of Akureyri, connects with the Skagafjörður road at Laugafell. This route is very pleasant, with few tourists, but it's more difficult to drive than the Bárðardalur Route.

Bárðardalur Approach

The route through Bárðardalur starts as Route 842 (near Goðafoss), then turns into F26 and carries on across Sprengisandur through 240km of inhospitable territory all the way to Þjórsárdalur (it meets up with the other two approaches about halfway through). It was used historically by the clergy from the southern bishopric at Skálholt when travelling to visit their flock in eastern Iceland. This is the route used by BSÍ Sprengisandur tours.

In Bárðardalur, between Goðafoss and Aldeyjarfoss, 23km south of the Ring Road, is the remote **Gistiheimilið Kiðagil** (☎ 464 3290; sb Ikr2000) open from June to August. At the end of Route 842 is **Aldeyjarfoss**, one of Iceland's most photogenic waterfalls. It flows over a layer of intriguing basalt columns on the Skjálfandafljót (Shivering River) in upper Bárðardalur. More basalt patterns can be seen in the shallow canyon above the falls.

Nýidalur & Tungnafellsjökull

Nýidalur (known as Jökuldalur), the range just south of the Tungnafellsjökull icecap, was discovered only in 1845. With a camp site, two Ferðafélag Íslands huts and lots of hiking possibilities, it makes a great break in a Sprengisandur journey. The huts have kitchen facilities and are open from 1 July to 31 August. Nights are particularly chilly here – something to do with the 800m elevation – so bring good warm gear.

Petrol isn't available. There are two rivers – the one 500m from the hut may be difficult to cross (even for a 4WD). Ask locally for advice.

Although there aren't any hiking tracks per se, the hiking is great. Soft options include strolling up the relatively lush **Nýidalur Valley** or wandering up the 150m-high hill east of the huts for a wide view across the desert expanses. A more challenging day hike will take you up to the colourful **Vonarskarð Pass**, a broad, 1000m-high saddle between Vatnajökull, Tungnafellsjökull and the green Ógöngur hills. This route also passes some active geothermal fields.

Versalir

Iceland's most remote farm, **Versalir** (☎ 852 2161; fax 487 5278; beds Ikr1800-2500; ⏲ Jul-Aug), lies on a bleak gravel plain, 18km north of Þórisvatn, along the Sprengisandur road. Although farming isn't really viable here, it's a well-used staging post with a restaurant, petrol and diesel pumps, and accommodation, including six-person cottages. If you're arriving with a tour, be sure to ask the driver to drop you at the right place.

With a 4WD vehicle or enough energy to walk up the Old Sprengisandur Route, you can visit the **Þjórsárver Nature Reserve**, in the grassy wetlands 25km north of Versalir.

Þórisvatn

Before water was diverted from Kaldakvísl into Þórisvatn from the Tungnaá hydroelectric scheme, it had a surface area of only 70 sq km. Now it's Iceland's second largest lake at 82 sq km. It lies 11km northeast of the junction between Route F26 and the Fjallabak Route.

Hrauneyjar

In the Hrauneyjar region, to the west of Þórisvatn, is **Hrauneyjar** (☎ 487 7782; fax 487 5278; sb/s/d Ikr1800/4000/6000), a guesthouse and restaurant in the bleakest position imaginable. It's readily accessible to many Interior attractions and staff can arrange excursions to sites of interest, including the beautiful **Dynkur waterfall**, which is a worthwhile 4WD excursion about 20km north. Petrol and diesel are available.

Veiðivötn

This beautiful area just northeast of Landmannalaugar is an entanglement of small desert lakes in a volcanic basin, a continuation of the same fissure that produced Laugahraun in the Fjallabak Nature Reserve. This is a wonderful area for wandering and you can spend quite a lot of time following 4WD tracks which wind across the tephra sands between the numerous lakes. On the hill to the northeast is a **view disc** pointing out the various lakes and peaks.

Veiðivötn lies 27km off the southern end of the Sprengisandur road south of Þórisvatn, via the F228 4WD road. Access from Landmannalaugar is thwarted by the substantial river Tungnaá, so you'll need private transport to get to Veiðivötn. At Tjaldvatn (Camping Lake), below Miðmorgunsalda (650m), is a camp site with huts.

Tours

From 15 July to 20 August, BSÍ buses travel the Sprengisandur Route from Landmannalaugar to Mývatn at 8.30am on Sunday, Tuesday and Thursday (Ikr6200, 10 hours). In the other direction, they depart from Mývatn at 8.30am on Monday, Wednesday and Friday. Although a scheduled bus, it's used as a tour, with brief stops at points of interest and accommodation places. A small discount is available to Omnibus and Full-Circle Passport holders.

A similar tour can be taken from Reykjavík at 8am on Wednesday and Saturday and from Mývatn to Reykjavík at 8.30am on Thursday and Sunday.

ÖSKJULEIÐ ROUTE (ASKJA WAY)

The Öskjuleið Route (Askja Way) leads to Herðubreið and Askja, the most popular wonders of the Icelandic desert. For much of the way it's a flat and dull journey, following the western bank of the Jökulsá á Fjöllum, meandering across tephra wasteland and winding circuitously through rough, tyre-abusing encounters with the 6000-sq-km lava flow Ódáðahraun (Evil Deeds Lava).

It then passes the oasis of Herðubreiðarlindir, which presents a superb close-up view of Iceland's most distinctive mountain, Herðubreið (unless, of course, you're greeted by a wall of blowing sand, as is often the case).

From Herðubreið, the Öskjuleið wanders southward through dunes and lava flows past Dreki hut and up the hill toward Askja, where vehicles may be halted by deep snowdrifts short of the road's end.

As with all Interior routes, the Öskjuleið is open only to 4WD vehicles, but it's still touch and go; sometimes you touch the pedal and only go deeper into the sand. Even the Askja Lunar tour has been known to get bogged, and in recent years a tour bus was swept away while attempting to ford a flooded river!

The usual access road is Route F88, which leaves the Ring Road 32km east of Mývatn, but Askja is also accessible further east from Route F910.

A Herðubreiðarlindir & Askja map/brochure is available for Ikr200.

Grafarlandaá

This tributary of the Jökulsá á Fjöllum is the first major stream to be forded on the southbound journey to Herðubreið and Askja. It has a reputation as the best-tasting stream in all of Iceland so fill your water bottle here. The banks also make a pleasant picnic spot.

Just past the second stream crossing near Ferjufjall, a short walk from the road takes you to a dramatic canyon being formed by Jökulsá á Fjöllum – a mini Jökulsárgljúfur in the making.

Herðubreiðarlindir

The grassy oasis of Herðubreiðarlindir was created by springs flowing from beneath the Ódáðahraun lava. This mini tourist

HERÐUBREIÐ ASKJA REGION

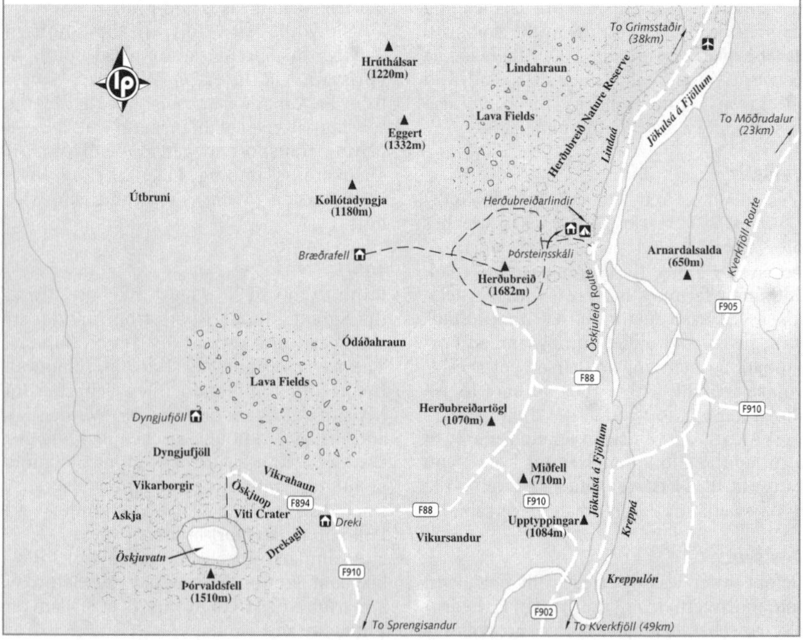

complex, 5km east of Herðubreið, has a nature reserve information office, a **camp site** (Ikr600) and the Ferðafélag Akureyrar 30-bed **Þórsteinsskáli hut** (members/nonmembers Ikr1100/1600; Jun-Aug). The hut has cooking facilities but no utensils.

Behind the hut is another Fjalla-Eyvindar shelter; this one is scarcely large enough to breathe inside. It was renovated in 1922 on the remains of the original, which had long since collapsed. Eyvindur is believed to have occupied it during the hard winter of 1774–75, when he subsisted on angelica root and raw horse meat stored on top of the hide-out to retain heat inside.

Herðubreið

It has been described as a birthday cake, a cooking pot, a lampshade and other things, but the more sophisticated tourist industry likes to call it the 'Queen of the Icelandic desert'. Whatever you see in Herðubreið's oddly symmetrical shape, it's certainly a welcome view after all those kilometres of desert you've crossed to reach it.

If Herðubreið (1682m) appears to have been made in a jelly mould, that's not far off base. It's another of those *móberg* mountains, the result of subglacial volcanic eruptions. In fact, if Vatnajökull was to suddenly be stripped of ice, Grímsvötn and Kverkfjöll would probably emerge looking more or less like Herðubreið.

HIKING

The Landmælingar Íslands topo sheet for this area is No 84, Herðubreið 1:100,000 (1986). If you don't require such great detail, use sheet No 8, Mid-Austurland 1:250,000.

From Þórsteinsskáli hut, a trail runs all the way around Herðubreið and can be hiked in a day. The mountain looks the same from all sides, so disorientation is a possibility, but if you remember that Kollótadyngja is west-northwest and Herðubreiðarlindir is east-northeast, orientation shouldn't be too difficult.

Under optimum conditions, Herðubreið can be climbed from Herðubreiðarlindir in a long day, but only because daylight isn't an issue in the Icelandic summer. The route to the top ascends the western slope, but it's quite steep and snow or bad weather may render it impossible without mountaineering gear. From the base to the top takes three to 3½ hours each way. Note the two cairns on the rim, which are there to show you the start of the route back down. Don't go alone, prepare for the foulest weather imaginable, and you'll probably be fine. Also, remember to inform the attendant at Herðubreiðarlindir of your intentions.

Kollótadyngja

The peak Kollótadyngja (1180m), 10km northwest of Herðubreið, is a textbook example of a shield volcano. Its broad, shieldlike cone oozed lava gently rather than exploded violently. At its base is the Ferðafélag Íslands Bræðrafell hut, which accommodates 12 people and has a coal stove but no running water. The best access is the trail leading west from the Herðubreið circuit.

Drekagil

The name of the gorge Drekagil, 35km southwest of Herðubreið, means 'dragon ravine', after the form of a dragon in the craggy rock formations that tower over it. The canyon behind the Ferðafélag Íslands 20-bed **Dreki hut** (members/nonmembers Ikr800/1200) resembles something out of Arizona or the Sinai; bitter winds and freezing temperatures just don't suit this desert landscape!

The Dreki hut is an ideal base for a day or two of exploring the area. Not only does the dramatic Drekagil ravine offer an easy stroll up to an impressive waterfall, but you can also walk 8km up the road to Askja. There are no cooking facilities, but the hut has a stove for heating, and water is available from the river. Camping (Ikr500) is also permitted, but the wind and cold can become oppressive.

At Dreki, the Gæsavatnaleið Route (F910) turns off the Öskjuleið to cross some intimidating expanses and connect with the Sprengisandur Route at Nýidalur. See p287.

Dyngjufjöll

The stark Dyngjufjöll range, which shelters the Askja caldera and the Drekagil gorge, is what remains of a volcanic system that collapsed into its magma chamber. Þórvaldsfell, the highest point along its southern rim, rises to 1510m.

This inhospitable territory may be intriguing, but it isn't terribly inviting to the

OUTLAW COUNTRY

Historically in Iceland, once a person had been convicted of outlawry they were beyond society's protection. Aggrieved parties were thereby given licence to take matters into their own hands. Many outlaws, or *útilegumenn*, such as the renowned Eiríkur Rauðe (Erik the Red), voluntarily took exile in another country. Others escaped revenge killing by fleeing into the mountains, valleys and broad expanses of the harsh Icelandic Interior, where few dared pursue them.

Undoubtedly, anyone who could survive the Icelandic Interior must have been extraordinary. Icelandic outlaws were credited with all sorts of fearsome feats, and the general populace came to fear the vast backlands, which they considered to be the haunt of superhuman evil. In fact, legends of a vile outlaw society in the heart of Kerlingarfjöll inspired so much fear that the range wasn't explored until modern times. The *útilegumenn* thereby joined the ranks of giants and trolls and provided the theme for popular tales, such as the fantastic *Grettis Saga*.

One particular outlaw, Fjalla-Eyvindar, has become a sort of Icelandic Robin Hood, Ned Kelly or Butch Cassidy. He had the unpopular habit of rustling sheep to support family, who had fled with him into the deserts. Throughout the Interior, you'll see shelters and hide-outs attributed to him and hear tales of his ability to survive in impossible conditions while always keeping one jump ahead of his pursuers. One of Iceland's best-known folk songs describes how his wife, Halla, threw their newborn child into a waterfall when food was scarce during one harsh winter.

casual hiker. If you come to explore beyond the tracks and footpaths, make careful preparations and take due precautions.

You'll find overnight accommodation at the remote and basic **Dyngjufell hut** (members/nonmembers Ikr800/1200), west of the caldera.

Askja

Askja is the main destination for all tours in this part of the Interior and shouldn't be missed. It's difficult to imagine what sort of forces created this immense 50-sq-km caldera, but this cold, windy and forbidding place sets one to thinking about the power of nature and who's in charge and all that.

The cataclysm that formed the original Askja caldera happened relatively recently (1875 to be exact) when two cu km of tephra was ejected from the volcano, making a mess as far away as mainland Europe. Activity continued over the next 30 years, culminating in another massive collapse of surface material, this time over an area of 11 sq km and 300m below the rim of the original. This new depression subsequently filled with water and became Öskjuvatn. What's most daunting is to realise that such cataclysmic events could be replayed at any time.

The deepest part of the collapsed magma chamber contains the sapphire-blue lake **Öskjuvatn**, the deepest in Iceland at 217m. It's thought to have some hazardous quirks, possibly odd currents or whirlpools, as suggested by the 1907 disappearance of German researchers Max Rudloff and Walther von Knebel, who'd taken a rowing boat onto the lake. There's a stone **cairn** and memorial to the men (who were never found) on the rim of the caldera.

In the 1875 eruption, one active vent, near the northeastern corner of the lake, exploded and formed the tephra crater **Viti**, which still contains a hot lake. Swimming in this turquoise-blue crater is a highlight for many visitors – the temperature (around 25°C) is ideal for swimming and the Icelandic way is to strip off and bathe naturally. If you're shy, bring a swimsuit. The route down is slippery but not as steep as it looks.

Askja has erupted frequently over the last century, and as recently as 1961 the vents at Öskjuop, near the road entrance to the caldera, exploded and formed the Vikraborgir crater row.

Tours

Plenty of tour operators run day and overnight tours from Akureyri and Mývatn (see p303). A good option is **Mývatn Tours** (☎ 464 4196; myvatntours@isholf.is; Ikr7500), which runs 12-hour day tours to Herðubreið and the Askja caldera at 8am from 15 June to 14 July and 16 August to 31 August on Monday, Wednesday and Friday (snow conditions permitting). From 15 July to 15 August, they leave daily. Bring your own lunch and a towel for swimming.

You can leave the tour at Herðubreiðarlindir or Drekagil and rejoin it later. Tell the driver when and where you want to be picked up so you'll have a seat going back to Mývatn.

Ferðafélag Akureyrar (☎ 462 2720; www.ffa.est.is) organises hut-based hiking tours from Þórsteinsskáli hut at Herðubreiðarlindir, along the Öskjuvegurinn Route to Svartárkot in upper Bárðardalur. The route runs via the huts at Bræðrafell, Dreki, Dyngjufell and Stóraflesja. The tour takes you over the vast Ódáðahraun lava flow and usually runs twice in July. With proper planning, this five-day trip may also be done independently.

GÆSAVATNALEIÐ ROUTE

The 120km-long Gæsavatnaleið Route (F910), also known as the Austurleið (it doesn't pass anywhere near its namesake Gæsavötn), connects the Sprengisandur Route and the Öskuleið. It's not nearly as treacherous as it once was, since a new road has been built north of the old one and the largest river is now bridged. However, it's still difficult to drive and you should attempt this route only if you have a lot of 4WD experience. There's little traffic but the scenery is excellent. The road crosses vast lava fields and sandy stretches, and there are always high icecaps in the background.

The bits over the lava fields are naturally slow going, so plan on one day to drive them. If you report to the warden in Askja that you're going this way, the main concern will be that you don't camp along the way, as much of the route lies inside a nature reserve.

Old Gæsavatnaleið

If anyone tells you the Gæsavatnaleið is impossible, they're speaking of the old southern route, which is best known as the road followed by the escaping hero, Alan Stewart, in the thriller *Running Blind*, by Desmond Bagley. In fact, it's not really impossible, but as yet no tour companies are willing to brave it and, with the opening of the new Gæsavatnaleið, the route isn't even being maintained. As a result, this is one of Iceland's roughest journeys, notorious for floods and deep sand drifts. It should be tackled only with at least two hardy 4WDs if you really know what you're doing, and it's imperative that you ask for advice before venturing out.

KVERKFJÖLL ROUTE

The 108km-long Kverkfjöll Route (F905, F910 and F902) connects Möðrudalur on the Ring Road with the Sigurðarskáli hut, 3km from the lower Kverkfjöll ice caves. Along the way are several sites of interest, including the twin pyramid-shaped Upptyppingar hills near the Jökulsá á Fjöllum bridge, and the Hvannalindir oasis where there is – you guessed it – another of good ol' Fjalla-Eyvindar's winter hideouts! He even constructed a rather high-tech (for those days) sheepfold at this one, so the sheep could visit the stream without having to face the elements. Hvannalindir lies about 30km north of the Sigurðarskáli hut.

With a 4WD vehicle you can link a trip to Askja with Kverkfjöll by driving south on Route 902.

Ask at information centres for the Kverkfjöll Mountains & the Hvannalindir Area brochure/map (Ikr200). The 85-bed **Sigurðarskáli hut** (members/nonmembers Ikr 1200/1700) or the camp site can be booked through Ferðelag Íslands.

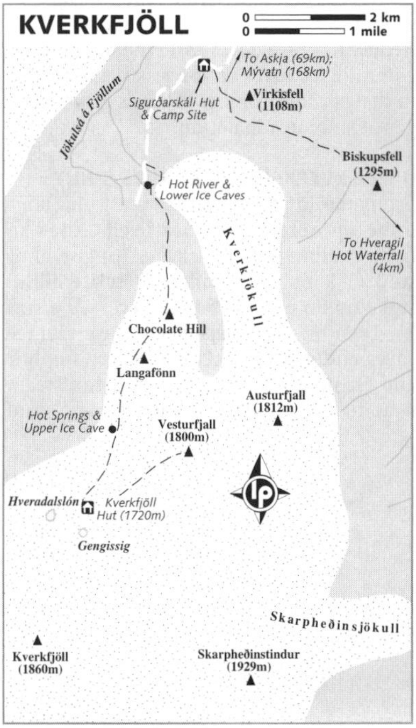

Kverkfjöll

Kverkfjöll is actually a mountain spur capped by the ice of Kverkjökull, a northern tongue of Vatnajökull. Through common usage, however, it has also come to refer to the hot-spring-filled ice caves that often form beneath the western margin of the Dyngjujökull ice.

When hiking in this area, be sure to carry plenty of water, as only silty glacial water is available higher up.

LOWER KVERKFJÖLL ICE CAVES

Besides being the source of the roiling Jökulsá á Fjöllum, central Iceland's greatest river, Kverkfjöll is also one of the world's largest geothermal areas. The 1.5km lower Kverkfjöll ice caves lie 3km from Sigurðarskáli hut, a half-hour return walk from the end of the 4WD track.

Here the hot river flows beneath the cold glacier ice, clouds of steam swirl over the river and melt shimmering patterns on the ice walls, and there you have it – a spectacular tourist attraction. Perhaps this was the source of the overworked fire-and-ice cliché that pervades almost everything ever written about Iceland. Huge blocks of ice frequently crash down from the roof – don't enter the ice caves or you risk being caught in their heated combat. There's also a danger of sulphur inhalation.

UPPER KVERKFJÖLL ICE CAVES & HUT

From the lower ice caves, the tours continue up onto the glacier itself. After an hour climbing up the glacier tongue, they stop at a nunatak called **Chocolate Hill** to stoke up on energy. From there, it's a stiff 1½-hour hike up **Langafönn** to the upper ice caves and geothermal area, where sulphur and rhyolite silt combine with the steam heat to create some of the gooiest mud imaginable. The caves here are larger than the lower ones – 2.5km long – but they aren't quite as impressive.

It's then a 40-minute climb to the Icelandic Glaciological Society's six-bunk **Kverkfjöll hut**, at 1720m. There's no water or heating, but it makes a viable icecap base. Nearby is the beautiful lagoon **Gengissig**, which was formed in a small volcanic eruption in 1961. Another hour beyond the hut will take you to the highest peak of western **Kverkfjöll** (1860m), with a fine view over the *kverk* (gap) through which the Kverkfjöll glacier passes.

HIKING

A one-hour marked hike from behind Sigurðarskáli hut will take you up **Virkisfell** (Fortress Mountain). At the top is an amazing natural bridge and a spectacular view over Kverkfjöll and the headwaters of the Jökulsá á Fjöllum.

There's a five-hour return hike from Sigurðarskáli hut to the 30°C hot river in **Hveragil**, where you can bathe in a hot waterfall. The wardens at the hut can provide specific directions.

Tours

Without a robust 4WD vehicle, the only way to visit Kverkfjöll is on a tour, and the most popular and easiest to join are **Ice & Fire Expeditions** (www.sba.is; 3-day tour Ikr18,700; Akureyri ☎ 5 500 700, Reykjavík ☎ 5 500 770), run by SBA-Norðurleið. The tours start from Akureyri (8.30am), Húsavík (9.45am) or Mývatn (11am) on Monday from 5 July to 23 August. The tours are essentially just transport and a guide – you must bring your own food and organise accommodation (either book a hut or bring a tent). Hiking boots or other strong footwear, a sleeping bag and warm clothing are essential.

Gateway to Greenland & the Faroe Islands

CONTENTS

If you enjoyed Iceland, why not continue on to Greenland or the Faroe Islands? With Air Iceland's regular flights to Kulusuk, Constable Point and Narsarsuaq, day tours or longer expeditions to Greenland can easily be tagged onto the end of an Iceland trip and there are also regular flights to Vágar in the Faroe Islands. Along with Iceland, these islands were the stepping stones of the great Viking push towards Vinland and America, but you'll need to be fairly prosperous to follow in the footsteps of these early explorers today, as travelling around the region is expensive even by Nordic standards.

GETTING THERE & AWAY

By far the easiest way to get from Iceland to Greenland or the Faroes is by air, but there are also summer ferry connections between Iceland and the Faroes.

Air

Several airlines provide air connections between Reykjavík's domestic airport and airstrips in Greenland and the Faroe Islands.

GREENLAND

Iceland's main domestic carrier, **Air Iceland** (Flugfélag Íslands; ☎ 570 3030 in Iceland; www.airiceland.is) also has flights from the domestic airport in Reykjavík to Kulusuk in east Greenland daily except Saturday from June to August, and twice weekly at other times. The full/promotional one-way fare is Ikr30,000/15,000 (two hours). Flights continue to Constable Point for the same fare. From 28 March to 30 September, there are also flights to Narsarsuaq in south Greenland (Ikr44,000 one way, three hours).

Internal flights by plane and helicopter link Kulusuk with Narsarsuaq in south Greenland and settlements all along the west coast. The national carrier, **Air Greenland** (www.airgreenland.gl), also flies to Copenhagen from Narsarsuaq or Kangerlussuaq in west Greenland; a return ticket on either route costs around Ikr6380.

FAROE ISLANDS

Air Iceland also has several weekly flights between Reykjavík and Vágar in the Faroes (full/promotional one-way fare Ikr28,400/11,700, two hours). The Faroese airline **Atlantic Airways** (www.atlanticairways.com) covers the route twice weekly for a similar fare. Heading on from Vágar, **Maersk Air** (www.maersk-air.com) and Atlantic Airways have flights to Copenhagen and Bilund. Atlantic Airways also flies to London, Aberdeen and Oslo.

Sea

The **Symril Line** (www.smyril-line.fo) car ferries link Iceland to Denmark and Norway, and travel via Tórshavn in the Faroe Islands. If you're travelling between Iceland and mainland Europe, you'll get a two-day stopover in the Faroes either there or back. See p308 for details of the ferry schedule and Smyril Line offices. Services from Hanstholm (Denmark) to Lerwick and Tórshavn continue through the winter.

TOURS

To see the best of Greenland or the Faroe Islands in a short time, there are several tour companies that specialise in air excursions from Reykjavík, and you'll have the satisfaction of knowing that dogsled teams and seakayaks will be waiting when you arrive.

One of the most popular options is the eight-hour Greenland day tour offered by **Air Iceland** (see p304). The trips run daily except Sunday from 26 May to 10 September and include return flights to Kulusuk and cultural activities laid on by local Inuit villagers. Prices start at Ikr29,900 (Ikr40,300 in peak season). If you want to stay longer, you could continue to Constable Point near Ittoqqoortoormiit, or transfer to the west coast with Air Greenland.

In Akureyri, **Nonni Travel** (☎ 461 1841; www.nonnitravel.is; Brekkugata 5, IS-602 Akureyri) has a great range of adventure tours around Greenland and the Faroe Islands. Tours in Greenland include dogsledding, ski-trekking and kayaking at Scoresby Sund, cultural tours at Ittoqqoortoormiit and Ammassalik, and walking tours at Narsarsuaq.

Several companies run tours from Iceland to the Faroe Islands, including Los Angeles–based **Scantours** (☎ 800 223 7226; www.scantours.com; 3439 Wade St, Los Angeles, CA 90066-1533), which offers four- to eight-day flying trips from Reykjavík or Copenhagen to the Faroe Islands, plus many other Greenland and Iceland tours.

The German company **Nordwind Reisen** (☎ 08331 87073; www.nordwindreisen.de; Maximilianstrasse 17, D-87700 Memmingen) offers a huge range of tours around Iceland, Greenland and the Faroes, with accommodation in hotels, farmhouses and hostels.

Other tour operators covering the region include:

Arctic Adventure (☎ 33 25 32 21; www.arctic-adventure.dk; 30 Reventlowsgade, DK-1651 Copenhagen V, Denmark) Offers well-organised hotel-based tours around Iceland and trips across to Greenland.

Discover the World (☎ 01737 214 214; www.arctic-discover.co.uk; 29 Nork Way, Banstead, Surrey, SM7 1PB, UK) This friendly agency is one of the most popular British tour operators to Iceland, Greenland and around Scandinavia, with plenty of adventure and wildlife itineraries.

Great Canadian Travel Company (☎ 204 949 0199; www.gctc-mst.com; 158 Fort St, Winnipeg, Manitoba RC3 1C9, Canada) This Canadian operator offers various activity-based tours to Iceland and Greenland.

Ijsland Tours & Travel (☎ 030 230 8010; www.ijsland.com/ijslandtours; Weteringstraat 132-C, NL-3581 EN Utrecht, Netherlands) This Dutch travel agency specialises in tours to Iceland, Greenland and the Faroes.

GREENLAND

Greenland is one huge, desolate snow plain, so why come here? To hear the call of the wild of course. Although impressive, the wilderness of Iceland is humble compared to the massive open spaces of Greenland. The landscape is scarred by mighty glaciers; snow-covered mountains soar above the tundra and the ocean is filled with creaking icebergs. Polar bears, reindeer, musk oxen and arctic foxes roam the frozen plains, whales breach in icy fjords and Inuit hunters fish from kayaks as they have for centuries.

Just 56,000 people live in this land of snow and silence, gathered in a few small settlements along the south and west coast. Travel in Greenland can feel like a real Arctic expedition and getting around can involve ski-trekking, helicopter rides, dogsledding and sea-kayaking. If you aren't quite ready for total immersion, many tour companies can arrange more comfortable trips where you can sample these activities without having to live out in the wilds.

The south of Greenland around Narsarsuaq is surprisingly green and temperate, while the icy east coast is home to just a few scattered Inuit communities. West Greenland has dozens of villages and fishing outposts – and the nation's tiny capital Nuuk – as well as the Arctic wastes of Disko Bay and the Inuit heartland of the far northwest.

For more information on Greenland, contact **Greenland Tourism** (☎ 45 33 69 32 00; www.greenland-guide.gl or www.greenland.com; PO Box 1139, Pilestræde 52, DK-1010, Copenhagen, Denmark).

FAROE ISLANDS

Hidden in the North Atlantic midway between Norway and Iceland, the Faroe Islands seem closer to their Viking roots than any of their neighbours. The 18 wind-scoured islands of the archipelago are home to a small but forcefully independent community of Danish-speaking farmers and fisherfolk. Their ancestors can be traced back to the first seafaring explorers who set out from southern Norway in the 9th century and claimed the Orkney and Shetland Islands, Iceland and Greenland – maybe even America.

The Faroes have a much more laid-back atmosphere than Iceland, and the villages are smaller and cosier – more like communities in the Scottish islands. The landscape is also very reminiscent of the Scottish highlands, with Munro-like peaks and towering grass-topped sea cliffs, mobbed by nesting seabirds. The capital Tórshavn is on the west coast of the largest island, Streymoy, while the airport is on Vágar, the next island south. Car ferries and tunnels link the various islands, providing access to remote fishing and farming villages and humbling ocean landscapes – somehow, this is exactly how you expect the North Atlantic to look.

For more information on the Faroe Islands, contact the **Faroe Islands Tourist Board** (☎ 298 31 60 55; www.tourist.fo; Bryggjubakka 17; FO-110 Tórshavn, Faroe Islands) or see the website www.faroeislands.com.

Directory

CONTENTS

ACCOMMODATION

Iceland has hundreds of accommodation options, from camp sites, guesthouses and hotels to farmhouse B&Bs and summer hotels in rural schools. Many places also offer inexpensive 'sleeping-bag space': a bed with a pillow but no sheets, duvet or blankets (designated 'sb' in this guide). Some places have dormitories but most just provide a bed without bedding in an ordinary room, however the cost is usually a fraction of what you would pay for the same bed with sheets.

For the purposes of this guide, places that offer rooms for less than Ikr3600 are classified as budget. Mid-range places offer singles for Ikr3600-8300 and Ikr4800-11,000 for doubles, while top-end places charge upwards of Ikr8300/11,000 (singles/doubles). To keep costs down, camp or bring a sleeping bag from home. If you intend to stay in B&B rooms and hotels, budget accordingly.

Camping

Camping is the cheapest accommodation option in Iceland, but make sure your tent is up to the weather conditions and bring a camping stove – butane cartridges and petroleum fuels are available from petrol stations and hardware stores in Iceland. *Tjaldsvæði* (organised camp sites) are found in most towns and at farmhouses in rural areas. The best council-run sites provide washing machines, cooking facilities and hot showers, but some of the simpler free sites may just have a cold-water tap and a toilet block. Camping with a tent or campervan/caravan costs around Ikr500 per person.

If you'd rather get off the beaten track, wild camping is possible in many wilderness areas and some farms will let you camp for free if you ask first. When wild camping, the standard rules apply – leave sites as you find them, carry out your rubbish and bury your toilet waste away from water sources.

Camping equipment can be rented from **Útilíf** (☎ 545 1500; www.utilif.is; Glæsibær, Alfheimer 74, Reykjavík, IS-101). Two-day rental rates start at Ikr1800 for a sleeping bag and Ikr3000 for a two-man tent.

Emergency Huts

ICE-SAR (Icelandic Association for Search & Rescue; www.icesar.is) and **Félag Íslenskra Bifeiðaeigenda** (Icelandic Automobile Association; www.fib.is) maintain orange-coloured survival huts along remote coastlines and on high mountain passes. They're stocked with emergency food, fuel and blankets and heaters and can only be used in an emergency. Users must sign the hut guest board stating which items have been used, so they may be replaced for future users.

Farmhouse Accommodation

In rural areas, there are loads of farmhouse guesthouses and B&Bs, which offer made-up beds, breakfast and, often, camping and sleeping-bag space. Many provide meals or

PRACTICALITIES

- Iceland is metric: distances are in kilometres and weights are in kilos.
- The electrical current is 240V AC 50Hz (cycles); North American electrical devices will require voltage converters.
- Most electrical plugs are of the European two-pin type.
- Iceland uses the PAL video system, like Britain and Germany, and falls within DVD Zone 2.
- The daily free paper *Morgunblaðið* is in Icelandic but features cinema listings in English.
- For tourist-oriented articles about Iceland in English, check out the glossy quarterly magazine *Iceland Review* (www.icelandreview.is).
- Iceland's two TV stations show Icelandic programmes during the day and American imports in the evening.
- Radio station RUV (Icelandic National Broadcasting Service; FM 92.4/93.5) has news in English at 7.30am weekdays.

have a guest kitchen, and some have hot pots (outdoor tubs), geothermal swimming pools and summer houses for rent. Prices are similar to guesthouses in towns, but sleeping-bag rates are reasonable. Most farmhouse B&Bs have signs by the road with icons depicting their facilities (such as made-up beds, sleeping bags, meals etc). From September to June, book accommodation in advance.

Example summer prices include:

Item	Cost
Breakfast	Ikr700-800
Dinner	Ikr1600-2500
Sleeping-bag accommodation (bed)	Ikr1500-2000
Made-up beds	per person Ikr2500-4500
Self-catering cottage or summer house	4 to 6 people Ikr5000-8000
Bed linen (daily)	per person Ikr500

Many farmhouse B&Bs are members of **Ferðaþjónusta Bænda** (Icelandic Farm Holidays; ☎ 570 2700; www.sveit.is; Síðumúli 13, IS-108 Reykjavík), which publishes an annual guide listing current member farmhouses.

Guesthouses

Iceland has many types of *gistiheimilið* (guesthouse). Some of these are simply private houses that let out rooms; others are custom-built minihotels. Guesthouses in converted houses usually offer rooms with shared bathrooms, but custom-built *gistiheimilið* may also have rooms with en suites. Some places also rent out self-contained flats with kitchens and bathrooms. Lots of them also offer sleeping-bag accommodation, usually with access to cooking facilities. These places are usually warm and comfortable, but many have had a visit from the chintz fairy and the décor can be a little over the top. Breakfast is either included in the price or you can buy it separately for around Ikr800.

As a general guide, sleeping-bag accommodation costs Ikr1500 to Ikr2500, double rooms from Ikr4000 to Ikr10,000 and self-contained units cost Ikr5000 to Ikr12,000 per night. Many Icelandic guesthouses are only open May to September (June to August in some cases). Guesthouses in Reykjavík often function as student houses from September to May (see Summer Hotels, p293).

Hotels

Every major city and town has at least one upmarket hotel. Most are fairly bland modern creations, but rooms are comfortable and the restaurants offer decent Icelandic food. Most offer rooms with private bathrooms, phones, TVs and sometimes minibars, and many have attached guesthouses containing cheaper rooms with shared bathrooms. There are also a few so-called 'country hotels' in rural areas. Summer prices for singles/doubles start at Ikr6000/7000. Most places offer discounts of between 15% and 30% outside the peak summer season (June to September). The Skanplus card (www.skanplus.com) will get you discounts at all hotels owned by **Fosshótel** (www.fosshotel.is).

Mountain Huts

Private walking clubs and touring organisations maintain *sæluhús* (mountain huts) on many popular hiking tracks around the country. The huts are open to anyone and offer sleeping-bag space in dormitories and guest kitchens; some also have camp sites and basic cafeterias. It's a good idea to book in advance with the relevant organisation. The huts at Landmannalaugar and Þórsmörk are accessible by 4WD vehicle, and you can get to the huts in Hornstrandir by boat, but most are only accessible to hikers.

The main organisation providing mountain huts is **Ferðafélag Íslands** (☎ 568 2533; www.fi.is; Mörkin 6, IS-108 Reykjavík), which maintains 22 huts around Iceland. The best huts have showers, kitchens, wardens and potable water; they cost Ikr1100/1600 for members/non-members (the popular Landmannalaugar hut costs Ikr1200/1700). Simpler huts cost Ikr850/1100 and usually just have bed space, toilets and a basic cooking area. Camping is available at some huts for around Ikr500 per person.

The following also provide huts:

Austurleið SBS (☎ 482 3400; www.austurleid.is) Húsadalur in Þórsmörk

Ferðafélag Akureyrar (Touring Club of Akureyri; ☎ 472 2720; www.ffa.est.is) Runs huts and most camp sites in the northeast, including the Akja Way.

Útivist (☎ 562 1000; www.utivist.is; Laugavegur 178, IS-101 Reykjavík) Básar & Fimmvörðuháls Pass in Þórsmörk

Summer Hotels

Iceland has 15 summer hotels in schools and colleges run by **Edda Hótels** (☎ 444 4000; www.hoteledda.is). They are only open during the school holidays (early June to late August) and all have simple but comfortable single and double rooms with a sink or attached bathroom. Sleeping-bag accommodation may also be available, either in rooms or on mattresses in classrooms at a bargain rate. All have attached restaurants; most have geothermal swimming pools. Discounted rates are available for children.

The standard Edda Hotel rates are:

Type of Accommodation	Cost
Single/double with sink and shared bathroom	Ikr5000/6400
Single/double with private bathroom	Ikr8500/10,700
Sleeping-bag accommodation in rooms	Ik1550-2000
Sleeping-bag accommodation in classrooms	Ikr1100
Extra bed or mattress	Ikr1500
Breakfast	Ikr850

A few hotels open a little longer (from May to September) and offer a 25% discount outside the main season. All the Edda hotels are perfectly comfortable, but the atmosphere of staying in a school can make it feel a bit like being on a school trip. Lots of town and village schools also operate as private summer hotels, including the main halls of residence at the University of Iceland in Reykjavík.

Summer Houses

The summer house is a national institution – many Icelanders maintain small self-catering summer cottages in natural beauty spots around the country. During the high season, some of these country cottages are rented to visitors for Ikr5000 to Ikr8000 per night, or Ikr30,000 upwards per week – many farmhouse B&Bs also offer summer-house rental.

For information contact the organisation **Icelandic Summer Houses** (☎ 482 3334; cottage@smart.is; X-Travel, Austurvegur 22, IS-800 Selfoss). Many also advertise on the website www.sumarbustadur.is.

Youth Hostels

Iceland has a good network of youth hostels, administered by the **Icelandic Hostel Association** (☎ 553 8110; www.hostel.is; Sundlaugavegur 34, IS-105 Reykjavík). All hostels offer hot showers, cooking facilities, luggage storage and dorm rooms or double bedrooms with space for sleeping bags. If you don't have a sleeping bag, sheets and blankets are available for Ikr400 per stay. All offer cheaper rates for members, and in some hostels you can pay a surcharge for a room to yourself.

At the time of writing the summer rates for members/nonmembers were Ikr1600/1950, with a surcharge of Ikr1000 if you want a room to yourself. Most hostels close in winter, but those that stay open charge slightly reduced rates. If you're planning to stay in hostels, it's wise to join **Hostelling International** (HI; www.hihostels.com) before you arrive in Iceland – to join locally, the only option is to buy a temporary card, which entitles you to member discounts after you've paid for six nights at the full rate.

At the time of writing, there were HI member hostels in Akureyri, Árnes (near Flúðir), Berunes (near Djúpivogur), Fljótsdalur (near Hvolsvöllur), Grundarfjörður,

Borgarnes, Húsey (Egilsstaðir), Hveragerði, Hvoll (Kirkjubæjarklaustur), Höfn, Kópasker, Laugarvatn, Njarðvík, Ósar (Hvammstangi), Reykjavík, Seyðisfjörður, Smiðsgerði, Stafafell, Stykkishólmur, Sæberg, Vagnsstaðir, Vík, Ytra Lón (Þórshöfn) and Önundarfjörður (Kirkjuból, near Flateyri).

There are also a few private hostels run by organisations such as the Boy Scouts Association, which charge similar rates but don't require you to be a member.

ACTIVITIES

With its vast areas of volcanic wilderness, Iceland is one big adventure playground. The rugged interior offers some fantastic opportunities for hiking – Þórsmörk, Landmannalaugar and Hornstrandir are particularly popular destinations – and if you'd rather be carried around, Icelandic ponies can be rented all over Iceland. The icecaps have loads of potential for snowmobile rides or ice-trekking (with crampons and axes) and attract plenty of serious ice climbers as well. Mighty rivers drain out from beneath the ice, providing lots of white water for rafting. You can go sea kayaking through dramatic fjordland scenery at many towns around the coast, and the light traffic makes cycling a viable proposition all round Iceland. Then there are the more leisurely activities such as swimming in geothermal pools (everywhere in Iceland), playing golf, bird-watching and whale watching – see p29 for more information on all these activities.

BUSINESS HOURS

The standard office hours in Iceland are 8am to 4pm Monday to Friday, but banks generally open from 9.15am to 4pm on weekdays. Shops typically open from 10am to 6pm or later, and some open until lunchtime on Saturday. Most rural towns have supermarkets that are open from 10am to 11pm daily. Post offices generally open from 9am to 4.30pm on weekdays. Some rural post offices also open on Saturday and Sunday.

Petrol station grills open from 9am to 9pm or later daily, but formal restaurants generally open from 11.30am to 9pm or 10pm. Restaurants that double as bars open until 1am on weekdays and 3am or later on Friday and Saturday. Almost all restaurants are open every day.

CHILDREN

Iceland is a fairly easy place to travel with children, and museums, tours, buses, internal airlines and hotels all offer discounts for little ones. However, wilderness activities often involve getting cold and damp – not every child's cup of tea! Icelanders are very family oriented, so things are generally set up to make travelling with kids as easy as possible. The town swimming pool is the focal point for children in most rural communities. However, spare a thought for Icelandic teenagers – riding your bike to the swimming pool every weekend must start to lose its gloss once you reach 16. Lonely Planet's *Travel with Children* gives all sorts of useful general advice on travelling with children.

Practicalities

Children are eligible for all sorts of discounts on transport and admission fees. On internal flights, children aged two to 11 years pay half fare and infants under two years pay 10% of the adult fare. BSÍ buses and tours charge half fare for children aged four to 11; children three and under travel free. Most tour companies and almost all museums and swimming pools offer 50% discounts for children under 12.

Accommodation in farmhouse B&Bs and hotels is usually free for children under two and half-price for those aged two to 12. Icelandair and Fosshótel make some effort for children in terms of cots and meals, but don't expect crèches or child-care facilities. Many restaurants in Reykjavík and larger towns also offer discounted kids meals. Child-care facilities for tourists are generally limited – ask at the tourist office in Reykjavík.

If you intend to hire a car, bring your own child seat to be safe – all cars in Iceland have front and rear seatbelts, including taxis. Buses sometimes have belts, but these are not compatible with child seats. Getting around Iceland can involve long journeys on bumpy dirt roads so be prepared for bouts of car sickness and tantrums from boredom.

Toilets at museums and other public institutions usually have dedicated nappy-changing facilities; elsewhere, you'll have to improvise. Attitudes to breast feeding in public are generally very relaxed; formula, nappies and other baby essentials are available everywhere.

Sights & Activities

Almost every village in Iceland has a warm geothermal swimming pool, often with a children's play pool, water slides, and hot pots where adults can relax while the children play – children usually pay Ikr100–120. At the Blue Lagoon (p95) children from 12 to 15 years pay half price and those under 12 are admitted free. Tiny Icelandic ponies appear to have been specifically bred with children in mind and horse farms all over the country offer riding by the hour from Ikr2000.

Reykjavík is the most child-friendly place in Iceland, with a highly recommended children's play park and zoo (p67) and some unusually colourful museums that should keep children entertained. Most kids will enjoy spotting whales on a whale-watching tour – top spots include Reykjavík, Húsavík, Hafnarfjörður, Keflavík and Ólafsvík.

Children will also enjoy some of the more lively geothermal areas – even those with short attention spans should be content to wait 10 minutes for the next eruption of the Strokkur geyser at Geysir (p105). The waterfalls just off Route 1 in Southwest Iceland are worthwhile detours to keep the children amused on drives around the coast, and the glaciers Sólheimajókull (near Skógar) and Vatnajökull are also right next to the main road. Children will find walks around lava fields more interesting if they think there might be elves and other little people about – dedicated elf-spotting tours are available in Hafnarfjörður. See p86 for more details.

CLIMATE CHARTS

Rainfall in Iceland is fairly consistent throughout the year, but because temperatures plummet in winter, it often falls as snow from September to May. Temperatures also drop considerably as you go up into the mountains, particularly around the icecaps. Areas with geothermal activity are often noticeably warmer than surrounding areas. Parts of the west coast, particularly Snæfellsnes and Reykjanes, get more than their fare share of rain in spring and autumn.

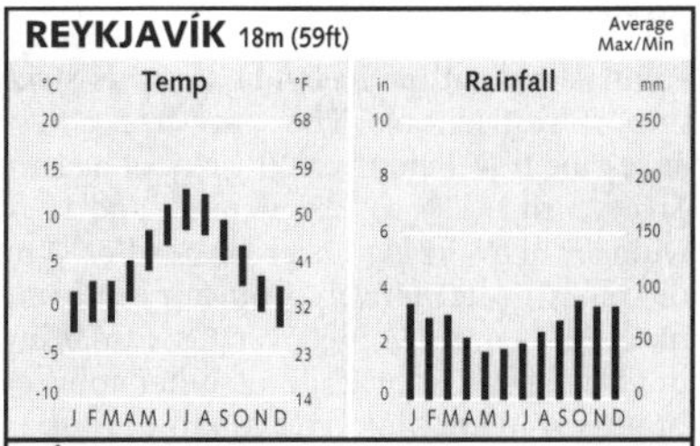

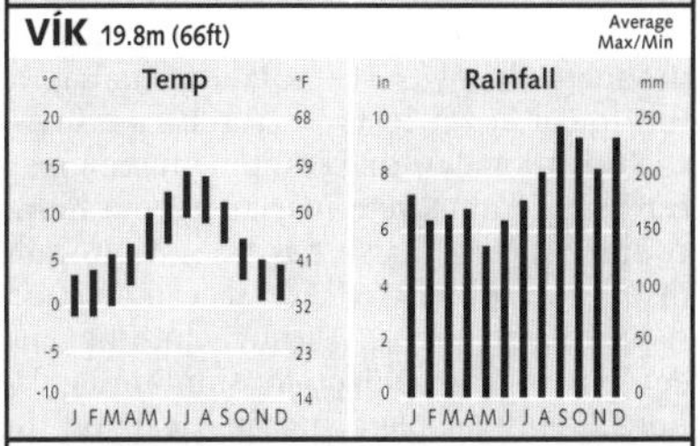

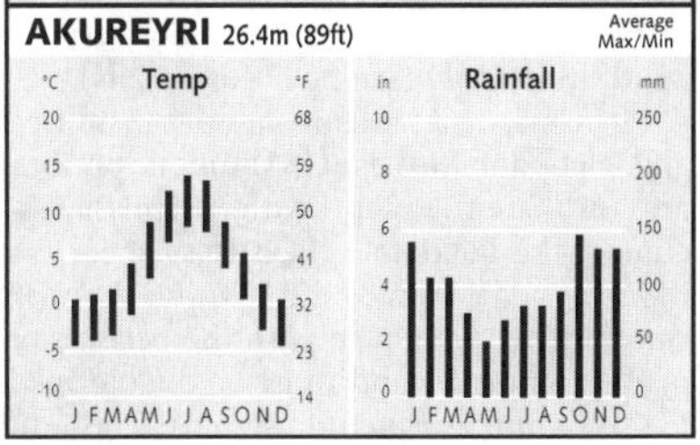

COURSES

It is possible to study in Iceland, but most of the courses on offer are only open to exchange students in the process of studying for a relevant academic qualification at a university overseas. One summer course that is open to nonstudents is the **Snorri Program** (☎ 551 0165; www.snorri.is; Óðinnsgata 7, Reykjavík, IS-101 Reykjavík), a residential study and work programme aimed at Americans with Icelandic ancestors. The Canadian organisation **Languages Abroad** (☎ 1-800 219 9924; www.languagesabroad.com; 413 Ontario St, Toronto, ON M5A 2V9, Canada) offers four-week residential programmes in Reykjavík – see their website for more information. The **Tækniháskóli Íslands** (Technical College of Iceland; ☎ 520 7400; www.ti.is/icelandicforforeigners) offers nine-week courses in Icelandic for foreigners (in English) costing Ikr14,000 – again, the details can be found on their website.

Lessons in skiing, horse riding and angling are sometimes available – see p29 for more information.

CUSTOMS

As an island nation, Iceland has rather strict import restrictions. The duty-free allowances for travellers over 20 years of age are 1L of spirits (22% to 79% alcohol) and 1L of wine, or 6L of foreign beer (instead of wine or spirits). Alternatively, you can just bring in 2L of wine. People over 18 can bring in 200 cigarettes or 250g of other tobacco products. In addition, you can import up to 3kg of food (except raw eggs, meat or dairy products). Many travellers take advantage of this to cut down costs when self-catering.

Recreational fishing equipment requires a certificate from a veterinarian in your home country stating that it has been chemically disinfected; otherwise officials can disinfect it when you arrive. Riding clothing and equipment are subject to similar regulations. Many people bring their cars on the ferry from Europe – special duty-waiver conditions apply (see p307 for details).

Firearms, drugs, plants, radio transmitters and telephones (except GSM mobile phones) are forbidden, except with permission – contact the **Directorate of Customs** (☎ 560 0300; www.tollur.is; Tryggvagötu 19, 150 Reykjavík). Animals can only be brought in with the permission of the authorities and must be quarantined. Plants, animals (including bird eggs and eggshells) and 'natural objects' (particularly stalagmites and stalactites) may not be taken out of Iceland.

VAT Refunds

Any purchases you make in Iceland over Ikr4000 including tax may be eligible for a 15% VAT refund. Shops offering VAT refunds display a special 'tax-free shopping' sign in the window. You'll need to fill out a form in the shop and present it to the Landsbanki bank in the departure lounge at Keflavík airport or at the Smyril Line terminal at Seyðisfjörður. If you are leaving Iceland by other means, see the website www.icelandrefund.com for details of other places where you can obtain refunds. Note that goods must be exported within 30 days of purchase.

DANGERS & ANNOYANCES

Crime is minimal in Iceland and probably the last major hitch in Iceland's political situation was the Reformation. However, there are a few risks to travellers, most of which are related to Iceland's inclement weather and turbulent geology.

The weather in Iceland can change without warning, particularly on the damp west coast. Always get a reliable weather forecast before you head off on any long treks – call ☎ 902 0600 for a daily forecast in English. Extreme cold can be dangerous when walking around glaciers and throughout the country in winter. Always wear proper winter clothing and carry food, water and blankets when driving in snowy conditions. Emergency huts are provided in places where travellers run the risk of getting caught in severe weather. Car hire companies can provide snow tyres or chains in winter.

On warm days, glacial run-off can turn trickling streams into raging torrents – be careful when crossing rivers on any treks. Many hiking paths in coastal areas are only accessible at low tide. Seek local advice or obtain the relevant tide tables from the **Icelandic Hydrographic Service** (☎ 545 2000; Seljaveg 32, Is-101 Reykjavík). High winds can cause dangerous sandstorms in areas where there is loose volcanic sand.

When visiting geothermal areas, stick to boardwalks or obviously solid ground and be careful of the water in hot springs and mud pots – it often emerges out of the ground at 100°C. Beware of dangerous quicksand at the end of glaciers, and never venture out onto the ice without crampons and ice axes (even then, watch out for crevasses). And it should go without saying that you should always get local advice before hiking around live volcanoes!

One risk most travellers must face is dangerous driving on Iceland's roads. Locals universally ignore the speed limit, cut corners and weave out of their lanes. Always give way if you meet another driver head on. A pair of 4WDs that collided head-on are displayed beside Route 1 just south of Reykjavík as a grisly warning about what can happen if you ignore this advice.

There are few scams in Iceland, though some guesthouse owners have been known to steer visitors towards more expensive made-up beds – be clear if you only want sleeping-bag space!

DISABLED TRAVELLERS

Iceland is on a par with most of northern Europe when it comes to access for disabled travellers. International and internal flights can accommodate most disabilities, but some flights use small aircraft that may be unsuitable for the mobility impaired. The car ferries *Baldur* and *Herjólfur* have facilities for wheelchairs, but public buses generally don't have lifts or ramps, with the exception of Reykjavík city buses. However, tours on specially equipped buses can be arranged by companies such as **Hopferdathjonusta Reykjavikur** (☎ 587 8030; Brunastodum 3, IS-112 Reykjavík). Discount fares for the disabled are available on the Smyril Line ferry from Europe to Iceland (see p308) and some internal flights.

For more details of facilities for the disabled – including disabled-friendly hotels and tours – contact the tourist office in Reykjavík and ask for the useful free brochure *Accessible Reykjavík*, or get in touch with **Sjálfsbjörg** (☎ 552 9133; www.sjalfsbjorg.is; Hátún 12, Reykjavík) and **ÖBÍ** (Organisation of Handicapped in Iceland; www.obi.is). There are reduced admission fees for most museums, galleries and tourist attractions (such as the Blue Lagoon).

The British-based **Royal Association for Disability & Rehabilitation** (Radar; ☎ 44 (0)20 7250 3222; www.radar.org.uk; 12 City Forum, 250 City Rd, London EC1V 8AF) produces a useful publication entitled *European Holiday & Travel* (£5), which presents an overview of facilities available to disabled travellers in Europe. In the USA, information can be obtained through the **Society for Accessible Travel & Hospitality** (☎ 212-447 7284; www.sath.org; 347 5th Ave, Suite 610, New York, NY 10016) or **Accessible Journeys** (☎ 610 521 0339; www.disabilitytravel.is; 35 West Sellers Ave, Ridley Park, PA 19078). **Access Able Travel** (www.access-able.com) has a worldwide travel bulletin board where you can post questions about disabled travel.

DISCOUNT CARDS

Students and the elderly qualify for discounts on internal flights, some bus fares, tours, museum entry fees etc, but you'll need to show proof of student status or age.

Senior Cards

Seniors (67 years or older) qualify for significant discounts on internal flights and ferry fares – any proof of age should suffice.

Student & Youth Cards

The **International Student Identity Card** (ISIC; www.isic.org) is the most widely recognised form of student identification. Card-holders under 26 get substantial discounts on internal flights (up to 50%), ferry fares, museum admissions and some bus fares. Some restaurants and bars also offer student discounts. All young people under 26 with proof of age can get special stand-by fares on internal flights.

EMBASSIES & CONSULATES

Iceland has representation around the world, and a few countries have reciprocal missions within Iceland. Up-to-date details of embassies and consulates within Iceland and overseas can be found (in English) on the Icelandic Ministry of Foreign Affairs website www.mfa.is.

Icelandic Embassies & Consulates

Here's a partial list of Icelandic embassies and consulates in other countries.

Australia (☎ 02-9365 7345; iceland@bigpond.net.au) 16 Birriga Road, Bellevue Hill, Sydney, NSW

Canada (☎ 613 482 1944; www.iceland.org/ca) 360 Albert St, Suite 710, Ottawa, ON K1R 7X7

Denmark (☎ 33 15 96 04; www.iceland.org/dk) Strandgade 89, 1401 Copenhagen K

Faroe Islands (☎ 31 11 55; info@faroeyard.fo) JC Svabosgöta 31, Box 65, Tórshavn

France (☎ 01 44 17 32 85; www.iceland.org/fr) 8 Ave Kléber, 75116 Paris

Germany (☎ 030 5050 4000; www.iceland.org/de) Rauchstrasse 1, D-10787 Berlin

Ireland (☎ 01 872 9299; jgg@goregrimes.ie) Cavendish House, Smitfield, Dublin

Japan (☎ 03 3447 1944; www.iceland.org/japan) 4-18-26 Takanawa, Minato-ku, Tokyo 108 0074

Netherlands (☎ 431 3114; wouter.jongepier@bdn.nl) PO Box 2508, 1000 CM Amsterdam Strawinskylaan 3037, Amsterdam

New Zealand (☎ 04-385 7934; denis@foot.co.nz) c/o Foot Law, Allen St, Courtenay Pl, Wellington

Norway (☎ 2323 7530; www.iceland.org/no) Stortingsgata 30, NO-0244 Oslo

Sweden (☎ 08 442 8300; www.iceland.org/se) Kommendörsgatan 35, 114 58 Stockholm

UK (☎ 020 7590 1100; www.iceland.org/uk) 2a Hans St, London, SW1 0JE

USA (☎ 202 265 6653; www.iceland.org/us) 1156 15th St NW, Suite 1200, Washington, DC 20005-1704

Embassies & Consulates in Iceland

Although many countries have some kind of representation in Iceland, you'll find that this is often just a trade representative who works for an Icelandic company. However, a handful of countries have formal embassies in Reykjavík, including:

Canada (☎ 533 5550; katrin.canada@mmedia.is) Túngata 14
Denmark (☎ 575 0300; rekamb@rekamb.um.dk) Hverfisgata 29
France (☎ 551 7621; amb.fran@itn.is) Túngata 22
Germany (☎ 530 1100; embager@li.is) Laufásvegur 31
Japan (☎ 510 8600; www.mofa.go.jp) Laugavegur 182
Norway (☎ 520 0700; www.noregur.is) Fjötugata 17
UK (☎ 550 5100; britemb@centrum.is) Laufásvegur 31
USA (☎ 562 9100; amemb@itn.is) Laufásvegur 21

FESTIVALS & EVENTS

True to their Viking roots, Icelanders relish any opportunity for a party and they hold enthusiastic celebrations throughout the year. The following list details the main national festivals, but there are also loads of lively regional festivals – see the individual destination chapters for further information. Reykjavík has a particularly hectic festival calendar.

January to March

Þorrablót (18 January to 16 February) The Viking Midwinter feast, when locals pick a day to chow down on Icelandic treats such as *svið* (singed lamb's head) and *hákarl* (putrid shark meat).

Bolludagur (Monday before Shrove Tuesday) In preparation for Lent, children are encouraged to pester adults with coloured sticks and solicit vast numbers of *bollur* (cream buns).

Sprengidagur (Shrove Tuesday) 'Bursting Day' is another pre-Lenten celebration, an excuse for a traditional feast of salted mutton and pea soup.

Öskudagur (Ash Wednesday) Another excuse for children to menace adults, this time by collecting money for goodies and tying small sacks of ash on their backs.

Beer Day (1 March) This is when locals celebrate the legalisation of beer in 1989 by drinking buckets of the stuff.

Easter (Last Sunday in April) Celebration of the crucifixion with the usual Easter-egg shenanigans followed by smoked lamb for dinner.

April/May

Sumardagurinn Fyrsti (25 April) Icelanders celebrate the First Day of Summer with carnival-type celebrations and street parades, particularly in Reykjavík.

June

Sjómannadagurinn (Sailors' Day, 1st Sunday in June) The biggest party of the year in fishing villages, with drinking, rowing and swimming contests, tugs-of-war, and mock-ups of sea rescues.

Independence Day (17 June) Icelanders get very patriotic as they commemorate Iceland's full independence from the Danish crown in 1944. Expect lots of drinking, dancing, music and parades.

Midsummer (24 June or thereabouts) The longest day of the year is celebrated with lots of partying. Some superstitious souls roll naked in the Midsummer dew for its 'magical' healing powers.

August/September

Verslunarmannahelgi (August Bank Holiday, first weekend in August) A long weekend where Icelanders flock to rural festivals around the country, from family barbecues to massive rock concerts. Vestmannaeyjar residents use this weekend for the massive Þjódhátíð Vestmannaeyja celebration of Iceland's constitution in 1874 (which local residents missed due to bad weather).

Réttir (September) Farmers around Iceland saddle up and ride out to corral a million sheep that have spent the summer grazing in the highlands, accompanied by general merriment.

October

Fyrsti Vetrardagur (third Saturday of October) The First Day of Winter, when families get together to mourn the passing of summer, is generally a low-key affair.

FOOD

Eating is going to be one of the main expenses of any trip to Iceland. A sit-down restaurant meal can easily cost as much as a hostel bed, or as much as an internal flight if you opt for one of Reykjavík's top restaurants. For the purposes of this book, meals priced under Ikr1000 are classified as budget, those from Ikr1000–3000 are mid-range and meals above Ikr3000 are top end.

If keeping costs down is important, self-catering is the way to go. Most places that offer hostel beds or sleeping-bag space have guest kitchens and supermarket prices are reasonable. The next cheapest option is to eat at fast-food grills and snack bars, found in most villages (usually at the petrol station). These places sell hot dogs, burgers, *samloka* (sandwiches) and *franskar* (chips) for Ikr200 to Ikr800.

If you eat at formal restaurants, expect to pay Ikr1200 to Ikr2500 for main dishes. Family restaurants in rural areas usually sell cheaper dishes such as burgers and sandwiches for under Ikr900 as well as proper meals. The food on offer is usually hearty and filling, but menus start to become tediously familiar. Fish is usually cheaper than meat, though not by as much as you might expect for a fishing nation. It's worth splurging on a meal at an upmarket restaurant every now and then for a bit of variety and to stave off scurvy with some salad or green vegetables.

Reykjavík is the best place in Iceland for a slap-up meal and there are restaurants here serving food from Iceland, Thailand, China, Mexico, Spain, Italy and India to name a few. There are also lots of gourmet seafood restaurants. Cafés and bars in Reykjavík often offer interesting light meals such as soups, noodles, pasta and salads for under Ikr1500. At the other end of the spectrum, you can easily spend Ikr3500 or more on a main course at many of Reykjavík's best eateries. Outside the capital, the best restaurants are normally at big hotels. To get gourmet food at bargain prices, keep an eye out for special lunch deals.

Try to find time for some of Iceland's specialties. Icelandic lobster soup and *hangikjöt* (smoked lamb) are delicious and other staples such as *svið* (singed lamb's head), *harðfiskur* (dried haddock) and *lundi* (roast or smoked puffin) will certainly give you a story to tell when you get back home. If you try *hákarl* (putrid shark meat), you'll never need to prove your bravery again. See p47 for more on the quirky tastes of Icelanders.

GAY & LESBIAN TRAVELLERS

Iceland has a relatively open gay scene, though low-key, and aggression against gays and lesbians is rare – see p71 for more information. The main gay and lesbian organisation is **Samtökin '78** (☎ 552 7878; www.samtokin78.is; Laugavegur 3, IS-101 Reykjavík). Other useful information sources are the websites http://gay.mis.is and www.gayiceland.com. Reykjavík has a gay bar and several gay-friendly guesthouses. Several companies offer tours to Iceland with a gay focus – try an Internet search using the terms 'gay tours iceland'. One gay-friendly local operator is **Eskimos** (☎ 566 4488; www.ekimos.is; Tunguháls 19, IS-110 Reykjavík).

HOLIDAYS

Various public holidays are observed in Iceland and any that occur on weekends or in summer provide an excuse for everyone to rush out to the countryside and camp. You should book camping areas, mountain huts and transport well in advance, particularly in popular areas such as Þórsmörk. Note that almost all Icelandic hotels and guesthouses shut down from Christmas Eve to New Year's Day.

Public Holidays

National public holidays in Iceland are listed following.

New Year's Day 1 January
Easter March/April (Maundy Thursday, Good Friday to Easter Monday; changes annually)
First Day of Summer Third Thursday in April
Labour Day 1 May
Ascension Day May/June (changes annually)
Whit Sunday and Whit Monday May/June (changes annually)
Independence Day 17 June
Shop & Office Workers' Holiday 1st Monday in August
Christmas 24–26 December
New Year's Eve 31 December

School Holidays

The main school summer holiday runs from June to August, which is when most of the Edda and summer hotels open up in schools and colleges around Iceland. There are big student parties when school breaks off (to celebrate graduation) and when school restarts (to initiate new students into school life), so popular camping areas may be packed out. Þórsmörk is the venue for a huge student bash in July, which is either a reason to come or a reason to stay away, depending on your mindset. There's another two- to three-week break over Christmas (December/January) but this rarely affects tourists.

INSURANCE

Although Iceland generally can be considered a very safe country, illness, accidents and theft occasionally happen and a travel insurance policy to cover theft, loss and medical problems is strongly recommended. Always check the small print to see if the policy covers any potentially dangerous sporting activities, such as trekking, rock climbing, horse riding, skiing or snowmobile rides. For more information on health aspects of travel in Iceland, including insurance, see p315. For information on motor insurance, see p312.

INTERNET ACCESS

By far the best place to check email and browse the Web in Iceland is at libraries – most offer Internet access for Ikr200 per 30 minutes and some even let you browse for free. Reykjavík and some larger towns also have private Internet cafés for around Ikr500 per hour. Some tourist offices, hotels and guesthouses also provide Internet terminals with usually fast and reliable connections. See the individual towns in this book for more details.

To access the Internet in Iceland with a laptop, you will need either a dial-up account with global access numbers – **AOL** (www.aol.com) and **CompuServe** (www.compuserve.com) both offer roaming accounts – or an account with a local Internet Service Provider (ISP). The main provider in Iceland is **Síminn** (www.siminn.is). Most hotels have telephones in the bedrooms, but you should bring an adapter with the correct type of telephone jack – Iceland uses RJ11 jacks like the USA.

For information on useful websites about Iceland, see (p11).

LEGAL MATTERS

You would really have to go out of your way to get into legal trouble in Iceland. Possession of drugs is illegal but there isn't much of a drug scene anyway. The most common way foreigners get into trouble with the police in Iceland is for drunk and disorderly behaviour – usually people are just escorted to the station to spend the night in a cell before being released in the morning. If you are involved in any traffic offences – speeding, driving without due care and attention etc – you may be asked to go to the station to pay the fines immediately.

In the incredibly unlikely event that you are arrested by the police, they can notify your embassy or consulate, or anyone else you specify, on your behalf. Lawyers are not provided by the state in Iceland, but the police can arrange a lawyer for you at your own expense. People can generally be held for 24 hours without being charged. The police can normally only search you if you give consent, unless they have reason to be suspicious.

ARE YOU OLD ENOUGH?

Iceland has legal minimum ages for many activities, including:

Voting	18 years
Drinking	20 years
Driving	18 years (20–21 years for car hire, depending on the company)
Sexual consent	14 years (heterosexual and gay sex)

MAPS

The best maps of Iceland are produced by **Landmælingar Íslands** (LMI; National Land Survey of Iceland; www.lmi.is), which covers the entire nation in fine detail. You can order any of these maps by mail order from the Landmælingar Íslands website, using your credit card. The best general map for driving around Iceland is the 1:500,000 *Ferðakort Touring Map* (Ikr1395), which includes all the larger villages and roads, and many small farms and B&Bs.

More detailed maps include the 1:250,000 maps of Westfjords & North Iceland, West & South Iceland and Northeast & East Iceland (Ikr1036); the 1:100,000 hikers maps for Hornstrandir, Húsavík/Lake Mývatn, Skaftafell National Park and Þórsmörk/Landmannalaugar (Ikr715); and the hiking maps of Þingvellir (1:25,000) and Vestmannaeyjar (1:50,000) – both Ikr602. There are also detailed topographic maps (Ikr538 per sheet) which cover all of Iceland at a scale of 1:100,000 or 1:50,000. LMI maps are sold in bookshops, tourist offices and souvenir shops across Iceland.

The tourist offices of the various regions produce useful maps showing sites of tourist interest. Town plans can be found in the Iceland Telecom phone book and the free tourist booklet *Around Iceland* available from tourist offices.

MONEY

Cash, travellers cheques and credit/debit cards are all viable options when travelling to Iceland.

ATMs

Banks in larger villages and towns, and some large petrol stations and shopping centres, have ATMs that accept major international credit and debit cards backed by Visa, MasterCard, Maestro, Electron or Cirrus and Eurocheque ATM-only cards. Cards issued by American Express, Diners Club, JCB etc tend only to be accepted in shops, restaurants and hotels. Be aware that your bank or credit-card issuer and the ATM provider in Iceland may both levy a charge.

Cash

The Icelandic unit of currency is the krónur (Ikr) and its value has been stable for years. One krónur is technically equal to 100 aurar, but coins only come in denominations of one, five, 10, 50 and 100 krónur. Notes come in 500, 1000, 2000 and 5000 krónur denominations. Stock up on krónur in Reykjavík if you're going to be relying on cash in rural areas.

Credit & Debit Cards

Icelanders are plastic mad and use credit and debit cards for even the smallest purchases. Major cards such as Visa, MasterCard, Maestro and Cirrus – and to a lesser extent American Express, Diners Club and JCB – are accepted in most shops, restaurants and hotels. If you intend to stay in rural farmhouse accommodation, carry sufficient cash. See ATMs (above) for information about electronic cash advances. You can also pay for the Flybus from the international airport to Reykjavík using plastic – handy if you've just arrived in the country.

Moneychangers

Foreign-denomination travellers cheques and banknotes can be exchanged for Icelandic currency without any commission at branches of Landsbanki Íslands and Sparisjoðurinn. Other banks may charge a small commission per transaction. Out of normal banking hours, you will have to rely on the poor rates of exchange offered by hotels and some guesthouses.

At Keflavík International Airport and Upplýsingamiðstöd (the main tourist office in Reykjavík), there are branches of the Change Group, a private moneychanger which opens longer hours (the airport branch is open 24 hours) and charges a punitive commission of 8.75% on all transactions – see p58 for more information.

Travellers Cheques

Travellers cheques in major currencies such as euros, US dollars, UK pounds and Danish krónur are accepted by all banks (Landsbanki Íslands and Sparisjoðurinn do not charge a commission) and by the commission-hungry Change Group – see above.

POST

The **Icelandic postal service** (Pósturinn; www.postur.is) is reliable and efficient, and rates are comparable to those in other Western European countries. Post office hours are 9am to 4.30pm on weekdays, but some rural post offices also open on Saturday and Sunday. The best place to receive poste restante is the central post office in Reykjavík – tell potential correspondents to capitalise your surname and address mail to Poste Restante, Central Post Office, Pósthússtræti 5, Reykjavík, Iceland.

Letters or postcards weighing up to 20g cost Ikr45 within Iceland. But *A-póstur* (airmail), postcards and letters under 20g cost Ikr60 to Europe and Ikr85 to the rest of the world. *B-póstur* (2nd class) mail is slightly cheaper but is much slower. *Bögglar* (overseas parcels) carry a flat charge and also a weight charge – eg airmail parcels to the USA cost Ikr800 plus Ikr685 per kilo, while parcels to northern Europe or the UK cost Ikr1480 plus an extra Ikr305 per kilo.

SOLO TRAVELLERS

Solo travelling is easy enough in Iceland, but meeting other travellers can be a problem in out-of-the-way places – remember that many people come specifically to Iceland to get away from other people. The Reykjavík City Hostel is an excellent place to hook up with other travellers and there's a noticeboard where you can leave messages. Another place you may be able to find travel companions is Lonely Planet's Thorn Tree message board (http://thorntree.lonelyplanet.com) – post a message on the Scandinavia branch and see if any other travellers are going to be in Iceland when you are.

If you stay in hotels or farmhouse B&Bs rather than hostels, you will be less likely to meet other travellers, though you may still bump into people in places with communal lounges or kitchens. One good way to meet travellers of a similar mindset is to join an organised adventure tour – guided treks, rafting and snowmobile tours usually have a good sense of camaraderie. Female travellers who are looking for other women to travel with stand the best chances at youth hostels, particularly in Reykjavík.

TELEPHONE & FAX

Iceland's Telecom is **Síminn** (www.siminn.is). The telephone directory and *Yellow Pages* are in Icelandic (apart from a section on what to do in the event of a natural disaster) but directory-enquiries operators usually speak English. The service numbers are:

Directory inquiries	☎ 118
Domestic operator	☎ 119
International inquiries	☎ 114
International operator	☎ 115

Coin-operated payphones can be found at post offices and public places such as bus stations. Reykjavík also has card-operated phones. The starting price for a three-minute local call is Ikr20. Public telephones in hotels, bars and restaurants eat up money at an incredible rate and some payphones cut out after three minutes on free calls. Public fax services are provided at telephone offices and some post offices, but it's very expensive at around Ikr200 per page.

Mobile Telephones

Iceland has two mobile phone networks: Reykjavík and larger settlements are covered by the GSM network, while the NMT network covers the interior and other remote areas. Visitors with compatible phones – most European phones are GSM compatible – will be able to make roaming calls, providing the service has been activated – contact your phone company for more information. American mobile phones use a different network and generally won't work in Iceland.

GSM and NMT phones can be rented from **Síminn** (☎ 550 7800; Ármúli 27, Reykjavík) for Ikr300 per day, with a Ikr10,000 credit-card deposit. If your mobile phone is not locked into a specific network, you may be able to use Frelsi, Síminn's pre-paid mobile phone service. You must buy a SIM card package for Ikr1250; cards with additional credits can then be obtained from petrol stations and some shops in Ikr500, Ikr1000 and Ikr2000 denominations.

Phone Codes

Phone numbers in Iceland have seven digits and there are no area codes. To phone Iceland from abroad, dial the local international access code, the country code (☎ 354) and the seven-digit phone number. Toll-free numbers in Iceland begin with ☎ 800 and seven-digit mobile phone numbers start with an '8'.

For calls within Iceland, dial the seven-digit number. International calls can be dialled directly from public and private phones and collect calls can be made to many countries. International call rates are the same around the clock. For international calling, first dial the international access code ☎ 00 then the country code (listed in telephone directories), the area or city code, and the telephone number. Using a Síminn phonecard, a three-minute phone call to the USA or Europe will cost around Ikr100; one to Australia will cost you around Ikr140.

The home-country direct service puts you in contact with your home-country operator and can be used for collect calls and charge-card calls. Access numbers in Iceland include:

Canada	
AT&T Canada	☎ 800 9011
Teleglobe	☎ 800 9010
Ireland	☎ 800 9353
New Zealand	☎ 800 9031
UK	
British Telecom	☎ 800 9044
Cable & Wireless	☎ 800 9088
US	
AT&T	☎ 800 9001
Global One	☎ 800 9111
MCII	☎ 800 9002
Sprint	☎ 800 9003

Phonecards

Card-operated payphones can be found in public places in Reykjavík, including the Lækjartorg and Hlemmur bus stands and they are useful for international calls.

The smallest-denomination phonecard is Ikr500, and cards are sold at post offices and Síminn telephone offices.

TIME

Iceland's time zone is the same as GMT/ UTC (London), but there is no daylight-saving time, which means that Iceland has the same time as the UK from 26 October to 24 March and is one hour behind from 25 March to 25 October. In summer, when it's noon in Reykjavík, it's 1pm in London, 2pm in Paris, 10pm in Sydney, 5am in Los Angeles and 8am in New York. See p318 for more on international time zones.

TOURIST INFORMATION

Icelandic tourist information offices are helpful and have stacks of free brochures and pamphlets. Employees usually speak Scandinavian languages, as well as English and some other European languages. Staff can arrange accommodation (for a Ikr400 booking fee), and book tours and transport.

Most tourist offices provide the useful booklets *Around Iceland* (a general tourist guide), *Iceland Independent Traveller* (a guide to Destination Iceland tours with information on public buses) and *Áning* (a guide to accommodation). All are published annually. If you plan to stay in farmhouse B&Bs, pick up a copy of *Upp Í Sveit*, a guide to farmhouse accommodation produced by the organisation Ferðaþjónusta Bænda (Icelandic Farm Holidays; p291).

The umbrella organisation in charge of tourism to Iceland is the **Icelandic Tourist Board** (☎ 535 5500; www.icetourist.is; Lækjargata 3, IS-101 Reykjavík). There's another office in Akureyri (☎ 461 2915; Strandgata 29, IS-600 Akureyri). This organisation can provide lots of general information on Iceland and publishes various promotional brochures designed to entice visitors to the country.

Icelandic Tourist Board offices overseas include:

Germany (☎ 06102 254 388; www.icetourist.de) Isländisches Fremdenverkehrsamt, City Center, Frankfurter Strasse 181, D-63263 Neu-Isenburg

USA (☎ 212-885 9700; www.icelandtouristboard.com) 655 Third Ave, New York, NY 10017

There are tourist offices at Keflavík International Airport (☎ 425-0330; www.reykjanes.is) and in Reykjavík at **Upplýsingamiðstöd** (Reykjavík Complete; ☎ 562 3045; www.visitreykjavik.is; Geysishús, Aðalstræti 2). Reykjavík also has several private tourist-information offices in Reykjavík, and there are council-run information offices in towns and villages around the country.

The main regional tourist offices are:

East Iceland (☎ 471 2320; www.east.is) Kaupangur 6, IS-700 Egilsstaðir

North Iceland (☎ 462 7733; www.eyjafjordur.is) Hafnarstræti 82, IS-600 Akureyri

Southeast Iceland (☎ 478 1500; www.east.is) Hafnarbraut 25, IS-780 Höfn

Southwest Iceland (☎ 483 4601; www.sudurland.net/info) Breiðamörk 2, IS-810 Hveragerði

Westfjords (☎ 456 5121; www.vestfirdir.is) Aðalstræti 7, IS-400 Ísafjörður

West Iceland (☎ 437 2214; www.west.is) Hyrnan Complex, IS-310 Borgarnes

TOURS

Many travellers baulk at the idea of joining an organised tour, but tours available in Iceland are a bit more adventurous than the tepid coach tours you may imagine. Many companies use huge 4WDs, off-road buses, snowmobiles or even light aircraft and it's often possible to tag on adventure activities such as white-water rafting, kayaking, snowmobile rides, horse riding and ice trekking. Many operate like informal bus services, allowing travellers to set their own agenda and get off and reboard at any time along the route. You'll need to make arrangements in advance to be picked back up. There are plenty of more conventional tours which will ferry you around in air-conditioned comfort. Children under 12 usually travel free with their parents and some companies offer 50% discounts to children from 12 to 15 years.

The following local operators offer some of the best tours in Iceland. Many tours and activities can now be booked through the website www.nat.is and discounts of up to 30% are available for online bookings. Specific tours are also covered in the destination chapters.

Activity Group (☎ 580 9900; www.activity.is; Tunguháls 8, IS-110 Reykjavík) This group of adventure-tour companies offers activities all over Iceland, including snowmobile tours, white-water rafting, dogsledding and ATR rides. They have a base at the Húsafell recreation centre in West Iceland.

Air Iceland (☎ 570 3030; www.airiceland.is; Reykjavík domestic airport, IS-101 Reykjavík) Iceland's largest domestic airline runs a wide range of combination air, bus, hiking, kayaking, rafting, horse riding, whale-watching and glacier day tours around Iceland from Reykjavík. It also runs day tours to Greenland and the Faroes from Reykjavík.

Arcanum Adventure Tours (☎ 487 1500; www.snow.is; Sólheimajókull, near Skógar) This adventure company offers ski-doo trips on the Sólheimajókull and Mýrdalsjökull glaciers – prices start at Ikr7200 for one hour.

Destination Iceland (☎ 552 2300; www.dice.is; BSÍ Bus Terminal, Vatnsmýrarvegur 10, IS-101 Reykjavík) Owned by the BSÍ bus consortium, Destination Iceland organises tours all over the country – many of which use scheduled bus services. There are dogsledding and rafting tours, bus tours, jeep tours, snowmobile tours and self-guided rental-car and trekking tours all over the country.

Dick Phillips (☎ 01434-381440; www.icelandic-travel.com; Whitehall House, Nenthead, Alston, Cumbria, CA9 3PS) British-based Dick Phillips has been organising small, custom-built hiking tours to Iceland since the 1960s and has decades of experience leading hiking and skiing trips through remotest Iceland.

Ferðafélag Íslands (☎ 568 2533; www.fi.is; Mörkin 6, IS-108 Reykjavík) The Icelandic Touring Club leads summer trekking trips along some of the most interesting tracks around the country, including Hornstrandir, Landmannalaugar and Þórsmörk, staying in tents and their own mountain huts.

Ferðaþjónustan Snjófell (☎ 435 6783; www.snjofell.is; IS-356 Arnarstapi) Based at Arnarstapi in Snæfellsnes, this company offers tours of the glacier Snæfellsjökull by snowcat (Ikr5200) and snowmobile (Ikr3500).

Guðmundur Jónasson Travel (☎ 511 1515; www.gjtravel.is; Borgartún 34, IS-105 Reykjavík) This ever-popular company offers bus and camping tours with light hiking. It's an excellent option for active people who'd rather not make their own arrangements. The 12-day highland walking adventures are recommended and there are also winter tours.

Highlanders (☎ 568 3030; www.hl.is; Suðurlandsbraut 10, IS-108 Reykjavík) This super-jeep operator offers tours up to Landmannalaugar, Hekla, Langjökull and along the south coast. It also offers rafting on the Þjórsá river in southwest Iceland.

Iceland Excursions (☎ 540 1313; www.icelandexcursions.is; Funahöfði 17, IS-110 Reykjavík) Offers various coach tours to the main tourist sites – the Golden Circle, Blue Lagoon, Snæfellsnes, Akranes, Landmannalaugar, Þórsmörk and the interior – as well as super-Jeep trips up to various glaciers, with optional snowmobile rides.

Mountain Guides (☎ 587 9999; www.mountainguides.is; Vagnhöfða, IS-110 Reykjavík) This adventurous company offers a wide range of hiking and climbing tours, including trips to Heiðmörk (near Reykjavík, Ikr4900), Hengill (Ikr8900), Sólheimajókull (Ikr14,900) and a series of ice-climbing and trekking tours around Skaftafell in the interior.

Mountaineers of Iceland (☎ 581 3800; www.mountaineers.is; Langholtsvegur 115, IS-104 Reykjavík) Specialises in adventure tours, including day trips by 4WD to Hekla and Landmannalaugar.

Mountain Taxi (☎ 565 5695; www.mountain-taxi.com; Álfholt 10, IS-220 Hafnarfjörður) This company runs all-year 4WD tours covering the popular tourist sites such as the Golden Circle but continuing up into the mountains. Some of the more interesting trips visit Landmannalaugar, the Þjórsárdalur valley, Hekla volcano and upper Borgarfjörður, and various adventure activities can be tagged on.

Nonni Travel (☎ 461 1841; Brekkugata 5, IS-602 Akureyri) The main tour agent in Akureyri, Nonni Travel offers a range of adventurous tours around Iceland, including bus tours, rafting, whale watching, horse riding and trips to Hrísey and Grímsey.

Reykjavík Excursions (☎ 562 1011; www.re.is; Hótel Loftleiðir, IS-101 Reykjavík) Reykjavík's most popular day-tour agency caters mainly to package tourists, but it's useful if you are short on time. There are tours to the Golden Circle, Reykjanes and the Blue Lagoon, Nesjavellir, Kaldidalur, Þjórsárdalur and loads of other possibilities.

Sæferðir (☎ 438 1450; www.saeferdir.is; Aðalgata 2, IS-340 Stykkishólmur) This company operates the ferry *Baldur* and also runs a variety of boat tours, including popular nature-watching cruises to the islands of Breiðafjörður (Ikr3600, 2¼ hours) and whale-watching trips from Ólafsvík (Ikr7950, four to seven hours).

This is Iceland (☎ 561 6010; www.this.is/iceland; Laugavegur 20, IS-101 Reykjavík) This company is a clearing house for tours and activities around Iceland, including Golden Circle tours, Landmannalaugar trips and rafting in southwest Iceland.

Touris (☎ 897 6196; www.tour.is; Frostaskjól 105, IS-107 Reykjavík) This super-Jeep operation offers Golden Circle tours with an off-road highland drive, and 4WD tours to Langjökull, Þórsmörk, Landmannalaugar and the volcano Helka.

Útivist (☎ 562 1000; www.utivist.is; Laugavegur 178, IS-101 Reykjavík) This recommended organisation runs friendly informal trekking trips and covers just about every corner of Iceland. It also runs one of the mountain huts at Þórsmörk.

Vestfjarðaleið (☎ 562 9950; www.vesttravel.is; Hestháls 10, IS-101 Reykjavík) This friendly company runs recommended day trips to Þórsmörk and also offers a five-day hiking trip from Reykjavík to Landmannalaugar and Þórsmörk.

Vesturferðir (☎ 456 5111; www.vesturferðir.is; Aðalstræti 7, IS-400 Ísafjörður) The main tour company in the Westfjords, Vesturferðir offers a huge range of tours in the surrounding area, including various day trips and multiday hikes to Hornstrandir.

Youth Hostel Travel Service (☎ 553 8110; www.hostel.is; Sundlaugavegur 34, IS-105 Reykjavík) In conjunction with other companies, the hostel association organises a wide range of tours, including sightseeing, horse riding, glacier trips, rafting, trekking and whale watching.

VISAS

Citizens of Schengen-Agreement nations (Austria, Belgium, Denmark, Finland, France, Germany, Greece, Italy, Luxembourg, the Netherlands, Norway, Portugal, Spain and Sweden) can enter Iceland as tourists for up to three months with a valid identity card. Other nationalities need a passport valid for at least three months from the date of arrival. Citizens of the European Economic Area (EEA), including Ireland and Great Britain, do not require visas for stays up to three months. To stay longer, you must apply for a residence permit, which is only available from Icelandic embassies or consulates overseas and requires evidence of sufficient funds to cover your stay.

American citizens can travel without a visa for up to three months within any six month period; the entry period is deemed to begin on the first entry to any Schengen Agreement nation. Similar agreements cover citizens of Australia, New Zealand, Japan and Canada. Other nationalities need a visa from an Icelandic consulate before arriving – see p297 for details of Icelandic embassies and consulates around the world. The fee varies depending on nationality, and the visa typically allows a three-month stay. Officials will usually request proof that you have sufficient funds for your visit and an onward plane or boat ticket.

WOMEN TRAVELLERS

Women travelling alone in Iceland will probably have fewer problems than they would travelling in their home country. Icelanders are generally polite and respectful towards women and gender equality is high – there's even a women's political party, Women's List, which forms part of the opposition Alliance coalition. The main women's rights association is **Kvenréttindafelag Íslands** (Icelandic Women's Rights Association; www.islandia.is/krfi), which campaigns against domestic violence and sexism, including some recent risqué advertising campaigns by Icelandair. The lingering sexism in Icelandic culture probably derives from the macho attitudes of a fishing culture and the traditional role of women in Viking legends – most Icelandic sagas involve noble men being undermined by scheming women!

Foreign women can usually travel alone without any problems and are generally treated with the same respect as local women. However, the usual precautions apply – walking around the streets alone after dark and hitching alone are not really recommended. You should also be prepared for some fairly forward behaviour by Icelandic men at bars and clubs in Reykjavík – if you feel your personal space is being infringed, don't be afraid to say so! Rural pubs tend to be both restaurants and drinking holes and attract mainly couples during the week, so single women should have few problems, though weekends are a bit more boisterous.

In Reykjavík, rape-crisis advice is available from the women's organisation **Stígamót** (☎ 562 6868), and legal advice for women can be obtained from **Women's Aid** (☎ 552 1500). If you are travelling alone and want to find other female travel companions, try putting up a note on the noticeboard in the Reykjavík youth hostel. Because it's such an easy place for women to travel, many international women's travel companies offer organised trips to Iceland; one possible operator is the American tour agent **Women Around the World** (☎ 800 890 4590; www.womenatw.com).

WORK

With its strong sense of national identity, the Icelandic government is rather resistant to the idea of employing foreigners. Traditionally, it used to be possible to find drudge work in canneries, fish-processing plants or on fishing boats, but the industry is currently in a slump and foreigners are unlikely to find work when Icelanders are being made redundant. There are sometimes seasonal shortages in certain skilled occupations – Icelandic embassies abroad can provide information on any current opportunities.

Technically, members of the EEA plus Norway, Iceland and Liechtenstein do not need a work permit to work in Iceland, but you must be able to support yourself financially until you find work. Be aware that Icelandic companies may not be keen to employ foreigners who cannot speak Icelandic. The website of **Vinnumalastofnun** (Directorate of Labour; ☎ 515 4800; www.vinnumalastofnun.is; Tryggvagata, IS-101 Reykjavík) has resources for EEA citizens who wish to work in Iceland.

All other nationalities require a work permit and residence permit before they arrive in Iceland. You need a residence permit to get a work permit, and you must have a firm job offer to apply for a residence permit. Work permits are generally only granted to fill seasonal job shortages or for highly skilled professions that are under-represented in Iceland.

Transport

CONTENTS

GETTING THERE & AWAY

AIR

Airports & Airlines

Iceland's main international airport is **Keflavík International Airport** (airport code KEF; www.keflavikairport.com), 48km southwest of Reykjavík on the Reykjanes peninsula. Flights to Greenland and the Faroe Islands use the small **Reykjavík Domestic Airport** (airport code REK) in central Reykjavík. Only four airlines fly to Iceland – Icelandair, Iceland Express, Atlantic Airways and Air Iceland – so getting to Iceland from anywhere in the world will involve a flight on one of these carriers.

The national flag carrier Icelandair has regular flights between Keflavík and London Heathrow, Glasgow, Copenhagen, Oslo, Stockholm, Paris, Frankfurt, Amsterdam, Barcelona, Milan, Baltimore, Boston, Minneapolis, New York, Orlando and Washington DC. The budget airline Iceland Express flies daily between Keflavík and London Stansted or Copenhagen.

Atlantic Airways flies twice weekly between Vágar in the Faroe Islands and the domestic airport in Reykjavík. The mainly domestic carrier, Air Iceland, has flights from Reykjavík to Vágar and to Kulusuk, Constable Point and Narsarsuaq in Greenland.

Contact details are:

Icelandair (airline code FI; www.icelandair.net; hub Keflavík, Iceland)
Iceland Express (airline code AEU; www.icelandexpress.com; hub Keflavík, Iceland)
Atlantic Airways (airline code RC; www.atlanticairways.com; hub Vágar, Faroes)
Air Iceland (airline code NY; www.airiceland.is; hub Reykjavík Airport, Iceland)

Departure Tax

The departure tax for domestic and international flights is included in the price of the plane ticket.

Tickets

All the airlines flying to Iceland allow you to pay for your tickets over the Internet using a credit or debit card. It's almost always cheaper to buy your ticket this way rather than through a travel agent. If you are coming from somewhere that doesn't have direct flights to Iceland, consider buying a ticket to Copenhagen or London through a travel agent and then arranging your onward to Iceland separately over the Internet. Note that online booked tickets are usually non-refundable and return dates are often fixed.

From Australia & New Zealand

To get to Iceland from Australia or New Zealand, you will need to connect through Europe or the USA, completing your journey on Icelandair or Iceland Express. Travel agents can book you all the way through to Keflavík, or you can buy a discount ticket to London, Copenhagen or New York and then arrange your onward ticket to Iceland online.

THINGS CHANGE

The information in this chapter is particularly vulnerable to change. Check directly with the airline or a travel agent to make sure you understand how fares and tickets work, as well as security requirements for international travel. Shop carefully. The details given in this chapter should be regarded as pointers rather than a substitute for your own careful, up-to-date research.

DISCOUNT TRAVEL AGENCIES

Tickets to Iceland are usually cheapest booked directly through the airline websites, but discount travel agencies can sometimes provide cheap seats. The online booking agent **Ebookers** (www.ebookers.com) has country-specific websites for France, Germany, Holland, Spain, Austria, Switzerland, Denmark, Finland, Norway and Sweden – just click on the links on the main website. **STA Travel** (www.statravel.com) has offices in the UK, USA, Canada, Australia, New Zealand, Germany, Austria, Switzerland, Finland, Denmark, Norway and Sweden. To find discount travel companies close to where you live, try looking in the travel sections of the weekend newspapers.

From Britain

Britain has hundreds of travel agents, but **Icelandair** (☎ 0870 787 4020) and **Iceland Express** (☎ 0870 850 0737) both fly directly from London to Keflavík and offer heavily discounted online fares – from UK£99/86 with Icelandair/Iceland Express. You might also consider making Iceland a stopover on the way from Britain to the USA.

If you're coming from Scotland, the best option is the Icelandair flight from Glasgow (around UK£140 return). From Ireland, you can connect through London or Glasgow. **Ryanair** (www.ryanair.com) has very cheap flights from Dublin to London Stansted, where you can pick up the Iceland Express flight.

From Continental Europe

Icelandair and Iceland Express fly daily between Keflavík and Copenhagen; online return fares start at Dkr1900 on Icelandair and Dkr1000 on Iceland Express. There are also direct Icelandair flights between Iceland and Paris, Frankfurt, Amsterdam, Milan, Barcelona, Stockholm and Oslo – these may be just as cheap booked with travel agents. From most of these places, you can find return fares of €400 to €500.

From the USA & Canada

Icelandair flies daily between Keflavík and Boston and several times a week between Keflavík and Baltimore, Minneapolis, New York, Orlando and Washington DC. You can also include Iceland as a free stopover on the way to Britain or continental Europe. Online return fares from New York to Reykjavík start at US$400. From the west coast or Canada, you'll need to connect through one of Icelandair's east coast hubs, or through Copenhagen or London.

SEA

Ferry

Smyril Line (www.smyril-line.fo) has a slow car ferry from Bergen in Norway or Hanstholm in Denmark to Seyðisfjörður in East Iceland, stopping on the way at Lerwick in the Shetland Islands and Tórshavn in the Faroe Islands. If you come from Hanstholm, you'll spend two days in the Faroes on the way to Iceland. If you come from Bergen, you'll spend two days in the Faroes on the way back. In winter, there are services only from Hanstholm to Lerwick and Tórshavn.

The ferry runs from mid-May to mid-September and offers all the usual restaurants, bars, shops, TV lounges and video games. The summer schedule is:

From	Departure	Duration
Hanstholm to Tórshavn	8pm Sat	9hrs
Bergen to Lerwick	3pm Tue	10hrs
Lerwick to Tórshavn	2am Wed	13hrs
Tórshavn to Seyðisfjörður	6pm Wed	14hrs
Seyðisfjörður to Tórshavn	noon Thu	14hrs
Tórshavn to Hanstholm	8.30am Fri	9hrs
Tórshavn to Lerwick	8.30am Mon	13hrs
Lerwick to Bergen	10.30pm Mon	10hrs

Passengers have a choice of couchettes (bed-seats), two- to four-berth cabins and suites. From Bergen to Seyðisfjörður, the one-way adult couchette fare is approximately Nkr2151/1578 in the low/high season; from Hanstholm the fare is Dkr2336/1730. The high season is from mid-June to mid-August. Significant discounts are available for children, students, seniors and disabled travellers. For cars there's an additional charge equivalent to about 75% of the adult couchette fare (40% for motorcycles). There's also a small charge for bicycles. If you are travelling from Britain, ferries from Kirkwall or Aberdeen to Lerwick connect with the Smyril ferries – see the website www.lerwickferry.co.uk for information.

Booking addresses for Smyril Line include:

DENMARK
Smyril Line Danmark (☎ +45 96 550 360; office@smyril-line.dk; Trafikhavnsgade 7, DK-7730, Hanstholm, Denmark)
NORWAY
Smyril Line Bergen (☎ +47 55 320 970; office@smyril-line.no; Slottsgt.1, PO Box 4135, Dreggen N-5835 Bergen, Norway)
SHETLAND
Smyril Line Shetland (☎ +44 1595 690845; office@smyril-line.co.uk; Holmsgarth Terminal, Lerwick, Shetland ZE1 0PR, UK)
FAROES
Smyril Line (☎ +298 345 900; office@smyril-line.fo; J Broncksgøta 37, PO Box 370, FO-110 Tórshavn, Faroe Islands)
ICELAND
Norræna Terra Nova/Smyril Line (☎ 587 1919; smyril-iceland@isholf.is; Stangarhyl 3a, IS-110 Reykjavík, Ísland)

Cargo Ship

The cargo carrier **Eimskip** (☎ 525 7009; www.eimskip.com; Pósthússtræti 2, Reykjavík), accepts passengers on its vessels *Detifoss* and *Godafoss*. Because the shipping route loops around, the shortest journey from Europe to Reykjavík is from Gothenburg or Fredrikstad (four days). If you are heading from Reykjavík to Europe, it takes four days to reach Rotterdam, five days to reach Hamburg, and eight days to reach Gothenburg or Fredrikstad. See the website for a full schedule.

One-way fares start at €410/574 for a single/double cabin and full board for the four-day run from Gothenburg to Reykjavík; the four-day trip from Reykjavík to Rotterdam costs Ikr39,200/55,000. You can transport your car for an additional €322 (Ikr30,800). Passengers are not accepted from 1 November to 31 February.

GETTING AROUND

AIR

Iceland has an extensive network of domestic flights, which are often the only way to get around during winter. However, be aware that winter schedules vary with the shrinking number of daylight hours and are heavily dependent on the weather. Big discounts are available for online booking and most flights are ticketless. Discount fares are sometimes available for young people, students, disabled travellers and seniors. See the Iceland Airline & Ferry routes map (p310) for the current routes operating in Iceland.

Air Iceland

Not to be confused with Icelandair, **Air Iceland** (☎ 570 3030; www.airiceland.is) is the main domestic carrier. In summer, there are flights between Reykjavík and Akureyri (45 minutes, around seven flights daily), Egilsstaðir (one hour, three or four daily) and Ísafjörður (45 minutes, two to four daily). From Akureyri, there are flights on to Grímsey (25 minutes, daily except Saturday), Vopnafjörður (45 minutes, Monday to Friday) and Þórshöfn (1¼ hours, Monday to Friday).

Air Passes

Air Iceland offers a couple of air passes which must be purchased outside Iceland. The Air Iceland Pass is available with four/five/six sectors for Ikr28,800/32,700/37,600. There's an extra tax of Ikr415/333 per adult/child for each departure and the maximum validity is one month. Fly As You Please gives 12 consecutive days of unlimited flights in Iceland for Ikr45,600, excluding airport taxes. Children under 12 pay half rates and rates drop by 15% in winter.

Íslandsflug

Flights to smaller airstrips in Iceland are provided by **Íslandsflug** (Icebird Airlines; ☎ 570 8090; www.islandsflug.is). In summer there are flights from Reykjavík to Vestmannæyjar (daily), Sauðárkrókur (daily except Saturday), Höfn (daily except Saturday), Bildudalur (daily except Saturday) and Gjögur (Monday and Thursday). A reduced schedule operates in winter.

Air Charters & Air Sightseeing

All of the domestic airlines can arrange air charters and sightseeing flights on request, but this is usually very expensive. **Flugfélag Vestmannaeyjar** (☎ 481 3255; www.eyjaflug.is; Bakki airport) runs charter flights to Vestmannæyjar from tiny Bakki airport, about 20km south of Hvolsvöllur. Other charter airlines include **Ernir Air** (☎ 562 4200; www.ernir.is; Reykjavík airport), with offices by the Hótel Loftleiðir in Reykjavík, and **Mýflug** (☎ 464 4400; www.myflug.is; Mývatn).

TRANSPORT

BICYCLE

Cycling through Iceland's dramatic landscape is a fantastic way to see the country, but you should be prepared for some harsh conditions along the way. The elements conspire against cyclists – sudden squalls are commonplace and gale-force winds blow up out of nowhere to cause blinding sandstorms in summer and driving sleet and snow in winter. Pack your things inside waterproof bags and bring the best waterproof clothing you can find. If things all get too much, you can always pack up your bike and travel by bus.

If you want to tackle the Interior, the Kjölur route through the Interior has bridges over all major rivers, making it fairly accessible to cyclists. A less challenging but still pleasantly rugged route is the F249 to Þórsmörk. The Westfjords also offer some wonderful cycling terrain, though the winding roads can make for slow progress. You'll need to be fairly self-sufficient in the Interior, but around the coast there are plenty of guesthouses, shops and restaurants.

Transporting Bicycles

Most airlines will carry your bike in the hold if you pack it up correctly. You should remove the pedals, lower the saddle, turn the handlebars parallel to the frame and deflate the tyres. Bicycles can be carried on long-distance buses if there's space. You'll normally pay a surcharge of around Ikr500; however, space can be an problem from July to August.

Many Icelandic roads are unsurfaced, so a sturdy mountain bike is a far more versatile option than a touring rig. Reykjavík has several well-stocked bike shops where you can find spares – the best is **Örninn** (☎ 588 9890; Skeifan 11, Reykjavík). Carry several puncture-repair kits to deal with the inevitable flat tyres caused by tortuous terrain.

Hire

Various places in Reykjavík and around Iceland rent out mountain bikes – see p314 for details – but these are generally intended for local use and aren't always up to long-haul travel. If you intend to go touring, bring a suitable bike from home.

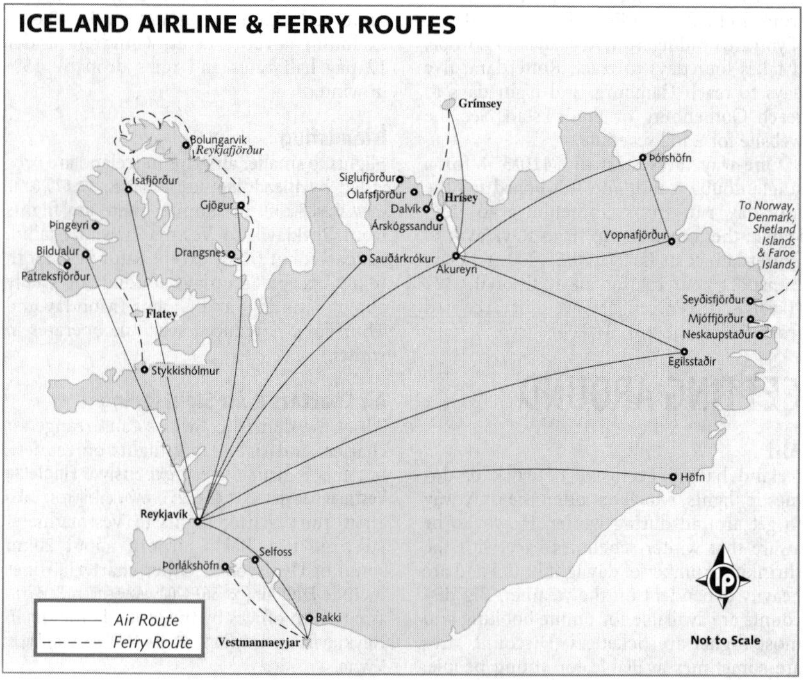

MOUNTAIN-BIKE CLUB

To learn about cycling in Iceland from locals who 'fear only a flat planet', contact the **Icelandic Mountain Bike Club** (Íslenska Fjallhjólaklúbburinn; ☎ 562 0099; ifhk@mmedia.is; PO Box 5193, IS-125 Reykjavík). Between late May and early September, the club organises cycling trips around the country, and visitors are welcome to join in.

BOAT

Ferry

Several public ferries operate in Iceland. The car ferry *Herjólfur* sails between Þorlákshöfn and Vestmannaeyjar and the *Baldur* sails between Stykkishólmur, Flatey and Brjánslækur – both run year-round. Passenger ferries include the *Sævar* between Árskógssandur and Hrísey; the *Sæfari* between Dalvík and Hrísey or Grímsey; and the *Anný* between Neskaupstaður and Mjóifjörður. Small summer-only ferries run from Reykjavík's Sundahöfn harbour to the island of Viðey, and from Ísafjörður and Drangsnes to Hornstrandir in the Westfjords.

Most ferry schedules are designed to coincide with bus arrival and departure times, and are outlined in the *Iceland Independent Traveller* bus timetable and tour guide, published by Destination Island/BSÍ. Holders of bus passes and (in winter) student cards are usually eligible for a 5% discount on fares.

BUS

Iceland has an extensive network of bus routes. In summer there are regular buses to most places on National Highway 1 and to larger towns in the Westfjords and the Reykjanes and Snæfellsnes peninsulas. Buses to the Westfjords run from 1 June to 31 August and buses around the east coast from Akureyri to Höfn from 21 May to 13 September. Bikes can be carried for a fee when there's space. As well as scheduled public buses, there are several bus tours which you can leave and rejoin as you like – see p303 for details. In small towns and villages, buses usually stop at the main petrol station.

All of Iceland's long-distance bus companies are members of the consortium **BSÍ** (Bifreiðastöd Íslands; ☎ 562 3320; www.bsi.is), which ensures an integrated bus network. The headquarters is the BSÍ Bus Terminal on Vatnsmýrarvegur in Reykjavík – the booking desk can provide tickets and timetables for buses to anywhere in Iceland. Full timetables and fares are published in the free booklet *Iceland Independent Traveller*, available from the BSÍ terminal and most tourist offices.

Bus Passes

BSÍ offers several bus passes that can save you money on longer journeys around Iceland, and also provides accommodation vouchers for HI hostels, farmhouses or camp sites. With any of the passes, you get a 5% discount on some Destination Iceland tours.

FULL-CIRCLE PASSPORT

The Full-Circle Passport (Hringmiði) allows you to make a complete circuit of the island on Route 1. You must complete the journey in one direction, but you can stop as often as you like. The pass is available from 21 May to 13 September and costs Ikr21,900. For an additional Ikr11,000, it can be extended to include Stykkishólmur in the Snæfellsnes peninsula, the ferry to Brjánslækur in the Westfjords and buses on to Þingeyri, Ísafjörður and Holmavík (1 June to 31 August).

OMNIBUS PASSPORT

The Omnibus Passport (Tímamiði) is available for one, two, three or four weeks and allows unrestricted travel on all but interior bus routes from 1 May to 13 September. This will cover you for the whole of National Highway 1, the Westfjords, the Reykjanes and Snæfellsnes peninsulas, the coast north of Akureyri and Mývatn, and the loop up to Gulfoss and Geysir in Southwest Iceland. The one-/two-/three-/four-week pass costs Ikr24,940/36,120/44,290/49,020. In winter a stripped-down version of the one-week Omnibus Passport costs Ikr14,620.

WEST ICELAND AND WESTFJORDS PASSPORT

This pass allows you to travel from Reykjavík to Borgarnes and on to Stykkishólmur, picking up the ferry to Brjánslækur and continuing through Þingeyri, Ísafjörður, Holmavík and back down to Reykjavík via Brú and Borgarnes. You can do the loop in either direction and there are no time restrictions. The pass costs Ikr14,395 and is available only when the Westfjords buses are running, from 1 June to 31 August.

CAR & MOTORCYCLE

Car hire is available everywhere in Iceland, or you can bring your own car or motorcycle on the car ferry service between Europe and Iceland – see p308. Petrol costs about Ikr96 per litre (95 octane); diesel is about Ikr43. Leaded petrol isn't available. There are regularly spaced petrol stations all the way around National Highway 1, but petrol stations are less common in the Interior and the Westfjords so make sure you have plenty of fuel before you leave National Highway 1. Some petrol stations require you to pay by credit card or petrol card – if you only have cash, you can usually buy petrol cards from the attendants inside.

Bring Your Own Vehicle

The Iceland government allows tourists to bring a motor vehicle into Iceland without paying import duty – customs officials will want to see the vehicle's registration, proof of international insurance valid in Iceland (known as a green card), and a driving licence from your home country. Import duty is initially waived for one month, so you must either re-export the vehicle within this period, or apply for an extension, which is valid for an additional two months. Vehicles must be less than 2.5m in width and 13m in length and have less than 200 litres of petrol in the fuel tank. Diesel vehicles also have to pay a weight tax on entry. For more information on importing vehicles into Iceland, contact the **Directorate of Customs** (☎ 560 0300; www.tollur.is; Tryggvagötu 19, 150 Reykjavík).

Driving Licence

You can drive in Iceland with a driving licence from the US, Canada, Australia, New Zealand and most European countries. If you have a licence from anywhere else, you may need to get an international driving licence, which is normally issued by the local automobile association in your home country.

Insurance

If you are bringing your own vehicle into Iceland, you'll need a so-called 'green card', which proves that you are insured to drive while in Iceland. Green cards are issued by

ROAD DISTANCES (KM)

	Akureyri	Borgarnes	Egilsstaðir	Höfn	Ísafjörður	Reykjavík	Selfoss	Seyðisfjörður	Stykkishólmur	Vík
Akureyri	---									
Borgarnes	315	---								
Egilsstaðir	265	580	---							
Höfn	512	519	247	---						
Ísafjörður	567	384	832	902	---					
Reykjavík	389	74	698	459	457	---				
Selfoss	432	117	640	402	500	57	---			
Seyðisfjörður	292	607	27	274	859	680	667	---		
Stykkishólmur	364	99	629	618	391	173	216	656	---	
Vík	561	246	511	273	630	187	129	538	345	---

insurance companies in your home country and rates vary according to the size of the vehicle and your driving history. Contact your existing car-insurance company for details. Cars are initially hired with just third-party insurance, which will only cover you for damage to other vehicles. We strongly recommend taking out the optional Collision Damage Waiver (CDW), which will cover you for damage to the hire car above Ikr50,000 for an additional daily fee.

Hire vehicles are not covered for damage to the tyres, headlights and windscreen, or damage caused to the underside of the vehicle by driving on dirt roads, through water or in sandstorms. Some policies also prohibit hirers from 'off-road driving'. This confuses many people as even main roads in Iceland are often unsurfaced. As a general rule, you should be fine on graded dirt roads that are not marked as 'back roads' on the Landmælingar Íslands maps of Iceland. Two-wheel drive vehicles are definitely not OK on mountain roads, including the road to Þórsmörk – these are designated with an 'F' prefix and are 4WD-only.

Hire

Hiring a car is the only way to get to many parts of Iceland, and although the rates are expensive by international standards, they compare quite well against the cost of buses and internal flights. Most car-hire companies can provide you with a Toyota Yaris or Nissan Micra for around Ikr6900 per day with unlimited mileage and CDW, and 23.4% VAT (value-added tax). You can hire the same vehicles on a per-kilometre basis but this will almost always work out more expensive. The usual discounts are available for long rentals. If you need a 4WD, you can rent Lada Nivas for as little as Ikr9900 per day including CDW and unlimited mileage, or pay Ikr9450 per day for a Suzuki Jimny, including CDW and 100km free (additional kilometres cost Ikr30 and upwards).

Rental cars are usually delivered to the customer and most companies allow you to drop the car off at Keflavík International Airport when you leave for a small surcharge. You must be at least 20 years old to rent a car. Most companies have their head offices in Reykjavík, but many companies have branches in Akureyri, Egilsstaðir, Höfn, Ísafjörður, Keflavík and Þórshöfn, among other places – see their websites for details or contact the local tourist office.

ALP (☎ 562 6060; www.alp.is; Vatnsmýrarvegur 10, IS-101 Reykjavík)
Avis (☎ 591 4000; www.avis.is; Knarrarvogur 2, IS-104 Reykjavík)
Eurorent/Bílaleiga Akureyrar/National (☎ 568 6915, www.eurorent.is; Skeifan 9, IS-108 Reykjavík)
Berg (☎ 577 6050; www.carrental-berg.com; Bíldshöfði 10, IS-112 Reykjavík)
Budget Car Rental (☎ 567 8300; www.budget.is; Duggovogur 10, IS-104 Reykjavík)
Europcar/ Bílaleiga Íslands (☎ 545 1300; www.europcar.is; Barónsstígur 2-4, IS-101 Reykjavík)
Hasso-Ísland (☎ 555 3330; www.hasso.is; Álfaskeið 115, IS-220 Hafnarfjörður)
Hertz (☎ 505 0600; www.hertz.is; Flugvallarvegur, IS-101 Reykjavík) Also has a discount subsidiary.
Geysir (☎ 893 4455; www.geysir.is)
Youth Hostel Travel Service (☎ 553 8110; www.hostel.is; Sundlaugavegur 34, IS-105 Reykjavík)

Road Rules

As in mainland Europe and North America, Icelanders drive on the right-hand side of the road. Seat belts are compulsory in the front and back seats and dipped headlights must be on at all times. Car-hire agreements do not cover damage to the hire car caused by collisions with animals, and if you do hit an animal, you may be required to compensate the owner. The speed limit is 50km an hour in built-up areas, 90km an hour on sealed roads, and 80km an hour on unsurfaced roads. Drink-driving laws are strict and the legal limit is 0.05% blood-alcohol content. Driving while using a mobile phone is also prohibited, though this is widely flouted.

There are a few Iceland-specific road signs that you need to watch out for. Signs with the warning *Malbik Endar* mark the transition from sealed to gravel roads – always slow down when you see these signs. The warning *Blindhæð* marks blind rises and *Einbreið Brú* marks a single-lane bridge – at either, slow down and be prepared to give way.

Dirt roads have occasional passing places where the road divides into two lanes, marked with a blue arrow showing you which side to pass on. Sites of tourist interest are marked with a '⌘' symbol. For further information on Icelandic road signs, ask tourist offices for the free brochure *Traffic Signs* or contact the **Icelandic Traffic**

Council (☎ 562 2000; www.umferd.is; Borgartún 33, IS-105 Reykjavík).

HITCHING

Although Iceland is remarkably crime free, hitching is never entirely safe in any country in the world, and we generally don't recommend it. Travellers who decide to hitch should understand that they are taking a small but potentially serious risk. People who do choose to hitch will be safer if they travel in pairs and let someone know where they are planning to go. Don't be afraid to refuse lifts which may seem suspicious. Traffic is fairly light in Iceland so expect some long waits.

LOCAL TRANSPORT

Apart from Reykjavík, the only places large enough to have their own local bus networks are Keflavík, Akranes, Akureyri and Ísafjörður. However, taxis are available in many smaller towns, including Heimaey in Vestmannæyjar.

Bicycle

You can hire bikes for local riding from some tourist offices, hotels, hostels and guesthouses in various places around the country, including in Reykjavík, Akureyri and Mývatn. Helmets are not a legal requirement, but most places will provide one if you ask. The standard daily charge is Ikr1600 per day, plus a deposit (a credit card imprint will usually suffice).

Bus

Reykjavík has an extensive network of local buses running out to all the suburbs, including Kópavogur and Hafnarfjörður. There are also local bus networks in Keflavík, Akranes, Akureyri and Ísafjörður.

Taxi

Most towns of any size will have some kind of taxi service, but expect to pay at least Ikr1000 for a short journey of around 3km.

Health

CONTENTS

Travel health depends on your predeparture preparations, your daily health care while travelling and how you handle any medical problem that does develop. If you do fall ill while in Iceland you will be very well looked after as health care is excellent.

BEFORE YOU GO

Prevention is the key to staying healthy while abroad. A little planning before departure, particularly for pre-existing illnesses, will save trouble later – see your dentist before a long trip, carry a spare pair of contact lenses and glasses, and take your optical prescription with you. Bring medications in their original, clearly labelled containers. A signed and dated letter from your physician describing your medical conditions and medications, including generic names, is also a good idea. If carrying syringes or needles, be sure to have a physician's letter documenting their medical necessity.

INSURANCE

If you're an EU citizen, an E111 form (available from health centres, or post offices in the UK) covers you for most medical care, except nonemergencies or emergency repatriation home. Citizens from other countries should find out if there is a reciprocal arrangement for free medical care between their country and the country visited. If you do need health insurance, strongly consider a policy that covers you for the worst possible scenario, such as an accident requiring an emergency flight home. Find out in advance if your insurance plan will make payments directly to providers or reimburse you later for overseas health expenditures. The former option is generally preferable, as it doesn't require you to pay out of pocket in a foreign country.

CHECK BEFORE YOU GO

It's usually a good idea to consult your government's travel-health website (if available) before departure:

Australia www.dfat.gov.au/travel
Canada www.travelhealth.gc.ca
United Kingdom www.doh.gov.uk/traveladvice
United States www.cdc.gov/travel

RECOMMENDED VACCINATIONS

The World Health Organization (WHO) recommends that all travellers should be covered for diphtheria, tetanus, measles, mumps, rubella and polio, regardless of their destination. Since most vaccines don't produce immunity until at least two weeks after they're given, visit a physician at least six weeks before departure.

ONLINE RESOURCES

The WHO's publication *International Travel and Health* is revised annually and is available online at www.who.int/ith. Other useful websites include www.mdtravelhealth.com (travel-health recommendations for every country, updated daily), www.fitfortravel.scot.nhs.uk (general travel advice), www.ageconcern.org.uk (advice on travel for the elderly) and www.mariestopes.org.uk (information on women's health and contraception).

FURTHER READING

Health Advice for Travellers (currently called the 'T6' leaflet) is an annually updated leaflet

HEALTH

by the Department of Health in the UK available free in post offices. It contains some general information, legally required and recommended vaccines for different countries, reciprocal health agreements and an E111 application form. Lonely Planet's *Travel with Children* includes advice on travel health for younger children. Other recommended references include *Traveller's Health*, by Dr Richard Dawood (Oxford University Press), and *The Traveller's Good Health Guide*, by Ted Lankester (Sheldon Press).

IN TRANSIT

DEEP VEIN THROMBOSIS (DVT)

Blood clots may form in the legs during plane flights, chiefly because of prolonged immobility – the longer the flight, the greater the risk. The chief symptom of DVT is swelling or pain of the foot, ankle or calf, usually but not always on just one side. When a blood clot travels to the lungs, it may cause chest pain and breathing difficulties. Travellers with any of these symptoms should immediately seek medical attention.

To prevent DVT on long flights you should walk about the cabin, contract leg muscles while sitting, drink plenty of fluids and avoid alcohol and tobacco.

JET LAG & MOTION SICKNESS

To avoid jet lag (common when crossing more than five time zones) try drinking plenty of nonalcoholic fluids and eating light meals. Upon arrival, get exposure to natural sunlight and readjust your schedule (for meals, sleep and so on) as soon as possible.

Antihistamines such as dimenhydrinate (Dramamine) and meclizine (Antivert, Bonine) are usually the first choice for treating motion sickness. A herbal alternative is ginger.

IN ICELAND

AVAILABILITY & COST OF HEALTH CARE

Good health care is readily available, and for minor, self-limiting illnesses, pharmacists can dispense valuable advice and over-the-counter medication. They can also advise when more specialised help is required. The standard of dental care is usually good; however, it is sensible to have a dental checkup before a long trip.

INFECTIOUS DISEASES

Tick-borne encephalitis is spread by tick bites. It is a serious infection of the brain and vaccination is advised for those in risk areas who are unable to avoid tick bites (such as campers, forestry workers and ramblers). Two doses of vaccine will give a year's protection; three doses up to three years.

TRAVELLER'S DIARRHOEA

To prevent diarrhoea, avoid tap water unless it has been boiled, filtered or chemically disinfected (with iodine tablets) and steer clear of ice. Eat fresh fruits or vegetables only if cooked or peeled; be wary of dairy products that might contain unpasteurised milk. Eat food which is hot throughout and avoid buffet-style meals. If a restaurant is full of locals the food is probably safe.

If you develop diarrhoea, be sure to drink plenty of fluids, preferably an oral rehydration solution (eg dioralyte). A few loose stools don't require treatment, but if you start having more than four or five stools a day, you should start taking an antibiotic (usually a quinoline drug) and an antidiarrhoeal agent (such as loperamide). If diarrhoea is bloody, persists for more than 72 hours or is accompanied by fever, shaking, chills or severe abdominal pain, you should seek medical attention.

ENVIRONMENTAL HAZARDS

Giardia

Giardia is an intestinal parasite which lives in the faeces of humans and animals and is normally contracted through drinking water. Problems can start several weeks after you've been exposed to the parasite and symptoms may sometimes remit for a few days and then return; this can go on for several weeks or even longer.

The first signs are a swelling of the stomach, followed by pale faeces, diarrhoea, frequent gas and possibly headache, nausea and depression. If you exhibit these symptoms you should visit a doctor for treatment.

Although most unpopulated lands in Iceland serve as sheep pastures, there seems to be very little Giardia; however, while most people have no problems drinking untreated surface water, there's still a possibility of contracting it. If you are unsure, purify your drinking water by boiling it for 10 minutes or use a chemical treatment such as iodine.

Hypothermia & Frostbite

Proper preparation will reduce the risks of getting hypothermia. Even on a hot day in the mountains, the weather can change rapidly – carry waterproof garments and warm layers, and inform others of your route.

Acute hypothermia follows a sudden drop of temperature over a short time. Chronic hypothermia is caused by a gradual loss of temperature over hours.

Hypothermia starts with shivering, loss of judgment and clumsiness. Unless rewarming occurs, the sufferer deteriorates into apathy, confusion and coma. Prevent further heat loss by seeking shelter, wearing warm, dry clothing, drinking hot, sweet drinks and sharing body warmth.

Frostbite is caused by freezing and subsequent damage to bodily extremities. It is dependent on wind-chill, temperature and length of exposure. Frostbite starts as frostnip (white, numb areas of skin) from which complete recovery is expected with rewarming. As frostbite develops, the skin blisters and becomes black. Loss of damaged tissue eventually occurs. Wear adequate clothing, stay dry, keep well hydrated and ensure you have adequate calorie intake to prevent frostbite. Treatment involves rapid rewarming. Avoid refreezing and rubbing the affected areas.

Insect Bites & Stings

Mosquitoes are found even in Iceland – they're not as ferocious as their southern cousins and may not carry malaria, but they can cause irritation and infected bites. Use a DEET-based insect repellent.

Bees and wasps cause real problems only to those with a severe allergy (anaphylaxis.) If you have such an allergy, carry EpiPen or similar adrenaline injections.

TRAVELLING WITH CHILDREN

All travellers with children should know how to treat minor ailments and when to seek medical treatment. Make sure the children are up to date with routine vaccinations and discuss any possible travel vaccines well before departure, as some vaccines are not suitable for children under a year.

Remember to avoid contaminated food and water. If your child has vomiting or diarrhoea, lost fluid and salts must be replaced. It may be helpful to take rehydration powders for reconstituting with boiled water.

Children should be encouraged to avoid and mistrust any dogs or other mammals because of the risk of rabies and other diseases. Any bite, scratch or lick from a warm-blooded, furry animal should immediately be thoroughly cleaned. If there is any possibility that the animal is infected with rabies, immediate medical assistance should be sought.

SEXUAL HEALTH

Condoms are widely available at *apótek* (pharmacies). When buying condoms, look for a European CE mark, which means they have been rigorously tested, and then keep them in a cool, dry place or they may crack and perish.

Emergency contraception is most effective if taken within 24 hours after unprotected sex. The International Planned Parent Federation (www.ippf.org) can advise about the availability of contraception in different countries.

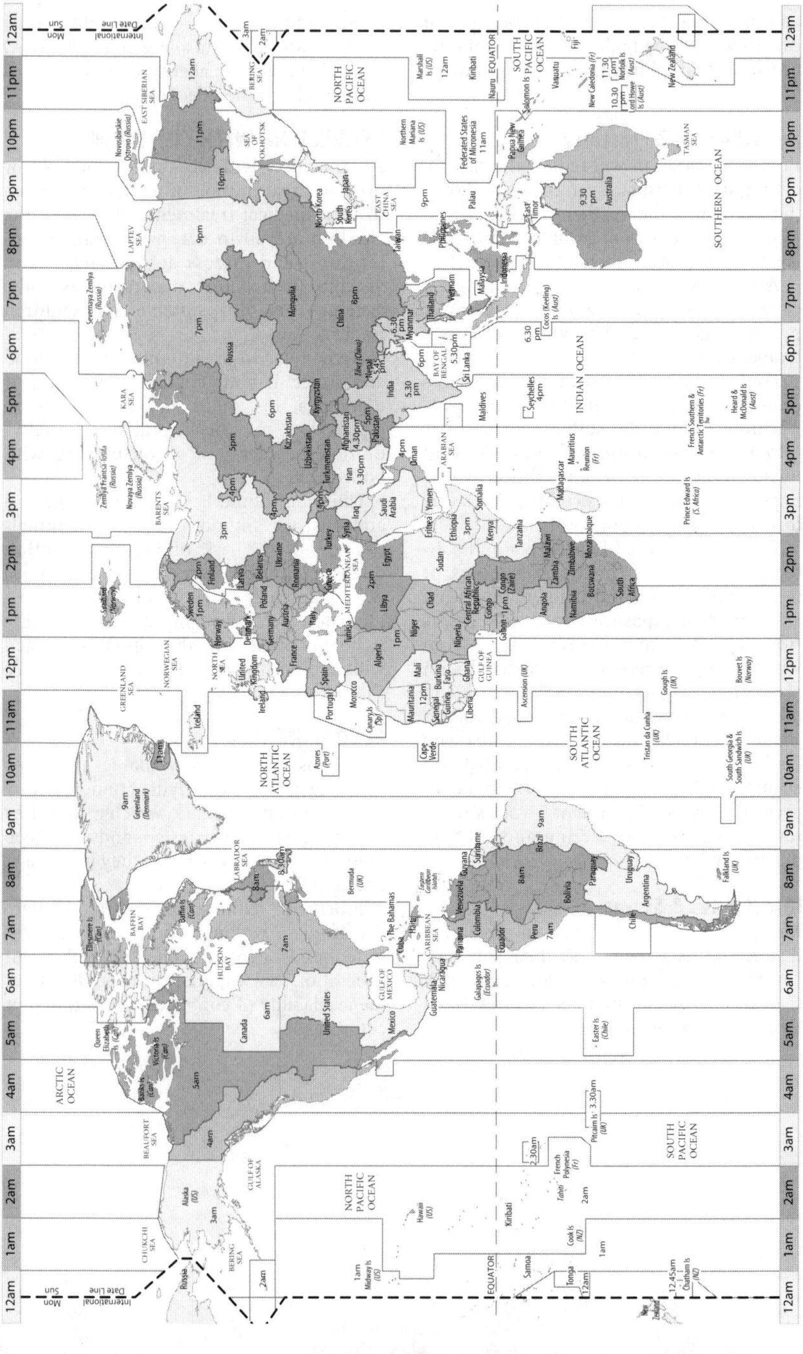
12am
1am
2am
3am
4am
5am
6am
7am
8am
9am
10am
11am
12pm
1pm
2pm
3pm
4pm
5pm
6pm
7pm
8pm
9pm
10pm
11pm
12am
International Date Line
Mon
Sun
ARCTIC OCEAN
NORTH PACIFIC OCEAN
SOUTH PACIFIC OCEAN
NORTH ATLANTIC OCEAN
SOUTH ATLANTIC OCEAN
INDIAN OCEAN
SOUTHERN OCEAN
EQUATOR
GULF OF ALASKA
BEAUFORT SEA
HUDSON BAY
BAFFIN BAY
LABRADOR SEA
GREENLAND SEA
NORWEGIAN SEA
NORTH SEA
BARENTS SEA
KARA SEA
LAPTEV SEA
EAST SIBERIAN SEA
SEA OF OKHOTSK
BERING SEA
EAST CHINA SEA
MEDITERRANEAN SEA
ARABIAN SEA
BAY OF BENGAL
GULF OF GUINEA
GULF OF MEXICO
CARIBBEAN SEA
TASMAN SEA
Alaska (US)
Canada
United States
Mexico
Greenland (Denmark)
Iceland
Brazil
Argentina
Chile
Russia
China
India
Australia
New Zealand

Language

CONTENTS

Icelandic is a Germanic language, one of the family which includes German, English, Dutch and all the Scandinavian languages except Finnish.

Most Icelanders speak English, and often as many as three or four other languages, so you'll have no problems if you can't muster any Icelandic. Of course, any attempts you do make to speak the lingo will be much appreciated. For a more in depth guide to Icelandic, pick ip a copy of Lonely Planet's *Scandinavian phrasebook*.

You should be aware that the complex grammar of Icelandic can lead to confusion, especially when you're trying to read bus timetables and find names of towns, which can be spelt several different ways. For example, the sign that welcomes visitors to the town of Höfn in the southeast reads *Velkomin til Hafnar*. In grammatical terms, Hafnar is the dative form of of Höfn.

PRONUNCIATION

Most letters are pronounced as they are in English. The trickier ones are listed below. Stress generally falls on the first syllable.

Vowels

á	as the 'ow' in 'cow'
é	as the 'ye' in 'yet'
i, y	as the 'i' in 'hit'
í, ý	as the 'i' in 'marine'
ó	as in 'note'
ö	as the 'er' in 'fern', without the 'r' sound
ú	as the 'oo' in 'cool'
æ	as th 'y' in 'cry'
au	as the word 'furry' without 'f' or 'rr'

Consonants

Ð ð	as the 'th' in 'lather'
Þ þ	as the 'th' in 'thin'
dj	as the 'j' in 'juice'
f	as in 'farm'; as the 'v' in 'van' between vowels or at the end of a word; as the 'b' in 'big' before **l** or **n**
hv	as 'kv'
j	as the 'y' in 'yes'
ll	as the 'ddl' in 'fiddle'
p	as in 'pit'; before **s** or **t**, it's as the 'f' in 'fit'
r	always trilled

ACCOMMODATION

Do you have any rooms available?	*Eru herbergi laus?*
May I see it?	*Má ég sjá það?*
I'd like (a) ...	*Gæti ég fengið ...*
single room	*einstklingsherbergi*
double room	*tveggjamannherbergi*
to share a dorm	*að deila herbergi með öðrum*
camping ground	*tjaldstæði*
guesthouse	*gistiheimili*
hotel	*hótel*
motel	*gistihús*
youth hostel	*farfuglaheimili*

CONVERSATION & ESSENTIALS

Hello.	*Halló.*
Good morning/afternoon.	*Góðan daginn.*
Good evening.	*Gott kvöld.*
Goodbye.	*Bless.*
Thank you.	*Takk fyrir.*
Yes.	*Jái.*
No.	*Nei.*
Do you speak English?	*Talar þú ensku?*
I understand.	*Ég skil.*
I don't understand.	*Ég skil ekki.*
How are you?	*Hvernig hefur þú það?*
Well, thanks.	*Gott, takk.*
Cheers!	*Skál!*
What's your name?	*Hvað heitir þú?*
My name is ...	*Ég heiti ...*
Where are you from?	*Hvaðan ert þú?*
I'm from ...	*Ég er frá ...*

HEALTH & EMERGENCIES

Help!	*Hjálp!*
I'm lost	*Ég er villt/villtur.* (f/m)
I'm sick	*Ég er veikur*
Go away!	*Farðu!*
antibiotics	*sótthreinsandi*
condoms	*smokkar*
contraceptive	*getnaðarvörn*
tampons	*vatttappar/tampónar*

Call ...!	*Náið í ...!*
a doctor	*lækni*
the police	*lögregluna*
an ambulance	*sjúkrabíl*

Where is a ...?	*Hvar er ...?*
chemist	*apótek*
dentist	*tannlæknir*
doctor	*læknir*
hospital	*sjúkrahús*

NUMBERS

0	*núll*
1	*einn*
2	*tveir*
3	*þrír*
4	*fjórir*
5	*fimm*
6	*sex*
7	*sjö*
8	*átta*
9	*níu*
10	*tíu*
11	*ellefu*
12	*tólf*
13	*þrettán*
14	*fjórtán*
15	*fimmtán*
16	*sextán*
17	*sautján*
18	*átján*
19	*nítján*
20	*tuttugu*
21	*tuttugu og einn*
30	*þrjátíu*
40	*fjörutíu*
100	*eitt hundrað*
1000	*eitt þúsund*

SHOPPING & SERVICES

I'm looking for (a/the) ...	*Ég er að leita að ...*
bank	*banka*
city centre	*miðbænum*
market	*markaðum*
police	*lögreglunni*
post office	*pósthúsinu*
public toilet	*almenningssalerni*
telephone centre	*símstöðinni*
tourist office	*upplýsingaþjónustu fyrir ferðafólk*

What time does it open/close?	*Hvenær er opnað/lokað?*
How much is it?	*Hvað kostar þetta?*
Where is the toilet?	*Hvar er snyrtingin/klósettið?*

TIME & DATES

Monday	*mánudagur*
Tuesday	*þriðjudagur*
Wednesday	*miðvikudagur*
Thursday	*fimmtudagur*
Friday	*föstudagur*
Saturday	*laugardagur*
Sunday	*sunnudagur*

What time is it?	*Hvað er klukkan?*
today	*í dag*
yesterday	*í gær*
tomorrow	*á morgun*

TRANSPORT

Where is a/the ...?	*Hvar er ...?*

airport	*flúgvöllur*
bus stop	*strætisvagnabiðstöð*
ferry	*ferja*
ticket office	*miðasala*

Is it far from here?	*Er það langt héðan?*
Go straight ahead.	*Farðu beint áfram.*
Turn left.	*Beygðu til vinstri.*
Turn right.	*Beygðu til hægri.*

Could you write the address, please?	*Gætir þú skrifað niður heimilisfangið?*

What time does the ... leave/arrive?	*Hvenær fer/kemur ...?*
boat	*báturinn*
bus	*vagninn*
plane	*flugvélin*
tram	*sporvagninn*

I'd like a ...	*Gæti ég fengið ...*
one-way ticket	*miða/aðra leiðina*
return ticket	*miða/báðar leiðir*

Glossary

A
á – river (as in Laxá, or Salmon River)
álfar – elves
alfhol – wooden cutouts of houses for elves, often placed in Icelandic gardens
alþing – ancient Icelandic parliament
Alþingi – modern Icelandic parliament

B
bær – farm
basalt – hard volcanic rock that often solidifies into hexagonal columns
bíó – cinema
bollur – cream buns
brennivín – local Schnapps

C
caldera – crater created by the collapse of a volcanic cone

D
dalur – valley

E
eddas – ancient Norse books

F
fjörður – fjord
foss – waterfall (as in Gullfoss, or Dettifoss)
franskar – chips
fumarole – vents in the earth releasing volcanic gas

G
gata – street
geyser – spouting hot spring
gistiheimilið – guesthouse
gisting – guesthouse
glíma – Icelandic wrestling
goðar – chieftan

H
hakarl – putrid shark meat
hamborgarar – hamburger
harðfiskur – dried fish
huldufólk – hidden people
hófn – harbour
hot pot – spa bath, found at public swimming pools and some hotels
hraun – lava field

I
icecap – permanently frozen glacier or mountaintop
Íslands – Iceland

J
jökull – glacier, icecap
jökulhlaup – glacial flooding caused by volcano erupting beneath an icecap

K
kirkja – church

L
lava tube – underground tunnel created by the flow of liquid lava under a solid crust
lón – lagoon

M
mörk – woods or forest
mud Pot – a bubbling pool of superheated mud

P
puffling – baby puffin
pylsur – hot dogs

R
reyk – geothermal steam or 'smoke' rising from the ground, as in 'Reykjavík ('Smoky Bay')
rift – crack between two geographical plates
runtur – 'round tour', Icelandic pub crawl or aimless driving around town by car

S
sagas – Icelandic legends
samloka – sandwiches
sandur – glacial sand plains
scoria – glassy volcanic lava
shield volcano – gently sloped volcano built up by fluid lava flows
skalinn – snack bar
skyr – Icelandic yoghurt
staðir – farm
sundlaug – heated swimming pool

T
tephra – rock and other material blasted out from a volcano
tjörn – pond
torg – square (as in town square)

V
vatn – lake (as in Mývatn, or Midge Lake)
vegur – road
vents – natural clefts where hot steam emerges from the ground
vogur – bay

Behind the Scenes

THIS BOOK

This is the 5th edition of *Iceland* (formerly *Iceland, Greenland & the Faroe Islands*). The 1st edition, published in February 1991 and was written by Deanna Swaney, who also updated the 2nd edition. The 3rd edition was updated by Graeme Cornwallis and Deanna Swaney. The 4th edition was updated by Graeme Cornwallis. We sent Paul Harding and Joe Bindloss on the road to update the 5th edition.

THANKS from the Authors

Paul Harding Many people helped to make my trip to Iceland a smooth one. Thanks to Valur and his friends at *Grapevine* magazine for advice and a few beers in Reykjavík's bars. Thanks to the staff at the Reykjavík tourist office, Icelandic Tourist Board and offices around the country, especially Akureyri, Egilsstaðir and Höfn. Thanks also to Trausti, Edda, Sylvia and Muff.

At Lonely Planet thanks to Amanda Canning, Fiona Christie, Mark Griffiths, Barb Benson and Simon Sellars.

Joe Bindloss First, my thanks to Linda Nylind for her tireless support and patience. Credit also to David Marshall, because it is long overdue. In Reykjavík, thanks to the various travellers who passed on top tips and the helpful staff at the Reykjavík City Hostel. Thanks also to Valur Gunnarson of *Grapevine* for the inside track on Reykjavík nightlife. Around Iceland, my thanks go to the owners of many farmhouse B&Bs for having a hot pot of coffee waiting for tired travellers.

CREDITS

This title was commissioned and developed by Amanda Canning in the London office. Fiona Christie carried out the manuscript assessment and Mark Griffiths developed the cartography.

In the Melbourne office, Simon Sellars coordinated the editing and Barbara Benson and Chris Thomas coordinated the cartography. Assisting with editing and proofing were Andrea Baster, Jackey Coyle, Simone Egger, Cathryn Game, Stephanie Pearson and Kalya Ryan. Mapping assistance was provided by Celia Wood and Christopher Crook.

Huw Fowles was the project manager, Cris Gibcus was the layout designer and Maria Vallianos designed the cover. Thanks also to Martin Heng and Quentin Frayne.

Series Publishing Manager Virginia Maxwell oversaw the redevelopment of the country guides series with help from Maria Donohoe. Regional Publishing Manager Katrina Browning steered the development of this title.

The series was designed by James Hardy, with mapping development by Paul Piaia. The series development team included Shahara Ahmed, Susie Ashworth, Gerilyn Attebery, Jenny Blake, Anna Bolger, Verity Campbell, Erin Corrigan, Nadine Fogale, Dave McClymont, Leonie Mugavin, Rachel Peart, Lynne Preston and Howard Ralley.

THE LONELY PLANET STORY

The story begins with a classic travel adventure: Tony and Maureen Wheeler's 1972 journey across Europe and Asia to Australia. There was no useful information about the overland trail then, so Tony and Maureen published the first Lonely Planet guidebook to meet a growing need.

From a kitchen table, Lonely Planet has grown to become the largest independent travel publisher in the world, with offices in Melbourne (Australia), Oakland (USA), London (UK) and Paris (France).

Today Lonely Planet guidebooks cover the globe. There is an ever-growing list of books and information in a variety of media. Some things haven't changed. The main aim is still to make it possible for adventurous travellers to get out there – to explore and better understand the world.

At Lonely Planet we believe travellers can make a positive contribution to the countries they visit – if they respect their host communities and spend their money wisely.

THANKS from Lonely Planet

Many thanks to the following travellers who used the last edition and wrote to us with helpful hints, useful advice and interesting anecdotes.

A Lisa Abrams, Dennis Akkerman, Anne Aldridge **B** Jean Baebler, Michaela Barber, Kate Barker, R Barkere, Catherine Becker, Mike Bodman, Marko Borko, Steven Boyd, Graeme Brock, Helen Bulakhtina, Chris Burge, Brian Burke **C** Roger Palau Capdevila, Wendy Chouinard, Geert de Coninck, Charlie Connelly, Richard Cook, George Coutts, Elisabeth Cox, John Cox **D** Per Danker, Sander van Dorp, John Drew, Louise Dillon, Jon Dunkelman **E** Clare Eccles, Richard Elberfeld, Kelly Eskridge, Cedric Evenepoel **F** Paul Fecteau, Berta Fernández, Margot Ferrier, Oliver Feste, Daniela de Fidio, Mike Frecklington, Jan Erik Fredriksen, Micha Frickenhaus **G** Richard Gardner, Christian Germain, Jóhanna Gunnlaugsdóttir, Katerina Gromanova, Menke de Groot **H** Joern Haase, Leo Hamulczyk, Cedric Hannedouche, Helga Härle, Andreas Hartel, Heike Heinrichs, Thrudur Helgadottir, Marese Hickey, Robert Hollingworth, Jurgen Horemans, Graham Hughes, Michael Hunter, Steve Hutton **J** Ludmila Johnsen, Adrian Jones, Jakob Busch Jürgensen, Dr David Jutson **K** Byron Karlevics, Kathrin Kappmeier, Faiz Kermani, Christoph Kessel, Isabel Kolic, Laurence Koster, Peter Koutsoukos, Sven Kreutz, Andri Kristjánsson **L** Leif Larsen, Peter Lawler, Carol Levy, Chris Louie **M** Keith Macleod, Mark Magielsen, Robert & Fiona Mahoney, Harold Mattie, Joy McNally, Kate McRae, Phil McCreery, E M McGileen, Edna Milano, Binnie Mobsy, Geraldine Moran, Steven Morrison **N** Paul Needham **O** Gavin O'Mahony **P** Sue Panno, Stephen Park, Andrew Perry, Bruce Pillard, Tullio Pitassi, Auke Pols, Tony & Jill Porco, Charles Postel, Eddie Powell, Holly Pyett **R** Thomas Rau, Anette Rehr, Lawrence Remmel, Michelle Rendle, Andrea Rogge, Nicola Romeo, Jana Rosqvist **S** Josette Sars, Bernard Sayer, Philip Scott, Thomas Siepert, Rosaria & Enrico Silva, Dr Mark Smith, Neil Smith, Joan Stace-Smith, Richard Stace-Smith, Marcia Stawarski, Don Stazic, Stephen Stewart, Michael Strange, Gretchen Stranger **T** Emanuela Tasinato, Steve Todmorden, Nils-Tore Torbergsen, Annabelle Truscitt, Thorir Tryggvason **V** Kristin Veighey, Peter Voigt **W** Aleksandra Wankiewicz, Kerstin Wasson, Dennis Waterman, J Welbank, Lesley Whitfield, John R Withers, Raanan Wlosko, Craig Woodcroft

SEND US YOUR FEEDBACK

We love to hear from travellers – your comments keep us on our toes and help make our books better. Our well-travelled team reads every word on what you loved or loathed about this book. Although we cannot reply individually to postal submissions, we always guarantee that your feedback goes straight to the appropriate authors, in time for the next edition. Each person who sends us information is thanked in the next edition – and the most useful submissions are rewarded with a free book.

To send us your updates – and find out about LP events, newsletters and travel news – visit our award-winning website: **www.lonelyplanet.com**.

Note: We may edit, reproduce and incorporate your comments in Lonely Planet products such as guidebooks, websites and digital products, so let us know if you don't want your comments reproduced or your name acknowledged. For a copy of our privacy policy visit www.lonelyplanet.com/privacy.

Index

The Icelandic characters **á**, **í**, **ó**, **ú** and **ý** are all ordered among the **a**, **i**, **o**, **u** and **y** listings, as is the practice in the local alphabets. The characters **ö** and **æ** appear among the **o** and **a** listings, while the character **ð** follows **d** and **þ** follows **z** in this listing.

000 Map pages
000 Location of colour photographs

000 Map pages
000 Location of colour photographs

INDEX

INDEX

LEGEND

ROUTES

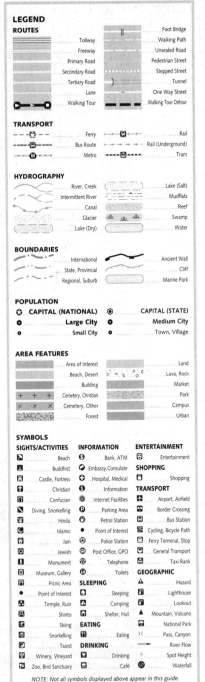

Tollway	Foot Bridge
Freeway	Walking Path
Primary Road	Unsealed Road
Secondary Road	Pedestrian Street
Tertiary Road	Stepped Street
Lane	Tunnel
Walking Tour	One Way Street
	Walking Tour Detour

TRANSPORT

Ferry	Rail
Bus Route	Rail (Underground)
Metro	Tram

HYDROGRAPHY

River, Creek	Lake (Salt)
Intermittent River	Mudflats
Canal	Reef
Glacier	Swamp
Lake (Dry)	Water

BOUNDARIES

International	Ancient Wall
State, Provincial	Cliff
Regional, Suburb	Marine Park

POPULATION

CAPITAL (NATIONAL)	CAPITAL (STATE)
Large City	**Medium City**
Small City	Town, Village

AREA FEATURES

Area of Interest	Land
Beach, Desert	Lava, Rock
Building	Market
Cemetery, Christian	Park
Cemetery, Other	Campus
Forest	Urban

SYMBOLS

SIGHTS/ACTIVITIES	INFORMATION	ENTERTAINMENT
Beach	Bank, ATM	Entertainment
Buddhist	Embassy,Consulate	**SHOPPING**
Castle, Fortress	Hospital, Medical	Shopping
Christian	Information	**TRANSPORT**
Confucian	Internet Facilities	Airport, Airfield
Diving, Snorkelling	Parking Area	Border Crossing
Hindu	Petrol Station	Bus Station
Islamic	Point of Interest	Cycling, Bicycle Path
Jain	Police Station	Ferry Terminal, Stop
Jewish	Post Office, GPO	General Transport
Monument	Telephone	Taxi Rank
Museum, Gallery	Toilets	**GEOGRAPHIC**
Picnic Area	**SLEEPING**	Hazard
Point of Interest	Sleeping	Lighthouse
Temple, Ruin	Camping	Lookout
Shinto	Shelter, Hut	Mountain, Volcano
Skiing	**EATING**	National Park
Snorkelling	Eating	Pass, Canyon
Taoist	**DRINKING**	River Flow
Winery, Vineyard	Drinking	Spot Height
Zoo, Bird Sanctuary	Café	Waterfall

NOTE: Not all symbols displayed above appear in this guide.

LONELY PLANET OFFICES

Australia
Head Office
Locked Bag 1, Footscray, Victoria 3011
☎ 03 8379 8000, fax 03 8379 8111
talk2us@lonelyplanet.com.au

USA
150 Linden St, Oakland, CA 94607
☎ 510 893 8555, toll free 800 275 8555
fax 510 893 8572, info@lonelyplanet.com

UK
72–82 Rosebery Ave,
Clerkenwell, London EC1R 4RW
☎ 020 7841 9000, fax 020 7841 9001
go@lonelyplanet.co.uk

France
1 rue du Dahomey, 75011 Paris
☎ 01 55 25 33 00, fax 01 55 25 33 01
bip@lonelyplanet.fr, www.lonelyplanet.fr

Published by Lonely Planet Publications Pty Ltd
ABN 36 005 607 983

Cover photographs: Falls at Gulfoss, Galen Rowell/CORBIS (front); Pair of puffins, Steve Hutton/LPI (back). Many of the images in this guide are available for licensing from Lonely Planet Images: www.lonelyplanetimages.com.

Printed by SNP Security Printing Pte Ltd, Singapore